PERFECT AWAKENING

Publisher's Acknowledgment

The publisher gratefully acknowledges the generous help of the Hershey Family Foundation in sponsoring the production of this book.

DĪRGHĀGAMA STUDIES, VOLUME 1

Perfect Awakening

An Edition and Translation of the *Prāsādika* and *Prasādanīya* Sūtras

Charles DiSimone

Wisdom

Wisdom Publications
132 Perry Street
New York, NY 10014 USA
wisdomexperience.org

Library of Congress Cataloging-in-Publication Data
Names: DiSimone, Charles, translator, editor.
Title: Perfect awakening: an edition and translation of the Prāsādika and Prasādanīya sūtras / Charles DiSimone.
Other titles: Tipiṭaka. Suttapiṭaka. Dīghanikāya. English.
Description: First edition. | New York: Wisdom Publications, 2024. | Series: Dīrghāgama studies; volume 1 | Includes bibliographical references and index.
Identifiers: LCCN 2023033215 (print) | LCCN 2023033216 (ebook) | ISBN 9781614296539 (hardcover) | ISBN 9781614296546 (ebook)
Subjects: LCSH: Buddhism—Sacred books. | Theravāda Buddhism—Doctrines.
Classification: LCC BQ1292.E53 D57 2024 (print) | LCC BQ1292.E53 (ebook) | DDC 294.3/82—dc23/eng/20231117
LC record available at https://lccn.loc.gov/2023033215
LC ebook record available at https://lccn.loc.gov/2023033216

ISBN 978-1-61429-653-9 ebook ISBN 978-1-61429-654-6

28 27 26 25 24
5 4 3 2 1

Cover and interior design by Gopa & Ted 2.

Printed on acid-free paper that meets the guidelines for permanence and durability of the Production Guidelines for Book Longevity of the Council on Library Resources.

Printed in the United States of America.

Contents

Preface

The central aim of this book is to present the *Prāsādika-sūtra* and the *Prasādanīya-sūtra*, two sūtras on confidence in the Buddha, from a witness of a Sanskrit *Dīrghāgama* (or Collection of Long Discourses) manuscript critically edited and translated into English, making this material widely available to both specialists and the interested readers for the first time. The *Dīrghāgama* manuscript was discovered around the Gilgit area of Pakistan in the 1990s, one of the many important new manuscript discoveries to come to light from the area of Greater Gandhāra starting in the late twentieth century and continuing to this day. It may be considered a counterpart to the already well-known *Dīgha-nikāya* of the Theravāda tradition transmitted in Pali and the *Cháng āhán jīng* (長阿含經) of the Dharmaguptaka transmission extant in Chinese. The finding of this *Dīrghāgama* manuscript represents the fabulous rediscovery of what had been an almost entirely lost corpus of canonical Buddhist sūtra literature. Since its discovery, it has been the subject of scholarly study primarily in Germany, where work to edit and translate its contents is now entering its third decade. Even after so many years have passed, the work to edit this manuscript continues and is still far from completed. The studies that have been published have mainly been dissertation projects in German and are rather notoriously difficult for those outside the orbit of the project to access. Indeed, this book has its roots in the doctoral dissertation I wrote at the University of Munich.

I am pleased to see my research on the *Prāsādika-sūtra* and the *Prasādanīya-sūtra* serve as the first volume in Wisdom's *Dīrghāgama Studies* series. The goal of this series is to make the philological research that has been conducted upon the *Dīrghāgama* manuscript widely available so that it may be easily accessed by those wishing to conduct research on the manuscript itself, the Long Discourses collections, or related issues within the field of Buddhist studies. In the first volumes this will be achieved through detailed critical editions allowing the reader to directly access the manuscript material as well as consult parallel material representing the rich tradition of Buddhist sūtra literature that is somehow simultaneously both an intricately woven quilt, each square its own unique work, and an interconnected city of towers made from shared phrases built over centuries of oral and, later, written transmission. The final volume of the series will result in a complete English translation of the manuscript, finally restoring this formerly lost collection of sūtras to the minds of this world. A global pandemic assured that the publication of this book was delayed, but it is my hope that the remaining volumes will come swiftly.

This book would not exist if not for the wisdom, help, research, friendship, and general energetic expenditure of people too numerous to list, but here I will nonetheless attempt to single out those who helped most. First, I must thank the good folk at Wisdom Publications for their diligent effort working with me in the publication of this book. My deep gratitude is directed toward David Kittlestrom and Alexander Gardner for their work editing the book, and to an anonymous reviewer. There is no doubt that the content has been much improved by the various suggestions of these three. In the *Prasādanīya-sūtra*, Śāriputra urges us to proclaim serene faith (*prasāda*) in the Teacher. Although he explicitly meant for this serene faith to be placed in the Buddha, I must express a similar sentiment for my own teacher, Jens-Uwe Hartmann. It was he who suggested, more than a few years ago, that I edit these sūtras from the Gilgit *Dīrghāgama* manuscript. I remember being a little disappointed at first, as I had wanted to continue my work on Mahāyāna sūtras. Little did I know I would discover that the roots of the Mahāyāna are found within this material and come to understand that to study the literature of the Mahāyāna one must also study the literature of the Śrāvakayāna as the two are inextricably related. Without his guidance I would remain blind to the intricacy and joys of philology and the practice of reading manuscripts. To my second advisor, Paul Harrison, I also owe a great deal for all he has taught me over the years, not least of which is that it was he who first taught me Buddhist philology over many pleasant hours reading sūtras together in the large-for-a-closet-but-cozy-for-a-room office at the Ho Center for Buddhist Studies at Stanford. It is difficult to describe how influential those hours upon hours of reading together were to the development and trajectory of my own understanding and research into the study of Buddhist textuality. Kazunobu Matsuda is owed a special thanks for providing me with photos that proved to be the keys to several formerly locked doors within the manuscript, as well as for countless other instances of help and genuine kindness he has graced me with over the years. Thanks are also owed to Klaus Wille, Somadeva

Vasudeva, and the late Lance Cousins, from whose early *Dīrghāgama* transliterations I was able to begin to learn and appreciate the Gilgit-Bamiyan Type II script. Reading this manuscript has led me to pick up my reading capacity in several other Brahmi scripts in the ensuing years, but I always return to the Gilgit-Bamiyan scripts rooted in my heart. I have had the pleasure of teaching the material discussed in this book at Mahidol University and thank my friends and former colleagues there, Mattia Salvini and Kengo Harimoto, for their assistance and insights on many issues and for their lasting friendship. I have also had the pleasure of closely reading and teaching this material at Ghent University and thank my colleagues there for making that so enjoyable. The final person I single out here for thanks is my wife and colleague, Jin kyoung Choi. She has done the most in helping with the creation of this book. Indeed, her own work on the *Dīrghāgama* manuscript will mark the second volume in this series, and our joint translation of the reminder of the *Dīrghāgama* will be the third.

I also extend my sincere thanks to the following people who, in one way or another, assisted me throughout my work: Ven. Anālayo, Stefan Baums, Cathy Cantwell, Ruixuan Chen, Seongho Choi, Oliver von Criegern, Ven. Dhammadinnā, Lewis Doney, Mamta Dwivedi, Franz-Karl Ehrhard, Elisa Freschi, Eric Greene, Hiromi Habata, Peter Harvey, Simone Heidegger, Ann Heirman, the late Seishi Karashima, Paulus Kaufmann, Evelyn Kindermann, Jowita Kramer, Youngjin Lee, Nathan McGovern, Gudrun Melzer, Yu Meng, Adelheid Mette, Tanni Moitra, Jason Neelis, Alexander von Rospatt, Andrea Schlosser, Marta Sernesi, Masanori Shono, Jonathan Silk, Daniel Stuart, Vincent Tournier, Ven. Vinitā Tseng, Vesna Wallace, Marco Walther, Fumi Yao, and Lixiang Zhang. All of these folk are luminous stars in the galaxy of my gratitude. Finally, I must thank my children, Haru DiSimone and later Maru DiSimone, neither of whom did anything to help in the production of this work and actively hindered my progress with glee yet proved somehow essential to this work.

The research conducted for this book was funded by the Deutscher Akademischer Austauschdienst (DAAD) and the Research Foundation – Flanders (FWO).

Technical Notes

The following tables in these technical notes contain explanations of the symbols used within the transliteration, reconstruction, and translation of the manuscript from which the editions of the *Prāsādika-sūtra* and *Prasādanīya-sūtra* were created. Following that is a list of abbreviations used in the book. While the reconstruction may be considered the edition proper by some, the transliteration provides invaluable information for those interested in studying the manuscript as it provides a faithful representation of the exact wording of the two sūtras as they were transmitted in this manuscript witness. The transliteration may be passed over by those whose interest lies mainly in the textual tradition of Buddhist literature. For such readers, the reconstruction and parallels will be of interest. Readers seeking to quickly engage with these two sūtras may profitably focus their attention upon the translations without overly concerning themselves with the transliteration, reconstruction, or parallels. However, to fully engage with the material the transliteration, reconstruction, translation, and parallels should each be consulted in tandem with one another. For those interested in the reconstruction, I would also strongly suggest to not ignore the footnotes where much contextualizing information is to be found.

Symbols Used in the Transliteration of the *Prāsādika* and *Prasādanīya* Sūtras

[ ] square brackets	damaged akṣaras or uncertain readings
<< >> double pointed brackets	addition in ms. by scribe
{{ }} double curly brackets	deletion in ms. by scribe
/// three oblique dashes	break in folio or fragment
+ cross	missing akṣara

<table>
<tr><td>.. two dots</td><td>illegible or damaged akṣara</td></tr>
<tr><td>. one dot</td><td>illegible or damaged inherent vowel, diacritic, or ligature of an akṣara</td></tr>
<tr><td>* asterisk</td><td>virāma</td></tr>
<tr><td>• higher dot</td><td>dot-like punctuation in ms.</td></tr>
<tr><td>○ circle</td><td>punch or string hole in ms.</td></tr>
<tr><td>◊ diamond</td><td>gap between akṣaras in ms.</td></tr>
<tr><td>| vertical bar</td><td>daṇḍa</td></tr>
<tr><td>= equal sign</td><td>filler mark left by scribe in ms.</td></tr>
<tr><td>|| double vertical bar</td><td>double daṇḍa</td></tr>
<tr><td>bold</td><td>start of new section in reconstruction</td></tr>
<tr><td><u>underline</u></td><td>fragments found laying atop or underneath other folios</td></tr>
<tr><td><u>double underline</u></td><td>restorations in ms. made from mirrored imprints or thin layers from one folio that had been transposed onto another folio</td></tr>
<tr><td>ḫ</td><td>upadhmānīya</td></tr>
<tr><td>ẖ</td><td>jihvāmūlīya</td></tr>
</table>

On the Edition

This portion of the book presents critical reconstructions of the *Prāsādika* and *Prasādanīya* sūtras, section by section, followed by English translations and parallel passages. The sections themselves are largely based upon the traditional topic division of the work outlined in the summary verses for both sūtras. Parallels are designated by the section number in bold placed between tildes (so: the parallels for **DĀ 15.1** would be under **~15.1~**). When available, direct fragment parallels from other Mūlasarvāstivāda transmission Central Asian witnesses of DĀ 15 and DĀ 16 are given first. Otherwise, parallels in order of counterpart Theravāda and Dharmaguptaka transmissions in Pali and Chinese are given directly after the translation. For DĀ 16, what are probably Mūlasarvāstivāda parallels extant in Chinese from T I 18 are given before the extant parallels from the other Long Discourses in Pali and Chinese. Parallels from the *Dīgha-nikāya* are given next, followed by any corresponding passages from the *Cháng āhán jīng* (長阿含經). The corresponding transmission parallels from the Theravāda and Dharmaguptaka Long Discourses that I have included are based upon the editions of the Pali Text Society and the Chinese recorded in the Taishō Shinshū Daizōkyō (大正新脩大藏經). Any other Sanskrit Central Asian fragments are placed after the Chinese, and followed finally by any remaining indirect parallels of related passages found in other, unrelated texts extant in the vast tradition of Buddhist literature surviving today. Indirect parallels are given in a slightly smaller font to indicate their secondary status after parallels from the Long Discourse transmissions.

I have endeavored to make a complete translation and only rarely leave a term in its original Sanskrit. While I have been largely successful, there are notable exceptions such as *arhat*, *nirvāṇadhātu*, *parinirvāṇa*, and *tathāgata*. I have also endeavored to standardize translations of terms. Sometimes this is impossible; for example, *dharma* is translated as both "doctrine" and "factor" depending on the usage of the term but is also often left untranslated, especially when it is used in conjunction with *vinaya*. On occasion, using a standard translation for a term can serve to limit the scope of a translation, such as my decision to translate *pūrvānta* and *aparānta* only as "the beginning" and "the end" although they also carry the force of "the past" and "the future." However, I concluded that this is ultimately necessary because it serves to distinguish the terms from the more general terms for the past and future, *atīta* and *anāgata*, which also appear in both sūtras. Throughout the translation one eye has been pointed on clarity so that even the general reader may understand the translation, but an important goal has been to preserve the features of the Sanskrit within the translation so that the specialist, by glancing at both the reconstruction and translation, may be able to correlate the grammar, syntax, and meaning of the words without undue effort.

Symbols Used in the Reconstruction

( ) parenthesis	restoration in ms.
< > pointed brackets	addition by editor
{ } curly brackets	deletion by editor
underline	emendation of individual akṣara by editor

+ cross	unreconstructed, missing akṣara
.. two dots	unreconstructed, illegible, or damaged akṣara
. one dot	unreconstructed, illegible, or damaged inherent vowel, diacritic, or ligature of an akṣara
* asterisk	*virāma*
• higher dot	dot like punctuation in the manusript.
; semicolon	punctuation added by editor where *sandhi* would make a *daṇḍa* impossible
| vertical bar	*daṇḍa*
|| double vertical bar	double *daṇḍa*
ḫ	*upadhmānīya*
ẖ	*jihvāmūlīya*
'aa	*avagraha* (*avagraha*s never appear in the manuscript. and are always supplied)
[a] **bold** letter in square brackets	a subsection of the text (not bolded when pointing out corresponding subsections in parallel passages)
[#] number in square brackets	numbering added by editor for clarity

Symbols Used in the Translation

( ) parenthesis	translation of words completely restored in ms.
< > pointed brackets	translation of words added by editor in ms.
[ ] square brackets	word or number interpolated into the translation for context or clarity
[...] ellipsis in square brackets	a damaged or destroyed section of ms. that cannot be translated
underline	uncertain translation (usually owing to an incomplete section)
[a] **bold** letter in square brackets	a subsection of the text

Abbreviations

The abbreviations are generally based on those found in Bechert 1990, except for Pali sources, which mainly follow the abbreviations of the Pali Text Society.

Abhidh-d	*Abhidharmadīpa*: ed. P. S. Jaini, see Jaini 1959.
Abhidh-k-bh(P)	Vasubandu, *Abhidharmakośabhāṣyam*: ed. P. Pradhan (= Pradhan 1975).
Abhidh-k-ṭ	Śamathadeva, *Abhidharmakośaṭīkopāyikā* (*Chos mngon pa'i mdzod kyi 'grel bshad nye bar mkho ba zhes bya ba*): Peking 5595, Derge 4094.
Abhidh-k-vy	Yaśomitra, *Abhidharmakośavyākhyā*: ed. Unrai Wogihara (= Wogihara 1932–36).
Abhidh-sam	Asaṅga, *Abhidharmasamuccaya*: ed. P. Pradhan (= Pradhan 1950).
Abhidh-sam-bh	*Abhidharmasamuccayabhāṣya*: ed. N. Tatia (= Tatia 1976).
AdSP(C)	*Aṣṭādaśasāhasrikā Prajñāpāramitā*: ed. Edward Conze (= Conze 1962/74).
AN	*Aṅguttara-nikāya*: ed. Richard Morris & E. Hardy (= Morris and Hardy 1885–1900).
ARIRIAB	*Annual Report of the International Research Institute for Advanced Buddhology at Soka University* (創価大学国際仏教学高等研究所年報 / 創価大学-国際仏教学高等研究所).
Arthav	Vīryaśrīdatta, *Arthaviniścaya-sūtra with Nibandhana*: ed. N. H. Samtani (= Samtani 1971).
Arthav(V)	*Arthaviniścaya-sūtra*: ed. P. L. Vaidya (= Vaidya 1961).
Avś(V)	*Avadānaśataka*: ed. P. L. Vaidya (= Vaidya 1958a).
BHSD	Franklin Edgerton, *Buddhist Hybrid Sanskrit Grammar and Dictionary* (= Edgerton 1972 (1953)).
Bl.	Blatt (= page).
BLSF	*The British Library Sanskrit Fragments: Buddhist Manuscripts From Central Asia*, ed. Seishi Karashima and Klaus Wille (= Karashima and Wille 2006, 2009, and 2015).
Brmj(W)	*Brahmajāla-sūtra*: ed F. Weller (= Weller 1934).

Brmj(W)tr	*Brahmajāla-sūtra*, German translation: F. Weller (= Weller 1935–36).
Caṅgī(UH)	*Caṅgī-sūtra*: Jens-Uwe Hartmann (= Hartmann 2002).
CASF	Ernst Waldschmidt, "Central Asian Sūtra Fragments and Their Relation to the Chinese Āgamas" (= Waldschmidt 1980).
CPD	V. Trenckner et al., ed. *A Critical Pali Dictionary* (= Trenckner et al. 1924–2011ff.).
CPS	*Catuṣpariṣatsūtra*: ed. Ernst Waldschmidt (= Waldschmidt 1952–62).
DĀ	Sanskrit (Mūla-)Sarvāstivāda *Dīrghāgama*.
DĀ 15	*Prāsādika-sūtra*: ed. Charles DiSimone (this publication).
DĀ 16	*Prasādanīya-sūtra*: ed. Charles DiSimone (this publication).
DĀ 17	*Pañcatraya-sūtra*: ms. currently unedited.
DĀ 20	*Kāyabhāvanā-sūtra*: ed. Liu Zhen (= Zhen 2008).
DĀ 24	*Mahāsamāja-sūtra*: ms. currently unedited.
DĀ 25	*Tridaṇḍi-sūtra*: ed. Jin kyoung Choi (= Choi 2016).
DĀ 27	*Lohitya-sūtra I*: ed. Jin kyoung Choi (= Choi 2016).
DĀ 28	*Kaivarti-sūtra*: ed. Chunyang Zhou (= Zhou 2008).
DĀ 31	*Maṇḍiśa-sūtra I*: ms. currently unedited.
DĀ 36	*Pṛṣṭhapāla-sūtra*: ed. Gudrun Melzer (= Melzer 2010).
DĀ 40	*Mahalla-sūtra*: ed. Gudrun Melzer (= Melzer 2010).
DĀ 44	*Rāja-sūtra*: ms. currently unedited.
DĀ 47	*Brahmajāla-sūtra*: ms. currently unedited.
DĀ^{c}	Chinese Dharmaguptaka *Dīrghāgama*, 長阿含經 (*Cháng āhán jīng*): T 1.
DĀ(U.H.)	Jens-Uwe Hartmann, *Untersuchungen zum Dīrghāgama der Sarvāstivādins* (=Hartmann 1992).
Daśa-bh	*Daśabhūmika-sūtra*: ed. Johannes Rahder (= Rahder 1926).

Daśo	*Daśottara-sūtra*: ed. Kusum Mittal, et al. (= Mittal, Schlingloff, and Stache-Rosen 1957/62).
DbSū(3)	*Daśabala-sūtra 3*: ed. Jin-il Chung (= Chung 2009).
DbSū(4)	*Daśabala-sūtra 4*: ed. Jin-il Chung (= Chung 2009).
Derge/Ju	Derge edition of the Tibetan Tripiṭaka.
DhskD	*Dharmaskandha*: ed. Siglinde Dietz (= Dietz 1984).
DhskM	*Dharmaskandha*: ed. Kazunobu Matsuda (= Matsuda 1986).
Div(V)	*Divyāvadāna*: ed. P. L. Vaidya (= Vaidya 1959).
DN	*Dīgha-nikāya*: ed. T. W. Rhys Davids & J. Estlin Carpenter (= Rhys Davids and Carpenter 2006 (1890–1911)).
EĀ	*Ekottarāgama.*
EFGH	C. B. Tripāṭhī, ed. *Ekottarāgama-Fragmente der Gilgit-Handschrift* (= Tripāṭhī 1995).
FrgmDĀ	Jens-Uwe Hartmann, "Fragmente aus dem Dīrghāgama der Sarvāstivādins" (= Hartmann 1989).
GBM	Raghu Vira and Lokesh Chandra, ed. *Gilgit Buddhist Manuscripts* (facsimile ed.) (= Vira and Chandra 1959–74).
Hs.	Handschrift (= manuscript).
JASB	Journal of the Asiatic Society (of Bengal), Calcutta.
JRAS	Journal of the Royal Asiatic Society of Great Britain and Ireland, London.
Khp	*Khuddakapāṭha*: ed. Helmer Smith (= Smith 1978 (1915)).
KP	*Kāśyapaparivarta*: ed. Alexander von Staël-Holstein (= von Staël-Holstein 1926).
KP(VD)	*Kāśyapaparivarta*: ed. M. I. Vorobyova-Desyatovskaya (= Vorobyova-Desyatovskaya 2002).
Lalv(V)	*Lalitavistara*: ed. P. L. Vaidya (= Vaidya 1958b).
LDB	*The Long Discourses of the Buddha* (*Dīgha-nikāya* translation): Maurice Walshe (= Walshe 1995 (1987)).
MĀ	*Madhyamāgama.*

MadhK	Nāgārjuna, *Mūlamadhyamakakārikā*: ed. Louis de La Vallée Poussin (= La Vallée Poussin 1903–13).
MAV	*Mahāvadāna-sūtra*: ed. Ernst Waldschmidt (= Waldschmidt 1953/56).
MN	*Majjhima-nikāya*: ed. V. Trenckner, R. Chalmers (= Trenckner and Chalmers 1993 (1888–99)).
MPS	*Mahāparinirvāṇasūtra*: Ernst Waldschmidt (= Waldschmidt 1986 (1950–51)).
ms.	manuscript.
MSjSū(Re-ed)	*Mahāsamāja-sūtra*, reissue (= Waldschmidt 1980, 150–62).
MSuAv	*Mahāsudarśanāvadāna*: ed. H. Matsumura (= Matsumura 1988).
MSV	Mūlasarvāstivādin *Vinayavastuvāgama*.
Mvu	*Mahāvastu*: ed. Émile Senart, *Mahāvastu-Avadāna* (= Senart 1882–97).
MW	Monier Monier-Williams' Sanskrit-English dictionary (= Monier-Williams et al. 1899).
NagSū (Hoernle)	*Nagaropasama-sūtra*: ed. A. F. R. Hoernle (= Hoernle 1897).
NagSū(VP)	*Nagaropasama-sūtra*: ed. Louis de La Vallée Poussin (= La Vallée Poussin 1911).
NidSa	*Nidānasaṃyukta*: ed. Chandrabhāl Tripāṭhī (=Tripāṭhī 1962).
no.	number.
Peṭ	*Peṭakopadesa*: ed. A. Barua (= Barua 1949).
Peking/Tu	The Tibetan Tripiṭaka, Peking Edition (repr.), ed. D. T. Suzuki (= Suzuki 1955–61).
Poṣ	*Poṣadhavastu*: ed. Haiyan Hu-von Hinüber (= Hu-von Hinüber 1994).
Pras	Candrakīrti, *Prasannapadā* (= La Vallée Poussin 1903–13).
Pravr-v	*Pravrajyāvastu* of MSV (Vastu 1 of the *Vinayavastvāgama*).

Pravr-v I	*Pravrajyāvastu* of MSV (Vastu 1 of the *Vinayavastvāgama*), folios 7–12 (= Vogel and Wille, 1984).
PvSP	*Pañcaviṃśatisāhasrikā Prajñāpāramitā*: ed. Nalinaksha Dutt (= Dutt 1934).
PvSP(K)	*Pañcaviṃśatisāhasrikā Prajñāpāramitā*: ed. Takayasu Kimura (= Kimura 1986–2009).
PTS	Pali Text Society.
PTSD	*The Pali Text Society's Pali-English Dictionary* (= Rhys Davids and Stede 1921–1925).
r	recto.
R	Rückseite (= verso).
repr.	reprint.
SĀ(H) I	*Saṃyuktāgama*: ed. N. Hosoda (= Hosoda 1989).
SĀ(VP)	*Saṃyuktāgama*: ed, Louis de La Vallée Poussin (= La Vallée Poussin 1913.
Saṅg	*Saṅgīti-sūtra*: ed. Valentina Stache-Rosen (= Stache-Rosen 1968).
SaṅgE	*Saṅgīti-sūtra*: ed. Ernst Waldschmidt (= Waldschmidt 1955).
Śay-v	*Śayanāsanavastu*, ed. R. Gnoli (= Gnoli 1978).
SBKN	Sanko Bunka Kenkyūjo Nenpo (Annual of the Sanko Research Institute for the Studies of Buddhism).
SBV	*Saṅghabhedavastu*: ed. R. Gnoli with the assistance of T. Venkatacharya (= Gnoli 1977–78).
SBVG	Gilgit Manuscript Witnesss of the *Saṅghabhedavastu*.
SHT	*Sanskrithandschriften aus den Turfan-Funden Teil 1–11* (= Waldschmidt et al. 1965ff.).
Śikṣ	Śāntideva, *Śikṣāsamuccaya*: ed. Cecil Bendall (= Bendall 1897–1902).
Skt.	Sanskrit.
ŚPrSū	*Śakrapraśna-sūtra*: ed. Ernst Waldschmidt (= Waldschmidt 1932).

SN	*Saṃyutta-nikāya*: ed. L. Feer (= Feer 1884–98).
Śrav-bh I	*Śrāvakabhūmi* (= Śrāvakabhūmi Study Group (The Institute for Comprehensive Studies of Buddhism, Taisho University)/大正大学綜合佛教研究所声聞地研究会 1998).
Śrāv-bh II	*Śrāvakabhūmi* (= Śrāvakabhūmi Study Group (The Institute for Comprehensive Studies of Buddhism, Taisho University)/大正大学綜合佛教研究所声聞地研究会 2007).
Śrāv-bh(Sh)	Asaṅga, *Śrāvakabhūmi*, ed. Karunesh Shukla (= Shukla 1973).
STT	Sanskrittexte aus den Turfanfunden. Vols. 1–9, Berlin 1955–68; vols. 10ff., Göttingen 1965ff.
SWTF	*Sanskrit-Wörterbuch der buddhistischen Texte aus den Turfan-Funden*. (= Waldschmidt et al. 1973ff.).
SWTF, Beiheft	Sanskrit-Wörterbuch der buddhistischen Texte aus den Turfan-Funden, Beiheft, Göttingen.
T	*Taishō Shinshū Daizōkyō* or *Taishō Issaikyō,* 100 vols (= Takakusu and Watanabe 1924ff.).
v	verso.
V	Vorderseite (= recto).
VAV(UH)	Mātṛceṭa, *Varṇārhavarṇastotra*: ed. J.-U. Hartmann (= Hartmann 1987).
Vibh	*Vibhaṅga*: ed. C. A. F. Rhys Davids (= Rhys Davids 1904).
Vin III	*Vinaya-pitaka* (vol. 3): ed. Hermann Oldenberg (= Oldenberg 1993 (1881)).
YBhū(Bh)	*Yogācārabhūmi*: ed. Vidushekhara Bhattacarya (= Bhattacarya 1957).
YL	Dieter Schlingloff, *Ein buddhistisches Yogalehrbuch* (= Schlingloff 1964).

Introduction

1. The Dīrghāgama Manuscript

The *Prāsādika-sūtra* (DĀ 15) and the *Prasādanīya-sūtra* (DĀ 16), which are the subject of this book, are two paired sūtras from the *Yuga-nipāta* (the section dealing with thematically paired sūtras) contained in the manuscript witness of the *Dīrghāgama* (Long Discourses) of the Mūlasarvāstivāda[1] tradition. The *Dīrghāgama* is a compilation of ancient, canonical Buddhist discourses transmitted in Sanskrit and written on birchbark folios in the Gilgit-Bamiyan Type II script, also known as Proto-Śāradā. This collection had been lost for centuries and was likely rediscovered somewhere within the border area of Afghanistan and Pakistan in the 1990s. Among the longest extant manuscripts found in the area, originally consisting of over 450 folios, it contains forty-seven individual texts. One cannot specify with certainty the location of the find spot of the manuscript because it only came to the attention of scholars after it had appeared on the rare book market in London, where it was identified by Kazunobu Matsuda and shortly thereafter subjected to preliminary examination by Lance Cousins, Somadeva Vasudeva, and Klaus Wille.

1. To be more precise, it is not certain whether this *Dīrghāgama* manuscript should be classified as belonging to the Sarvāstivāda or Mūlasarvāstivāda tradition. While it is clear in terms of *vinaya* that the Sarvāstivāda and Mūlasarvāstivāda traditions had unique transmission, it is not clear whether this was the case with their *āgama* transmissions nor what, if anything, the distinctions between these traditions may have been if they shared *āgama*s or had separate *āgama* transmissions. Hartmann has discussed this issue in the past (see Hartmann 2014, 140n5) and has suggested the hyphenated term (Mūla-)Sarvāstivāda to make this ambiguity clear. Anālayo, however, rejects such terms and suggests that differences in *āgama* transmissions between Sarvāstivāda and Mūlasarvāstivāda traditions may be explained as resulting from the transmission lineages of these traditions having been formed regionally following ordination lineages and that the oral transmission of these works played a key role in these distinctions (see Anālayo 2020a, 404ff.). It might be noted that the beginning of the *Prasādanīya-sūtra* edited here is quoted within Śamathadeva's *Abhidharmakośaṭīkopāyikā* (see DĀ 16.1–2 below), which suggests to me that this *Dīrghāgama* manuscript may cautiously be considered as Mūlasarvāstivāda. For reasons such as this, throughout this book I refer to the *Dīrghāgama* manuscript witness as a Mūlasarvāstivāda work but the inherent ambiguity in such terminology should be implicitly understood by the reader.

While it is regrettable that the provenance remains unknown, it is believed to be either another part of the cache of manuscripts found in the 1930s at the Gilgit site in Pakistan, which was historically part of the area we refer to as Greater Gandhāra, or to have been found nearby within the vicinity. Based on paleographical analysis and radiocarbon dating, the manuscript is thought to date from between 676–776 CE,[2] and the script, suggesting a production after the sixth century, allows us to conclude that it may have been copied sometime around the eighth century of the Common Era.[3] While this particular manuscript witness of the Mūlasarvāstivāda *Dīrghāgama* was likely created in the eighth century, the *Dīrghāgama* as a work of oral literature is much older and was likely composed centuries before.[4]

Currently, over half of the *Dīrghāgama* manuscript is split into four private collections, two in Japan and one each in Norway and the United States. The whereabouts of the rest of the manuscript remain a mystery, one that will hopefully be solved in time. The folios in three of the four private collections, while fragmentary in many places, have fortunately been subjected to high-resolution scans,[5] allowing scholars to study the texts independently of the physical folios, which remain housed with their respective owners.

2. Personal correspondence via email between the author, Kazunobu Matsuda, Jens-Uwe Hartmann, and Jin kyoung Choi on November 19, 2019. This new radiocarbon dating has resulted from current research being conducted by Fumi Yao. Yao also had the *Bhaiṣajyavastu-Uttaragrantha* manuscript she has worked on tested, with a remarkably similar result of 671–770 CE. This may speak to a strong relationship in the production of the *Dīrghāgama* manuscript and the Mūlasarvāstivāda *Vinayavastvāgama* manuscripts found in Gilgit.

3. Cf. Hartmann and Wille 2014, 137, and Hartmann 2014, 155. Previous radiocarbon dating of the *Dīrghāgama* manuscript discussed in these two publications give a range of 764–1000 CE. These ranges are based on testing commissioned by the Sam Fogg dealer (first reported in Allon et al. 2006, 279) and are now superseded by the new radiocarbon dating performed in 2019 as part of Yao's research described in note 2 above.

4. The Long Discourse collections are held to be *buddhavacana* by all Buddhist traditions and are therefore considered to have been spoken by the historical Buddha Gautama, transmitted orally for generations, and only later compiled in writing as a distinct collection and eventually translated into various languages. This of course makes discussion of composition somewhat complicated. In this process of textual transmission, many manuscript witnesses of these texts were produced via a copying tradition that spanned hundreds of years.

5. Unfortunately, the folios in the Hirayama Collection are only available in low-resolution images.

While we are fortunate that high-quality photos of the manuscript are available, the folios comprising the *Prāsādika* and *Prasādanīya* sūtras are damaged throughout, in some places quite heavily, and the text itself is often problematic, displaying instances of negation where there should be none and the opposite along with no small amount of textual ambiguity. As Hartmann notes:

> At first sight the manuscript looks very good, but it does not hold what it seems to promise. As soon as one starts reading the texts it becomes obvious that the textual transmission has already deteriorated to a degree that turns its perusal into quite a challenge for the modern academic reader.[6]

This has compounded the already philologically complicated process of creating the reconstruction, much like piecing together a jigsaw puzzle. However, I have been successful in fitting together damaged sections of the manuscript and have been able to reconstruct the missing passages based on the many Sanskrit and Pali parallels to the text that may be found within extant Buddhist literature; whenever I have a textual parallel, I have been able to reconstruct the text with a reasonable degree of confidence, and the great majority of both have been reconstructed. However, in the rare instances when both the manuscript is damaged and there are no extant parallels, such portions of the text must remain lost until either the missing part of the manuscript is found or a similar parallel is discovered.

The *Prāsādika-sūtra* and *Prasādanīya-sūtra* together run to twenty-six folios, with the *Prāsādika-sūtra* spanning seventeen (fols. 274v5–290r4) and the *Prasādanīya-sūtra* ten (fols. 290r5–299v3). The folios of the *Prasādanīya-sūtra*, while damaged throughout, are all extant. The *Prāsādika-sūtra* on the other hand was missing nearly a quarter of its folios when I began working on it. I have been able to identify and partially restore all of the folios and partially or completely reconstruct the text of all previously missing folios. Some I was able to piece together: some folios from various fragments were missing their folio numbers; others I discovered were obscured by other folios due to the folios being stuck together. The reason so many folios were stuck together was made clear to me when Kazunobu Matsuda kindly sent me pictures of the folio bundles he had

6. Hartmann 2014, 155.

managed to photograph when he first encountered them in the possession of the Sam Fogg rare bookseller in London where the *Dīrghāgama* manuscript first became known to scholars. One of those pictures (fig. 1) shows that the manuscript bundle had been separated into at least three smaller bundles at some point in its history. It is not clear whether the manuscript was divided after it was found or some time in the centuries before that, but the bundles must have been together in one bundle for a long period in the past, since layers of adjacent folios are fused together and stuck to the topmost folios in the bundles. This fusing of birchbark folios is not uncommon in recovered manuscripts from Greater Gandhāra, especially for folios at the top or bottom of a manuscript bundle.

The *Prāsādika-sūtra* was split between the top and bottom of two of the bundles, where folios seem to have been especially in danger of becoming fused together, due perhaps to exposure to the elements. Due to their being so close to the top and bottom of these bundles, they appear to have suffered an unusual amount of damage compared to those of some other sections of the manuscript when the individual folios were eventually separated. Fortunately, my digital restoration of the manuscript via Photoshop has been successful in allowing for the majority of the damaged folios to be restored. However, several folios still remain fused and should be reexamined by a skilled conservator.

Due to the damaged and fragmentary quality of the manuscript folios making up the two sūtras, I have had to spend considerable time and effort identifying fragments from folios that were present on other, unrelated folios and digitally restoring these fragments to their correct place in the manuscript. As noted, I have had great success using Adobe Photoshop as my main tool for digital restoration of folios. Of the twenty-six folios containing the *Prāsādika-sūtra* and *Prasādanīya-sūtra*, well over half have undergone digital restoration, ranging from small fragments of a few *akṣaras* (the graphemes used in Brahmic scripts) to an entire folio (see figs. 2–4). The most common digital restoration consists of fragments from one line up to one fourth of the folio in length being moved from the folio on which they rested to their correct folio in the manuscript. Fragments that have been digitally restored are generally not commented upon in the transliteration, which reads the folios in their most complete state. Indeed, the digital restorations I have created supersede all other images of the folios they represent. While I have identified the correct location and digitally restored some fragments to their proper folio, in the transliteration

I have also retained them as fragments in the place where they were found in the manuscript, as removing them from the folio on which they rested would have damaged the fidelity of that folio. In such cases, these fragments are noted in the transliteration with their proper location given. Fragments that remain unidentified are naturally also noted in the transliteration. Such fragments are generally quite short, often consisting of no more than a few illegible akṣaras.

FIGURE 1. Folio bundles of the *Dīrghāgama* manuscript with the uppermost folios fused together. Photo courtesy of Kazunobu Matsuda.

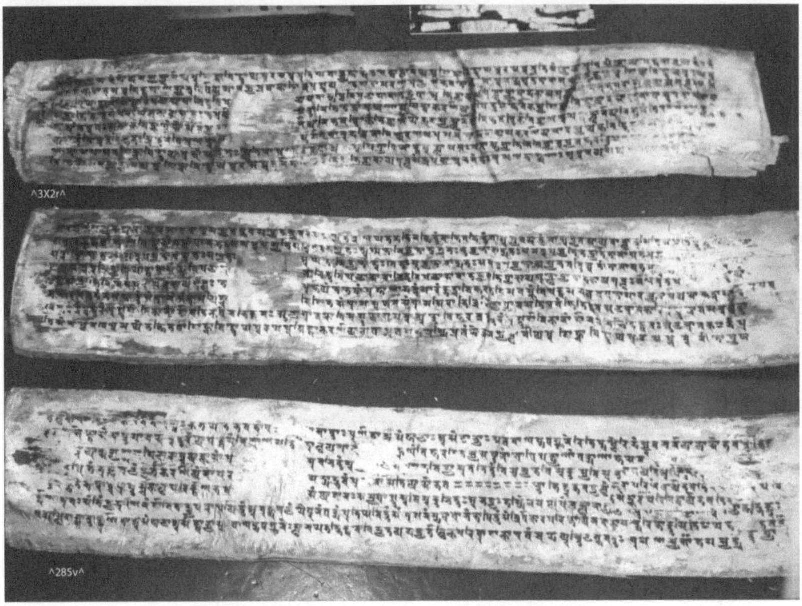

FIGURE 2. Damaged section of folio 298r7.

Figure 3. Digital restoration of folio 298r7 using fragment that had been fused to 299r7.

Figure 4. Partially restored folio 285r restored from five disparate fragments found in different locations of the manuscript and birchbark cells that had been transposed onto other folios. Note that the akṣaras in the upper right corner are upside down due to their having been restored from transposed birchbark layers.

2. Paleographical and Codicological Features[7]

On Techniques Used by Scribes C and D of the *Dīrghāgama* Manuscript Scriptorium

The *Dīrghāgama* manuscript from Gilgit was produced in a scriptorium, and in the *Prāsādika-sūtra* one sees evidence of multiple hands with two different scribes. Gudrun Melzer, whose research on the paleography of the *Dīrghāgama* has uncovered that the manuscript is most likely the work of no more than five to seven scribes, has named the two hands that copied the *Prasādika-sūtra* as scribe C and scribe D. She hypothesizes that they frequently sat together, with one writing the recto and the other the verso in turn for spans of folios throughout the various sections of the *Dīrghāgama* manuscript, including many in the *Prāsādika-sūtra*.[8] In the course of editing the *Prāsādika-sūtra*, I have been able to confirm that it is almost certainly the work of these two scribes working collaboratively. In table 1 below, I list the folios that scribes C and D have written that I have been able to directly observe.[9]

Table 1. Folios written by scribes C and D in DĀ 15, DĀ 16, and surrounding folios.

Scribe C	Scribe D
262v (unidentified sūtra) 264v (unidentified sūtra) 274v (*Prāsādika-sūtra* begins.) 275v	262r (unidentified sūtra) 264r (unidentified sūtra) 274r (*Govinda-sūtra*) 275r

7. A version of this chapter was published in DiSimone 2019.

8. Melzer 2010, 79, and Melzer 2014, 249–51.

9. This table expands upon Melzer's previous table of the distribution of the *Dīrghāgama* scribes across the manuscript (Melzer 2014, 248).

276v	276r
277v	277r
278v	278r
279v	279r
280v	(probably 280r, but folio is obscured)
	281r
281v1–2 (Scribe C begins the folio.)	281v3–8 (Scribe D finishes 281v, imitating style of scribe C.)[10]
282v	282r
283v	283r
284r	284v
285v	285r
	286r, 286v
287r–299v (*Prasādanīya-sūtra* ends.) 300r–319 (*Pañcatraya-*, *Māyājāla-*, and beginning of *Kāmaṭhika-sūtras*)	

After prolonged exposure to the manuscript, discerning the hand of the scribes becomes less a task of great effort in observation and more akin to a conversation with a familiar friend. Even so, one must rely on certain clues found within the handwriting of the various scribes' styles. As Melzer notes, scribe C's "handwriting is characterized by a clear and even flow of lines. All *akṣara*s are carefully placed below the upper line," while "the script of scribe D is stocky and uneven."[11] This fundamental gap between the two scribes in their level of precision in penmanship makes it possible to differentiate between them. Certain quirks of calligraphy, such as a way of writing a conjunct consonant, especially reveal the identity of a scribe. One of the clearest examples of such a difference is that of the *-ṣṭ-* ligature. Scribe C's *-ṣṭ-* is, like his handwriting generally, elegant and clear; a long line descending diagonally from the right lateral side of the ligature above the hook of the *-ṭ-* is a clear continuation of the lower diagonal stoke of the *-ṣ-*, as can be seen in figures 5 and 6. Scribe D's *-ṣṭ-* is rather scrunched up, with

10. Melzer (2014, 248) writes that 281v is the work of scribe D alone, but I do not think this is the case.

11. Melzer 2014, 240 and 241.

the diagonal line descending from the upper diagonal line of the -*ṣ*- while the hook of the -*ṭ*- resembles *ṛ* more than -*ṭ*-, as is seen in figures 7 and 8.

FIGURE 5. Scribe C *dṛṣṭī* (282v2).

FIGURE 6. Scribe C *pṛṣṭa* (291v4).

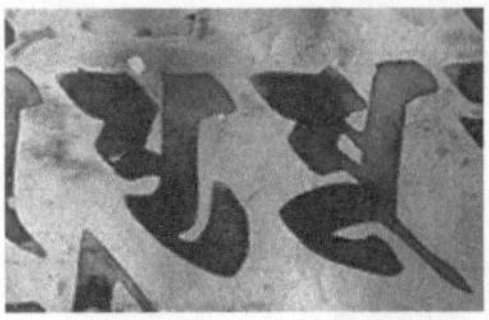

FIGURE 7. Scribe D *dṛṣṭī* (282r2).

FIGURE 8. Scribe D *dṛṣṭa* (282r2).

Although scribe C usually copied the verso side of a folio and scribe D the recto, sometimes they switched. In 281v scribe C copied the first two lines and scribe D the rest. Interestingly, on this folio alone, scribe D eschews an aspect of his usual style in order to imitate scribe C. This is made apparent when we see the telltale -*ṣṭ*- ligature written by both scribes. While scribe C's remains unchanged, as seen in figures 9 and 10, scribe D's are awkwardly contorted to mimic the style of scribe C, as shown in figures 11 and 12. The reason the two scribes worked together on the same side of this folio remains unclear. My own suspicion is that one was the master and the other an apprentice or at least one with less experience. Perhaps scribe C was setting an example for scribe D to study and emulate. Another possibility is that there was some sort of mix up in the workload for the day, and once scribe C realized he was writing the wrong side of the folio he handed it to scribe D to finish.

Figure 9. Scribe C *dṛṣṭa* (281v1).

Figure 10. Scribe C *dṛṣṭa* (281v1).

Figure 11. Scribe D *dṛṣṭa* (281v4).

Figure 12. Scribe D *dṛṣṭa* (281v5).

Starting at folio 287r we find a small number 1 in the margin of the lower lefthand corner written in what was at the time of the copying of the manuscript the new numeration system that is very similar to numbers in modern Devanāgarī and the basis of Hindu-Arabic numeration in use throughout the world today (figs. 13–24).[12] This number marks the first folio in a series of an alternate numeration system used in some sections of the manuscript. This particular series of numbers, first detected by Gudrun Melzer, runs in sequence in the lower margin to the left of the last line of the recto side of every folio throughout the manuscript from 287r–316r, marking off thirty folios. These folios span the end of the *Prāsādika-sūtra* and the entirety of the *Prasādanīya-*, *Pañcatraya-* (DĀ 17, 299v3–306r5), and *Māyājāla-* (DĀ 18, 306r5–317v5) sūtras.[13] With these numbers we see the end of scribe C and D's collaboration in this section of the manuscript. The purpose of this series seems to have been to mark off a certain section for scribe C to copy alone.

Figure 13. 287r7 #1.

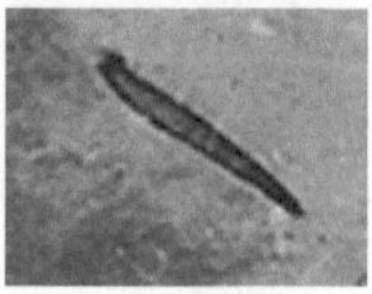

Figure 14. 288r8 #2.

Figure 15. 289r8 #3.

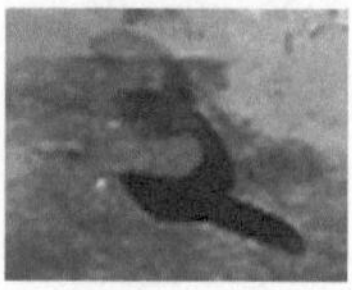

12. The number 4 is not preserved in the manuscript.

13. See Melzer 2014, 252–56 for further remarks on this numeration system used by the scribes.

FIGURE 16. 291r8 #5.

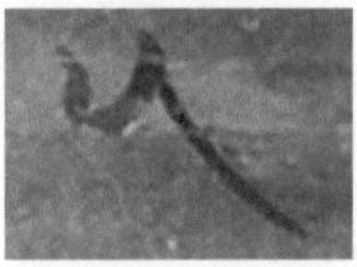

FIGURE 17. 292r8 # 6.

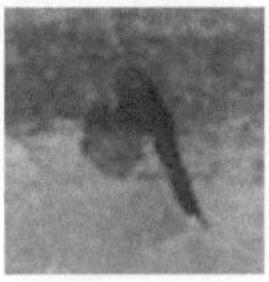

FIGURE 18. 293r8 #7.

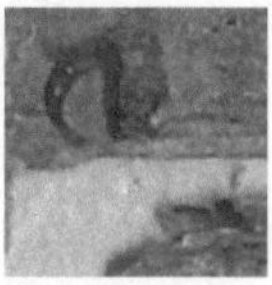

FIGURE 19. 294r8 #8.

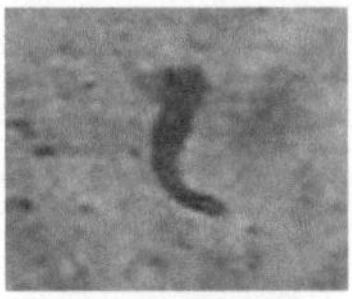

FIGURE 20. 295r8 #9.

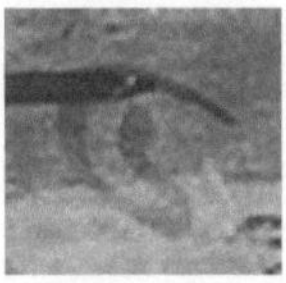

FIGURE 21. 296r8 # 10.

FIGURE 22. 297r8 #11.

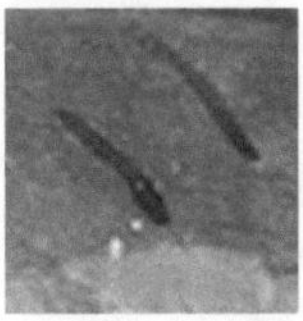

FIGURE 23. 298r8 #12.

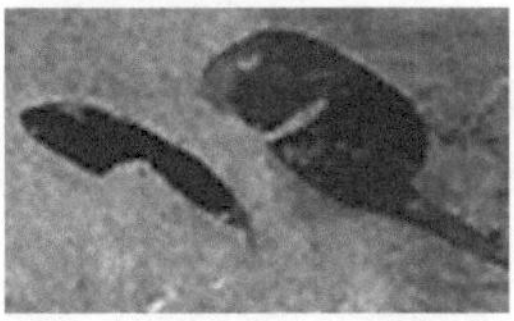

FIGURE 24. 299r8 #13.

The *Prasādanīya-sūtra* and the two immediately following texts, the *Pañcatraya-sūtra* and *Māyājāla-sūtra*, appear to be the work of scribe C alone. Reading scribe C's much more accurate solo efforts, it becomes clear that collaborative work between scribes may have led to some of the textual problems in the *Prāsādika-sūtra* that could have been avoided had the scribes each focused on their own portions of the text, and it raises the question of why the trading of folios between scribes was practiced. This collaborative effort may have served some purpose of efficiency or utility. Perhaps a scribe would write the recto side of a folio and set it aside to dry, moving on to another folio's recto side, and then the other scribe would continue on the verso side once it dried. As the two scribes traded back and forth in this way, one can imagine that not having to wait for the ink to dry allowed the copying to progress quickly, even if this was at the expense of clarity and continuity in the text. Indeed, from the numerous mistakes and textual problems seen throughout the manuscript, it would not be surprising to learn that speed was held in greater esteem than accuracy, for a certain carelessness is often evident. The numerous omissions of negations that are demanded by the content's context suggest either a lack of comprehension or a transmission that had become corrupted by the time the manuscript was copied—or perhaps both. One also finds corrections inscribed in the manuscript, but these are relatively rare and appear to be the result of a scribe either catching his own mistake or correcting an error already present in the witness he was copying, but including it in his copy in order to maintain the akṣara count for that line. The rather poor state of the copied composition of the content in the manuscript suggests that by the time the manuscript was copied, the *Dīrghāgama* as a text was possibly no longer as significant a work within the community[14] that held the manuscript as it might have been in previous centuries, and that the manuscript may have been copied either for making merit or for the sake of maintaining a library.[15]

Scribal Marks

One further paleographical issue I will touch upon here is the existence of what may be described as scribal marks in the manuscript. It is common to observe various marks and smudges on the birchbark owing to the general deterioration of the folios over the centuries, and also perhaps to rough handling when the manuscript was found. This is most often from the ink of one folio, or even of the uppermost layers of the birchbark, transferring onto another folio over centuries of lying atop one another. However, if one observes closely, it becomes apparent that there are also marks written by the scribes. Generally, these marks consist of dots or small ticks or dash-like strokes usually to the left of the lower-left quadrant of an akṣara. Both scribes C and D made these marks at various points throughout the manuscript, although it seems that scribe D made more of them. Many of them are likely drops of ink that dripped from the scribes' writing nibs either without them noticing or not caring (figs. 25–27). Occasionally, we see multiple dots that appear to be intentional (figs. 28, 37, and 38). Figure 28 shows a triangle of dots made by scribe D, while scribe C seems to have preferred making lines of dots, as seen in figures 37 and 38. These are likely attempts to adjust the ink on the writing nib, just as today one might draw a squiggle to discharge the ink in a ballpoint pen. Other marks (figs. 29 and 30) appear to have been made by the scribes, but it is not entirely clear for what

14. We cannot say with absolute certainty if this community was even affiliated with the Mūlasarvāstivāda tradition.

15. See Hartmann 2014, 156–57.

purpose. They may be "practice strokes" to clear excess ink from the nib in preparation for writing the often extremely thin lines used in portions of the akṣaras. This may explain why scribe D, apparently the less accomplished scribe, made them more often. Scribe D is also seen making similar but thicker strokes on the left and right sides of akṣaras, as can be seen in figure 32 and above in figure 7, where the top stroke of the *-dṛ-* akṣara is marked in this way. One also often sees a particular "broken slash" that I have only observed used by scribe D (figs. 33–36). These strokes were likely also a way to offload excess ink on the writing instrument, but the space in these strokes is puzzling. More research is needed, but this may be a peculiar habit developed by scribe D and may be useful in identifying his work in other sections of the manuscript or perhaps even in other manuscripts.

After a somewhat cursory examination of other Gilgit manuscripts, I can confirm that they contain similar scribal marks. Figure 39 reveals a mark in the manuscript of the *Saṅghabhedavastu* part of the *Vinayavastu* of the Mūlasarvāstivāda Vinaya that bears a striking resemblance to the marks we have seen used by scribe D. This is especially true when compared to figure 40, which shows a detail of the same mark found in figure 32. While it is tempting to speculate further, a more in-depth study of this phenomenon in other manuscripts from the Gilgit area is needed. For the time being I simply wish to point out the possibility that such marks may help identify the scriptoriums or even individual scribes that produced these manuscripts.

FIGURE 25.
273r3 scribe D.

FIGURE 26.
274r5 scribe D.

FIGURE 27.
273r7 scribe D.

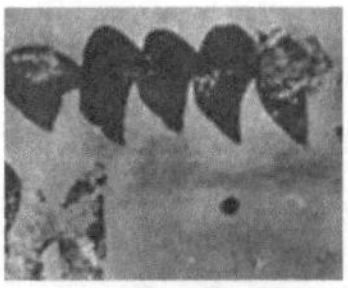

FIGURE 28.
277r8 scribe D.

FIGURE 29.
281r3 scribe D.

FIGURE 30.
281r4 scribe D.

FIGURE 31. 285r5 scribe D.

FIGURE 32. 281r4 scribe D.

FIGURE 33. 274r6 scribe D.

FIGURE 34. 277r2 scribe D.

FIGURE 35. 279r6 scribe D.

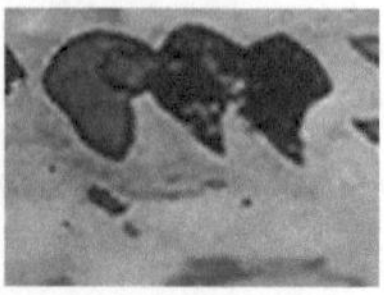

FIGURE 36. 286v6 scribe D.

FIGURE 37. 271r8 scribe C.

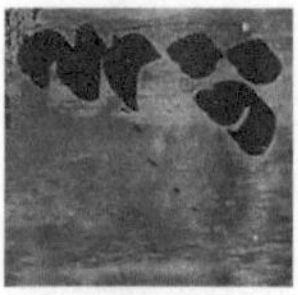

FIGURE 38. 297v8 scribe C.

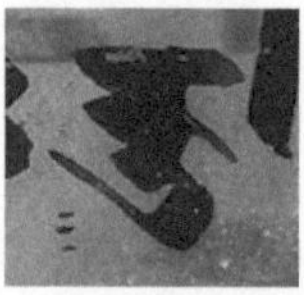

FIGURE 39. *Saṅghabhedavastu* 327a6, detail of mark near the string hole.[16]

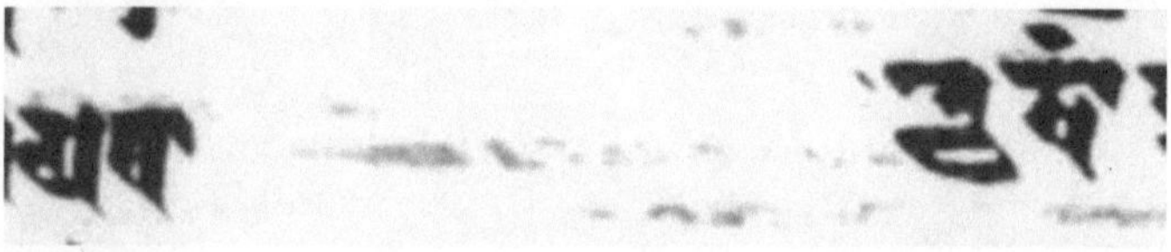

FIGURE 40. 281r4 scribe D, detail of mark near the string hole.

16. Photo detail of the *Saṅghabhedavastu* of the Mūlasarvāstivāda *Vinayavastvāgama* manuscript taken by Giuseppe Tucci; image courtesy Francesco Sferra.

On Repair to the Manuscript

If, as noted above, the *Dīrghāgama* manuscript witness from Gilgit under consideration here was somewhat carelessly copied, it is somewhat surprising to find multiple instances where the manuscript has been repaired. In the middle of 285v we find a birchbark patch applied over portions of lines 4 and 5 (fig. 41). In 285v4 the scribe wrote eight filler marks on the patch in the middle of the word *bhavanto*.[17] However, the patch is also applied to a smaller part of 285v5 where the scribe seemed content to continue writing the proper akṣaras of *ttaḥ abhavyaḥ* over the patch.[18] It appears that filler marks were only used on 285v4 and not 285v5, as the patch was likely applied to cover either a crack in the folio that already existed or a flaw in the bark that was judged to be in danger of eventually cracking. We find just such a crack on the reverse side of the patch on 285r4 (fig. 42). Indeed, the crack is even now apparent in the patch itself. No patch is observed on the reverse side of the folio at 285r4–5[19] (fig. 42), which may suggest that the damage was considered to be more severe on 285v4–5. Seven akṣaras into 295v8[20] there is a birchbark patch that is clearly seen to be pasted atop the manuscript (fig. 43). Just as in the patch found on 285v4 above, instead of the content of the sūtra, six filler marks are written on the patch. Filler marks appear regularly in the manuscript for a variety of reasons, especially (but not always) where the birchbark is warped or otherwise unsuitable to write on. However, the patch to the manuscript does not appear to be

17. 285v4: + + *r uṣitaṃ bra[hm]acaryaṃ kṛtaṃ karaṇīyaṃ nāpara*○*m asmād bhavaṃ prajānāmīti yo sau bhava* = = = = = = = = *nto bhikṣur bhavaty arthaṃ .ī* + + + + + + + + + + + + + +.

18. 285v5: *y. .. [h]ṛt. bhāro nuprāptasvakārtha parikṣīṇabhava*○*saṃyojanaḥ samyagājñāsuvimuktacittaḥ abhavyaḥ tasmiṃ samaye paṃcasthānāny [a] .y. .. [tu]. [k].* + + + + + *[abh]. .y[o] rhad bhikṣuḥ.*

19. 285r4: + ○ *.y. ..* + *.. ti bhavaṃto vyākṛtam itīdaṃ duḥkhasamudayo yam idaṃ duḫkhanirodham iy.[ṃ] .u. kh[a] .[i] .. [dh]. g[ā]mi[nī] pra[t]i .. .. ..* + + + +
285r5: + ○ *.. parivrājakā evaṃ vadeyuḥ kasmād bhavantaḥ śramaṇena gautamena ime dharmā ekāṃ .. na vyākṛtā iti pṛṣṭair idaṃ sy. r vacan. y[āḥ].*

20. 295v8: *[śat]i [cetasā]m api* = = = = = = *dharmān nādiśati yac ca tathā ādiśati tat sarvaṃ tat tathaiva bhavati nānyathā bhagavā[n] bhadanta paraṃ paśyaty av[i]tarkam avicāraṃ samādhiṃ samāpannaṃ dṛṣṭvā ca puna<<s te evaṃ bhavati>>.*

faulty. The bottom of the *-ṛ-* from *rahatkṛtaṃ* in line 7[21] has even been written on the patch, as it obscured that akṣara, suggesting that the repair to the manuscript was made before the copying process began, and the only reason for the filler marks seems to be to indicate the damage that had been repaired. In figure 44 we see 295r1,[22] the reverse side of folio 295v8 where the patch was made. There was no repair made to the recto side of the folio, and beyond a vertical line that appears to be an imprint from the repair on the verso, there is no sign of repair.

The repair to the manuscript here has even affected the akṣara count on at least one line of the manuscript. Figure 45 shows the right side of 295v8, on the right side of the folio with the repaired patch seen in figure 43. There the final six akṣaras of *s te evaṃ bhavati* are added underneath the bottom of the line, thus connecting to the last words on the line proper, *dṛṣṭvā ca puna*, in order to maintain the fidelity of the akṣara count so that the copying could continue without diverging from the exemplar. In 296v1–2,[23] seen in figure 46, we see another patch repairing the beginning of the line (see figure 47 for the reverse side of the repaired folio). Unfortunately, the latter portion of the folio is damaged and the final akṣaras of 296v1–2 are missing, so we cannot confirm that akṣaras were added interlinearly to keep the akṣara count. Conversely, the beginning of 287v8[24] (fig. 48) is damaged and the first six akṣaras are lost, but we find *kāmaguṇaiḥ* added below the end of the line, suggesting that there was a repair made to the manuscript at the beginning of the line.[25] A fourth patch is seen in the *Māyājāla-sūtra*

21. 295v7: *bhāṣitam a[py ā]diśati rahatkṛtaṃ rahobhāṣitam apy ādiśati dūre 'py ādiśaty antike py ādiśati atīt{{ānā}}m apy ādiśaty anāg[a]tam apy ādiśati pūrvavac cittam apy ādi.*

22. 295r1: *[bhagavata ṛ]ddhir ity ucyate bhagavān bhadanta sarvaśa ākiṃcanyāyatanaṃ samatikramya naiva saṃjñānāsaṃjñāyatanam upasaṃpadya viharatīyaṃ bhadanta bhagavata riddhir ity ucyate bhagavān bhadanta.*

23. 296v1: = = = *[=]gato vā āta .t. .v. .. [p]rahāṇānvayā bhāvanānvayā bahulīkārānvayā .. m. [ṅma]nasikārātayā tadrūpaṃ śāntaṃ cetaḥsamādhi .[e] .. sa[m]ādhiṃ spṛśati ..* + + + + + + + +

296v2: = = = = *tvāriṃśataṃ saṃvarttavivarttakalpān samanusmarati .. syaivaṃ bhavati etāvad .. .. lokaḥ saṃvarttiṣyate ca vivarttiṣyate ca yāvad e[v]. .. yānvayam a .i ..* + + + + + + + + +.

24. 287v8: + + + + + + .. *.ātmā uc[ch]id[ya]te na vinaśyati na bhavati paraṃ maranād etāvad ayam ātmā samyaksamucchinno bhavati saṃti bhikṣava eke śramaṇabrāhmanā evaṃdṛṣṭaya evaṃvādino yataś cāyam ātmā paṃcabhiḥ <<kāmaguṇaiḥ>>.*

25. While the smaller lettering of *kāmagunaiḥ* may appear at a glance as another hand, there is no evidence that such interlinear writings in this *Dīrghāgama* manuscript witness were

on folio 307v2 toward the middle of the folio about sixteen akṣaras from the end of the line (fig. 49). This patch offers the clearest evidence of corresponding repair to the reverse side of the folio on 307r8 (fig. 50), where it appears that both sides of the manuscript have been repaired.

These repairs were probably implemented before or during the copying process, for if they were repaired after the copying process, there would be no need to add akṣaras interlinearly. Or, if they were made to the manuscript while it was blank, the use of filler marks may suggest that the scribe chose not to write on the repaired areas out of concern for the structural integrity of the manuscript where it had been patched. In either case, these repairs indicate that a certain level of care was taken in the manuscript's copying, at least regarding the birchbark the sūtras were written upon. The reasons for this type of repair remain unclear. We have seen that while filler marks are usually written on these patches, a few akṣaras, or parts of akṣaras, are also often included. Whether akṣaras were written on these repaired sections appears to have been based on the judgment of the scribe, who might not have found them too fragile to risk writing text upon. Holes, warps, and knots in the birchbark are seen frequently throughout the manuscript. While it is quite probable that the holes found in the manuscript were made in the ensuing centuries following its production, the members of the scriptorium did not seem overly concerned with warps and knots in the folios themselves and generally used filler marks over such impurities or simply avoided writing on those areas (figs. 51 and 52).[26] Therefore, it seems most probable that these repairs were made to patch holes or structural problem points that were present in the manuscript folios when they were first produced, further suggesting that they were made before the scribes began copying the text of the manuscript. However, this is difficult to substantiate when we look at the reverse side of the patches. Evidence of the repair is visible. However, no filler marks are used and evidence of damage on the reverse of these repaired folios is not always immediately apparent. A close examination of the physical folios is required in order to shed light

added later by anyone beyond the copying scriptorium or that there were any later textual corrections made (this further suggests that the manuscript was not used for active study). In fact, this is not even a separate script but rather an example of Gilgit-Bamiyan Type II script written so small that the calligraphic elements are not present.

26. Filler marks were additionally used, as their name indicates, simply to fill empty space and were additionally used for ending lines in order to provide symmetry to the manuscript. This is also seen commonly in later Buddhist manuscripts from other areas.

on the situation as it stands. Although it seems most likely that these repairs were made to the birchbark during the creation of the folios themselves by whomever manufactured them, it is perhaps worth noting that the patches to the manuscript thus far uncovered all occur on folios copied by scribe C, but an exhaustive search for other patches must be made throughout the entirety of the manuscript before we can speculate if the repairs have anything to do with this particular scribe.

FIGURE 41. 285v4–5, repair to the manuscript with eight filler signs (line 4) and *ttaḥ abhavyaḥ* (line 5).

FIGURE 42. 285r4–5, reverse side of the patch on 285v4–5 (fig. 41).

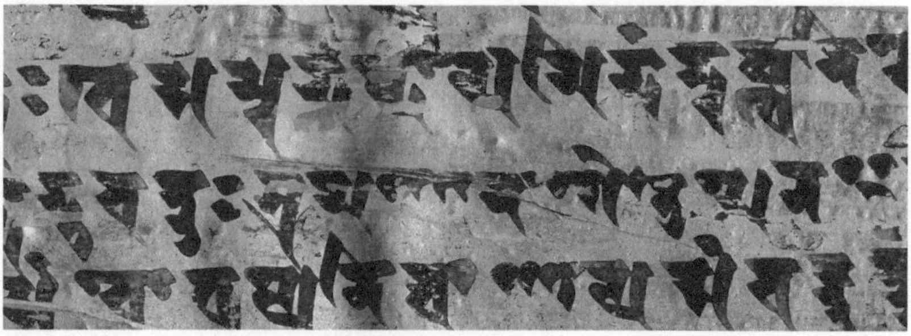

FIGURE 43. 295v8, repair to the ms. with six filler signs.

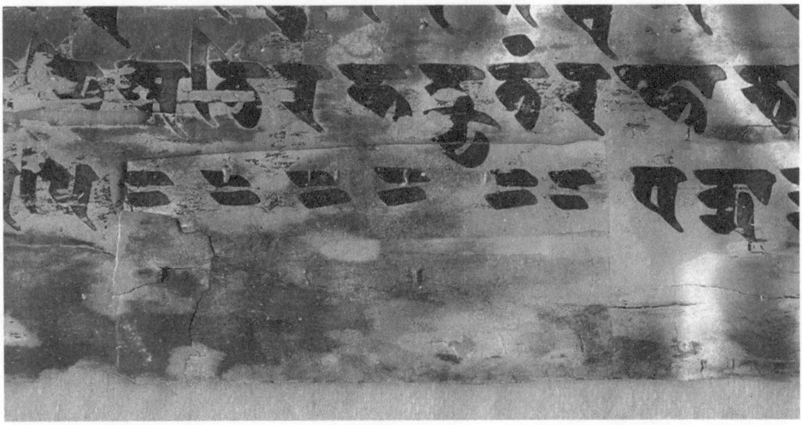

FIGURE 44. 295r1, the reverse of the patch on 295v8 (fig. 43).

FIGURE 45. 295v8, *puna<<s te evaṃ bhavati>>* (six akṣaras) added to ms. to compensate for damage.

FIGURE 46. 296v1–2 repair to the manuscript.

FIGURE 47. 296r7–8, reverse side of repaired patch on 296v1–2 (fig. 46).

FIGURE 48. 287v8, <<*kāmaguṇaiḥ*>> written below bottom line.

FIGURE 49. Patch on folio 307v2: *bhavati* = = =.

FIGURE 50. Patch on 307r8: *'ham asmīti manye*. Repair on the reverse side of repair on 307v2 (fig. 49).

FIGURE 51. Example of a knot in the birchbark where the scribe used filler marks.

FIGURE 52. Example of a knot in the birchbark where the scribe simply wrote around the knot.

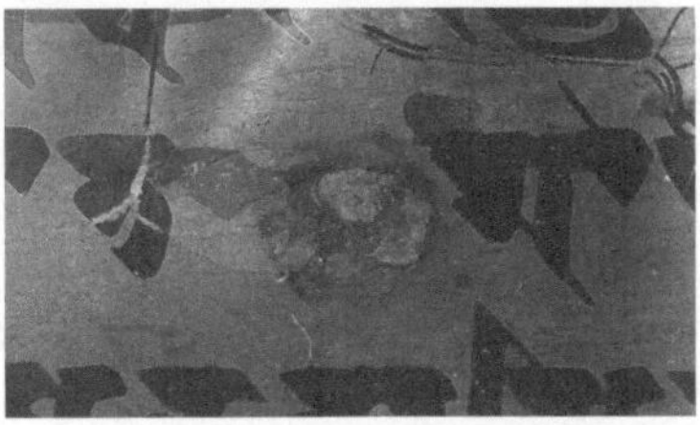

Repair to the manuscript folios can be observed in other manuscripts produced in the Gilgit area to a greater or lesser extent. While an exhaustive examination of all extant Gilgit material remains a desideratum, I have made a preliminary examination of five facsimile editions of the Gilgit manuscripts preserved at the National Archives of India, each containing either a long manuscript or multiple shorter manuscripts.[27]

Only one of these collections of manuscript images failed to contain evidence of repair to a manuscript: Kudo's *Avadānas and Miscellaneous Texts*, which contains multiple shorter texts copied on what appear to have been rather high-quality birchbark folios when the manuscripts were produced.[28] The manuscript of the *Samādhirāja-sūtra*, a lengthy Mahāyāna sūtra of nearly two hundred folios, contains just two instances of repair that I was able to discern, figures 53 and 54. Beyond that the manuscript appears to be generally free from structural issues that might make repair necessary. The birchbark folios even seem to have only a small number of knots present throughout the manuscript.

Of the four manuscripts collected in Mette and company's *Further Mahāyānasūtras*, I only found repair in two instances in the *Kāraṇḍavyūha* (figs. 55 and 56), a relatively long text spanning around eighty folios, although the manuscript folios are of the shorter type often used for less lengthy texts as opposed to the longer folios used in the *Dīrghāgama* and other manuscripts of extensive length. The patches made to the *Kāraṇḍavyūha* are not visible on the reverse side of the folios to which they were made. The patch in figure 56 is of special note, for on the upper lefthand side of the patch on line 6 we see a clear instance of a darker lenticel, ubiquitous in birchbark manuscripts, being cut off.

The *Vinaya Texts* facsimile volume edited by Shayne Clarke represents only a portion of the very lengthy Mūlasarvāstivāda *Vinayavastvāgama* manuscript. It is clear from the facsimiles that the quality of the manuscript folios is very good, and I have observed patches in only five of the extant 212 folios, with two of the patches exemplified here in figures 57–60. The repair to this manuscript appears to use a different technique, or perhaps was designed to solve a different problem, than the repair seen in other manuscripts from Gilgit. These patches all appear to show a lighter portion of birchbark in the center surrounded by a cut birchbark square of a darker color. It is unclear why this type of repair is seen exclusively in this manuscript. I did not find any patches in the thirty-eight *Prātimokṣa* folios and nineteen *Karmavācanā* folios also contained in the *Vinaya Texts* volume.

The final facsimile edition I have consulted is Karashima and company's

27. Specifically, I have examined Clarke 2014, Karashima et al. 2016, Kudo 2017, Kudo, Fukita, and Tanaka 2018, and Mette et al. 2017.

28. Kudo 2017.

Mahāyāna Texts: Prajñāpāramitā Texts (1). This volume contains only two sūtra manuscripts, the *Larger Prajñāpāramitā* and the *Vajracchedikā*. The *Vajracchedikā*, a brief manuscript of just twelve folios of which seven are extant, does not appear to contain any instances of repair. If we accept that repairs were most commonly performed on blank folios before the manuscripts were copied, then this may provide some support to the idea that shorter manuscripts were made with better quality birchbark and were thus not often subjected to such repair. The *Larger Prajñāpāramitā*, a very long and mostly intact manuscript of 307 folios with only ten folios no longer extant, however, contains numerous instances of repair, often continuously from folio to folio throughout large spans of the manuscript. Several examples from among the many instances can be seen in figures 61–69. Interestgingly, it appears that the first half of the manuscript contains more repairs than the second. Those who made the repairs often seemed to be concerned with the aesthetic nature of the repairs, apparently trying to match up the horizontal level of the darker birchbark lenticels in the patches with underlying lenticels in the manuscript, as we see, for example, in figure 61. Less commonly, we find rather haphazardly applied patches where the birchbark lenticel is radiating at a 20-degree southeast angle, such as in figure 63. Curiously, the bottom line of the patch in figure 63 (fol. 15r6) appears to be written atop the patch, and the lower quadrants of these akṣaras appear to be obscured by the repair. This would suggest that the repair had been made *after* the sūtra had been copied; it is the only such instance I have uncovered. All other instances of repair I have examined seem to have been made before the copying process began. In figure 66 we find the lenticels, somewhat shockingly, at a 90-degree angle, rising vertically, when the folios of these manuscripts were designed nearly exclusively so that the dark lenticels run horizontally along the folios. This was likely the surest way to obtain the birchbark in the necessary lengths for manuscript production. In figure 67, the corresponding patch on the verso side of the repair seen in figure 66, we see that a second patch seems to have been applied that does not correspond in shape or size to the patch on the recto side of the folio. Perhaps most noteworthy, we find instances where a patch running the entire vertical length of the folios is applied. In figures 68 and 69, the recto and verso of the same folio, we see such repair and find that again the darker lenticels of the birchbark are vertical to the rest of the folio. Such repair indicates that the structural integrity of such folios had been completely lost and are perhaps examples of a broken folio being made whole.

Figure 53.
Samādhirāja-sūtra 431v1–2.[29]

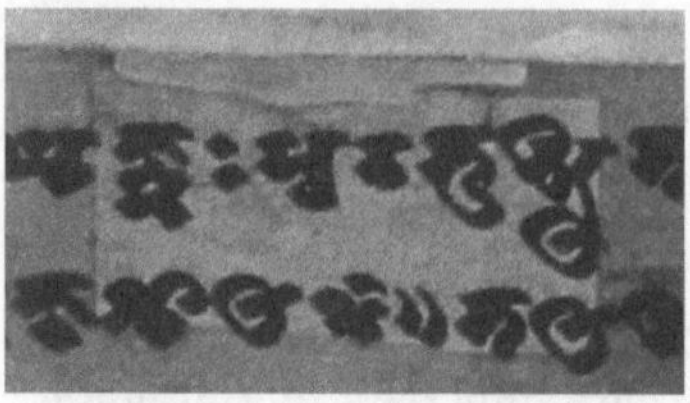

Figure 54.
Samādhirāja-sūtra 115v4–5.[30]

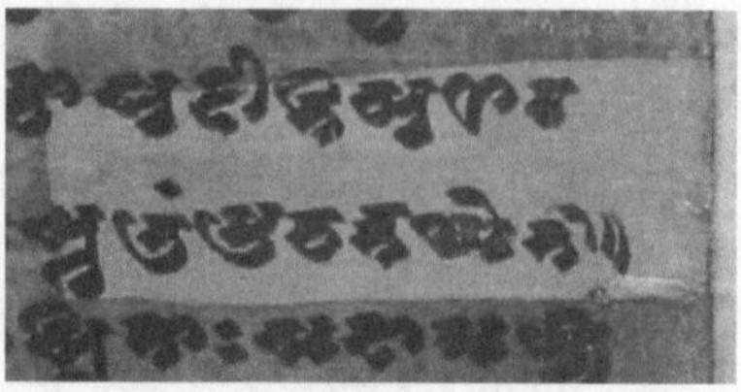

Figure 55. *Kāraṇḍavyūha* 22r3.[31]

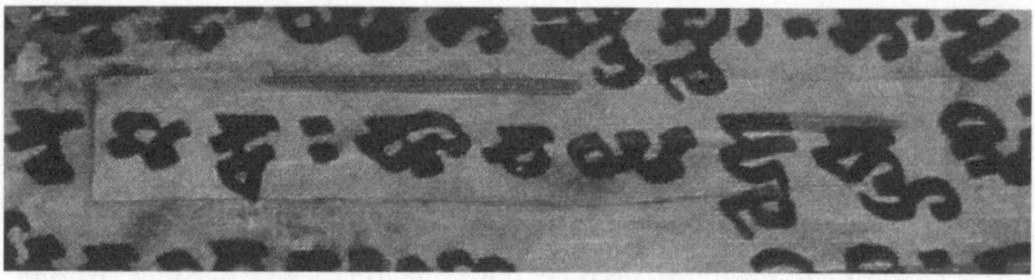

Figure 56.
Kāraṇḍavyūha 23r6–8.[32]

Figure 57.
Bhaiṣajyavastu 205rL<?>6.[33]

29. Kudo 2017, 39.
30. Kudo 2017, 110.
31. Mette et al. 2017, 77.
32. Mette et al. 2017, 78.
33. Clarke 2014, 100.

FIGURE 58.
Bhaiṣajyavastu 205vL<?>5.[34]

FIGURE 59.
Kaṭhinavastu 277r6–7.[35]

FIGURE 60.
Kaṭhinavastu 277r6–7.[36]

FIGURE 61.
Larger Prajñāpāramitā 13r3–4.[37]

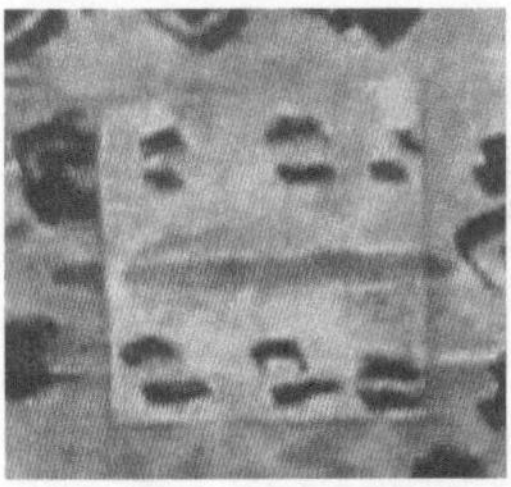

FIGURE 62. *Larger Prajñāpāramitā* 13v8–9, reverse of figure 61.[38]

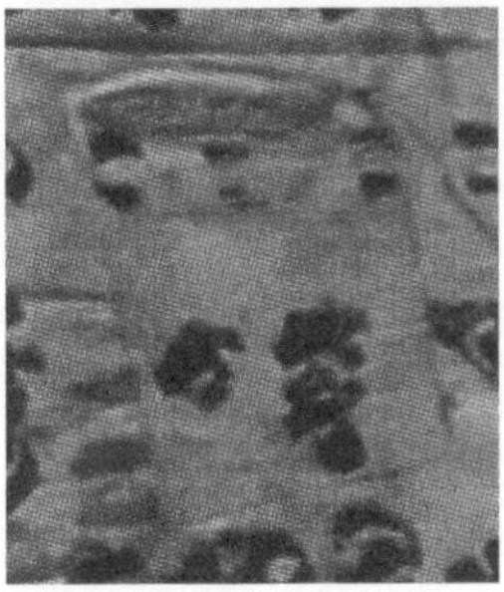

FIGURE 63. *Larger Prajñāpāramitā* 15r4–6.[39]

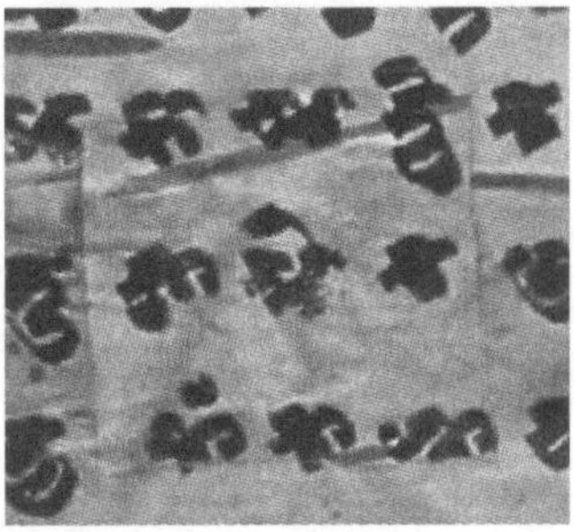

34. Clarke 2014, 101.
35. Clarke 2014, 172.
36. Clarke 2014, 172.
37. Karashima et al. 2016, 13.
38. Karashima et al. 2016, 13.
39. Karashima et al. 2016, 15.

Figure 64. *Larger Prajñāpāramitā* 15r4–5.[40]

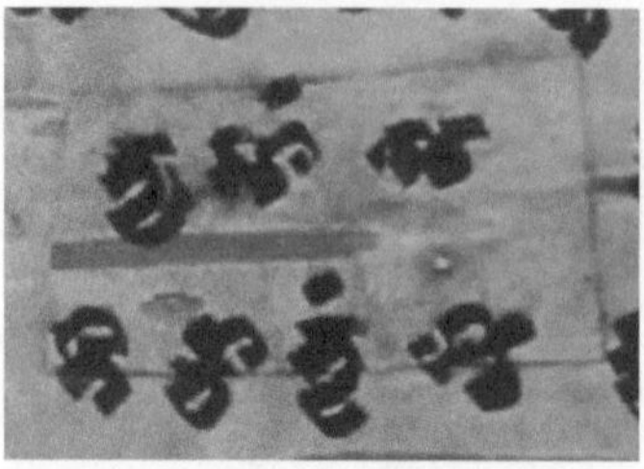

Figure 65. *Larger Prajñāpāramitā* 21r10–11.[41]

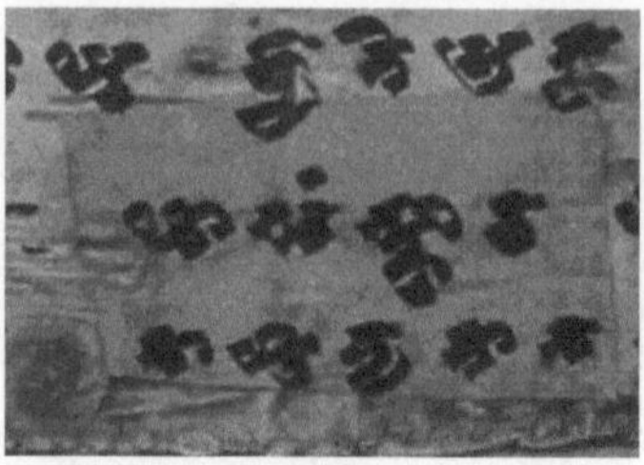

Figure 66. *Larger Prajñāpāramitā* 23r6.[42]

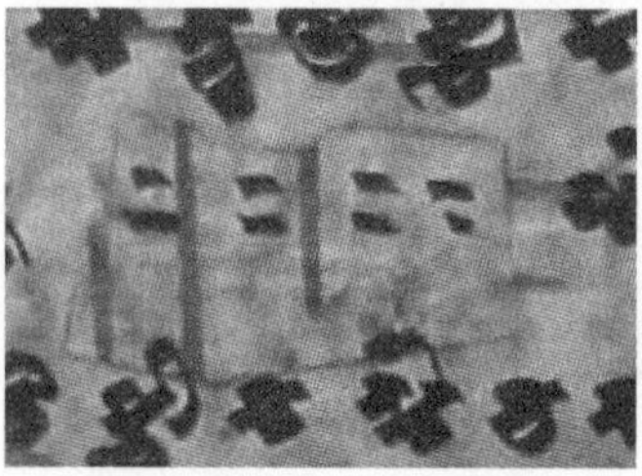

Figure 67. *Larger Prajñāpāramitā* 23v6, reverse of figure 66.[43]

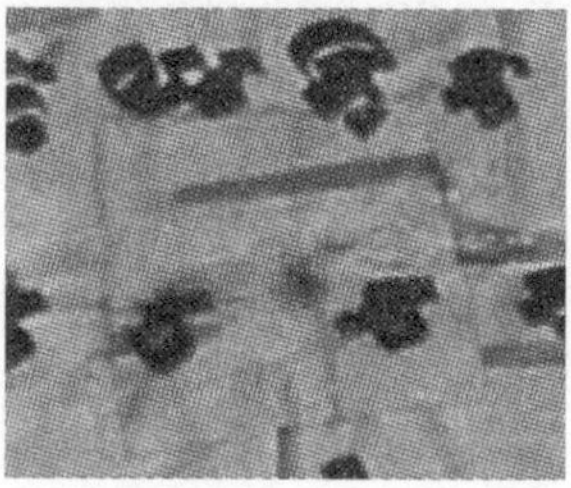

40. Karashima et al. 2016, 15.

41. Karashima et al. 2016, 21.

42. Karashima et al. 2016, 23.

43. Karashima et al. 2016, 23.

Figure 68.
Larger Prajñāpāramitā 61r1–14.[44]

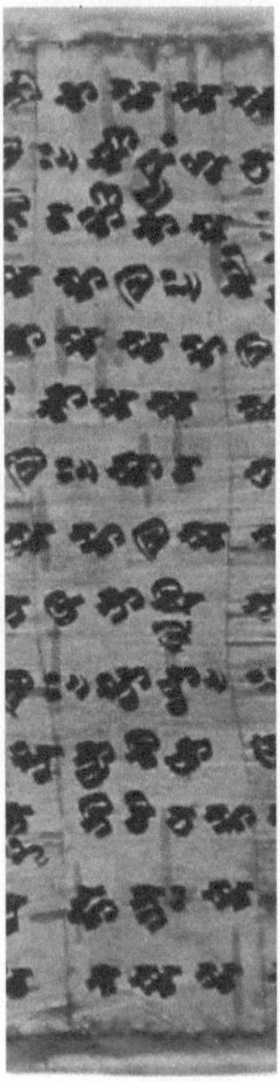

Figure 69.
Larger Prajñāpāramitā 61v1–13, reverse of figure 68.[45]

Conclusions

Where does this leave us? When contemplating the production of the *Dīrghāgama* manuscript witness from Gilgit, we must imagine a group of scribes working in tandem. Either this group had only a minimal knowledge of the material being copied and/or its language of transmission, or if they did have knowledge of the material and its language, they were more concerned with the pace of copying than with its content. They planned their work ahead and divvied up the number of folios to be copied between them, sometimes marking folio spans with marginal numeration.

44. Karashima et al. 2016, 60.

45. Karashima et al. 2016, 60.

Sometimes the work was dispersed by the length of the component sūtras, but other times they worked in teams with little apparent regard for breaks between sūtras. They often traded folios back and forth by verso and recto, which may have been the fastest way to copy a span of folios. They only rarely seemed to share the same side of a folio, and this may be an example of some confusion in the copying process or of the resumption of work after a pause. We may speculate that the scriptorium consisted of scribes of both greater and lesser accomplishment and provided some aspect of training to the less accomplished scribes. Individual scribes appear to have made unique marks on the folios in the course of their copying. Further study of such marks may allow scholars to deduce information about the skill level of a particular scribe or even help to identify the work of a scribe or scriptorium across multiple manuscripts.

The folios appear to have undergone repair prior to copying, although we cannot say that patches were never added after copying. We also cannot be certain what criteria warranted this preemptive repair, as irregularities in the birchbark material were generally worked around. Such repair has been witnessed in other manuscripts from the region and appears to have been implemented by whomever produced the birchbark folios. It is unclear if the scribes of the scriptorium were trained only to copy the texts or also to prepare the folios. In either case, it appears that longer manuscripts, which consist of more folios that are generally larger in size than those of shorter manuscripts, contained more instances of repair. Whoever commissioned a given manuscript may have gotten a better financial deal on more folios by accepting lower quality material. Perhaps the supply of birchbark serving as a raw material was not steady and, for whatever reason, it was not possible to ensure a consistent quality of the birchbark folios. The cost or ease of obtaining birchbark folios would have been less for the smaller quantities necessary for shorter texts, which were often several centimeters shorter in length or thinner than the folios traditionally used for longer texts. One might also speculate that some texts were considered of particular importance or value and the production of their manuscripts were expressly commissioned with finer material. This might be a factor in how similarly lengthy texts such as the Mūlasarvāstivāda *Vinayavastvāgama* and *Larger Prajñāpāramitā* manuscripts would have such disparate amounts of repair. If this were indeed a consideration in manuscript production, it would raise further questions, such as to whom would certain manuscripts be considered more important than others:

the artisans producing the folios, the scribes (if they were a separate group from the folio manufacturers), the donor/s, or a community of monastics?

The instances of repaired patches discussed here indicate that the practice of manuscript repair appears to have been widespread in the Gilgit region. However, these examples are merely the tip of the iceberg, and a thorough analysis of the entire Gilgit corpus and, indeed, Gilgit-Bamiyan type manuscripts produced throughout the whole of the area of Greater Gandhāra still needs to be undertaken. Such a study may one day allow us to place specific manuscripts into groups discerned by the material they were made from and the type of repair they were subjected to, fine-tuning our understanding of the networks of Buddhist groups in that area and time. Ideally, a thorough examination of the entirety of elements of production would have been made in tandem with the editing of the texts. However, the portions of the *Dīrghāgama* manuscript that have been edited were completed by scholars with disparate levels of interest in such matters. This makes the situation somewhat difficult, but such aspects should at least be examined with the portions remaining to be edited. The physical manuscript should also be reexamined by a skilled conservator who might be able to finally separate the folios that are fused together. The anonymous owner of the largest collection of folios has not expressed an interest in pursuing such an action. Still, it may be possible if the proper funding is raised.

Ultimately, all such marks and manuscript repair that have been discussed here should be noted not just in the *Dīrghāgama* manuscript but throughout the entirety of the Gilgit-Bamiyan type manuscripts from Greater Gandhāra so that we may make some sense of them in total, perhaps allowing us to definitively say whether these repairs and aspects of sūtra copying are just individual quirks in the writing styles of certain scribes and elements of manuscript production used solely by this scriptorium, or whether they were common throughout the region in the production of Buddhiṣt and other textual material. This renders more acute the already overdue need to re-edit and translate the Gilgit material that was discovered in the 1930s as well as the need to create new images of these manuscripts with modern equipment. As for images, endeavors such as the facsimile series of the material at the National Archives of India make it much easier for scholars to examine this material, but much more needs to be done in coming years to locate the collections that remain lost and digitize such material in high resolution and in color so that it may be made widely available. Finally, as new material from the area occasionally comes to light, we should be mindful of these issues in the hope of understanding where these manuscripts were produced and by whom, perhaps down to the individual scribe.

3. Structure and Synopsis

Structure and Synopsis of DĀ 15, the *Prāsādika-sūtra*

The structure of the *Prāsādika-sūtra* takes the form of a consultation between Cunda and Ānanda and then the Buddha. However, although Manné, in her study of the various categories of suttas in the Nikāyas, identifies the *Pāsādika-sutta* as a consultation—indeed, the only consultation in the *Dīgha-nikāya*[46]—the greater portion of the *Prāsādika-sūtra*'s content actually consists of an imagined debate between hypothetical wanderers who are adherents of another faith (*anyatīrthikaparivrājaka*) questioning Buddhist doctrine, and faithful monks defending their doctrines narrated by the Buddha. From the summary verse (*antaroddāna*) of the *Prāsādika-sūtra*, we see that the content is divided into thirteen[47] general topics that are each fleshed out over several passages:

> *durākh)yāt(a)ś ca svākhyāto n(a)vaś śāstā* (**290r4**) *tathāgat(a)ḥ*
> *u(dra)ko ye te dharmā nā(nādṛṣṭiś ca cīvaram)*
> *(su)khālaya(saptaphalā v)y(ākṛtāvyākṛtena ca)*
> \+ + + +[48] .. *(p)ū(r)v(ā)ntāparāntena paṃcakāḥ* (||) ||

These keywords represent the following subjects:

DĀ 15.4–5: Ill-Proclaimed Dharma and Vinaya (*durākhyātaḥ*)
DĀ 15.6–7: Well-Proclaimed Dharma and Vinaya (*svākhyātaḥ*)

46. Manné 1990, 75.

47. Or possibly fourteen depending on whether the small, unreconstructed gap in the fourth line contains another keyword or is merely some metrical filler. See the note below.

48. For discussion on this lacuna, please see the notes 917 and 920 in the body of the edition below.

DĀ 15.8–15: A Tathāgata Who Is a New Teacher (*navaś śāstā tathāgataḥ*)
DĀ 15.16: Udraka Rāmaputra (*udrakaḥ*)
DĀ 15.17: Those Doctrines That Are Conducive to Dwelling Happily (*ye te dharma*)
DĀ 15.18–21: Monks of Various Views (*nānādṛṣṭiḥ*)
DĀ 15.22: Robes and That Which Is Allowed by the Buddha (*cīvaram*)
DĀ 15.23–25: Devotion to Pleasure (*sukhālayaḥ*)
DĀ 15.26: Seven Fruits (*saptaphalāḥ*)
DĀ 15.27–36: That Which Is and Is Not Explained by the Ascetic Gautama (*vyākṛtāvyākṛtena*)
DĀ 15.37, 15.38, 15.40, and 15.42: The Beginning (*pūrvāntaḥ*)
DĀ 15.37, 15.39, 15.41 and 15.42: The End (*aparāntaḥ*)
DĀ 15.39.d and 15.41.d:[49] The Fivefold Fallacy of Nirvāṇa in the Present Existence (*paṃcakāḥ*)

The first half of the sūtra is generally clear and flows relatively seamlessly from topic to topic, but as can be seen by the sometimes disparate section numbers under some topics, the presentation of the topics in the latter half is somewhat complex in that some topics are spread across multiple sections and some sections encompass multiple topics. The topic on the fivefold fallacy of nirvāṇa in the present state of existence is discussed seemingly in passing in subsections of sections devoted to other topics: DĀ 15.39d and 15.41d. These are, respectively, in the sections on the beginning and the end, while the five sensual pleasures, which make up a great part of this topic, are also discussed in DĀ 15.24b and 15.25b, which both fall under broader sections dealing with devotion to pleasure. The sections on the beginning and the end are themselves blended together, switching from one to another while generally repeating the same content for each topic. The topics themselves are surrounded by a frame story involving the death of Nirgrantha Jñātiputra. The introductory frame is rather detailed, repeating the same events thrice in the span of three sections, the first time as it is experienced by Cunda, the second as relayed to Ānanda, and the third as relayed to the Buddha. The sūtra, however, ends quite abruptly, and the concluding frame

49. Also note DĀ 15.24b and 15.25b, which discuss the same five sensual pleasures (*kāmaguṇa*) referred to here.

is very short. While the manuscript is heavily damaged and the concluding frame is mostly lost, it is clear that it cannot have been more than a few cursory lines.

The *Prāsādika-sūtra* begins with the novice named Cunda going to Pāpā[50] to spend the rainy season, only to find that Nirgrantha Jñātiputra, widely known as Mahāvīra, the founder of Jainism, has recently died and the Nirgranthas (Jains) have fallen into dispute because their doctrines were ill-proclaimed and their teacher was not a buddha. Cunda goes to where the Buddha is staying among the Śākyans and informs Ānanda of Nirgrantha Jñātiputra's death, and Ānanda in turn informs the Buddha. After this frame story sets up the scene, the Buddha proceeds to deliver the sūtra, which primarily consists of debate scenarios in which a monk may find himself and how to respond (DĀ 15.1–3).

The Buddha explains to Cunda that a disciple who correctly practices an ill-proclaimed dharma and vinaya (doctrine and discipline) espoused by one who is not a buddha is blameworthy, as is the teacher and the dharma, while a disciple who does not correctly practice an ill-proclaimed dharma is praiseworthy (DĀ 15.4–5). Conversely, a disciple who incorrectly practices a well-proclaimed dharma espoused by a buddha is blameworthy while the teacher and the dharma are praiseworthy, and a disciple who correctly practices a well-proclaimed dharma is praiseworthy (DĀ 15.6–7).

The Buddha then explains the various states of the dharma and vinaya of a tathāgata throughout his teaching career from a recently awakened buddha with poor students to a buddha who is senior, whose fame and holy life (*brahmacarya*) have spread widely, and who has capable disciples (DĀ 15.8–15). After uttering what is perhaps the line most indicative of the *Prāsādika-sūtra*: "Certainly, Cunda, insofar as there are those regarded as teachers, I do not consider even a single teacher equal to myself,"[51] the Buddha proceeds to discuss his former teacher, Udraka Rāmaputra, and his inferior (yet enigmatic) teaching of "seeing, one does not see" (DĀ 15.16). The Buddha then reveals the doctrines that are conducive to benefit and happiness in this and the next existence: *sūtra*, *geya*, *vyākaraṇa*, *gāthā*, *uddāna*, *nidāna*, *avadāna*, *itivṛttaka*, *jātaka*, *vaipulya*, *adbhutadharma*, and *upadeśa*, which together make the *dvādaśāṅga dharma pravacana* (the twelvefold classification of

50. Pāvā in Pali, one of the capital cities of the Malla republics.

51. *Yāvantaḥ khalu cunda{ḥ} śāstriṃsaṃmatā nāham eka<ṃ> śāstāram (apy āt)m(a)nā samasamaṃ samanup(a)ś(yām)i.*

[Buddhist] instruction)[52] and should be recited so that the Buddha's holy life might be maintained (DĀ 15.17).

At this point the Buddha stops addressing Cunda, whose name ceases to appear in the sūtra, and instead addresses all the monks assembled, "who are of various views, various abilities, various inclinations, and various opinions" about how they should deal with problems involving the meaning and wording (*artha* and *vyañjana*) of his dharma. He does this by explaining the proper way to correct other monks if they were to grasp the meaning of the dharma but not the wording, the wording and not the meaning, both incorrectly, or both correctly, which of course does not need correction (DĀ 15.18–21). The Buddha then lays out the items he allows the community of monks to use and the proper way of using them: a robe, food, lodging, and medicine (DĀ 15.22).

From here a large portion of the sūtra is devoted to the Buddha, who in continuing to address the assembled monks delves into possible critiques by wanderers who are adherents of other faiths. He begins this rhetorical debate with a hypothetical opponent accusing the ascetic followers of the Śākya of being devoted to pleasure. The Buddha explains that there are two types of addiction to pleasure: one to be feared and one not to be feared. The ascetics who follow the Śākya are devoted in the correct way, which should not be feared, in that they reject pleasure that is dependent on the five sensual pleasures (*kāmaguṇa*) and five negative acts: intentionally taking life, stealing, engaging in sexual misconduct, lying, and ingesting intoxicants (DĀ 15.23–25). The Buddha then instructs the monks to explain the seven fruits expected from such positive devotion to pleasure, ranging from highest knowledge in the present existence to traveling upward in the stream of transmigration in future births (DĀ 15.26).

The focus of the hypothetical non-Buddhist disputants now shifts to that which the Buddha does and does not explain. They ask if the Buddha explains whether the world is eternal, whether life is different from embodiment, and whether a tathāgata exists after death. The answer to these questions is "no" (DĀ 15.27). Then the monks are asked why the Buddha does not explain these things. The answer is that they are not associated with the goal of salvation (DĀ 15.28). The disputants ask what the Buddha does explain, and the answer is, of course, the four noble truths (DĀ 15.29). Why have those doctrines been explained by the Buddha? They are explained

52. Although they are not referred to as such in the text.

because they are associated with the goal of salvation (DĀ 15.30). The hypothetical opponent then claims that Buddhist doctrines are uncertain, as some things are explained by the Buddha and some are not. The Buddhist retort: "Our doctrines are certain" (DĀ 15.31). What are these certain doctrines? They are being liberated from negative influences of existence and ignorance by proper mental attention to the seven factors of awakening (*saptabodhipakṣa*). Such a person is an arhat, unable to intentionally kill, steal, engage in sexual misconduct, deliberately lie, or derive pleasure from amassing possessions (DĀ 15.32). The disputant then asks why some things are explained at different points in time while other things are not. The Buddha's response is that things from the past, future, and present are only explained if they are associated with the goal (DĀ 15.33–34). The Buddha then explains that this is all known, perceived, learned, understood, and completely, fully, perfectly realized by the Tathāgata,[53] which is why he is called the Tathāgata (DĀ 15.35). The next section ends the hypothetical debate, stating that the Tathāgata roars a complete lion's roar, and like a lotus rising from the water is unsullied by that water, the Tathāgata rises from the world and yet is unsullied by the world (DĀ 15.36).

At this point the Buddha states that he has correctly explained all views associated with the beginning and end of existence and goes on to explain how they are incorrectly stated by other groups of ascetics and brahmins (DĀ 15.37). Incorrect views regarding the beginning concern the eternality of the self and the world, eternality of the self and suffering, the creation of the self and the world, and the creation of the self and suffering (DĀ 15.38). The Buddha restates these incorrect views about the beginning and, after confirming that some ascetics and brahmins actually hold such views, explains that he does not accept them because different ascetics and brahmins hold different opinions and there is no consensus (DĀ 15.40). Incorrect views regarding the end of existence concern the *saṃjñīvāda*, *asaṃjñīvāda*, *naivasaṃjñīnāsaṃjñīvāda*, *ucchedavāda*, and *dṛṣṭadharmanirvāṇavāda* views[54] (DĀ 15.39). The Buddha restates these incorrect views about the end and, after confirming that some ascetics and brahmins actually hold such views, explains that he does not accept them because different ascetics and brahmins hold different opinions and there is no consensus (DĀ 15.41).

53. Note the similarity to the statement made by Śāriputra in DĀ 16.18 below.

54. The names of these various views are not explicitly stated in the *Prāsādika-sūtra*.

The final folios of the manuscript are heavily damaged, but the sūtra ends with the Buddha making a brief, final refutation before a very short conclusion to the frame story, the only part that survives, again states the location: the mango forest of the Śākyan named Medha (DĀ 15.42).

Structure and Synopsis of DĀ 16, the *Prasādanīya-sūtra*

The structure of the *Prasādanīya-sūtra* is rather straightforward and less complex than that of the *Prāsādika-sūtra*. Like the *Prāsādika-sūtra*, this sūtra largely takes the form of a hypothetical debate, this one between Śāriputra and the Buddha. This debate starts off in a dialogue but lacks the flowing, conversational nature of the hypothetical debate of the *Prāsādika-sūtra*; it consists mainly of the Buddha questioning Śariputra, who responds with succinct replies. After the first two sections of the text, the pretense of debate is dropped, and Śāriputra spends the bulk of the sūtra reciting the supremacies of the Buddha in a formulaic fashion as he would explain it to a hypothetical person previously suggested by the Buddha. We see from the summary verse of the *Prasādanīya-sūtra* that the content is divided into seventeen general topics, each fleshed out in their respective passages:

> *saṃbodhikuśalāyatanaṃ pudgalā bhāṣyadarśanam*
> *pratiprahāṇam ṛddhiś ca nivāsādeśanena ca •*
> *śāśvatam cānuśāstiś ca ga(rbhā)vakrānti pudgalā*
> *(puruṣaśīlaviśuddhim ādhicai)(299v2)tasikena ca •* || ||

The keywords in the summary verse represent these topics:

DĀ 16.1–2: Perfect Awakening (*saṃbodhiḥ*)
DĀ 16.3: The Classification of Wholesome Factors (*kuśalaḥ*)
DĀ 16.4: The Classification of the Sense Spheres (*āyatanam*)
DĀ 16.5: The Classification of Individuals (*pudgalāḥ*)
DĀ 16.6: Conduct in Speech (*bhāṣyaḥ*)
DĀ 16.7: Attainments of Discernment (*darśanam*)
DĀ 16.8: Practices (*pratipad*)
DĀ 16.9: Efforts (*prahāṇam*)
DĀ 16.10: Knowledge of the Range of Supernormal Power (*ṛddhiḥ*)

DĀ 16.11: Knowledge of the Recollection of Former States of Existence (*nivāsaḥ*)
DĀ 16.12: The Method of Reading Minds (*ādeśanena*)
DĀ 16.13: Theories of Eternalism (*śāśvatam*)
DĀ 16.14: The Method of Instruction (*anuśāstiḥ*)
DĀ 16.15: Descent into the Womb (*garbhāvakrāntiḥ*)
DĀ 16.16: Knowledge of the Liberation of Other People (*pudgalāḥ*)
DĀ 16.17: Knowledge of the Purity of Moral Conduct of Men (*puruṣaśīlaviśuddhim*)
DĀ 16.18: Higher Mental States (*ādhicaitasikena*)

Unlike in the *Prāsādika-sūtra* each topic here is contained, often quite handily, within one section. Starting in DĀ 16.3 these sections always begin and end with two formulaic phrases with the content of the section, and the bulk of the sūtra, sandwiched between them. The beginning formula is "For me, sir, there is another supremacy of the Blessed One when the Blessed One teaches me dharma regarding (the topic of the section),"[55] and the end formula is "Sir, this is the supremacy of the Blessed One regarding the classification of (topic of section). The Blessed One knows this in its entirety. For you, knowing this in its entirety, there is nothing further to be known from the knowledge of which another ascetic or brahmin could be more knowledgeable than the Blessed One in regard to perfect awakening."[56]

The *Prasādanīya-sūtra* begins with the Buddha dwelling in Nālandā. Śāriputra declares to him that he has serene faith that in the past, future, and present no other ascetic or brahmin could know more of perfect awakening (*saṃbodhi*) than the Buddha. The Buddha acknowledges that Śāriputra has roared a lion's roar but questions how Śāriputra knows this. Does he know the minds of tathāgatas of the past, future, and present? Śāriputra admits that no, he does not know this; however, he does know the dharma discourses (*dharmaparyāya*), and as such he is able to understand or abandon dharmas appropriately via supernormal knowledge (*abhijñā*), and he

55. *Aparam api me bhadanta bhagavata ānuttaryaṃ yadā me bhagavāṃ dharmaṃ deśayati yad uta* _____.

56. *Etad ānuttaryaṃ bhadanta bhagavato yad uta* _____ | *tad bhagavān aśeṣam abhijānāti* | *tat te 'śeṣam abhijānata uttare 'bhijñeyaṃ nāsti yasyābhijñānād anyaḥ śramaṇo vā brahmaṇo vā bhagavato 'ntikād bhūyo 'bhijñataraḥ syād yad uta saṃbodhaye.*

is therefore perfect regarding dharma. At this point Śāriputra utters what is the crux of the sūtra: "One should proclaim serene faith in the Teacher. I know: 'The Blessed One is certainly a complete, perfect buddha'"[57] (DĀ 16.1).

After Śāriputra's statement the Buddha questions him further. The Buddha asks Śāriputra if someone were to approach him asking if in the past, future, or present there were, are, or will be any ascetics or brahmins more knowledgeable than he, the Buddha, regarding perfect awakening, how he would respond. Śāriputra tells the Buddha that he would say "no." The Buddha then asks how Śāriputra would respond if asked whether in the past, future, or present there are any ascetics or brahmins equal to the Buddha regarding perfect awakening. Śāriputra tells the Buddha that he would respond "yes" to the questions concerning the past and future and "no" concerning the present. The Buddha asks why Śāriputra would respond this way. Śāriputra answers that there have been ascetics and brahmins equal to the Buddha in the past and there will be in the future (i.e., previous and future buddhas) but it is impossible for two buddhas to exist in the world simultaneously. This is why the Buddha is supreme regarding perfect awakening (DĀ 16.2).

Śāriputra then proceeds to state that the Blessed One is supreme regarding the remaining topics outlined in the summary verse. In the process of laying out these supremacies of the Blessed One, Śāriputra sometimes explains the topics in question and other times explains why the Buddha is supreme (DĀ 16.3–17). After Śāriputra completes his enumerations of the Buddha's supremacies, he explains that whatever is to be known, all that is already known, perceived, learned, understood, and completely, fully, perfectly realized by the Tathāgata[58] and that the Buddha has not come to the world for ignoble enjoyment but is one who dwells having reached the fourth dhyāna (DĀ 16.18).

From here we return to the frame story for its conclusion. The monk, Nāgasapāla, who had been fanning the Buddha, exclaims that if any wanderers who are adherents of another faith were to possess any of the supreme qualities that Śāriputra had just explained that the Buddha possessed, they would parade themselves all over Nālandā claiming how great they are while the Buddha, on the other hand, is modest and does not boast

57. *Śāstari ca prasādaṃ pravedayet; samyaksa(ṃb)uddh(o) b(a)t(a) bhagavāṃn ity api jāne.*

58. Note the similarity to the statement the Buddha makes in DĀ 15.35 above.

of his excellent qualities. Nāgasapāla suggests that Śāriputra's discourse should constantly appear in mind in order to be preached to monks, nuns, laypeople, and various ascetics, brahmins, and wanderers who are adherents of another faith so that their doubt may be allayed and their view corrected. In this way, they will ultimately proclaim serene faith in the Teacher and know that the Blessed One is a complete, perfect buddha, just as Śāriputra proclaimed at the beginning of the sūtra in section 16.1, bringing the frame story full circle. The Buddha then addresses Śāriputra, telling him to enact Nāgasapāla's request just as it has been outlined. While the discourse is being preached, a large crowd surrounding the Buddha is inspired to serene confidence (DĀ 16.19).

4. Similarities between DĀ 15 and DĀ 16

The fact that the *Prāsādika* and *Prasādanīya* sūtras are paired together in the *Yuga-nipāta* implies a relationship between the two texts. The link is only bolstered by their Pali and Chinese counterparts also being placed next to one another (although not necessarily in the same order) in both the *Dīgha-nikāya* and the *Cháng āhán jīng* (長阿含經). To a greater or lesser extent, the two texts do share multiple similarities.

Perhaps the most obvious is the similarity of their names, *Prāsādika* and *Prasādanīya*. Both stem from the word *prasāda*, which, unlike *śraddhā* or *śrāddha* ("believing" or "faith"), carries the force of meaning both "faith" and "tranquility," a "serene faith" as I translate the term. The usage is clear in the term *prasādanīya*, and while I prefer not to translate titles of sūtras, a fair translation of the *Prasādanīya-sūtra* would be *The Sūtra Inspiring Serene Faith*.[59] Though the term *prāsādika* is also derived from *prasāda*, it connotes something pleasing or beautiful, and the *Prāsādika-sūtra* may be translated as *The Delightful Sūtra*.[60] In the case of the *Prāsādika-sūtra* it is delightful in that the reader is delighted by the faith that is inspired from learning that the Buddha's doctrines are complete and that no others are their equal.

Another obvious similarity between the two sūtras is the timing of their preaching. Both take place late in the Buddha's career and reflect the doctrinal concerns of his mature teachings. The death of Nirgrantha Jñātiputra, considered a contemporary of the Buddha, in the *Prāsādika-sūtra* indicates the later phase of the Buddha's own career. Additionally, while not present in the *Prāsādika-sūtra*, the Pali *Pāsādika-sutta* contains a passage where the Buddha states: "But now I am an aged teacher of long standing,

59. Walshe (LDB) translates the *Sampasādanīya-sutta* as *Serene Faith*, while Rhys Davids and Rhys Davids (1965) translate it as *The Faith That Satisfied*.

60. Walshe (LDB) translates the *Pāsādika-sutta* as *The Delightful Discourse*, while Rhys Davids and Rhys Davids (1965) translate it as *The Delectable Discourse*.

who went forth a long time ago, and my life is coming to its close."[61] The setting of Pāvārika's mango grove in Nālandā in the *Prasādanīya-sūtra* is one of the locations where he spent his final days, as depicted in the *Mahāparinibbāna-sutta*. Indeed, the beginning of the *Prasādanīya-sūtra* is recounted as part of the *Mahāparinibbāna-sutta*.[62]

As noted above, both texts assume the format of a debate. The *Prāsādika-sūtra* takes the form of a hypothetical debate where the Buddha repeatedly offers: "If someone were to say that, you should say this." The *Prasādanīya-sūtra* revolves around an actual debate between the Buddha and Śāriputra, with the Buddha questioning the depth of Śāriputra's lion's roar about the supremacy of the Buddha's *saṃbodhi*. Although the narrative structure takes the shape of a debate, the stakes are quite low in both texts, for the possibility that other religious leaders or their doctrines could exceed the Buddha or his doctrines is never taken seriously.

The greatest similarity between the two texts is that they share the theme of the nature of teachers and of the importance of placing one's faith in a proper teacher—that is to say, the Buddha. Set in a time when the era of Buddhism without the Buddha was looming, both sūtras are concerned with establishing the supremacy of the Buddhist faith over others to nullify doubts among the faithful. The *Prāsādika-sūtra* implicitly states that while the Nirgranthas fell into dispute after their founder's death, the Buddhist doctrines are complete, and as long as they are memorized and conveyed correctly, there cannot be confusion, even without a buddha. Both sūtras have the goal of making it absolutely clear that no one can replace the Buddha for leadership of the saṅgha. In the *Prāsādika-sūtra*, the intent is to show that non-Buddhists are inherently incorrect and should not be followed, be they the Nirgranthas or the previous teachers of the Buddha such as Udraka Rāmaputra. In making Śāriputra the interlocutor, the intent of the *Prasādanīya-sūtra* is to show that not even other Buddhists are worthy of replacing the Buddha after his death. Śāriputra was considered foremost in insight and was the chief disciple of the Buddha along with Mahāmaudgalyāyana. Śāriputra was known as the Second Teacher, or second King of the Dharma, and was even recognized in the *Sutta-nipāta* as the successor to the Buddha.[63] Just as he preached the *Prasādanīya-sūtra*, it is no surprise

61. LDB 430. Cf. DN III 125.15–17 (DN 29.14): *ahaṃ kho pana cunda etarahi satthā thero rattaññū cira-pabbajito addh-agato vaya anuppatto.*

62. Cf. DN II 81.28 (*Mahāparinibbāna-sutta*, DN 16.15ff.).

63. Li 2019, 412. See 412ff. for a discussion on Śāriputra's role as a leader in the saṅgha.

that Śāriputra is the one recorded as having delivered the *Saṅgīti-sutta* when the Buddha was afflicted with back pain and not disposed to teach.[64] Had anyone been considered the Buddha's heir, it would have been Śāriputra. However, the *Prasādanīya-sūtra* makes clear that Śāriputra cannot know the mind of the Buddha or of any buddha. As the expounder of the sūtra, he is made to state that no one is equal to the Buddha and all should have faith in the Buddha alone as the supreme teacher. The *Prasādanīya-sūtra* takes pains to show how the founder of Buddhism is supreme above all others, with the explicit purpose of inspiring the faithful, and the *Prāsādika-sūtra* posits that when the Buddha is gone, only his dharma and vinaya (*dharmavinaya*)—that is, his religious doctrine and monastic discipline—may be relied upon for guidance. Even when the founder is no longer living, one can assume that a disciple who believes that his teacher surpasses all others and that his teachings may be trusted as a guide will be less likely to have a crisis of confidence than one who does not believe as such. This is a serious concern for the Buddhists, owing to the Buddha's position on the impossibility of more than one buddha existing in a world system (*lokadhātu*) at a time, as seen in DĀ 16.2. In the *Prasādanīya-sūtra*, the answer is to maintain faith in the Buddha. For later Buddhists, however, for whom the Buddha was only a memory, we see creative solutions to this impossibility, such as the Pure Land idea that one might meet and learn from living buddhas residing in other world systems.

The *Prāsādika-sūtra* engages in ideological confrontation with other views to prove the supremacy of Buddhist doctrine and its teacher and satisfy the concerns of the faithful, while in the *Prasādanīya-sūtra* the battle has already been won; the faithful are appeased and rewarded with a satisfying paean where Śāriputra triumphantly trumpets the already accepted supremacy of the Buddha and, thereby, of his doctrines. The two texts can rightly be seen as a pair with each reinforcing the arguments of the other so that they can together present a unified vision of the excellence of a complete Buddhist doctrine as presented by a complete Buddha.

If we follow the theory that the discourses in the *Dīrghāgama* were compiled to illustrate how Buddhism is superior to any other systems of thought in order to gain converts,[65] then the *Prāsādika* and *Prasādanīya*

64. DN III 209.13–15. The *Saṅgīti-sutta* also takes place just after the death of Nirgrantha Jñātiputra, suggesting a period around the time of the *Prāsādika-sūtra* and, by association, the *Prasādanīya-sūtra*.

65. Cf. Hartmann 2014, 151 and 153.

sūtras can certainly be considered useful tools in such a project. The *Prāsādika* lays out how any system of thought not originating from a proper teacher (i.e., a buddha) is doomed to fail, and the *Prasādanīya* goes on to explain the superior qualities a buddha has in the role of teacher. This theme of what makes a good teacher is what ties these two sūtras together as a pair in the *Yuga-nipāta*.

Another somewhat compelling shared feature of the two sūtras is what appear to be narrative callbacks from one text to the other. In the *Prāsādika-sūtra* the Buddha states that he does not consider any other teachers to be his equal, and in the *Prasādanīya-sūtra* we find Śāriputra saying that one should proclaim serene faith in the Buddha as their teacher, knowing he is a perfectly awakened teacher without equal. Section 15.36 of the *Prāsādika-sūtra* is heavily damaged, but we can make out what appears to be a reference to a lion's roar, and in the *Prāsādanīya-sūtra* the whole discourse is set off by Śāriputra's lion's roar. Questions are posed throughout the *Prāsādika-sūtra* by wanderers who are adherents of another faith, and in the *Prasādanīya-sūtra* (DĀ 16.19a) the monk Nāgasapāla mocks those very wanderers who hold other beliefs.

Table 2. Narrative callbacks between DĀ 15 and DĀ 16.

DĀ 15 *Prāsādika-sūtra*	DĀ 16 *Prasādanīya-sūtra*
DĀ 15.16a Certainly, Cunda, however many are those regarded as teachers, I do not consider (even) a single teacher equal to myself: (one who) is thus (endowed with the highest gain and the highest fame). Right now, I [am] (just such) a teacher.[66]	DĀ 16.1.5b One should proclaim serene faith in the Teacher. I know: 'The Blessed One is certainly a complete, perfect buddha.'[67]

66. *Yāvantaḥ khalu cunda{ḥ} śāstriṃsaṃmatā nāham eka<ṃ> śāstāram (apy āt)m(a)nā samasamaṃ samanup(a)ś(yām)i <|> (ya eva)ṃ (lābhāgra)*(280v8)(yaśogreṇa samanvāgatas; tadyathā aha)m etarhi *śāstā*.

67. *Śāstari ca prasādaṃ pravedayet; samyaksa(ṃb)uddh(o) b(a)t(a) bhagavāṃn ity* api jāne.

DĀ 15.36 Monks saying, "Lion" [...] this, in that case, for that Tathāgata who roars a (complete lion's) roar [...].[68]	DĀ 16.1.5a Rather, how is it that you say this lofty bull's speech of yours in the assembly in this way, unequivocally roaring a complete lion's roar?[69]
DĀ 15.24a[70] It is possible, monks, that wanderers who are adherents of another faith might speak in this way.[71]	DĀ 16.19a Sir, if these wanderers who are adherents of another faith were to see one or another of these qualities [...] present in themselves, immediately raising a great cloth banner, they would wander about the whole of Nālandā [...] [saying] "We are of such great supernormal power, we are the ones whose power is so great."[72]

Finally, reading the two sūtras one occasionally finds what appear to be textual similarities beyond the structural and thematic similarities. For example, we see a phrase concerning the omniscience of the Buddha appearing in very similar circumstances in DĀ 15.35 and DĀ 16.18 and a phrase regarding concern with frequent practice and proper mental attention in both DĀ 15.35 and several instances of DĀ 16:

68. *Siṃha (i)ti bhikṣavo v(a)d(a)nto .ā* .. + + + ... + + + + + + (286v3) .. + + + + + + + + + + + + + + + *id(aṃ) tatra tathāg(a)t(as)ya (samyaksiṃhan)ādaṃ nā*ditasya.

69. *Atha kin nu te {sa}tvayā iyam ev(aṃ)rū*(290v7)*pā udārā ārṣabhī vāg bhāṣitā ekāṃśa udgṛhītaḥ parṣadi samyaksiṃhanādo nāditaḥ.*

70. This phrase occurs regularly throughout the text.

71. *{A}sthānam etad bhikṣavo vidy(ate) y(a)d anyatīrthikaparivrajakā evam vadeyuḥ.*

72. *Ime bhadanta anyatīrthika*(299r1)*parivrājakā eṣām aṃgānām anyatamānyata(m). saṃ .. m ātmanaḥ saṃmukhībhūtaṃ paśyeyur apīdānī<ṃ> mahatī cailap(a)tākā (u)cchrayitvā sarvāṃ nālandāṃ anvāhiṇḍata<ṃ>ty ā .. .. n ity a(p)i vaya*(299r2)*(m evaṃ)mahardhikā evaṃmahānubhāvā iti.*

Table 3. Textual similarities between DĀ 15 and DĀ 16.

DĀ 15 *Prāsādika-sūtra*	DĀ 16 *Prasādanīya-sūtra*
DĀ 15.35 *yat t(ad) bh(ik)ṣ(ava)s sarvaśaḥ sarvatra bhāyai samyak tat sarvaṃ tathāgatena jñātaṃ dṛṣṭaṃ viditaṃ vijñāt(aṃ sam)y(ag evābh) i(saṃb)uddh(am |)*	DĀ 16.18 *(yat tad bhadanta śrāddhena)* **(298v4)** *kulaputreṇa jñātavyaṃ draṣṭavyaṃ prāptavyaṃ boddhavyaṃ tat sa(rv)aṃ bha(ga)vatā jñātaṃ dṛṣṭaṃ viditaṃ vijñātaṃ samyag evābhisaṃbuddhaṃ*
DĀ 15.35 Monks, whatever perfection shines wholly [and] entirely, that is all known, perceived, learned, understood, and completely, fully, perfectly realized by the Tathāgata.	DĀ 16.18 (Sir, whatever) is to be known, to be perceived, to be obtained, and to be realized (by a faithful son of a good family), that is all known, perceived, learned, understood, and completely, fully, perfectly realized by the Blessed One.
DĀ 15.32b tasya saptānāṃ bodhipakṣyāṇāṃ dharmāṇām āsev(anānvayāt* bhavanānvayat)* (bahu)**(285v3)**-(līkārā)nvayāt samyaṅmanasikārānvayāt kāmā{ṃpra}sravā<c> cittaṃ <vi>mucyate <|> bhavāsravād avidyāsravā<c>[73] cittaṃ vimucyate <|>	DĀ 16.3[74] iha bhadantaika<ḥ> śramaṇo vā brāhmaṇo vāraṇyagato vā (vṛkṣamūlagato v)ā śūnyāgāra **(292r5)**gato vā ātaptānvayāt prah(ā)ṇ(ā)nvayāt* bhāvanānvayād bahulīkārānvayāt samyaṅmanasikārānvayāt tadrūpaṃ śānta<ṃ> cetaḥsamādhi<ṃ> spṛśati yathā (samāhite cit)te anekavi**(292r6)**dhān pāpakā<n> akuśalā<n> dharmān abhinivarjya anekavidhān kuśalān dharmān samādāya varttate sākṣādbhavyatāyāṃ na ca pari(ta)syati <|>

73. Ms. reads *avidyāsravacittaṃ*.

74. Cf. very similar phrases in DĀ 1613a–c.

DĀ 15.32b	DĀ 16.3
His mind, due to concern with the following, (concern with cultivating), concern with frequently performing, and concern with properly mentally attending to the seven factors related to awakening, is liberated from the [negative] influence of sensual pleasure. [His] mind is liberated from the [negative] influence of existence, from the [negative] influence of ignorance.	In this case, sir, an ascetic or brahmin, or one who has gone to the wilderness, (or one who has gone to the foot of a tree), or one who has gone to a solitary place, due to concern with ardor, concern with effort, concern with cultivation, concern with intense practice, and concern with proper mental attention, he experiences such a calm concentration of mind that when his mind (is settled), having cast away numerous evil, unwholesome factors and having taken up numerous wholesome factors, he abides in direct cultivation and will not be disturbed.

While it is tempting to conclude that such textual similarities indicate an inherent relationship between the two sūtras on the most basic level, similar phrases can also be seen in other texts,[75] both within the *Dīrghāgama* and elsewhere, including both the *āgama* and non-*āgama* genres. Therefore, I am hesitant to draw any firm conclusions besides the fact that such phrases may have served as a kind of shared idiomatic resource drawn on in the creation of certain scriptures. Nonetheless, I have noted all instances of such similar phrasing in the editions of the *Prāsādika* and *Prasādanīya* sūtras when I have encountered them.

75. Note for example, DĀ 20.179 (*Kāyabhāvanā-sūtra*) (Zhen 2008, 132): *tasya mamaivaṃ jānata evaṃ paśyataḥ kā*(338v2)*māsravāc cittaṃ vimucyate bhavāsravād avidyāsravāc cittaṃ vimucyate* <|> *vimuktasya vimuktam eva jñānadarśanaṃ bhavati* <|> *kṣīṇā me jātir uṣitaṃ brahmacaryaṃ* *<kṛtaṃ karaṇīyaṃ>* *nāparam asmād bhavaṃ prajānāmi* | *iti* <|> and DbSū(4) 6.2 (cf. DbSū(4) 6.1 & 6.3–10, which are very similar): *taṃ c(ai)naṃ tathāgataṃ karmasv(a)kajñānabale praśnaṃ pṛccheyu(ḥ ya)thā ta(t tathā)g(a)tena karmasvakajñānabalaṃ jñātaṃ dṛṣṭaṃ viditaṃ vijñātaṃ samyag evābhisaṃbuddhaṃ tathā t(a)t tathā(gataḥ praśnaṃ pṛṣṭo vy)ākuryāt**.

5. Textual Parallels to DĀ 15 and DĀ 16

Buddhavacana, the canonical literature held to be the words of a buddha, is the product of a developmental process spanning centuries that began as an oral tradition and moved to a written one. This process surely created waves of memorization and muddling, elaboration and contraction, and entailed a codification that resulted in textual reuse in the production of texts. Indeed, this body of literature is very much disposed to textual repetition and the use of standard lists, especially the sūtra literature, with its highly modular nature of stock vernacular phrases and specialized expressions that appear in multiple texts set in different times and places. Thus in any particular sūtra, one is nearly guaranteed to encounter a large volume of parallel passages shared with other texts. This becomes all the more intricate when one takes into consideration the textual transmission of the Buddhist faith in the multiple languages of ancient India by different Buddhist transmissions, each of which acted as redactors of corpora they considered correct while viewing the material transmitted by other traditions as faulty. Nonetheless, this tapestry of material is a great asset for the philologist in the preparation of critical editions, and such parallel material has proven to be a key tool in the reconstruction of the missing material in the *Dīrghāgama* manuscript.

I have used three types of textual parallels in the production of the critical edition of the *Prāṣādika* and *Prasādanīya* sūtras: the Theravāda and Dharmaguptaka Long Discourse parallel counterparts from the other transmissions of the works extant in Pali and Chinese; direct, word-for-word (or nearly so) parallels from the only other surviving Sanskrit witness of the Mūlasarvāstivāda transmission of the Dīrghāgama in the few recovered fragments of the Sanskrit *Dīrghāgama* manuscript found in Central Asia, of which only small fragments are extant; and finally indirect, although often word-for-word, parallel passages in disparate Buddhist texts from a variety of Buddhist *āgama*, *nikāya*, commentarial, and even Mahāyāna sūtra corpora that, while often not directly related to the *Prāsādika* and *Prasādanīya* sūtras, or even to the *Dīrghāgama*, display undeniable textual similarities.

Parallels in Long Discourse Collections

The *Prāsādika* and *Prasādanīya* sūtras both have counterpart parallel versions from the Long Discourse transmissions of the Theravāda *Dīgha-nikāya* preserved in Pali and the Dharmaguptaka *Cháng āhán jīng* (長阿含經) preserved in Chinese, and the *Prasādanīya-sūtra* has an additional parallel from what is likely a Mūlasarvāstivada transmission translated into Chinese:

Table 4. Extant counterpart parallel transmissions to DĀ 15 and DĀ 16.

DĀ 15: *Prāsādika-sūtra*	DĀ 16: *Prasādanīya-sūtra*
Pali parallel: *Pāsādika-sutta*, sutta 29 of the Theravāda *Dīgha-nikāya*, DN III 117–41. Chinese parallel: *Qīngjìng jīng* (清净經), sūtra 17 of the Dharmaguptaka *Dīrghāgama* (*Cháng āhán jīng*), T No. 1(17): Vol. I 72c10–76b22.	Pali parallel: *Sampasādanīya-sutta*, sutta 28 of the Theravāda *Dīgha-nikāya*, DN III 99–116 Chinese parallels: *Zì huānxǐ jīng* (自歡喜經), sūtra 18 of the Dharmaguptaka *Dīrghāgama* (*Cháng āhán jīng*), T No. 1(18): Vol. I 76b24–79a28. *Fó shuō xìn fó gōngdé jīng* (佛說信佛功德經), T No. 18: Vol. I 255a11–258a4. Almost surely from a Mūlasarvāstivāda transmission.

The *Cháng āhán jīng* was translated by Buddhayaśas (佛陀耶舍) and Zhu Fonian (竺佛念) in 413 CE.[76] The *Qīngjìng jīng* and *Zì huānxǐ jīng* share the same placement with regard to one another in the *Cháng āhán jīng* as do the *Prāsādika-sūtra* and *Prasādanīya-sūtra* in the *Dīrghāgama*, while the order is switched in the *Dīgha-nikāya*, with the *Sampasādanīya-sutta* appearing

76. The mechanics of the translation effort likely consisted of the sūtra being recited by

before the *Pāsādika-sutta*. In addition to the *Zì huānxǐ jīng* there is another, a translation by Fǎxián (法賢) (337–422 CE) of the Chinese version of the *Prasādanīya-sūtra*, the *Fó shuō xìn fó gōngdé jīng*. Fǎxián's Taishō 18 translation is very similar to the *Prasādanīya-sūtra* of DĀ 16. The sections basically match, and there are only slight variations in content. This strongly suggests that the *Fó shuō xìn fó gōngdé jīng* is a translation of the *Prasādanīya-sūtra* as transmitted within the Mūlasarvāstivāda tradition, representing a complete witness to the *Prasādanīya-sūtra* created several centuries before the Sanskrit witness preserved as DĀ 15 within the Gilgit *Dīrghāgama* manuscript.

The parallels from the *Dīgha-nikāya* and the *Cháng āhán jīng* share similar structures with the *Prāsādika-sūtra* and *Prasādanīya-sūtra*. However, the content of corresponding sections is often different. Sometimes the Sanskrit and Pali are quite similar, but other times they are very different even when the topic is the same. Likewise, the Sanskrit and Chinese will occasionally be similar, but just as often this is not the case. Other times, the Pali and Chinese will be similar while the Sanskrit diverges. Owing perhaps to its more straightforward structure, the *Prasādanīya-sūtra* appears to contain more sections in common with its Pali and Chinese counterparts than does the *Prāsādika-sūtra*, where entire sections are sometimes unique to only one of the three versions. I have included the Pali and Chinese parallels for every corresponding section available in the editions of the *Prāsādika* and *Prasādanīya* sūtras directly after the translations. Complete correlations of the related sections of the *Prāsādika* and *Prasādanīya* sūtras with their Pali and Chinese counterparts are given in the tables below:

Buddhayaśas and then translated into Chinese by Zhu Fonian with the consultation and approval of Buddhayaśas. See the text's preface for more information on the date of the translation, T I 1b1. For information on the circumstances of the translation, see the catalogue, *Chū sānzàng jì jí* (出三藏記集), T 2145 at LV 11b1.

Table 5. Correlations between the *Prāsādika* and its counterpart parallel transmissions.

DĀ 15: *Prāsādika-sūtra*	DN 29: *Pāsādika-sutta*	DĀ[c] 17 of T I 1: *Qīngjìng jīng*
15.1	DN III 117.1–118.5 (DN29.1)	(1) T I 1 72c13–28
15.2	DN III 118.6–20 (DN29.2)	
15.3	DN III 118.21–119.2 (DN 29.3)	(2) T I 1 72c28–73a7
15.4	DN III 119.24–120.14 (DN 29.5)	(5) T I 1 73a23–73b2
15.5	DN III 119.3–23 (DN 29.4)	(3) T I 1 73a07–17
15.6	DN III 120.15–35 (DN 29.6)	(4) T I 1 73a17–23
15.7	DN III 121.1–20 (DN 29.7)	(6) T I 1 73b2–9
15.8a	DN III 121.21–122.12 (DN 29.8)	(7) T I 1 73b9–17
15.8b	DN III 122.13–123.2 (DN 29.9)	(8) T I 1 73b17–23
15.9a	DN III 123.3–6 (DN 29.10)	(9) T I 1 73b23–25
15.9b	DN III 123.6–10 (DN 29.10)	(10) T I 1 73b25–26
15.10a	DN III 123.11–18 (DN 29.11)	(16) T I 1 73c16–17
15.10b	DN III 123.11–18 (DN 29.11)	(17) T I 1 73c17–19
15.11a	DN III 123.19–124.22 (DN 29.12)	(13–15) T I 1 73c6–16
15.11b	DN III 124.23–125.8 (DN 29.13)	(13–15) T I 1 73c6–16
15.12a	DN III 123.19–124.22 (DN 29.12)	(11) T I 1 73b27–73c2
15.12b	DN III 124.23–125.8 (DN 29.13)	(12) T I 1 73c2–6
—	DN III 123.19–124.22 (DN 29.12)	(13) T I 1 73c6–10
—	DN III 124.23–125.8 (DN 29.13)	(14) T I 1 73c10–14
—	DN III 123.19–124.22 (DN 29.12) DN III 124.23–125.8 (DN 29.13)	(15) T I 1 73c14–16
15.13a	DN III 123.19–124.22 (DN 29.12)	(13–15) T I 1 73c6–16

DĀ 15: *Prāsādika-sūtra*	DN 29: *Pāsādika-sutta*	DĀ^{c} 17 of T I 1: *Qīngjìng jīng*
15.13b	DN III 124.23–125.8 (DN 29.13)	(13–15) T I 1 73c6–16
15.14a	DN III 123.19–124.22 (DN 29.12)	(13–15) T I 1 73c6–16
15.14b	DN III 124.23–125.8 (DN 29.13)	(13–15) T I 1 73c6–16
15.15a	DN III 123.19–124.22 (DN 29.12)	(18) T I 1 73c19–21
15.15b	DN III 124.23–125.8 (DN 29.13)	(19) T I 1 73c21–23
—		(20) T I 1 73c23
—	DN III 125.9–17 (DN 29.14)	—
—	DN III 125.18–126.5 (DN 29.15)	—
15.16a	DN III 126.6–17 (DN 29.16)	(21) T I 1 73c23–74a5
15.16b	DN III 126.17–23 (DN 29.16)	(22) T I 1 74a5–7
15.16c	DN III 126.17–23 (DN 29.16)	(23) T I 1 74a7–8
15.16d	DN III 126.24–127.14 (DN 29.16)	(24) T I 1 74a8–13
15.17a	DN III 127.15–20 (DN 29.17)	(5) T I 1 74a13–15
15.17b	DN III 127.21–26 (DN 29.17)	(25) T I 1 74a13–15
15.17c	DN III 127.27–128.7 (DN 29.17)	(25) T I 1 74a13–15 & (29) T I 1 74b19–24
15.18a	DN III 129.9–20 (DN 29.20)	(28) T I 1 74a25–74b1
15.18b		(29) T I 1 74b1–5
15.19a	DN III 128.24–129.8 (DN 29.19)	(30) T I 1 74b5–10
15.19b		(31) T I 1 74b10–14
15.20a	DN III 128.8–18 (DN 29.18)	(26) T I 1 74a16–20
15.20b		(27) T I 1 74a20–25
15.21	DN III 129.21–29 (DN 29.21)	(28) T I 1 74b14–19
—		(29) T I 1 74b19–24

DĀ 15: *Prāsādika-sūtra*	DN 29: *Pāsādika-sutta*	DĀ^c 17 of T I 1: *Qīngjìngjīng*
15.22a	DN III 129.30–130.9 (DN 29.22)	(30) T I 1 74b24–26
15.22b		(31) T I 1 74b26–28
15.22c		(32) T I 1 74b28–74c3
15.22d		(33) T I 1 74c3–5
15.23a–c	—	(34) T I 1 74c5–9
15.24a	DN III 130.22–131.10 (DN 29.23)	(35) T I 1 74c9–10
15.24b		(36) T I 1 74c10–23
15.24c–e		(36) T I 1 74c23–75a5
15.25a	DN III 131.11–132.8 (DN 29.24) (but is much closer to DN III 130.22–131.10 (DN 29.23))	(37) T I 1 75a5–7
15.25b		(38) T I 1 75a7–18
15.25c		(39) T I 1 75a18–26
15.25d		—
15.25e		—
15.26a	DN III 132.9–32 (DN 29.25)	(40) T I 1 75a26–27
15.26b		(41) T I 1 75a27–28
15.26c		(42) T I 1 75a28–75b4
—		(43) T I 1 75b4–75b21
—		(44) T I 1 75b21–25
15.27a	DN III 135.23–136.16 (DN 29.30)	(48) T I 1 75c12–28
15.27b		(49) T I 1 75c28–76a1
15.28	DN III 136.16–25 (DN 29.31)	—
15.29	DN III 136.26–33 (DN 29.32)	—
15.30	DN III 137.1–8 (DN 29.33)	—
15.31	DN III 132.33–133.10 (DN 29.26)	—

DĀ 15: *Prāsādika-sūtra*	DN 29: *Pāsādika-sutta*	DĀ^{c} 17 of T I 1: *Qīngjìngjīng*
15.32a	—	—
15.32b	—	—
15.32c	DN III 133.10–27 (DN 29.26)	—
15.33	DN III 134.1–13 (DN 29.27)	(45) T I 1 75b25–28
15.34a	DN III 134.14–135.6 (DN 29.28)	(46) T I 1 75b28–75c7
15.34b		
15.34c		
15.34d		—
15.35	DN III 135.7–22 (DN 29.29)	(47) T I 1 75c7–12
15.36	—	—
15.37	DN III 137.9–14 (DN 29.34)	—
15.38a	DN III 137.15–17 (DN 29.34)	—
15.38b	DN III 137.17–138.11 (DN 29.34)	(52) T I 1 76a20–23 [b3 & b4]
15.38c	DN III 139.17–20 (DN 29.36)	—
—		(53) T I 1 76a23–76b5
15.39a	DN III 139.21–140.5 (DN 29.37)	—
15.39b		(50) T I 1 76a1–12
15.39c	—	—
15.39d	—	—
15.39e	DN III 140.34–141.2 (DN 29.39)	—
15.40a	DN III 138.12–21 (DN 29.35)	(51) T I 1 76a12–20
15.40b	DN III 138.22–139.17 (DN 29.36)	—
15.40c		—
15.41a	DN III 140.6–16 (DN 29.38)	—

DĀ 15: *Prāsādika-sūtra*	DN 29: *Pāsādika-sutta*	DĀ^c 17 of T I 1: *Qīngjìng jīng*
15.41b	[b] DN III 140.17–34 (DN 29.39)	—
15.41c	—	—
15.41d	—	—
15.41e	—	—
15.42	DN III 141.3–14 (DN 29.40) DN 141.15–25 (DN 29.41)	(54) T I 1 76b5–22
15.43	—	—

Table 6. Correlations between the *Prasādanīya* and its counterpart parallel transmissions.

DĀ 16: *Prasādanīya-sūtra*	DN 28: *Sampasādanīya-sutta*	DĀ^c 18 of T I 1: *Zì huānxǐ jīng*	T I 18 *Fó shuō xìn fó gōngdé jīng*
16.1.1	DN III 99.2–11 (DN 28.1)	(1) T I 1 76b24–76c3	T I 18 255a15–23
16.1.2	DN III 99.12–100.3 (DN 28.1)	(1) T I 1 76c3–8	T I 18 255a24–b6 = 1.2a, 1.3a, 1.4a T I 18 255b6–12 = 1.2b, 1.3b, 1.4b
16.1.3	DN III 100.4–10 (DN 28.1)	(1) T I 1 76c8–10	
16.1.4	DN III 100.11–15 (DN 28.1)	(1) T I 1 76c11–13	
16.1.5a	DN III 100.16–22 (DN 28.1)	(1) T I 1 76c13–19	T I 18 255b12–17
16.1.5b	DN III 100.23–102.9 (DN 28.2)	T I 1 76c19–26	

DĀ 16: *Prasādanīya-sūtra*	DN 28: *Sampasādanīya-sutta*	DĀ^{c} 18 of T I 1: *Zì huānxǐ jīng*	T I 18 *Fó shuō xìn fó gōngdé jīng*
16.2.1a	DN III 113.25–114.4 (DN 28.20)	—	T I 18 255b18–20
16.2.1b	DN III 113.28–114.1 (DN 28.20)		T I 18 255c1
16.2.2	DN III 113.28–114.1 (DN 28.20)		—
16.2.3	DN III 114.1–4 (DN 28.20)		—
16.2.4	DN III 114.4–8 (DN 28.20)	T I 1 78c19–21	—
16.2.5	DN III 114.8–11 (DN 28.20)		T I 18 255b21–23
16.2.6	DN III 114.11–14 (DN 28.20)		T I 18 255b24–26
16.2.7a	DN III 114.14–115.9 (DN 28.20)	T I 1 78c28–29	T I 18 255b27–29
16.2.7b		T I 1 78c29–79a08 cf. (1) T I 1 76c26–28	T I 18 255c1–6
16.3	DN III 102.10–22 (DN 28.3)	(2) T I 1 76c28–77a3	T I 18 255c7–15
16.4	DN III 102.23–103.2	(3) T I 1 77a3–11	T I 18 255c16–22
16.5	DN III 105.25–30 (DN 28.8)	—	T I 18 255c23–29
16.6	DN III 106.20–25 (DN 28.11)	(7) T I 1 77b5–11	T I 18 256a1–6
16.7a	DN III 104.15–105.24 (DN 28.7)	(8) T I 1 77b11–16	T I 18 256a7–11

DĀ 16: *Prasādanīya-sūtra*	DN 28: *Sampasādanīya-sutta*	DĀ[c] 18 of T I 1: *Zì huānxǐ jīng*	T I 18 *Fó shuō xìn fó gōngdé jīng*
16.7b	DN III 104.28–105.13 (DN 28.7)	(8) T I 1 77b16–18	T I 18 256a12–14
16.7c	DN III 105.13–18 (DN 28.7)	(8) T I 1 77b18–22	T I 18 256a15–17
16.7d	DN III 105.18–24 (DN 28.7)	(8) T I 1 77b22–26	T I 18 256a18–20
16.7e		(8) T I 1 77b26–77c1	T I 18 256a21–24
16.7f		(8) T I 1 77c1	T I 18 256a25–28
16.8	DN III 106.6–19 (DN 28.10) (content actually parallels DN III 105.31–106.5)	(5) T I 1 77a17–23	T I 18 256a29–b5
16.9	DN III 105.31–106.5 (DN 28.9) (content actually parallels DN III 106.6–19)	(6) T I 1 77a23–77b5	T I 18 256b6–10
16.10	DN III 112.6–113.15 (DN 28.18)	(16) T I 1 78b16–26	T I 18 256b11–20 = 10a T I 18 256b21–26 = 10b T I 18 256b27–c13 = 10c
16.11	DN 110.24–111.14 (DN 28.16)	(14) T I 1 78b6–16	T I 18 256c14–21

DĀ 16: *Prasādanīya-sūtra*	DN 28: *Sampasādanīya-sutta*	DĀ[c] 18 of T I 1: *Zì huānxǐ jīng*	T I 18 *Fó shuō xìn fó gōngdé jīng*
16.12a	DN III 103.20–104.14 (DN 28.6)	(10.1) T I 1 77c25–28	T I 18 256c22–28
16.12b		(10.2) T I 1 77c28–78a1	T I 18 256c29–257a3
16.12c		(10.3) T I 1 78a1–5	T I 18 257a4–9
16.12d		(10.4) T I 1 78a5–11	T I 18 257a10–14
16.13a	DN III 108.20–109.11 (DN 28.15)	cf. (9.1) T I 1 77c3–10 (9.2) T I 1 77c10–17	T I 18 257a15–21
16.13b		—	T I 18 257a22–27
16.13c		(9) T I 1 77c17–25	T I 18 257a28–b6
16.14a	DN III 107.7–27 (DN 28.13)	(11.4) T I 1 78a 19–21	T I 18 257b07–11
16.14b		(11.3) T I 1 78a 16–18	T I 18 257b11–14
16.14c		(11.2) T I 1 78a15–16	T I 18 257b14–17
16.14d		(11.1) T I 1 78a11–15; T I 1 78a21–23	T I 18 257b17–21
16.15	DN III 103.3–19 (DN 28.5)	(4) T I 1 77a11–17	T I 18 257b22–27

DĀ 16: *Prasādanīya-sūtra*	DN 28: *Sampasādanīya-sutta*	DĀ^{c} 18 of T I 1: *Zì huānxǐ jīng*	T I 18 *Fó shuō xìn fó gōngdé jīng*
16.16a	DN III 108.1–19 (DN 28.14)	(13) T I 1 78b1–6	T I 18 257b28–c1
16.16b			
16.16c			
16.16d			
16.17	DN III 106.26–107.6 (DN 28.12)	(12) T I 1 78a23–78b1	T I 18 257c2–7
16.18	DN III 113.16–24 (DN 28.20)	(17) T I 1 78c12–19	T I 18 257c8–14
16.19a	DN III 115.10–29 (DN 28.21)	T I 1 79a8–23	T I 18 257c15–20
16.19b	DN III 116.1–10 (DN 28.22)	T I 1 79a23–29	T I 18 257c21–258a5
16.20a	—	—	—
16.20b	—	—	—

Direct Parallels in Central Asian Fragment Witnesses and Quotations in Later Works

In addition to the texts extant in Pali and Chinese, there are several fragments of different Central Asian Sanskrit witnesses of the *Prāsādika-sūtra* and *Prasādanīya-sūtra*. There are seventeen confirmed fragments of the *Prāsādika* and *Prasādanīya* sūtras in the *Sanskrithandschriften aus den Turfan-Funden* (SHT), in *The British Library Sanskrit Fragments* (BLSF), and in Hartmann's habilitation (DĀ(U.H.)) as well as an additional potential fragment in SHT (V) corresponding to DĀ 15.32.[77] The corresponding fragments in the SHT, BLSF, and DĀ(U.H.) are almost all identified under sūtra titles other than *Prāsādika* and *Prasādanīya*: fragments from

77. This possible fragment of the *Prāsādika-sūtra* is found in a section that parallels several other texts, and thus it may belong, for example, to the *Saṅgīti-sūtra*.

the *Prāsādika-sūtra* are designated as being from the *Prasādanīya-sūtra*, and the fragments from the *Prasādanīya-sūtra* are designated as being from the *Saṃprasādanīya-sūtra*. I have included all the Central Asian Sanskrit fragments I have found immediately after the Pali and Chinese parallels in editions of the *Prāsādika-sūtra* and *Prasādanīya-sūtra*. There are also a limited number of instances where one of the sūtras appears to have been quoted in a later exegetical work. Of note is a passage in the *Abhidharmakośabhāṣya* that is almost certainly a direct quote from the *Prasādanīya-sūtra* (DĀ 16.2.7) and a relatively long passage from the *Abhidharmakośaṭīkopāyikā* extant in Tibetan translation in which Śamathadeva appears to be quoting from a witness of the *Prasādanīya-sūtra* corresponding to sections DĀ 16.1–2.[78]

Table 7. Central Asian fragments and quotations corresponding to DĀ 15 & DĀ 16.

DĀ section	Fragment
15.1	SHT (IV) 165 (43) (*Prāsādika-sūtra*)
15.7	SHT (VIII) 1870 (*Prāsādika-sūtra*)
15.8	BLSF III.1 Or.15015/105 (*Prāsādika-sūtra*)
15.8	SHT (VIII) 1870 (*Prāsādika-sūtra*)
15.9	SHT (VIII) 1870 (*Prāsādika-sūtra*)
15.22–23	DĀ(U.H) Hs. 129 (*Prāsādika-sūtra*)
15.25–27	DĀ(U.H.) Hs. 130 (=BLSF III.1 Or.15009/565) (*Prāsādika-sūtra*)
15.32	SHT (V) 1123 M 644, sūtra fragment with a discussion of "five impossible states" (*fünf unmöglichen Zustände*) (possibly from *Prāsādika-sūtra*)
15.42–43	SHT (IV) 32 fragment 66, Bl. 183 (*Prāsādika-sūtra*)
15.43	DĀ(U.H.) Hs. 131 (= BLSF III.1 Or.15009/406) (*Prāsādika-sūtra*)
16.1–16.2	Abhidh-k-ṭ where Śamatha quotes the *Prasādanīya-sūtra*

78. Abhidh-k-bh(P) 184.16–185.2 and Abhidh-k-ṭ Derge Ju 3a4–5a5.

16.2.7	Abhidh-k-bh(P) where Vasubandhu quotes the *Prasādanīya-sūtra*
16.2.2–7	BLSF III.1 Or.15007/548 (*Prasādanīya-sūtra*)
16.2.6–16.4	BLSF III.1 Or.15007/235 (*Prasādanīya-sūtra*)
16.6–7	BLSF II.1 Or.15009/59 (*Prasādanīya-sūtra*)
16.12–13	BLSF II.1 Or.15009/137 (= DĀ(U.H.) Hs. 136) (*Prasādanīya-sūtra*)
16.13–14	BLSF III.1 Or.15009/408 (= DĀ(U.H.) Hs. 137) (*Prasādanīya-sūtra*)

Indirect Parallels in Buddhist Literature

Beyond the texts directly corresponding to the *Prāsādika* and *Prasādanīya* sūtras, numerous parallel passages can be found in otherwise unrelated texts. I will describe the most relevant parallels from other texts below and list all the texts with passages paralleling the *Prāsādika* and *Prasādaniya* sūtras found to date in table 8.

As both the *Prāsādika* and *Prasādanīya* sūtras document the Buddha's later life, it is not surprising that the two sūtras contain many sections that are paralleled in both the Sanskrit *Mahāparinirvāṇa-sūtra* (MPS) and Pali *Mahāparinibbāna-sutta* (DN 16). As noted above, the frame story of the *Prasādanīya-sūtra* partially appears in the *Mahāparinibbāna-sutta* as well. The other text that appears to share parallels with both the *Prāsādika* and *Prasādanīya* sūtras is the *Saṅghabhedavastu*. This is not surprising considering that the *Saṅghabhedavastu* is an extensive, narrative Mūlasarvāstivāda Vinaya text that contains parallels consistently with the sūtras of the *Dīrghāgama*.

The frame story of the *Prāsādika-sūtra* occurs in the *Saṅgīti-sūtra* in both its Sanskrit (Saṅg and SaṅgE) and Pali (DN 33) versions as well as in the *Sāmagāma-sutta* (MN 104). In addition to the frame story, parallels from the *Saṅgīti-sūtra* consistently appear throughout the *Prāsādika-sūtra*. Walshe even suggests that the *Saṅgīti-sutta* was inspired by the frame story in the *Prāsādika-sūtra* and by the exhortation by the Buddha in DN 29.17 to recite the doctrines he espoused.[79] This phrase is found in the cor-

79. LDB 479 and 615–16n1012.

responding section of the *Prāsādika-sūtra*, DĀ 15.17: "These doctrines ... having been grasped and comprehended by monks in this way, they are to be held in mind, familiarized with, and recited so that this holy life might have a long existence."[80] Along with the *Mahāparinirvāṇa* and *Saṅgīti* sūtras, the text with the most relevant parallels to the *Prāsādika-sūtra* is the *Brahmajāla-sūtra*, which parallels several passages in its various Sanskrit, Pali, and Tibetan translations.[81] The last sections of the *Prāsādika-sūtra* (DĀ 15.39 and 15.41) deal heavily with the views of non-Buddhists. They parallel passages from the various versions of the *Brahmajāla-sūtra* nearly verbatim. While parallels can be found between the *Prāsādika-sūtra* and other *Dīrghāgama* sūtras besides the *Brahmajāla-sūtra*—such as the *Pañcatraya-sūtra* (DĀ 17), *Kāyabhāvanā-sūtra* (DĀ 20), *Mahāsamāja-sūtra* (DĀ 24), *Tridaṇḍi-sūtra* (DĀ 25), *Lohitya-sūtra I* (DĀ 27), *Kaivarti-sūtra* (DĀ 29), *Maṇḍiśa-sūtra I* (DĀ 31), *Śroṇatāṇḍya-sūtra* (DĀ 33), *Mahalla-sūtra* (DĀ 40), and *Rājan-sūtra* (DĀ 44)—only the *Pṛṣṭhapāla-sūtra* (DĀ 36) has parallels with several of the later sections in the *Prāsādika-sūtra*. The *Catuṣpariṣat-sūtra* manuscript witness recovered from Turfan also contains several parallels to the *Prāsādika-sūtra*.

While there are some texts that parallel both the *Prāsādika-sūtra* and the *Prasādanīya-sūtra*, as noted above, most of the parallels are to one or the other. Generally, there are fewer known parallels to the *Prasādanīya-sūtra* than to the *Prāsādika-sūtra*, or at least fewer close parallels. The *Prasādanīya-sūtra*'s unique formulaic way of presenting the Buddha's supremacies may have rendered it less susceptible to repurposing. There are also several parallels in Yaśomitra's *Abhidharmakośavyākhya* and a fair number of parallels from the *Śrāvakabhūmi*. However, despite the fact that these appear in commentarial works, they do not appear to be direct quotations from the *Prāsādika-sūtra and the Prasādanīya-sūtra*. One other text with frequent parallels to the *Prasādanīya-sūtra* is the *Pañcaviṃśatisāhasrikā Prajñāpāramitā*.

80. *Ye te dharmā ... te bhikṣu{ā}bhir udgṛhya paryavāpya tathā tath(ā dhāray)i(tavyā) <grāhayitavyā> (v)ācayitavyā yathedaṃ brahmacaryaṃ cirasthitikaṃ syāt.* For a discussion of the terms *ud√grah*, *√dhṛ*, and *pari-ava-√āp* as they appear in Mahāyāna literature, see Drewes 2015. Cf. DN 29.17 and T I 1 74a13–15 for Pali and Chinese instances. Note that the Pali reads *tattha sabbeh' eva saṅgāyitabbaṃ na vivaditabbaṃ, yathayidaṃ brahmacariyaṃ addhaniyaṃ assa cira-ṭṭhitikaṃ* with the emphasis on *saṅgāyitabbam* as opposed to *dhārayitavyāḥ*, *grāhayitavyāḥ*, and *vācayitavyāḥ*.

81. DĀ 47 (the currently unedited *Brahmajāla-sūtra*), DN 16, and Weller's edition of the Tibetan translation, Brmj(W).

I have tried to be exhaustive in collecting these parallels, though I harbor no illusions that I have found every one. The modular, intertextual nature of Buddhist sūtra literature suggests that the only sure way to accumulate a complete collection of parallels for any given text would be to digitally mine all of the extant canons to create a comprehensive database. Such a project, while daunting, would be a sure desideratum in the field of Buddhist studies and a fine digital humanities project.

TABLE 8. Indirect parallels to DĀ 15 and DĀ 16

Text containing parallels	DĀ 15: *Prāsādika-sūtra*	DĀ 16: *Prasādanīya-sūtra*
Abhidh-d		16.9
Abhidh-k-bh(P)	15.23–25, 15.27	16.9
Abhidh-k-vy	15.26, 15.39	16.3, 16.8, 16.11, 16.13, 16.14, 16.16
Abhidh-sam		16.9
Abhidh-sam-bh	15.39	
AdSP(C)		16.10
AN II (*Cakka-vagga*)	15.36	
AN III (*Brāhmaṇa-vagga*)		16.12
AN IV (*Mahā-vagga*)	15.32	
AN V (*Thera-vagga*)	15.36	
Arthav	15.36	
Arthav(V)	15.36	16.7, 16.8, 16.9
Avś(V)	15.32	
BLSF II.1 Or.15009/59[82]		16.6, 16.7
BLSF II.1 Or.15009/68	15.1–3	

82. This and the following BLSF entries are fragments of other witnesses of the *Prāsādika* and *Prasāsadīya* sūtras.

Text containing parallels	DĀ 15: *Prāsādika-sūtra*	DĀ 16: *Prasādanīya-sūtra*
BLSF II.1 Or.15009/137 (= DĀ(U.H.) Hs. 136)		16.12, 16.13
BLSF III.1 Or.15007/235		16.2, 16.3, 16.4
BLSF III.1 Or.15007/548		16.2
BLSF III.1 Or.15009/406 (= DĀ(U.H.) Hs. 131)	15.43	16.20
BLSF III.1 Or.15009/408 (= DĀ(U.H.) Hs. 137)		16.13, 16.14
BLSF III.1 Or.15009/565 (= DĀ(U.H) Hs. 130)	15.25, 15.26, 15.27	
BLSF III.1 Or.15015/105	15.8	
Brmj(W)	15.39, 15.41	
Caṅgī(U.H.)	15.40, 15.41	
CPS	15.12, 15.23–25, 15.29, 15.32	
DĀ 17 (*Pañcatraya-sūtra*)	15.39, 15.41	
DĀ 20 (*Kāyabhāvanā-sūtra*)	15.29, 15.32	
DĀ 24 (*Mahāsamāja-sūtra*)	15.32	
DĀ 25 *(Tridaṇḍi-sūtra)*	15.1–3, 15.29	16.11
DĀ 27 (*Lohitya-sūtra I*)	15.1–3, 15.29, 15.36	16.10
DĀ 29 (*Kaivarti-sūtra*)		16.12
DĀ 31 (*Maṇḍiśa-sūtra I*)	15.39	
DĀ 33 (*Śroṇatāṇḍya-sūtra*)	15.24–25, 15.32	
DĀ 36 (*Pṛṣṭhapāla-sūtra*)	15.27, 15.28, 15.29, 15.30, 15.39, 15.41	16.14, 16.16
DĀ 40 (*Mahalla-sūtra*)	15.24–25	
DĀ 44 (*Rājan-sūtra*)	15.39, 15,41	

Text containing parallels	DĀ 15: *Prāsādika-sūtra*	DĀ 16: *Prasādanīya-sūtra*
DĀ 47 (*Brahmajāla-sūtra*)	15.39, 15.41	
DĀ(U.H.) Hs. 13[83]	15.39, 15.41	
DĀ(U.H) Hs. 14		16.3, 16.13
DĀ(U.H.) Hs. 93	15.39	
DĀ(U.H.) Hs. 127	15.37	
DĀ(U.H.) Hs. 128	15.37	
DĀ(U.H) Hs. 129	15.22	
DĀ(U.H) Hs. 130 (= BLSF III.1 Or.15009/565)	15.25, 15.26, 15.27	
DĀ(U.H) Hs. 131(= BLSF III.1 Or.15009/406)	15.43	16.20
DĀ(U.H.) Hs. 136 (= BLSF II.1 Or.15009/137)		16.12, 16.13
DĀ(U.H.) Hs. 137 (= BLSF III.1 Or.15009/408)		16.13, 16.14
Daśa-bh		16.11
DbSū(3)		16.14, 16.16
DbSū(4)	15.35	16.14, 16.16
DhskD	15.24–25, 15.27, 15.39	
DN I (DN 1 *Brahmajāla-sutta)*	15.1–3, 15.39, 15.41	16.11, 16.13
DN I (DN 2 *Sāmaññaphala-sutta*)	15.1–3	
DN II (DN 14 *Mahāpadāna-sutta*)	15.36	16.14

83. This and the following DĀ(U.H.) entries are fragments of other witnesses of the *Prāsādika* and *Prasādanīya* sūtras.

Text containing parallels	DĀ 15: *Prāsādika-sūtra*	DĀ 16: *Prasādanīya-sūtra*
DN II (DN 14 *Mahānidāna-sutta*)		16.10
DN II (DN 16 *Mahāparinibbāna-sutta*)	15.11–15, 15.17, 15.18–21, 15.35	16.1, 16.8, 16.10, 16.14, 16.16
DN II (DN 21 *Sakkapañha-sutta*)	15.40, 15.41	
DN II (DN 22 *Mahāsatipaṭṭhāna-sutta*)		16.7
DN III (DN 33 *Saṅgīti-sutta*)	15.1–3, 15.4–7, 15.17, 15.24–25, 15.26, 15.32	16.5, 16.8
EFGH	15.4–7, 15.29	
FrgmDĀ (*Brahmajāla-sūtra*)	15.39, 15.41	
Khp		16.7
KP	15.36	
KP(VD)	15.36	
Lalv(V)		16.8
MN I (MN 13 *Mahādukkhakkhanda-sutta*)	15.24–25	
MN I (MN 14 *Cūḷadukkhakkhandha-sutta*)	15.24–25	
MN I (MN 4 *Bhayabherava-sutta*)	15.32	
MN I (MN 36 *Mahāsaccaka-sutta*)	15.29, 15.32	
MN I (MN 76 *Sandaka-sutta*)	15.24–25, 15.32	
MN II (MN 104 *Sāmagāma-sutta*)	15.1–3	

Text containing parallels	DĀ 15: *Prāsādika-sūtra*	DĀ 16: *Prasādanīya-sūtra*
MN III (MN 112 *Chabbisodhana-sutta*)	15.32	
MPS	15.12, 15.17, 15.18–21, 15.35, 15.39, 15.41	16.8, 16.14, 16.16
MSuAv	15.39, 15.41	
NidSa	15.29, 15.38, 15.40, 15.41	16.19, 16.20
Poṣ		16.7
Pras	15.27	
Pravr-v	15.39	
PvSP		16.8, 16.10, 16.11 16.14, 16.16
PvSP(K)		16.8, 16.10, 16.11, 16.14, 16.16
SĀ(H) I	15.27	
SĀ(VP)	15.32	
Saṅg	15.1, 15.2, 15.3, 15.6–7, 15.17, 15.24–25, 15.26, 15.32	16.5, 16.8
SaṅgE	15.1, 15.2, 15.3, 15.6–7, 15.17	
SBV I	15.23–25, 15.29,	
SBV II	15.1–3 15.29, 15.32, 15.36, 15.39, 15.40	16.10, 16.11, 16.14, 16.16
SHT (I) 790	15.22	
SHT (IV) 32 (66)	15.42, 15.43	16.20
SHT (IV) 165 (43)	15.1	

Text containing parallels	DĀ 15: *Prāsādika-sūtra*	DĀ 16: *Prasādanīya-sūtra*
SHT (IV) 412	15.3, 15.37	
SHT (V) 1118		16.18
SHT (V) 1123	15.32	
SHT (V) 1152	15.22	
SHT (VI) 1248	15.39	
SHT (VII) 1689		16.19
SHT (VIII) 1870 (177)	15.7, 15.8, 15.9	
Śikṣ		16.7
SN I (*Brahma-saṃyutta*)	15.36	
SN III (*Khanda-saṃyutta*)	15.36	
SN V (*Ānāpāna-saṃyutta*)	15.26	
SN V (*Bojjhaṅga-saṃyutta*)	15.26	
SN V (*Iddhipāda-saṃyutta*)	15.26	
SN V (*Indriya-saṃyutta*)	15.26	
SN V (*Nālanda-saṃyutta*)		16.1
Śrāv-bh I	15.22	
Śrāv-bh II	15.24–25, 15.32	16.7, 16.9, 16.10, 16.14, 16.16
Śrāv-bh(Sh)	15.24–25, 15.32	16.7
Vibh	15.32, 15.39	
Vin III (Suttavibhaṅga)	15.32	
YBhū(Bh)	15.39	
YL	15.35	

Text containing parallels	DĀ 15: *Prāsādika-sūtra*	DĀ 16: *Prasādanīya-sūtra*
Zá āhán jīng (雜阿含經) (Chinese *Saṃyuktāgama*, T 99), discourse 498 (*Nà luó jiāntuó* 那羅犍陀), T II 130c07–131a24		16.1

Transliteration

Transliteration of the *Prāsādika-sūtra* (DĀ 15), Folios 274v5–290r4

274v

v5 dya bhagavataḥ pā[d]au śira[s]ā vandi[tvā] tatr[ai]vāntarhitaḥ || O || **bhagavāṃc chākyeṣu**[84] va[rṣā u]pagataḫ puṣkariṇīprāsād. [m]. dhya .y. śākyasyāśra[v]. ṇe[na t]e[na] khal[u s]a[m]aye .. .u .. .[ram]. ṇoddeśaḥ

v6 [pāpāyā]ṃ .. .. [upag]ato ja[l]ūkāvanaṣaṇḍe taṃ khaO[l]u varṣāvāsa[ṃ] pāpāyāṃ [n]irgrantho jñātiputraḫ kālagato yasya kālakriyāyā [n]irgran[th]āj[ñā]tiputrīyā bhinnā dvidhājātā

v7 viharaṃti k[a] .. .. [j]. tā bhaṇḍanajātā vigṛhītā vivādam ā[pa] .nā[ḥ t]adyathā .. m enaṃ dharma[v]inaya[m] ājānāmi na tvam enaṃ dharmavinayam ājā .[ās]i ya[th]āha[ṃ] cāh. .. [n]. dharmavine

v8 [yam ā]jānāmi yathā .. tvam [e]naṃ dharmavinayam ājānāsi y[u]ktaṃ ma[m]āy[u]ktaṃ t. .. .. .i ..[ṃ ma]māsahitaṃ tava iti .. rvaṃ va[c]a[n]īyaṃ pa[ś]cād avocat* p. + + + [nī] ..[ṃ] .ūrvam avocat* {{abhi}}

275r

r4 ṣpravedi[t]. .. .. ///

r5 vārṣikāṇāṃ mā[s]ā[nām]. .y. .. .ṛ ///

r6 m anuprāpto medhyasya śākyasya pra[vaṇa a] .. .[u] ..[ḥ] [ś]r. [m]. ///

r7 sya pādau śirasā vanditvaikānte sthād ekāntasthitaṃ cundaṃ .. /// .. pāpā

r8 yāṃ varṣā uṣita tata etarhy āgacchāmi pāpāyāṃ cāsmi va .ā + .. .[ā]

84. Imprint from previous folio looks similar to an *anusvāra* here (i.e., *chāṃkyeṣu*).

275v

v1 vih. [r]. nt. kalahajātā bhaṇḍanajā[t]. .. [g]ṛh. t[ā] [v]. .. +

v2 [m] ājānāmi yathā [c]a [ta t]vam enaṃ dharmavinayam ājā[n]. .i .. +

v3 abhitūrṇaṃ [te v]i .. r[ā] .[ṛṣṭa] .ā .[o] .i .. .. vādo [v]ā +

v4 .yaṃ .[ukh]aśa[k]tika[y]ā [v]i[ra] .. .[i] .[i] + ///

v5 .. .. ///

v6 .. .. .. ///

276r

r1 + + + + + .. **[m]** idam avocat* ayaṃ [bh]adanta cun[d]a[ḥ] śramaṇ[o]-ddeś[o] ye[nā]ṃha te[no]pasaṃkrānta u[pa] .. [kr]. .y. .. + + + ...[i] [r]. .. [v]. .. .. .. + + + + + + + + + + + + + +

r2 + + + + + .. tarhy āgaccha[si] kutra [c]āsi [varṣā] .. [ṣ]. ta iti sa eṣa evam āha • pāpāto haṃ bha[da]nt[ā]nandaitarhy āgacch[ā] .i pā .. .. .[āsmi] varṣā uṣita iti pāpāyā .. .. + + + + + + + + + + +

r3 + + + + + + + .i .. .{{e}} j.ā [t]ip. t.īyā [bh]i .. ○ [d].idhājā[t]ā vihara[nt]i kalahajātā bhaṇḍanajā .. .i .. .. .. vivādam āpannā[s **ta]dyathāham enaṃ** dharmavin[a]y[a]m ā .. + + + +

r4 + + + + + + + + + + + + + + + + [m]. [n]. [dh]. .[m]. [vin]. ○[a][yam ājā]-nā[m]i yathā ca tvam [e]naṃ dharmavinaya[m ā]jānāsi y. ktaṃ tava sahitaṃ samāhitaṃ tava iti pū[r]vaṃ vacanīyaṃ p. [ś]c. [d]. v. [c]. [t*]

[a] 276v2 /// .. [v]. [na]yo bhavati du[ṣ].r. .[e] .i .. ///[85]

85. This fragment belongs to 276v2.

r5 + + + + + + ... [vo] .. .. [abh]. .ū[rṇ].ṃ te viparā○ + + + + [pitas]-.[e] vādo vādārthāya apaharavādaṃ vād[av]ipram. [k].āya ni[g]ṛhīto si nirveṭhaya yady uttaraṃ prajānāsi [b]rūhi pṛ

r6 + + + + ... [khaś]a[kt]i[kayā v]i[t]uda[n]ti [v]irujanti vi○ .. [a]+ + + .. [dh]v[aṃs]a[yaṃ]ti vada[ko] py e[dā]ṃ na prajñāyate yad uta sahadharmeṇa **y[e] pi** te ni[rg]ranthasya jñātiputrasya śrāvakā gṛhiṇo v[a]dā

[a] .ṛ[śā]d. ..

r7 + ...[ā]ṃ [p]ra[t]i[va]santi te pi ni[r]grantheṣu jñātipu[trī] .. .u + ... [a]+ + + + .. .i .. .. .. kalahajāteṣu bhaṇḍanajāteṣu vi .. hīteṣu v[i]vādam āpanneṣu nirviṣaṇṇāḥ [p]r. [ti] .. .. + + [b]+ + +

[a] [d]e[ś]. mā [y]. [b] 275r7 /// .. pāpā[86]

r8[87] + + [nt]. yathāpi tad durākhyātād dha[rm]a[v]i .. [y]ād [du]ṣ[p]r. [v]e .i .. .. .āmi[n]. bh. [n]nād as[tūp]. [d] a[pr]atisaraṇā[c ch]ās[t]ā ca tathāgato rhan samyaksaṃbu[d]dhas tam ena[ṃ] .. [v]. .. + + + + + [a]+ +

[a] 275r8 /// .. .[ā][88]

276v

v1 .. [p].[ā]bhṛtam bhagavantaṃ darśanāyo[p]. ..ṃ .r[a][m]i[t]u + + ..ṃ + ... gavāṃ[s] tenopa[s].[ṃ]kr[a] .āvaḥ apy eva labhemahi bhagavato ntikāt kāṃcid eva gaṃbhīragaṃbhīrāṃ dhar[m]y[ā]ṃ .. + + + ...

v2 + + ..ṃ .. ..ṃ ś[r]a .aṇoddeśam āmantrayate | **iha bha .. ..** [v]i[na]yo bhavati du[ṣ]pr[a]v[e][d]ito nairyāṇiko saṃ[bo]dhigāmī • bhinnastūpo prati[s]raṇa śāst[ā] .. [n]a .. .. + + ..

86. This fragment belongs to the end of 275r7.

87. There are four inverted and mirrored akṣaras reading .. .*i te* on the lower-right corner of this folio. They do not appear to be an overlapping fragment but rather an imprint from another folio entirely, the most likely candidate being the currently lost verso of folio 275.

88. This fragment belongs to the end of 275r8.

v3 + + + + .. [sm]iṃ [kh]alu [c]unda dharmavinaye śrāvako bha○[va]ti dharmānudharmapratipannaḥ sāmīcīpratipanno nudharmacārī **evaṃrūpaś cu[nd]a** .r. .. .. [ga]rhyo bhavati dha .m. .v. [a] + + + + ..

[a] .i .. .i .o

v4 + + + + + ... [to] .[u] .[ā] .[y]. [t]o [dh]armavinayo ○ .. .. tivedi .o nairyāṇiko saṃbodhigāmī bhinno stūpo pratisaraṇaḥ [śās]t[ā] ca na .. .. [g]ato rhan samyaksaṃbu .dh. [ḥ] **[t]. .[m]. ..v.** ..

v5 + + + + + + + + + + + + + + + + ...ī .ī○pr. [t]i [p]. nn. .udharmacā .ī .. .. .u .cunda taṃ śrāvakam eva[ṃ] praśaṃsitavyaṃ manye .. .. .. ṣ.āyuṣmann{{ā}}kām. [a][k]o duḥkhasaha

[a] .. ..

v6 + + + + + + + + + .[y]. .. .. .. [ṣ]. s. .yā[y]yaṃ [dha]○[rm]a[ṃ[89] k]uśala[m] i[t]i **[t]atra cunda** yaś ca praśaṃsati yaś ca praśaṃsyate yaś ca praśasyamāna[s ta] .[ā] tathā[a] pratip. dy. t[e] .. + + + +

[a] .. + .i + + + + ..

v7 + + + + + + + + + .. cunda bh. [v]. ti yathāpi [t]ad du .ākhyāto dharmavinayo duṣpravedito nairyāṇiko saṃbo[dh]i[gā]mī bhinn[o] stūpo pratisaraṇīyaḥ śā .. + + + + + + + + +

v8 + + + + + + + + .. nda dharmavinaye [śā] .[tā]pi garhyo dharmo pi śrāvako py anenāṃgena garhyaḥ **punar aparaṃ** cun[da] durā .. .o[90] dharm[a]vinayo .. [v]. ti [d]. + + + + + + + + + + +

277r

r1 [n]. ryāṇiko sambodhigāmī bhinno stūpo pratisaraṇaḥ śāstā ca na tathāgatho rhaṃ samyaksaṃbuddhaḥ tasmin khalu cunda dharmavinaye śrāvako bhavati na dharmānudharmapra[t]ipanno [na] sāmīcīpratipanno nānudharmacārī

89. This *anusvāra* is completely obscured by a fragment above it. However, the fragment is thin enough to be somewhat translucent.

90. This is a relatively uncommon formation of the *-o-* diacritic for this particular manuscript.

r2 **evaṃrūpaś c[u]nda** [ś]rāvakaḥ na praśasyo bhava[t]i dharmeṣu evaṃ ca punaḥ praśasyo bhavati dharmeṣv āyuṣmato dharmavinayo durākhyāto dharmavi[na]yo [d]u[ṣp]rati[v]edito nairy[ā]ṇiko saṃbodhigāmī bhinno st[ū]pa[91] pratisaraṇaḥ

r3 śā[s]tā [c]a na .. .. .. [t]o [r]han samyaksaṃbuddhas **ta[s]miṃs tvam** āyuṣman dha○.[m]avi[n]aye dharmānudharmapratipan.o na sāmīcīpratipa[n]no nānudharmacārī yat khalu cu[nd]a ta[ṃ] śrāvakam evaṃ samādāpayit. vy.. manyeta dharme

r4 ṣv eva āyu[ṣ]man n[a] te dha.[m]ā [śās]tr[ā]dh]i .. .. ..[ṃ] .[t]v.ṃ [s]ādhu ca suṣṭhu ○ c[a] s[a]mā[d]. y[a] .. .[ta] .. .. + + + + + + + ṣyasi nyāyyaṃ dharmaṃ kuśalam iti **ta[t]ra [cu]nda** yaś ca samād. .. .. .i .. ..[ā]dāpyate

r5 yaś ca samādāpyamāna[s] tathā [ta] .ā .r[a t]i .. .[y]. .. [s]arve te ba○hu-[p]uṇya[ṃ] prasūya .. [ev]. .[e] .. .. [ti y]. [thā]p. tad durākhyāto dharmavinayo [d]uṣpravedito nairyāṇiko sa[ṃ]b[o]dhigāmī bhinno stūpo

r6 pratisaraṇaḥ śāstā ca na tathā[g]ato rhan samya[k]saṃ[b]uddhaḥ evaṃ ○.[ū]p[e] .. .. .i + y. + [s]t .i garhyo dharmo pi śrāvakas tv ane[n]āṃgena praśasya | **[i]ha cunda** svākhyāto dharmavinayo .. .. .i .. .. .i .{{.i}} ..

r7 .ito nairyāṇikaḥ ..ṃbhodigāmī abhinnaḥ sas[tū]paḥ pratisara[ṇ]. + + + + + + ... [n samya]k[sa]ṃbuddhaḥ [t]. [s].i .[kh]a[l]u[r] .unda dharmavinaye śrāvako bhavati dharmā[n]udh[a] .[m]. [p]r. t. panno [n..] sāmīcī .r. .i + + + + +

r8 rmacārī[92] **evaṃrūpaś cunda** śrāvako bhavati gar[h]y. .. .[m]. [ṣ]v evaṃ ca .[u] .. + + + + + + + + + + + + ...[ā] .y[a]t[o] dharmavinayaḥ [s]upravedi[t]o nairyāṇikaḥ saṃbodhigāmī a[bh]i + + + + + + + + + +

277v

v1 [s]t[ā] [c]a tathāgato [r]han samyaksaṃbuddhas **tasmiṃ[s] tv[a]** .. yuṣmaṃ dha[r]mavi .. + + + + + + + + + + + + + .. + + + + + + + + + + + t [kh]. lu {{[t]aṃ}} .unda taṃ śrāva[k]am evaṃ samādā pa .i + + + + + + + +

91. Note the small tick to the lower left of *pa*.

92. Note the small marks around the *rma* conjunct *akṣara*, especially what appears to be three dots in the shape of a triangle to the lower right of the akṣara.

v2 [a]ddhā āyuṣman ye te dharmāḥ śāstrādhigatā tāṃs tvaṃ sādhu ca s[u] ṣ.[u] c[a] s. .. + + + + + + + + + .i [ṣyasyā] .[ādh]ayi[ṣ]y. si ny[ā]yya. dh[a]rma. kuṣala{{ṃ}}m iti **tatra**[a] **cunda** yas samā[d]. + + + + + + +

[a] .. .. ..[93]

v3 dāpyate yaś ca samādāpyamānaḥ tathā ta[thā p]ratiO.. .y. .. + + ... + + + ... ya[nt]e evam etac cunda bhavati yathāpi tathā[p]i [t]a .sv. [kh]yāto dharmavinay. [ḥ] .u .. + + + +

v4 nairyāṇikaḥ saṃbodhigāmī a[bh]i .. .. .tūpaḥ saOpratisaraṇaḥ ś. [s]t[ā c]. .. .. .. [t]o [rhan] s[a]myaksaṃbuddha e[v]aṃ[a] [r]ū[p]. [ṣ]u cunda dharmavinaye śāstāpi praśasyo dharmo pi śrāv[a]kas tv [a]n[e]

[a] [k]. [vi] [r]. ..

v5 nāṃgena garh[y]aḥ **i[h]a [c]un[d]a** svā .y. .. .. rmavinayo O bh[a]v[a]ti suprati .. .i .. + + + + + + + + .. gāmī abhinnaḥ sastupaḥ sapratisaraṇa śāstā = ca tathāg. [t]o r[h]an samyaksaṃ

v6 buddhaḥ .. .. .. [lu] dharmavinaye śrāvakā bhavaṃti O [dh]ar[m]ānudharmapratipannaḥ s.[m]. [c]. [pr]. [ti] p. nno nudharmacārī **evaṃrūpa cundaḥ** śrāvakaḥ [p]r[a]śasyo bhavati dharmeṣv eva[ṃ] ca punaḥ

v7 pra[ś]. [s]y[o] bhavati dharmeṣv āyuṣmata svākhyāto dharmavinayaḥ suprativedito nairyāṇikaḥ saṃbodhigāmī abhinnaḥ sastūpaḥ pratisaraṇaḥ śāstā ca tathāgato rhan samyaksaṃbuddhas **tasmiṃ**

v8 **tva[m]** āyuṣmaṃ dharmavinaye dharmānudharmapratipanna samīcīpratipanno nudharmacārī yat khalu cundaṃ śrāvakam evaṃ praśaṃsitavyaṃ manyeta dharmeṣu addhāyuṣmaṃ lajjī kaukṛtikaḥ saṃvṛtāḥ {{śi}}

278r

r1 śikṣākāmaḥ ārādhako bhaviṣyasy ārādhayiṣyasi nyāyyaṃ dharmaṃ[94]

93. This small fragment partially covers *tra cunda*.

94. Note the irregular *anusvāra* formation on *nyāyyaṃ* and *dharmaṃ*.

kuśalam iti • **tatra cunda** yaś ca praśaṃsati yaś ca praśa{{ṃ}}syate yaś ca pra[ś]asyamānas [t]athā [tath]ā...[i] + + .. sarve te bahupuṇyaṃ prasūyante eva .. +

r2 c cunda bhava[a]ti yathāpi tat svākhyāto dharmavinayaḥ supratipanno nairyāṇikaḥ saṃbodhigāmī abhinna sastūpaḥ sapratisaraṇaḥ śā[st]ā ca tathāg[a]t[o] .r. s. .y. .[s]. .[u] .[dh]. + ..ṃrūpe c[u]n[d]a dharmavinaye .. + +

[a] .. ..

r3 praśasyo [dh]a .. .i śrāvako py anenāṃgena praśaṃsyaḥ **iha cu○nda** [n]a śā[s]tā loka utpanno bha[a]va[t]. a[c]irābhisaṃbuddhaḥ avijñātārthāś cāsya śrāvakā bhavanti dharmeṣv atha ca punas tasya śāstuḥ kṣi[p]r. + + + +

[a] .. .. ..

r4 ntar[dh]ānaṃ bhavati[a] evaṃrūpa[ś] cu .[d]. .[āst]ā anutāpyo bha○vati dharme evaṃ ca punar ananu[t].[b] [p]yo bhavati dharmeṣu navaḥ śāstā loka utpannaḥ acirābhisaṃbuddhaḥ avijñātārthāś cā .y. .r .. ..

[a] .[e] [b] .[ā] ..

r5 bhavanti dharmeṣv atha ca punas tasya śāstu[ḥ] [a].i .. [m]. va lo○ke [n]t[a]rdhānaṃ bhavati • **iha cun[da]** navaḥ śās[t]ā loka utpan[n]o bhavaty acirābhisaṃbuddhaḥ vijñātārthāś cāsya śrāvakā bhavanti dharmeṣv atha ca pu

[a] .. .y ..

r6 nas tasya[95] śāstuḥ k[ṣ]ipram evāntardhānaṃ bhavati evaṃ[r]ūpaś [cu]nda[96] ○ śāstā [anan]u[t]. .y. [bh]. .. .i .. .. [ṣv]. vaṃ [c]a punar ananutāpyo bhavati na dharmeṣu na dharmaḥ śāstā loka utpanno cirābhis[a]ṃb. ..[ḥ] .i .. .[ā]

95. Note the small mark to the left of the bottom of *sya*.

96. The triple conjunct *ṣcu* here goes all the way down into the next line, something that is generally avoided by the scribes in the ms.

r7 rthāś cāsya śrāvakā bhavanti dharmeṣv atha ca punas tasya śāstuḥ k[ṣ]i-pra[m e] + + + + + ..ṃ [bha] .. [t]i .. .. .[u] [a].. .. ..[t]. [lo]k[a] ut[pa]nno bhavati tathāgato rhan samyaksaṃbu[d]dho vi[d]y[ā]car. + + + + + + + + + +

[a] .[r]. .. .. ..

r8 vid a[nutt]araḥ puruṣadamyasārathiḥ śāstā [d]e .a[m]a[n]u[ṣ]y[ā]ṇāṃ[97] .u .[dh]. .. ..[a c]a [n]a bhavati vṛddho jīrṇo [m]. .. .. + + + + + + + + + + y. [n]e[n]āṃ[g]e[n]ā paripūrṇo bhavati **i** .. + + + + + + + +

278v

v1 nno bha[v]ati tathāgato rhan samyaksaṃbuddho vidyācara[ṇa]saṃ-[pa]nna[ḥ] .. .. .[o lok]. vid anuttaraḥ puruṣadamyasārathiḥ śāstā deva-manu .y. + ... [bh]agavāṃ bhavati jīrṇo vṛddho .. + + + + + + +

v2 dharmavinayo nenāṃgena paripūrṇo bhavati **iha cunda** śāstā [l]. + + + + ...i .. [thāgat]o[98] .. ..ṃ .. .[o] vi[d]yācaraṇasaṃpannaḥ sugato lokavid anuttaraḥ .. + + + + + + + +

v3 śāstā devamanuṣyāṇāṃ buddho bhagavāṃ sa ca bhavati ○ j. rṇo [v]ṛddho [m]a[h]alakaḥ sa ca na bhaveti lābhāgrayaśogreṇa sama[n]v[ā] gataḥ evam asya dharmavinayo n. n[ā] .. .. + + ..

v4 vati **iha cunda** śāstā loka ut[p]anno bhavati tathāga○to rhan samyak-sa[ṃ]buddho vidyā[c]araṇasaṃ[p]annaḥ sugato [l]o[k]a[v]id anuttaraḥ puruṣadamyasārathiḥ śāstā devamanuṣyāṇā[ṃ] bu[ddh].

v5 bh[ag]avāṃ sa ca [bha] .. [t]i .ī .. .[ṛ] .[dh]. [m]ahallakaḥ sa ○ ca bh[a]-vati khābhāgrayaś[o]greṇa samanvāgataḥ evam asya dharmavinayo nenāṃ-gena paripūrṇo bh[av]. .i .. **[h].** .**[u] .d.** .. stā l.

97. The ms. was pieced together here, and some akṣaras are are misaligned; note especially the *ṣyā*.

98. The ms. is cracked here, and the akṣaras are split horizontally and somewhat misaligned.

v6 ka utpa .n. [bh]a[v]a[t]i tathāga[t]o .ha[n] sa[m]yaksaṃbuddho vi◯dyāc[a]raṇasaṃpannaḥ sugato lokavid anuttaraḥ puruṣadamyasārathiḥ śāstā devamanuṣyaṇāṃ [b]. .dh[o bh]a .. + +

v7 ca bhavati jīrṇo vṛddho mahallakaḥ sa ca bhavati lābhāgrayaśogreṇa[99] samanvāgato na vāsya vaistārikaṃ brahmacaryaṃ bhavati | bāh[u]ja[n]yaṃ pṛthubhūtaṃ yāvad ev[a]m. [n]. .e .. [ḥ] .a .ya .[s]u [pr]akāśi ..ṃ + +

v8 sya dharmavinayo nenāṃgena paripūrṇo bhavati **iha cundaḥ** śāstā loka utpanno bhavati tathāgato rhan samyaksaṃbuddho vi[d]yācaraṇa[sa]ṃ .. .. .. + + + + + + d anuttaraḥ {{puru}}ṣa +[100]

279r

r1 puruṣadamyasārathiḥ śāstā devamanuṣyāṇā[ṃ] b[u]ddho bh[a]gavāṃ sa na bhavati jīrṇo vṛddho mahallaka sa ca bhavati lābhāgr[e]ṇ[ay]. [ś]. .r. ṇa sama[n]vagat[o] [vais]tārika [n]. .[y]. + + + + + + + + + + + + +

r2 bhūtaṃ yāvad evamanuṣyebhyaḥ samyaksu[p]rak[āś]it[a]ḥ evam asya sadharmavinayo nenāṃgena paripūrṇo bhavati |[101] **iha cunda** śāstā loka utpanno bhavati tathāga[to] .han samyaksaṃbu[d]dho vi .y. .. .. + + + + + + + +

r3 kavi[d] anu[t]ta[raḥ] puruṣadamyasārathiḥ śastā devamanu◯ṣy[āṇā]ṃ buddho bhagavān sa ca bhavati jīrṇo vṛddho mahallakaḥ sa ca bhavati lābhā[g]rayaśogreṇa samanvaga .[o] [vai]s[t]arikaṃ [c]. + + +

r4 caryaṃ [bh]avati bāhu[j]a[n]yaṃ .ṛ[th]u[bh]ū[ta]ṃ .. .. d [de]vamanuṣyebhyaḥ ◯ samyaksuprakāśitaṃ na cāsya śrāvakāḥ sthavirā navyā navakā paṇḍitā bhavanti vyaktā medhāvino lam utpanno[tp]annānā[ṃ][a] sahadh. .. .. ..

[a] .. .[y]. .. .. ..

99. Note the small tick mark extending from the left side of *lā* here.

100. Although the ms. is damaged after *ṣa*, it is clear that the scribe had written *{{puruṣada}}*, ending this line with the decision to delete all four akṣaras and preferring to start *puruṣadamyasārathiḥ* anew in 279r1.

101. Note the small dot underneath the *daṇḍa* here.

r5 gṛhītāro la [s]vādasya paryavadā[p]ayi[tā]raḥ evam asya ○ dha .[m] avinayo nenāṃgena paripūrṇo bhavati || **iha cunda** śāstā loka utpanno bhavati tathāgato [r]han sa .ya .s.ṃ .u .dh. .i .y. .. ..

r6 nnaḥ sugato lokavid[102] anuttaraḥ puruṣadamyasārathiḥ ○ śās[t]ā [d] e .a[m]a[n]u[ṣy]āṇā[ṃ] buddho bha[g]avā[n sa c]a bhavati jīrṇo vṛddho mahallakaḥ sa ca bhavati lābhāgrayaśogreṇa[103] saman[v]āg[ato v]ais. .i

r7 kaṃ cā[s]ya brah[m]acaryaṃ bhavati bāhujanyaṃ pṛthubhūtaṃ yāvad devaman[u]ṣy[e] + + + + ... [t]. śrāvakā cā[s]ya s[th]avirā madh[y]ā navakāḥ paṇḍitā bhavanti vyaktā medhāvino lam utpanno[tp]an.ā .āṃ [p]. .. + + + +

r8 sahadharmeṇa nigṛhītāro laṃ svasya vāda .ya [par]yavadāpayitāraḥ evam a .. dh[armav]i .. y. [ne]nā[ṃ]gena pa[r]i[pūr]ṇo bh[a]vati • **iha cunda** śāstā loka utpanno bhavati tathāgato r[h]. .. + + + + + + + + +

279v[104]

v1 sampann. + ... [r]. + + + + + + + + +

v2 [cā] .. +

v3 + .. + .. +

v4 + [ma] .[u] .[y]. ṇāṃ

102. Note the irregular form of *lo*.

103. Note the small tick under the left side of *ṇa*.

104. Unfortunately folios 279 and 280 are stuck together, so only small parts of 279v are visible, and 280r is completely obscured.

v5 + tam̩ yā + +

v6 + + .. [ṣye] .y. + [m]yaksuprakā[ś]i + ... + + + + + + + + + + + + +

v7 .. .y. [vādā]sya paravadāyitāra[ḥ] .. + .[i] .. .. .. +

v8 .. [to] .hansamyaksaṃbuddho vidyācaraṇasaṃpanna +

280r[105]

280v

v1 + + m[e]dhāvino[106] lam utpannotpannānāṃ parapravādānāṃ sahadharmeṇa nigṛhītāro la[ṃ] svasya vādasya paryavadāpayitāraḥ śrāvak. [s]. [gh]. [ś] c. .y. .[ṛ] .. + + + + + + + + + + + + +

v2 + + + .y. stha[v]i[rarā]janyatayā samanvāgato bhavati na cāsya [śrā] .. .. [s].ṃ[gho] na lābhāgrayaśogreṇa samanvāgato bhavaty evam asya dharmavinayo nāṃgena paripūrṇo [bha]v. .. + + + + + +

v3 l. ka [u]tpanno bhavati tathāgato rhan samyaksaṃbuddho vi○.y. .. .. ṇasaṃpannaḥ sugato lokakavid anuttaraḥ puruṣadamyasārathiḥ śāstā devamanuṣyāṇāṃ buddho bhagavāṃ [sa] .. .. .. + + +

v4 vṛddho mahallakaḥ sa [c]a bhavati lābhāgrayaśogreṇa ○ samanvāgato vaistarikaṃ cāsya brahmacaryaṃ bhavati bāhujanyaṃ pṛthubhūtaṃ yāvad devamanuṣyebhyaḥ samyaksuprak. ..[a].. [ś].[ā] v. +

105. Though this side of the folio is completely lost, I have been able to almost entirely reconstruct its content.

106. The *e* in *medhāvino* here is confirmed by a mirrored imprint below in 281r8.

[a] 279v4 /// [ma] .[u] .[y]. ṇāṃ[107]

v5 [ś c]āsya s[th]avirā [m]a[dh]yā navak[āḥ] paṇḍitā vyaktā medhā○vino lam utpannotpannānāṃ parapravādo sahadharmeṇa nigṛhītāro laṃ svasya vādasya paryavadāpa[y]i [a]+ + + +

[a] 279v5 /// taṃ yā + +[108]

v6 [a]va.. ..[ṃ]ghaś cā[s]. .. .. ..i [vai]pu[l]yāṃ gato bhava○ti śrāvakasaṃghaś cāsya sthavirarājany{{ā}}tayā samanvāgato bhavati śravakasaṃghaś cāsya lābhāgrayaś[o] + + + + + +

[a] 279v6 /// + + .. [ṣye] .y. + [m]yaksuprakā[ś]i

v7 [a].[o] + + + + + + + + .i[na]yo nenāṃgena paripūrṇo bhavati **yāvantaḥ khalu** cundaḥ śāstriṃ[109] saṃmatā nāham eka śāstāra[m]. + .[m]. [nā] [s]amasamaṃ samanup. [ś]. .i .. .. ..ṃ + + +

[a] 279v7 /// .. .y. [vādā]sya paravadāyitāra[ḥ]

v8 [a]+ + + + + + + + + + + + + + m etarhi śāstā yāvantaḥ khalu cunda saṃghā vā gaṇā vā parṣado vā aham eka śrāvaka [s].[ṃgh]. [m a]py ātmanā samasamaṃ .. + + + + + + + +

[a] 279v8 /// .. [to] .hansamyaksaṃbuddho vidyācaraṇasaṃpanna

281r

r1 ya evaṃ lābhāgrayaśogreṇa samanvāgatas tadyathā aham etarhi śrāvakasaṃgha iti cunda śāstāraṃ śrāvakasaṃgham asmākam evāgacchet parataḥ sahadharmeṇa praśaṃsāsthānīyo[110] dharm[a] .. + + + ... + + + + + + +

107. Belongs to end of 279v4.

108. Belongs to end of 279v5.

109. Note the small ink dot on the lower left of *striṃ*.

110. Note the small ink tick between *yo* and *dha*.

r2 **ntrayate sma** • udrako bhikṣavo rāmaputra evaṃdṛṣṭir evaṃvādī paśyan na paśyati • kiṃ paśyan na paśyati bhikṣur asya satatalikhitasya yo dhārāṃ paśyati sa [ph]alaṃ na paśyati yaḥ phalaṃ paśyati sa dhārā. na paśyati iti [s]. + + +

r3 śyan pha ..[ṃ] .. [ś]yati phalasya pa[ś]yaṃ [dh]ārān na paśyati | **sa khalu** bhi◯kṣava udrakasya rāmaputrasya[111] vāṇīhīnāyāṃ kṣuradhārāyām upasitāy[a] evam āha paśyan na paśyati kiṃ paśyan na paśyati kṣurasya satata .i + + +

r4 yo dhār[āṃ] paśyati sa phalaṃ paśyati | y[aḥ] [ph]. .aṃ paśyati sa dhārā◯n[112] na paśyati[113] iti dhārān paśyati phalaṃ paśyan dhārān na paśyati kṣurasya bhikṣavaḥ satatalikhitasya yo dhārāṃ paśyati sa phalaṃ paśya[t]i + + +

r5 paśyati sa dhārāṃ paśyati iti sa dhārā[n] paśyan phalaṃ paśyati ◯ phalasya paśyan dhārāṃ paśyatīti | **yad bhikṣavaḥ** samyagvadanto vadeyuḥ paśyan na paśyatīti iha tat samyagvadanto vadeyus tat kasya he[to] .. + + +

r6 paripūrṇaṃ brahmacaryam ane[n]āṃgena paripūrṇaṃ [t]ad aṅ[ga]ṃ pari◯pūrayiṣyām i[t]y apy en[a]ṃ[114] n[a] p[a]śyati kārapari[ś]uddhaṃ brahmacaryam ity apy enaṃ paśyati tat khalu sarvākārapariśuddhaṃ brahmacaryam ane ..ṃ .. + + + +

r7 ddhaṃ tad a[ṅgam] a[p]anīyānyat [p]aśutara[m] aṃ[g]am[115] upasaṃhariṣyāmevam idaṃ bhūyasya mā[t]r. + + + + + + .[y]. vadātaṃ ca bhavatīty apy enaṃ na paśyati **tasmāt khalu** bhikṣavo ye te dharmā dṛṣṭadharmasukhavihārāya s[a]ṃ + + + + + + + +

111. Note the small ink tick under the *ma*.

112. Note the small ink tick here to the left of the *-n-* ligature.

113. Note the small ink tick below the *-i-* diacritic in *ti* here.

114. There is a small mark extending from the tip of the *-e-* diacritic that could be construed as a deletion mark. However, I do not think that is the case here, considering that this phrase is used again in this very line.

115. Note the ink mark under the *saṃ* here. It is very similar to the marks found on line 4 of this folio.

r8 khāya saṃparāyahitāya saṃparāyasukhāya te bhikṣuābhir[116] udgṛhya paryavāpya tathā ta[th]. . . . . .i . . .ā .ācayitavyā yathedaṃ brahmacaryaṃ cirasthitikaṃ syāt tad bhaviṣyati bahujanahitāya [b]a[hu] + + + + + + +

281v

v1 nukaṃpāyai a[rth]āya hitāya sukhāya d[e]va[m]a[n]u[ṣ]yāṇāṃ **kat[ame] t[e]** [bhi] .. + + + + + + .. dṛṣṭadharmahitāya saṃvarttate[117] dṛṣṭadharmasukhāya [sa]ṃparāyajitāya saṃp[a] + + + + + + +

v2 kṣubhir udgṛhya pavāpya tathā tathā dhārayitavyā grāhayitavyā vācayi[t]. .. + + + ... caryaṃ cira .i [t]ikaṃ syāt tad bhaviṣyati bahujanahitāya bahujanasukhāya lokānu .. .[ā] + + + + + +

v3 ya sukhāya devamanuṣyānāṃ | **tadyath[ā]** [s]ū[tr]aṃ [g]e[y]aṃ vyā○k. r. ṇ.. [g]. .. .[d]. .. .i .ānāva .ānetivṛttakajātakavaipulyādbhutadharmopadeśā iyam ete bhikṣavo dharmm[ā] .. + + + + +

v4 ya saṃvarttaṃte dṛṣṭadharmmasukhā[y]a saṃparāyahitāya ○ saṃparāyasukhāyeti udgṛhya paryavāpya tathā tathā dhārayitavyā grāhayitavyā vāca yathedaṃ brahmacaryaṃ cir[a] .thitik. + + +

v5 viṣyati bahujanasukhāya lok. .ukaṃ[p]āyai arthāya ○ hitāya sukhāya devamanuṣyāṇāṃ **api tu khalu** yūyaṃ bhikṣavas sarve nānādṛṣṭayo nānākṣāntayo nānārucayo nānā .i + +

v6 s te ..ṃ bhikṣavo nānādṛṣṭīnāṃ nānākṣāntīnāṃ nānā○cīnāṃ nānābhiprāyāṇāṃ bhikṣur upasaṃkramya dharmaṃ bhāṣeta sa s[am]yañ cārtham upasaṃh[a]ren [m]i[th]y[ā] ca vyajanaṃ nirūpayet a[s]y. .. +

v7 d bhāṣitaṃ naivotsāhayitavyaṃ nāvasādayitavyam* anutsahyānavasādya śrotram avadadhāya dharmapadavyaṃjanān udgṛhya ta ..i .. .. .. [a]nyad yuktata[r]aṃ ..ṃjana[m] upasaṃhṛtya ev[a]ṃ .y. + +

116. The *-ā-* diacritic is quite strange. It is possibly just a messy akṣara and not meant as an *-ā-* at all.

117. Note that in this script *rta* is always written as *rtta*.

v8 nīyaḥ asmiṃ «tva»m āyuṣma{{anta}} nn arthe katarad yuktaraṃ vyaṃjanaṃ samanupaśyasy etad vā idaṃ veti sacet sa evaṃ vaded **asminn aham** āyu[ṣ]manto rthe i ..ṃ .uktataraṃ ..[ṃ] + ..[ṃ] + + + + + + + +

282r[118]

r1 samanupaśyāmi na tathedam iti sa bhikṣur idaṃ syād vacanīyo tena hi tvam āyuṣmaṃ caitad vyaṃjanaṃ chorayitvā anena vyaṃjanenaitam arthaṃ dhanaya evam atra pa[r]e saṃj[ñ]apa[y]itavyā yad ut. + + + + + + + .u .. .. +

r2 sarve nānādṛṣṭayo nānākṣāntayo nānārucayo nānābhiprāyās teṣāṃ vo bhikṣavo nānādṛṣṭīnāṃ nānākṣāntīnāṃ nānāṃrūcīnāṃ nānābhiprāyāṇāṃ bhikṣur upasaṃ[k]ra .y[a] [dh]a[r]m[a]ṃ [bh]āṣeta sa mi .. .[ā]rtham upasaṃharet samyañ ca vyaṃ[ja] + + +

r3 payet [t]. [s]ya [bh]ikṣos tad bhāṣitaṃ naivotsāhayitavyaṃ nāvasādaOyitavyaṃ[119] anutsāhyānavasādya[120] śrotram avadhāya dharmapadavyaṃjanāny udgṛhya tasmin vyaṃjane anyad yuktataram artham upasaṃhṛ .y. [t] i ..[ṃ] + +

r4 syād vacanīyaṃ **asmiṃs tvam** āyuṣmad vyaṃjane katarad yuktararam aOrthaṃ samanupaśyasy enaṃ vā idaṃ veti sacet sa evaṃ vadet tasminn aham āyuṣ[m]a[n]to vyaṃjane idaṃ yukta[ta]ram arthaṃ [s]a[m]anupaśyāmi .. + + + +

r5 ti sa idaṃ syād vacanīyas tena hi tva .. y. ṣmann imam arthenaiOtad vyaṃjanaṃ dhāraya eva[m] a[t]ra pare saṃjñapayitavyā yad utārthaśaḥ **api khalu** yūyaṃ bhikṣavaḥ sarve nānādṛṣṭayo[121] nānāk.. .. .o [n]ā[n]. .. .. ..

118. A substantial part of the last quarter of 282r1–8 became stuck to 283r at some point. I have been able to digitally restore the sections that were stuck above 283r to their proper places in 282r. However, everything from 283r that was underneath these fragments is lost without access to the physical ms. Additionally, although a few akṣaras are still visible, the corresponding sections from 282v are mostly lost underneath 283v.

119. Note the irregular *-ā-* in *sā* here.

120. Again note the irregular *-ā-* in *sā*.

121. Note the irregular *-o-* diacritic in *yo* here.

r6 nānābhipr[ā]yās teṣāṃ v[o] bhi[k]ṣavo nānā[d]ṛṣṭ. nā. nānākṣānt[ī]nā. ○ nānārucīnāṃ nānābhiprā .[ā]ṇ[ā]ṃ bhik[ṣ]u .. pasaṃkramya dharmaṃ bhāṣeta sa mithyā cārtham upasaṃhare .i .[ā] .. .y[a]ṃjanaṃ nirūpaye[t] .. + + + + + +

r7 taṃ naivotsāhayitavyaṃ nāvasādayitavyaṃ anutsāhyānavasādya śro .ram ava .. + + + + [a].. .. ..ṃ[ja]nān [u]d[g]ṛh.. tasminn arthapadavyaṃja .. [a]nu[d] yu[k]ta[t]ara[ṃ] arthav..ṃ[jan]am upasa. hṛ[t]y[a] [bh] .ṣu. .. .. + + + + +

[a] .. .. .y.

r8 **katama tvam** āyu[ṣ]mann arthavyaṃjanaṃ yuktataraṃ sama[n]upaśyasy etad vā [i] ..ṃ + + + .. + + + + ... [h]a[m]āyu .m. [n]t. [rth]. .y. [ja] naṃ [yu] .t. [t]araṃ [a] [sam]. nu .. .y. .i [ti] sa bhikṣubhir idaṃ syād va .. + + + + + + +

282v

v1 yuṣmann etad avyaṃjanaṃ cchorayitvā idaṃ artha{{ṃ}}vyaṃjanaṃ dhāra[y]a .. + + + ... + ...i [t]. .[yā] yad utārthaśo vyaṃjanaśaś ca • **a .i khal. .. ..ṃ** bhik[ṣav]. s.. ..e .[ā] .ā .. .. + + + + + + + + +

v2 rucayo nānābhiprāyā teṣāṃ vo bhikṣavo nānādṛṣṭīnāṃ nānākṣānt. .. + + + + ... + + .āy[ā]ṇāṃ bhikṣur upasaṃkramya dha ..ṃ bhāṣe[t]. [s]. [s]. .y. .[c]. + + + + + + + + + + + + + + + + + + +

v3 t tasya bhikṣos tad bhāṣitaṃ sādhv abhiṇ[a]n.itav[ya]ṃ sādhv anumo○ditavya. sādhv abhinaṃdyaṃ [sā]dhva{{bhi}}numodya uttare idaṃ syād vacanīya evaṃ hy āyuṣma[n]. .. + + + + .[t]. .. .. [c]. .[u] .. + + + + + +

v4 bhavati **yad yuṣmākaṃ** bhikṣavo ma .[ā] [c].varam anujñātaṃ ya○di vā pāṃsukūlaṃ yadi [v]ā gṛhapaticīvaram alaṃ vas tat pratisevituṃ na dravārthaṃ na .. .. + + + ṇ.. nārthaṃ na vi[bhūṣ]. + + + + + + + +

v5 gamaśakavātātapasarīsṛpasa[ṃsp]a[rś]ānāṃ pratighā○tārthaṃ hrīkaupīnapra[c]chā[d]anārthaṃ ca **yad yuṣmākaṃ** bhikṣavo mayā bhojana[m a] .ujñātaṃ y. + + + + + + + .i + + ...i + +

v6 ṇakaḥ alaṃ vas tat pratisevituṃ na dravārthaṃ na madā○rthaṃ na maṇḍanārthaṃ na vibhūṣaṇārthaṃ yāvad eva kāyasya [s]thi[t]a[y]. [yāp]anāyai ji[gh]. .. + + + + + + + + + + + + + + +

v7 purāṇīṃ ca vedanā pratihaniṣyāmi navā ca vedanā notpādayiṣyāmi yātrā ca me bhaviṣyati balaṃ ca sukhaṃ cānavadyatāṃ [c]a .. .. vihāra .. + + + + + + + + + + + + + + +

v8 m anujñātaṃ yadi vā vṛkṣamūlaṃ yadi vā layanam anyāni vā mā .ā vā kūṭāgārāṃ vā alaṃ vastavyaṃ pratisevituṃ na dravārthaṃ na madārthaṃ na ma[ṇḍa] .. [rtha]ṃ [n]a vibhuṣ. ṇā[rtha]ṃ .. + + + + + + + + +

283r[122]

r1 [p]rati[gh]. [t]ā[r]thaṃ pratisaṃl[a]yanaparamatāyai ca **yad yuṣmākaṃ** mayā bhikṣavo .[lā] n[a] .[aiyajṣ]a [s]amanujñātaṃ yadi vā [p]ūti[m]uktaṃ yadi vā sarpistailamadhuphāṇi[t]. [m] a[l]aṃ vas tat pratis[e]vi .u + + + ..[ṃ] .. .. + ..[ṃ] .. .. [ṇ].. .[ā]rthaṃ na

r2 vibhūṣaṇārthaṃ yāvad evotpannotpannānāṃ śārīrikāṇāṃ vedanānāṃ duḥkhānāṃ tīvrāṇāṃ kharāṇ[ā]ṃ ka[ṭ]. [k]ā[n]ā[m]. [m]. nāpānāṃ prāṇahāriṇīnāṃ pratighātā[rth]am avya .. .aparama[tā]yai [c]. .. + + + + + + + + + + + nyatīrthi

r3 kaparivrājakā evaṃ vadeyuḥ sukhālayānuyogam anuyu○ktāḥ śramaṇāś śākyap[u]trīyā viharantīti t[ac] ca sukhasya ta[c] ca sukh[asya t]ad idaṃ .. ..ṃ tad idaṃ ka[th].ṃ .. .. ..ṃ .[i] + + + + + + + + + + .. nta eka

r4 eva sukh[ā]layānuyoga ukto bhagavatā **api tv asti** sukhā○layā[n]u-yo[go] h[ī] .. .. ..[ḥ] .r. kṛtaḥ pārthagjaniko rogasya mūlaṃ gaṇḍasya mūlaṃ śa[l]yasya .. .. [m]. + + + + + + + + + [r]yaḥ sāmi

r5 ṣaḥ so[va]dhiko nāsevitavyo na bhāvayitavyo na bahulīka○[rttavyo yasmāt sukhā]layān[u]yo .. .. tavyam iti vadāmi **asti** sukhā[la]yānuyogaḥ a .[ī] .. .. .y. .. + + + + + + + + + + + k. na ro

122. A large portion of fourth quarter of lines 1–8 are obscured by pieces of 282r1–8 where the two folios are stuck together.

r6 gasya mūlaṃ na gaṇḍasya mūlaṃ na śalyasya mū[l]. [n]. .. .. maraOṇasya pratyayaḥ āryo nirā .[i] .. .[i]r[o]padhikhaḥ asevayitavyo bhāvayitavya bahulīka[rtt]a .y. .. .. .. khālayān. yo[gā] + + + + .i .i

r7 vadāmi • **asthānam etad** bhikṣavo vi[d]y. .. y. d anyatīrthikapari-[v]rājakā evaṃ vadeyuḥ katamaḥ sa.... [ntaḥ su]khālayānuyogo hīno grāmyaḥ [p]rāk[ṛ]taḥ pārthagjani .yo + + ...[ṃ] .. .. + + + + +

r8 jarāmaraṇasya pr. ty. y. ḥ .. [nāryaḥ sām]i[ṣa]ḥ sopadhiko nāsevitavyo na bh[ā]vayitavyo [n]a bahulī[k]arttavyo yasmāt sukhālayānuyogā[d] bh[e]tavyam iti vadata[ḥ] **.. .. .. ..yu** .. .. .. + + + + + + + + + + +

283v[123]

v1 .[uṇ]. .. [t]. .. .. .. + + + + + + .[ūpāṇ]. [ṣ]ṭ. .. .. [p]ṛy[āṇi] manāpāni kāmopabhogasaṃhitāni raṃjanīyāni śrotravijñeyāḥ śabdāḥ ghrāṇ. .i .[e]yā [g]. ◊ .. .. .. v. [jñ]. .. ..

v2 [s]ā[ḥ] .. .. .i .. .. [ṣ]. [vy]. nīṣṭāni kāntāni [p]ri .. .. [pā]ni .[ā] .[o] pa[s]aṃhitāni raṃja[n]ī .. .i iti **ya im[ā]ṃ** paṃ[c]a k[āmag]uṇāṃ pratītomutpa .. .. .. [kh]. .. .. + +

v3 ty. + + + + + .. y. nuy. .. .. [nu] .. ..[ḥ] .. .. ṇāḥ O śākyaputrīyā viharaṃta iti y. [e]vaṃ vade na samyak sa evaṃ vadan vaded asamanuyu[kt].[ḥ] .. .. ..[ḥ] ś. .. .[u] .r. y. .. + + + + + +

v4 **vaṃ** v[a] .. .. .. .y. .s. .. [v].ṃ vad. .. [d]. .* y. [thā] .. .[v ih]. [k]. .y. Os saṃcintya prāṇinaṃ jīvitād vy[apa]ropyādattam ādāya kāmeṣu mithyā caritvā saṃprajānaṃ .[ṛ] .. + + + + + + .. [pānaṃ][a] p.

[a] ::

v5 + + + ..[ḥ] ..ṃ .[o] .. [v]i .. [rī] .. .i .. cchet sukham adhiOga .[che]t saumanasyam ity evaṃrūpe sukhālayānuyoge anuyuktāḥ śramaṇāḥ śākyaputrīy.[ḥ] .i .. ..ṃtīti .. .. [de] n. sa

123. Double underlined akṣaras in this folio occurring between lines 2–6 were restored via Photoshop by mirroring the thin birchbark layer of 283v that is lying atop 284r2–7.

v6 + ... va[ṃ] vadan [v]. ded anuyu[k]tā viharantīti **ya e○vaṃ** vade samyak sa evaṃ vadan vadet* ayaṃ sa bhavantaḥ sukhālayānuyogo hīn[o] grā .yaḥ [p]r. .[ṛ] ..ḥ pārthag[j]. nik[o] [m]aṃg[a]sya

v7 m[ū]l.. .. [a]ṇ.. s.. mūlaṃ śalyasya mūlaṃ jarāmaraṇasya pratyayaḥ anāryaḥ sāmiṣaḥ sopadhiko nāsevitavyo na bhāvayitavyo na bahulīkarttavyo yasmāt sukhālayānuy[og]. d [ṛ]t. .y. [m iti] v. d. [m]i

[a] [bh]. [v].

v8 .. .. .[e] .. .[i] .. .. [y]a[d] anyatīrthikaparivrājakā evaṃ [v]a[de]yu[ḥ] .. [t]. [maḥ] [s]. bhavantas sukhālayānuyogaḥ ahīnaḥ a grāmya aprākṛto pārtagjaniko na rodhasya mūlaṃ gaṇ[ḍ]asya mūl.ṃ ..{{ṃ}} «.y.» .. .. «la»[124] [ja]m[a]ṇa[s]ya [p]ratyayaḥ

284r

r1 + ...i .o .i .. .. [dh]ik. [ā] .. .i [t]. .. ba h[u]līkar[tt]a[a] .o yas[m]āt sukhālayānuyogān na bhettavyam iti vadatān **pṛṣṭair idaṃ** syur vacanīyāḥ paṃceme bhav. [n]t.[ḥ] k. .. guṇā katame paṃca cakṣurvijñē

[a] [s]. ..

r2 yā[ni][a] .. .. .. [ṣ]ṭ[ā]ni kāntāni priyāṇi manāpāni kāmopasaṃhitā[n]i r.ṃjanīyāni śro[t]avijñeyāṃ śabdhāṃ ghrāṇavijñeyāṃ gandhāṃ jih[v]āvijñeyān rasāṃ kāyavijñ. yāni spraṣṭavyānīṣṭāni

[a] .. ..ḥ [śr]. [m]. ṇ.

r3 kāntāni priyāṇi manāpā[n]i .. .. [p]asaṃhitāni ○ ..ṃ + + + + + + + + + **n paṃca** kāmagunā[n] pratītyotpadyate sukham utpadyate saumanasyam iti vi .itvā tac ca prahāya vivi

r4 [k]..ṃ + + + [v]ac caturthaṃ [dhy]ā[n]. [m]. .. .. viharatīty e○.. .. .. .[u] .. .. [y]. [n]uy. [g]. anuyuktāḥ śramaṇāḥ śākyaputrīyā viharaṃtīti ya evaṃ vade na samyak sa evam vade [n]uyu .t. vi

124. The *.y.* and *la* are written in small letters interlinearly under the line.

r5 haraṃtīti y[a] **ev.ṃ** [v]. [det].. .. .. ev. v. d. vade yathā ○ khalv ihaikasya saṃciṃtya prāṇi ..ṃ jī[v]itād [v]yap[a]ropyādattam ā[dā]y[a] k[ā]meṣu mithyā caritvā saṃprajānaṃ mṛ[ṣ]āvā[d]aṃ bhāṣitvā

r6 [m]ad[y]a[p]ān[a]ṃ pī[t]vā prama[t]..ḥ [pa]ṃ .o .. .i .. .ī .. .. ga○cchet sukham adhigacchet saumanasyam iti viditvā tac ca prahāya viviktaṃ kāmair yāvac caturthaṃ dhyānam upasaṃpa[d]y[a] .[i] .. .. .ī .. ..ṃ ..

r7 .. .. [la]y[ā] .[u] .. .. .. .u[y]u .t.[ḥ] .r. .. ṇā śākyap[u]trīyā viharantīti **ya** evaṃ vaden na sam[y]a[k] sa evaṃ vadaṃn vaded anuyuktā viharaṃtīti **ya** **eva[ṃ]** vadet sam. k[s]. e ..ṃ .. .. .. + + + + + [bh]. ..

r8 n[ta]ḥ s[u]khālayān[u]y[o] .. ..[ḥ] .. [g].ām..ḥ [a]prākṛto .. .. gjaniko na rogasya mūlaṃ n[a] g. ṇ[ḍ]. s.. m. l.ṃ n.. .ā [r]. [m]. .. ..ṃ +

284v[125]

v1 ā [a]+ + [t]. [v]y[o bh]. [v]i [t]. .. .. .. .ī .. .. + + + + + + + .. bhe [t]. .y. .. .. **.th.** .. ..[bh]. .. .. +

[a] 285v1 tīrthi + + + + + + + + ... yu[ḥ] katame te bhavatā dh. rm[a] .. ///[126]

v2 [bh.] [a].. .. ..ṃ + .[i] + + + + + + + + + + + + + + + .. **[ṣṭ]. r idaṃ** syu .vacanīyāḥ evaṃ sukhālayān[u]yogam anuyuktānā[m]. sm[ā]k. [bh]. [v]. [nto] [v]. h. r. t. [s]. .[t]. [ph]. .. + .. .[t]. .. + + + + + + + + + +

[a] 285v2 [r bh]. .. .i .. .ṣ. s. prāptamānas[o n]uttaraṃ y[o]gakṣemaṃ nirvāṇa[m]. .i ///

125. The left side of this folio up to the string hole is almost completely covered by 285v.

126. The fragments that obscure the left side of this folio belong to 285v, a folio that is still extant in a picture kindly provided to me by Kazunobu Matsuda. The photo was taken of the manuscript bundles before the folios were separated, a process that unfortunately and unavoidably caused a great deal of damage to the surrounding folios for this part of the *Prāsādika-sūtra*.

v3 [**me** s]. [a].. .. .. + + + + + + + + + + + + + + + + + + ..○yati [no] tra maraṇasa[may]e || p[un]a .. para bhikṣur na haiva dṛṣṭa eva dharme pratiyatyevājñām ārāgayati a[p]i [tu] .. .. + + + + ... [ra]

[a] 285v3 .. .. .. nvayāt samyaṅ[m]anasikārānvayāt kāmāṃ pra○ ///

v4 paraṃ [a]bhik[ṣ]. + y[a]○ti [n]āpi maraṇasamay[e] a .i [tu] ..ṃ .. .[ā]m ava[rabh]ā[gī]yānāṃ saṃyojanānāṃ prahāṇād a[n]tarāparinirvāyī bhavati .. .. [p]. ri

[a] 285v4 + + r uṣitaṃ bra[h]macaryaṃ kṛtaṃ karaṇīyaṃ nāp. r.○ ///

v5 .i [a].. + .. ○ [tv]. .. .i ..ṃ .. .. [p]a[r]i-ni[r]vāyī bhavati na haivābhiparinirvāyī bhavati • api tu sābhisaṃskārapa-rinirvāyī bhavati n. h. v[a] sābhi

[a] 285v5 y. .. [h]ṛt. bhāro nuprāptasvakārtha parikṣīṇabhava○ ///

v6 + [a]+ ○ + + + + + + + + + + ..
nām asmākaṃ bhavanto viharatām imāni saptaphalāni ime saptānuśaṃsāḥ pratik[ā]ṃ[k]ṣit[av]y[ā]ḥ

[a] 285v6 kṣīṇāsravaḥ saṃciṃtya prāṇinaṃ jīvitātād vyaparopayituṃ abrahmaca[r]y.ṃ .. .. ///

v7 + [a]+ .. ..[t]. .[r]. .. .. .. [gau]tamena śāśvato [l]. k.ḥ idam eva satyaṃ moham anyad iti aśāśvataḥ śāśvataś cāś[āś]vataś[127] ca

[a] 285v7 /// .. .. .i .ā .[ā] .ā ḫ.. ṇī .[ā a]s.ṃ .ā .ā [a]s.ṃk.obh.ā s. [rv]. bāl[a]-pṛth[a]g. naiḥ s.ān. [m]. ///

127. Note the tick on the lower left side of *śa*.

v8 .. va śāśv[a]to nāśā[ś]v. .. .[c]. | a[nt]. [v]. .. .. .. ḥ [a]nt. v. .c. .. .t. .. .c. .. [vān] t. .. .. nantavān* sa jīvas tac charīram[128] a[n]yo jīvo nyac charīraṃ bhavati tathāgataḥ paraṃ[129] maraṇ[ā n]. [bh]a .[at]i [t]. [thā]gataḥ paraṃ maraṇā

285r

r1 ..[130] + ... satyaṃ moham anyad iti pṛṣṭair naiti syur vasanīyāḥ **sthānam etad** bhikṣavo vidyate y. .. .. ri .rā[jak]. .. ..

r2 ..[131] + ... sy[u]r vacanīyāḥ eterhi bhavanto dharmānārthopasaṃhitā na dharmopasaṃhitā na brahmacaryo[p]. [s]. hi .. .. + + + + + + + + + + +

r3 [s]. + + + + + .. [132] + + + + + + + + + + + + + + ○ .. .. .[ā kṛ]tā iti **sthānam etad** bhikṣavo vidyate yad a[n]y[a]tīrthika parivrājakā evaṃ vad[eyu] + + + + + + + + + + + + + +

r4 + ○ .y. [a].. + .. ti bhavaṃto vyākṛtam itīdaṃ duḥkhasamudayo yam idaṃ duḥkhanirodham[133] iy.[ṃ] .u. kh[a] .[i] .. [dh]. g[ā]mi[nī] pra[t]i .. .. .. + + + +

[a] [rū]pe ..

r5 + ○ .. parivrājakā evaṃ vadeyuḥ kasmād bhavantaḥ śramaṇena gautamena ime dharmā ekāṃ[134] .. na vyākṛtā iti **pṛṣṭair idaṃ** sy. r vacan. y[āḥ]

128. Note the alternate style *rī* with a very long *ī* diacritic often seen in later scripts.

129. Note the small interlinear mark here beside the lower left quadrant of *pa*.

130. Supplied from the fragment found at the beginning of 286r1 in the photo provided by Kazunobu Matsuda.

131. Supplied from the fragment found at the beginning of 286r2 in the photo provided by Kazunobu Matsuda.

132. *[s].* + + + + + .. supplied from the fragment found at the beginning of 286r3 in the photo provided by Kazunobu Matsuda.

133. Note the *jihvāmūlīya*.

134. Note the small tick to the lower left of the *-e-* diacritic.

r6 .. + + + + + + + + + + + + + + + + + + + ○ tāḥ brahmacaryopasaṃhitāḥ abhi[jñā]yai saṃbodhaye nirvāṇāya saṃvarttanta iti tasmād ime dharmā bhagavatā ekāṃ .. [a] .. ..

[a] [b]. [h].[135]

r7 + ..ṃ v. deyur asthiradharmāṇaḥ śramaṇāḥ śākyaputrīyāḥ na sthiradharmāṇas tathā hy eṣām ekaṃ vyākṛtam ekan n[ā] [v]yā[k]. [t]. .i .. .. + +

r8 + ti santy asmākaṃ dharmāḥ sthirāḥ śāntāḥ praṇītāḥ asaṃhāryā asaṃkṣobhyāḥ [s]. .. .. .. + ... [n]aiḥ .. .. **m** [e] .. + + + + + + + + +

285v[136]

v1 t[ī]rth[i]ka [a].. + + + k[ā e]v. v. d. yuḥ katame te bhavatāṃ dha rm. ..i .. śāntāḥ praṇītā [a]saṃhāryāḥ asaṃk.obhyāḥ sarvabālapṛthagjanair iti **pṛṣṭair idaṃ** syur vacanīyā yo sau bhavant[o] bhik[ṣ].

[a] 284v1 /// .. .. .i .. + + + .ī ///[137]

v2 r [bh]. .. .i śaikṣo saṃprāptamānas[o] nuttaraṃ yogakṣemaṃ nirvāṇam abhiprārthayamāna .. .o .a hulaṃ viharati tasya saptānāṃ bodhipakṣyāṇāṃ dharmāṇā hase[v]. [a].. + ... + + + ... * .. +

[a] 284v2 /// .t. + ... ///[138]

135. It is unclear where this fragment belongs, as it does not fit with the reconstructions of either 285r6 or 286r5. It may possibly belong to 288r, as with the fragments found on 286r1: .. *[t]. ..* and 286r2: *ātmalo ..*

136. There are only seven lines on 285v. This folio has been transcribed taking into account both the reconstructed folio I have prepared in Photoshop from photos of the Virginia Collection fragments and a photo generously provided by Kazunobu Matsuda that shows a nearly complete image of the folio. I have also consulted the left half of 285v that is lying atop 284v in the photo from the Virginia Collection.

137. This fragment belongs near the beginning of 284v1.

138. This fragment belongs to 284v2.

v3 .. .. .. nvayāt samyaṅ[m]anasikārānvayāt kāmāṃ pra○sravacittaṃ [m]u[a][c]y[ate] bhavāsravād avidyā sravacittaṃ vimucyate vimuktasya vimu[kt]. [b]+ + + + + [c]+ + + + ... + +

[a] 284v3 ///.. .. [ry]. [s]. .. .. /// [b] 285v3 /// rāgayati a[p]i [tu] .. .. ///[139]
[c] 285v3 /// .. .. ///

v4 + + r uṣitaṃ bra[hm]acaryaṃ kṛtaṃ karaṇīyaṃ nāpara○m asmād bhavaṃ prajānāmīti **yo sau** bhava = = = = = = = nto bhikṣur bhavaty arthaṃ .ī[a]+ + + + + + + + + + + + + +

[a] 284v4 /// .. rāparinirvāyī bhavati .. .. r. pa ri ///[140]

v5 y. .. [h]ṛt. bhāro nuprāptasvakārtha parikṣīṇabhava○saṃyojanaḥ samyagājñāsuvimuktacittaḥ abhavyaḥ tasmiṃ samaye paṃcasthānāny [a][a] .y. .. [tu]. [k]. [b]+ + + + + [abh]. .y[o] rhad bhikṣuḥ

[a] 284v5 /// bh.saṃskāraparinirvāyī bhavati n. .. ///[141] [b] 285v6 /// .. .. ..ṃ[s]ā[ḥ] .. ///[142]

v6 kṣīṇāsravaḥ saṃciṃtya prāṇinaṃ jīvitād vyaparopayituṃ abrahmacaryaṃ maithunaṃ dharmaṃ pratisevituṃ saṃprajānaṃ mṛṣāvācaṃ bhāṣituṃ sa{{ṃ}}nnidhīkāraparibhogena vā kāmā[n] paribhoktum iti ime [te] .. .. [bh]av[a] .o

v7 dharmāsthirāś śāntāḥ praṇītā asaṃhāryā asaṃkṣobhyās .. [rv]. bālapṛthagjanaiḥ **sthānam etad** bhikṣavo vidyate yad anyatīrthikaparivrājakā evaṃ vadeyus tiryag bhavantaḥ śramaṇasya gautamasya ..[a] + + + +

[a] .. rttavyā

139. This fragment belongs to 284v3.

140. This fragment belongs to 284v4.

141. This fragment belongs to 284v5.

142. This fragment belongs to 284v6.

286r[143]

r1 [tā] .. [na]da .. naṃ pravarttate anāgate na tathāgatā hy anenaikaṃ vyākṛtaḥm ekaṃ na vyākṛtam iti tad idaṃ bhikṣavo anyatīrthikaparivrājakā anyathābhāgīyena jñānena aryabhāgīyajñā ..ṃ[a] .. .i[b] .ā[na]yi

[a] 285r1 .. ///[144] [b] .. [t]. ..[145]

r2 [a]tavyaṃ manyeta tat teṣāṃ asadṛśaṃ | **atītaṃ cāpi** bhikṣavo bhavati tac ca bhavaty abhūtam atatvam anarthopasaṃhitaṃ sarvathā tat tathāgato na vyākaroti • atītaṃ cāpi bhikṣavo bha [b].. + .. + bha

[a] 285r2 .. ///[146] [b] ātma lo ..[147]

r3 [a]+ .. bhūtaṃ ta .. [b]m a[rtho]pasaṃhitaṃ tad api tathāga◯to na vyākaroti | atītaṃ cāpi bhikṣavo bhavati tac ca bhavati bhūtaṃ ta[tv]am[148] [b]arthopasaṃhi ..ṃ + ◊ ◊ ◊[149] [t]r. k[ā]lajñas ta

[a] 285r3 [s]. + + + + + .. ///[150] [b] 285r4 /// .. .[i] .. [dh]. g[ā]mi[nī] pra[t]i .. .. .. ///[151]

r4 [th]āgata[s t]asya vyākaraṇāya smṛtaḥ saṃprajā◯naṃ **anā .. taṃ pratyutpannaṃ cāpi** bhikṣavo bhavati tac ca bhavaty abhūtam atatvam[a] anarthopasaṃhitaṃ .. .. .ā .. .. to na vyā

143. There are only seven lines on both the recto and verso sides of folio 286. This side of the folio has been transcribed taking into account both the photo of the folio 286r that is a part of the Virginia Collection as well as the more complete image of 286r that is visible in a photo provided by Kazunobu Matsuda of the manuscript bundles before the folios were separated.

144. This fragment starts 285r1.

145. This fragment likely belongs to 288r.

146. This fragment belongs to the beginning of 285r2.

147. This fragment likely belongs to 288r.

148. Compare with 286r4 and 286r. The *tva* akṣara is slightly different here, possibly displaying an example of *ttva*.

149. There is a knot in the birchbark here, leaving a gap of around three akṣaras that the scribe left blank.

150. This fragment belongs to the beginning of 285r3.

151. This fragment belongs to the latter half of 285r4.

[a] 285r5 /// .. na vyākṛtā iti pṛṣṭair idaṃ sy. r vacan. y[aḥ][152]

r5 [a][k]. roti [b]pratyutpanna[ṃ] cāpi bhikṣavo bhavati tac ca ○ bhava .i .. [c]..ṃ .. .. .. .th[o]pasaṃhitaṃ tad api tathāgato na vyākaroti pratyu [d].. .. .. .i bhik[ṣa] .. .. [e].. .. ..[153]

[a] ..[154] [b] .. .i ..[155] [c] .āni tā .[i][156] [d] 285r6 /// .. dharmā bhagavatā ekāṃ .. [e] [b]. [h].[157]

r6 t[a]tva[m] a[rtho]pasaṃhitaṃ ta[t]r. [k]ālajñas tathāgato[s ta]thāgatasya vyākaraṇasmṛt[aḥ] .. .. .. [n]. **atīte bhikṣa[vas** t]athāgatasya smṛtyanusārijñānaṃ yena tathāgat.[a] .. .. [dh].ṃ .. .. + + + + + + + + ...

[a] 285r7 /// .. .ā [k]. [t]. .i .. ..[158]

r7 .. + + + + ...[ṃ] .. .. ntimā jātir iyaṃ m[e] bhave .. .i .. .. tir iti **yat t.** .[bh]. .[ṣ]. .. s sarvaśaḥ sarvatra [bhā]yai samyaktvaṃ sarvaṃ tathāgatena jñātaṃ dṛṣṭaṃ[159] viditaṃ vijñāt.. ..y.. .. .. .[i] .. .u[ddh]. [a]+ + + + +

[a] .. t[a]m. [s].

286v[160]

v1 ..ṃ + + + + ..ṃ + + .iṃ + + + + + + + + ...ṃ .. .i .. .i ..ṃ .[u]ddho ya .y.[ṃ] .. .. tr[au] tathā[gato n]irupadhi[ś]eṣe nirvāṇadhātau [p]a[r]i[n]i .v[ā] .y. [t]y atrāntar[e] .y.. .. .. + ... + + + + + + + + +

152. This fragment belongs to the end of 285r5.

153. This fragment finishes 285r6.

154. This fragment likely belongs to the beginning of 285r6.

155. This fragment likely belongs in the first half of 285r6.

156. This is not a fragment but actually akṣaras from 287r4 just after the string hole as seen through a hole in 286r. This is evident in the picture of the folio provided by Matsuda.

157. It is unclear where this fragment belongs, as it does not fit with the reconstructions of either 285r6 or 286r5. It may possibly belong to 288r, as with the fragments found on 286r1: *.. [t]. ..* and 286r2: *ātmalo ..*

158. This fragment finishes 285r7.

159. Note the irregular *-ṭ-* ligature in *dṛṣṭaṃ* here, a strong signifier of scribe D's hand.

160. Like 286r, this half of the folio only has seven lines.

v2 .. + .. + ...v. .. .. .. .i[p]. [rīt]. m avipa[ry] s..ṃ .. .. .[ta] .. gata ity ucyate || **siṃh[a] .ti** bhikṣavo v. [d]. n[t]o .ā .. + + + ... + + + + + +

v3 .. + + + + + + + + + + + + + + + + id.. t[a]tr[a] t[a]◯thāg. [t]. .y[a] .. ..[ā]da na[d]i[tas]y[a] tadyathā utpalāni vā padmāni vā kumudā[n]i .. puṇḍ[a]r[īk]. .. + + + + + + + +

v4 + + + + + + + + + + + ...[ṭh]. [nt]y. [nu]paliptā[n]y u◯[da] .e .. .. t[a]thāgato loke jāto lo[ke] ..[ddh]o lokād abhyud.. ta .[t]i[ṣṭh]atyanupalipto loke .. + + + + + + + + +

v5 + + + + + + + + + + + + + + ... te anupali◯[p]t[o] .. .. + + + **.i** bhikṣavaḥ pūrvāntasa[h]a .. .. .. .ṛ[ṣṭ]igatāni vyākṛtāni mayā yathā tā .i .y[āk]. .[t]t[a] .y. .[i] .. .[ā] tāni

v6 + + + + + + + + + + + + + + [vy]ākariṣye yāni tāny aparāntasahagatāni [d]ṛṣṭigatāni vyā[k]ṛtāni tāni mayā .. .. .[ā] .i .. .. .. v.āni yathā tāni na[161] vyā[k]. [rtta]◊[162]vyāni kim aha[ṃ]

v7 + + + + + + + + + + + **[m]āni tāni** bhikṣavaḥ pūrvāntasahagatāni dṛṣṭigatāni yāni mayā vyākṛtāni [y]. .. .. .i .. .y. .. .ta .[yā] .i + + + .i na vyāka .. .. ni[163]

287r[164]

r1 + + + + + + .y. .[i] [k]. .. ..[ṃ tān]i tathā vyākariṣye **santi bhikṣava** eke śramaṇabrāhmaṇāḥ pūrvāntakalpakā evaṃdṛṣṭaya evaṃvādinaḥ śāśvataḥ ātmā lokaś ca aśāśvataḥ śāśva

161. Note the small tick under *na*.

162. There is a three-akṣara gap here that the scribe chose to avoid writing on because of a knot in the birchbark.

163. The spaces between the akṣaras grow in last quarter of this line, something often seen in the last line of a folio.

164. Like the folios preceding it, 286v has only seven lines.

r2 + + + + ...[aiv]. śāś.[a] .[o n]āśāśvataḥ ātmā lokaś ca śā[ś]vataḥ ātmā duḫkhaṃ[165] ca śāśvataḥ śāśvataś cāśāśvataś ca n[ai]va śāśvato nāśāśvataḥ ātmā duḫkhaṃ[166] ca svayaṃkṛta ātmā loka

r3 + + + + + + + + + + [a]+ + + + + .. .[cā]svayaṃkā○rāparakārahetusamutpannaḥ ātmā lokaś ca svayaṃkṛta ātmā duḫkhaṃ[167] ca parakṛtaḥ svayaṃkṛtaś ca parakṛtaś cāsvayaṃkā

[a] .. s. hi

r4 + + + + + + + + + + + ḥ [ātm]ā duḫkhaṃ[168] ca **i○māni tā[n]i** .[i]kṣavaḥ pūrvāntasahagatāni [d]ṛ[ṣ]ṭigatāni yāni mayā vyākṛtāni yathā tāni karttavyāni yathā tā

r5 + + + + + + + + + + + + + + + + .. ○riṣye **katamāni tāni** bhikṣavo pūrvāntasahagatāni dṛṣṭigatāni ◊[169] yāni mayā vyākṛt[ā] .i + + + + + + + +

r6 vyā [a].i + + + + + + + + + + + + + + + + [b]+ + + + + [m]. [ṇ]. .r[ā]hmaṇāḥ aparāntakalpakā evaṃdṛṣṭaya evaṃvādino rūpī ātmā bhavaty a[t]a[ḥ pa]raṃ [saṃ] .. + + + + + + + + +

[a] .. .. .. sth. p. s. [hi][b] .. [thā]

r7[170] .. .[ai] + + ...[ūp]. ā[t]m. [bh]. .. .[y]. + + + + + + .. [nt]. [v]. nātmā bhavaty ataḥ paraṃ saṃjñī anantaḥ anantavāṃś cānantavāṃś ca [nai]vānantavāṃś cānantavān ānya bhavaty ata[ḥ] .. + + + +

165. Note *jihvāmūlīya.*

166. Note *jihvāmūlīya.*

167. Note *jihvāmūlīya.*

168. Note *jihvāmūlīya.*

169. There is a knot in the birchbark here. It can also be seen on the other side of the folio at 287v4.

170. Marginalia to left of line: *1*, representing the first folio in a series of an alternate numeration system used in some sections of the ms. This particular series of numbers runs in sequence to the left of the last line of the recto side of every folio throughout the ms. from 287r–316r. There should presumably be an instance of marginalia stating "*4*" on 290r as well, but that folio is obscured.

287v

v1 kat[v]asaṃj[ñ]ī nānāt[v]asaṃjñī parīttasa[ṃ]j.. .. + + + + + + k. [nta]-sukhī ekāntaduẖkhī[171] sukhaduẖkhī[172] aduẖkhāsukhī[173] ātmā bhavaty ataḥ paraṃ saṃjñī rūpī {{bha}} ātmā bhavaty ataḥ paraṃ saṃj.ī + + + + + + + + + + +

v2 rū [p]. .. [rū] .. [ā] .. .. + + + + + + + + + + + + + + ...[y]. [t]aḫ paraṃ naiva saṃjñī anantataḥ anantavāṃś cānantavāṃś ca naivānantavān nānan-tavāṃn ātmā bhava[t]y. .. .. + + + + + + + + +

v3 [t]. .. .. .[ai] .. [s].ṃ .ī .. .. + + + + + + + + + + + + [a]◯ .. [rū] .ī [nā]rūpī ātmā bhavaty ataḥ paraṃ naivasaṃjñīnāsaṃjñī antavān ātmā bhavaty [b]a .. .. + + + + +

[a] .. [b] .. .t. [id]. .. [v].

v4 + ◯ vaty ataḥ paraṃ naivasaṃ-jñīnāsaṃjñī **santi bhikṣava** eke śramaṇabrāhmaṇāḥ a◊[a]parāntakalpakā[174] evaṃ .[ṛṣṭ]. + + + + + + +

[a] [ṇa]brāh[ma]nā ..

v5 + + + + + + + + + + + + + ... [hā]bhūti◯ko jīvati tiṣṭhati dhṛyate[175] yāpayati tāvat sarogaḥ sagaṇḍaḥ saśalyaḥ sajvaraḥ saparidāho yata[c] cāyam āt[m]ācchidya

v6 + + + + + + + + + + + ... ṇād etāvad a◯yam ātmā samyaksusamuc-chinno bhavati divyaẖ[176] kāmāvacaro divyo rūpāvacaraḥ arūpi ākāśā-naṃtyāyatanopago rū

171. Note *jihvāmūlīya*.

172. Note *jihvāmūlīya*.

173. Note *jihvāmūlīya*.

174. There is a knot in the birchbark here. It can also be seen on the other side of the folio at 287r5.

175. Note the irregular usage of *ṛ* for *ri*.

176. Note *jihvāmūlīya*.

v7 + + + + + + + + ... rūpī ākiṃcanyāyatanopago rūpī naivasaṃjñānāsaṃjñāyatanopago jīvati tiṣṭhati dhṛyate[177] yāpayati tāvat sarogaḥ sagaṇḍas saśalyas sajvaraḥ sapa

v8 + + + + + + .. .ātmā uc[ch]id[ya]te na vinaśyati na bhavati paraṃ maranād etāvad ayam ātmā samyaksamucchinno bhavati **saṃti bhikṣava** eke śramaṇabrāhmanā evaṃdṛṣṭaya evaṃvādino yataś cāyam ātmā paṃcabhiḥ <<kāmaguṇaiḥ>>[178]

288r

288r1 samar[p]itaḥ samanvaṃgībhūtaḥ krīḍati ramate paricārayati etāvad ayam ātmā dṛṣṭadharmanirvāṇaprāpto bhavati yataś cātmā vivikta kāmai pūrvavat* [yā]vac .aturthaṃ dhyāna{{ṃ}}m upasaṃpa

r2 saṃpadya viharati etāvad ayam ātmā paramadṛṣṭadharmanirvāṇaprāpto bhavati **imāni tāvad** bhikṣavo parān[t]asahagatāni dṛṣṭigatāni yāni mayā = = = vyākṛtāni yathā tā

r3 [n]i v[y]ākarttavyāni yathā tāni na vyākarttavyāni ○ kim ahaṃ tāni ta[thā] vyākariṣye **tatra bhikṣavo** te śramaṇ{{ā}}brāhmaṇāḥ pūrvāntakalpakā = = = evaṃdṛṣṭaya evamvādi

r4 no śāśvata ātmā lokaś [ce]ty abhiv[a]dan[t]o bhiv[a]danti ○ tān aham upasaṃkra .ā .y upasaṃkramyaivaṃ vadāmi satyaṃ kila bhavanti evaṃdṛṣṭaya evaṃvādinaḥ śāśvataḥ ātmā loka

r5 [ś c]eti te mama pṛṣṭā o[m] i .. ..○ham evaṃ vadā .i .. .y. ta[d] bhavant[a]ḥ evaṃ ucyate yat punar atra bhavantaḥ sthānaśaḥ parāmṛśyābhiniviśyānuvyav. h. ranti i

r6 .. .. va satyaṃ moham an[y]ad iti idam [a]trāha[ṃ] nā○nujānāmi t[at ka]sy[a] h[e]t. + [a] .[y]. .. [sa]ṃjñino hi bhavanta ihaike śramaṇa[b]rā[h].. ṇā .. .. .i + .. + + + + + + +

177. Note the irregular usage of *ṛ* for *ri*.

178. *Kāmaguṇaiḥ* has been written in interlinearly underneath the akṣaras *mātmāpaṃ* at the end of the line.

r7 ṇāḥ aśāś[v]a[t]aḥ .[ā] .v. .. [ś c]āśāś[v]ataś ca naiva .. + .[o] nāś[ā] + ..[ḥ] [āt].ā lokaś ca śāśvataḥ .. t.[ā] [d]uḥkhaṃ ca śāśvataś śāśvataś cāśāśvataś ca nai .. .. .[v]. + + + + + + + + + + + +

r8[179] [lo]kaś ca parakṛtaḥ svayaṃkṛtaś ca p[ar]. .. [t]. .[c]āsvaya[ṃkā]rāp[a] r. k[ā]r[ā]h. tus. mutpannaḥ ātmā lokaś ca svayaṃkṛta ātmā du[ḥ]khaṃ ca parakṛtaḥ svayaṃkṛtaś ca pa .. .[ṛ] + + + + + + + + + + +

288v

v1 hetusamutpannāḥ ātmā duḫkhaṃ[180] ca **tān a[ha]m**. pasaṃkramy upakramyaivaṃ vadāmi satyaṃ kila bhavanta evaṃdṛ[ṣ]ṭaya evaṃvādinaḥ asvayaṃkārāparakārāhetusamut.. .. + + + + + + + + + + +

v2 yā pṛ[ṣ]ṭā om iti prajānante tān aham eva[ṃ] vadāmy apy etad bhavantaḥ evam u[c]yate yat [p]unar atra bh[a]va[n]taḥ [s]th[ā]maśaḥ parāmṛśyābhiniviśyānuvyavahara[n].i [i] .. .. + + + + + + + + + + + +

v3 da .atrāhaṃ nānujānāmi tat kasya hetor anya◯thā[s]aṃjñino hi bhavanta ihaikena śr[a] .aṇabrā[h]maṇā **tatra bhikṣavo** y[e] te [ś]ramaṇ. .. .. + + + + + + + + + + + + + +

v4 evaṃ .ādino rūpī ātmā bhavaty ataḫ pa[ra s]aṃjī◯ti tān aham [u]pasaṃkramāmy .pasaṃkra[m]y. vaṃ vadāmi satyaṃ kila bhavantaḥ evaṃdṛṣṭayo eva. vādin.[a] + + + + + + + taḥ

[a] .. .. [t]. .. ..[181]

v5 paraṃ saṃjñīti mayā pṛṣṭā om iti pratijāna◯te tān aham eva. vadā .y asty etad bha{{ga}}vanta[182] evam ucyate ya. punar atra bhavanta sthāmaśaḥ parāmṛ .y. [bh]. .[i] .[i][a] .[y]. [nu] .y. .. [h]a

179. Marginalia to left of line: *2*. See note 170 above.

180. Note *jihvāmūlīya*.

181. This fragment likely belongs to 289v, possibly on either line 4 or 5.

182. The *nta* akṣara here is slightly different from the standard formation. It is almost as if the scribe added the bottommost stroke as an afterthought, which gives the *-t-* ligature the slight appearance of an *-ṛ-*.

[a] .. ..ṃ [t]a[183]

v6 ranti ida[m e]va [s]atya moham anyad iti idam atrā[h]aṃ nānujānāmi ta[t] kasya hetor anyathāsaṃjñino hi bhavanta i[h]aike śramaṇabrāhmaṇāḥ **tatra bhi[k]ṣa** .. ye

v7 te śramaṇabrāhmaṇā evaṃdṛṣṭaya evaṃvādino arūpī rūpī cārūpī ca naiva rūpī nārūpī ā .[m]ā bhavaty ataḥ [p]araṃ saṃjñī antavān ātmā bhavaty ataḥ paraṃ saṃjñī = anantaḥ anantavāṃ

v8 ś cānantavāṃ[ś] ca nai[v]āna[n]tavāṃ nā[n]a[n]tavā bhavaty ataẖ para saṃjñī ekatvasaṃjñī nānātvasaṃjñī parīttasa[ṃ]jñī apramaṇasaṃjñī ekāntasukhī ekāntaduẖkhī[184] sukhaduẖkhī[185] aduẖkhāsukhī[186] ātmā bhava

289r[187]

r1 [a].y. .. .. + ..[ṃ] .ī + .ī + + + + .. taḥ paraṃ saṃjñī arūpī rūpi cārūpī ca naiva rūpī nārūpī [ā]tmā bhavaty ataḥ paraṃ saṃjñī anta[v]ān ātmā bhavaty a[t]aḥ paraṃ naiva saṃjñī anantaḥ anantavāṃś cāna

[a] 290r1 .. [p]r[ā]pto bh[a]v[a]ti t[a]d .[p]i [rm]. [s]. .t. .y.[188]

r2 [a]+ + + + + + + .t. .. .. nantavān ātmā bha◊vaty ataḥ paraṃ naiva saṃjñī rūpī ātmā bhavaty a .. [p]araṃ naivasaṃjñīnāsaṃjñī arūpī rūpi cārūpī ca naiva rūpī nārūpī bhavaty ataḥ paraṃ nai

[a] 290r2 m a[nutp]ā[d]ā .. t[v]āri s. .. ..[189]

183. This fragment likely belongs to 289v, possibly on either line 5 or line 6.

184. Note *jihvāmūlīya*.

185. Note *jihvāmūlīya*.

186. Note *jihvāmūlīya*.

187. Folios 289 and 290 are stuck together. Folio 289r lies above 290v, and thus 290v is only partially visible. Folios 289v and 290r are almost wholly obscured from view, with very few akṣaras visible as fragments or as outer layers of birchbark that have been transposed, mirrored onto the their adjacent folio sides.

188. This is 290r1 obscured underneath 289r1.

189. This is 290r2 obscured underneath 289r2.

r3 + + .. [n]ā[s]aṃjñī anan[t]avā[n] ātmā bhavaty ata◊ḥ ○ paraṃ naivasaṃjñīnāsaṃ[jñ]. + + .[ā]n ātmā bhavaty ataḥ paraṃ naivasaṃjñīnāsaṃjñī anantaḥ[a] [a]nantavāṃś cān[a]nt[a]v[aṃ] + + .[ā]

[a] .y[ā]t. [ś] c[a] [s]vākhy[ā]to n. vaś śāstā[190]

r4 [a]+ + .. + + + + + + + + + + + + naiva◊saṃ○j.ī [b].. ..ṃ ..ī .. .. ś.ā y[a]**m** ātmā rūpī audārikaś cāturmahābhūtik[o] jī ..[c] [t]i [t]i .. + + + + + + + + + +

[a] 290r4 t[a]thāg[a]t.[ḥ u] .. [ko] ye te dharmā nā .. .. + + + + ○ + + [b] khālaya + + + .y. + + + + + + + + + + + + + + + + + [c] .. .ū .v. [ntā]parāntena paṃcakā[ḥ] + + ||[191]

r5 [a]sar. g[a]ḥ sag[aṇ]ḍa[ḥ s]. .. .y.. .. .[v]. .. .. .. .i .. ○ h. y. t. [ś]c. y. [m ā] .[m]. .. .. .. te vinaśyati na bhavati • paraṃ maraṇād etā[va]d [a] [b].. + + + + + + + + + +

[a] 290r5 bh. g. [vā]ṃ .. + + .. .[ih]. [ra] .i [p]ā[v]ā .[i] .. + + ○ + + + + + + p[u]tr[a]ḥ .. + ..ṃ + + + + + + + + + + +[192] [b] 289r3 /// [a]nantavāś. cānantav[ā] .. .. ///[193]

r6 v. t[i] divyaḥ kā[m]āvacaro divyo rūpāvacaraḥ ○ arūpī ātmākāśānaṃ .[yā] .. t[a]nopagaḥ arūpīvijñānāna[ṃ]tyāyatananop.[a] g. + + + + + + + + +

[a] 290r6 /// ..ṃ .. da .. ///[194]

r7 [a][p]. .. [rū]pī naivasamjñānāsaṃjñāyatan[o]pa[g]. jīvati tiṣ[ṭh]ati dhriyate yāpaya[t]i tāvat [s]a[r]ogaḥ sagaṇdaḥ sa[śa]lyaḥ sajvaraḥ saparidāho yataś [c]ātmā u + + + + + + + + + +

190. This is 290r3 obscured underneath 289r3. It is part of the *antaroddāna*.

191. This is 290r4 obscured underneath 289r4. It should be part of the *antaroddāna*, and the double *daṇḍa*s mark the end of the *Prāsādika-sūtra*.

192. This is 290r5 obscured underneath 289r5. It marks the beginning of the *Prasāsadanīya-sūtra*.

193. This fragment belongs to 289r3.

194. This is 290r6 obscured underneath 289r6.

[a] 290r7 /// .y. .. + + .. ///[195]

r8[196] ti[a] paraṃ mar[a]ṇād etāvad ayam ātmā .. .y. .[s]u samucchinno bhavati **santi bhikṣava** eke śramaṇābrāh.[a]ṇā evaṃdṛṣṭaya [ev]aṃvā[d]i .. .. tāś cāyam ātmā paṃca [b].. + + + + + + + + + + + + +

[a] 290r8 /// .. + + ... ///[197] [b] 290r8 /// .. .. ///[198]

289v[199]

v1 +

v2 .. .. + + + + + + + + + + + + ... + .. +

v3 + + + + + + + + + + + + + + + + ... ○ .. .. + + + + + + + + + + ... +

v4 .. .. + + + + + + + + + + + + + + + + ○ + + + + + + + .. [v]. [s]. .. +

v5 .. .. + + + [k]. śra[m]. [ṇabra] .. [ṇ]. tatra [bh]i + + ○ .. [te ś]. [m]. [ṇa] .. [h]. [ṇ]. .. .. .. +

v6 .. .. + + .. + + + + + .i + + + + ○ + + + + + + + + ... + + + + + + + + + + + + + + + ... + + + + + .. .[vā] ṇ. [p]r[ā]pto bhav. [t]i • tad.

195. This is 290r7 obscured underneath 289r7.

196. Marginalia to left of line: *3*. See note 170 above.

197. This is likely 290r8 obscured underneath 289r8.

198. This is likely 290r8 obscured underneath 289r8.

199. As 289r and 290r are currently stuck together, 289v is largely lost to analysis until the two folios can be separated. Only a few parts of 289v remain visible underneath 290v. Additionally, in some places the thin layers of the outer cells of the birchbark of 289v have been transferred in a mirrored state onto the small areas where 290v is visible under 289r. From these mirrored layers, I have been able to sucessully reconstruct some sections 289v.

v7 .i .. .. .. [s]. .. +
.i + ...[o] k[aś] c. ti [t].
[d a]

v8 pi s[p]. .. + + ..[ṃ] .. .. + ... + + + + + + + + + + + + + + + + + + +
+ + + + + .. + .. m ātmā
parama[dṛṣṭa]dharmanirvā

290r[200]
r1 .. [p]r[ā]pto bh[a]v[a]ti t[a]d .[p]i [rm]. [s]. .r. .y. + + + + + + + + + + +
+ +
+ .. .. d[ṛ]ṣṭigatānā

r2 m a[nutp]ā[d]ā .. t[v]āri s.. .. .. + + + + + + + + + + + + + + + + + +
+ .. [dh]. .y.
śākyasyāśra

r3 + + + + + + + + + + + + + + + + ○ + + + + + + + + + + + + + + + + +
+ + + + + + + + + + + + .y[ā]t. [ś] c[a] [s]vākhy[ā]to n. vaś śāstā

r4 t[a]thāg[a]t.[ḥ u] .. [ko] ye te dharmā nā .. .. + + + + ○ + + khālay[a]
+ + + .. .y. .. + + + + + + + + + + .. .ū .v. [ntā]parāntena paṃcakā[ḥ] + + ||

200. As 289r and 290r are currently stuck together, 290r is unfortunately lost to analysis until the two folios can be separated. However, in some places 290v is visible under 289r.

Transliteration of the *Prasādanīya-sūtra* (DĀ 16), Folios 290r5–299v3

290r

r5 **bh. g. [vā]ṃ** .. + + .. .[ih]. [ra] .i [p]ā[v]ā .[i] .. + + ○ + + + + + +
p[u]tr[a]ḥ .. + + + + + + + + + + + + + + + + + + + ..ṃ + + + + + + + +
+ + +

r6 + + + + + + + + + + + + + + + ○ + + + + + + + + + + + + + + + + + +
+ + + + + + + + ..ṃ .. da .. + + + + + + + + + +

r7 .y. .. + + .. +
+ +

r8 .. + + ... +
+ + + + + + + + + + + + + + + + + + + ... + + + + + + + + + + +

290v

v1 d bhūyo bhijñatara syād yad uta saṃbodhāya iti kiṃ punas te śā[r]i-
[pu]tra ye abhūvaṃ atīte dhvani tathāgatārhantaḥ samyaksaṃbuddhās te
tvayā buddhā bhaga[v]antaś cetasā s. .i .. + + + + + + + + +

v2 t[e] bu .[o] bhagavanto bhūvaṃn ity apy evaṃdharmāṇaḥ e[va]ṃpra[-
jñā] .. .. [m]abhi[jñā] evaṃvimuktayaḥ evaṃbahulavihāriṇo bata te buddhā
bhagavanto nity api **no [bhada] .. ..** + + + + + + + + + + +

v3 tathāgatārhantaḥ samyaksaṃbuddhās te tvayā buddhā bha○ga[v]
antaś cetasā spharitvā viditā evaṃśīlā bata te buddhā bhagavaṃto bhā[v]i-
[ṣ]yaṃ[t]y anāga[te] .v. + + + + + + + + +

v4 ṇaḥ evaṃprajñā evamabhijñā evaṃvimuk[t]iṃya evaṃ○bahulavi-
hāriṇo bata te buddhā bhagavaṃto bhaviṣyaṃty anāgate dhvanīti **no bhadanta ahaṃ [t]ā**[a] .. + + + + + + + + +

[a] 289v6 /// . . .[vā]ṇ. [p]r[ā]pto bhav. [t]i • tad.[201]

v5 thāgato 'rhan samyaksaṃbuddhaḥ evaṃ cetasā spharitvā ○ viditaḥ evaṃśīlo batāyaṃ buddho bhagavānn ity api evaṃdharmā evaṃprajña evamabhijña [e] . . . . .[u]. [kti] . . . . + [a].. + + + +

[a] 289v7 /// .[o] + . . .i . . ..[202]

v6 batāyaṃ buddho bhagavāṃ ity api **no [bh]adanta na te** ○ śāriputrātītānāgatapratyutpannānāṃ ma samyaksaṃbuddhānāṃ cetaḥparyā[y]o viditaḥ atha kin nu te satvāya i[ya]m ev. rū

v7 pā udārā ārṣabhī vāg bhāṣitā ekāṃśa udgṛhītaḥ parṣadi samyak siṃhanādo naditaḥ evaṃ sati prasanno haṃ bhadanta bhagavato yan nābhūn na bhaviṣ[y]ati nāp[y] etarhi vid[y]ate[a] yad anyaḥ

[a] 289v7 /// . . . . k[aś] c. [ti t]. [d].[203]

v8 śramaṇo vā brāhmaṇo vā bhagavato ntikād bhūyo bhijñatara syād yad uta saṃbodhaya iti **na me** bhadantātītānāgatapratyutpannānāṃ tathāgatānām a .[ha]tā [a].. + + ... paryāyo

[a] 289v8 /// . . m ātmā parama[dṛṣṭa]dharmanirvā[204]

291r[205]

r1 vidito pi dharmaparyāyo me vidita iha mama bhagavāṃ dharmaṃ de[ś]ayaty[206] uttarād uttarataraṃ praṇītāt praṇītataraṃ hīnapraṇītakṛṣṇaśukle sapratibh[āg]apra[t]ī .y. . . [mutpa]nnā[n dh]armān vista[re]ṇa saṃpra

201. This fragment belongs to the end of 289v6.

202. This fragment belongs to the end of 289v4.

203. This fragment belongs to the *Prāsādika-sūtra* at the end of 289v7.

204. This fragment belongs to the *Prāsādika-sūtra* at the end of 289v8. Cf. similar usage in 288r1 and 288r2.

205. There are multiple elision marks on this folio. Parts of the birchbark appear to be warped and were perhaps not to the scribe's liking.

206. The -*ś*- here is rather odd. Compare with the same word in the next line.

r2 kāśayati yathā yathā me bhagavāṃ dharmaṃ deśayaty uttarād uttarataraṃ [pr]aṇīta = = taraṃ hīnapraṇītakṛ[ṣ]ṇa[ś]uklasapratibhāgapratītyasamutpannāṃ dha[rm]āṃ vistareṇa saṃprakā[ś]ay[a]ti tathā [ta]

r3 thānekāṃ dharmān abhijñayā parijā[nā] .. .[ā]ṃ dhar[m]ā○n abhijñayā = pratijahāmi ekāṃ dharmān abhijñayā sākṣāt karomy ekāṃ dharmān abhijñayā bhāvayāmi dharmeṣu ca niṣṭhāṃ gacchāmi

r4 śāstari ca prasādaṃ pravedayet* samyaksa .[uddh]. [b]. [t]. ○ bhagavāṃ=n ity api jāne **sace tvā** śāriputra kaśc[i]d upasaṃkramyaivaṃ pṛcched abhūvad bho śāriputrātīte dhvany aśramaṇabrāhmaṇā[207]

r5 ye śramaṇasya gautamasyāntikād bhūyo bhijñatara ○ yad uta saṃbodhaya iti ev[a]ṃ .ṛṣṭas tvaṃ śāriputra kiṃ vākuryāḥ **sacen mā** bhadanta kaś[c]id upas. + ... [a]+ + + .. syāhaṃ .ṛṣṭo

[a] .. .. .r.

r6 neti vyākuryāṃ **sace tvā** śāriputra kaścid upasaṃ○kram[y]aivaṃ p[ṛ]cche◊d[208] bha[v]i .y. .ti .u bhoḥ śāriputr{{ā}}rājate dhvany eke śramaṇa .[ā h]. [ṇ]. [ye] .. .. [ṇ]. [a]+ + [s]. g[au]tama. y. .ti .. .. [yo]

[a] .[t]. ..

r7 bhijñatarā yad uta saṃbodhāya iti | evaṃ pṛṣṭas [tv]aṃ [ś]āri .. [tr]a kiṃ vyākuryāḥ **sacen mā** bhadanta ka[c]cid upasaṃkramyaivaṃ pṛcche tasyāhaṃ pṛṣṭo ne[t]i .y. .u + + + + + + + + + + + + + +

r8[209] myaivaṃ pṛcchat*d asti nu bhoḥ śāriputra kaccid etarhi pratyut[p]anne śramaṇo brāhmaṇo vā yaḥ śramaṇasya gautamasyāntikā[d] bhūyo bhijñataro yad uta saṃbodh[a] + + + + + + + + + + +

207. Note the stylized *ṇā* where its end forms a slight swirl.

208. The gap in *pṛcched* appears along the warped section of the bark on which the scribe had been using filler marks in previous lines.

209. Marginalia to left of line: *5*. See note 170 above.

291v

v1 putra kiṃ vyākuryā **sacen mā** bhadanta kaccid upasaṃkramyaivaṃ pṛcche tasyāhaṃ pṛṣṭo neti vyākuryāṃ = = = = **sac[e tv]ā** [ś]āriputra kaccid upasaṃkramyaivaṃ pṛcched abhūv. bh[o] + + + + + + + + + +

v2 maṇabrāhmaṇā ye mama saha śramaṇena gautame[na] ya[d]. ta saṃbodhāya iti evaṃ pṛṣṭas tvaṃ śāriput[ra] vaṃ kiṃ vyāku .y.{{ṃ}} **s. c. tv[ā]** {{śāriputra}} bhadan[ta] ka .i[d]. .. .. + + + + + + + + + +

v3 {{riputrā}} om iti vyākuryāṃ **sace tvā** śāriputra kaści◯[d] upasaṃ-[k]ramyaivaṃ pṛcched bha[v]i .[y]ati nu bhoḥ [ś]āriputra anāgate dhvany eke śra[m]. + + + + + ... [a].. .. [ś]r. .. .. .. +

[a] 292v3 /// .. ///[210]

v4 t. [m]. na yad uta saṃbodhaya iti evaṃ pṛṣṭas tvaṃ śāri◯putra kiṃ vyāku◊[211]ryāḥ **sacen mā** bhadanta kaścid upasaṃkramyaivaṃ pṛcchet tasyāha[ṃ p]ṛṣṭa [o]m i[t]i vyāku[ry]. .. + + + + + + [ka]ści

v5 d upasaṃkramyaivaṃ pṛcche[d] asti nu bhoḥ śāriputra kaści◯d etarhi = = pratyutpanne dhvani śramaṇo vā brāhmaṇo vā yas sama[s]amaḥ śramaṇena gau .. .. + saṃ[b]odhaya i

v6 ti evaṃ pṛṣṭa[s t]vaṃ śāriputra kiṃ vyākuryā **sacen mā** ◯ bhadanta = kaścid upasaṃkramyaivaṃ pṛcche[t] tasyāhaṃ pṛṣṭo neti vyākuryāṃ **sace tvaṃ** śāripu[t]ra kaś. id upasaṃ[k]ramy. vaṃ pṛcchet ka

v7 [smā t]va[ṃ] bhoḥ śāriputrātītānāgatapratyutpannāṃ śramaṇabrā=hmaṇā[212] brāhma= = =ṇān ekān anyanumoda .. [e]kāṃ nānya .umoda iti e[va]ṃ [p]ṛṣṭas tvaṃ śāriputra kiṃ vy[āk]u ..[ā]ḥ **sacen mā** bhada

210. This small fragment belongs to 292v3.

211. A warp in the bark occurs here, which continues down through lines 5–7, where the scribe used filler marks.

212. Looks like *ṇa*, but the birchbark is folded over itself here obscuring the akṣara, which actually reads *ṇā*. This is also true of the elision sign marking a gap—it is folded over itself, making it appear somewhat truncated.

v8 nta kaścid upaṃkramyaivaṃ pṛcchet tasyāhaṃ pṛṣṭa evaṃ vyākuryā abhū[t]ad bhadantotīte dhvany eke [ś]ra[m]aṇabrāhmaṇāḥ y. mama sa[m]ā bhagavatā yad u[ta] saṃbo[dhā]yeti bhaviṣyat[y] an[ā] .. te 'dhvany eke śra

292r

r1 maṇabrāhmaṇā ye mama samā bhagavatā saṃbodhaya iti • saṃ[m]ukhaṃ me bhadanta bhagavato ntikāc chrutaṃ saṃmukham udgṛhītaṃ a[s]thānam anava .āśo ya[d] apū[r]vācara[m]au dvau tathāgatāv arha

r2 n[t]au samyaksaṃbuddhau loka utpadyate[213] evaṃ sthānaṃ vidyate • sthānam etad vidyate yad eka etad ānuttaryaṃ bhadanta bha[g]avataḥ yad[u]ta saṃbodhaye tad bhagavān aśeṣam abhijānāti tat te śeṣam a

r3 .i[jā] .. [t]aḥ [utt]aro 'bhijñ[e]yaṃ nāsti yasyābhijñā○nād anyaḥ śramaṇena vā brāhmaṇena vā bhagavato ntikād bhūyo bhijñatara [s]yād yad uta saṃbodh[a]ye **[a]param api** [y]e bhadanta bha

r4 gav[a]t[o] ānu[t]ta[ryaṃ] yadā me bh[a]gavāṃ dharmaṃ deśaya○ti yad uta kuśaladharmaprajñaptiṣṭhā iha bhadantaika śramaṇo vā brāhmaṇo vāraṇyagato vā + + + + + + .[ā] śūnyāgāra

r5 gato vā ātaptānvayāt* prah. ṇ. nvayād bhavanatva○yād bahulīkarātvayāt samyaṅmanasikāratvayāt tadrūpaṃ śānta cetaḥ[sa]māvi[214] spṛśati yathā + + + + .. [te] anekavi

r6 [dhān] pāpakā akuśalādharmān abhinivarjya a○[n]ek[a]vidhān [k]uśalān dharmān [s]amādāya varttate [s]āk[ṣ]ādbhavyatāyāṃ na ca pa[r]i .. sya [t]i [e] + + + + + + + + + + + + + + +

r7 ta kuśaladharmaprajñaptiṣu tad bhagavān aśeṣam a .[i] .. .. .[i ta]t te śeṣam abhinati uttare bhijñeyaṃ nāsti yasyābhijñānyaḥ śramaṇo vā brā[h]ma[215] .. .. + + + + + + + + + + + + + +

213. Note stray ink stroke radiating northeast from the *-e-* diacritic.

214. Note the tick to the left of *ce*.

215. Note the tick to the left of *hma*.

r8[216] d yad uta saṃbodhāya iti **aparam api** y[e] bhada[n]ta bhagavata ānuttaryaṃ yadi me bhagavāṃ dharmaṃ deśayati ya[du]tāyatanaprajñapt[i]ṣu ye kecid bhadanta [ś]ra + + + + + + + + + + + + + +

292v

v1 ni prajñāpayantaḥ [p]ra[j]ñāpayanti sarve te dvādaśā[y]atanāni • katamāni dvādaśa cakṣurāyatanaṃ rūpāyatanaṃ vrotrāyatanaṃ śabdāyatanaṃ ghrāṇāyatanaṃ [g]+ + + + + + + + + + + + + + + + + +

v2 naṃ spraṣṭavyāyatanaṃ mana āyatanaṃ dharmāyatana[ṃ] etad ā[n]u[ttar]yaṃ bhadanta bhagavato yad utāyatanaprajñaptiṣu tad bhagavāṃn aśeṣam abhijānati tat t. [ś]. ṣ[am] + + + + + + + + + + + + + +

v3 ya. yā[bh]ijñānād anyaḥ śramaṇo vā brāhmaṇo vā bhaOgavato ntikād bhūyo bhijñataraṃ syād bata saṃbodhaye • **aparam api** te bhadanta .. .. .. [ta] [ā] .. + + + + + + + + + + + + + +

v4 ti y. [d] uta ◊ pudgalaprajñaptiṣu ye kecid bhadanta śraOmaṇā vā brāhmaṇā vā sataḥ pudgalaḥ prajñāpayanti sarve te saptapudga[l]āḥ śraddhānusāri[ṇ]. dh[armā] .. .āriṇaṃ śra .. .i .. kt. dṛ

v5 ṣṭiprāptaṃ kāyasākṣiṇaṃ prajñāvimuktam ubhayatobhāOgavimukta etad ānutt[ar]yaṃ bhabhadanta bhagavato yad uta pudgalaḥ prajñaptiṣu tad bhagavān aśe .. + + + + + .. t t[e a]śe[ṣa]

v6 [m] a[bh]ijñānata uttare bhijñeyaṃ nāsti yasyābhijñāOnād anyaḥ paiśunyam arthamatīṃ dharatīn niruktivatī[ṃ] kālenātiprakīrṇāsāvadānāṃ sopade[ś]. .. .y. .. .th. .. sahitāṃ vācaṃ

v7 .. .. t. t[a]d **ānuttaryaṃ bhadanta** bhagavāṃ dharmaṃ deśayati yad uta bhāṣyasamudācāratāyāṃ na bhagavāṃn saṃprajānaṃ mṛṣāvācaṃ bhāṣate na saṃrambhahetoḥ paiśunyam arthamatīṃ dharmamatīṃn niruktivatīṃ kāle

216. Marginalia to left of line: *6*. See note 170 above.

v8 nātiprakīrṇā{{ṃ}}sāvadānāṃ sopadeśāṃ dharmyāṃ arthopasaṃhitāṃ vācaṃ bhāṣate tad ānuttaryaṃ bhadanta bhagavatā yad bhāṣyasamudācāratāyāṃ tad bhagavān aśeṣam abhijānāti tat te aśeṣa[217]

293r

r1 [m] abhijñānata uttare bhijñeyaṃ nāsti yasyābhi[jñ]. .. [n]yaḥ śramaṇo[218] vā bhagavato ntikād bhūyo 'bhijñata[r]a syād yad uta saṃbodhaye | **aparam api** me bhadanta bhagavat. ān[u]t[t]aryaṃ yadā me bhagavāṃ dharmaṃ de

r2 ś[a]y[a]ti yad[uta darś]anasamāpattiṣu paṃcem. n[i] bhadanta samāpattayaḥ iha bhadanta ke śramaṇā [vā brā]hmaṇā vā imam eva kāya pūrvaṃ pādatalād adhaḥ keśamastaka .. kparyantaṃ yathāsthitaṃ yathā

r3 + + .. [t]. pūrva. n[ān]āprakārasyāśucinaḥ pratyavekṣa○te saṃty asmiṃ kāye keśā romāṇi nakhā dantā rajo malaṃ tvaṅ*[219] m[ā]ṃsam asthi snāyu śira vṛkkā hṛdayaṃ plīhā klomaśa ā{{ṃ}}ntrāṇya

r4 ntr. guṇ. āmāśayaḥ pa[kv]ā[ś]ayaḥ audaryakaṃ yatkṛt [pū]○ṣam aśrūṇi svedaḥ kheṭaḥ śiṃghaṇako vasā lasīkā majjā medaḥ pittaṃ śleṣmā pūyaṃ śoṇitaṃ [m]. [t]. ..[ṃ ma]stakaluṃgaṃ

r5 prasrāva iti yasy[ai]va [s]yād [i]yaṃ [p]ra .. ..[ṃ] .. .[ś]. .. sa○māpatti **punar aparaṃ** bhadanta ihaika śramaṇo vā brāhmaṇo vā imam evaṃrūpaṃ kāyaṃ yāva[t p]r. .. + + .i .i .ā .i .i .ya

r6 tva ..[ṃsa] .. ṇitam asthipuruṣakaṃ pratyavekṣate vi○jñānasrota [i]ti yasyaivaṃ syād iyaṃ dvitīyaṃ darśanasamāpatti • **punar aparaṃ** bh. d. n.. i .ai ..ḥ .. .. + + + + + .. ima

r7 m evaṃ kāyaṃ yāvat [p]rasrāvaḥ adhividhyādhividhya tvaṃmāsa-[ś]oṇit. m [as]thiṣu puru[ṣ]akaṃ pratyavekṣate vijñānasrotaḥ pratyavekṣate • iha lok[e] pratiṣṭhi .. .. + + + + + + + + + + + + + +

217. Note the dot slightly below *śe*.

218. The ms. was broken here and perhaps pieced together; note the *ṇo* and *vā* akṣaras are both partially missing and seemingly pressed together.

219. This is an interesting conjunct cluster in the ms. that appears to read *ṅ*maṃ*, where the *-ṅ-* and *-m-* are conjoined with the *-m-* below the *-ṅ-*. Cf. 293r8 and 293v1.

r8[220] .iyaṃ tṛtīyaṃ dar[ś]anasamāpattiḥ **punar aparaṃ** [bh]a[d]anta ihaika śramaṇo vā brāhmaṇo vā yāvad adhividhyādhividhyā tvaṅ*[221] māṃsaśoṇitam asthipuruṣaka[ṃ] pra[t]yave[a]+ + + + + + + + + + + + + +

[a] .. ṇ. .. ..

293v

v1 i.. loke pratiṣṭhitam iti yasyaivaṃ syād iyaṃ [catu]rthī darśanasamāpatti **punar aparaṃ** bhadanta ihaikaḥ śramaṇo vā [br]āhmaṇo vā imam eva kāyaṃ yāvad adhividhya tvaṅ*[222] [m]. ṃ + + + + + + + + +

v2 kaṃ [p]ratyavekṣate vijñānasrotaḥ pratyavekṣa[t]e iha [lok]. .. [pr]atiṣṭhite paraloke apratiṣṭhitam apratiṣṭhite vā punaḥ kvacit pariśuddhaṃ paryavadātam iti ya .. .. + + + + + + + + + + +

v3 pattiḥ **bhagavāṃ bhadanta** divyena cakṣuṣā [yāvad] d. veṣūpa○pa .. .. iti etad ānuttaryaṃ bhadanta bhagavato yad uta darśanasamāpa[tt]i .. .. + + + + + + + + + + + + ...

v4 bhijānata uttare bhijñeyaṃ nā .i .. .ābhijñā[n]ād anya○ḥ śramaṇo vā brāhmaṇo vā bhagavato ntikād bhū◊yo bhijñatara syād yad uta .. .. + + + + + .. [t]aḥ ā

v5 nuttaryaṃ yā me bhagavāṃ dharmaṃ deśayati yad uta prati○pa[t]su ye kecic chramaṇā vā [b]rāhmaṇā vā sataḥ pratipadaḥ prajñāpa[yan. aḥ] prajñāpa .. .[i] .. .. [t]. .. .. [b]. dhya[ṃ]g[āni •] k.

v6 .. .. ni sapta smṛtisaṃbo .yaṃga dharmavicayavīrya○prītiprasrabdhisamādhyupekṣāsaṃbodhyaṃgam etad ānuttaryaṃ bhadanta bhaga[vato] ya[duta] prat[ipats]u tad bhagavā[n] aśeṣam abhi

220. Marginalia to left of line: *7*. See note 170 above.

221. Note again the strange *virāma*-like adition to this conjunct cluster. Cf. *tvaṅ* m[ā]ṃsam* in 293r3 and 293v1. Also for example *samyaṅmanasikāratvayāt* in 292r5 for the expected form of *ṅma*.

222. Cf. 293r3 and 293r8 for more intact examples of this uncommon akṣara cluster.

v7 .. .. .t. [a]śeṣam abhijānata uttare bhijñeyaṃ nāsti yasyābhijñānād anyaḥ śramaṇo vā brāhmaṇo vā bhagavato ntikād bhū{{n}}yo bhijñatara syād yad uta saṃbodhaye **aparam api** bhadanta bha

v8 gavata ānuttaryaṃ yadā me bhagavāṃ dharmaṃ de[śa] .. ti ya[d]uta prahaṇā catvārīmāni bhadanta [p]rahaṇāni katamāni catvāri asmiṃ prahāṇaṃ duẖkhaṃ[223] vaṃdhābhijñam asti prahāṇaṃ duẖkhaṃ[224] kṣiprābhijñā[225]

294r

r1 + + + .. [ṇaṃ sukh]aṃ dhaṃdhābhijñam[226] asti prahāṇaṃ sukhaṃ kṣiprābhijña na bahujanyaṃ pṛthībhūtaṃ na yāvad eva deva[man]uṣyebhyaḥ samyak .. .. [ta]tra bhadanta ya .i ..ṃ .. hāṇaṃ duẖkhaṃ dhandhābhi[jñ]aṃ

r2 + + + + + .. [tv]ād dhīnam ākhyātaṃ tatra yad idaṃ prahāṇaṃ duẖkh{{ā}}ṃ[227] {{bhi jñaṃ}} kṣiprābhijñaṃ tadduḥkhat[v]ād [dh]īnam ākhyātaṃ [ta]tra y[a]d idaṃ prahāṇaṃ [du]ẖkh[a] dhandhābhijñaṃ dhandhatva dhī .. + .ātaṃ tatra yad idaṃ prahā

r3 + .. kh. kṣ. prā[bhi]jñaṃ na ba[hu]janyaṃ pṛthubhūtaṃ na yā○vad devamanuṣyebhyaḥ samyaksupra[kā]śitaṃ ta[d a]bahujanyatvād apṛthubhūta[tvā] na yāv[d] evama[n]uṣye .. [ḥ] samyak.. prakāśita

r4 tv[ā]d dh[ī]nam ākhyātaṃ bhagavato bhadanta prahāṇaṃ su○khaṃ kṣiprābhijñaṃ bahujanyaṃ pṛth. bhūtaṃ [yā]vad evamanuṣye[bhyaḥ sa]myaksuprakā .ita .[e] [a]+ + + + + + + + + + + + + + +

[a] vi .. .. .. + .. + .. + + dh. rm. +[228]

223. Note *jihvāmulīya*.

224. Note *jihvāmulīya*.

225. Note the dot to the lower left of *bhi*.

226. Note how the scribe uses an *anusvāra* here and in 293v8 while this is not seen in the rest of the section.

227. Note *jihvāmulīya*.

228. This fragment likely belongs to DĀ 17 (*Pañcatraya-sūtra*).

r5 prahāṇāt tad bhagavānn aśeṣaḥ .. .i .. .. .. tat te ◯ aśeṣam abhijānata uttare [bhi] .[ñ]. yaṃ nāsti yasyā[bh]ijñānād anyaḥ [śra] .. .. [a]+ + + + + + + + + + + + + +

[a] .. vaṃ caivaṃ ca pretya bhaviṣyāma iti[229]

r6 jñatara syād yad uta saṃbodhaye **aparam api** bha◯[dan]ta bhagavata ānuttaryaṃ yadā me bhagavāṃ dharmaṃ deśaya[ti] yad uta .. .i .. + + + [a]+ + + + + + + + + + + +

[a] ..ḥ paridāho yataś cāyam ātmā[230]

r7 ṇo vā anekavidham ṛddhiviṣayaṃ pratyanubhavaty e[k]. [bh]ūtvā bahudhā bhavati yāvad imau vā punaḥ sūryacandramasāv evaṃmahardhikāv eva. m. h. .u .. [a]+ + + + + + + + + + +

[a] .ucched eva vādina ucchidyate[231]

r8[232] asty eṣā bhadanta ṛddhi[n a]haṃ nāstīti dadāmi • sā caiṣā hīnā grāmyā prākṛtā pārthagjanikā nālāmāryānālamārya saṃkhyātā nābhijñāyai na saṃ[b]. .. .. + + + + + + + + +

294v

v1 **bhagavān bhadanta** ye loke [priyar]ūpaṃ sātarū[p]am ākāṃkṣaṃs tatra tathāgataḥ pratikūlaṃsaṃjñī viharati kūlasaṃjñī tatra tathāgato viharataḥ smṛtas saṃprajānaṃ .i .. + + + + + + + + + +

v2 m ucyate **bhagavān bhadanta** ye loke apriyarūpam asātatarūpam ākāṃkṣas tatra tathāgato pratikūlasaṃjñī viharaty apratikūlasaṃjñī ta[tra] t. [th]āg. .o [a]+ + + + + + + + + + + +

[a] t. • yathābhūta prajānāti • ye te[233]

229. This fragment likely belongs to DĀ 17 (*Pañcatraya-sūtra*).

230. This fragment likely belongs to DĀ 17 (*Pañcatraya-sūtra*).

231. This fragment likely belongs to DĀ 17 (*Pañcatraya-sūtra*).

232. Marginalia to left of line: *8*. See note 170 above.

233. This fragment likely belongs to DĀ 17 (*Pañcatraya-sūtra*).

v3 yaṃ bhadanta bhagavata riddhir[234] ity ucyate .. **g. vān bha○danta** ye lloke priyarūpaṃ cāpy apṛyarūpaṃ ca sātarūpaṃ cāsātarūpaṃ .. + + + + + [a]+ + + + + + + + + + + +

[a] .. naḥ saṃjñī ātmā bhavaty ataḥ para[235]

v4 smṛtaḥ saṃprajānan iyaṃ bhadanta .. + + .. ṛddhi○r ity ucyate **bhagavāṃ bhadanta** rūpī rūpāṇi paśyatīyaṃ bhadanta bhagavata ṛddhi .i .. [a]+ + + + + + + + + + + + +

[a] taḥ param ity eve bhivadaṃto bhivada[236]

v5 saṃjñībahirdhā rūpāṇi paśyatīyaṃ .. .. .. bha○gavata ṛddhir ity ucyate **bhagavān bhadanta** śubhaṃ vimokṣaṃ kāyena sākṣātkṛtv. .. [a]+ + + + + + + + + + + + + + +

[a] .. m etat praṇītaṃ ya[d u]ta naivasaṃ[jñā] ..[237]

v6 + + [d]dhir it. .cyate **bhagavān bhadanta** sarva .o rūpa○saṃjñānāṃ samatikramāt pratighasaṃjñānām astagamā nānātvasaṃjñānām amanasikārād atram ākā[śam i]ty ā .. ..

v7 + + + + + + + [s]aṃpadya vihara[t]īyaṃ bhadanta bhagavataḥ ṛddhir ity ucyate **bhagavān bhadanta** sarvaśa ākāśānaṃtyāyatanaṃ samatikramyānantaṃ vijñānam iti vijñānānaṃtyāyata

v8 + + + ...y. .. h. r. [t]i [i]yaṃ [bhadanta] bhagavata ṛddhir ity ucyate **bhagavān bhadanta** sarvaśo vijñānānaṃtyāyatanaṃ samatikramya .. .[ti] .iṃcid ity ākiṃcanyāyatana[m] u[p]a[s]aṃ[pa] .ya viharati iyaṃ bhadanta

234. Note the use of *ri* for *ṛ*.

235. This fragment likely belongs to DĀ 17 (*Pañcatraya-sūtra*).

236. This fragment likely belongs to DĀ 17 (*Pañcatraya-sūtra*). Cf. 299v8.

237. This fragment likely belongs to DĀ 17 (*Pañcatraya-sūtra*).

295r

r1 [bhagavata ṛ]ddhir ity ucyate **bhagavān bhadanta** sarvaśa ākiṃcanyāyatanaṃ samatikramya naiva saṃjñānāsaṃjñāyatanam upasaṃpadya viharatīyaṃ bhadanta bhagavata riddhir ity ucyate **bhagavān bhadanta**

r2 .. .. .. [n]aivasaṃjñā]nāsaṃjñāyatanaṃ samatikramya saṃjñāveditanirodhaṃ kāyena sākṣātkṛtvopasaṃpadya viharati iyaṃ bhadanta bhagavata ri ty ucyate etād vāvuttaryaṃ bhadanta bhagavato

r3 yad uta ṛddhiviṣayajñān etad bhagavā[n] a[ś]roṣa○m abhijānāti tat te aśeṣam abhijānata uttare bhijñeyaṃ nāsti yasyābhijñānād anyaḥ śramaṇo vā brā[hm]aṇo vā bhagava

r4 to ntikād bhūyo bhijñatarata syād yad uta [sa]ṃbo○dhaye **aparam api** bhadanta bhagavata ānutta = = ryaṃ yadā me bhagavāṃ dharmaṃ de .. .. .i .. .. .. [a]+ + .i + ... ti

[a] 296r3 /// d. nt. + g.

r5 jñāne iha bhadantaika śramaṇo vā [b]r[āhma[ṇo vā ○ anekavidhaṃ pūrvanivāsaṃ samanusmarati tadyathā ekām api jā tisraḥ catasraḥ [yā]vad ih[otpanna] [a].. .. .[i] [khalv ahaṃ bhada]

[a] .. .. ..

r6 nta varṣā ugrakoṭīgaṇanasaṃkhyāmā[trake]na ○ satvānām āyuṣparyantaṃ vadāmi **bhagavāṃ bhadanta** yatra tatra uṣitapū .o .. .. [a].. .i .. .. [p]i [ṣ]. .. di vā [arūp]i[ṣ]. .. di

[a] .. .. [jñā] ..

r7 vā saṃjñiṣu yadi vā asaṃjñiṣu yadi vā naivasaṃjñānāsaṃjñiṣu tatra tatra bhagavāṃ nātmākāraṃs sodaśam anekavidhaṃ pūrvanivāsaṃ sama[nu] [a].. .. .. + + + + + + + + + + +

[a] .. .. [bh]. vo [pā] .. ..

r8[238] duta pūrvanivāsānu[smṛt]ijñānena tad bhagavān aśeṣam abhijānāti tat te aśeṣam abhijānataḥ uttare abhijñeyaṃ nāsti yasyābhijñānād anyaḥ .r. .. .. .. + + + + + + +

295v[239]

v1 to ntikād bhūyo bhijñatara syād yad uta saṃbodhaye **aparam api** me bhadanta bhaga[vata] ānuttaryaṃ yadā me bhagavāṃ dharmaṃ deśayati yad uta ā .. .. [a]+ + + + + + .. + + + + + + + + +

[a] 296v1 /// [samādhiṃ spṛśati] .. ///[240]

v2 vā nimittena vā parikathayā vā ādiśaty evaṃ ma .. .. tthaṃ te mana anyathā te manu ciraṃ kṛtaṃ cirabhāṣitam apy ādiśati rahaḥkṛta[ṃ] .. [a]+ +

[a] 296v2 /// .. yānvayam a .i .. ///[241]

v3 gataṃ pratyutpanna{{ṃ}}m apy ādiśati • atīgatapratyutpa◯[n]nam apy ādiśati cittam apy ādiśati caitasām api dharmān nādi[śa] .i [y]. .[c]. [t]. [a]+ + + + + + + + + + + + + + + + + +

[a] 296v3 /// .c. t[i] s. n. .. .. .. + .y. .. .[y]. .t. .. ś. [bh]. .. ..[242]

v4 **nar aparam** ihaiko na haiva nimittena vā pa◯rikathayā v[ā] ādiśati api tu de .. [nāṃ vā] .. nu[ṣ]yāṇāṃ vā śa[bdaṃ śrutvā] ā .[i][243] [a]+ + + .. te .. .. + + + + + + + + + + ... = =

238. Marginalia to left of line: *9*. See note 170 above.

239. Throughout this folio one finds imprints from another folio transposed on the birchbark in the form of faint, upside-down akṣaras. There also appear to be several lines where the latter half has been covered by imprints (in the correct orientation) from another folio or section. The overlapping fragments appear to correspond to gaps in 296v.

240. This fragment belongs to 296v1.

241. This fragment belongs to 296v2.

242. This fragment belongs to 296v3.

243. Here the new akṣaras appear slightly above the line and continue to the end. They seem to be imprinted from another folio.

[a] 296v4 /// haikaḥ śr. .. .. vā [brāhmaṇ. vā] a .. .. ///[244]

v5 d ādiśanti sarvaṃ tat tathaiva bhavati [nān]yathā **puna◯r aparam** ihaiko na haiva nimittena vā pa .. .. rikathayā vā ādi[śati] .. [a]+ + + [dev]. + + + + ... [vā] śabdaṃ

[a] 296v5 /// .. drū .. .. ..ṃ .. .. ///[245]

v6 śrutvā ādiśati api tu parasatvānāṃ para◯pudgalānāṃ vitarkitaṃ manasā mānasaṃ [jñātvā] ādiśati evaṃ [t]. .. .. [itthaṃ te] .. [nā]nyathā te naḥ cirakṛtaṃ cira

v7 bhāṣitam a[py ā]diśati rahatkṛtaṃ rahobhāṣitam apy ādiśati dūre 'py ādiśaty antike py ādiśati atīt{{ānā}}m apy ādiśaty anāg[a]tam apy ādiśati pūrvavac cittam apy ādi

v8 [śat]i [cetasā]m api = = = = = =[246] dharmān nādiśati yac ca tathā ādiśati tat sarvaṃ tat tathaiva bhavati nānyathā **bhagavā[n] bhadanta** paraṃ paśyaty av[i]tarkam avicāraṃ samādhiṃ samāpannaṃ dṛṣṭvā ca puna<<s te evaṃ bhavati>>[247]

296r[248]

r1 .. .. + + .. vitarkayati na vicārayati yathā praṇihitāś cāsya manaḥsaṃskārāḥ pravarttante idānīm ayam āyuṣmāṃ tasmāt s. .. [dher] vy[u]tthāya imāṃś cemāṃś ca vitarkān vitarkayi

r2 .y. .. [t]i .. .. .. .samādhe[r] vyutthāya tāṃs tāṃ vita .kān vitarkayati etad ānuttaryaṃ bhadanta .. .. [va]to ādeśa .. .. [dhau tad bhagavā] .. .. [ṣ]. [m]. .i .. nāti [t]. + [a] .. ṣam abhijānata uttare bhi

244. This fragment belongs to 296v4.

245. This fragment belongs to 296v5.

246. Here the ms. has been patched over with birchbark. The six akṣaras lost here are made up for by the scribe adding six akṣaras interlineally at the end of the line. See next note.

247. These are the six akṣaras added interlinearly. See preceding note.

248. This folio is pieced together from several fragments. The first lines are generally readable, but large chunks are missing from the latter lines. Lines 5–8 are each missing at least ten to fifteen akṣaras at the end.

r3 jñeyaṃ nāsti yasyābhijñānād anyaḥ śramaṇo vā brā○hmaṇo vā bhagav. + + + + + ... tara . [y]. .. . [ut]a saṃbo[dha]ye **a .. .. .. [p]i** + + ... [v]. [t]. [ānu] .. ryaṃ yadā bhaga

r4 vāṃ dharmaṃ deśayati yad uta śāsvata .. . [i]tāyāṃ ○ iha bhadantai + + + + + + + [ṇ]. .. [a] .. [ṇy]agato vā vṛkṣamūla .. .. .. [v]. + + + + + + + + + + + + + .. ṇ[ā]

r5 nvayā bhāvanānvayā bahulīkārānva[yā] samyaṅma○ .. .i .. [r]. [nva]y. [t]. [drū] + + + + + + [samā]dhi[ṃ] spṛśati yathā [sam]. .. .. + + + + + + + + + + + + + + +

r6 rati tasyaivaṃ bhavati[249] etāvad ayaṃ [lo]ka saṃvṛ○ .. .c. vivṛta[ś] ca [yā]vad eva may[ānva]yam abhisaṃbaddha it{{i}}ḥ [p]ū .. .. ..ṃ + + + + + + + + + + + + + + + + + +

r7 = itaḥ paścād a[h]aṃ ca jāna etāvad ayaṃ lo[k]. ..[ṃ] .. [r]ttayiṣyate ca viva[r].. .i . [y]ate .eti sa na haiva lokasya pa[r]ya[n]tadarśī [bh]. .. + + + + + + + + + + + + + + + +

r8[250] +[251] = aparānte .. .. .. [m] iti pasyaivaṃ syād iyaṃ prathamā śāśvata-vādi[t]. **.u[nar] aparaṃ** bhadanta ihaikaḥ śramaṇo vā b. āhmaṇo v[ā a] .. + + + + + + + + + + + + + + + +

296v[252]

v1 = = = [=][253] gato vā āta .t. .v. .. [p]rahāṇānvayā bhāvanānvayā bahulīkārānvayā .. m. [ṅma]nasikārātayā tadrūpaṃ śāntaṃ cetaḥsamādhi .[e] .. sa[m]ādhiṃ spṛśati .. + + + + + + + +

249. Note the small mark on the top of the *va* in *bhavati*.

250. Marginalia to left of line: *10*. See note 170 above.

251. The only thing legible here is a mirrored imprint of *to*, the first akṣara of 295v1. From the placement of filler marks directly above this akṣara in 296r7 and directly next to it in 296r8, we can deduce that there was a problem with this part of the birchbark and the scribe likely (or should have) placed a filler mark here, and this lacuna is thus not included in the akṣara count to be reconstructed for this line.

252. This folio has imprints from other folios on the lower left quadrant in lines 4–7. These imprints correspond to 297r2–5.

253. The ms. appears to be repaired here with a birchbark patch.

v2 = = = =[254] tvāriṃśataṃ saṃvarttavivarttakalpān samanusmarati .. syaivaṃ bhavati etāvad .. .. lokaḥ saṃvarttiṣyate ca vivarttiṣyate ca yāvad e[v]. .. yānvayam a .i .. + + + + + + + + +

v3 d ahaṃ jāne etāvad vayaṃ lokaḥ saṃvarttiṣya[te] ca viva○.i .. te ceti itaḥ pūrvam ahaṃ jāne etāvad ayaṃ lokaḥ sa[ṃ]vṛtaś ca [vi] [.ṛ] .. .c. t[i] s. n. .. .. .. + .y. .. .[y] .t. .. ś. [bh]. .. ..

v4 api tv aparānte jñānadarśanaṃ pravarttate + .. nte a○jñ[ā] .. .. .. [y]asyaivaṃ [sy]ā .i .. .i .[ī] .. .. .. [śv]atavādināṃ **punar aparaṃ** bhadanta ihaikaḥ śr. .. .. .ā [brāhmaṇ. vā] a .. .. + +

v5 vā vṛkṣamūlagato vā śunyāgāragato vā ātaptā○nvayāt prahāṇānvayād bhāvanānvayā bahu .īkārānvayā samyaṅmanasikārānvay. .. d rū .. .. ..ṃ .. ..[ṛ] .. .. .. [th].

v6 samāhite citte aśītiṃ saṃva[r]ttakalpān samanusma○rati tasyaivaṃ bhavati etāvad ayaṃ loka .. [v]. rttate <<ca>>[255] vivarttate ca yāvad eva mayā .v. y. .. bhijñayābhisa[ṃ]buddha ita pūrva

v7 .. ..[ṃ] .. [ne] etāvad ayaṃ lokaḥ saṃvṛttaś ca vivṛttaś ca itaḥ paścād apy ahaṃ jāne etāvad ayaṃ lokaḥ saṃvartti .yate na vivarttiṣyate c. ti [s]. [na] haiva lokasya paryantadarśī bhavati api tu pū

v8 .. .. .. [rānte] .[y]. [jñā]na .. .. naṃ pravarttata iti yasyaivaṃ syād iyaṃ tṛtayā śāśvatavāditā **bhagavāṃ bhadanta** divyena cakṣuṣā yāvat sugatau svargaloke deveṣūpapadyata iti etad ānuttaryaṃ bhada

297r

r1 nta bhagavato yad uta śāśvatavāditāyāṃ tad bhagavān aśeṣam abhijānāti tat te aśeṣam abhijānata uttare bhijñeyaṃ nāsti yasyābhijñānād anyaḥ śramaṇo vā brāhmaṇo vā bhagavato

254. The ms. appears to be repaired here, as with the line above.

255. This added *ca* is very small and wedged between its neighboring akṣaras, with a supplemental sign (a small cross) above indicating its inclusion.

r2 nti[k]ād [bh]ūyo bhijñatara syād yad uta saṃ[b]odhaye [a]**param api** me bha[d]anta bhagavata anuttaryaṃ yadā[256] me bhagavāṃ dharmaṃ deśayati yad uta anu[ś]āsanavidhau jānāti bhagavāṃn aya pudgalaḥ kālya

r3 [m] aveditaḥ sāyaṃ[257] vi[śeṣā]ya paraiṣyati sāyaṃ ◯ vā avoditaẖ[258] kālyaṃ viśeṣāya pareṣyatīti sa evaṃ yathānuśiṣ[ṭ]a samyak pratipadyamā[n]o [n]acirād eva trayāṇāṃ saṃyo

r4 ja[n]ānāṃ pra[h]āṇāt [s]rota-āpanno bhavat{{i}}y avinipā◯ta = = dharmā niyataṃ saṃbodhiparāyaṇaḥ satvakṛtvobhavati paramaḥ saptakṛtvo devāṃ[ś]. . .anuṣyāṃś ca saṃ[dh]ā[vy]. [s]aṃ[s]ṛ[ty]. [d].

r5 khasyāntaṃ kariṣyatīti • ity api bhagavāṃ jānāti ◯ **jānāti [bh]a[g]avāṃ** nāyaṃ pudgalaḥ kālyam avoditaḥ sāyaṃ viśeṣāya paraiṣyati sā ..ṃ .. . . .o .i ..ḥ .. + + + + + +

r6 raiṣyatīti sa evaṃ yathānuśiṣṭaḥ [s]amyak pratimā◯ .[o n]acirād eva trayāṇāṃ saṃyojanānāṃ prahāṇād rāgadveṣamoh[ā] ..[ṃ] .. .. [n]. [t].[ā] .. + + + + + + + + + + + + +

r7 lokam āgatya duḥkhasyāntaṃ kariṣyatīti ity api bhagavāṃ jānāti **bhagavā{{ṃ}}n** ayaṃ pudgalaḥ kālyam aviditaḥ sāyaṃ viśeṣāya parai[ṣ]ya[t]i [s]. .. .. .. + + + + + + + + + + + +

r8[259] ṣyatīti sa vevaṃ yathānu[ś]i .. [ḥ] samyak pratipadyamāno nacirād eva paṃcānā{{ṃ}}m avarabhāgīyānāṃ saṃyojanānāṃ prahāṇād upapāduko bhaviṣyati [t]a .r. + + + + + + + + + + +

256. Note the odd, small smudge or stroke of what appears to be ink radiating out from the upper left quadrant of the *ya*.

257. Note that with each instance of the word *sāyam* in this section, the scribe employs a less common way of writing *sā*.

258. Note *jihvāmūlīya*.

259. Marginalia to left of line: *11*. See note 170 above.

297v[260]

v1 anāvṛttikadharmā punar imaṃ loka ity api bhagavāṃ jānāti **bhagavān** ayaṃ pu[dg]alaḥ kālyam avoditaḥ sāyaṃ viśeṣāya paraiṣyati .. [a]+ + + + + + + + + + + + + + +

[a] .. .. [ṭaṃ] nira .i

v2 tīti sa evaṃ yathānuśiṣṭaḥ samyak pratipadyamāno nacirād evāsravāṇāṃ cet[o]vimuktiṃ prajñāvimuktiṃ dṛṣṭa eva dharme svayam abhi[jñ]a[y]ā {{.i}}[261] + + + + + + + + + + + + + +

v3 te • kṣīṇā me jātir uṣitaṃ brahmacaryaṃ kṛtaṃ karaṇīyaṃ ◯ [n]. param [asmā]d bhavaṃ prajānīāmīti[262] ity api bhagavāṃ jānāti etad ā .u .. .. [a]+ + + + .. + + + + + + + + + + + + + +

[a] [t]. [sm]. [je t].

v4 d bhagavān aśeṣam abhijānāti uttara bhijñeyaṃ nā◯sti [ya] .yābhijñād a[n]yaḥ śramaṇo vā brāhmaṇo vā bhagavato ntikād bhūyo bhijña[tara][263] .yā .ya[d] u[t]. [s]. [bodh]. y. [**a**] + + + +

260. 297v is mostly intact, only missing substantial portions in the upper right-hand quadrant, unfortunately leaving the ends of lines 1–4 destroyed. The destroyed ends of lines 1 and 3 are obscured by small fragments of three to six akṣaras from another folio. Imprints from 298r can be seen throughout the folio but most clearly on the lower left quadrant.

261. It is unclear if the scribe omitted this akṣara. There appears to be a deletion mark above it, but this is not at all certain. As it is, this akṣara does not fit in the expected reading (*abhijñayā sākṣātkṛtvopasaṃpadya pravedayiṣyate*) but does contribute to the expected akṣara count, which together can be taken as good evidence that it was meant to be deleted. Another option would be to assume that the scribe had meant for its inclusion and read this akṣara as a particle such as *hi*.

262. This surely should be read *prajānāmīti*, where the scribe mistakenly wrote the diacritics for both *ī* and *ā* on to the base *-n-* of *prajānāmi*.

263. It is likely that the lower part of the fragment in the previous line is obscuring the tops of the akṣaras here.

v5 me [bh]adanta bha[gavat]a[264] anuttaryaṃ yadā [m]e bhagavāṃ ○ dha◊rmaṃ[265] deśayati yad uta bhavākrāntiṣu[266] catasraḥ imā garbhāvakrāntayaẖ[267] katamā [c]atasraḥ a[s]ti [g]ar[bh]o s[a]. pra[jān]a.

v6 [m]ātuḥ ku[kṣim[268] a]vakrāmat[y] ayaṃ saṃprajānaṃs tiṣṭha○ty asaṃprajāna niṣkramati asti garbhas saṃpra[jā]na[n m]ātuḥ kukṣi[m a]vakrāmati saṃprajānaṃ tiṣṭhati saṃprajānaṃ niṣkrāmati

v7 asa[ṃ]prajānaṃ niṣkrāmati | asti ga .bhaḥ saṃprajānan mātuḥ kukṣim avakrāmati saṃprajānaṃs tiṣṭhaty asaṃprajānaṃ niṣkrāmati | asti garbhaḥ saṃpra .. nan mātuḥ kukṣim avakrāmati saṃprajā

v8 na. tiṣṭhati saṃprajānaṃ niṣkrāmati bodhisatvo bhagavāṃ saṃprajānaṃ mātuḥ[269] kukṣim avakrāntaḥ saṃprajānaṃ sthitaḥ saṃprajānan niṣkrāntaḥ eta[d u]tta[rya]ṃ bhadanta bhagavato yad. ta garbhā

298r

r1 .. krāntiṣu tad bhagavān aśeṣam abhijānāti tat te aśeṣam abhijānataḥ uttare 'bhijñeyaṃ nāsti bhijñānād anyaḥ śramaṇo vā brāhmaṇo vā bhagav[a]to 'ntikād bhūyo 'bhijñatara syād ya .uta saṃbo

r2 dha[ye] .. **param api** [me] bhadanta [bha]gava[ta] ānuttaryaṃ yadā me bhagavāṃ dharmaṃ deśayati yad uta pudgalaḥ āsravāṇāṃ kṣayād anāsravā cetovimuktiṃ prajñā[vi]muktiṃ dṛṣṭa eva dharme svayam abhijñayā

264. The *ga* here is quite blotchy, and what could be mistaken for an *anusvāra* over the *va* is actually ink from inversed ghost imprint of 298r.

265. There is a hole in the ms. here between *dha* and *rma* that must have been there before the scribe wrote this line.

266. Note the very small fragment intersecting the bottom of the *-u-* diacritic in *ṣu*.

267. Note *jihvāmūlīya*. Note also the strange squiggle connecting the lower halves of *nta* and *ya*.

268. Note that the upper left portion of the *va* is slightly detached and moved to the left into the upper right portion of *ma*, giving it the deceptive appearance of *mā*.

269. Note the three very small dots or strokes in the lower section between *mātuḥ* and *kukṣim*.

r3 s. .ṣ. [t]kṛtvo .. ..ṃ[p]adya pravedayiṣyate kṣīṇā me ◯ jātir uṣitaṃ brahmacaryaṃ kṛtaṃ karaṇīyaṃ nā[p]aram asmād bhavaṃ prajānāmīti ity api bhagavāṃ jānāti **bhagavān** ayaṃ pudgalaḥ

r4 paṃ .. .[ā]m [a]v. r. [bh]. [gīyā] .[āṃ] saṃyoja[n]. nāṃ .rahā◯ṇād upapāduko bhaviṣyati tatra sa parinirvāyī anāgāmī anāvṛttikadharmā puna[r] i[maṃ lo]kam i[ty] api bhavāṃ jānāti

r5 **bhagavān** āyaṃ pudgalaḥ trayāṇāṃ saṃyojanānāṃ ◯ pra .. .ā[d r]āga-[dveṣ]amohānāṃ ca tanutvāt sakṛdāgāmī bhaviṣyati sa[kṛd] i[ma]ṃ [a].. .. .. .. [lo] .. .[āga]tya duḥkhasyā[nt]aṃ[270] .. .iṣ.atīti

[a] .. .y. .. ..

r6 ity api bhagavāṃ jānāti **bhagavān** ayaṃ pudgalaḥ ◯ .. [yā]ṇāṃ .. .. janā[n]āṃ prahāṇāt srota-āpanno bhaviṣyati vi .i .. [a]+ + + + + + + + + + + + + + + + +

[a] .ā .[i] ..

r7 tvo bhavaparamasaptakṛtvo devāṃś ca manuṣyāṃś ca saṃdhāvya saṃsṛtya du[ḥkh]asyān[t]aṃ kariṣyatīti ity api bhagavāṃ jānīte etad ānuttaryaṃ bha + .. +

r8[271] gavā .. .[e] .. m abhijānāti tat te aśeṣam abhijānata uttare bhijñe[ye n]āsti y. .y[ā]bhijñānād anyaḥ śramaṇo vā brāhmaṇo vā bhagava .. ..i .. ..ū .. .. jñ. + + + + + + + + + +

298v
v1 **apa[ra] .. .i** [m]. bhadanta bhagavata ānuttaryaṃ yadā me bhagavāṃ dharmaṃ de[ś]a[y]ati y. .. ta p. [ru]ṣaśīlaviśuddhijñāne śrāddha syāt satyaś ca a[śuddh]. + + .[i] + .[i] .. + + + + + + + + +

270. Note *jihvāmūlīya*.

271. Marginalia to left of line: *12*. See note 170 above.

v2 ko na ca kāmeṣu avam āpadyeta n[a] ca satv[e]ṣu mithyā pratipadyeta smṛta[ś cāna] + ... + + + + + + ... nta bhagavato yad uta puru[ṣa] .ī .. + + + + + + + + + + + + + + + + + + +

v3 t te aśeṣam abhijānata uttare bhijñeyaṃ[272] nāsti yasyā○[bh]ijñ. nād any.. śramaṇ. vā brāhmaṇ[o] vā bhagavato ntikād bhūyo bhijñ. [t]. .. + + + + + + + + + + + + + + + +

v4 kulaputreṇa [jñā]tavyaṃ draṣṭavyaṃ prāptavyaṃ boddhavyaṃ tat sa○. aṃ [bha].. [va]to jñānaṃ dṛṣṭaṃ viditaṃ vijñātaṃ samyag evābhisaṃbuddhena bhagavān kā[m]. .[ukh]. .. .. .. yoga [hīne] .. .y. .. ..

v5 kṛte [p]ā[rth]. g[j]ani[ke] gar[ba]m[273] āpanno nātmaklamathānu○yoge duḥkhe nārye anar[ś]opasaṃhite caturṇāṃ ca bhagavān ādhicaitasikānāṃ [dṛṣ]ṭ. .. [rma] .u .. vihā[r]i[ṇāṃ] ni.[ā] .. .[ā]

v6 bhī [kṛcchr]alābhī katameṣāṃ caturṇāṃ bhagavāṃ bhadanta ○ viviktaṃ kāmair yāvac caturthaṃ dhyānam upasaṃ .. + .[i] + + .i .. .. .. [bh]a[g]avāṃ kāmasukhālayānuyoge hīne grāmye prākṛ

v7 te pā[r].. [g]ja[ni]ke ga[r]bham āpanno nātmaklamathānu[y]o[g]e duḫkhe[274] anārye anarthopasaṃhite eṣāṃ ca bhagavā catur[ṇ]ā[m ā]+ + + + + + .[ṛ]ṣ[ṭ]adharmasukhavihā[rāṇā]ṃ nikāmalābhy akṛcchralābhī **tena kha**

v8 .. .. .. y. nāyu[ṣm]ān nāgasapālo bhagavataḥ pṛ .. ta[sth]ito 'bhūd vyajanaṃ gṛhītvā bhagavantaṃ vījayamānaḥ athāyu .m. .. [g]. .. [pā]lo bhagavantam idam avocat* ime bhadanta [a]nyatīrthika{{pa}}

299r

r1 parivrājakā eṣām aṃganām anyatamānyata .. [sa]ṃ .. [m] ātmanaḥ saṃmukhībhūtaṃ [pa]śyeyur apī[d]ānī ma[ha]tī caila[p]. [tākā] .. cchrayitvā sarvāṃ nālandāṃ anvāhiṇ[ḍ]ita[n] yā .. .. ni[t]y[a]. iva ya

272. Note the odd, small stroke under the *-i-* in *bhijñeyaṃ*.

273. Note the small dot-like stroke emanating from the top of the *-m-* before the *-ā-* diacritic.

274. Note *jihvāmūlīya*.

r2 .. .. mahardhikā evaṃmahānubhāvā iti a[th]a [ca] punar bhavāṃ mahardhika eva mahānubhāvo [ne]cchati pa[re] .. [m] a .. + + + + .. .[y]. tra bhagavāṃn alpe[cch]aḥ s[ā]dhu bhadanta āyu[ṣm]ataḥ ś[āripu]

r3 tr[a] .yāha[ṃ] dhar[m]aparyāyo bhīkṣṇaṃ bhāṣituṃ pratibhāyaOd bhikṣubhyo bhikṣuṇībhyaḥ upāsakebhyaḥ upāsi[k]. + + + + .. [t]īrthikaśra[m]aṇabrāhmaṇacarakaparivrājakebhyas ta

r4 [tr]a [yeṣ]āṃ [bhav]i[ṣya]ti bhagavato ntike kāṃkṣā vā viOmatir vā te kāṃkṣā pra[hās]yanti dṛṣṭim ṛjvīkariṣyanti dharmeṣu ca niṣṭhāṃ gacchiṣya[nt]i śās[t]ari [ca pr]a .āda]ṃ [pr]a .e[d]a[y]iṣ[y]a[ṃt]e

r5 [s]amyaksaṃbuddho bata bhagavān ity api jñāsyanti **taO[t]ra bhagavān** āyuṣmantaṃ śāriputram āmantrayate tasmā[t] tarhi śāriputrāyaṃ dharmaparyā .. .īk. [bhā]ṣi[tuṃ pra]ti[bh]ā[tu] bhik ..

r6 bhyo bhikṣuṇībhyaḥ upāsakebhya upāsikābhyo O .. .. nānātīrthikaśramaṇabrāh[m]aṇac. rakaparivrājakebhyas [t]atra [y]e ..ṃ .. .i .. .i .. .. + + + + + + + + + +

r7 r vā te kāṃkṣā prahāsyanti dṛṣṭim ṛjvī[k]ariṣyanti dharmeṣu ca niṣṭhāṃ [g]ami .ya .i + + + + + + + + + dayiṣyante samyaksaṃbuddho bha .. + + + + + + + + + + + + + + + + + + +

r8[275] putras tūṣṇīṃ .āvena asmiṃ khalu dharmaparyāye bhāṣyamāṇe mahājana .āyasya bhagav. t[o nt]ike cittam abhiprasannaṃ tasmād asya dharmaparyāyasya prasad[a] .. .. + + + + + + + + + +

299v

v1 **anta .. [d]dānam*** || saṃbodhiku[ś]alāyatanaṃ pudgalā bhāṣyada[rś]anam* pratiprahāṇam ṛddhiś ca nivāsādeśanena ca • śāśvatam cānuśāstiś ca ga .. vakrāntipudgalā + + + + + + + + + + + + +

v2 tasikena ca • || || **apannakaḥ sarveko** bhārgavaḥ śalyāvabhaya-[bh]ai[ra]vo ro[m]a[harṣa]ṇo jina[y]abhaś ca .ovindaḥ prāsādikaḥ prasādanīye [d]. + + + + + + + + + + + + + + + + + + +

275. Marginalia to left of line: *13*. See note 170 above.

v3 maṭhikaḥ kāya◊bhāvanā bodhaḥ saṃkaraś caiva ā○.. .. ṭamahāsamājena bhavati paścimaṃ || || bhagavāṃ cchrāvastyām [v]i .. .. .. + + + + + + + + + + + + + + +

Reconstruction, Translation, and Parallels

The *Prāsādika-sūtra*

Introductory Frame: The Death of Jñātiputra (DĀ 15.1–3)

DĀ 15.1

[**a**] bhagavāṃc chākyeṣu varṣā upagataḥ puṣkariṇīprāsād(e) m(e)dhya-(s)y(a)[276] śākyasyāmrav(a)ṇe{na}[277] <|> tena khalu samaye(na) (c)u(nda ś)ram(a)ṇoddeśaḥ (**274v6**) pāpāyāṃ (varṣā)[278] upagato jalūkāvanaṣaṇḍe <|> taṃ khalu varṣāvāsaṃ pāpāyāṃ nirgrantho jñātiputraḥ kālagato; yasya kālakriyayā[279] nirgranthā jñātiputrīyā bhinnā dvidhājātā (**274v7**) viharaṃti ka(laha)j(ā)tā[280] bhaṇḍanajātā vigṛhītā vivādam āpannāḥ <|>

[**b**] tadyathā(ha)m enaṃ dharmavinayam ājānāmi na tvam enaṃ dharmavinayam ājā(n)āsi <|> yathā{haṃ} cāh(am e)n(aṃ)[281] dharmavina(**274v8**)-yam[282] ājānāmi yathā (ca)[283] tvam enaṃ dharmavinayam ājānāsi <|> yuktaṃ mamāyuktaṃ t(ava sah)i(ta)ṃ mamāsahitaṃ tava iti <|> (pūr)vaṃ vacanīyaṃ paścād avocat* p(aścād vaca)nī(ya)ṃ (p)ūrvam avocat* <|>[284]

276. Cf. 275r6. This is the name of the family hosting the Buddha, corresponding to the Pali *vedhañña* in DN III 117.1.

277. Ms. reads *śākyasyāśrav(a)ṇena*. Cf. 275r6: *pravaṇa(ṃ)*, "hillside grove," which would work just as well. However, note the reading in SHT IV 32 fragment 66 V2: *medhyasya śākyasy=āmravane*, which refers to a mango forest as opposed to a hillside. I emend to the reading above, as the Pali states it is a mango forest and not a hillside. DN III 117.2: *ambavane pāsāde*. In any case, in this manuscript, this appears to be the site where the Buddha delivered this discourse.

278. Cf. DN III 118.6: *atha kho cundo samaṇuddeso pāvāyaṃ vassaṃ vuttho*.

279. Ms. reads *kālakriyāyā*. Cf. 275r8.

280. Cf. 276r3 and DN III 117.7: *kalaha-jāta*.

281. Unfortunately, the ms. is damaged here and in its corresponding sections (DĀ 15.2b and DĀ 15.3b). It seems that the scribe had added *aham* twice. I have emended accordingly.

282. Ms. reads *dharmavineyam*. This supposed *-e-* may in fact be an imprint from the 275r2, but the majority of this folio is unfortunately missing, making it impossible to verify.

283. Cf. 275v2 and 276r4.

284. Cf. 276r4–5.

(275r1) (abhitūrṇaṃ te viparāmṛṣṭam āropitas te vādo vādārthāya apahara vādaṃ vādavipramokṣāya nigṛhīto 'si | nirveṭhaya yady uttaraṃ prajānāsi | brūhi pṛṣṭa | ity anyonyaṃ mukhaśaktikayā vitudanti viru)(~275r2)(janti | vi) .. + + . (anudhvaṃsayaṃti vadako 'py eṣāṃ na prajñāyate yad uta sahadharmeṇa |)[285]

[c] (ye 'pi te nirgranthasya jñātiputrasya śrāvakā gṛhiṇo 'vadātavasanāḥ prativasanti te 'pi nirgrantheṣu jñātiputrīyeṣu) (~275r3) (bhinneṣu dvidhājāteṣu viharanti kalahajāteṣu bhaṇḍanajāteṣu vigṛhīteṣu vivādam āpanneṣu nirviṇṇāḥ prativāṇayo 'samānā apakrāntā yathāpi tad durākhyātād dharmavinayād du)(275r4)ṣpravedit(ād anairyāṇikād asaṃbodhigāmino bhinnād astūpād apratisaraṇāc; chāstā ca na tathāgato 'rhan samyaksaṃbuddhaḥ |)[286] ///

DĀ 15.1

[a] The Blessed One retired for the rainy season among the Śākyans at the Lotus Pond mansion along the mango forest of the Śākyan [named] Medhya. At that time, the novice Cunda had retired to the Jalūkā Grove in Pāpā[287] for the rainy season. Just then the Nirgrantha Jñātiputra[288] died at the monsoon residence in Pāpā. With his death the Nirgranthas, the followers of Jñātiputra, dwelled split, divided, contentious, quarrelsome, aggressive, and fallen into dispute.

285. Cf. 275v3–4 and 276r5–6, DĀ 25.29 (*Tridaṇḍi-sūtra*, 363v5) and DĀ 27.45 (*Lohitya-sūtra I*, 374r6), SBV II 236.13–23, and SaṅgE 312 (=44) para 23 (=x).

286. Cf. 276r6–8, SaṅgE 312–13 (= Saṅg 44–45), paragraph 24 (= Saṅg x): *(ye 'pi) n(ir)gr(an)thasya jñ(āti)*(12.3/14.3)*(pu)trasya śrāvakā gṛh(iṇo 'vadātavasa)*(13.2/14.3)*nā pāpāyāṃ prativasaṃti te 'pi ni(r)gra(ntheṣu jñātiputrikeṣu bhinneṣu vivādam āpanneṣu kalahajāteṣu)* (12.4/14.4) *bhaṇḍana(jā)teṣu vigṛhīt(eṣu nirviṇṇarūpāḥ prativāṇirūpā a)*(13.3/16.3) *samānarūpā apakrāntā yathā (dharmavinayād durākhyātād duṣpraveditād a)*(12.5/14.5) *niryāṇikād asaṃbodhagāmino bhinnād as(aṃstūpād apratiśaraṇāt |)*, and DN III 117.17–118.5: *ye pi nigaṇṭhassa nāthaputtassa sāvakā gihī odāta-vasanā, te pi nigaṇṭhesu nāthaputtiyesu nibbiṇṇarūpā viratta-rūpā paṭivāna-rūpā, yathā taṃ durakkhāte dhamma-vinaye duppavedite aniyyānike anupasamasaṃvattanike asammā-sambuddha-ppavedite bhinnathūpe appaṭisaraṇe.* Additionally, s.v. *sa-stūpa* in SWTF; while the definition is for the opposite meaning, the entry gives similar references for the *a-stūpa* usage here.

287. Pāvā in Pali. A Malla city.

288. Jñātiputra is a common epithet for Mahāvīra, the founder of Jainism.

[**b**] [They spoke] as follows: "I know this dharma and vinaya; you do not know this dharma and vinaya. How I know this dharma and vinaya is like this, and how you know this dharma and vinaya is like this. My [understanding] is consistent and yours is inconsistent; mine is coherent and yours is incoherent." One said afterward what is to be said beforehand; another said beforehand what is to be said afterward. [They spoke further, saying]: ("What you have adhered to is totally refuted; your theory has been taken up for the sake of argument. For release from this argument, cast it aside; you are rebuked. Reveal if you know the answer. You have been asked, speak up."[289] In this way they strike and injure one another with sharp words. They accuse [...] their speech is not especially understood even by those who are in agreement with their dharma.)

[**c**] (Even the white-clad householder disciples of the Nirgrantha Jñātiputra reside feeling revulsion, aversion, disagreement, and alienation toward the Nirgranthas, the followers of Jñātipūtra who dwell split, divided, contentious, quarrelsome, aggressive, and fallen into dispute, obviously a result from this dharma and vinaya being ill-proclaimed), poorly imparted, (not conducive to emancipation, not leading to perfect awakening, broken, incohesive, and unreliable. The teacher is not a tathāgata, not an arhat, nor a complete, perfect buddha.) [...]

~15.1~

SHT IV 165 (43) (*Prāsādika-sūtra*)

A	B
a /// u[y].t. ///	a /// ya bha ///
b /// ṣu dvaidhajā ///	b /// pāyāṃ varṣā ///
c /// ḥ śrama ///	c /// [y]ābhinnāṇ=vai ///
	d /// m=ājāt. ///

DN III 117.1–118.5 (DN 29.1)

[a] 1. ekaṃ samayaṃ bhagavā sakkesu viharati. (vedhaññā nāma sakyā, tesaṃ ambavane pāsāde). tena kho pana samayena nigaṇṭho nāthaputto pāvāyaṃ adhunā kālakato hoti. tassa kālakiriyāya bhinnā nigaṇṭhā dvedhikajātā bhaṇḍana-jātā kalaha-jātā vivādāpannā aññamaññaṃ mukha-sattīhi vitūdantā viharanti—

289. These phrases are characterzed in the *Brahmajāla-sutta* (DN I 8.16–17) as quarrelsome speech (*viggāhikakathā*).

[b] na tvaṃ imaṃ dhamma-vinayaṃ ājānāsi, ahaṃ imaṃ dhamma-vinayaṃ ājānāmi, kiṃ tvaṃ imaṃ dhamma-vinayaṃ ājānissasi?—micchā-paṭipanno tvam asi, aham asmi sammā-paṭipanno,—sahitam me, asahitan te,—pure vacanīyaṃ pacchā avaca, pacchā vacanīyaṃ pure avaca,—aviciṇṇan te viparāvattaṃ—āropito te vādo, niggahīto 'si—cara vādappamokkhāya, nibbeṭhehi vā sace pahosīti. vadho yeva kho maññe nigaṇṭhesu nāthaputtiyesu vattati.

[c] ye pi nigaṇṭhassa nāthaputtassa sāvakā gihī odāta-vasanā, te pi nigaṇṭhesu nāthaputtiyesu nibbiṇṇarūpā viratta-rūpā paṭivāna-rūpā, yathā taṃ durakkhāte dhamma-vinaye duppavedite aniyyānike anupasamasaṃvattanike asammā-sambuddha-ppavedite bhinna-thūpe appaṭisaraṇe.

T I 1 72c13–28 (= DĀ 15.1–15.2)[290]
如是我聞。一時佛在迦維羅衛國緬祇優婆塞林中。與大比丘千二百五十人俱。時有沙彌周那在波波國。夏安居已執持衣鉢。漸詣迦維羅衛緬祇園中。至阿難所頭面禮足於一面立。白阿難言。波波城內有尼乾子命終未久。其諸弟子分爲二分。各共諍訟。面相毀罵無復上下。迭相求短競其知見。我能知是汝不能知。我行眞正汝爲邪見。以前著後以後著前。顚倒錯亂。無有法則。我所爲妙。汝所言非。汝有所疑當諮問我。大德阿難。時彼國人民事尼乾者。聞諍訟已生厭患心。阿難語周那沙彌曰。我等有言欲啓世尊。今共汝往宣啓此事。若世尊有所戒勅當共奉行。爾時沙彌周那聞阿難語已。即共詣世尊。頭面禮足在一面立。

~15.1a–c~[291]
SaṅgE 311–13 (= Saṅg 44–45) paragraphs 22–24 (= Saṅg v–x)
22/v (nirgrantho jñātiputraḥ kālakṛtaḥ pā)(11.c)(pā)y(āṃ | tasya kā)lakriyayā nir(gra)nthā jñātipu(t)r(ikā bhinnāḥ kalahakārakā viharanti bhaṇḍanakārakā vigṛhītā vivādam āpannāḥ |)
23/w–x (naitaṃ tvaṃ dharmavinaya)(11.d)m ājān(āsi |) aham etaṃ (dharmavinayam ājānāmi | kim etaṃ dharmavinayaṃ tvam ājānāsi |) .. .. .(sahitaṃ mama | asahi)(7.a)t(aṃ) t(a)v(a | pū)rvaṃ vacanīyaṃ paścād avocaḥ | paścād vacanīyaṃ pū(rvam avocaḥ | abhicīrṇaṃ te) .. .. (apahara vādaṃ vāda)(7.b)vipramokṣāya .. .. (ity anyonyaṃ) (13.1/16.1) mukh(aśak)t(i)k(ayā) v(i)tud(anto viharanti |) .. ..

290. The content cannot easily be separated between the sections.
291. The following parallel passages are also relevant for DĀ 15.2 and DĀ 15.3 below.

24/x (ye ’pi) n(ir)gr(an)thasya jñ(āti)(12.3/14.3)(pu)trasya śrāvakā gṛh(iṇo ’vadātavasa)(13.2/14.3)nā pāpāyāṃ prativasaṃti te ’pi ni(r)gra(ntheṣu jñātiputrikeṣu bhinneṣu vivādam āpanneṣu kalahajāteṣu) (12.4/14/4) bhaṇḍana(jā)teṣu vigṛhīt(eṣu nirviṇṇarūpāḥ prativāṇirūpā a)(13.3/16.3)samānarūpā apakrāntā yathā (dharmavinayād durākhyātād duṣpraveditād a)(12.5/14.5)niryāṇikād asaṃbodhagāmino bhinnād as(aṃstūpād apratiśaraṇāt |)

DN III 209.24–210.17 (*Saṅgīti-sutta*, DN 33.6)
6. tena kho pana samayena nigaṇṭho nātha-putto pāvāyaṃ adhunā kālakato hoti. tassa kāla-kiriyāya bhinnā nigaṇṭhā dvedhika-jātā bhaṇḍana-jātā kalahajātā vivādāpannā aññamaññaṃ mukha-sattīhi vitudantā virahanti—na tvaṃ imaṃ dhamma-vinayaṃ ājānāsi! ahaṃ imaṃ dhamma-vina-vinayaṃ ājānāmi! kiṃ tvaṃ imaṃ dhamma-vinayaṃ ājānissasi? micchā-paṭipanno tvam asi, aham asmi sammā-paṭipanno, sahitam me asahitan te, pure vacanīyaṃ pacchā avaca, pacchā vacanīyaṃ pure avaca, aviciṇṇan te viparāvattaṃ, āropito te vādo, niggahīto ’si cara, vāda-ppamokkhāya nibbeṭhehi vā sace pahosī ti. vadho yeva kho maññe nigaṇṭhesu nātha-puttiyesy vattati. ye pi te nigaṇṭhassa nāthaputtassa sāvakā gihī odāta-vasanā, te pi nigaṇṭhesu nātha-puttiyesu nibbiṇṇa-rūpā paṭivāna-rūpā, yathā taṃ durakkhāte dhamma-vinaye duppavedite aniyyānike anupasama-saṃvattanike asammāsambuddha-ppavedite bhinna-thūpe appaṭisaraṇe.

MN II 243.15–244.9 (*Sāmagāma-sutta* MN 104)
[a] ekaṃ samayaṃ bhagavā sakkesu viharati sāmagāme. tena kho pana samayena nigaṇṭho nātaputto pāvāyaṃ adhunā kālakato hoti. tassa kālakiriyāya bhinnā nigaṇṭhā dvedhikajātā bhaṇḍanajātā kalahajātā vivādāpannā aññamaññaṃ mukhasattīhi vitudantā viharanti:
[b] na tvaṃ imaṃ dhammavinayaṃ ājānāsi, ahaṃ imaṃ dhammavinayaṃ ājānāmi; kiṃ tvaṃ imaṃ dhammavinayaṃ ājānissasi, micchāpaṭipanno tvam asi, aham asmi sammāpaṭipanno; sahitam me, asahitan te; pure vacanīyaṃ pacchā avaca, pacchā vacanīyaṃ pure avaca; aviciṇṇan te viparāvattaṃ; āropito te vādo; niggahīto sī; cara vādappamokkhāya; nibbeṭhehi vā sace pahosīti. vadho yev’; eko maññe nigaṇṭhesu nātaputtiyesu vattati.
[c] ye pi nigaṇṭhassa nātaputtassa sāvakā gihī odātavasanā, te pi nigaṇṭhesu nātaputtiyesu nibbindarūpā virattarūpā paṭivāṇarūpā yathā taṃ durakkhāte dhammavinaye duppavedite aniyyānike anupasamasaṃvattanike asammāsambuddhappavedite bhinnatthūpe appaṭisaraṇe.

~15.1b~[292]

BLSF II.1: Or.15009/68 (Unidentified Sūtra (of the *Dīrghāgama*?) with passages from the śīlaskandha section)

verso

1 /// + .. dharma[vi]nay.

2 ///+ya[p].....voca•

3 /// [pa]hara vād. vā

4 /// hyakathāsa[m]ār.

5 /// .. mithyājīvena

6 ///++.o[v]auteyaṃgṛ

DĀ 27.45 (*Lohitya-sūtra I*) (Choi 2016)

(**374r5**) tadyathāham enaṃ dharmavinayam ājānāmi na tvaṃm enaṃ dharmavinayam ājānāsi <|> yathā cāham enaṃ dharmavinaya<ṃ> prajānāmi yathā na tvam enaṃ dharmavinayam ājānāsi <|> yuktaṃ ma(**374r6**)māyuktaṃ tava <|> sahitaṃ <mamāsahitaṃ> tava iti <|> pūrvvaṃ vacanīyaṃ paścād avocaḥ paścād vacanīyaṃ pūrvam avocaḥ <|> atitūrṇaṃ[293] te parāmṛṣṭam <|> āropitas te vādo vādārtham ¦ apahara vādaṃ (vāda)(**374r7**)(v)i(p)ramok(ṣ)āya <|> nigṛhīto 'si (n)i(rve)ṭhaya saty uttaraṃ prajānāsi <|> brūhi pṛṣṭa ⁝

DĀ 25.29 (*Tridaṇḍi-sūtra*) (Choi 2016)

yathāpi ta<t> tṛdaṇḍinn eke śramaṇabrāhmaṇāḥ śraddhādeyaṃ paribhujya vividhavigrahasamāra- mbhānuy(ogam anuyukt)ā vi(**363v4**)(ha)ranti <|> tadyathāham enaṃ dharmavinaya(m) ājānāmi na tva{ha}m ena<ṃ> dharmavinayam ājānāsi <|> yathā cāham enaṃ dharmavinayam ājānāmi yathā <ca> tvam enaṃ dharmavinayam ājānāsi <|> yu(k)t(aṃ) mamāyu(**363v5**)ktaṃ {samāyuktaṃ} tava <|> sahitaṃ mamā<sa>hitaṃ tava iti <|> pūrva<ṃ> vacanīyaṃ paścād avocaḥ paścād vacanīyaṃ pūrvam avocaḥ <|> abhitūrṇaṃ te viparāmṛṣṭam ¦ ā<ro>pitas te vādo vādārthāya <apa>hara vādaṃ (**363v6**) vādavipramokṣāya <|> nigṛhīto 'si <|> nirveṭhaya <sa>ty uttaraṃ prajānāmi <|> brūhi pṛṣṭa ⁝ ity apy evaṃrūpā<c> chramaṇo vividhavigrahasamārambhānuyogāt prativirato bhavati <|>

SBVG 510r6–9 (found in DĀ 27.45, Choi 2016) (= SBV II 236.13–23)

292. As with the immediately preceding passage (see note 291 above), the following passages are also relevant to the two subsequent sections. Even if they are not direct parallels, they reflect similar usage.

293. Ms. *apitūrṇaṃ*.

yathāpi tan mahāraja eke śramaṇabrāhmaṇā<ḥ> śraddhādeyāni paribhujya <vividha>vigṛhyakathāsamaraṃbhānu(yo)<gam anuyuktā> (G510r7) viharanti <|> tadyathā na tvam enaṃ dharmavinayam ājānāsi; aham enaṃ dharmavinayam ājānāmi; yathā cā{tva}ham enaṃ dharmavinayam ājānāmi; yathā ca tva{ha}m enaṃ dharmavinayam ājānāsi; yuktaṃ mamāyuktaṃ tava; sahitaṃ mamāsahitaṃ <tava iti; pūrvaṃ> (G510r8) vacanīyaṃ paścād avocaḥ; paścād vacanīyaṃ pūrvam avocaḥ; atitūrṇaṃ te parāmṛṣṭam; āropitas te vādo vādārthāya; apahara vādaṃ vādavipramokṣāya; <ni>gṛhīto 'si; nirveṭhaya saty uttaraṃ prajānāsi; brūhi pṛṣṭa ⁝ ity apy evaṃ- rūpāc chramaṇo vividhavi(gṛhyakathāsamāra)(G510r9)mbhānuyogāt) <prativirato bhavati |>

DN I 8.9–16 (*Brahmajāla-sutta*, DN 1.18)
na tvaṃ imaṃ dhamma-vinayaṃ ājānāsi, ahaṃ imaṃ dhamma-vinayaṃ ājānāmi, kiṃ tvaṃ imaṃ dhamma-vinayaṃ ājānissasi?—micchā-paṭipanno tvam asi, aham asmi sammā-paṭipanno—sahitam me, asahitan te—pure vacanīyaṃ pacchā avaca, pacchā vacanīyaṃpure avaca—aviciṇṇan te viparāvattaṃ—āropito te vādo, niggahīto 'si—cara vāda-ppamokkhāya, nibbeṭhehi vā sace pahosīti.

DN I 66.28–35 (*Sāmaññaphala-sutta*, DN 2.53)
na tvaṃ imaṃ dhamma-vinayaṃ ājānāsi, ahaṃ imaṃ dhamma-vinayaṃ ājānāmi, kiṃ tvaṃ imaṃ dhamma-vinayaṃ ājānissasi?—micchā-paṭipanno tvam asi, aham asmi sammā-paṭipanno—sahitam me, asahitan te—pure vacanīyaṃ pacchā avaca, pacchā vacanīyaṃ pure avaca—aviciṇṇan te viparāvattaṃ—āropito te vādo, niggahīto 'si—cara vāda-ppamokkhāya, nibbeṭhehi vā sace pahosīti.

■ ■ ■ ■ ■

DĀ 15.2

[a] (275r5) vārṣikāṇāṃ māsānām. .y.. ..ṛ /// (275r6)m anuprāpto medhyasya śākyasyāmravaṇa(ṃ)[294] a(tha c)u(nda)ḥ śr(a)m(aṇoddeśaḥ)[295] /// (ānanda)(275r7)sya pādau śirasā vanditvaikānte 'sthād; ekāntasthitaṃ cundaṃ (śramaṇoddeśam)[296] /// pāpā(275r8)yāṃ varṣā uṣita <|> tata etarhy āgacchāmi <|> pāpāyāṃ cāsmi va(rṣ)ā[297] (uṣyamāṇaḥ[298] pāpāyāṃ

294. Cf. 274v6. See note 277 above.

295. Cf. 274v5 and DN III 118.6–7: *atha kho cundo samaṇuddeso pāvāyaṃ vassaṃ vuttho.*

296. Cf. DN III 118.10: *ekamantaṃ nisinno kho cundo samaṇūddeso.*

297. Cf. 276r2.

298. This reconstruction is not based on a direct parallel. If it were, it would be recon-

nirgrantho jñātiputraḥ kālagato; yasya kālakriyayā nigranthā jñātiputrīya bhinnā dvidhājāt)ā[299] (275v1) vih(a)r(a)nt(i) kalahajātā bhaṇḍanajāt(ā vi)gṛh(ī)tā v(ivādam āpannāḥ |)[300]

[b] (tadyathāham enaṃ dharmavinayam ājānāmi na tvam enaṃ dharmavinayam ājānāsi | yathā cāham enaṃ dharmavinaya)(275v2)m[301] ājānāmi yathā ca {ta} tvam enaṃ dharmavinayam ājān(ās)i (| yuktaṃ mamāyuktaṃ tava sahitaṃ mamāsahitaṃ tava iti | pūrvaṃ vacanīyaṃ paścād avocat paścād vacanīyaṃ pūrvam avocat |)[302] (275v3) abhitūrṇaṃ[303] te

structed as *uṣita iti*, as seen in 276r2 below. However, that reading in the ms. is not without its own trouble, as the *iti* is rather awkward (see note 314 below). Thus I have chosen the present participle *uṣyamāṇaḥ* as the reconstruction instead of *uṣita iti*, as this captures what may likely have been the meaning and keeps the akṣara count with *uṣita iti*. This is not ideal and should be regarded as an educated guess.

299. Cf. 274v6, 276r2, and 276r3.

300. Cf. 274v7 and 276r3.

301. Cf. 274v7, 274v8, 276r3, and 276r4.

302. Cf. 274v8 and 276r4.

303. The ms. is clear, but this is an obscure word. The *Pāsādika-sutta* reads *aviciṇṇan* (DN III 117.14). *Aviciṇṇa*, according to CPD, is a wrong reading for *adhiciṇṇa* (s.v. *aviciṇṇa* in CPD and *viciṇṇa* in PTSD), and Ramers states that the commentaries give priority to such an interpretation (Ramers 1996, 262–63). Regardless, this does not parallel the readings found in Sanskrit. Following SBV II 236 and the Tibetan reading of *ha cang myur ba* (in the Tibetan translations of the *Saṅghabhedavastu*, *Bhaiṣajyavastu*, and *Kṣudrakavastu*), Choi (2016, 247) emends *apitūrṇaṃ* to *atitūrṇaṃ* in the *Lohitya-sūtra I* (DĀ 27.45). And if one looks at the actual ms. (SBV 510r7–8) Gnoli worked on for his edition, it is clear that he emended *abhitūrṇaṃ* to *atitūrṇaṃ* without any notation of this action. The reading in the *Tridaṇḍi-sūtra* (DĀ 25.29) (Choi 2016, 106) agrees with the reading in the ms. here, and SaṅgE reads *abhicīrṇa* in reconstruction. While *abhicīrṇa* can theoretically be translated as "totally refuted" (s.v. *abhicīrṇa* and *abhicūrṇa* in SWTF), *abhitūrṇa* equals *abhitunna* in Buddhist Hybrid Sanskrit and Pali in the sense of "afflicted," "overwhelmed," or "overpowered" (s.v. *abhitūrṇa* and *abhitunna* in BHSD and *abhitunna* in PTSD and CPD), and *atitūrṇa* is only found in Schmidt's *Nachträge zum Sanskrit-Wörterbuch in kürzerer Fassung von Otto Böhtlingk* with a very brief entry of *sehr -x-, allzu rasch* (very -x-, too quickly) (s.v. *atitūrṇa* in Schmidt and Boehtlingk, 1924). Despite its definition only being found in Schmidt's *Nachträge*, I have been tempted to emend to *atitūrṇaṃ* following Choi (2016, 106) but am hesitant after reading what were to my eyes very clear *bhi* akṣaras in the *Tridaṇḍi-sūtra* (DĀ 25.29) and the ms. on which Gnoli based his edition (SBV 5107–8). My translation of this phrase is "What you have adhered to is totally refuted…" (taking some liberty with the sense of *abhitūrṇa*), and Choi renders her translation as "What you have considered was [done] too quickly…" Perhaps there were (at least) two separate understandings of this passage based on received traditions of *abhitūrṇa* and *atitūrṇa* in the texts, or perhaps

vi(pa)rā(m)ṛṣṭa(m) ā(r)o(p)i(tas te) vādo vā(dārthāya apahara vādaṃ vāda-vipramokṣāya nigṛhīto 'si | nirveṭhaya yady uttaraṃ prajānāsi | brūhi pṛṣṭa | ity anyo)(**275v4**)(n)yaṃ (m)ukhaśaktikayā vitu(danti[304] v)i(rujanti | vi .. + + . anudhvaṃsayaṃti vadako 'py eṣāṃ na prajñāyate yad uta sahadharmeṇa |)[305]

[c] (ye 'pi te nirgranthasya jñātiputrasya śrāvakā) (**~275v5**) (gṛhiṇo 'vadātavasanāḥ prativasanti te 'pi nirgrantheṣu jñātiputrīyeṣu bhinneṣu dvidhājāteṣu viharanti kalahajāteṣu bhaṇḍanajāteṣu vigṛhīteṣu vivādam) (**~275v6**) (āpanneṣu nirviṇṇāḥ prativāṇayo 'samānā apakrāntā yathāpi tad durākhyātād dharmavinayād duṣpraveditāt anairyāṇikād asaṃbodhigāmino bhinnād astūpād[306] apratisa)(**~275v7**)(raṇāc; chāstā ca na tathāgato 'rhan samyaksaṃbuddhas |)[307] /// (**275v8**) ///[308]

DĀ 15.2

[a] [...] for the rainy season [...]. [...] the novice Cunda arrived at the mango forest of the Śākyan [named] Medhya [...]. [...] having paid homage by

---

the few witnesses we have before us disagree for another reason, but for the time being it must be left to the reader to decide which reading is preferred.

304. Ms. reads *[v]i[ra] .. .[i] .[i]*.

305. Cf. 274v7–275r2 and 276r5–6, DĀ 25.29 (*Tridaṇḍi-sūtra*, 363v5), and DĀ 27.45 (*Lohitya-sūtra I*, 374r6), SBV II 236.13–23, and SaṅgE 312 (= Saṅg 44) paragraph 23 (= Saṅg x).

306. Cf. 276r7, 277r1, 277r5, 277v3, and 278r2.

307. Cf. 276r6–8, SaṅgE 312–13 (= Saṅg 44–45) paragraph 24 (= Saṅg x): *(ye 'pi) n(ir)gr(an)thasya jñ(āti)*(12.3/14.3)*(pu)trasya śrāvakā gṛh(iṇo 'vadātavasa)*(13.2/14.3)*nā pāpāyāṃ prativasaṃti te 'pi ni(r)gra(ntheṣu jñātiputrikeṣu bhinneṣu vivādam āpanneṣu kalahajāteṣu)* (12.4/14.4) *bhaṇḍana(jā)teṣu vigṛhīt(eṣu nirviṇṇarūpāḥ prativāṇirūpā a)*(13.3/16.3)-*samānarūpā apakrāntā yathā (dharmavinayād durākhyātād duṣpraveditād a)*(12.5/14.5)-*niryāṇikād asaṃbodhagāmino bhinnād as(aṃstūpād apratiśaraṇāt |)*, and DN III 118.11–13: *nigaṇṭho bhante nāthaputto pāvāyaṃ adhunā kālakato. tassa kālakiriyāya bhinnā nigaṇṭhā dvedhika-jātā ... pe ... bhinna-thūpe appaṭisaraṇe ti*, which abbreviates DN III 117.17–118.5: *ye pi nigaṇṭhassa nāthaputtassa sāvakā gihī odāta-vasanā, te pi nigaṇṭhesu nāthaputtiyesu nibbiṇṇarūpā viratta-rūpā paṭivāna-rūpā, yathā taṃ durakkhāte dhamma-vinaye duppavedite aniyyānike anupasamasaṃvattanike asammā-sambuddha-ppavedite bhinna-thūpe appaṭisaraṇe.*

308. This folio is highly fragmentary, and the final line (275v8) is not extant. I have not found any relevant parallel passages that would allow a reconstruction of this line. It would seem to have indicated that Ānanda went to the Buddha to tell him what he had learned from Cunda.

placing his head at Ānanda's feet, he stood to the side. Standing to the side, the novice Cunda [...]. "[...] I spent the rainy season in Pāpā. I have come from there now. (While) I (was spending) the rainy season in Pāpā, (the Nirgrantha Jñātiputra died in Pāpā. With his death the Nirgranthas, the followers of Jñātipūtra), dwelled (split, divided), contentious, quarrelsome, aggressive, and (fallen) into dispute.

[b] "[They spoke] (as follows: 'I know this dharma and vinaya; you do not know this) dharma and vinaya. How I know this dharma and vinaya is like this, and how you know this dharma and vinaya is like this. (My [understanding] is consistent and yours is inconsistent; mine is coherent and yours is incoherent.' One said afterward what is to be said beforehand; another said beforehand what is to be said afterward. [They spoke further, saying]: ('What you have adhered to is totally refuted; (your) theory has been taken up for the sake of argument. (For release from this argument, cast it aside; you are rebuked. Reveal if you know the answer. You have been asked; speak up.' In this way) they strike and injure one another with sharp words. (They accuse [...] their speech is not especially understood even by those who are in agreement with their dharma.)

[c] ("Even white-clad householder disciples of the Nirgrantha Jñātiputra feel revulsion, aversion, disagreement, and alienation toward the Nirgranthas, the followers of Jñātipūtra who dwell split, divided, contentious, quarrelsome, aggressive, and fallen into dispute, obviously a result from this dharma and vinaya being ill-proclaimed, poorly imparted, not conducive to emancipation, not leading to perfect awakening, broken, incohesive, and unreliable. The teacher is not a tathāgata, not an arhat, nor a complete, perfect buddha.") [...]

~15.2~

DN III 118.6–20 (DN 29.2)

2. atha kho cundo samaṇuddeso pāvāyaṃ vassaṃ vuttho, yena sāmagāmo yen' āyasmā ānando ten' upasaṃkami, upasaṃkamitvā āyasmantaṃ ānandaṃ abhivādetvā ekamantaṃ nisīdi. ekamantaṃ nisinno kho cundo samaṇuddeso āyasmantaṃ ānandaṃ etad avoca:

nigaṇṭho bhante nāthaputto pāvāyaṃ adhunā kālakato. tassa kālakiriyāya bhinnā nigaṇṭhā dvedhika-jātā ... pe ... bhinna-thūpe appaṭisaraṇe ti.

evaṃ vutte āyasmā ānando cundaṃ samaṇuddesaṃ etad avoca: atthi kho idaṃ āvuso cunda kathā-pābhataṃ bhagavantaṃ dassanāya, āyām' āvuso cunda, yena bhagavā ten' upasaṃkamissāma, upasaṃkamitvā etam atthaṃ bhagavato ārocessāmāti.

evaṃ bhante ti kho cundo samaṇuddeso āyasmato ānandassa paccassosi.

T I 1 72c13–28 (= DĀ 15.1–15.2)[309]

如是我聞。一時佛在迦維羅衛國緬祇優婆塞林中。與大比丘千二百五十人俱。時有沙彌周那在波波國。夏安居已執持衣鉢。漸詣迦維羅衛緬祇園中。至阿難所頭面禮足於一面立。白阿難言。波波城内有尼乾子命終未久。其諸弟子分爲二分。各共諍訟。面相毀罵無復上下。迭相求短競其知見。我能知是汝不能知。我行眞正汝爲邪見。以前著後以後著前。顛倒錯亂。無有法則。我所爲妙。汝所言非。汝有所疑當諮問我。大徳阿難。時彼國人民事尼乾者。聞諍訟已生厭患心。阿難語周那沙彌曰。我等有言欲啓世尊。今共汝往宣啓此事。若世尊有所戒勅當共奉行。爾時沙彌周那聞阿難語已。即共詣世尊。頭面禮足在一面立。

~15.2a–c~[310]

▪ ▪ ▪ ▪ ▪

DĀ 15.3

[a] **(276r1)** + + (bhagavanta)m[311] idam avocat* <|> ayaṃ bhadanta cundaḥ śramaṇoddeśo yenāhaṃ[312] tenopasaṃkrānta upa(saṃ)kr(am)y(ā) .. + + (mama padau ś)ir(asā vanditvaikānte 'sthād; ekāntasthitaṃ cundaṃ śramaṇoddeśam)[313] **(276r2)** + + + (kutas e)tarhy āgacchasi <|> kutra cāsi varṣā (u)ṣ(i)ta iti <|> sa eṣa evam āha • pāpāto 'haṃ bhadantānandaitarhy āgacchā(m)i <|> pā(pāyāṃ c)āsmi varṣā uṣita iti[314] <|> pāpāyā(ṃ nirgrantho jñātiputraḥ kālagato); **(276r3)** (yasya kālakriyayā n)i(rgranthā) j(ñ)ātip(u)t(r)īyā bhi(nnā) d(v)idhājātā viharanti kalahajātā bhaṇḍanajā(tā v)i(gṛhītā)[315] vivādam āpannās;

309. The content cannot easily be separated between the sections.

310. See above in DĀ 15.1 for relevant parallel passages. See notes 291 and 292.

311. Cf. DN III 118.24.

312. Ms. reads *yenāṃha*.

313. Cf. 275r7.

314. This *iti* is not in a felicitous location, as one would expect the remainder of this section to be part of the Ānanda's quotation of what Cunda told him. I have translated the section as one quotation, taking the *iti* for the entire account.

315. Cf. 274v6.

[b] tadyathāham enaṃ dharmavinayam ā(jānāmi na tva)(**276r4**)(m enaṃ dharmavinayam ājānāsi | yathā cāha)m (e)n(aṃ) dh(ar)m(a)vin(a)yam[316] ājānāmi yathā ca tvam enaṃ dharmavinayam ājānāsi <|> y(u)ktaṃ <mamāyuktaṃ>[317] tava sahitaṃ mamā<sa>hitaṃ[318] tava iti <|> pūrvaṃ vacanīyaṃ p(a)śc(ā)d (a)v(o)c(a)t* (**276r5**) (paścād vacanīyaṃ pūrvam a)vo(cat)[319] <|> abh(it)ūrṇ(a)ṃ[320] te viparā(mṛṣṭam āro)pitas (t)e vādo vādārthāya apahara vādaṃ vādavipram(o)k(ṣ)āya nigṛhīto 'si <|> nirveṭhaya yady uttaraṃ prajānāsi <|> brūhi pṛ(**276r6**)(ṣṭa | ity anyonyaṃ mu)khaśaktikayā[321] vitudanti virujanti <|> vi .. + + . (anu)dhvaṃsayaṃti vadako 'py eṣāṃ[322] na prajñāyate yad uta sahadharmeṇa <|>

[c] ye 'pi te nirgranthasya jñātiputrasya śrāvakā gṛhiṇo 'vadā(**276r7**)(tavasan)āḥ[323] prativasanti te 'pi nirgrantheṣu jñātiputrī(yeṣ)u (bhinneṣu dvidhājāteṣu v)i(haranti)[324] kalahajāteṣu bhaṇḍanajāteṣu vi(gṛ)hīteṣu vivādam āpanneṣu nirvi{ṣa}ṇṇāḥ pr(a)ti(vāṇayo 'samānā a)(**276r8**)(pakrā)nt(ā)[325] yathāpi tad durākhyātād dharmavi(na)yād duṣpr(a)ve(d)i(tād anairyāṇikād asaṃbodhig)āmin(o) bh(i)nnād astūp(ā)d[326] apratisaraṇāc; chāstā ca <na>[327] tathāgato 'rhan samyaksaṃbuddhas;[328] tam enaṃ .. v.

316. Cf. 274v6–8.

317. Cf. 274v8 and 275v2.

318. Ms. reads *samāhitaṃ*. Cf. 274v8 and 275v2.

319. Cf.274v8.

320. Cf. 275v3. See also discussion in note 303.

321. Cf. 275v3, DĀ 25.29 (*Tridaṇḍi-sūtra*, 363v5–6), DĀ 27.45 (*Lohitya-sūtra I*, 374r6–7), and SBV II 236.13–23.

322. Ms. reads *edāṃ*.

323. Cf. DN III 118.1. Ms. reads *vadā + ...āṃ*.

324. Cf. 274v6–7, 275r8–275v1, and 276r2–3.

325. Cf. SaṅgE 312–13 (= Saṅg 44–45) paragraph 24 (= Saṅg x): *(ye 'pi) n(ir)gr(an)thasya jñ(āti)*(12.3/14.3)*(pu)trasya śrāvakā gṛh(iṇo 'vadātavasa)*(13.2/14.3)*nā pāpāyāṃ prativasaṃti te 'pi ni(r)gra(ntheṣu jñātiputrikeṣu bhinneṣu vivādam āpanneṣu kalahajāteṣu)* (12.4/14.4) *bhaṇḍana(jā)teṣu vigṛhīt(eṣu nirviṇṇarūpāḥ prativāṇirūpā a)*(13.3/16.3)-*samānarūpā apakrāntā yathā (dharmavinayād durākhyātād duṣpraviveditād a)*(12.5/14.5)-*niryāṇikād asaṃbodhagāmino bhinnād as(aṃstūpād apratiśaraṇāt |).*

326. Cf. 276r7, 277r1, 277r5, 277v3, and 278r2.

327. Cf. 276r7, 277r1–2, 277r5, 277v3, and 278r2.

328. Note that the scribe applies *sandhi* here between *samyamsaṃbuddhaḥ* and *tam* that would not appear had the scribe used punctuation. Generally, *sandhi* is not used in the ms. at the end of this phrase, suggesting unwritten punctuation. Cf. 276r8, 277v1, 277v4, and

.. + + + + + .. .ā(**276v1**) .. p(r)ābhṛtam bhagavantaṃ darśanāyop(asa)ṃ(k)ramitu(m) . + + ..ṃ (yena bha)gavāṃs tenopas(a)ṃkra(m)āvaḥ apy eva labhemahi bhagavato 'ntikāt kāṃcid eva gaṃbhīragaṃbhīrāṃ dharmyāṃ (kathāṃ)[329] + + ...

DĀ 15.3

[**a**] [...] [Ānanda] said this to the Blessed One. "Sir, the novice Cunda approached me, and having approached me [...] (having paid homage by placing his) head (at my feet, he stood to the side. Standing to the side, the novice Cunda) [...] '(From where) have you now come, and where did you spend the rainy season?' He spoke thus: 'Reverend Ānanda, now I have come from Pāpā, and I spent the rainy season in Pāpā. (The Nirgrantha Jñātiputra died) in Pāpā. (With his death) the Nirgranthas, the followers of Jñātipūtra, dwelled split, divided, contentious, quarrelsome, aggressive, and fallen into dispute.'

[**b**] '[They spoke] as follows: "I know this dharma and vinaya; (you do not know this dharma and vinaya. How I) know this dharma and vinaya (is like this), and how you know this dharma and vinaya is like this. My [understanding] is consistent and yours is inconsistent; mine is coherent and yours is incoherent." One said afterward what is to be said beforehand; (another said beforehand what is to be said afterward). [They spoke further, saying]: ("What you have adhered to is totally refuted; (your) theory has been taken up for the sake of argument. (For release from this argument, cast it aside; you are rebuked. Reveal if you know the answer. You have been asked; speak up." (In this way) they strike and injure (one another) with sharp words. They accuse [...] Their speech is not especially understood even by those who are in agreement with their dharma.

[**c**] 'Even white-clad householder disciples of the Nirgrantha Jñātiputra feel revulsion, aversion, disagreement, and alienation toward the Nirgranthas, the followers of Jñātipūtra who dwell (split, divided), contentious, quarrelsome, aggressive, and fallen into dispute, obviously a result from this dharma and vinaya being ill-proclaimed, poorly imparted, (not conducive

---

277v7, where *sandhi* is employed, and 276v3, 276v4, 276v8, 277r1, 277r3, and 277r6, where it is not.

329. *Dharmyām* here can only be followed by *kathām*. S.v. [3]*dharma* in BHSD and [2]*dhārma* in SWTF.

to emancipation), not leading to perfect awakening, broken, incohesive, and unreliable. The teacher is not a tathāgata, an arhat, a complete, perfect buddha.' That [...] to approach in order to behold the gift that is the Blessed One,[330] [...] we approach the Blessed One, hoping we may find in the presence of the Blessed One some profound lecture on dharma [...]."

~15.3~

DN III 118.21–119.2 (DN 29.3)

3. atha kho āyasmā ca ānando cundo ca samaṇuddeso yena bhagavā ten' upasaṃkamiṃsu, upasaṃkamitvā bhagavantaṃ abhivādetvā eka-m-antaṃ nisīdiṃsu. eka-m-antaṃ nisinno kho āyasmā ānando bhagavantam etad avoca:

ayaṃ bhante cundo samaṇuddeso evam āha—nigaṇṭho nāthaputto pāvāyaṃ adhunā kālakato. tassa kālakiriyāya bhinnā nigaṇṭhā dvedhika-jātā ... pe ... bhinna-thūpe appaṭisaraṇe ti.

evaṃ h' etaṃ cunda hoti durakkhāte dhamma-vinaye duppavedite aniyyānike anupasama-saṃvattanike asammāsambuddha-ppavedite.

T I 1 72c28–73a7

爾時阿難白世尊曰。此沙彌周那。在波波國夏安居已。執持衣鉢漸來至此。禮我足語我言。波波國有尼乾子命終未久。其諸弟子分爲二分。各共諍訟。面相毀罵無復上下。迭相求短競其知見。我能知是。汝不能知。我行眞正。汝爲邪見。以前著後以後著前。顛倒錯亂無有法則。我所言是。汝所言非。汝有所疑當諮問我。時彼國人民事尼乾者。聞諍訟已。生厭患心。

~15.3a–c~[331]

330. This feels like an odd turn of phrase but seems to be what is stated. Of course, the lacunae before and after this phrase complicate any confident translation.

331. See above for relevant parallel passages. See notes 291 and 292.

⁝ Ill-Proclaimed Dharma and Vinaya (DĀ 15.4–5)

DĀ 15.4

[a] (**276v2**) (bhagavā)ṃ[332] (cunda)ṃ śra(m)aṇoddeśam āmantrayate | iha bha(danta durākhyāto dharma)vinayo bhavati duṣpra<ti>vedito[333] 'nairyāṇiko 'saṃbodhigāmī {•} bhinno[334] 'stūpo 'pratisaraṇa<ḥ |> śāstā (ca) na (tathāgato 'rhan samya)(**276v3**)(ksaṃbuddhaḥ | ta)smiṃ[335] khalu cunda dharmavinaye śrāvako bhavati dharmānudharmapratipannaḥ sāmīcīpratipanno 'nudharmacārī[336] <|>

[**b**] evaṃrūpaś cunda (ś)r(āvako) garhyo bhavati dha(r)m(eṣ)v; (evaṃ ca punar) (**276v4**) (garhyo dharmeṣv āyuṣma)to[337] (d)u(r)ā(kh)yāto dharmavinayo (duṣpra)tivedi(t)o[338] 'nairyāṇiko 'saṃbodhigāmī bhinno 'stūpo 'pratisaraṇaḥ <|> śāstā ca na (tathā)gato 'rhan samyaksaṃbu(d)dh(a)ḥ[339] <|>

[c] t(as)m(iṃs t)v(am ā)(**276v5**)(yuṣman dharmavinaye dharmānudharmapratipannaḥ sām)ī(c)īpr(a)tip(a)nn(o 'n)udharmacā(r)ī[340] <|> (yat khalu c)unda[341] taṃ śrāvakam evaṃ praśaṃsitavyaṃ[342] manye(ta

332. Cf. 276v1.

333. Cf. 277r1, 277r2, 277r5, 277v7, 278r2, and 278r8.

334. Ms. reads *bhinnastūpo*.

335. Cf. 277r1, 277r7, and 277v5–6.

336. DhskD 18v10 does not parallel but reads this phrase similarly: *dharmānudharmapratipanno bhavati sāmīcīpratipanno 'nudharmacār* [sic].

337. Cf. 277r2, 277r8, and 277v6–7.

338. Cf. 276r8, 276v2, 276v7 276v8, 277r2, and 277r5.

339. Cf. 277r3.

340. Cf. 276v3, 277r3, 277v1, and 277v8.

341. Cf. 277r3.

342. Throughout the text both *praśas*° and *praśaṃs*° are used interchangeably. This usage of

dharme)ṣ(v)āyuṣmann[343] akām(a)ko 'duḥkhasaha(**276v6**)(+ + + + + bhaviṣyas)y (ārādhayi)ṣ(ya)s(i n)yāyyaṃ[344] dharmaṃ kuśalam iti <|>

[**d**] tatra cunda yaś ca praśaṃsati yaś ca praśaṃsyate yaś ca praśasyamānas ta(th)ā[345] tathā pratip(a)dy(a)te (sarve te bahv a)(**276v7**)(puṇyaṃ[346] prasūyante | evam etac)[347] cunda bh(a)v(a)ti[348] yathāpi tad du(r)ākhyāto[349] dharmavinayo duṣpratívedito 'nairyāṇiko 'saṃbodhigāmī bhinno 'stūpo 'pratisaraṇīyaḥ <|> śā(stā ca na tathāgato 'rhan samya)(**276v8**)(ksaṃbuddhaḥ | evaṃrūpe cu)nda dharmavinaye śā(s)tāpi[350] garhyo dharmo 'pi śrāvako 'py anenāṃgena garhyaḥ <|>

DĀ 15.4

[a] The Blessed One addressed the novice Cunda. "In this case, sir, there is a dharma and vinaya that is ill-proclaimed, poorly imparted, not conducive to emancipation, not leading to perfect awakening, broken, incohesive, and unreliable. The teacher is not (a tathāgata, not an arhat, nor a complete, perfect buddha). Now then, Cunda, regarding such a dharma and vinaya, there is a disciple who practices according to the true method of the dharma, practices with propriety, and behaves according to dharma.

[**b**] "Regarding dharmas, a disciple of this kind, Cunda, is blameworthy. (And thus, further regarding dharmas, the dharma and vinaya) of that venerable one (is blameworthy): [it is] ill-proclaimed, poorly imparted, not conducive to emancipation, not leading to perfect awakening, broken,

---

the word with and without the *anusvāra* is seen often in Buddhist literature. S.v. *praśaṃs*, *praśaṃsiya*, and *praśasya* in SWTF.

343. Cf. 277r3–4, 277v3, and 277v8.

344. Cf. 277r4, 277v2, and 278r1.

345. Cf. 278r1.

346. EFGH 13.14 reads *bahuśaḥ pāpaṃ*, but *bahv apuṇyaṃ* seems more likely, considering 277r5 was probably mistakenly written as *bahu puṇyaṃ* instead of *bhav apuṇyaṃ* as *hva* and *hu* are so similar in appearance.

347. Cf. 277r5, 277v3, 278r1, and EFGH 13.14.

348. Cf. 278r2.

349. Cf. 277v5.

350. Cf. 277r6, 277v4, and 278r2.

incohesive, unreliable. The teacher is not a tathāgata, not an arhat, nor a complete, perfect buddha.

[c] "'Regarding this (dharma and vinaya, venerable sir, you practice according to the true method of the dharma), you practice with propriety, and you behave according to the dharma.' Cunda, that disciple is to be praised in this way: 'Please be informed,[351] venerable sir, regarding dharmas, unwilling [...] you will be. You will accomplish this correct, wholesome dharma.'

[d] "In that case, Cunda, one who praises, one who is praised, and one who is being praised, in whatever manner one practices, (they all produce much demerit. This is so), Cunda, obviously because there is a dharma and vinaya that is ill-proclaimed, poorly imparted, not conducive to emancipation, not leading to perfect awakening, broken, incohesive, and unreliable. The teacher (is not a tathāgata, not an arhat, nor a complete, perfect buddha). Regarding a dharma and vinaya (of this kind), Cunda, the teacher is blameworthy, as is the dharma, and by this aspect, the disciple too is blameworthy."

~15.4~

DN III 119.24–120.14 (DN 29.5)

5. idha pana cunda satthā ca hoti asammā-sambuddho, dhammo ca durakkhāto duppavedito aniyyāniko anupasamasaṃvattaniko asammāsambuddha-ppavedito, sāvako ca tasmiṃ dhamme dhammānudhamma-paṭipanno viharati sāmīci-paṭipanno anudhamma-cārī, samādāya taṃ dhammaṃ vattati. so evam assa vacanīyo—tassa te āvuso alābhā, tassa te dulladdhaṃ, satthā ca te asammāsambuddho, dhammo ca durakkhāto duppavedito aniyyāniko anupasama-saṃvattaniko asammāsambuddha-ppavedito, tvañ ca tasmiṃ dhamme dhammānudhammapaṭipanno viharasi sāmīci-paṭipanno anudhamma-cārī, samādāya taṃ dhammaṃ vattasīti. iti kho cunda satthā pi tattha gārayho, dhammo pi tattha gārayho, sāvako pi tattha evaṃ gārayho. yo kho cunda evarūpaṃ sāvakaṃ evaṃ vadeyya—addhā yasmā ñāya-paṭipanno ñāyam ārādhessatīti, yo ca pasaṃsati yañ ca pasaṃsati yo ca pasattho bhiyyoso-mattāya viriyaṃ ārabhati, sabbe te bahuṃ apuññaṃ pasavanti. taṃ kissa hetu? evaṃ h' etaṃ cunda hoti durakkhāte

351. *Yat khalu ... manyeta,* taking √*man* for √*jñā*. S.v. *yat khalu* or *yaṃ khalu* in BHSD: "with a 2d (or polite 3d) person form of *jñā* (regularly opt[ative]), the whole phrase meaning please be informed; allow me to inform you." S.v. *khalu* (e) in SWTF as well.

dhamma-vinaye duppavedite aniyyānike anupasama-saṃvattanike asammā-sambuddha-ppavedite.

T I 1 73a23–73b2
佛告周那。彼雖有師然懷邪見。雖復有法盡不眞正。不足聽採不能出要。非三耶三佛所說。猶如朽塔不可汙色。彼諸弟子法法成就。隨順其行起諸邪見。周那。若有人來語其弟子言。汝師法正汝所行是。今所修行勤苦如是。應於現法成就道果。彼諸弟子信受其言者。則二俱失道獲無量罪。所以者何。以法不眞正故。

EFGH 13.14[352]
durākhyāte dharma-vinaye *(a)* yaś ca samādāpayati, *(b)* yaś ca samādāpyate, *(c)* yaś ca samā(dāpitas tathatāṃ pratipadyate sarve te bahuśaḥ pāpaṃ pra)(*DlV5*) savanti, evam etad bhavati yathāpi tad durākhyāto dharma-vinayaḥ |

svākhyāte dharma-vinaye *(a)* yaś ca samādāpayati, *(b)* yaś ca samādāpyate, *(c)* y(aś ca samādāpitas tathatāṃ pratipadyate, sarve te bahuśaḥ) (*DlV6*) [p](u)ṇ(y)aṃ prasavanti, evam etad bhavati yathāpi tad svākhyāto dharma-vinayaḥ ||

DN III 210.18–23 (*Saṅgīti-sutta*, DN 33.7)
7. atha kho āyasmā sāriputto bhikkhū āmantesi:
nigaṇṭho āvuso nātha-putto pāvāyaṃ adhunā {kālakato.} tassa kāla-kiriyāya bhinnā nigaṇṭhā dvedhika-jātā ... pe ... bhinna-thūpe appaṭisaraṇe. evaṃ h' etaṃ āvuso durakkhāte dhamma-vinaye duppavedite aniyyānike anupasama-saṃvattanike asammāsambuddha-ppavedite.

▪ ▪ ▪ ▪ ▪

DĀ 15.5
[a] punar aparaṃ cunda durā(khyāt)o[353] dharmavinayo (bha)v(a)ti[354] d(uṣprativedito) + + + + + + (**277r1**) 'n(ai)ryāṇiko[355] 'sambodhigāmī bhinno 'stūpo 'pratisaraṇaḥ <|> śāstā ca na tathāgato 'rhaṃ samyaksaṃbuddhaḥ <|> tasmin khalu cunda dharmavinaye śrāvako bhavati na dharmānudharmapratipanno na sāmīcīpratipanno nānudharmacārī <|> (**277r2**)

352. This and the following passage also parallel DĀ 15.5.

353. Cf. 276r8, 276v2, 276v4, 276v7, 277v2, and 277v5.

354. Cf. 276v2 and 277r6.

355. Cf. 276r8, 276v2, 276v4, 276v7, 277v2, and 277v5.

[**b**] evaṃrūpaś cunda śrāvakaḥ {na} praśasyo bhavati dharmeṣu <|> evaṃ ca punaḥ <na> praśasyo bhavati dharmeṣv āyuṣmato {dharmavinayo} durākhyāto dharmavinayo duṣpratived ito 'nairyāṇiko 'saṃbodhigāmī bhinno 'stūpo[356] 'pratisaraṇaḥ <|> (**277r3**) śāstā ca na (tathāga)to[357] 'rhan samyaksaṃbuddhas;

[**c**] tasmiṃs tvam āyuṣman dha(r)mavinaye[358]<na>[359] dharmānudharma-pratipan(n)o[360] na sāmīcīpratipanno nānudharmacārī <|> yat khalu cunda taṃ śrāvakam evaṃ samādāpayit(a)vy(aṃ)[361] manyeta dharme(**277r4**)ṣv eva āyuṣman na te dha(r)mā<ḥ> śāstrādhi(gatās tāṃs) tv(a)ṃ[362] sādhu ca suṣṭhu ca samād. ya .. .ta .. .. (bhaviṣyasy ārādhayi)ṣyasi[363] nyāyyaṃ dharmaṃ kuśalam iti <|>

[**d**] tatra cunda yaś ca samād(āpayat)i[364] (yaś ca sam)ādāpyate[365] (**277r5**) yaś ca samādāpyamānas tathā ta(th)ā[366] (p)rati(pad)y(ate)[367] sarve te bahv apuṇyaṃ[368] prasūya(nte)[369] <|> ev(am)[370] e(tac cunda bhava)ti[371] y(a)thāp(i) tad durākhyāto dharmavinayo duṣpravedito 'nairyāṇiko 'saṃbodhigāmī bhinno 'stūpo (**277r6**) 'pratisaraṇaḥ <|> śāstā ca na tathāgato

356. Ms. reads *stūpa*. Cf. 277r1.

357. Cf. 276r8, 276v2, 276v4, 276v7, 277r1, 277v4, and 277v7.

358. Cf. 276v3, 276v5, 277r1, 277v6, and 277v8.

359. Cf. 277r1.

360. Cf. 276v3, 276v5, 277r1, 277v6, and 277v8.

361. Cf. 276v5 and 277v8.

362. Cf. 277v2.

363. Cf. 276v6, 277v2, and 278r1.

364. Cf. 277v2 and EFGH 13.14.

365. Cf. 276v6, 277v2, 278r1, and EFGH 13.14.

366. Cf. 276v6 and 278r1. Note, however, *tathatāṃ pratipadyate* in EFGH 13.14.

367. Cf. 276v6, 278r1, and EFGH 13.14.

368. Ms reads *bahu puṇyaṃ* but this is contextually incorrect and one can imagine it being very easy for a scribe to mistakenly write *hu* for *hva* as they are so similar. Cf. DN III 120.10–11: *sabbe te bahuṃ apuññaṃ pasavanti* and EFGH 13.14.

369. Cf. 276v6–7, 277v3, 278r1, and EFGH 13.14. Note that the EFGH reads *prasavanti*, the *parasmaipada* form of the same root, *pra √sū*, while the *Prāsādika-sūtra* uses the *ātmanepada* conjugation.

370. Cf. 277v3 and EFGH 13.14.

371. Cf. 276v7, 277v3, 278r1, and EFGH 13.14.

'rhan samyaksaṃbuddhaḥ <|> evaṃ(r)ūpe (cunda dharmav)i(na)y(e śā)st(āp)i[372] garhyo dharmo 'pi śrāvakas tv anenāṃgena praśasya<ḥ>[373] |

DĀ 15.5

[a] [Buddha:] "Moreover, Cunda, there is a dharma and vinaya that is ill-proclaimed, poorly imparted, [...] not conducive to emancipation, not leading to perfect awakening, broken, incohesive, and unreliable. The teacher is not a tathāgata, not an arhat, nor a complete, perfect buddha. Now then, Cunda, regarding such a dharma and vinaya, there is a disciple who does not practice according to the true method of the dharma, does not practice with propriety, and does not behave according to dharma.

[b] "Regarding dharmas, a disciple of this kind, Cunda, is praiseworthy. And thus, further regarding dharmas, the dharma and vinaya of that venerable one is <not> praiseworthy among dharmas: [it is] ill-proclaimed, poorly imparted, not conducive to emancipation, not leading to perfect awakening, broken, incohesive, and unreliable. The teacher is not a tathāgata, not an arhat, nor a complete, perfect buddha.

[c] "'Regarding this dharma and vinaya, venerable sir, you do not practice according to the true method of the dharma, you do not practice with propriety, and you do not behave according to dharma.' Cunda, that disciple is to be urged in this way: 'Please be informed,[374] venerable sir, surely regarding dharmas, those dharmas that are not found within the precepts, you, those wonderful and excellent [...] (you will be). You will accomplish this correct, wholesome dharma.'

[d] "In that case, Cunda, one who urges, (one who) is urged, and one who is being urged, in whatever manner one practices, they all produce much demerit. This is so, (Cunda,) because there is obviously a dharma and vinaya that is ill-proclaimed, poorly imparted, not conducive to emancipation,

372. Cf. 276v8, 277v4, and 278r2.

373. The irregular usage of *sandhi* and punctuation in the ms. is illustrated here as *sandhi* is used between *praśasyaḥ* and the *iha* that begins the next section (making *praśasya iha*) even though the two words are separated by a *daṇḍa* while a very similar passage in 277v5 (*garhyaḥ iha*) takes the opposite approach where a *daṇḍa* separating the two words is omitted and *sandhi* is not applied, which is used to mark punctuation instead.

374. *Yat khalu* [...] *manyeta*, see note 351 above.

not leading to perfect awakening, broken, incohesive, and unreliable. The teacher is not a tathāgata, not an arhat, nor a complete, perfect buddha. Regarding a dharma and vinaya of this kind, (Cunda), the teacher is blameworthy, as is the dharma, but by this aspect, the disciple is praiseworthy."

~15.5~[375]

DN III 119.3–23 (DN 29.4)

4. idha cunda satthā ca hoti asammā-sambuddho; dhammo ca durakkhāto duppavedito aniyyāniko anupasamasaṃvattaniko asammāsambuddha-ppavedito; sāvako ca tasmiṃ dhamme na dhammānudhamma-paṭipanno viharati na sāmīci-paṭipanno na anudhamma-cāri, vokkamma ca tamhā dhammā vattati. so evam assa vacanīyo—tassa te āvuso lābhā, tassa te suladdhaṃ, satthā ca te asammāsambuddho, dhammo ca durakkhāto duppavedito aniyyāniko anupasama-saṃvattaniko asammāsambuddha-ppavedito, tvañ ca tasmiṃ dhamme na dhammānudhammapaṭipanno viharasi na sāmīci-paṭipanno na anudhammacārī, vokkamma ca tamhā dhammā vattasīti. iti kho cunda satthā pi tattha gārayho, dhammo pi tattha gārayho, sāvako ca tattha evaṃ pāsaṃso. yo kho cunda evarūpaṃ sāvakaṃ evaṃ vadeyya—et' āyasmā tathā paṭipajjatu yathā te satthārā dhammo desito paññatto ti, yo ca samādapeti yañ ca samādapeti yo ca samādapito tathattāya paṭipajjati, sabbe te bahuṃ apuññaṃ pasavanti. taṃ kissa hetu? evaṃ h' etaṃ cunda hoti durakkhāte dhamma-vinaye duppavedite aniyyānike anupasama-saṃvattanike asammāsambuddha-ppavedite.

T I 1 73a7–17

世尊告周那沙彌曰。如是周那。彼非法中不足聽聞。此非三耶三佛所說。猶如朽塔難可汙色。彼雖有師盡懷邪見。雖復有法盡不眞正。不足聽採不能出要。非是三耶三佛所說。猶如故塔不可汙也。彼諸弟子有不順其法。捨彼異見。行於正見。周那。若有人來語彼弟子。諸賢。汝師法正當於中行。何以捨離。其彼弟子信其言者。則二俱失道獲無量罪。所以者何。彼雖有法。然不眞正故。

375. Further parallel passages may be found in ~15.4~ above. See note 352.

: Well-Proclaimed Dharma and Vinaya (DĀ 15.6–7)

DĀ 15.6

[**a**] iha cunda svākhyāto dharmavinayo (bhavat)i[376] (suprat)i(ve)(**277r7**) (d)ito[377] nairyāṇikaḥ (sa)ṃbhodigāmī[378] abhinnaḥ sastūpaḥ[379] <sa>pratisaraṇ(aḥ | śāstā ca tathāgatho 'rha)n samyaksaṃbuddhaḥ | t(a)s(m)i(n) khalu{r} (c)unda dharmavinaye śrāvako bhavati <na>[380] dharmānudha(r)m(a)pr(a)t(i)panno n(na) sāmīcī(p)r(at)i(panno nānudha)(**277r8**)rmacārī[381] <|>

[**b**] evaṃrūpaś cunda śrāvako bhavati garhy(o)[382] (dhar)m(e)ṣv;[383] evaṃ ca (p)u(naḥ praśasyo bhavati dharmesv āyuṣmataḥ sv)ā(kh)y(ā)to dharmavinayaḥ suprativedito nairyāṇikaḥ saṃbodhigāmī abhi(nnaḥ sastūpaḥ sapratisaranaḥ | śā)(**277v1**)stā[384] ca tathāgato 'rhan samyaksaṃbuddhas;[385]

[**c**] tasmiṃs tva(m ā)yuṣmaṃ dharmavi(naye na dharmānudharmapratipanno na sāmīcīpratipanno nānudharmacārī <|> ya)t[386] kh(a)lu (c)

376. Cf. 276v2, 276v8, and 277v5.

377. Cf. 277v5 and 277v7.

378. Cf. 276r8, 276v2, 276v4, 276v7, 277r1, 277r2, 277r5, 277v5, 277v7, and 278r2.

379. *Sastūpaḥ* apprears to be an alternate for *saṃstūpa*. S.v. *saṃstūpa* in BHSD.

380. Cf. 277r1.

381. Cf. 276v2–3 and 277r1.

382. Cf. 276v3 and 277v5.

383. Cf. 276v3, 277r2, 277v6.

384. Cf. 277v7.

385. Note that the scribe applies *sandhi* here between *samyaksaṃbuddhaḥ* and *tasmin* that would not appear had the scribe used punctuation. Generally, *sandhi* is not used in the ms. at the end of this phrase, suggesting unwritten punctuation. Cf. 276r8, 277v1, 277v4, and 277v7, where *sandhi* is employed, and 276v3, 276v4, 276v8, 277r1, 277r3, and 277r6, where it is not.

386. Cf. 276v5, 277r3, and 277v8.

unda taṃ śrāvakam evaṃ samādāp(y)i(tavyaṃ manyeta dharmeṣu)[387] (**277v2**) addhā āyuṣman ye te dharmāḥ śāstrādhigatā<s> tāṃs tvaṃ sādhu ca suṣ(ṭh)u[388] ca s(amā + + + + + + + + bhav)iṣyasy ā(r)ādhayiṣy(a)si nyāyya(ṃ) dharma(ṃ)[389] kuṣalam iti <|>

[**d**] tatra cunda yas samād(āpayati yaś ca samā)(**277v3**)dāpyate[390] yaś ca samādāpyamānas[391] tathā tathā prati(pad)y(ate sarve te bahu puṇyaṃ prasū)yante[392] <|> evam etac cunda bhavati yathāpi {tathāpi}[393] ta(t)[394] sv(ā)khyāto dharmavinay(a)ḥ[395] (s)u(pratīvedito) (**277v4**) nairyāṇikaḥ saṃbodhigāmī abhi(nnaḥ sas)tūpaḥ[396] sapratisaraṇaḥ <|> ś(ā)stā[397] c(a tathā-ga)to[398] 'rhan samyaksaṃbuddha;[399] evaṃrūp(e){ṣu}[400] cunda dharmavinaye śāstāpi praśasyo dharmo 'pi śrāvakas tv ane(**277v5**)nāṃgena garhyaḥ <|>

DĀ 15.6

[a] [Buddha:] "In this case, Cunda, there is a dharma and vinaya that is well proclaimed, properly imparted, conducive to emancipation, leading to per-

387. Cf. 277r3 and 277v8.

388. Cf. 277r4.

389. Cf 276v6, 277r4, and 278r1.

390. Cf. 276v6, 277r4, 278r1, and EFGH 13.14.

391. Ms reads *samādāpyamānaḥ*.

392. Cf. 276v6–7, 277r5, 278r1, and EFGH 13.14. Note that EFGH reads *prasavanti*, the *parasmaipada* form of the same root, *pra√sū*, while the *Prāsādika-sūtra* uses the *ātmanepada* conjugation.

393. This is not found in 276v7, 277r5, or 278r1.

394. Cf. 276v7, 277r5, and 278r2.

395. Cf 277v7 and 278r2.

396. Cf. 277r7–8, 277v7, and 278r2. Note however that 278r2 reads *abhbinnasastūpa* in the ms.

397. Cf. 276v3, 276v4, 276v7, 277r1, 277r3, 277r6, 277r7, 277r8–277v1, 277v7, and 278r2.

398. Cf. 277r7, 277r8, 277v7, and 278r2.

399. Note that the scribe applies *sandhi* here between *samyaksaṃbuddhaḥ* and *evaṃ* that would not appear had the scribe used punctuation. Generally, *sandhi* is not used in the ms. at the end of this phrase, suggesting unwritten punctuation. Cf. 276r8, 277v1, 277v4, and 277v7, where *sandhi* is employed, and 276v3, 276v4, 276v8, 277r1, 277r3, and 277r6, where it is not.

400. Cf. 276v8, 277r6, and 278r2.

fect awakening, intact, cohesive, and reliable. (The teacher is a tathāgata, an arhat, a complete, perfect buddha). Now then, Cunda, regarding such a dharma and vinaya, there is a disciple who does <not> practice according to the true method of the dharma, does not practice with propriety, and does not behave according to dharma.

[**b**] "Regarding dharmas, a disciple of this kind, Cunda, is blameworthy. And thus, further regarding dharmas, the dharma and vinaya (of that venerable one is praiseworthy): [it is] well proclaimed, properly imparted, conducive to emancipation, leading to perfect awakening, intact, (cohesive, and reliable). The teacher is a tathāgata, an arhat, a complete, perfect buddha.

[**c**] "'Regarding this dharma and vinaya, venerable sir, you (do not practice according to the true method of the dharma, you do not practice with propriety, and you do not behave according to dharma).' Cunda, that disciple is to be urged in this way: 'Please be informed,[401] venerable sir, certainly (regarding dharmas), those dharmas that are obtained by the teacher, those you wonderfully and excellently[402] [...] you will be. You will accomplish this correct, wholesome dharma.'

[**d**] "In that case, Cunda, one who urges, one who is urged, and one who is being urged, in whatever manner one practices, (they all) produce (much merit). This is so, Cunda, because there is obviously a dharma and vinaya that is well proclaimed, properly imparted, conducive to emancipation, leading to perfect awakening, intact, cohesive, and reliable. The teacher is a tathāgata, an arhat, a complete, perfect buddha. Regarding a dharma and vinaya of this kind, Cunda, the teacher is praiseworthy, as is the dharma, but by this aspect, the disciple is blameworthy."

401. *Yat khalu* [...] *manyeta*, see note 351 above.

402. *Sādhu ca suṣṭhu*... The phrase *sādhu ca suṣṭhu* is often associated with hearing (often appearing with the root √*śru*) and is taken adverbially. There is no testament to the act of hearing in the manuscript, although it may appear in the lacuna. Since we cannot be sure what lies in the lacuna, the translation must remain unclear.

~15.6~

DN III 120.15–35 (DN 29.6)

6. idha pana cunda satthā ca hoti sammā-sambuddho dhammo ca svākkhāto suppavedito niyyāniko upasamasaṃvattaniko sammāsambuddhappavedito, sāvako ca tasmiṃ dhamme na dhammānudhamma-paṭipanno viharati na sāmīci-paṭipanno na anudhamma-cārī, vokkamma ca tamhā dhammā vattati. so evam assa vacanīyo—tassa te āvuso alābhā, tassa te dulladdhaṃ, satthā ca te sammāsambuddho, dhammo ca svākkhāto suppavedito niyyāniko upasama-saṃvattaniko sammāsambuddha-ppavedito, tvañ ca tasmiṃ dhamme na dhammānudhamma-paṭipanno viharasi na sāmīci-paṭipanno na anudhamma-cārī, vokkamma ca tamhā dhammā vattasīti. iti kho cunda satthā pi tattha pāsaṃso, dhammo pi tattha pāsaṃso, sāvako ca tattha evaṃ gārayho. yo kho cunda evarūpaṃ sāvakaṃ evaṃ vadeyya—et' āyasmā tathā paṭipajjatu yathā te satthārā dhammo desito paññatto ti,' yo ca samādapeti yañ ca samādapeti yo ca samādapito tathattāya paṭipajjati, sabbe te bahuṃ puññaṃ pasavanti. taṃ kissa hetu? evaṃ h' etaṃ cunda hoti svākkhāte dhammavinaye suppavedite niyyānike upasamasaṃvattanike sammāsambuddha-ppavedite.

T I 1 73a17–23

周那。若師不邪見其法眞正。善可聽採能得出要。三耶三佛所說。譬如新塔易可汙色。然諸弟子於此法中。不能勤修不能成就。捨平等道入於邪見。若有人來語彼弟子。諸賢。汝師法正當於中行。何以捨離入於邪見。其彼弟子信其言者。則二俱見眞正獲無量福。所以者何。其法眞正。

EFGH 13.14[403]

durākhyāte dharma-vinaye *(a)* yaś ca samādāpayati, *(b)* yaś ca samādāpyate, *(c)* yaś ca samā(dāpitas tathatāṃ pratipadyate sarve te bahuśaḥ pāpaṃ pra)(*DlV5*)savanti, evam etad bhavati yathāpi tad durākhyāto dharma-vinayaḥ |

svākhyāte dharma-vinaye *(a)* yaś ca samādāpayati, *(b)* yaś ca samādāpyate, *(c)* y(aś ca samādāpitas tathatāṃ pratipadyate, sarve te bahuśaḥ) (*DlV6*) [p](u)ṇ(y)aṃ prasavanti, evam etad bhavati yathāpi tad svākhyāto dharma-vinayaḥ ||

SaṅgE 313–14 (= Saṅg 45) paragraph 25 (= Saṅg y)

25/y (ayaṃ khalu tathā)(13.4/16.4)gato 'rhan samyaksaṃbuddho 'smakaṃ (śāstā | svākhyātaś cāyaṃ dharmavinayaḥ suprave)(12.6/14.6)d(i)to naiyāṇikaḥ

403. The following passages also parallel DĀ 15.7 below.

saṃbodhagāmy abhinnaḥ sa(ṃstūpaḥ sapratiśaraṇaḥ | śāstā cāsya tathā)(13.5/16.5)-gato 'rhan samyaksaṃbuddhaḥ |

DN III 211.1–14 (*Saṅgīti-sutta*, DN 33.7)
ayaṃ kho pan' āvuso asmākaṃ bhagavatā dhammo svākkhāto suppavedito niyyāniko upasama-saṃvattaniko sammāsambuddha-ppavedito. tattha sabbeh' eva saṃgāyitabbaṃ na vivaditabbaṃ, yathayidaṃ brahmacariyaṃ addhaniyaṃ assa cira-ṭṭhitikaṃ, tad assa bahujana-hitāya bahujana-sukhāya lokānukampāya atthāya hitāya sukhāya deva-manussānaṃ.

katamo c' āvuso asmākaṃ bhagavatā dhammo svākkhāto suppavedito niyyāniko upasama-saṃvattaniko sammāsambuddha-ppavedito, yattha sabbeh' eva saṅgāyitabbaṃ na vivaditabbaṃ yathayidaṃ brahmacariyaṃ addhaniyaṃ assa cira-ṭṭhitikaṃ, tad assa bahujana-hitāya bahujanasukhāya lokānukampāya atthāya hitāya sukhāya devamanussānaṃ?

▪ ▪ ▪ ▪ ▪

DĀ 15.7

[**a**] iha cunda svā(kh)y(āto dha)rmavinayo[404] bhavati suprati(ved)i(to nairyāṇikaḥ saṃbodhi)gāmī[405] abhinnaḥ sastupaḥ sapratisaraṇa<ḥ |> śāstā ca tathāg(a)to[406] 'rhan samyaksaṃ(**277v6**)buddhaḥ <|> (tasmiṃ kha)lu[407] dharmavinaye śrāvako[408] bhava{ṃ}ti dharmānudharmapratipannaḥ s(ā)m(ī)c(ī)pr(a)tip(a)nno[409] 'nudharmacārī <|>

[**b**] evaṃrūpa<ś> cunda{ḥ}[410] śrāvakaḥ praśasyo bhavati dharmeṣv; evaṃ ca punaḥ (**277v7**) praś(a)syo[411] bhavati dharmeṣv āyuṣmata<ḥ> svākhyāto dharmavinayaḥ suprativedito nairyāṇikaḥ saṃbodhigāmī

404. Cf. 277r6, 277v3, 277v7, and 278r2.

405. Cf. 277r6–7, 277r8, 277v3–4, 277v7, and 278r2.

406. Cf. 276r8, 276v4, 277r1, 277r6, 277r7, 277v1, 277v7, and 278r2.

407. Cf. 276v3, 277r1 and 277r7. Note that *tasmiṃ khalu* is not followed by *cunda* here as in the other two instances of this phrase.

408. Ms. reads *śrāvakā*. Cf. 276v3, 277r1, and 277r7.

409. Cf. 276v3, 277r1, and 277r7.

410. Cf. 276v3, 277r2, and 277r8.

411. Cf. 277r2 and 277r8.

abhinnaḥ sastūpaḥ <sa>pratisaraṇaḥ[412] <|> śāstā ca tathāgato 'rhan samyaksaṃbuddhas <|>

[c] tasmiṃ(**277v8**)<s>[413] tvam āyuṣmaṃ dharmavinaye dharmānudharmapratipanna<ḥ>[414] samīcīpratipanno 'nudharmacārī <|> yat khalu cunda{ṃ}[415] śrāvakam evaṃ praśaṃsitavyaṃ manyeta dharmeṣu addhāyuṣmaṃ lajjī kaukṛtikaḥ saṃvṛtaḥ[416] (**278r1**) śikṣākāmaḥ ārādhako bhaviṣyasy ārādhayiṣyasi nyāyyaṃ[417] dharmaṃ kuśalam iti •

[d] tatra cunda yaś ca praśaṃsati yaś ca praśasyate yaś ca praśasyamānas tathā tathā (prat)i(padyate) sarve te bahu puṇyaṃ prasūyante | eva(m eta)(**278r2**)c[418] cunda bhavati yathāpi tat svākhyāto dharmavinayaḥ supratipanno nairyāṇikaḥ saṃbodhigāmī abhinna<ḥ>[419] sastūpaḥ sapratisaraṇaḥ <|> śāstā ca tathāgato '(r)h(an) s(am)y(ak)s(aṃb)u(d)dh(aḥ | eva)ṃrūpe cunda dharmavinaye (śāstāpi) (**278r3**) praśasyo dhar(mo 'p)i[420] śrāvako 'py anenāṃgena prāśaṃsyaḥ[421] <|>

DĀ 15.7

[a] [Buddha:] "In this case, Cunda, there is a dharma and vinaya that is well-proclaimed, properly imparted, conducive to emancipation, leading to perfect awakening, intact, cohesive, and reliable. The teacher is a tathāgata, an arhat, a complete, perfect buddha. Now then, regarding such a dharma and vinaya, there is a disciple who practices according to the true method of the dharma, practices with propriety, and behaves according to dharma.

412. Cf. 277v4, 277v5 and 278r2.

413. Cf. 277r3 and 277v1.

414. Cf. 276v3 and 277v6.

415. Cf. 276v5, 277r3, and 277v1.

416. Ms. reads *saṃvṛtāḥ*.

417. The Pali would suggest *nyāyam* here (DN III 121.15: *ñāya-paṭipanno ñāyaṃ ārādhessatī ti*). However, one would imagine that *dharma* takes that connotation here and *nyāyya* serves as an adjective.

418. Cf. 276v6–7, 275r5, 277v3, and EFGH 13.14. Note that EFGH reads *prasavanti*, the *parasmaipada* form of the same root, *pra√sū*, while the *Prāsādika-sūtra* uses the *ātmanepada* conjugation.

419. Cf. 277r7, 277v5, and 277v7.

420. Cf. 276v8, 277r6, and 277v4.

421. Ms. reads *praśaṃsyaḥ*. S.v. *prāśaṃsyaḥ* in SWTF.

[**b**] "Regarding dharmas, a disciple of this kind, Cunda, is praiseworthy. And thus, further regarding dharmas, the dharma and vinaya of that venerable one is praiseworthy: [it is] well proclaimed, properly imparted, conducive to emancipation, leading to perfect awakening, intact, cohesive, and reliable. The teacher is a tathāgata, an arhat, a complete, perfect buddha.

[**c**] "'Regarding this dharma and vinaya, venerable sir, you practice according to the true method of the dharma, you practice with propriety, and you behave according to dharma.' Cunda, that disciple is to be praised in this way: 'Please be informed,[422] venerable sir, certainly regarding dharmas, you will be conscientious, scrupulous, self-restrained, anxious to observe the teaching, one who has accomplished his undertaking. You will accomplish this correct, wholesome dharma.'

[**d**] "In that case, Cunda, one who praises, one who is praised, and one who being praised, in whatever manner one practices, (they all produce much merit). This is so, Cunda, because there obviously is a dharma and vinaya that is well proclaimed, properly imparted, conducive to emancipation, leading to perfect awakening, intact, cohesive, and reliable. The teacher is a tathāgata, an arhat, a complete, perfect buddha. (Regarding a dharma and vinaya of this kind, Cunda, the teacher) is praiseworthy, as is the dharma, and by this aspect, the disciple, too, is praiseworthy."

~15.7~[423]

SHT (VIII) 1870 (*Prāsādika-sūtra*)

V

1[424] /// maḥ ārādhako bhaviṣyati ārādhayi[t]. ///

2[425] /// + bahv=apuṇyaṃ prasavaṃti evam=eta .. + ///

3 /// + [g]ato 'rhāṃ samyaksaṃbuddhaḥ e[v]aṃ .. + + ///

DN III 121.1–20 (DN 29.7)

7. idha pana cunda satthā ca hoti sammā-sambuddho, dhammo ca svākkhāto suppavedito niyyāniko upasama-saṃvattaniko sammāsambuddhappavedito, sāvako ca tasmiṃ dhamme dhammānudhamma-paṭipanno

422. *Yat khalu* [...] *manyeta*, see note 351 above.

423. Further related passages may be found at ~15.6~ above. See note 403.

424. DĀ 15.7c

425. DĀ 15.7d.

viharati sāmīci-paṭipanno anudhamma-cārī, samādāya taṃ dhammaṃ vattati. so evam assa vacanīyo—tassa te āvuso lābhā, tassa te suladdhaṃ, satthā ca te arahaṃ sammā-sambuddho dhammo ca svākkhāto suppavedito niyyāniko upasama-saṃvattaniko sammāsambuddha-ppavedito, tvañ ca tasmiṃ dhamme dhammānudhamma-paṭipanno viharasi, sāmīci-paṭipanno anudhamma-cārī, samādāya taṃ dhammaṃ vattasīti. iti kho cunda satthā pi tattha pāsaṃso, dhammo pi tattha pāsaṃso, sāvako pi tattha evaṃ pāsaṃso. yo kho cunda evarūpaṃ sāvakaṃ evaṃ vadeyya—addhā yasmā ñāya-paṭipanno ñāyaṃ ārādhessatīti, yo ca pasaṃsati yañ ca pasaṃsati, yo ca pasattho bhiyyosomattāya viriyaṃ ārabhati, sabbe te bahuṃ puññaṃ pasavanti. taṃ kissa hetu? evaṃ h' etaṃ cunda hoti svākkhāte dhamma-vinaye suppavedite niyyānike upasamasaṃvattanike sammāsambuddha-ppavedite.

T I 1 73b2–9

周那。若師不邪見。其法眞正。善可聽採能得出要。三耶三佛所說。譬如新塔易爲汙色。又其弟子法法成就。隨順修行而生正見。若有人來語其弟子言。汝師法正汝所行是。今所修行勤苦如是。應於現法成就道果。彼諸弟子信受其言。二俱正見獲無量福。所以者何。法眞正故。

A Tathāgata Who Is a New Teacher (DĀ 15.8–15)

DĀ 15.8

[**a**] iha cunda na<vaḥ>[426] śāstā loka utpanno bhavat(y) acirābhisaṃbuddhaḥ <|> avijñātārthāś cāsya śrāvakā bhavanti dharmeṣv; atha ca punas tasya śāstuḥ kṣipr(am eva loke)[427] (**278r4**) 'ntardhānaṃ bhavati <|> evaṃrūpaś cu(n)d(a ś)āstā anutāpyo bhavati dharme <|> evaṃ ca punar a{na}nut(ā)pyo[428] bhavati dharmeṣu navaḥ śāstā loka utpannaḥ acirābhisaṃbuddhaḥ avijñātārthāś cā(s)y(a ś)r(āvakā)[429] (**278r5**) bhavanti dharmeṣv; atha ca punas tasya śāstuḥ (kṣ)i(pra)m (e)va[430] loke 'ntardhānaṃ bhavati •

[**b**] iha cunda navaḥ śāstā loka utpanno bhavaty acirābhisaṃbuddhaḥ <|> vijñātārthāś cāsya śrāvakā bhavanti dharmeṣv; atha ca pu(**278r6**)nas tasya śāstuḥ kṣipram eva[431] <loke>[432] 'ntardhānaṃ bhavati <|> evaṃrūpaś cunda śāstā ananut(āp)y(o) bh(avat)i (dharme)ṣv; (e)vaṃ[433] ca punar ananutāpyo bhavati na dharmeṣu nava{rma}ḥ[434] śāstā loka utpanno 'cirābhisaṃb(uddha)ḥ (v)i(jñāth)ā(**278r7**)rthāś cāsya śrāvakā bhavanti dharmeṣv; atha ca punas tasya śāstuḥ kṣipram e(va loke 'ntardhāna)ṃ bha(va)ti <|>

DĀ 15.8

[**a**] [Buddha:] "In this case, Cunda, a new teacher is arisen in the world, one who has just had perfect awakening. His disciples are not proficient

426. Cf. 278r4 and 278r5.
427. Cf.278r5, 278r6, and 278r7.
428. Cf. 278r6.
429. Cf. 278r3.
430. Cf.278r4, 278r6, and 278r7.
431. Ms. reads *evāntardhānaṃ*.
432. Cf. 278r4–5, 278r5, and 278r7
433. Cf. 278r4.
434. Ms. reads *na dharmaḥ*.

regarding dharmas. Moreover, this teacher disappears (very) quickly (from[435] the world). Regarding [his] dharma, a teacher of this kind, Cunda, is to be regretted. Further, regarding dharmas, this is to be regretted: a new teacher arisen in the world, one who has just had perfect awakening and whose disciples are not proficient regarding dharmas. Moreover, this teacher disappears very quickly from the world.

[**b**] "In this case, Cunda, a new teacher is arisen in the world, one who has just had perfect awakening. His disciples are proficient regarding dharmas. Moreover, this teacher disappears very quickly <from the world>. Regarding [his] dharma, a teacher of this kind, Cunda, is not to be regretted. Further, regarding dharmas, this is not to be regretted: a new teacher arisen in the world, one who has just had perfect awakening and whose disciples are proficient regarding dharmas. Moreover, this teacher disappears very quickly (from the world)."

~15.8~

BLSF III.1 Or.15015/105 (*Prāsādika-sūtra*)

A	B
a /// + + ... ///	a /// + v[e]d[i] + ///
b /// + (n)[no] bha[v]. ///	b /// rūpe cu[nd]. ///
c /// [n]ta[r]dhāna ///	c /// + + ci[r]. ///
d /// + .. vi + ///	

SHT (VIII) 1870 (*Prāsādika-sūtra*)

V

4[436] /// + [c]irābhisaṃbuddhaḥ avi[j](ñ)[ā] + + + + + ///

5 /// evaṃ ca p(u)nar=ānutā[pyo] + + + + + + ///

R

1 /// (n)[t](ar)dh(ā)nam* iha tu cu[n](da) + + + + ///

2 /// + antardhānaṃ bhavati eva .. + + + ///

3[437] /// + [t]ārthāś=c=āsya srāvakā dharmeṣu .. + + ///

435. *Loke* is locative but is translated as an ablative.

436. DĀ 15.8a.

437. DĀ 15.8b.

DN III 121.21–122.12 (DN 29.8)

[a] 8. idha pana cunda satthā ca loke udapādi arahaṃ sammā-sambuddho, dhammo ca svākkhāto suppavedito niyyāniko upasama-saṃvattaniko sammā-sambuddha-ppavedito, aviññāpitatthā c' assa honti sāvakā saddhamme, na ca tesaṃ kevalaṃ paripūraṃ brahmacariyaṃ āvikataṃ hoti uttāni-kataṃ sabba-saṅgāha-pada-kataṃ sappāṭihīra-kataṃ yāvad eva manussehi suppakāsitaṃ, atha nesaṃ satthuno antaradhānaṃ hoti. evarūpo kho cunda satthā sāvakānaṃ kālakato anutappo hoti. taṃ kissa hetu? satthā ca no loke udapādi arahaṃ sammāsambuddho, dhammo ca svākkhāto suppavedito niyyāniko upasama-saṃvattaniko sammā-sambuddha-ppavedito, aviññāpitatthā c' amha saddhamme, na ca no kevalaṃ paripūraṃ brahmacariyaṃ āvikataṃ hoti uttāni-kataṃ sabba-saṅgāha-pada-kataṃ sappāṭihīra-kataṃ yāvad eva manussehi suppakāsitaṃ, atha no satthuno antaradhānaṃ hotīti. evarūpo kho cunda satthā sāvakānaṃ kālakato anutappo hoti.

DN III 122.13–123.2 (DN 29.9)

[b] 9. idha pana cunda satthā ca loke udapādi arahaṃ sammā-sambuddho, dhammo ca svākkhāto suppavedito niyyāniko upasama-saṃvattaniko sammā-sambuddha-ppavedito, viññāpitatthā c' assa honti sāvakā saddhamme, kevalañ ca tesaṃ paripūraṃ brahmacariyaṃ āvikataṃ hoti uttāni-kataṃ sabba-saṅgāha-pada-kataṃ sappāṭihīra-kataṃ yāvad eva manussehi suppakāsitaṃ, atha nesaṃ satthuno antaradhānaṃ hoti. evarūpo kho cunda satthā sāvakānaṃ kālakato ananutappo hoti. taṃ kissa hetu? satthā ca no loke udapādi arahaṃ sammā-sambuddho, dhammo ca svākkhāto suppavedito niyyāniko upasama-saṃvattaniko sammā-sambuddha-ppavedito, viññāpitatthā c' amha saddhamme, kevalañ ca no paripūraṃ brahmacariyaṃ āvikataṃ hoti uttāni-kataṃ sabba-saṅgāha-pada-kataṃ sappāṭihīra-kataṃ yāvad eva manussehi suppakāsitaṃ, atha no satthuno antaradhānaṃ hotīti. evarūpo kho cunda satthā sāvakānaṃ kālakato ananutappo hoti.

T I 1 73b9–17

[a] 周那。或有導師出世使弟子生憂。或有導師出世使弟子無憂。云何導師出世使弟子生憂。周那。導師新出世間成道未久。其法具足梵行清淨。如實眞要而不布現。然彼導師速取滅度。其諸弟子不得修行。皆愁憂言。師初出世。成道未久其法清淨。梵行具足。如實眞要竟不布現。而今導師便速滅度。我等弟子不得修行。是爲導師出世弟子愁憂。

T I 1 73b17–23

[**b**] 云何導師出世弟子不憂。謂導師出世。其法清淨。梵行具足。如實眞要而廣流布。然後導師方取滅度。其諸弟子皆得修行不懷憂。言師初出世成道未久。其法清淨。梵行具足。如實眞要而不布現。而今導師便速滅度。使我弟子不得修行。如是。周那。導師出世弟子無憂。

▪ ▪ ▪ ▪ ▪

DĀ 15.9

[**a**] (iha c)u(nda śās)t(ā)[438] loka utpanno bhavati tathāgato ’rhan samyaksaṃbuddho vidyācar(aṇasaṃpannaḥ sugato loka)(**278r8**)vid[439] anuttaraḥ puruṣadamyasārathiḥ śāstā de(v)amanuṣyāṇāṃ[440] (b)u(d)dh(o bhagavaṃ; s)a[441] ca na bhavati vṛddho[442] jīrṇo m(ahallakaḥ | evaṃ nāsya dharmavina)y(o)[443] ’nenāṃgena paripūrṇo bhavati

[**b**] i(ha cunda śāstā loka utpa)(**278v1**)nno bhavati tathāgato ’rhan samyaksaṃbuddho vidyācaraṇasaṃpannaḥ (sugat)o[444] lok(a)vid[445] anuttaraḥ puruṣadamyasārathiḥ śāstā devamanu(ṣ)y(āṇāṃ buddho)[446] bhagavaṃ; bhavati jīrṇo vṛddho (mahallakaḥ | evam asya)[447] (**278v2**) dharmavinayo ’nenāṃgena paripūrṇo bhavati <|>

DĀ 15.9

[**a**] [Buddha:] “In this case, Cunda, a teacher is arisen in the world: a tathāgata, an arhat, a complete, perfect buddha, one who is perfect in knowledge and conduct, a (sugata), world-knowing, an unsurpassed charioteer of men to be tamed, a teacher of gods and men, a buddha, (a blessed

438. Cf. 278r3, 278r4, 278r5, 278v2, 278v4, 278v5–6, 278v8, 279r2, 279r5, and 279r8. This section of the ms. is obscured by a fragment that makes reconstruction difficult, but fortunately this reading is attested to in numerous instances.

439. Cf. 278v2, 278v4, 278v6, 278v8, 279r2, 279r5–6, and 280v3.

440. Cf. 278v1, 278v3, 278v4, 278v6, 279r1, 279r3, 279r6, 280v3.

441. Cf. 278v1, 278v3, 278v4–5, 278v6, 279r1, 279r3, 279r6, 280v3.

442. Note that *vṛddho* comes before *jīrṇo* here, which is rare in this common stock phrase.

443. Cf. 278v1–2 and 278v5.

444. Cf. 278v2, 278v4, 278v6, 278v8, 279r2, 279r6, and 280v3.

445. Cf. 278v2, 278v4, 278v6, 278v8, 279r2, 279r6, and 280v3.

446. Cf.278r8, 278v3, 278v4, 278v6, 279r1, 279r3, 279r6, and 280v3.

447. Cf. 278v3 and 278v5.

one). [However], he is not aged, old, and senior. (Thus), by this aspect, (his) dharma and vinaya are (not) fulfilled.

[b] "In this case, (Cunda, a teacher) is arisen (in the world): a tathāgata, an arhat, a complete, perfect buddha, one who is perfect in knowledge and conduct, a (sugata), world-knowing, an unsurpassed charioteer of men to be tamed, a teacher of gods and men, (a buddha), a blessed one. He is aged, old, and (senior. Thus), by this aspect, (his) dharma and vinaya are fulfilled."

~15.9~

SHT (VIII) 1870 (*Prāsādika-sūtra*)
R
4[448] /// + raṇasaṃpa<ṃ>naḥ sugato lokavi[d]=(a) + ///
5 /// [n]=āṅgen=āparipū{•}rṇ[o] bhavati • i .. ///

DN III 123.3–10 (DN 29.10)
[a] 10. etehi ce pi cunda aṅgehi samannāgataṃ brahmacariyaṃ hoti, no ca kho satthā hoti thero rattaññū cirapabbajito addha-gato vayo anuppatto, evaṃ taṃ brahmacariyaṃ aparipūraṃ hoti ten' aṅgena.

[b] yato ca kho cunda etehi c' eva aṅgehi samannāgataṃ brahmacariyaṃ hoti, satthā ca hoti thero rattaññū cira-pabbajito addhagato vayo anuppatto, evan taṃ brahmacariyaṃ paripūraṃ hoti ten' aṅgena.

T I 1 73b23–25
[a] 佛告周那。此支成就梵行。謂導師出世。出家未久。名聞未廣。是謂梵行支不具足。

T I 1 73b25–26
[b] 周那。導師出世出家既久。名聞廣遠。是謂梵行支具足滿。

▪ ▪ ▪ ▪ ▪

DĀ 15.10

[a] iha cunda śāstā l(oka utpanno bhavat)i (ta)thāgato ('rhan samyaksa)ṃ-(buddh)o vidyācaraṇasaṃpanna(ḥ s)ugato lokavid anuttaraḥ (puruṣadamyasārathiḥ)[449] **(278v3)** śāstā devamanuṣyāṇāṃ buddho

448. DĀ 15.9a.

449. Cf. 278r7, 278r8–278v1, 278v4, 278v5–6, 278v8, 279r2–3, 278r5–6, 279r8, and 280v3.

bhagavāṃ; sa ca bhavati j(ī)rṇo[450] vṛddho mahal<l>akaḥ <|> sa ca na bhavati[451] lābhāgrayaśogreṇa samanvāgataḥ <|> evaṃ <n>āsya[452] dharmavinayo 'n(e)nā(ṃgena paripūrṇo bha)(278v4)vati[453] <|>

[**b**] iha cunda śāstā loka utpanno bhavati tathāgato 'rhan samyaksaṃbuddho vidyācaraṇasaṃpannaḥ sugato lokavid anuttaraḥ puruṣadamyasārathiḥ śāstā devamanuṣyāṇāṃ buddh(o)[454] **(278v5)** bhagavāṃ; sa ca bha(va)ti (j)ī(rṇo v)ṛ(d)dh(o)[455] mahallakaḥ <|> sa ca bhavati lābhāgrayaśogreṇa[456] samanvāgataḥ <|> evam asya dharmavinayo 'nenāṃgena paripūrṇo bhav(at)i

DĀ 15.10

[a] "In this case, Cunda, a teacher is (arisen) in the world: a tathāgata, an arhat, a complete, perfect buddha, one who is perfect in knowledge and conduct, a sugata, (world-knowing, an unsurpassed charioteer of men to be tamed), a teacher of gods and men, (a buddha), a blessed one. He is aged, old, and senior. [However], he is not endowed with the highest gain and the highest fame. Thus, by this aspect, his dharma and vinaya are not fulfilled.

[**b**] "In this case, Cunda, a teacher is arisen in the world: a tathāgata, an arhat, a complete, perfect buddha, one who is perfect in knowledge and conduct, a sugata, world-knowing, an unsurpassed charioteer of men to be tamed, a teacher of gods and men, a buddha, a blessed one. He is aged, old, and senior. He is endowed with the highest gain and the highest fame. Thus, by this aspect, his dharma and vinaya are fulfilled."

~15.10~

DN III 123.11–18 (DN 29.11)

11. etehi ce pi cunda aṅgehi samannāgataṃ brahmacariyaṃ hoti, satthā ca hoti thero rattaññū cira-pabbajito addha-gato vayo anuppatto, no ca kho

450. Cf. 278r8, 278v3, 278v5, 278v7, 279r1, and 279r3.

451. Ms. reads *bhaveti.*

452. Ms. reads *evam asya* but the content and context suggest a negative.

453. Cf. 278v2, 278v5, 278v8, 279r2, 279r5, 279r8, and 279v1.

454. Cf. 278v3, 278v6, 279r1, 279r3, 279r6, and 279v3.

455. Cf. 278r8, 278v1, 278v3, 278v7, 279r1, 279r3, 279r6, and 280v3.

456. Ms. reads *khābhāgrayaśogreṇa. Khā* and *lā* bear a resemblance, and it seems one was mistaken for the other here.

assa therā bhikkhū sāvakā honti vyattā vinītā visāradā patta-yogakkhemā, alaṃ samakkhātuṃ saddhammassa, alaṃ uppannaṃ parappavādaṃ sahadhammena suniggahītaṃ niggahetvā sappāṭihāriyaṃ dhammaṃ desetuṃ; evaṃ taṃ brahmacariyaṃ aparipūraṃ hoti ten' aṅgena.

T I 1 73c16–17
[a] 周那。若導師不在世。無有名聞利養損減。則梵行支不具足滿。

T I 1 73c17–19
[b] 若導師在世名聞利養皆悉具足無有損減。則梵行支爲具足滿。

▪ ▪ ▪ ▪ ▪

DĀ 15.11
[a] (i)h(a c)u(n)d(a śā)stā l(o)(**278v6**)ka utpa(n)n(o) bhavati tathāgato ('r)han[457] samyaksaṃbuddho vidyācaraṇasaṃpannaḥ sugato lokavid anuttaraḥ puruṣadamyasārathiḥ śāstā devamanuṣyaṇāṃ b(ud)dho bha(gavāṃ; sa)[458] (**278v7**) ca bhavati jīrṇo vṛddho mahallakaḥ <|> sa ca bhavati lābhāgrayaśogreṇa samanvāgato; na cāsya[459] vaistārikaṃ brahmacaryaṃ bhavati | bāhujanyaṃ pṛthubhūtaṃ yāvad <d>evam(a)n(uṣy)e(bhya)ḥ[460] (s)a(m)ya(k)suprakāśi(ta)ṃ;[461] (evaṃ nā)(**278v8**)sya[462] dharmavinayo 'nenāṃgena paripūrṇo bhavati <|>

457. Cf. 278r7, 278r8–278v1, 278v2, 278v4, 278v6, 278v8, 279r2, 279r5, 279r8, and 280v3.

458. Cf. 278r8, 278v3, 278v5, 278v6, 279r1, 279v3, 279r6, and 280v3.

459. Ms. reads *vāsya* but *cā* and *vā* look very similar.

460. Cf. 279r4, 279r7, and 279v4. We are left with a choice regarding the instances of *yāvad devamanuṣyebhaḥ* in these sections. We can read this phrase as presented above or as *yāvad eva manuṣyebhaḥ*. Making a decision is difficult, for in 278v7 and 279r2 the ms. reads *yāvad eva* while in 279r4, 279r7, and 279v4 we find *yāvad deva°*. Rhys Davids seems to be alone in adopting the reading of *yāvad eva*, but I do not follow that reading here. S.v. *yāva* in PTSD and especially the following remarks: "Note. In the stock phrase of the Buddha's refusal to die until his teaching has been fully proclaimed (*Mahāparinibbānasutta*) among gods and men D II.106 (= 114, 219; III.122; A IV.311) '*yāva-deva-manussehi suppakāsitaṃ*' (trsl (n) Dial. II.113: 'until, in a word, it shall have been well proclaimed among men') we are inclined to consider the reading *yāva deva°* as original and better than yāvad-eva, although Rhys Davids (Dial. II.236) is in favour of the latter being the original." Cf. Rhys Davids & Rhys Davids 1910, 236 (referred to as Dial. II.236 in PTSD).

461. Cf. 279r2, 279r4 279r7, and 280v4.

462. Cf. 278v5, 279r2, 279r5, 279r8, and 280v2.

[**b**] iha cunda{ḥ} śāstā loka utpanno bhavati tathāgato ’rhan samyaksaṃbuddho vidyācaraṇasaṃ(pannaḥ sugato lokavi)d anuttaraḥ[463] (**279r1**) puruṣadamyasārathiḥ śāstā devamanuṣyāṇāṃ buddho bhagavāṃ; sa na bhavati jīrṇo vṛddho mahallaka<ḥ |> sa ca bhavati lābhāgra̲{ṇa}y(a)ś(og)r(e)ṇa[464] samanvagato; vaistārika<ṃ> c̲(ās)y(a[465] brahmacaryaṃ bhavati | bāhujanyaṃ pṛthu)(**279r2**)bhūtaṃ yāvad <d>evamanuṣyebhyaḥ[466] samyaksuprakāśitaṃ̲[467] <|> evam asya {sa}dharmavinayo ’nenāṃgena paripūrṇo bhavati |

DĀ 15.11

[a] [Buddha:] “In this case, Cunda, (a teacher) is arisen in the world: a tathāgata, an arhat, a complete, perfect buddha, one who is perfect in knowledge and conduct, a sugata, world-knowing, an unsurpassed charioteer of men to be tamed, a teacher of gods and men, a buddha, a blessed one. (He) is aged, old, and senior. He is endowed with the highest gain and the highest fame. [However], his holy life is not widespread, [not] widely known to many people and properly taught to gods and men. (Thus), by this aspect, his dharma and vinaya are not fulfilled.

[b] “In this case, Cunda, a teacher is arisen in the world: a tathāgata, an arhat, a complete, perfect buddha, one who is perfect in knowledge and conduct, (a sugata, world-knowing, an unsurpassed) charioteer of men to be tamed, a teacher of gods and men, a buddha, a blessed one. (He) is aged, old, and senior. He is endowed with the highest gain and the highest fame. His (holy life is widespread), widely known (to many people) and properly taught to gods and men. Thus, by this aspect, his dharma and vinaya are fulfilled.”

▪ ▪ ▪ ▪ ▪

DĀ 15.12

[**a**] iha cunda śāstā loka utpanno bhavati tathāgato ’(r)han samyaksaṃbuddho vi(d)y(ācaraṇasaṃpannaḥ sugato lo)(**279r3**)kavid[468] anut-

463. Cf. 278v4.

464. Cf. 278v3, 278v5, 278v7, 279r3, 279r6, and 280v4.

465. Ms. reads n. .. y.

466. Cf. 279r4, 279r7, and 280v4.

467. Ms. reads *samyaksuprakāsitaḥ*.

468. Cf. 278r7–8, 278v2, 278v4, 278v6, 278v8, 279r2–3, 278r5–6, 279r8, and 280v3.

taraḥ puruṣadamyasārathiḥ śastā devamanuṣyāṇāṃ buddho bhagavān sa ca bhavati jīrṇo vṛddho mahallakaḥ <|> sa ca bhavati lābhāgrayaśogreṇa samanvaga(t)o; vaistarikaṃ c(āsya brahma)**(279r4)**caryaṃ bhavati <|> bāhujanyaṃ (p)ṛthubhūtaṃ (yāva)d[469] devamanuṣyebhyaḥ samyaksuprakāśitaṃ; na cāsya śrāvakāḥ sthavirā madhyā[470] navakā<ḥ> paṇḍitā bhavanti vyaktā medhāvino; 'lam utpannotpannānāṃ <parapravādānāṃ> sahadh(armeṇa ni)**(279r5)**gṛhītāro;[471] 'la<ṃ> sv<asya v>ādasya[472] paryavadāpayitāraḥ <|> evaṃ <n>āsya[473] dha(r)mavinayo 'nenāṃgena paripūrṇo bhavati ||

[**b**] iha cunda śāstā loka utpanno bhavati tathāgato 'rhan sa(m)ya(k)s(a)ṃ(b)u(d)dh(o v)i(d)y(ācaraṇasampa)**(279r6)**nnaḥ[474] sugato lokavid anuttaraḥ puruṣadamyasārathiḥ śāstā de(v)amanuṣyāṇāṃ buddho bhagavān sa ca bhavati jīrṇo vṛddho mahallakaḥ <|> sa ca bhavati lābhāgrayaśogreṇa samanvāgato; vais(tar)i**(279r7)**kaṃ cāsya brahmacaryaṃ bhavati <|> bāhujanyaṃ pṛthubhūtaṃ yāvad devamanuṣye(bhyaḥ samyaksuprakāśi)t(aṃ);[475] śrāvakā<ś> cāsya sthavirā madhyā navakāḥ paṇḍitā bhavanti vyaktā medhāvino; 'lam utpannotpan(n)ā(n)āṃ p(arapravādānāṃ)[476] **(279r8)** sahadharmeṇa nigṛhītāro; 'laṃ svasya vāda(s)ya paryavadāpayitāraḥ <|> evam a(sya) dharmavi(na)y(o)[477] 'nenāṃgena paripūrṇo bhavati •

DĀ 15.12

[**a**] [Buddha:] "In this case, Cunda, a teacher is arisen in the world: a tathāgata, an arhat, a complete, perfect buddha, one who is perfect in knowledge and conduct, (a sugata), world-knowing, an unsurpassed charioteer of men to be tamed, a teacher of gods and men, a buddha, a blessed one. He is aged, old, and senior. He is endowed with the highest gain and the highest fame. His holy life is widespread, widely known to many people

469. Cf. 278v7, 279r1–2, 279r6–7, and 280v4.

470. Ms. reads navyā.

471. 279r7–8 and 280v5.

472. Cf. 279r8, 278v5, and 280v1.

473. Ms. reads *evam asya* but the content and context suggest a negative.

474. Cf. 278r7, 278v1, 278v2, 278v4, 278v6, 278v8, 278r2, 279r8, and 280v3.

475. Cf. 278v7, 279r1–2, 279r3–4, and 280v4.

476. Cf. 280v1.

477. Cf. 279r5 and 280v5.

and properly taught to gods and men. [However], his elder, middle, and novice disciples are not wise, clever, or learned. They are not capable in employing dharma to refute false dharmas that repeatedly arise. They are not capable purifiers of their own speech. Thus, by this aspect, his dharma and vinaya are not fulfilled.

[b] "In this case, Cunda, a teacher is arisen in the world: a tathāgata, an arhat, a complete, perfect buddha, one who is perfect in knowledge and conduct, a sugata, world-knowing, an unsurpassed charioteer of men to be tamed, a teacher of gods and men, a buddha, a blessed one. He is aged, old, and senior. He is endowed with the highest gain and the highest fame. His holy life is widespread, widely known to many people and properly taught to gods and men. His elder, middle, and novice disciples are wise, clever, and learned. They are capable in employing dharma to refute false dharmas that repeatedly arise. They are capable purifiers of their own speech. Thus, by this aspect, his dharma and vinaya are fulfilled."

▪ ▪ ▪ ▪ ▪

DĀ 15.13

[a] iha cunda śāstā loka utpanno bhavati tathāgato 'rh(an samyaksaṃbuddho vidyācaraṇa)(**279v1**)saṃpann(aḥ sugato lokavid anuttaraḥ puruṣadamyasārathiḥ śāstā devamanuṣyāṇāṃ buddho bhagavān sa ca bhavati jīrṇo vṛddho mahallakaḥ | sa ca bhavati lābhāgrayaśog) r(eṇa samanvāgato; vaistarikaṃ) (**279v2**) cā(sya brahmacaryaṃ bhavati | bāhujanyaṃ pṛthubhūtaṃ yāvad devamanuṣyebhyaḥ samyaksuprakāśitaṃ; śrāvakāś cāsya sthavirā madhyā navakāḥ paṇḍitā bhavanti vyaktā medhāvino; 'lam utpannotpannānāṃ) (**~279v3**) (parapravādānāṃ sahadharmeṇa nigṛhītāro; 'laṃ svasya vādasya paryavadāpayitāraḥ | na cāsya śrāvakasaṃghaḥ .ṛ .. .. .(i)[478] vaipulyāṃ gato bhavaty; evaṃ nāsya dharmavinayo 'nenāṃgena paripūrṇo bhavati |)[479]

[b] (**~279v4**) (iha cunda śāstā loka utpanno bhavati tathāgato 'rhan samyaksaṃbuddho vidyācaraṇasaṃpanna sugato lokakavid anuttaraḥ puruṣadamyasārathiḥ śāstā deva)ma(n)u(ṣ)y(ā)ṇāṃ (**279v5**) (buddho bhagavān sa ca bhavati jīrṇo vṛddho mahallakaḥ | sa ca bhavati

478. Cf. 280v6.

479. Cf. 278r7–279r8 and 279v4–280v6.

lābhāgrayaśogrena samanvāgato vaistarikaṃ cāsya brahmacaryaṃ bhavati | bāhujanyaṃ pṛthubhū)taṃ yā(vad de)(**279v6**)(vamanu)ṣye(bh)y(aḥ sa)myaksuprakāśi(taṃ; śrāvakāś cāsya sthavirā madhyā navakāḥ paṇḍitā bhavanti vyaktā medhāvino; 'lam utpannotpannānāṃ parapravādānāṃ sahadharmeṇa nigṛhītāro; 'laṃ) (**279v7**) (svas)y(a) vādāsya paravadā<pa>yitāraḥ (| śrāvakasaṃghaś cāsya .ṛ .. .. .i[480] vaipulyāṃ gato bhavaty; evam asya dharmavinayo 'nenāṃgena par)i(pūrṇo bhavati |)[481]

DĀ 15.13

[**a**] [Buddha:] "In this case, Cunda, a teacher is arisen in the world: a tathāgata, an arhat, (a complete, perfect buddha), one who is perfect in knowledge and conduct, (a sugata, world-knowing, an unsurpassed charioteer of men to be tamed, a teacher of gods and men, a buddha, a blessed one. He is aged, old, and senior. He is endowed) with the highest gain and the highest fame. His (holy life is widespread, widely known to many people and properly taught to gods and men. His elder, middle, and novice disciples are wise, clever, and learned. They are capable in employing dharma to refute false dharmas that repeatedly arise. They are capable purifiers of their own speech. [However], his community of disciples [...] does not become abundant. Thus, by this aspect, his dharma and vinaya are not fulfilled.)

[**b**] ("In this case, Cunda, a teacher is arisen in the world: a tathāgata, an arhat, a complete, perfect buddha, one who is perfect in knowledge and conduct, a sugata, world-knowing, an unsurpassed charioteer of men to be tamed, a teacher) of gods and men, (a buddha, a blessed one. He is aged, old, and senior. He is endowed with the highest gain and the highest fame. His holy life is widespread), widely known (to many people) and properly taught to gods and men. (His elder, middle, and novice disciples are wise, clever, and learned. They are capable in employing dharma to refute false dharmas that repeatedly arise. They are) capable purifiers of their own speech. (His community of disciples [...] becomes abundant. Thus, by this aspect, his dharma and vinaya are fulfilled.")

▪ ▪ ▪ ▪ ▪

480. Cf. 280v6.

481. Cf. 278r7–279v3 and 279v8–280v6.

DĀ 15.14

[a] (iha cunda śāstā loka utpanno bhavati tathā)(279v8)(ga)to ('r)han samyaksaṃbuddho vidyācaraṇasaṃpanna(ḥ sugato lokavid anuttaraḥ puruṣadamyasārathiḥ śāstā devamanuṣyāṇāṃ buddho bhagavān sa ca bhavati jīrṇo vṛddho mahallakaḥ | sa ca bhavati) (~280r1) (lābhāgrayaśogreṇa samanvāgato vaistarikaṃ cāsya brahmacaryaṃ bhavati | bāhujanyaṃ pṛthubhūtaṃ yāvad devamanuṣyebhyaḥ samyaksuprakāśitaṃ; śrāvakāś cāsya sthavirā madhyā navakāḥ paṇḍitā bhavanti vyaktā medhāvino; 'lam) (~280r2) (utpannotpannānāṃ parapravādānāṃ sahadharmeṇa nigṛhītāro; 'laṃ svasya vādasya paryavadāpayitāraḥ | śrāvakasaṃghaś cāsya .ṛ .. .. .i[482] vaipulyāṃ gato bhavati | na cāsya śrāvakasaṃghaḥ sthavirarājanyatayā) (~280r3) (samanvāgato bhavaty; evaṃ nāsya dharmavinayo 'nenāṃgena paripūrṇo bhavati |)[483]

[b] (iha cunda śāstā loka utpanno bhavati tathāgato 'rhan samyaksaṃbuddho vidyācaraṇasaṃpanna sugato lokavid anuttaraḥ puruṣadamyasārathiḥ) (~280r4) (śāstā devamanuṣyāṇāṃ buddho bhagavān sa ca bhavati jīrṇo vṛddho mahallakaḥ | sa ca bhavati lābhāgrayaśogrena samanvāgato vaistarikaṃ cāsya brahmacaryaṃ bhavati | bāhujanyaṃ pṛthubhūtaṃ yāvad devamanuṣyebhyaḥ) (~280r5) (samyaksuprakāśitaṃ; śrāvakāś cāsya sthavirā madhyā navakāḥ paṇḍitā bhavanti vyaktā medhāvino; 'lam utpannotpannānāṃ parapravādānāṃ sahadharmeṇa nigṛhītāro; 'laṃ svasya vādasya paryavadāpayitāraḥ |) (~280r6) (śrāvakasaṃghaś cāsya .ṛ .. .. .i[484] vaipulyāṃ gato bhavati | śrāvakasaṃghaś cāsya sthavirarājanyatayā samanvāgato bhavaty; evam asya dharmavinayo 'nenāṃgena paripūrṇo bhavati |)[485]

DĀ 15.14

[a] [Buddha:] ("In this case, Cunda, a teacher is arisen in the world): a tathāgata, an arhat, a complete, perfect buddha, one who is perfect in knowledge and conduct, (a sugata, world-knowing, an unsurpassed charioteer of men to be tamed, a teacher of gods and men, a buddha, a blessed one. He is aged, old, and senior. He is endowed with the highest gain and the highest fame. His holy life is widespread, widely known to many people

482. Cf. 280v6.

483. Cf. 278r7–279v7 and 280v1–280v6.

484. Cf. 280v6.

485. Cf. 278r7–279v8 and 280v3–280v6.

and properly taught to gods and men. His elder, middle, and novice disciples are wise, clever, and learned. They are capable in employing dharma to refute false dharmas that repeatedly arise. They are capable purifiers of their own speech. His community of disciples [...] becomes abundant. [However], his community of disciples is not endowed with a royalty of elders.[486] Thus, by this aspect, his dharma and vinaya are not fulfilled.)

[**b**] ("In this case, Cunda, a teacher is arisen in the world: a tathāgata, an arhat, a complete, perfect buddha, one who is perfect in knowledge and conduct, a sugata, world-knowing, an unsurpassed charioteer of men to be tamed, a teacher of gods and men, a buddha, a blessed one. He is aged, old, and senior. He is endowed with the highest gain and the highest fame. His holy life is widespread, widely known to many people and properly taught to gods and men. His elder, middle, and novice disciples are wise, clever, and learned. They are capable in employing dharma to refute false dharmas that repeatedly arise. They are capable purifiers of their own speech. His community of disciples [...] becomes abundant. His community of disciples is endowed with a royalty of elders. Thus, by this aspect, his dharma and vinaya are fulfilled.")

■ ■ ■ ■ ■

DĀ 15.15

[**a**] (iha cunda śāstā loka utpanno) (~**280r7**) (bhavati tathāgato 'rhan samyaksaṃbuddho vidhyacaraṇasaṃpannaḥ sugato lokavid anuttaraḥ puruṣadamyasārathiḥ śāstā devamanuṣyāṇāṃ buddho bhagavān sa ca bhavati jīrṇo vṛddho mahallakaḥ |) (~**280r8**) (sa ca bhavati lābhāgrayaśogrena samanvāgato vaistarikaṃ cāsya brahmacaryaṃ bhavati | bāhujanyaṃ pṛthubhūtaṃ yāvad devamanuṣyebhyaḥ samyaksuprakāśitaṃ; śrāvakāś cāsya sthavirā madhyā navakāḥ paṇḍitā bhavanti) (**280v1**) (vyaktā) medhāvino; 'lam utpannotpannānāṃ parapravādānāṃ sahadharmeṇa nigṛhītāro; 'laṃ svasya vādasya paryavadāpayitāraḥ <|> śrāvak(a)s(aṃ)gh(a)ś c(ās)y(a) ṛ. .. + .(i[487] vaipulyāṃ gato bhavati |

486. *Sthavirarājanyatayā* above. This refers not to monks of royal lineage but to the saṅgha having its own form of royalty in its elder monks who are arhats. Śāriputra and Mahāmaudgalyāyana would be the two foremost members of this group. See a similar usage in the *Pāsādika-sutta*, DN III 123: *thero rattaññū*.

487. Cf. 280v6.

śrāvaka)(280v2)(saṃghaś cās)y(a) sthavirarājanyatayā samanvāgato bhavati <|> na cāsya śrā(vaka)s(a)ṃgho {na} lābhāgrayaśogreṇa samanvāgato bhavaty; evaṃ <n>āsya[488] dharmavinayo <'ne>nāṃgena paripūrṇo bhav(ati |)[489]

[**b**] (iha cunda śāstā) (**280v3**) l(o)ka utpanno bhavati tathāgato 'rhan samyaksaṃbuddho vi(dh)y(acara)ṇasaṃpannaḥ sugato lokakavid anuttaraḥ puruṣadamyasārathiḥ śāstā devamanuṣyāṇāṃ buddho bhagavāṃ sa (ca bavati jīrṇo) (**280v4**) vṛddho mahallakaḥ <|> sa ca bhavati lābhāgrayaśogreṇa samanvāgato vaistarikaṃ cāsya brahmacaryaṃ bhavati <|> bāhujanyaṃ pṛthubhūtaṃ yāvad devamanuṣyebhyaḥ samyaksuprak(āśitaṃ); ś(r)āv(akā)(**280v5**)ś cāsya sthavirā madhyā navakāḥ paṇḍitā vyaktā medhāvino; 'lam utpannotpannānāṃ parapravādā<nāṃ>[490] sahadharmeṇa nigṛhītāro; 'laṃ svasya vādasya paryavadāpayi(tāraḥ | śrā)(**280v6**)va(kasa)ṃghaś cās(ya) .(ṛ) .. .. .i vaipulyāṃ gato bhavati <|> śrāvakasaṃghaś cāsya sthavirarājanyatayā samanvāgato bhavati <|> śravakasaṃghaś cāsya lābhāgrayaśo(greṇa samanvāga)(**280v7**)(t)o (bhavaty; evam asya dharmav)inayo 'nenāṃgena paripūrṇo bhavati <|>[491]

DĀ 15.15

[**a**] [Buddha:] "In this case, Cunda, a teacher is arisen in the world: a tathāgata, an arhat, a complete, perfect buddha, one who is perfect in knowledge and conduct, a sugata, world-knowing, an unsurpassed charioteer of men to be tamed, a teacher of gods and men, a buddha, a blessed one. He is aged, old, and senior. He is endowed with the highest gain and the highest fame. His holy life is widespread, widely known to many people and properly taught to gods and men. His elder, middle, and novice disciples are wise, clever, and learned. They are capable in employing dharma to refute false dharmas that repeatedly arise. They are capable purifiers of their own speech. His community of disciples [...] becomes abundant. His community of disciples is endowed with a royalty of elders. [However], his community of disciples is not endowed with the highest gain and the highest fame. Thus, by this aspect, his dharma and vinaya are not fulfilled."

488. Ms reads *evam asya*, but content and context suggest a negative.

489. Cf. 278r7–279v8 and 289v3–280v6.

490. Ms. reads *parapravādo*.

491. Cf. 278r7–279v8 and 280v1–2.

[**b**] "In this case, Cunda, a teacher is arisen in the world: a tathāgata, an arhat, a complete, perfect buddha, one who is perfect in knowledge and conduct, a sugata, world-knowing, an unsurpassed charioteer of men to be tamed, a teacher of gods and men, a buddha, a blessed one. He is aged, old, and senior. He is endowed with the highest gain and the highest fame. His holy life is widespread, widely known to many people and properly taught to gods and men. His elder, middle, and novice disciples are wise, clever, and learned. They are capable in employing dharma to refute false dharmas that repeatedly arise. They are capable purifiers of their own speech. His community of disciples [...] becomes abundant. His community of disciples is endowed with a royalty of elders. His community of disciples is endowed with the highest gain and the highest fame. Thus, by this aspect, his dharma and vinaya are fulfilled."

~15.12~

T I 1 73b27–73c2

[a] 周那。導師出世。出家既久。名聞亦廣。而諸弟子未受訓誨。未具梵行。未至安處。未獲己利。未能受法分布演說。有異論起不能如法而往滅之。未能變化成神通證。是爲梵行支不具足。

T I 1 73c2–6

[b] 周那。導師出世。出家既久。名聞亦廣。而諸弟子盡受教訓。梵行具足。至安隱處已獲己利。又能受法分別演說。有異論起能如法滅。變化具足成神通證。是爲梵行支具足滿。

MPS 16.8 (= CPS 4.6) and 16.9

[a] 16.8 (na tāvat pāpīyan parinirvā)sy(ā)mi yāvan na me śrāvakāḥ paṇḍitā bhaviṣyanti vyaktā medhāvinaḥ || alam u(tpannotpannānāṃ parapravādināṃ saha dharmeṇa nigrahītāraḥ || alaṃ svasya vādasya pa)ryavadātāro bhikṣavo bhikṣuṇya upāsakā upāsikā vaistārikaṃ ca me bra(hmacaryaṃ cariṣyanti bahujanyaṃ pṛthubhūtaṃ yāvad devamanuṣyebhyaḥ samyaksaṃpra)kāśitam |

[b] 16.9 etarhi bhadanta bhagavataḥ śrāvakāḥ paṇḍitā vyaktā medhāvinaḥ | a(lam utpannotpannānāṃ parapravādināṃ saha dharmeṇa nigrahītāraḥ svasya vādasya pa)ryavadātāro bhikṣavo bhikṣuṇya upāsakā upāsikā vaistārikaṃ ca te brahma(-caryaṃ bāhujanyaṃ pṛthubhūtaṃ yāvad devamanuṣyebhyaḥ samyaksaṃprakāśitam |)

CPS 4.6 (= MPS 16.8)
[a] na tāvat pāpīyan parinirv(āsyāmi yāvan na me śrāvakāḥ paṇḍitā bhaviṣyanti vyaktā me)(44.2)dhāvinaḥ | a(lam utpannotpannānāṃ para)pravādinā(ṃ saha dha)rmeṇa ni(grahī(127.6)tāraḥ | alaṃ svasya vādasya parya(vadātāro bhikṣavo bhikṣunya upāsakā upāsikā vaistārikaṃ ca) (44.3) me (bra)hmacaryaṃ bh(aviṣyati bahujanyaṃ p)ṛthubhutaṃ (yāvad devama)(127.7)nuṣuebhuaḥ samya(ks)upr(a)-kāṣi(tam |)

~15.11a, 15.12a, 15.13a, 15.14a, 15.15a~
DN III 123.19–124.22 (DN 29.12)
12. yato ca kho cunda etehi c' eva aṅgehi samannāgataṃ brahmacariyaṃ hoti, satthā ca hoti thero rattaññū cira-pabbajito addha-gato vayo anuppatto, therā c' assa bhikkhū sāvakā honti ... pe ... no ca khv assa majjhimā bhikkhū sāvakā honti ... pe ... majjhimā 'ssa bhikkhū sāvakā honti ... pe ... no ca khv assa navā bhikkhū sāvakā honti ... pe ... navā c' assa bhikkhū sāvakā honti ... pe ... no ca khv assa therā bhikkhuniyo sāvikā honti ... pe ... therā c' assa bhikkhuniyo sāvikā honti ... pe ... no ca khv assa majjhimā bhikkhuniyo sāvikā honti ... pe ... majjhimā c' assa bhikkhuniyo sāvikā honti ... pe ... no ca khv assa navā bhikkhuniyo sāvikā honti ... pe ... navā c' assa bhikkhuniyo sāvikā honti ... pe ... no ca khv assa upāsakā sāvakā honti gihī odāta-vasanā brahmacārino ... pe ... upāsakā c' assa sāvakā honti gihī odāta-vasanā brahmacārino ... pe ... no ca khv assa upāsakā sāvakā honti gihī odāta-vasanā kāma-bhogino ... pe ... upāsakā c' assa sāvakā honti gihī odāta-vasanā kāmabhogino ... pe ... no ca khv assa upāsikā sāvikā honti gihiniyo odāta-vasanā brahmacāriniyo ... pe ... upāsikā c' assa sāvikā honti gihiniyo odāta-vasanā brahmacāriniyo ... pe ... no ca khv assa upāsikā sāvikā honti gihiniyo odāta-vasanā kāma-bhoginiyo ... pe ... upāsikā c' assa sāvikā honti gihiniyo odāta-vasanā kāmabhoginiyo ... pe ... no ca khv assa brahmacariyaṃ iddhañ c' eva hoti phītañ ca vitthārikaṃ bāhu-jaññaṃ puthu-bhūtaṃ yāvad eva-manussehi suppakāsitaṃ ... pe ... brahmacariyaṃ c' assa hoti iddhañ c' eva phītañ ca vitthārikaṃ bāhu-jaññaṃ puthu-bhūtaṃ yāvad eva manussehi suppakāsitaṃ, no ca kho lābhagga-yasagga-ppattaṃ, evan taṃ brahmacariyaṃ aparipūraṃ hoti ten' aṅgena.

~15.11b, 15.12b, 15.13b, 15.14b, 15.15b~
DN III 124.23–125.8 (DN 29.13)
13. yato ca kho cunda etehi c' eva aṅgehi samannāgataṃ brahmacariyaṃ hoti satthā ca hoti thero rattaññū cirapabbajito addha-gato vayo anuppatto,

therā c' assa bhikkhū sāvakā honti vyattā vinītā ... pe ... sappāṭihāriyaṃ dhammaṃ desetuṃ, majjhimā c' assa bhikkhū sāvakā honti, navā c' assa bhikkhū sāvakā honti, therā c' assa bhikkhuniyo sāvikā honti, majjhimā c' assa bhikkhuniyo sāvikā honti, navā c' assa bhikkhuniyo sāvikā honti, upāsakā c' assa sāvakā honti gihī odāta-vasanā brahmacārino, upāsakā c' assa sāvakā honti gihī odāta-vasanā kāma-bhogino, upāsikā c' assa sāvikā honti gihiniyo odātavasanā brahmacāriniyo, upāsikā c' assa sāvikā honti gihiniyo odāta-vasanā kāma-bhoginiyo, brahmacariyaṃ c' assa hoti iddhañ c' eva phītañ ca vitthārikaṃ bāhujaññaṃ puthu-bhūtaṃ yāvad eva manussehi suppakāsitaṃ lābhagga-yasagga-ppattañ ca, evaṃ taṃ brahmacariyaṃ paripūraṃ hoti ten' aṅgena.

~15.11, 13–14~ cf. the following:

(13) T I 1 73c6–10

周那。導師出世。出家亦久。名聞亦廣。諸比丘尼未受訓誨。未至安處未獲己利。未能受法分布演說。有異論起不能以法如實除滅。未能變化成神通證。是爲梵行支未具足。

(14) T I 1 73c10–14

周那。導師出世。出家亦久。名聞亦廣。諸比丘尼盡受教訓。梵行具足。至安隱處已獲己利。復能受法分別演說。有異論起能如法滅。變化具足成神通證。是爲梵行支具足滿。

(15) T I 1 73c14–16

周那。諸優婆塞優婆夷廣修梵行。乃至變化具足成神通證。亦復如是。

~15.15~

T I 1 73c19–23

[a]若導師在世。名聞利養皆悉具足。而諸比丘名聞利養不能具足。是爲梵行支不具足。

[b] 若導師在世。名聞利養具足無損。諸比丘衆亦復具足。則梵行支爲具足滿。

Cf. T I 1 73c23

比丘尼衆亦復如是。

Cf. DN II 104.12–106.15 (*Mahāparinibbāna-sutta*, DN 16.3.7–8) for similar discussion:

7. atha kho māro pāpimā acira-pakkante āyasmante ānande yena bhagavā ten' upasaṃkami, upasaṃkamitvā ekamantaṃ aṭṭhāsi. ekamantaṃ ṭhito kho māro pāpimā bhagavantaṃ etad avoca: parinibbātu dāni bhante bhagavā, parinibbātu sugato, parinibbāna-kālo dāni bhante bhagavato. bhāsitā kho pan' esā bhante bhagavatā vācā: na tāvāhaṃ pāpima parinibbāyissāmi yāva me bhikkhū na sāvakā bhavissanti viyattā vinītā visāradā bahussutā dhamma-dharā dhammānudhamma-paṭipannā sāmīci-paṭipannā anudhamma-cārino, sakaṃ ācariyakaṃ uggahetvā ācikkhissanti desessanti paññāpessanti paṭṭhapessanti vivarissanti vibhajissanti uttāni-karissanti, uppannaṃ parappavādaṃ saha dhammena suniggahītaṃ niggahetvā sappāṭihāriyaṃ dhammaṃ desessantīti.

8. etarahi kho pana bhante bhikkhū bhagavato sāvakā viyattā vinītā visāradā bahussutā dhamma-dharā dhammānudhamma-paṭipannā sāmīci-paṭipannā anudhammacārino sakaṃ ācariyakaṃ uggahetvā ācikkhanti desenti paññāpenti paṭṭhapenti vivaranti vibhajanti uttāni-karonti, uppannaṃ parappavādaṃ saha dhammena suniggahītaṃ niggahetvā sappāṭihāriyaṃ dhammaṃ desenti. parinibbātu dāni bhante bhagavā, parinibbātu sugato, parinibbāna-kālo dāni bhante bhagavato.

bhāsitā kho pan' esā bhante bhagavatā vācā: na tāvāhaṃ pāpima parinibbāyissāmi yāva me bhikkhuniyo na sāvikā bhavissanti viyattā vinītā ... pe ... yāva me upāsakā na sāvakā bhavissanti viyattā vinītā visāradā bahussutā dhamma-dharā dhammānudhamma-paṭipannā sāmīci-paṭipannā anudhamma-cārino, sakaṃ ācariyakaṃ uggahetvā ācikkhissanti desessanti paññāpessanti paṭṭhapessanti vivarissanti vibhajissanti uttāni-karissanti, uppannaṃ parappavādaṃ saha dhammena niggahītaṃ niggahetvā sappāṭihāriyaṃ dhammaṃ desessantīti. etarahi kho pana bhante upāsakā bhagavato sāvakā viyattā vinītā visāradā bahussutā dhamma-dharā dhammānudhammapaṭipannā sāmīci-paṭipannā anudhamma-cārino sakaṃ ācariyakaṃ uggahetvā ācikkhanti desenti paññāpenti paṭṭhapenti vivaranti vibhajanti uttāni-karonti, uppannaṃ parappavādaṃ saha dhammena suniggahītaṃ niggahetvā sappāṭihāriyaṃ dhammaṃ desenti. parinibbātu dāni bhante bhagavā, parinibbātu sugato, parinibbāna-kālo dāni bhante bhagavato.

bhāsitā kho pan' esā bhante bhagavatā vācā: na tāvāhaṃ pāpima parinibbāyissāmi yāva me upāsikā na sāvikā bhavissanti viyattā vinītā vinītā visāradā bahussutā dhamma-dharā dhammānudhamma-paṭipannā sāmīci-paṭipannā anudhammacāriniyo, sakaṃ ācariyakaṃ uggahetvā ācikkhissanti desessanti paññāpessanti paṭṭhapessanti vivarissanti vibhajissanti uttāni-karissanti, uppannaṃ parappavādaṃ saha dhammena suniggahītaṃ niggahetvā sappāṭihāriyaṃ dhammaṃ desessantīti. etarahi kho pana bhante upāsikā bhagavato sāvikā viyattā vinītā visāradā bahussutā dhamma-dharā dhammānudhammapaṭipannā sāmīcipaṭipannā anudhamma-cāriniyo, sakaṃ ācariyakaṃ uggahetvā ācikkhanti desenti paññāpenti paṭṭhapenti vivaranti vibhajanti uttāni-karonti, uppannaṃ parappavādaṃ saha dhammena suniggahītaṃ niggahetvā sappāṭihāriyaṃ dhammaṃ desenti. parinibbātu dāni bhante bhagavā, parinibbātu sugato, parinibbāna-kālo dāni bhante bhagavato.

bhāsitā kho pan' esā bhante bhagavatā vācā: na tāvāhaṃ pāpima parinibbāyissāmi yāva me idaṃ brahmacariyaṃ na iddhañ c' eva bhavissati phītañ ca vitthārikaṃ bāhu-jaññaṃ puthu-bhūtaṃ, yāvad eva manussehi suppakāsitan ti. etarahi kho pana bhante bhagavato brahmacariyaṃ iddhañ c' eva phītañ ca vitthārikaṃ bāhujaññaṃ puthu-bhūtaṃ yāvad eva manussehi suppakāsitaṃ. parinibbātu dāni bhante bhagavā, parinibbātu sugato, parinibbāna-kālo dāni bhante bhagavato ti.

⁝ Udraka Rāmaputra (DĀ 15.16)

DĀ 15.16

[a] yāvantaḥ khalu cunda{ḥ} śāstriṃsaṃmatā nāham eka<ṃ> śāstāram (apy āt)m(a)nā[492] samasamaṃ samanup(a)ś(yām)i[493]<|> (ya eva)ṃ (lābhāgra)(**280v8**)(yaśogreṇa samanvāgatas; tadyathā aha)m[494] etarhi śāstā <|> yāvantaḥ khalu cunda saṃghā vā gaṇā vā parṣado vā nāham[495] eka<ṃ> śrāvakas(a)ṃgh(a)m apy ātmanā samasamaṃ (samanupaśyāmi) + + +[496] (**281r1**) ya evaṃ lābhāgrayaśogreṇa samanvāgatas; tadyathā aham etarhi śrāvakasaṃgha; iti cunda śāstāraṃ śrāvakasaṃgham asmākam evāgacchet <|> parataḥ sahadharmeṇa praśaṃsāsthānīyo dharma .. + + + ... +[497]

[b] .. .. + + + + +[498] (āma)(**281r2**)ntrayate[499] sma • udrako bhikṣavo rāmaputra evaṃdṛṣṭir evaṃvādī paśyan na paśyati • kiṃ paśyan na paśyati <|> {bhi}kṣurasya[500] satatalikhitasya yo dhārāṃ paśyati sa phalaṃ[501] na paśyati

492. Cf. 280v8.

493. Cf. 282r1 and DN III 126.7: *samanupassāmi*.

494. Cf. 280v8–281r1.

495. Ms. reads *aham*.

496. Cf. 280v7. There are extraneous akṣaras here that cannot be accounted for, as the reconstruction appears complete.

497. Owing to the damage to the ms., it is impossible to say where DĀ 15.16a ends and DĀ 15.16b begins. Thus the unreconstructed akṣaras ending DĀ 15.16a and beginning DĀ 15.16b are estimates.

498. Same problem as discussed above in note 497.

499. Cf. 276v2 and 299r5.

500. Cf. 281r3 and 281r4. Confusing *bhikṣur asya* with *kṣurasya* is a very easy mistake to make.

501. *Phala* is seen exclusively in these lines, while the Pali of the *Pāsādika-sutta* reads *tala*; cf. DN III 126.19–20: *khurassa sādhu-nisitassa talam assa passati, dhārañ ca kho tassa na passati.*

<|> yaḥ phalaṃ paśyati sa dhārā(ṃ) na paśyati <|> iti s(a dhārān pa)(281r3)-śyan pha(la)ṃ (na pa)śyati[502] phalasya paśyaṃ dhārān na paśyati <|>

[c] sa khalu bhikṣava udrakasya rāmaputrasya vāṇīhīnāyāṃ kṣuradhārāyām upasitāya[503] evam āha <|> paśyan na paśyati <|> kiṃ paśyan na paśyati <|> kṣurasya satata(l)i(khitasya)[504] **(281r4)** yo dhārāṃ paśyati sa phalaṃ <na> paśyati | yaḥ ph(al)aṃ paśyati sa dhārān na paśyati <|> iti dhārān paśyati phalaṃ paśyan dhārān na paśyati <|> kṣurasya bhikṣavaḥ satatalikhitasya yo dhārāṃ paśyati sa phalaṃ paśyati (| yaḥ phalaṃ)[505] **(281r5)** paśyati sa dhārāṃ paśyati <|> iti sa dhārān paśyan phalaṃ paśyati phalasya paśyan dhārāṃ paśyatīti |

[**d**] yad bhikṣavaḥ samyagvadanto vadeyuḥ paśyan na paśyatīti <|> iha tat samyagvadanto vadeyus; tat kasya heto .. + + + **(281r6)** paripūrṇaṃ brahmacaryam anenāṃgena paripūrṇaṃ; tad aṅgaṃ paripūrayiṣyāmīty[506] apy; enaṃ n[a] paśyati <|> <sarvā>kārapariśuddhaṃ brahmacaryam ity apy enaṃ paśyati <|> tat khalu sarvākārapariśuddhaṃ brahmacaryam ane(nā)ṃ-(gena pariśu)**(281r7)**ddhaṃ; tad aṅgam apanīyānyat pa<ri>śu<d-dha>taram[507] aṃgam upasaṃhariṣyāmaivam[508] idaṃ bhūyasyā[509] mātr(ayā) + + + + + .y. vadā taṃ ca bhavatīty apy enaṃ na paśyati <|>

DĀ 15.16

[a] [Buddha:] "Certainly, Cunda, insofar as there are those regarded as teachers, I do not consider (even) a single teacher equal to myself: (one who) is thus (endowed with the highest gain and the highest fame). Right now, I [am] (just such) a teacher. Certainly, Cunda, insofar as there are

Both words refer here to a blade or a knife's edge. S.v. *phala* in MW: "a blade (of a sword or knife)."

502. Cf. 281r5.

503. The meaning of *upasitāya* is unclear. Perhaps something like *upaśikṣita* ("learned, studied"; s.v. in MW) was intended here?

504. Cf. 281r2 and 281r4.

505. Cf. 281r2 and 281r4.

506. Ms. reads *paripūrayiṣyām ity*.

507. Cf. 281r6.

508. Ms. reads *upasaṃhariṣyāmevam*.

509. Ms. reads *bhūyasya*.

communities, or multitudes, or assemblies, I do not (consider) even a single community of disciples to be equal to my own—that which is thus endowed with the highest gain and the highest fame. Right now, I [have] just such a community of monks. Therefore, Cunda, one should truly have recourse to the community of monks and the teacher. Afterward, this dharma, legitimately having its place in praise [...]

[**b**] [...] he addressed:[...]. "Monks, Udraka Rāmaputra was one who held such a view, one who professed so: 'Seeing, he does not see.'[510] On seeing, what does he not see? One who sees the edge of a razor frequently used for shaving, he does not see the flat of the blade. One who sees the flat of the blade, he does not see the edge. Therefore, on seeing (the edge) he does (not) see the flat of the blade, and on seeing of the flat of the blade he does not see the edge.

[**c**] "Certainly, monks, regarding Udraka Rāmaputra's inferior speech [about] the edge of a razor, [...][511] he spoke thus: 'Seeing, he does not see. On seeing, what does he not see? One who sees the edge of a razor frequently used for shaving, he <does not> see the flat of the blade. One who sees the flat of the blade, he does not see the edge. Therefore he sees the edge, and on seeing the flat of the blade he does not see the edge.' Monks, one who sees the edge of a razor frequently used for shaving, he sees the flat of the blade. One who sees the flat of the blade, he sees the edge. Therefore, on seeing the edge he sees the flat of the blade, and on seeing of the flat of the blade he sees the edge.

[**d**] "Monks, saying it properly they should say: 'Seeing, he does not see.' In this case, saying it properly they should say: 'Why is this? [...] the holy life is fulfilled by this aspect.' [Thinking]: 'I will fulfill that aspect,' he does not see it. [Thinking]: 'The holy life is perfected in every way,' he sees it. Certainly, the holy life that is perfected in every way is perfect by this aspect. [Thinking]: 'Having removed that aspect, I will include another, more perfect aspect; in this way it is more [...],' he does not see it."

510. On this phrase, see Wynne 2007, 40–43.

511. *Upasitāya* in ms., which I have been unable to decipher. See note 503 above.

~15.16~

DN III 126.6–17 (DN 29.16)

[a] 16. yāvatā kho cunda etarahi satthāro loke uppannā, nāhaṃ cunda aññaṃ ekaṃ satthāram pi samanupassāmi evaṃ lābhagga-yasagga-ppattaṃ yatharivāhaṃ. yāvatā kho cunda etarahi saṃghā vā gaṇā loke uppannā, nāhaṃ cunda aññaṃ ekaṃ saṃghaṃ pi samanupassāmi evaṃ lābhagga-yasagga-ppattaṃ yathariva cunda bhikkhusaṅgho. yaṃ kho taṃ cunda sammā-vadamāno vadeyya—sabbākāra-sampannaṃ sabbākāra-paripūraṃ anūnaṃ anadhikaṃ svākkhātaṃ kevala-paripūraṃ brahmacariyaṃ suppakāsitan ti, idam eva taṃ sammā-vadamāno vadeyya—sabbākāra-sampannaṃ ... pe ... brahmacariyaṃ suppakāsitan ti.

DN III 126.17–23 (DN 29.16)

[b&c] uddako sudaṃ cunda rāmaputto evaṃ vācaṃ bhāsati: passan na passatīti. kiñ ca passan na passatīti? khurassa sādhu-nisitassa talam assa passati, dhārañ ca kho tassa na passati. idaṃ vuccati cunda—passan na passatīti. taṃ kho pan etaṃ cunda—uddakena rāmaputtena bhāsitaṃ hīnaṃ gammaṃ pothujjanikaṃ anariyaṃ anattha-saṃhitaṃ khuram eva sandhāya.

DN III 126.24–127.14 (DN 29.16)

[d] yañ ca taṃ cunda sammā-vadamāno vadeyya—passaṃ na passatīti, idam eva taṃ sammā-vadamāno vadeyya—passaṃ na passatīti. kiñ ca passaṃ na passatīti? evaṃ sabbākāra-sampannaṃ sabbākāra-paripūraṃ anūnaṃ anadhikaṃ svākkhātaṃ kevala paripūraṃ brahmacariyaṃ suppakāsitan ti. iti h' etaṃ passati, idam ettha apakaḍḍheyya, evan taṃ parisuddhataraṃ assāti. iti h' etaṃ na passati, idam ettha upakaḍḍheyya, evan taṃ paripūraṃ assāti. iti h' etaṃ na passati, idaṃ vuccati passaṃ na passatīti.' yaṃ kho taṃ cunda sammāvadamāno vadeyya—sabbākāra sampannaṃ ... pe ... brahmacariyaṃ suppakāsitan ti, idam etaṃ sammāvadamāno vadeyya—sabbākāra-sampannaṃ sabbākāraparipūraṃ anūnaṃ anadhikaṃ svākkhātaṃ kevala-paripūraṃ brahmacariyaṃ suppakāsitan ti.

T I 1 73c23–74a5

[a] 周那。我出家久。名聞廣遠。我諸比丘已受教誡。到安隱處自獲己利。復能受法爲人説法。有異論起能如法滅。變化具足成神通證。諸比丘比丘尼優婆塞優婆夷皆亦如是。周那。我以廣流布梵行。乃至變化具足成神通證。周那。一切世間所有導師。不見有得名聞利養如我如來至眞等正覺者也。周那。諸世

間所有徒衆。不見有名聞利養如我衆也。周那。若欲正說者。當言見不可見。云何見不可見。一切梵行清淨具足宣示布現。是名見不可見。

T I 174a5–8

[b] 爾時世尊告諸比丘。欝頭藍子。在大衆中而作是說。有見不見。云何名見不見。如刀可見刃不可見。

T I 174a7–8

[c] 諸比丘彼子乃引凡夫無識之言。以爲譬喩。

T I 174a8–13

[d] 如是周那。若欲正說者。當言見不見。云何見不見。汝當正欲説言。一切梵行清淨具足宣示流布。是不可見。周那。彼相續法不具足而可得。不相續法具足而不可得。周那。諸法中梵行。酪酥中醍醐。

Doctrines That Are Conducive to Dwelling Happily (DĀ 15.17)

DĀ 15.17

[**a**] tasmāt khalu bhikṣavo ye te dharmā dṛṣṭadharmasukhavihārāya saṃ(-vartante dṛṣṭadharmasu)(**281r8**)khāya saṃparāyahitāya saṃparāyasukhāya <|> te bhikṣu{ā}bhir udgṛhya paryavāpya tathā tath(ā dhāray)i(tavyā) <grāhayitavyā> (v)ācayitavyā yathedaṃ brahmacaryaṃ cirasthitikaṃ syāt <|> tad bhaviṣyati bahujanahitāya bahu(janasukhāya lokā)(**281v1**)-nukaṃpāyai arthāya hitāya sukhāya devamanuṣyāṇāṃ |[512]

[**b**] katame te bhi(kṣavo dharmā) + + + .. [513] dṛṣṭadharmahitāya saṃvartta<ṃ>te dṛṣṭadharmasukhāya saṃparāyahitāya saṃpa(rāyāsukhāya <|> te bhi)(**281v2**)kṣubhir udgṛhya pa<rya>vāpya tathā tathā dhārayitavyā grāhayitavyā vācayit(avyā yathedaṃ brahma)caryaṃ cira(sth)tikaṃ syāt <|> tad bhaviṣyati bahujanahitāya bahujanasukhāya lokānu(kaṃp)ā(yai arthāya hitā)(**281v3**)ya sukhāya devamanuṣyānāṃ;[514]

[**c**] tadyathā sūtraṃ geyaṃ vyāk(a)r(a)ṇ(aṃ) g(āthod)d(ānan)i(d)ānāva(d)ānetivṛttakajātakavaipulyādbhutadharmopadeśā <|> i{ya}-me te bhikṣavo dharmmā (dṛṣṭadharmahitā)(**281v4**)ya saṃvarttaṃ-te dṛṣṭadharmmasukhāya saṃparāyahitāya saṃparāyasukhāyeti <|> udgṛhya paryavāpya tathā tathā dhārayitavyā grāhayitavyā vāca<yitavyā> yathedaṃ brahmacaryaṃ cira(s)thitik(aṃ syāt | tad bha)(**281v5**)viṣyati

512. Cf. 281v1–2, 281v4–5, and MPS 19.7 and 40.60.

513. This reconstruction leaves an unexplained gap that is not consistent with the very close parallels found in MPS 19.8: *katame te dharmā dṛṣṭadharmahitāya* and MPS 40.61: *katame te dharmā dṛṣtad(harma)h(i)tāya.*

514. Cf. 281r8, 281v4, and MPS 19.8 and 40.61

<bahujanahitāya>[515] bahujanasukhāya lok(ān)ukaṃpāyai arthāya hitāya sukhāya devamanuṣyāṇāṃ;[516]

DĀ 15.17

[**a**] [Buddha:] "Therefore indeed, monks, those doctrines—those that are conducive to dwelling happily in this present state of existence, to happiness in this present state of existence, to benefit in the next state of existence, and to happiness in the next state of existence—having been grasped and comprehended by monks, the more they are to be held in mind, familiarized with, and recited, the more this holy life might have a long existence. It will be for the benefit of many people, for the happiness of many people, for compassion for the world, for the sake, benefit, and happiness of gods and men.

[**b**] "Monks, what are these (doctrines) [...] that are conducive to benefit in this present state of existence, to happiness in this present state of existence, to benefit in the next state of existence, and to happiness in the next state of existence; that having been grasped and comprehended by monks, the more they are to be held in mind, familiarized with, and recited (the more this) holy life might have a long existence; that will be for the benefit of many people, for the happiness of many people, for compassion for the world, for the sake, benefit, and happiness of gods and men?

[**c**] "Namely, they are: *sūtra*, *geya*, *vyākaraṇa*, *gāthā*, *uddāna*, *nidāna*, *avadāna*, *itivṛttaka*, *jātaka*, *vaipulya*, *adbhutadharma*, and *upadeśa*.[517] These, monks, are 'those doctrines that are conducive to benefit in this present state of existence, to happiness in this present state of existence, to

515. Omission due to haplographical error.

516. Cf. 281r8, 281v1, and 281v2, MPS 19.9–10 and 40.62, and SaṅgE 314 (= Saṅg 45) para. 26 (= Saṅg z).

517. The *dvādaśāṅga dharma pravacana* (the twelvefold classification of [Buddhist] instruction) as enumerated in the *Mahāvyutpatti* (no. 1267–1278 in Sakaki 1916 and no. 1272–1283 in Ishihama and Fukuda 1989). For more on this list and its relation to the *navāṅga* classification see Lamotte 1980, Tome V, 2281–2305, Lamotte 1988a, 143–47, Hikata 1983, 55–58, Hirakawa 1963, 61–65, Hirakawa and Groner 1990, 74–75, Burnouf 2010, 97–110 and these articles that deal with these classifications: von Hinüber 1994, Nattier 2003, Anālayo 2020b, Anālayo and Travagnin 2020, and Choong 2020. For the specific term *vaipulya* found in the *dvādaśāṅga* see Skilling 2013, (esp. 86 and 157 for the *dvādaśāṅga*), and Karashima 2015.

benefit in the next state of existence, and to happiness in the next state of existence.' Having been grasped and comprehended by monks, the more they are to be held in mind, familiarized with, and recited, the more this holy life might have a long existence. It will be for the benefit of many people, <for the happiness of many people>, for compassion for the world, for the sake, benefit, and happiness of gods and men."

~15.17~

DN III 127.15–128.7 (DN 29.17)

[a] 17. tasmāt iha cunda ye vo mayā dhammā abhiññā desitā, tattha sabbeh' eva saṅgamma samāgamma atthena atthaṃ vyañjanena vyañjanaṃ saṅgāyitabbaṃ na vivaditabbaṃ, yathayidaṃ brahmacariyaṃ addhaniyaṃ assa cira-ṭṭhitikaṃ, tad assa bahujana-hitāya bahujana-sukhāya lokānukampāya atthāya hitāya sukhāya deva-manussānaṃ.

[b] katame ca te cunda mayā dhammā abhiññā desitā yattha sabbeh' eva saṅgamma samāgamma atthena atthaṃ vyañjanena vyañjanaṃ saṅgāyitabbaṃ na vivaditabbaṃ, yathayidaṃ brahmacariyaṃ addhaniyaṃ assa cira-ṭṭhitikaṃ, tad assa bahujana-hitāya bahujana-sukhāya lokānukampāya atthāya hitāya sukhāya deva-manussānaṃ?

[c] seyyathīdaṃ cattāro satipaṭṭhānā, cattāro samma-ppadhānā, cattāro iddhi-pādā, pañc' indriyāni, pañca balāni, satta bojjhaṅgā, ariyo aṭṭhaṅgiko maggo. ime kho te cunda dhammā mayā abhiññā desitā, yattha sabbeh' eva saṃgamma samāgamma atthena atthaṃ vyañjanena vyañjanaṃ saṅgāyitabbaṃ na vivaditabbaṃ, yathayidaṃ brahmacariyaṃ addhaniyaṃ assa cira-ṭṭhitikaṃ, tad assa bahujana-hitāya bahujana-sukhāya lokānukampāya atthāya hitāya sukhāya deva-manussānaṃ.

T I 1 74a13–15

[a–c] 爾時世尊告諸比丘。我於是法躬自作證。謂四念處四神足四意斷四禪五根五力七覺意賢聖八道。

T I 1 74b19–24

[c] 是故比丘。於十二部經自身作證當廣流布。一曰貫經。二曰祇夜經。三曰受記經。四曰偈經。五曰法句經。六曰相應經。七曰本緣經。八曰天本經。九曰廣經。十曰未曾有經。十一曰譬喻經。十二曰大教經。當善受持稱量觀察廣演分布。

~15.17a~

MPS 19.7

19.7 tasmāt tarh(i) bhikṣavo ye te dharm(ā) dṛṣṭadharmahitāya saṃva(r)tante dṛṣṭadharmasukhāya saṃparāy(ahitāya saṃpa)rāyasukhāya te bhikṣubhir udgṛhya paryavāpya (tathā ta)th(ā) dhārayitavyā grāhayitavyā vācayitavyā yathedaṃ brahmacaryaṃ cirasthitikaṃ syāt tad bhaviṣ(yati bahu)janahitāya bahujanasukhāya lo(kānukam)pāyārthāya hitāya sukhāya devamanuṣyāṇāṃ |

DN II 119.25–30 (*Mahāparinibbāna-sutta*, DN 16.50)

tasmāt iha bhikkhave ye vo mayā dhammā abhiññāya desitā, te vo sādhukaṃ uggahetvā āsevitabbā bhāvetabbā bahulī-kātabbā, yathayidaṃ brahmacariyaṃ addhaniyaṃ assa ciraṭṭhitikaṃ, tad assa bahujana-hitāya bahujana-sukhāya lokānukampāya atthāya hitāya sukhāya deva-manussānaṃ.

MPS 40.60

40.60 (tasmāt ta)rhi bhikṣavo ye te dharmā dṛṣṭadharmahitāya s(aṃ)vartante dṛṣṭadharmasukhāya sāṃp(arāyahitāya) sāṃparāyasukhāya te bhikṣubhir udgṛhya paryavāpya ta(thā tathā dhā)rayitavyā grāhayitavyā vācayitavyā yathedaṃ brahmacaryaṃ cirasthitikaṃ bha)viṣyati bahujanahitāya bahujanasukhāya (lokānu)kaṃpāyārthāya hitāya sukhāya devamanuṣyāṇām |

DN III 211.15–20 (*Saṅgīti-sutta*, DN 33.7)

atthi kho āvuso tena bhagavatā jānatā passatā arahatā sammā-sambuddhena eko dhammo sammad-akkhāto. tattha sabbeh' eva saṅgāyitabbaṃ na vivaditabbaṃ, yathayidaṃ brahmacariyaṃ addhaniyaṃ assa cira-ṭṭhitikaṃ, tad assa bahujana-hitāya bahujana-sukhāya lokānukampāya atthāya hitāya sukhāya deva-manussānaṃ.

~15.17b~

MPS 19.8

19.8 katame te dharmā dṛṣṭadharmahitāya (saṃvartante dṛ)ṣṭadharmasukhāya sa(ṃ)parāyahitāy(a saṃparā)y(a)s(u)khāya te bhikṣubhir udgṛhya pūrvavad yāvad devamanuṣyāṇām |

DN II 119.30–120.3 (*Mahāparinibbāna-sutta*, DN 16.50)

katame ca te bhikkhave dhammā mayā abhiññāya desitā, ye vo sādhukaṃ uggahetvā āsevitabbā bhāvetabbā bahulī-kātabbā yathayidaṃ brahmacariyaṃ addhaniyaṃ assa ciraṭṭhitikaṃ, tad assa bahujana-hitāya bahujana-sukhāya lokānukampāya atthāya hitāya sukhāya deva-manussānaṃ?

MPS 40.61
40.61 katame te dharmā dṛṣṭad(harma)h(i)tāya saṃvartante pūrvavad yāvad devamanuṣyāṇām |

DN III 211.2–212.3 (*Saṅgīti-sutta*, DN 33.8)
8. Katamo eko dhammo? Sabbe sattā āhāra-ṭṭhitikā, sabbe sattā saṃkhāraṭṭhitikā. Ayaṃ kho āvuso tena Bhagavatā jānatā passatā arahatā Sammā-Sambuddhena eko dhammo sammadakkhāto. Tattha sabbeh' eva saṅgāyitabbaṃ na vivaditabbaṃ, yathayidaṃ brahmacariyaṃ addhaniyaṃ assa cira-ṭṭhitikaṃ, tad assa bahujana-hitāya bahujana-sukhāya lokānukampāya atthāya hitāya sukhāya deva-manussānaṃ.

~15.17c~
MPS 19.9 and 19.10
19.9 tadyathā catvāri smṛtyup(asthānāni catvāri) s(a)myakprahāṇāni catvāra ṛddhipādāḥ pañcendri(yāṇi pañca ba)lāni sapta bodhyaṅgāny āryāṣṭāṅgo mārgaḥ |

19.10 ime te dharmā dṛṣṭadharmahitāya saṃvart(ante pūrvavad yāvad devamanu)ṣyāṇām |

DN II 120.3–11 (*Mahāparinibbāna-sutta*, DN 16.50)
seyyathīdaṃ cattāro satipaṭṭhānā, cattāro samma-ppadhāna, cattāro iddhipādā, pañc' indriyāni, pañca balāni, satta bojjhaṅgā, ariyo aṭṭhaṅgiko maggo. ime kho bhikkhave dhammā mayā abhiññāya desitā, te vo sādhukaṃ uggahetvā āsevitabbā bhāvetabbā bahulī-kātabbā yathayidaṃ brahmacariyaṃ addhaniyaṃ assa ciraṭṭhitikaṃ, tad assa bahujana-hitāya bahujana-sukhāya lokānukampāya atthāya hitāya sukhāya deva-manussānan ti.

MPS 40.62
40.62 tadyathā sūtraṃ geyaṃ svyā)karaṇaṃ gāthodānanidānāvadānetivṛttakajātakavaipulyādbhutadharmopadeśāḥ | ime te dharmā dṛṣṭadharmahitāya saṃvartante pūrvavad yāvad devamanuṣyāṇām |

SaṅgE 314 (= Saṅg 45) para. 26 (= Saṅg z)
te vayam sa(ṃhitāḥ samagrāḥ saṃmodamānā bhūtvā saṃśayāya na viva)dāmahe yathedaṃ brahmacaryam c(ira)sthi(tikaṃ syāt | tad bhaviṣya)(14.1/18.1)ti bahujanahitā(13.6/16.6)ya bahujanasukhāya lokānu(kaṃpāyārthāya hitāya sukhāya devamanuṣyāṇām |)

DN III 212.4–7 (*Saṅgīti-sutta*, DN 33.9)

9. atthi kho āvuso tena bhagavatā jānatā passatā arahatā sammā-sambuddhena dve dhammā sammadakkhātā. tattha sabbeh' eva saṅgāyitabbaṃ ... pe ... atthāya hitāya sukhāya deva-manussānaṃ.

Monks of Various Views (DĀ 15.18–21)

DĀ 15.18

[**a**] api tu khalu yūyaṃ bhikṣavas sarve nānādṛṣṭayo nānākṣāntayo nānārucayo[518] nānā(bh)i(prāyā)(**281v6**)s te(ṣā)ṃ <vo> bhikṣavo nānādṛṣṭīnāṃ nānākṣāntīnāṃ nānā<ru>cīnāṃ nānābhiprāyāṇāṃ bhikṣur upasaṃkramya dharmaṃ bhāṣeta <|> sa samyañ cārtham upasaṃharen mithyā ca vya<ṃ>-janaṃ nirūpayet <|> asy(a bhikṣos ta)(**281v7**)d bhāṣitaṃ naivotsāhayitavyaṃ nāvasādayitavyam* <|> anutsāhyānavasādya[519] śrotram avadadhāya dharmapadavyaṃjanān<y> udgṛhya ta(sm)i(n vyaṃjane) anyad yuktataraṃ (vya)ṃjanam upasaṃhṛtya <bhikṣum> evaṃ (s)y(ād vaca)(**281v8**)-nīyaḥ <|>[520]

[**b**] asmiṃ tvam āyuṣmann arthe katarad yuktataraṃ vyaṃjanaṃ samanupaśyasy etad vā idaṃ veti <|> sacet sa evaṃ vaded asminn aham āyuṣmanto 'rthe i(da)ṃ (y)uktataraṃ (vya)ṃ(jana)ṃ + + + + + + + + (**282r1**) samanupaśyāmi na tathedam iti sa bhikṣu<bhi>r idaṃ syād vacanīyo; tena hi tvam āyuṣmaṃ caitad vyaṃjanaṃ chorayitvā anena vyaṃjanenaitam arthaṃ dhāraya[521] <|> evam atra pare saṃjñapayitavyā yad ut(a vyaṃjanaśaḥ |)[522]

518. Note a similar use of these three phrases, *dṛṣṭi*, *kṣānti*, and *ruci*, in DhskM 22v10: *śrotravijñānānubhūtaṃ śrotravijñānaprativijñaptaṃ sa vinidhāya saṃjñāṃ vinidhāya kṣāntiṃ ruciṃ matiṃ prekṣāṃ dṛṣṭiṃ na me śrutam ity āha*. Here we see that *dṛṣṭi*, *kṣānti*, and *ruci* are joined by *abhiprāya* as opposed to *mati*.

519. Ms. reads *anutsahyānavasādya*.

520. Cf. 282r2, 282r3, 282r4, 282r5, 282v1, 282v2, and 282v3 and MPS 24.6, 24.12, 24,18, 24.24, 24.29, 24.35, 24.41, and 24.47.

521. Ms. reads *dhanaya*.

522. Cf. 282r2, 282r3, 282r4, 282r5, 282v1, 282v2, and 282v3.

DĀ 15.18

[a] [Buddha:]"However, all you monks who are of various views, various abilities, various inclinations, and various opinions, suppose a monk having approached all you monks of various views, various abilities, various inclinations, and various opinions were to speak about dharma. Suppose he were to declare[523] the meaning correctly and state the wording incorrectly.[524] The speech of this (monk) is to be neither encouraged nor is it to be rebuked. Having neither encouraged nor rebuked, having paid heed, having comprehended the wording of the dharma sayings, and having declared the wording that is more suitable than others regarding the (wording), that <monk> should be addressed in this way:

[b] "'Venerable sir, which wording do you consider more suitable in regard to the meaning, this or that?' If he were to say this: 'Venerable sirs, I consider [...] this wording more suitable in regard to the meaning and not so that,' he should be addressed by the monks like this: 'Now then, venerable sir, having renounced that wording, hold in mind the meaning along with this [correct] wording.' Thus, in this respect, others are made to agree in regard to wording."

DĀ 15.19

[a] (api khal)u (yūyaṃ bhikṣavas) **(282r2)** sarve nānādṛṣṭayo nānākṣāntayo nānārucayo nānābhiprāyās teṣāṃ vo bhikṣavo nānādṛṣṭīnāṃ nānākṣāntīnāṃ nānā{ṃ}rūcīnāṃ nānābhiprāyāṇāṃ bhikṣur upasaṃkra(m)ya dharmaṃ bhāṣeta <|> sa mi(thyā c)ārtham upasaṃharet samyañ ca vyaṃja(naṃ nirū)**(282r3)**payet <|> t(a)sya bhikṣos tad bhāṣitaṃ naivotsāhayitavyaṃ nāvasādayitavyaṃ; anutsāhyānavasādya śrotram ava<da>dhāya dharmapadavyaṃjanāny udgṛhya tasmin vyaṃjane anyad y(u)ktataraṃ artham upasaṃhṛ(t)ya bhi(kṣu){ṃ}(r evaṃ)[525] **(282r4)** syād vacanīyaḥ;[526]

523. S.v. *upasaṃharati* (esp. definitions 4 and 5) in BHSD and *upasaṁharati* (esp. definition 3) in CPD.

524. *Artha* and *vyañjana*. For information on the use of these terms broadly within sūtra literature see Lamotte 1988b, 13–16, and Potter 1996, 99–100.

525. Cf. 281v5, 281v6, 281v7, 282r2, 282v2, and 282v3 and MPS 24.6, 24.12, 24,18, 24.24, 24.29, 24.35, 24.41, and 24.47.

526. Ms. reads *vacanīyaṃ*.

[**b**] asmiṃs tvam āyuṣman[527] vyaṃjane katarad yuktataram arthaṃ samanupaśyasy enaṃ[528] vā idaṃ veti <|> sacet sa evaṃ vadet tasminn aham āyuṣmanto vyaṃjane idaṃ yuktataram arthaṃ samanupaśyāmi (na tathedam i)(**282r5**)ti sa <bhikṣubhir> idaṃ syād vacanīyas; tena hi tva(m ā)y(u)ṣmann imam <arthaṃ chorayitvā anena>[529] arthenaitad vyaṃjanaṃ dhāraya <|> evam atra pare saṃjñapayitavyā yad utārthaśaḥ <|>[530]

▪ ▪ ▪ ▪ ▪

DĀ 15.19

[a] [Buddha:] "Moreover, all (you monks) who are of various views, various abilities, various inclinations, and various opinions, suppose a monk having approached all you monks of various views, various abilities, various inclinations, and various opinions were to speak about dharma. Suppose he were to declare the meaning incorrectly and state the wording correctly. The speech of this monk is to be neither encouraged nor is it to be rebuked. Having neither encouraged nor rebuked, having paid heed, having comprehended the wording of the doctrinal sayings, and having declared the meaning that is more suitable than others regarding the wording, that monk should be addressed (in this way):

[**b**] "'Venerable sir, which meaning do you consider more suitable in regard to the wording, that or this?' If he were to say this: 'In this case, venerable sirs, I consider this meaning more suitable in regard to the wording (and not so that),' he should be addressed by the monks like this: 'Now then, venerable sir, <having renounced> that <meaning> hold in mind the wording along with this [correct] meaning.' Thus, in this respect, others are made to agree in regard to meaning."

▪ ▪ ▪ ▪ ▪

DĀ 15.20

[a] api khalu yūyaṃ bhikṣavaḥ sarve nānādṛṣṭayo nānāk(ṣāntay)o nān(ārucayo) (**282r6**) nānābhiprāyās teṣāṃ vo bhikṣavo nānādṛṣṭ(ī)nā(ṃ)

527. Ms. reads *āyuṣmad*.

528. Note the usage of *enam* here as opposed to *etat* in the other instances. *Etat* is preferable as it maintains the proper, neuter gender of both *artha* and *vyañjana* while *enam* is masculine.

529. Cf. 282r1.

530. Cf. 281v5, 281v6, 281v7, 282r2, 282v2, and 282v3.

nānākṣāntīnā(ṃ) nānārucīnāṃ nānābhiprā(y)āṇāṃ bhikṣu(r u)pasaṃkramya dharmaṃ bhāṣeta <|> sa mithyā cārtham upasaṃhare(n m)i(thy)ā (ca v)yaṃjanaṃ nirūpayet (| tasya bhikṣos tad bhāṣi)(**282r7**)taṃ naivotsāhayitavyaṃ nāvasādayitavyaṃ; anutsāhyānavasādya śro(t)ram ava(dadhāya dharmapadavya)ṃjanān<y> udgṛh(ya) tasminn arthapadavyaṃja(ne) anyad[531] yuktataraṃ arthav(ya)ṃjanam upasa(ṃ)hṛtya bhi(k)ṣu(ṃ evaṃ syād vacanīyaḥ|)[532]

[**b**] (**282r8**) katama<ṃ> tvam āyuṣmann arthavyaṃjanaṃ yuktataraṃ samanupaśyasy etad vā i(da)ṃ (veti | sacet sa evaṃ vadet tasminn a)ham āyu(ṣ)m(a)nt(o) 'rth(av)y(aṃ)janaṃ yu(k)t(a)taraṃ sam(a)nu(paś)y(ām)īti[533] sa bhikṣubhir idaṃ syād va(canīyas; tena hi tvam ā)(**282v1**)yuṣmann etad a<rtha>vyaṃjanaṃ cchorayitvā idaṃ arthavyaṃjanaṃ dhāraya <|> (evam atra pare saṃjñāpay)it(av)yā yad utārthaśo vyaṃjanaśaś ca •[534]

DĀ 15.20

[a] [Buddha:] "Moreover, all you monks who are of various views, various abilities, various inclinations, and various opinions, suppose a monk having approached all you monks of various views, various abilities, various inclinations, and various opinions were to speak about dharma. Suppose he were to declare the meaning incorrectly and state the wording incorrectly. (The) speech (of this monk) is to be neither encouraged nor is it to be rebuked. Having neither encouraged nor rebuked, having paid heed, having comprehended the wording of the doctrinal sayings, and having declared the meaning and wording that is more suitable than others regarding the meaning and wording, that monk (should be addressed in this way):

[**b**] "'Venerable sir, which meaning and wording do you consider more suitable, this (or) that?' (If he were to say this): 'In this case, venerable sirs, I consider [this] meaning and wording more suitable,' he should be addressed by the monks like this: 'Now then, venerable sir, having renounced that

531. Ms. reads *anud.*

532. Cf. 281v5, 281v6, 281v7, 281v8, 282r1, 282r2, 282r3, 282r4, 282r5, 282v1, 282v2, and 282v3 and and MPS 24.6, 24.12, 24.18, 24.24, 24.29, 24.35, 24.41, and 24.47.

533. Ms reads *samanupaśyāmi ti.*

534. Cf. 281v5, 281v6, 281v7, 281v8, 282r1, 282r2, 282r3, 282r4, 282r5, 282v1, 282v2, and 282v3.

meaning and wording, hold in mind this [correct] meaning and wording.' (Thus, in this respect, others) are made to agree in regard to meaning and wording."

DĀ 15.21

a(p)i khal(u yūya)ṃ bhikṣav(a)s (sarv)e (n)ā(n)ā(dṛṣṭayo nānākṣāntayo nana)(282v2)rucayo nānābhiprāyā<s> teṣāṃ vo bhikṣavo nānādṛṣṭīnāṃ nānākṣānt(īnāṃ nānārucīnāṃ nānābhipr)āyāṇāṃ bhikṣur upasaṃkramya dha(rma)ṃ bhāṣet(a) <|> s(a) s(am)y(añ) c(ārtham upasaṃharet samyañ ca vyaṃjanaṃ nirūpaye)(282v3)t <|> tasya bhikṣos tad bhāṣitaṃ sādhv abhinan(d)itavyaṃ sādhv anumoditavya(ṃ) sādhv abhinaṃdya{ṃ} sādhv anumodya uttare idaṃ syād vacanīya<ḥ |> evaṃ hy āyuṣman. .. + + + + .t. .. .. c. .u .. + + + + + (282v4) bhavati <|>[535]

DĀ 15.21

[Buddha:] "Moreover, all you monks who are of various views, various abilities, various inclinations, and various opinions, suppose a monk having approached all you monks of various views, various abilities, (various inclinations), and various opinions were to speak about dharma. (Suppose he were to declare) the meaning (correctly and) state (the wording correctly). The speech of this monk is to be applauded as wonderful and to be happily accepted as wonderful. Having applauded it as wonderful and having happily accepted it as wonderful, it should be addressed further: 'Thus indeed, venerable sir, it is [...].'"

~15.18~

DN III 129.9–20 (DN 29.20)

[a] 20. aparo pi ce cunda sabrahmacārī saṅghe dhammaṃ bhāseyya, tatra ce tumhākaṃ evam assa—ayaṃ kho āyasmā atthaṃ hi kho sammā gaṇhāti, vyañjanāni micchā ropetī ti, tassa n' eva abhinanditabbaṃ na paṭikkositabbaṃ. anabhinanditvā appaṭikkositvā so evam assa vacanīyo—

[b] imassa nu kho āvuso atthassa imāni ca vyañjanāni etāni vā vyañjanāni, katamāni opāyikatarānīti? so ce evaṃ vadeyya—imassa nu kho āvuso atthassa imān eva vyañjanāni opāyikatarāni, yāni c' eva etānī ti, so n' eva

535. Cf. 281v5, 281v6, 282r1, 282r2, 282r3, 282r5, and 282r6.

ussādetabbo na apasādetabbo. anussādetvā anapasādetvā so yeva sādhukaṃ saññāpetabbo tesaṃ ñeva vyañjanānaṃ nisantiyā.

T I 1 74a25–74b1

[a] 如是盡共和合勿生諍訟。同一受同一師同一乳於如來正法。當自熾然快得安樂。得安樂已。若有比丘說法。中有比丘作是言。彼所說句不正義正。比丘聞已。不可言是不可言非。當語彼比丘言。

T I 1 74b01–5

[b] 云何比丘。我句如是汝句如是。何者爲是。何者爲非。若彼比丘報言。我句如是汝句如是汝句亦勝。彼比丘說此。亦不得言是不得言非。當諫彼比丘。當呵當止當共推求。

~15.19~

DN III 128.24–129.8 (DN 29.19)

[a] aparo pi ce cunda sabrahmacārī saṅghe dhammaṃ bhāseyya. tatra ce tumhākaṃ evam assa — ayaṃ kho āyasmā atthaṃ hi kho micchā gaṇhāti, vyañjanāni sammā ropetī ti, tassa n' eva abhinanditabbaṃ na paṭikkositabbaṃ. anabhinanditvā appaṭikkositvā so evam assa vacanīyo —

[b] imesaṃ nu kho āvuso vyañjanānaṃ ayaṃ vā attho eso vā attho, katamo opāyikataro ti? so ce evaṃ vadeyya — imesaṃ kho āvuso vyañjanānaṃ ayam eva attho opāyikataro, yo c' eva eso ti, so n' eva ussādetabbo na apasādetabbo. anussādetvā anapasādetvā so yeva sādhukaṃ saññāpetabbo tass' ev' atthassa nisantiyā.

T I 1 74b05–10

[a] 如是盡共和合勿生諍訟。同一師受同一水乳。於如來正法。當自熾然快得安樂。得安樂已。若有比丘說法。中有比丘作是言。彼所說句正義不正。比丘聞已。不可言是不可言非。當語彼比丘言。

T I 1 74b10–14

[b] 云何比丘。我義如是汝義如是。何者爲是何者爲非。若彼報言。我義如是汝義如是。汝義而勝。彼比丘說此已。亦不得言是亦不得言非。當諫彼比丘。當呵當止當共推求。

~15.20~

DN III 128.8–18 (DN 29.18)

[a] 18. tesañ ca vo cunda samaggānaṃ sammodamānānaṃ avivadamānānaṃ sikkhitabbaṃ, aññataro sabrahmacārī saṅghe dhammaṃ bhāseyya. tatra ce tumhākaṃ evam assa—ayaṃ kho āyasmā atthañ c' eva micchā gaṇhāti, vyañjanāni ca micchā ropetī ti, tassa n' eva abhinanditabbaṃ na paṭikkositabbaṃ. anabhinanditvā appaṭikkositvā so evam assa vacanīyo—

[b] imassa nu kho āvuso atthassa imāni vā vyañjanāni etāni vā vyañjanāni, katamāni opāyikatarāni; imesaṃ vā vyañjanānaṃ ayaṃ vā attho eso vā attho, katamo opāyikataro ti? so ce evaṃ vadeyya—imassa kho āvuso atthassa imān eva vyañjanāni opāyikatarāni yāni c' eva etāni, imesaṃ vyañjanānaṃ ayam eva attho opāyikataro yo c' eva eso ti, so n' eva ussādetabbo na apasādetabbo. anussādetvā na apasādetvā so va sādhukaṃ saññāpetabbo, tassa ca atthassa tesañ ca vyañjanānaṃ nisantiyā.

T I 1 74a16–20

[a] 汝等盡共和合勿生諍訟。同一師受同一水乳。於如來正法當自熾然快得安樂。得安樂已。若有比丘說法中有作是言。彼所說句不正義理不正。比丘聞已。不可言是不可言非。當語彼比丘言。

T I 1 74a20–25

[b] 云何諸賢。我句如是汝句如是。我義如是汝義如是。何者爲勝何者爲負。若彼比丘報言我句如是我義如是。汝句如是汝義如是。汝句亦勝汝義亦勝。彼比丘說此。亦不得非亦不得是。當諫彼比丘。當呵當止當共推求。

~15.21~

DN III 129.21–29 (DN 29.21)

21. aparo pi ce cunda sabrahmacārī saṅghe dhammaṃ bhāseyya, tatra ce tumhākaṃ evam assa—ayaṃ kho āyasmā atthaṃ ñeva sammā gaṇhāti, vyañjanāni sammā ropetī ti, tassa sādhū ti bhāsitaṃ abhinanditabbaṃ anumoditabbaṃ. tassa sādhū ti bhāsitaṃ abhinanditvā anumoditvā so evam assa vacanīyo—lābhā no āvuso, suladdhaṃ no āvuso, ye mayaṃ āyasmantaṃ tādisaṃ sabrahmacāriṃ passāma evaṃ atthūpetaṃ vyañjanūpetan ti.

T I 1 74b14–19

如是比丘盡共和合勿生諍訟。同一師受同一水乳。於如來正法當自熾然快得安樂。得安樂已。若有比丘說法。中有比丘。作如是言。彼所說句正義正。比丘聞已不得言非。當稱讚彼言。汝所言是汝所言是。

~15.18a, 15.19a, & 15.20a~

MPS 24.6 (=24.12, 24.18, 24.24, 24.29, 24.35, 24.41, 24.47)

24.6 t(asya bhikṣavas tan) notsāhayit(a)vyaṃ nāvasādayitavyam | anutsāhayitvānavasādayitvā śrotram avadhā(ya tāni pa)davyaṃjanāny udgṛhya sūtre 'vatār(ayitavyaṃ vina)y(e) saṃdarśayitavyaṃ | yadi sūtr(e) 'vatāryamāṇā vinaye saṃdarśyamānāḥ sūtre nāvataran(ti vinaye) na saṃdṛśyante dharmatāṃ ca vilomayanti (sa eva)ṃ syād vacanīyaḥ |

DN II 124.3–19 (*Mahāparinibbāna-sutta*, DN 16.4.8)

8. idha bhikkhave bhikkhu evaṃ vadeyya: sammukhā me taṃ āvuso bhagavato sutaṃ sammukhā paṭiggahītaṃ, ayaṃ dhammo ayaṃ vinayo idaṃ satthu sāsanan ti, tassa bhikkhave bhikkhuno bhāsitaṃ n' eva abhinanditabbaṃ na paṭikkositabbaṃ. anabhinanditvā appaṭikkositvā tāni pada-vyañjanāni sādhukaṃ uggahetvā sutte otāretabbāni vinaye sandassetabbāni. tāni ce sutte otāriyamānāni vinaye sandassiyamānāni na c' eva sutte otaranti na vinaye sandissanti, niṭṭham ettha gantabbaṃ: addhā idaṃ na c' eva tassa bhagavato vacanaṃ, imassa ca bhikkhuno duggahītan ti, iti h' etaṃ bhikkhave chaḍḍeyyātha. tāni ce sutte otāriyamānāni vinaye sandassiyamānāni sutte c' eva otaranti vinaye ca sandissanti, niṭṭham ettha gantabbaṃ: addhā idaṃ tassa bhagavato vacanaṃ imassa ca bhikkhuno suggahītan ti. idaṃ bhikkhave paṭhamaṃ mahā-padesaṃ dhāreyyātha.

Robes and That Which Is Allowed by the Buddha (DĀ 15.22)

DĀ 15.22

[**a**] yad yuṣmākaṃ bhikṣavo ma(y)ā c(ī)varam anujñātaṃ yadi vā pāṃsukūlaṃ yadi vā gṛhapaticīvaram alaṃ vas tat pratisevituṃ na dravārthaṃ na (madārthaṃ na ma)ṇ(ḍa)nārthaṃ na vibhūṣ(aṇārthaṃ yāvad eva daṃ)-(**282v5**)ṣamaśakavātātapasarīsṛpasaṃsparśānāṃ[536] pratighātārthaṃ hrīkaupīnapracchādanārthaṃ ca <|>[537]

[**b**] yad yuṣmākaṃ bhikṣavo mayā bhojanam a(n)ujñātaṃ y(adi vā piṇḍapāto yad)i (vā) + ... (n)i(mantra)(**282v6**)ṇakaḥ[538] alaṃ vas tat pratisevituṃ na dravārthaṃ[539] na madārthaṃ na maṇḍanārthaṃ na vibhūṣaṇārthaṃ yāvad eva kāyasya sthitay(e) yāpanāyai jigh(atsoparatаye brahmacaryānugrahāya iti |) (**282v7**) purāṇīṃ ca vedanā<ṃ>

536. Ms. reads *gamaśaka*°.

537. Cf. 282v6, 282v7, 282v8, 283r1, and 283r2 as well as Śrāv-bh I 9*: (I)-A-II-4-b-(7) and Śrāv-bh I 73*: (I)-C-III-6-b-(3)-(b).

538. Cf. DĀ(U.H) Hs. 129 Vx, which is reconstructed to read: *p(i)ṇḍapāto yadi vā n(i)mantraṇam al(am)*. This is a very similar reading but the text of the *Prāsādika* here seems to have another word that I have not been able to reconstruct. Cf. also DN III 130.9: *piṇḍapāto aññāto*, which corresponds to *bhojanam anujñātaṃ* above. However, such a reconstruction would be in keeping with the listing of the *niśraya*s occurring here and in the surrounding sections that compliments the concurrent listing of the *pariṣkāra*s (personal belongings) of monks that makes up the primary topic of these sections. S.v. *niśraya* in BHSD, especially where Edgerton writes, "... in Mvy 8669 °*yaḥ* (Tib. *gnas*), of the four technical '*requisites*' or *supports, supplies*, which a Buddhist monk needs and is allowed, listed 8670–3 as *vṛkṣamūlam* (for sleeping), *piṇḍapātaḥ* (for food), *pāṃsukūlaṃ* (for garments), *pūtimukta-* (q.v.) *-bhaiṣajyam* (for medicine); the same four in Pali (*nissaya*)." Also, s.v. *nissaya* in PTSD. It should be noted that *piṇḍapātaḥ* appears to be used somewhat interchangeably as a *pariṣkāra* and *niśraya*. This seems to have been dealt here by using *bhojanam* as the representative element of *pariṣkāra*.

539. Note how Śrāv-bh I 9*: (I)-A-II-4-b-(7) reads *darpārthaṃ* here while Śrāv-bh I 73*: (I)-C-III-6-b-(3)-(b) reads *dravārthaṃ*, agreeing with the text of the *Prāsādika-sūtra*.

pratihaniṣyāmi navā<ṃ> ca vedanā<ṃ> notpādayiṣyāmi <|> yātrā ca me bhaviṣyati balaṃ ca sukhaṃ cānavadyatā{ṃ} ca (sparśa)vihāra(tā ca[540] |)[541]

[c] (yad yuṣmākaṃ bhikṣavo mayā śayanāsana)(**282v8**)m[542] anujñātaṃ yadi vā vṛkṣamūlaṃ yadi vā layanam anyāni vā mā(ḍ)ā vā kūṭāgārāṃ vā alaṃ vas tat[*543] pratisevituṃ na dravārthaṃ na madārthaṃ na maṇḍa(na)rthaṃ na vibhuṣ(a)ṇār(tha)ṃ (yāvad eva ṛtuparisravānāṃ)[544] (**283r1**) pratigh(ā)tārthaṃ pratisaṃlayanaparamatāyai ca <|>[545]

[**d**] yad yuṣmākaṃ mayā bhikṣavo (g)lāna(bh)aiṣajya<ḥ>[546] samanujñātaṃ[547] yadi vā pūtimuktaṃ yadi vā sarpistailamadhuphāṇit(a)m alaṃ vas tat pratisevi(t)u(ṃ na dravārtha)ṃ (na madārtha)ṃ (na ma)ṇ(dan)ārthaṃ na (**283r2**) vibhūṣaṇārthaṃ yāvad evotpannotpannānāṃ śārīrikāṇāṃ vedanānāṃ duḥkhānāṃ tīvrāṇāṃ kharāṇāṃ kaṭ(u)kānām (a)m(a)nāpānāṃ prāṇahāriṇīnāṃ pratighātārtham avyā(bādh)aparamatāyai[548] c(a |)[549]

DĀ 15.22

[**a**] [Buddha:]"The robe, monks, which I have allowed to you, whether it is rags sewn together or the clothes of a householder, it is to be used not for the sake of sport, not (for the sake of pride, not) for the sake of ornamenta-

540. Cf. MPS 50.19 *(yātrāñ ca balaṃ va sukhaṃ cānavadyatāṃ ca sparśaviharatāṃ ca)* and SHT (I) 790 R1: *yā[trā]ṃ [ca] balaṃ ca sukhaṃ [va]dya[tāṃ ca spa]rsavihā[ra](tṃ) [c](a)*. Note however that I follow Śrāv-bh I 9*: (I)-A-II-4-b-(7), which reads these terms in the nominative case: *yātrā ca me bhaviṣyati balaṃ ca sukhaṃ cānavadyatā ca sparśavihāratā ca*.

541. Cf. 282v4, 282v8, 283r1, and 283r2 as well as as well as Śrāv-bh I 9*: (I)-A-II-4-b-(7) and Śrāv-bh I 73*: (I)-C-III-6-b-(3)-(b).

542. Cf. DN III 130.14: *senāsanaṃ*.

543. Ms. reads *vastavyaṃ*.

544. Cf. DN III 130.16: *yāvad eva utu-parissaya-vinodakaṃ*.

545. Cf. 282v4, 282v5, 282v6, 282v7, and 283r2 as well as as well as Śrāv-bh I 9*: (I)-A-II-4-b-(7) and Śrāv-bh I 73*: (I)-C-III-6-b-(3)-(b).

546. Cf. DN III 130.18: *gilānapaccaya-bhesajja-parikkhāro*.

547. Note here we see *samanujātam* as opposed to *anujñātam* as in other instances. The meaning is not changed.

548. Ms. reads *avya°*. Cf. DN III 130.20: *abhyāpajjhaparamatāyā*.

549. Cf. Cf. 282v4, 282v5, 282v6, and 282v7 as well as Śrāv-bh I 9*: (I)-A-II-4-b-(7), Śrāv-bh I 73*: (I)-C-III-6-b-(3)-(b), Śrāv-bh I 108*: (I)-C-III-9-a-(1)-vi, and Śrāv-bh I 144*: (I)-C-III-13-a-(15).

tion, and not for the sake of adornment, but only (simply) for the sake of protection against gadflies, mosquitos, wind, heat, and reptiles and for the sake of concealing one's private parts out of modesty.

[**b**] "The food, monks, which I have allowed you, whether (alms-food or whether) [...] (an invited feast), it is to be used not for the sake of sport, not for the sake of pride, not for the sake of ornamentation, and not for the sake of adornment but only simply for maintenance of the body, for sustenance, for the quieting of hunger, and (for the advancement of the holy life, saying): 'I will eliminate that former sensation and I will not produce a new sensation.[550] Well-being will be mine along with strength, happiness, blamelessness, and comfort.'

[**c**] "(The) lodging, (monks, which I) have allowed you, whether at the foot of a tree, or a cell, or another place, or a pavilion, or the upper room of a house, it is to be used not for the sake of sport, not for the sake of pride, not for the sake of ornamentation, and not for the sake of adornment but only (simply) for the sake of protection against (the dangers of the seasons) and excellent seclusion.

[**d**] "The medicine for sickness, monks, which I have permitted you, whether a decoction of urine[551] or ghee, sesame oil, honey, or cane juice, it is to be used (not) for the sake of sport, (not) for the sake of pride, (not) for the sake of ornamentation, and not for the sake of adornment but only simply for the sake of protection against repeatedly arising bodily sensations that are painful, intense, piercing, sharp, unpleasant, or life-threatening, and for the utmost health."

~15.22~

DĀ(U.H.) Hs. 129 (*Prāsādika-sūtra*)

V

t[552] /// + + + + ... + + + + .. + + ///

550. The former sensation of hunger and any new sensation of overeating, etc.

551. *Pūtimuktam*, while the exact substance referred to is somewhat unclear it appears to be a drug made from cattle urine, a common ingredient in Ayurvedic medicine to this day. It is perhaps worth noting that fermented urine is explicitly allowed to monastics, see Salguero 2014, 175 note 70, for example, in the Therevāda *vinaya*.

552. DĀ 15.22a.

u /// + + + .. .[y]. [sā] .[v]. .. m[o]d. [n]. .. + + ///
v /// (ṣ)[m](ā)[k](aṃ) [m](a)[yā] cīvaram anujñāta[ṃ] ya///[553]
w /// + .. yāvad eva daṃśamaśakavātā[t]. [p]. ///
x[554] /// [p]. [ṇḍap]ā[to] yadi vā n. mantra[ṇ]am a[l]. .. ///
y /// .. .. .. [rata]ye brahmacaryā .. .. hā[y]. ///
z /// + + + sparśavihāratāṃ ca + .. [ṣ]mā ///
R
1[555] /// + + + vāṇāṃ [pra]t[igh]. t. .. + + [t]. [saṃ] ///
2[556] /// .. m alaṃ vas tat pratiṣevituṃ .. .. [d]. v. ///
3 /// danārtham avyā[b]ādhaparamatayā ca .[th]. ///

DN III 129.30–130.9 (DN 29.22)
[a] 22. navaṃ ahaṃ cunda diṭṭha-dhammikānaṃ yeva āsavānaṃ saṃvarāya dhammaṃ desemi. na panāhaṃ cunda samparāyikānaṃ yeva āsavānaṃ paṭighātāya dhammaṃ desemi, diṭṭha-dhammikānaṃ c' evāhaṃ cunda āsavānaṃ saṃvarāya dhammaṃ desemi samparāyikānañ ca āsavānaṃ paṭighātāya. tasmā-t-iha cunda yaṃ vo mayā cīvaraṃ anuññātaṃ, alaṃ vo taṃ yāvad eva sītassa paṭighātāya, uṇhassa paṭighātāya, ḍaṃsa-makasa-vātātapasiriṃsapa-samphassānaṃ paṭighātāya yāvad eva hirikopīna-paṭicchādanatthaṃ.

[b] yo vo mayā piṇḍapāto anuññāto, alaṃ vo so yāvad eva imassa kāyassa ṭhitiyā yāpanāya vihiṃsūparatiyā brahmacariyānuggahāya—iti purāṇañ ca vedanaṃ paṭihaṅkhāmi navañ ca vedanaṃ na uppādessāmi, yātrā ca me bhavissati anavajjatā ca phāsuvihāro cā ti.

[c] yaṃ vo mayā senāsanaṃ anuññātaṃ, alaṃ vo taṃ yāvad eva sītassa paṭighātāya uṇhassa paṭighātāya daṃsa-makasa-vātātapa-siriṃsapa-samphassānaṃ paṭighātāya yāvad eva utu-parissaya-vinodakaṃ paṭisallāṇārāmatthaṃ.

[d] yo vo mayā gilāna-paccaya-bhesajja-parikkhāro anuññāto, alaṃ vo so yāvad eva uppannānaṃ veyyābādhikānaṃ vedanānaṃ paṭighātāya abyāpajjhaparamatāyā ti.

553. Reconstructed in SWTF: 27 page 500 (s.v. *anujñāta*).

554. DĀ 15.22b.

555. DĀ15.22c.

556. DĀ 15.22d.

T I 1 74b24–26
[a] 諸比丘。我所制衣。若塚間衣若長者衣麤賤衣。此衣足障寒暑蚊虻。足蔽四體。

T I 1 74b26–28
[b] 諸比丘。我所制食。若乞食。若居士食。此食自足。若身苦惱衆患切已。恐遂至死故聽此食。知足而已。

T I 1 74b28–74c3
[c] 諸比丘。我所制住處。若在樹下。若在露地。若在房内若樓閣上。若在窟内若在種種住處。此處自足爲障寒暑風雨蚊虻。下至閑靜懈息之處。

T I 1 74c3–5
[d] 諸比丘。我所制藥。若大小便。酥油蜜黒石蜜。此藥自足。若身生苦惱衆患切已。恐遂至死故聽此藥。

~15.22b~
Śrāv-bh I 9*: (I)-A-II-4-b-(7)
bhojane mātrajñatā katamā | sa tathā saṃvṛtendriyaḥ pratisaṃkhyāyāhāram āharati, na darpārthaṃ na madārthaṃ na maṇḍanārthaṃ na vibhūṣaṇārthaṃ, yāvad evāsya kāyasya sthitaye yāpanāyai jighatsoparataye brahmacaryānugrahāya iti | paurāṇāṃ ca vedanāṃ prahāsyāmi, navāṃ ca notpādayiṣyāmi | yātrā ca me bhaviṣyati balaṃ ca sukhaṃ cānavadyatā ca sparśavihāratā ca | iyam ucyate bhojane mātrajñatā ||

Śrāv-bh I 73*: (I)-C-III-6-b-(3)-(b)
tatra yat tāvad āha | "pratisaṃkhyāyāhāram āharati | na dravārthaṃ, na madārthaṃ, na maṇḍanārthaṃ na vibhūṣaṇārtham", yāvad eva, "asya kāyasya sthitaye, yāpanāyai", anena tāvad abhojanaṃ ca pratikṣipati |
yat punar āha | "jighatsoparataye, brahmacaryānugrahāya" vistareṇa yāvat "sparśavihāratāyai", anena viṣamabhojanaṃ pratikṣipati |

~15.22d~
Śrāv-bh I 108*: (I)-C-III-9-a-(1)-vi
kathaṃ kṣamāvān bhavati | ākruṣṭo na pratyākrośati | roṣito na pratiroṣayati | tādito na pratitāḍayati | bhaṇḍito na pratibhaṇḍayati | ākoṭānapratyākoṭānakṣamo bhavati | pragāḍheṣv api bandhaneṣu rodhaneṣu tāḍaneṣu kutsaneṣu tarjaneṣu chedaneṣv ātmāparādhī bhavati | karmavipākaṃ ca pratisarati | na pareṣām antike kupyati | nāpy anuśayaṃ vahati | iti vimānito 'pi vivarṇito 'pi vijugupsito 'pi na

vikṛtim āpadyate | nānyatrārthāyaiva cetayate | kṣamaś ca bhavati śītasyoṣṇasya jighatsāyāḥ pipāsāyā daṃśamaśakavātātapasarīsṛpasaṃsparśānām | parato duruktānām durāgatānāṃ vacanapathānām *utpannānāṃ śārīrikāṇāṃ vedanānāṃ duḥkhānāṃ tīvrāṇāṃ kharāṇāṃ kaṭukānām amanaāpānāṃ prāṇahāriṇīnāṃ* kṣamo bhavaty adhivāsanajātīyaḥ | evaṃ kṣamāvān bhavati ||

SHT (V) 1152 R2–3 (*Saṃyuktāgama* Fragment)

R

2 /// pratiseṃvedayet=tīvram eva khara ○ m=eva kaṭukam=eva amanā[p] + ///

3 /// kham=eva pratisaṃvedayati tīvra ○ m=eva kharam=eva kaṭukam=eva ///

Devotion to Pleasure (DĀ 15.23–25)

DĀ 15.23

[**a**] (sthānam etad bhikṣavo vidyate yad a)nyatīrthi(**283r3**)kaparivrājakā[557] evaṃ vadeyuḥ <|>[558] sukhālayānuyogam[559] anuyuktāḥ śramaṇāś śākyaputrīyā viharantīti <|> tac ca sukhasya tac ca sukhasya tad idaṃ .. ..ṃ tad idaṃ kath(a)ṃ .. .. ..ṃ .i + + + + + + + + + + .. nta eka (**283r4**) eva sukhālayānuyoga ukto bhagavatā <|>[560]

[**b**] api tv asti sukhālayānuyogo hī(no grāmya)ḥ (p)r(ā)kṛtaḥ pārthagjaniko[561] rogasya mūlaṃ gaṇḍasya mūlaṃ śalyasya (mūlaṃ jarā)m(araṇasya pratyayaḥ anā)ryaḥ sāmi(**283r5**)ṣaḥ sopadhiko[562] nāsevitavyo na bhāvayitavyo na bahulīkarttavyo; yasmāt sukhālayānuyo(gād bhe)tavyam iti vadāmi <|>[563]

557. This phrase, *anyatīrthikaparivrājakāḥ*, besides occurring regularly throughout the *Prāsādika-sūtra*, also occurs in the *Prasādanīya-sūtra*: DĀ 16.19a 298v8–299r1.

558. Cf. 283r7, 283v8, 284v1, 285r1, 285r3, 285r5, 285r7, 285r8–v1, and 285v7.

559. The *Prāsādika-sūtra* and *Prasādanīya-sūtra* exclusively use the phrase *sukhālayānuyoga* (*Prāsādika-sūtra*: 283r3, 283r4, 283r5, 283r7, 283r8, 283v4, 283v6, 283v8, 284v1, 284v8 and *Prasādanīya-sūtra*: 299v4 and 299v6), which does not occur in SWTF, BHSD, or MW (nor its Pali counterpart in PTSD) instead of the much more common *sukhallikānuyoga* (s.v. SWTF: *kāmasukhalikā*, *kāmasukhalikānuyoga*, *sukhalikā*, *sukhallikā*, and *sukhallikānuyoga*; BHSD: *sukhallikā*; MW: *sukhallikā*; and PTSD: *kāma* and *sukhallikānuyoga)*, which frequently occurs in Buddhist texts. Outside of the DĀ, I have only found this usage in a parallel in the SBV (SBV I 134, confirmed in ms. (391a4). Based on the consistent usage in the *Prāsādika-sūtra* and *Prasādanīya-sūtra* and the parallel in the SBV, I believe this is a variant usage local to the Gilgit area.

560. Cf. 283r7, 283v8, 285v1, and 285v7.

561. This phrase similarly occurs in the *Prasādanīya-sūtra*, DĀ 16.18 (298v6–7): *kāmasukhālayānuyoge hīne grāmye prākṛte pār(tha)gjanike.*

562. Ms. reads *so[va]dhiko.*

563. Cf. 283r6, 283r8, 283v6, 283v7, 283v8, 284r8, 285v7, CPS 11.14, SBV I 134 (391a4), and Abhidh-k-bh(P) 153.23.

[c] asti sukhālayānuyogaḥ a(h)ī(naḥ agrām)y(aḥ aprākṛtaḥ apārthagjani) k(o) na ro(**283r6**)gasya mūlaṃ na gaṇḍasya mūlaṃ na śalyasya mūl(aṃ) n(a jarā)maraṇasya pratyayaḥ āryo nirā(m)i(ṣo n)iropadhikhaḥ āsevi{yi}tavyo[564] bhāvayitavya bahulīkartta(v)y(o; yasmāt su)khālayān(u)yogā(n na bhetavyam) i(t)i (**283r7**) vadāmi •[565]

DĀ 15.23

[a] [Buddha:] "(It is possible, monks, that) wanderers who are adherents of another faith might speak in this way: 'Those ascetics who follow the Śākya dwell addicted to devotion to pleasure.' It has been said by the Blessed One that this of pleasure and that of pleasure that [...] there, how is it that [...] very one devotion to pleasure.

[b] "However, there is a devotion to pleasure that is inferior, vulgar, simple, characteristic of common folk, the root of disease, the root of ulcers, (the root) of torment,[566] (the cause) of old age and death, ignoble, worldly, attached to the substratum of existence, not to be followed, not to be cultivated, not to be made much of. Therefore, I say that the devotion to pleasure is to be feared.

[c] "There is a devotion to pleasure that is not inferior, not vulgar, (not simple), not characteristic of common folk, not the root of disease, not the root of ulcers, not the root of torment, not the cause of old age and death, noble, free from worldliness, free from attachment to the substratum of existence, to be followed, to be cultivated, to be made much of. (Therefore), I say that the devotion to pleasure (is not to be feared)."

▪ ▪ ▪ ▪ ▪

564. Ms. reads *āsevayitatvyo*.

565. Cf. 283r4, 283r7, 283r8, 283v6, 283v7, 283v8, 284r1, CPS 11.14, SBV I 134 (391a4), and Abhidh-k-bh(P) 153.23.

566. *Śalyasya mūlam* would literally translate to "root of arrows" but *śalyaḥ* carries the additional, figurative meaning of anything tormenting or causing pain. S.v. *śalya* in SWTF and MW and *saśalya* in MW.

DĀ 15.24

[a] {a}sthānam etad bhikṣavo vidy(ate)[567] y(a)d anyatīrthikaparivrājakā evaṃ vadeyuḥ <|>[568] katamaḥ sa (bhava)ntaḥ[569] sukhālayānuyogo hīno grāmyaḥ prākṛtaḥ pārthagjani(k)yo (rogasya mūla)ṃ (gaṇḍasya mūlaṃ śalyasya mūlaṃ) **(283r8)** jarāmaraṇasya pr(a)ty(a)y(a)ḥ (a)nāryaḥ sāmiṣaḥ sopadhiko nāsevitavyo na bhāvayitavyo na bahulīkarttavyo; yasmāt sukhālayānuyogād bhetavyam iti vada<n>taḥ <|>[570]

[b][571] (pṛṣṭair evaṃ[572] s)yu(r vacanīyāḥ |[573] paṃceme bhavantaḥ kāma)-**(283v1)**(g)u(ṇāḥ | ka)t(ame paṃca <|> [1] cakṣurvijñeyāni r)ūpāṇ(ī)ṣṭ(āni kāntāni) pṛyāṇi[574] manāpāni kāmopa{bhoga}saṃhitāni raṃjanīyāni [2] śrotravijñeyāḥ śabdāḥ [3] ghrāṇ(av)i(jñ)eyā g(andhā [4] ji̱hvā)v(i)jñ(eyā[575]

567. Cf. 285v7 and DN III 131.11: *vijjati*.

568. Cf. 283r1–2, 283v8, 284v1, 285r1, 285r3, 285r5, 285r7, 285r8–v1, and 285v7.

569. Cf. 283v6 and 283v8.

570. Cf. 283r4, 283r5, 283v6, 283v7,283v8, 284r8, 285v7, CPS 11.14, SBV I 134 (391a4), and Abhidh-k-bh(P) 153.23.

571. Compare with DĀ 15.39d and DĀ 15.41d regarding *kāmaguṇa*.

572. Ms. reads *idaṃ* in all instances (283r8, 284r1, 284v2, 285r5, and 285v1). However, cf. Or.15009/565 verso 1 in BLSF III.1, 394: */// pṛ[ṣ]ṭair evaṃ syur vacanīyā + + + + ///* Note that information in BLSF regarding parallels from the DĀ *Prāsādika-sūtra* is not completely accurate. Or.15009/565 is erroneously reported to belong to the *Prasādanīya-sūtra* when it is definitely from the *Prāsādika-sūtra*. This is an understandable error considering that the two texts run one after the other in the DĀ and that the folios consisting of the *Prāsādika-sūtra* had only been partially identified until their identification by myself in this study. However, there are further errors involving the parallels from the DĀ *Prāsādika-sūtra* listed for the British Library *Prāsādika-sūtra* fragments. Inexplicably, what is quoted as 284v1: *iti pṛṣṭair idaṃ syur vacanīyā yo 'sau*, is actually from 285v1 and what is quoted as 284v2: *tasya saptānāṃ bodhipakṣāṇāṃ dharmāṇā ha ///*, is actually from 285v2. Folios 284v and 285v are both damaged and joined together, to be sure, but it is impossible to read *tasya saptānāṃ bodhipakṣāṇāṃ dharmāṇā ha* anywhere and conclude that it came from 284v, as that part of 285v is lost in the Virginia Collection folios and only becomes clear when one examines the photo taken by Kazunobu Matsuda of the folio bundles before they were separated.

573. Cf. 284r1, 284v2, 285r1, and 285v1.

574. Note the use of the vocalic r (*ṛ*) for *ri*.

575. Where I reconstruct *ji* in *jihvavijñeyā* the ms. appears to read either *.e*, *.ai*, *.o*, or *.au*. where only the uppermost part of the diacritic remains, making it impossible to know for certain what the proper vowel might have been. This reconstruction assumes a scribal error where *je*, *jai*, *jo*, or *jau* was written for *ji*.

ra)(**283v2**)sāḥ [5] (kāyav)i(jñeyāni spra)ṣ(ṭa)vy(ā)nīṣṭāni kāntāni pri(yāṇi manā)pāni (k)ā(m)opasaṃhitāni raṃjanī(yān)i iti <|>[576]

[c] ya imāṃ paṃca kāmaguṇāṃ pratītyo{mu}tpa(dyate[577] su)kh(am utpadyate saumanasyam i)(**283v3**)ty; (evaṃ kāmasukhāla)y(ā)nuy(oge a)nu(yuktā)ḥ (śrama)ṇāḥ śākyaputrīyā viharaṃti[578] iti <|> y(a) evaṃ vade<n> na samyak sa evaṃ vadan vaded {asam}anuyukt(ā)ḥ (śramaṇā)ḥ ś(ākyap)u(t)r(ī)y(ā viharantīti |)[579]

[**d**] (ya e)(**283v4**)vaṃ va(den na sam)y(ak) s(a e)v(a)ṃ vad(an va)d(e)t* <|> y(a)thā (khal)v ih(ai)k(at)y(a){s} saṃcintya prāṇinaṃ jīvitād vyaparopyādattam ādāya[580] kāmeṣu mithyā caritvā saṃprajānaṃ (m)ṛ(ṣāvādaṃ bhāṣitvā madya)pānaṃ p(ī)(**283v5**)(tvā pramatta)ḥ ..ṃ .o .. vi .. rī . (adh)igacchet sukham adhiga(c)chet saumanasyam ity; evaṃrūpe sukhālayānuyoge anuyuktāḥ śramaṇāḥ śākyaputrīy(ā)ḥ (v)i(hara)ṃtīti <|>[581] (ya evaṃ va)de<n> n(a) sa(**283v6**)(myak sa e)vaṃ vadan v(a)ded anuyuktā viharantīti <|>[582]

[e] ya evaṃ vade<t> samyak sa evaṃ vadan vadet* <|> ayaṃ sa bhavantaḥ sukhālayānuyogo hīno grā(m)yaḥ pr(āk)ṛ(ta)ḥ pārthagj(a)niko rogasya[583] (**283v7**) mūl(aṃ ga)ṇ(ḍa)s(ya) mūlaṃ śalyasya mūlaṃ jarāmaraṇasya pratyayaḥ anāryaḥ sāmiṣaḥ sopadhiko nāsevitavyo na bhāvayitavyo na bahulīkarttavyo; yasmāt sukhālayānuyog(ā)d bhet(av)y(a)m[584] iti v(a)d(ā)mi <|>[585]

576. Cf. 284r1, 284r2, 285v1, and DĀ 40.8 (*Mahalla-sūtra*).

577. Ms. reads *pratītomutpa* . . . .

578. Ms. reads *viharaṃta*.

579. Cf. 284r3, 284r4, 284r5, 298v6, and DĀ 40.9 (*Mahalla-sūtra*).

580. Note the following slightly similar phrase in Śrāv-bh II 232-234: -II-12-b-(6)-i: *na saṃprajāno mṛṣāṃ vācaṃ bhāṣate, na saṃcintya prāṇinaṃ jīvitād vyaparopayati, nādattam ādatte,* (234) *na kāmeṣu mithyā carati.*

581. Cf. 283r3, 283v2, 283v3, 284r4, 284r5, 284r6, and 284r7.

582. Cf. 283v3, 284r4, 284r5, and 284r7.

583. Ms. reads *[m]aṃg[a]sya*.

584. Ms. reads *[r]t. .y. [m]*.

585. Cf. 283r4, 283r5, 283r7, 283r8, 283v8, 284r1, 284r8, CPS 11.14, SBV I 134 (391a4), and Abhidh-k-bh(P) 153.23.

DĀ 15.24[586]

[**a**] [Buddha:] "It is possible, monks, that wanderers who are adherents of another faith might speak in this way, saying: 'Sirs, which is this devotion to pleasure that is inferior, vulgar, simple, characteristic of common folk, the root (of disease, the root of ulcers, the root of torment),[587] the cause of old age and death, ignoble, worldly, attached to the substratum of existence, not to be followed, not to be cultivated, not to be made much of?' Saying: 'Therefore, devotion to pleasure is to be feared.'

[**b**] "They are to be addressed thus by those questioned: 'These, sirs, are the five sensual pleasures. What are the five? [1] Objects perceptible to the eye that are delightful, related to sensual pleasure, charming, beloved, pleasing, and desirable, [2] sounds perceptible to the ears, [3] scents perceptible to the nose, [4] tastes perceptible to the tongue, and [5] tactile sensations perceptible to the body that are delightful, related to sensual pleasure, charming, beloved, pleasing, and desirable.'

[**c**] "'He who produces pleasure dependent upon these five sensual pleasures (produces cheerfulness).' Thus, 'The ascetics who follow the Śākya dwell addicted to devotion to pleasure.' He who might speak in this way is not correct; speaking thus he might say: 'The ascetics who follow the Śākya (dwell) addicted.'

[**d**] "(He who) might speak in this way is not correct; speaking this way, he might say: 'Certainly, as in this case one [1] having intentionally deprived a living creature of life, [2] having taken what was not given, [3] having engaged in sexual misconduct, [4] having deliberately (told) lies, [5] having drunk intoxicating beverages, careless [...] he should acquire pleasure and he should acquire cheerfulness. The ascetics who follow the Śākya dwell addicted to devotion to pleasure of this kind.' (He who) might speak in this way is not correct; speaking thus, (he) might say: 'They dwell addicted.'

[**e**] "He who might speak in this way is correct; speaking this way, he might say: 'Sirs, this devotion to pleasure is inferior, vulgar, simple, characteristic

586. DĀ 15.24 and DĀ 15.25 mirror one another with 15.24 stating its content negatively and 15.25 stating its content positively.

587. See note 566 above.

of common folk, the root of disease, the root of ulcers, the root of torment, the cause of old age and death, ignoble, worldly, attached to the substratum of existence, not to be followed, not to be cultivated, not to be made much of.' Therefore, I say that the devotion to pleasure is to be feared."

▪ ▪ ▪ ▪ ▪

DĀ 15.25a–c

[a] **(283v8)** (sthānam) e(tad bh)i(kṣavo vidyate) yad anyatīrthikaparivrājakā evaṃ vadeyuḥ <|>[588] (ka)t(a)maḥ s(a)[589] bhavantas[590] sukhālayānuyogaḥ ahīnaḥ agrāmya aprākṛto 'pārtagjaniko na rogasya[591] mūlaṃ <na> gaṇḍasya mūl(a)ṃ <na> (śal)y(asya mū)la<ṃ na> ja<rā>ma<ra>ṇasya pratyayaḥ **(284r1)** (āryo nirām)i(ṣ)o (n)i(ropa)dhik(aḥ) ā(sev)it(avyo) <bhāvayitavyo> bahulīkartta(vy)o;[592] yasmāt sukhālayānuyogān na bhe{t}tavyam iti vada<n>taḥ{n};[593]

[b][594] pṛṣṭair evaṃ[595] syur vacanīyāḥ <|> paṃceme bhav(a)nt(a)ḥ k(āma)guṇā<ḥ |> katame paṃca <|> [1] cakṣurvijñē**(284r2)**yāni (rūpāṇī)ṣṭāni[596] kāntāni priyāṇi manāpāni kāmopasaṃhitāni r(a)ṃjanīyāni [2] śrotavijñeyāṃ śabdhāṃ [3] ghrāṇavijñeyā{ṃ} gandhā{ṃ} [4] jihvāvijñeyā{n} rasāḥ[597] [5] kāyavijñ(e)yāni spraṣṭavyānīṣṭāni **(284r3)** kāntāni priyāṇi manāpāni (kāmo)pasaṃhitāni (rā)ṃ(janīyāni iti |)[598]

588. Cf. 283r1–2, 283r7, 284v1, 285r1, 285r3, 285r5, 285r7, 285r8–v1, and 285v7.

589. Cf. 283r2, 283r7, 285v1, and 285v7.

590. Note the irregular *sandhi* here where the *visarga* becomes an *-s-* before an *-s-* initial word.

591. Ms. reads *rodhasya*.

592. Cf. 283r4, 283r5, 283r6, 283r8, 283v6, 284r8, CPS 11.14, SBV I 134 (391a4), and Abhidh-k-bh(P) 153.23.

593. Ms reads *vadatān*, a word that has no meaning. Cf. 283r8 (*vada<n>taḥ*), which while still in need of emendation, is more plausible than what we find here in the ms.

594. Compare with DĀ 15.39.d and DĀ 15.41.d regarding *kāmaguṇa*.

595. See note 572 above.

596. While the ms. is damaged where I reconstruct *ṇī* in *rūpāṇīṣṭāni*, the original akṣara is legible enough that we can conclude with reasonable certainty that *ṇī* was not what was written. However, the reconstruction is likely correct, as this passage occurs previously in the ms. and is attested in a parallel from the *Mahalla-sūtra*. Perhaps the scribe wrote *nī* instead of *ṇī* here, or some similar error.

597. Ms. reads *rasāṃ*.

598. Cf. 283r8, 283v1, 283v2, and DĀ 40.8 (*Mahalla-sūtra*).

[**c**] (ya imā)n[599] paṃca kāmagunān pratītyotpadyate sukham utpadyate saumanasyam iti vi(d)itvā tac ca prahāya vivi(**284r4**)k(ta)ṃ (kāmair yā) vac caturthaṃ dhyān(a)m (upasaṃpadya) viharatīty; e(vaṃ kāmas)u(khā-la)y(ā)nuy(o)g(e) anuyuktāḥ śramaṇāḥ śākyaputrīyā viharaṃtīti <|> ya evaṃ vade<t> {na} samyak sa evam <vadan> vade<d a>nuyu(k)t(ā) vi(**284r5**)haraṃtīti <|>[600]

DĀ 15.25a–c[601]

[**a**] [Buddha:] "(It is possible), monks, that wanderers who are adherents of another faith might speak in this way, saying: 'Sirs, which is this devotion to pleasure that is not inferior, not vulgar, not simple, not characteristic of common folk, not the root of disease, <not> the root of ulcers, <not> the root of torment,[602] <not> the cause of old age and death, (noble), free from worldliness, free from attachment to the substratum of existence, to be followed, <to be cultivated>, to be made much of?' Saying: 'Therefore, the devotion to pleasure is not to be feared.'

[**b**] "They are to be addressed thus by those questioned: 'Those, sirs, are the five sensual pleasures. What are the five? [1] Objects perceptible to the eye that are delightful, related to sensual pleasure, charming, beloved, pleasing, and desirable, [2] sounds perceptible to the ears, [3] scents perceptible to the nose, [4] tastes perceptible to the tongue, and [5] tactile sensations perceptible to the body that are delightful, related to sensual pleasure, charming, beloved, pleasing, and desirable.'

[**c**] "'He (who) produces pleasure dependent upon these five sensual pleasures produces cheerfulness.' Having understood and having rejected this [statement], he dwells free (from passion, having reached) up to the fourth dhyāna. Thus, 'The ascetics who follow the Śākya dwell addicted to devotion to pleasure.' He who might speak in this way is correct, <speaking> thus he might say: 'They dwell addicted.'"

599. Cf. 283r8, 283v1, 283v2, and DĀ 40.9 (*Mahalla-sūtra*).

600. 282v2, 282v3, 284r6, 284r7, 298v6: *viviktaṃ kāmair yāvac caturthaṃ dhyānam upasaṃ(padya v)i(harat)i*, and DĀ 40.9 (*Mahalla-sūtra*).

601. DĀ 15.24 and DĀ 15.25 mirror one another with 15.24 stating its content negatively and 15.25 stating its content positively.

602. See note 566 above.

DĀ 15.25d–e

[**d**] ya ev(a)ṃ v(a)det (samyak sa) ev(aṃ) v(a)d(aṃ) vade<t* |> yathā khalv ihaikat̲ya[603] saṃciṃtya prāṇi(na)ṃ jīvitād vyaparopyādattam ādāya[604] kāmeṣu mithyā caritvā saṃprajānaṃ mṛṣāvādaṃ bhāṣitvā (**284r6**) madyapānaṃ pītvā pramat(ta)ḥ paṃ .o .. .i .. .ī . (adhi)gacchet sukham adhigacchet saumanasyam iti viditvā tac ca prahāya viviktaṃ kāmair yāvac caturthaṃ dhyānam upasaṃpadya (v)i(harat)ī(ty;[605] eva)ṃ(rū)(**284r7**)(pe kāmasukhā)layā(n)u(yoge an)uyu(k)t(ā)ḥ (ś)r(ama)ṇā<ḥ> śākyaputrīyā viharantīti <|>[606] ya evaṃ vadet̲[607] {na} samyak sa evaṃ vadaṃn vaded anuyuktā viharaṃtīti <|>

[**e**] ya evaṃ vadet sam(ya)k s(a) e(va)ṃ (vadan vadet* | ayaṃ sa) bh(ava)(**284r8**)ntaḥ sukhālayānuyo(gaḥ ahīna)ḥ (a)g(r)ām(ya)ḥ aprākṛto ('pārtha)gjaniko na rogasya mūlaṃ na g(a)ṇḍ(a)s(ya) m(ū)l(a)ṃ n(a) (ś)a̲(lyasya[608] mūla)ṃ (na jarāmaraṇasya pratyayaḥ āryo nirāmiṣo niropadhikaḥ) (**284v1**) ā(sevi)t(a)vyo bh(ā)<va>y̲i(tavyo[609] bahul)ī(kartavyo yasmāt sukhālayānuyogān na) bhet(av)y(am it)i (vadām)i <|>[610]

DĀ 15.25d–e

[**d**] [Buddha:] "He who might speak in this way is (correct). Speaking this way, he might say: 'Certainly, as in this case one [1] having intentionally deprived a living creature of life, [2] having taken what was not given, [3] having engaged in sexual misconduct, [4] having deliberately (told) lies, [5] having drunk intoxicating beverages, careless [...] he should acquire plea-

603. Ms. reads *ihaikasya.*

604. Note the following slightly similar phrase in Śrāv-bh II 232-234: -II-12-b-(6)-i: *na saṃprajāno mṛṣāṃ vācaṃ bhāṣate, na saṃcintya prāṇinaṃ jīvitād vyaparopayati, nādattam ādatte, na kāmeṣu mithyā carati.*

605. Cf. 283v2, 283v3, 284r4 and 298v6: *viviktaṃ kāmair yāvac caturthaṃ dhyānam upasaṃ(padya v)i(harat)i.*

606. Cf. 282v2, 282v3, and 283v5.

607. Ms reads *vaden.*

608. Ms. reads *.ā [r]. [m].*, which would most likely be reconstructed as *(j)ār(a)m(a).* However, even if that is what was written in the ms. (although it is too damaged to say with certainty), it should be emended to read as above.

609. Ms. reads *[bh]. [v]i [t]. ..*

610. Cf. 283r5, 283r6, 283r7, 283v5, 283v6, 283v7, 283v8, 284r1, CPS 11.14, SBV I 134 (391a4), and Abhidh-k-bh(P) 153.23.

sure and he should acquire cheerfulness.' Having understood and having rejected this, he dwells free from passion, having reached up to the fourth dhyāna. Regarding [a statement] of this kind: 'The ascetics who follow the Śākya dwell addicted to devotion to pleasure.' He who might speak in this way is correct; speaking thus, he might say: 'They dwell addicted.'

[e] "He who might speak in this way is correct; (speaking) this way, (he might say): 'Sirs, I say (this) devotion to pleasure is not inferior, not vulgar, not simple, not characteristic of common folk, not the root of disease, not the root of ulcers, not the root of torment, not the cause of old age and death, noble, free from worldliness, free from attachment to the substratum of existence, to be followed, to be cultivated, to be made much of.' Therefore, I say that the devotion to pleasure is not to be feared."

~15.23~

DĀ(U.H.) Hs. 129 (*Prāsādika-sūtra*)

R

4[611] /// .. yā viharaṃti tad idaṃ kathaṃ syāt pr̥ .ai ///

5[612] /// + .. [g].ām[y]aḥ prākr̥taḥ pārthagjaniko [ro] + ///

6 /// + + + + .. [sukh]. [l].i[k]ā[n]. [yo]g. + ///

7 /// + + + + ... + + + + ... + ///

DN —

T I 1 74c5–9

佛言。或有外道梵志來作是語。沙門釋子以衆樂自娛。若有此言。當如是報。汝等莫作此言。謂沙門釋子以衆樂自娛。所以者何。有樂自娛如來呵責。有樂自娛如來稱譽。

~15.24~

DN III 130.22–131.10 (DN 29.23)

[a] 23. ṭhānaṃ kho pan' etaṃ cunda vijjati, yaṃ añña-titthiyā paribbājakā evaṃ vadeyyuṃ—sukhallikānuyogam anuyuttā samaṇā sakya-puttiyā viharantīti. evaṃ vādino cunda añña-titthiyā paribbājakā evam assu vacanīyā—katamo so āvuso sukhallikānuyogo? sukhallikānuyogā pi hi

611. DĀ 15.23a.

612. DĀ 15.23b.

bahū aneka-vihitā nāna-ppakārakā ti. cattāro 'me cunda sukhallikānuyogā hīnā gammā pothujjanikā anariyā anattha-saṃhitā na nibbidāya na virāgāya na nirodhāya na upasamāya na abhiññāya na sambodhāya na nibbānāya saṃvattanti.

[d] katame cattāro? idha cunda ekacco bālo pāṇe vadhitvā attānaṃ sukheti pīṇeti, ayaṃ paṭhamo sukhallikānuyogo. puna ca paraṃ cunda idh' ekacco adinnaṃ ādiyitvā attānaṃ sukheti pīṇeti, ayaṃ dutiyo sukhallikānuyogo. puna ca paraṃ cunda idh' ekacco musā-bhaṇitvā attānaṃ sukheti pīṇeti, ayaṃ tatiyo sukhallikānuyogo.

[b–c] puna ca paraṃ cunda idh' ekacco pañcahi kāma-guṇehi samappito samaṅgi-bhūto parivāreti, ayaṃ catuttho sukhallikānuyogo.

[e] ime kho cunda cattāro sukhallikānuyogā hīnā gammā pothujjanikā anariyā anattha-saṃhitā na nibbidāya na virāgāya na nirodhāya na upasamāya na abhiññāya na sambodhāya na nibbānāya saṃvattanti.

T I 1 74c9–10
[a] 若外道梵志問言。何樂自娛瞿曇呵責。設有此語。

T I 1 74c10–23
[b] 汝等當報。五欲功德。可愛可樂人所貪著。云何爲五。眼知色。可愛可樂人所貪著。耳聞聲鼻知香舌知味身知觸。可愛可樂人所貪著。諸賢。猶是五欲緣生喜樂。此是如來至眞等正覺之所呵責也。猶如有人故殺衆生自以爲樂。此是如來至眞等正覺之所呵責。猶如有人私竊偸盜自以爲樂。此爲如來之所呵責。猶如有人犯於梵行自以爲樂。此是如來之所呵責。猶如有人故作妄語自以爲樂。此是如來之所呵責。猶如有人放蕩自恣。此是如來之所呵責。猶如有人行外苦行非是如來所說正行。自以爲樂。此是如來之所呵責。

T I 1 74c23–75a5
[c–e] 諸比丘。呵責五欲功德人所貪著。云何爲五。眼知色。可愛可樂人所貪著。耳聞聲鼻知香舌知味身知觸可愛可樂人所貪著。如此諸樂沙門釋子無如此樂。猶如有人故殺衆生以此爲樂。沙門釋子無如此樂。猶如有人公爲盜賊自以爲樂。沙門釋子無如是樂。猶如有人犯於梵行自以爲樂。沙門釋子無如是樂。猶如有人故作妄語自以爲樂。沙門釋子無如是樂。猶如有人放蕩自恣自以爲樂。沙門釋子無如是樂。猶如有人行外苦行自以爲樂。沙門釋子無如是樂。

~15.25~

DĀ(U.H.) Hs. 130 (=BLSF III.1 Or.15009/565) (*Prāsādika-sūtra*)

V

1[613] ///+ nuyogaḥ ahīnaḥ agrāmya +++ ///

2[614] /// + kāmaguṇāḥ katame paṃca | c. [kṣu] .[v]. [jñ]. ///

3[615] /// + ○ ditvā tac ca prahāya [vi]vi .. ///

4[616] /// + ○ [saṃ]ci[ṃ]tya prāṇināṃ [jīv]i[t]. ///

5 /// [ti] ○ viditvā tac ca prahāya + ///

6[617] ///.. sukhallikānuyogaḥ ahī[na] .. ++ ///

DN III 131.11–132.8 (DN 29.24)[618]

24. ṭhānaṃ kho pan' etaṃ cunda vijjati, yaṃ aññatitthiyā evaṃ puccheyyuṃ—ime cattāro sukhallikānuyoge anuyuttā samaṇā sakya-puttiyā viharantīti? te mā h' evan ti 'ssu vacanīyā, na vo te sammā vadamānā vadeyyuṃ, abbhācikkheyyuṃ vo te asatā abhūtena. cattāro 'me cunda sukhallikānuyogā ekanta-nibbidāya virāgāya nirodhāya upasamāya abhiññāya sambodhāya nibbānāya saṃvattanti. katame cattāro? idha cunda bhikkhu vivicc' eva kāmehi vivicca akusalehi dhammehi savitakkaṃ savicāraṃ vivekajaṃ pīti-sukhaṃ paṭhamajjhānaṃ upasampajja viharati. ayaṃ paṭhamo sukhallikānuyogo. puna ca paraṃ cunda bhikkhu vitakkavicārānaṃ vūpasamā ajjhattaṃ sampasādanaṃ cetaso ekodibhāvaṃ avitakkaṃ avicāraṃ samādhijaṃ pīti-sukhaṃ dutiya-jjhānaṃ upasampajja viharati. ayaṃ dutiyo sukhallikānuyogo. puna ca paraṃ cunda bhikkhu pītiyā ca virago ... pe ... ayaṃ tatiyo sukhallikānuyogo.

puna ca paraṃ cunda bhikkhu sukhassa ca pahānā ... pe ... ayaṃ catuttho sukhallikānuyogo. ime kho cunda cattāro sukhallikānuyogā ekanta-nibbidāya virāgāya nirodhāya upasamāya abhiññāya sambodhāya nibbānāya saṃvattanti. ṭhānaṃ kho pan' etaṃ cunda vijjati yaṃ aññatitthiyā paribbājakā evaṃ vadeyyuṃ—ime cattāro sukhallikānuyoge anuyuttā

613. DĀ 15.25a.

614. DĀ 15.25b.

615. DĀ 15.25c.

616. DĀ 15.25d.

617. DĀ 15.25e.

618. The content of the DN here differs rather extensively from that of the DĀ. DN III 130.22–31.10 (DN 29.23), which corresponds to DĀ 15.24, better parallels the content of DĀ 15.25, as 15.25 is nearly identical in content with 15.24.

samaṇā sakya-puttiyā viharantīti. te evan ti 'ssu vacanīyā, sammā vo te vadamānā vadeyyuṃ, na vo te abbhācikkheyyuṃ asatā abhūtena.

T I 1 75a5–26
[a] 若外道梵志作如是問何樂自娛。沙門瞿曇之所稱譽。

[b] 諸比丘。彼若有此言。汝等當答彼言。諸賢。有五欲功德可愛可樂人所貪著。云何爲五。眼知色乃至意知法。可愛可樂人所貪著。諸賢。五欲因縁生樂當速除滅。猶如有人故殺衆生自以爲樂。有如此樂應速除滅。猶如有人公爲盜賊自以爲樂。有如此樂應速除滅。猶如有人犯於梵行自以爲樂。有如此樂應速除滅。猶如有人故爲妄語自以爲樂。有如此樂應速除滅。猶如有人放蕩自恣自以爲樂。有如此樂應速除滅。猶如有人行外苦行自以爲樂。有如是樂應速除滅。

[c] 猶如有人去離貪欲無復惡法。有覺有觀。離生喜樂入初禪。如是樂者佛所稱譽。猶如有人滅於覺觀。內喜一心。無覺無觀。定生喜樂入第二禪。如是樂者佛所稱譽。猶如有人除喜入捨。自知身樂。賢聖所求。護念一心入第三禪。如是樂者佛所稱譽。樂盡苦盡憂喜先滅。不苦不樂。護念清淨入第四禪。如是樂者佛所稱譽。

~15.23b–c, 15.24a&e, & 15.25a&e~
CPS 11.14
dvāv imau bhiksavo [sic] 'nṭau pravrajtena na sevitavau na bhajitavyau na paryupāsitavyau | yaś ca kāmeṣu k(ā)masukhallikānuyogo hī(no) gr(ā)myaḥ prākṛ(ta)ḥ pārthagjanikaḥ | yaś cātmaklamathānuyogo duḥkho 'nāryo 'nārthopasaṃhitaḥ |

SBVG (391a4–5) (cf. SBV I 134) (ms. checked and emended as necessary)
(391a4)m etad āyuṣmaṃ gautama. tatra bhagavāṃ paṃcakān bhikṣūn āmantrayate sma: ◯ dvāv imau bhikṣavo 'ntau pravrajitena na sevitavyau, na vaktavyau, na paryupāsitavyau; katamau dvau; yaś ca kāmeṣu kāmasukhālayānuyogo hīno grāmyaḥ prākṛtaḥ pārthagjanikaḥ; ya(ś cātmakla)**(391a5)**mathānuyogo duḥkho 'nāryo 'narthopasaṃhita<ḥ>;

Abhidh-k-bh(P) 153.23
uktaṃ hi bhagavatā catvāra ime āhārā rogasya mūlaṃ gaṇḍasya śalyasya jarāmaraṇasya pratyaya iti |

~15.24b & 15.25b~

Saṅg V.3
(pañca kāmaguṇāḥ | cakṣuvijñeyāni rūpanīṣṭāni kāntāni manāpāni priyarūpāṇi kāmopasaṃhitāni raṃjanīyāni | śrotravijñeyāḥ śabdā iṣṭāḥ kāntā manāpāḥ priyarūpāḥ kāmopasaṃhitā rañjanīyāḥ | ghrāṇavijñeyā gandhā iṣṭāḥ kāntā manāpāḥ priyarūpāḥ kāmopasaṃhitā rañjanīyāḥ | jihvāvijñeyā rasā iṣṭāḥ kāntā manāpāḥ priyarūpāḥ kāmopasaṃhitā rañjanīyāḥ | kāyavijñeyāni spraṣṭavyānīṣṭāni kāntāni manāpāni priyarūpāṇi kāmopasaṃhitāni rañjanīyāni |)

DN III 234.3–7 (*Saṅgīti-sutta*, DN 33.2.3)
pañca kāma-guṇā. cakkhu-viññeyyā rūpā iṭṭhā kantā manāpā piya-rūpā kāmūpasaṃhitā rajanīyā, sotaviññeyyā saddā ... ghāna-viññeyyā gandhā ... jivhā-viññeyyā rasā ... kāya-viññeyyā phoṭṭhabbā iṭṭhā kantā manāpā piya-rūpā kāmūpasaṃhitā rajanīyā.

DĀ 40.8 (*Mahalla-sūtra*) (Melzer 2010, 370)
paṃceme brāhmaṇa kāmaguṇāḥ <|> katame paṃca <|> cakṣurvijñeyāni rūpāṇī(**428r6**)ṣṭāni kāntāni priyāṇi manāpāni kāmopasaṃhitāni raṃjanīyāni śrotravijñeyāś śabdāḥ ghrāṇavijñeyā gandhā jihvāvijñeyā rasā<ḥ> kāyavijñeyāni spraṣṭavyāni iṣṭā(**428r7**)ni kāntāni priyāṇi manāpāni kāmopasaṃhitāni (raṃja)nīyāni iti <|>

MN I 85.22–28 (*Mahādukkhakkhanda-sutta*, MN 13)
pañc' ime kāmaguṇā, katame pañca: cakkhuviññeyyā rūpā iṭṭhā kantā manāpā piyarūpā kāmūpasaṃhitā rajanīyā, sotaviññeyyā saddā—pe—ghānaviññeyyā gandhā—jivhāviññeyyā rasā—kāyaviññeyyā phoṭṭhabbā iṭṭhā kantā manāpā piyarūpā kāmūpasaṃhitā rajanīyā. ime kho bhikkhave pañca kāmaguṇā.

MN I 92.13–19 (*Cūḷadukkhakkhandha-sutta*, MN 14)
pañc' ime kāmaguṇā, katame pañca: cakkhuviññeyyā rūpā iṭṭhā kantā manāpā piyarūpā kāmūpasaṃhitā rajanīyā, sotaviññeyyā saddā—pe—ghānaviññeyyā gandhā—jivhāviññeyyā rasā—kāyaviññeyyā phoṭṭhabbā iṭṭhā kantā manāpā piyarūpā kāmūpasaṃhitā rajanīyā. ime kho bhikkhave pañca kāmaguṇā.

~15.24c & 15.25c ~

DĀ 40.9 (*Mahalla-sūtra*) (Melzer 2010, 370)
yad imān paṃca kāmaguṇā pratītyotpadyate sukham utpadyate saumanasyam

ayaṃ brāhmaṇa kāmeṣv āsvāda<ḥ>; alpatara eṣāsvāda<ḥ>; api (**428r8**) tv ādīnavo bhūyān*;

MN I 85.28–29 (*Mahādukkhakkhanda-sutta*, MN 13)
yaṃ kho ime pañca kāmaguṇe paṭicca uppajjati sukhaṃ somanassam, ayaṃ kāmānaṃ assādo.

MN I 92.19–20 (*Cūḷadukkhakkhandha-sutta*, MN 14)
yaṃ kho ime pañca kāmaguṇe paṭicca uppajjati sukhaṃ somanassam, ayaṃ kāmānaṃ assādo.

MN I 91.25–26, 31–32, 92.2–3, 7–8 (*Cūḷadukkhakkhandha-sutta*, MN 14)
appassādā kāmā bahudukkhā bahupāyāsā, ādīnavo ettha bhiyyo ti

DhskD 11r2–4
yad bhikṣavo rūpaṃ *pratīty[ot]padyate* (11r3) *sukham utpadyate saumanasyam* ayaṃ rūpe āsvādaḥ (|) ity etad rūpāsvādavedayitaṃ pratītya yāvat tṛṣṇā (|) tad ucyate vedanāpratyayā tṛṣṇā (|) yad bhikṣavo vedanāsaṃjñāsaṃskārān yad vijñānaṃ *pratītyotpadyate sukham utpadyate saumanasyam* (11r4) ayaṃ vijñāne āsvāda (|)

~15.24d & 15.25d~
Saṅg V.16
(pañcābhavyasthānāni | abhavyo 'rhad bhikṣuḥ kṣīṇāsravaḥ saṃcintya prāṇinaṃ jīvitād vyaparopitum | abhavyo 'dattaṃ steyasaṃkhyātam ādātum | abhavyo maithunaṃ dharmaṃ pratisevitum | abhavyaḥ saṃprajānan mṛṣā vaditum |) .. ..

DN III 235.4–11 (*Saṅgīti-sutta*, DN 33.2 I (x))
(x) pañca abhabba-ṭṭhānāni. abhabbo āvuso khīṇāsavo bhikkhu sañcicca pāṇaṃ jīvitā voropetuṃ. abhabbo khīṇāsavo bhikkhu adinnaṃ theyyasaṃkhātaṃādātuṃ. abhabbo khīṇāsavo bhikkhu methunaṃ dhammaṃ paṭisevituṃ. abhabbo khīṇāsavo bhikkhu sampajāna-musā bhāsituṃ. abhabbo khīṇāsavo bhikkhu sannidhi-kārakaṃ kāme paribhuñjituṃ, seyyathā pi pubbe agāriya-bhūto.

Śrāv-bh(Sh) 509–10[619]

619. Unfortunately, the reading of the text as edited by Shukla here is very problematic. Indeed, Shukla states (Śrāv-bh(Sh) xlv–xlvi) that the single ms. he worked from was dam-

[4] ..... parinirvṛt(o) bhavati | yathā na saṃsṛto/(tau) nānyatra yad duḥkhaṃ tan niruddhaṃ tavyupaśāntaṃ tac chītībhūtaṃ bhava iṃ [sic] gataṃ | śāntaṃ śāntam idaṃ padaṃ | yad uta sarvopadhipratiniḥsarvasaṃjñākṣayo virāgo nirodho nirvāṇaṃ tasyemāni liṃgān yevaṃ bhāgīyāni veditavyāni | [510] pañcasthānāny u .... bhikṣuḥ kṣīṇāsravaḥ prati | vi vine | kta [sic] manyamasaṃ tathā [5] prāpayituṃ mandadātram abrahmacaryaṃ maithunaṃ dharmaṃ pratiṣevituṃ | saṃprajānā(no) mṛṣāpa [sic] bhāṣitum abhavyaḥ mandavikāreṇa kāmān paribhoktuṃ | tathā bhavyaḥ svayaṃ kṛtaṃ sukhaṃ duḥkhaṃ pratyetuṃ | pūrvavad yāvat svayaṃkāyakāro (')hetusamutpannam ugraduḥkhaṃ praṇītam amavyāya kṛtastubhiḥ-(tiḥ) | satrāsaṃ māṃsaṃ bhakṣya(vya) ....

Śrāv-bh II 232–234: -II-12-b-(6)-i
yo 'py āryakāntāni śīlāny ucyante | kena kāraṇena | dīrghakālaṃ hy etad āryāṇāṃ satāṃ samyaggatānām iṣṭaṃ kāntaṃ priyaṃ mana-āpaṃ "kaccid ahaṃ tad vāgduścaritasya kāyaduścaritasya mithyājīvasyākaraṇaṃ saṃvaraṃ pratilabheyam" | yad asya dīrgharātram iṣṭaṃ kāntaṃ priyaṃ mana-āpaṃ tad anena tasmin samaye pratilabdhaṃ bhavati | tasmād āryakāntam ity ucyate | tathā hi sa labdheṣv āryakānteṣu śīleṣu, na saṃprajāno mṛṣāṃ vācaṃ bhāṣate, na saṃcintya prāṇinaṃ jīvitād vyaparopayati, nādattam ādatte, (Śrāv-bh II 234) na kāmeṣu mithyā carati, na cādharmeṇa cīvarādīni paryeṣate | iti tāny āryakāntāni śīlāny adhipatiṃ kṛtvā mārgabhāvanākāle yā vāk pravartate yac ca kāyakarma yaś cājīvaḥ, te 'pi samyagvākkarmāntājīvā ity ucyante |

MN I 523 (MN 76 *Sandaka-sutta* 3.6)
yo so sandaka bhikkhu arahaṃ khīṇāsavo vusitavā katakaraṇīyo ohitabhāro anuppattasadattho parikkhīṇabhavasaṃyojano samma-d-aññā vimutto, abhabbo so pañca ṭhānāni ajjhācarituṃ: abhabbo khīṇāsavo bhikkhu sañcicca pāṇaṃ jīvitā voropetuṃ, abhabbo khīṇā-savo bhikkhu adinnaṃ theyyasaṅkhātaṃ ādātuṃ, abhabbo khīṇāsavo bhikkhu methunaṃ dhammaṃ patisevituṃ, abhabbo khīṇāsavo bhikkhu sampajānamusā bhāsituṃ, abhabbo khīṇāsavo bhikkhu sannidhikārakaṃ kāme paribhuñjituṃ seyyathā pi pubbe agāriyabhūto. yo so sandaka

aged and often rife with problematic readings and scribal errors or, perhaps more accurately, a strong Middle-Indic influence. It should be noted, however, that de Jong wrote a rather scathing review of Shukla's work where, after comparing Shukla's work on this text with previous work by Wayman, he concluded that the problems with the edition do not originate from the manuscript, but rather from the editor (de Jong 1976a).

bhikkhu arahaṃ khīṇāsavo vusitavā katakaraṇīyo ohitabhāro anuppattasadattho parikkhīṇabhavasaṃyojano samma-d-aññā-vimutto, abhabbo so imāni pañca ṭhānāni ajjhācaritun-ti.

Seven Fruits (DĀ 15.26)

DĀ 15.26

[**a**] (s)th(ānam etad) bh(ikṣavo vidyate yad anyatīrthikaparivrājakā evaṃ vadeyuḥ |)[620] + + + + + + + + + + + + + + (**284v2**)bh. .. ..ṃ + .i + + + + + + + + + + + + + + + <|>[621]

[**b**] (pṛ)ṣṭ(ai)r evaṃ[622] syu(r) vacanīyāḥ <|>[623] evaṃ sukhālayānuyogam anuyuktānām (a)smāk(aṃ) bh(a)v(a)nto v(i)h(a)r(a)t(āṃ) s(ap)t(a)-ph(alāni sap)t(ānuśaṃsāḥ pratikāṃkṣitavyāḥ |)[624]

[**c**] (kata)(**284v3**)me[625] s(aptāḥ | iha[626] [1] bhikṣur dṛṣṭa eva dharme pratiyaty' evājñām ārāga)yati[627] nātra[628] maraṇasamaye || [2] puna(r a)para<ṃ>[629] bhikṣur na haiva dṛṣṭa eva dharme pratiyaty'[630] evājñām

620. Cf. 283r1–2, 283r7, 283v8, 285r1, 285r3, 285r5, 285r7, 285r8–v1, and 285v7 as well as BLSF III.1 Or.15009/565 (= DĀ(U.H.) Hs. 130) r7.

621. While the DĀ and DN diverge in content here and I have not been able to reconstruct this passage, we can expect wording similar to DN III 132.10–12: *ime pana āvuso cattāro sukhallikānuyoge anuyuttānaṃ viharataṃ kati phalāni kat' ānisaṃsā pāṭikaṅkhā ti?* which Walshe translates as: "Well then, those who are given to these four forms of pleasure-seeking—how many fruits, how many benefits can they expect?" (LDB, 424). Of course, the DĀ refers to seven fruits and benefits as opposed to four as seen on 284v6: *imāni sapta-phalāni ime saptānuśaṃsāḥ*.

622. See note 572 above.

623. Cf. 283r8, 284r1, 285r1, and 285v1.

624. Cf. 284v6.

625. Cf. SN V 69 no. 12, SN V 237 no. 2, SN V 285 no. 3, and SN V 314 no. 12.

626. Cf. BLSF III.1 Or.15009/565 verso 2 (= DĀ(U.H.) 130R2: */// katame saptaḥ iha bh. kṣu. [d]ṛ.[ṭ]. + + ///.*

627. Cf. 283v3 (later in this same line).

628. Ms. reads *notra*.

629. Cf. 276v8.

630. Interestingly, the parallel in Abhidh-k-bh(P) 72.3–4 reads: *sa na haiva dṛṣṭa eva dharme pratipattyevājñām ārāgayati nāpi maraṇakālasamaye*, which translates to: "surely he

ārāgayati <|> api tu (maraṇasamaye | [3] puna)r a(284v4)paraṃ bhikṣ(ur na haiva dṛṣṭa eva dharme pratiyaty' evajñām ārāga)yati[631] nāpi maraṇasamaye <|> a(p)i tu (pa)ṃ(cān)ām avarabhāgīyānāṃ saṃyojanānāṃ prahāṇād antarāparinirvāyī bhavati <|>[632] [4] (na haivāntarā)p(a)ri(284v5)(n)i(rvāyī bhavati | api tūpapadyaparinirvāyī bhavati |)[633] [5] <na haivopapadyaparinirvāyī bhavati |>[634] (api) tv (anabh)i(sa)ṃ(skāra)parinirvāyī bhavati <|> [6] na haivā<na>bhi<saṃskāra>parinirvāyī bhavati • api tu sābhisaṃskāraparinirvāyī bhavati <|> [7] n(a) h(ai)va sābhi(284v6)(saṃskāraparinirvāyī bhavati |[635] api tūrdhvaṃsrotā bhavati |[636] evaṃ sukhālayānuyogam anuyuktā)nām[637] asmākaṃ bhavanto viharatām imāni saptaphalāni ime saptānuśaṃsāḥ pratikāṃkṣitavyāḥ <|>

DĀ 15.26

[a] [Buddha:] "It (is possible), monks, (that wanderers who are adherents of another faith might speak in this way): [...][638]

---

does not in this very existence acquire perfect insight just by good behavior." Furthermore, Pradhan notes an alternate reading of *pratipadye°* (Abhidh-k-bh(P) 72. note 3). However, *pratiyaty* is attested in the British Library fragment corresponding to this part of the text, Or.15009/565 verso 3 (BLSF III.1, 394): */// dha◯rme pratiyaty(') eva ājñā[m]. + ///.* S.v. *pratiyatya* in SWTF for an explanation of the *avagraha*: *meist gefolgt von eva unter Ausfall des auslautenden a* (usually followed by *eva* under termination of the final *a*). Note also a similar usage in Hartmann's forthcoming edition and translation of the *Pravāraṇā-sūtra*: *so 'pi bhagavatā prati(26.1)ya(5.b)ty eva vyākṛtaḥ.* de Jong and Brough (de Jong 1976b, 325f. (= de Jong 1979, 280f.) and Brough 1962, 278) both suggest *pratiyatya* may be a corrupted or not clearly understood usage of the prakrit *paḍiyacca* related to the Pali *paṭikacca* or *paṭigacca.*

631. Cf. 284v3.

632. Cf. Abhidh-k-vy 270–271. A similar phrase occurs twice in the *Prasādanīya-sūtra*, 297r8: *paṃcānām avarabhāgīyānāṃ saṃyojanānāṃ prahāṇād upapāduko bhaviṣyati <|> ta(t)r(a sa parinirvāyī anāgamī)...* and 298r4: *paṃ(cān)ām av(a)r(a)bh(ā)gīyā(n)āṃ saṃyojan(ā)nāṃ (p)rahāṇād upapāduko bhaviṣyati <|> tatra sa parinirvāyī anāgamī...*

633. Cf. Abhidh-k-vy 273.24–33 and 274.12–19.

634. Cf. Abhidh-k-vy 273.27–28 and 274.14.

635. Cf. BLSF III.1 Or.15009/565 (= DĀ(U.H.) Hs. 130): v5 */// skā◯raparinirvāyī bhavat[i] ///* and Abhidh-k-vy 273.24–33 and 274.12–19.

636. Cf. Abhidh-k-vy 273.24–33 and 274.12–19.

637. Cf. 284v2.

638. See note 621 above.

[**b**] "They are to be addressed thus by those questioned: Thus, sirs, for us dwelling addicted to devotion to pleasure, seven fruits and seven benefits (are to be expected).

[**c**] "What are these seven? [1] (In this case, a monk) acquires (highest knowledge immediately in this very existence), not at the time of death. [2] Moreover, a monk definitely does not acquire highest knowledge immediately in this very existence. Nonetheless, [he acquires it] at the time of death. [3] Moreover, a monk (definitely does not) acquire (highest knowledge in this very existence) nor at the time of death. Nonetheless, due to his abandonment of the five lower fetters he is one who attains parinirvāṇa in the intermediate state.[639] [4] He is (definitely not) one who attains parinirvāṇa in the intermediate state. Nonetheless, he is one who attains parinirvāṇa at birth. [5] <He is definitely not one who attains parinirvāṇa at birth.> Nonetheless, he is one who attains parinirvāṇa without exertion. [6] He is definitely not one who attains parinirvāṇa without exertion. Nonetheless, he is one who attains parinirvāṇa with exertion. [7] He (is definitely not) one who attains parinirvāṇa with exertion. (Nonetheless, he is going upward in the stream of transmigration. Thus), sirs, for us dwelling addicted (to devotion to pleasure), these seven fruits and these seven benefits are to be expected."

~15.26~

DĀ(U.H.) Hs. 130 (=BLSF III.1 Or.15009/565) (*Prāsādika-sūtra*)

V

7[640] /// .. kapari[vrāj]akā evaṃ va + + + + + ///

R

639. *Antarāparinirvāyī* describes a state that could be taken two ways. As Edgerton notes, it may refer to an intermediate state between death and birth, as it is taken in Tibetan sources (an idea that is heterodox to Theravāda tradition), or a state before having passed the first half of life as it is understood in Theravāda orthodoxy. S.v. *antarāparinirvāyin* and *antarābhava* in BHSD. As the Buddhist thought and *vinaya* that was transmitted into the Himalayan regions was that of the Mūlasarvāstivāda tradition, the intermediate state between death and birth seems plausible in this context. However, it must be noted that this phrase occurs often in the SN (SN V 69, SN V 237, SN V 285, and SN V 314) where the Theravāda interpretation would have been intended.

640. DĀ 15.26a.

1[641] /// pṛṣṭair evaṃ syur vacanīyā + + + + ///
2[642] /// katame saptaḥ iha bh. kṣu. [d]ṛ.[ṭ]. + + ///
3 /// dha◯rme pratiyaty eva ājñā[m]. + ///
4 ///.. ◯rāparinirvāyī [bh]. [v]. + ///
5 ///skā◯raparinirvāyī bhava[ti] ///
6 /// + m asmākaṃ viharatāṃ imā .. [s]. ///

DN III 132.9–32 (DN 29.25)
[a] 25. ṭhānaṃ kho pan' etaṃ cunda vijjati yaṃ añña titthiyā paribbājakā evaṃ vadeyyuṃ—

[b] ime pana āvuso cattāro sukhallikānuyoge anuyuttānaṃ viharataṃ kati phalāni kat' ānisaṃsā pāṭikaṅkhā ti? evaṃ-vādino cunda añña-titthiyā paribbājakā evam assu vacanīyā—

[c] ime kho āvuso cattāro sukhallikānuyoge anuyuttānaṃ viharataṃ cattāri phalāni cattāro ānisaṃsā pāṭikaṅkhā. katame cattāro? idh' āvuso bhikkhu tiṇṇaṃ saṃyojanānaṃ parikkhayā sotāpanno hoti avinipāta-dhammo niyato sambodhi-parāyano. idaṃ paṭhamaṃ phalaṃ paṭhamo ānisaṃso. puna ca paraṃ āvuso bhikkhu tiṇṇaṃ saṃyojanānaṃ parikkhayā rāga-dosa-mohānaṃ tanuttā sakadāgāmī hoti sakid eva imaṃ lokaṃ āgantvā dukkhass' antaṃ karoti. idaṃ dutiyaṃ phalaṃ dutiyo ānisaṃso. puna ca paraṃ āvuso bhikkhu pañcannaṃ orambhāgiyānaṃ saṃyojanānaṃ parikkhayā opapātiko hoti tattha parinibbāyī anāvatti-dhammo tasmā lokā. idaṃ tatiyaṃ phalaṃ tatiyo ānisaṃso. puna ca paraṃ āvuso bhikkhu āsavānam khayā anāsavaṃ ceto-vimuttim paññā-vimuttiṃ diṭṭhe va dhamme sayaṃ abhiññā sacchikatvā upasampajja viharati. idaṃ catutthaṃ phalaṃ catuttho ānisaṃso. ime kho āvuso cattāro sukhallikānuyoge anuyuttānaṃ viharataṃ imāni cattāri phalāni cattāro ānisaṃsā pāṭikaṅkhā ti.

T I 1 75a26–27
[a] 若有外道梵志作如是問。汝等於此樂中求幾果功德。

T I 1 75a27–28
[b] 應答彼言。此樂當有七果功德。

641. DĀ 15.26b.
642. DĀ 15.26c.

T I 1 75a28–75b4
[c] 云何爲七。於現法中得成道證。正使不成臨命終時當成道證。若臨命終復不成者當盡五下結。中間般涅槃。生彼般涅槃。行般涅槃。無行般涅槃。上流阿迦尼吒般涅槃。諸賢。是爲此樂有七功德。

~15.26c~
Saṅg V.22
(pa)(71.7)ñ(cā)nāg(ā)(69.3)minaḥ | katame pañca | anta(111.7)rāparinirvāyī | upapa(dyaparinirvāyī | sābhisaṃskāraparinirvāyī | anabhisaṃskāraparinirvāyī | ūrdhvasrotaḥ |)

DN III 237.21–23 (*Saṅgīti-sutta*, DN 33.2.18)
pañca anāgāmino. antarā-parinibbāyī, upahacca-parinibbāyī, asaṃkhāra-parinibbāyī, sasaṃkhāraparinibbāyī, uddhaṃsoto akaniṭṭha-gāmī.

SN V 314:[643] SN V, 54(10).5(5).3–14 *Mahāvagga: Ānāpāna-saṃyutta: Phalā 2*
3. Ānāpānasati bhikkhave bhā° bahu° mahapphalā hoti mahānisaṃsā || katham bhāvitā ca bhikkhave katham bahumahapphalā hoti mahanisaṃsā || ||

4—10. Idha bhikkhave bhikkhu araññagato vā rukkhamūlagato vā suññāgāragato vā nisīdati° vitthāro || yāva° °sikkhati paṭinissaggānupassī Passasissāmīti sikkhati || ||

11. Evam bhāvitā kho bhikkhave ānāpānasati evambahulīkatā mahapphalā hoti mahānisaṃsā || ||

12. Evam bhāvitāya kho bhikkhave ānāpānasatiyā evam bahulīkatāya satta phalā sattānisaṃsā paṭikaṅkhā || katame satta phalā sattānisaṃsā || ||

13. Diṭṭheva dhamme patihacca aññam ārādheti || || No ce diṭṭheva dhamme paṭihacca aññam ārādheti || atha maraṇakāle aññam ārādheti || || No ce maraṇakāle aññam ārādheti || atha pañcannaṃ orambhāgiyānaṃ saṃyojanānam parikkhayā antarāparinibbāyī hoti || upahaccaparinibbāyī hoti || asaṅkhāraparinibbāyī hoti || sasaṅkhāraparinibbāyī hoti || uddhaṃsoto hoti akaniṭṭhāgāmī || ||

14. Evam bhāvitāya kho bhikkhave ānāpānasatiyā evam bahulīkatāya ime satta phalā sattānisaṃsā paṭikaṅkhā ti || ||

643. Cf. also SN V 69, SN V 237, and SN V 285.

Abhidh-k-vy 270.31–271.32 (italics signify root text)

evam eva tasya tāvan mānāvaśeṣasyāprahāṇād aparijñānāt *paṃcānām avarabhāgīyānāṃ saṃyojanānāṃ prahāṇād antarā-parinirvāyī bhavati.* iyaṃ *prathamā satpuruṣa-gatir* ākhyātā. [271] punar aparaṃ bhikṣur evaṃ pratipanno bhavati. no ca syām iti pūrvavat yāvat syuḥ praṣṭāra iti. *tadyathā* 'yo-guḍānāṃ vā 'yas-phālānāṃ vā pradīptāgni-saṃtprataptānām ayo-ghanena hanyamānānām *ayas-prapāṭikā utpataṃty eva nirvāyāt. evam eva* tasya pūrvavat yāvat *paṃcānām avarabhāgīyānāṃ saṃyojanānāṃ prahāṇād antarā-parinirvāyī bhavati.* iyaṃ *dvitīyā satpuruṣa-gatiḥ.* punar aparaṃ bhikṣur evaṃ pratipanno bhavati. pūrvavad yāvad *ayas-prapāṭikā utplutyāpatitvaiva pṛthivyāṃ nirvāyāt. evam eva* tasya pūrvavat yāvad antarā-parinirvāyī bhavati. iyaṃ *tṛtīyā satpuruṣa-gatiḥ.* punar aparaṃ bhikṣur evaṃ pratipanno bhavatīti pūrvavat yāvad ayas-prapāṭikā utplutya patitamātraiva pṛthivyāṃ nirvāyāt. evam eva tasya pūrvavad yāvat *paṃcānām avarabhāgīyānāṃ saṃyojanānāṃ prahāṇād upapadya-parinirvāyī bhavati.* iyaṃ caturthī satpuruṣa-gatiḥ. punar aparaṃ bhikṣur evaṃ pratipanna iti pūrvavad yāvad ayas-prapāṭikā utplutya parītte tṛṇa-kāṣṭhe nipatet. sā tatra dhūmam api kuryāt. arcir api saṃjanayet. sā tatra dhūmam api kṛtvā 'rcir api saṃjanayya tad eva parīttaṃ tṛṇa-kāṣṭaṃ dagdhvā paryādāya nirupādānā nirvāyāt. evam eva tasya pūrvavad yāvat *paṃcānām avarabhāgīyānāṃ saṃyojanānāṃ prahāṇād anabhisaṃskāraparinirvāyī bhavati.* iyaṃ paṃcamī satpuruṣa-gatiḥ. punar aparaṃ bhikṣur evaṃ pratipanna iti pūrvavad yāvad ayas-prapāṭikā utplutya mahati vipule tṛṇa-kāṣṭhe nipatet. sā tatra dhūmam api kuryāt. arcir api saṃjanayet. sā tatra dhūmam api kṛtvā 'rcir api saṃjanayya tad eva mahad vipulam tṛṇa-kāṣṭhaṃ dagdhvā paryādāya nirupādānā nirvāyāt. evam eva tasya pūrvavad yāvat *paṃcānām avarabhāgīyānāṃ saṃyojanānāṃ prahāṇāt sābhisaṃskāraparinirvāyī bhavati.* iyaṃ ṣaṣṭhī satpuruṣa-gatiḥ. punar aparaṃ bhikṣur evaṃ pratipanna iti pūrvavad yāvad ayas-prapāṭikā utplutya mahati vipule tṛṇa-kāṣṭhe nipatet. sā tatra dhūmam api kuryāt arcir api saṃjanayet. sā tatra dhūmam api kṛtvā 'rcir api saṃjanayya tad eva mahad vipulaṃ tṛṇa-kāṣṭahaṃ dagdhvā grāmam api dahed grāma-pradeśam api nagaram api nagara-pradeśam api janapadam api janapada-pradeśam api kakṣam api dāvam api dvīpam api ṣaṇḍam api dahet. grāmam api dagdhvā yāvad ṣaṇḍam api dagdhvā mārgāntam āgamya udakāntaṃ vā 'lpa-haritakaṃ vā pṛthivī-pradeśam āgamya paryādāya nirypādānā nirvāyāt. evam eva pūrvvad yāvat *paṃcānām avarabhāgīyānāṃ saṃyojanānāṃ prahāṇāt ūrdhvaṃ-srotā bhavati.* iyaṃ saptamī satpuruṣa-gatir ākhyātā.

Abhidh-k-vy 273.24–33 (repeats on 274.12–19)

2. etad eva ca sūtram uktvā no tu vimucyate.

api tu tenaiva dharmacchandena tenaiva dharmasnehena tenaiva dharmapremnā tayaiva dharmābhiratyā antarāparinirvāyī bhavati.

3. na haivāntarāparinirvāyī bhavati.
api tūpapadyaparinirvāyī bhavati.

4. na haivopapadyaparinirvāyī bhavati.
api tv anabhisaṃskāraparinirvāyi bhavati

5. na haivanabhisaṃskāraparinirvāyī bhavati
api tu sābhisaṃskāraparinirvāyī bhavati.

6. na haiva sābhisaṃskāraparinirvāyī bhavati.
api t' ūrdhvaṃ-srotā bhavati.

7. na haivordhvaṃ-srotā bhavati.
api tu tenaiva dharmacchandena pūrvavat yāvat tayaiva dharmābhiratyā mahābrahmaṇāṃ devānāṃ sabhāgatāyām upapadyate.

That Which Is and Is Not Explained by the Ascetic Gautama (DĀ 15.27–36)

DĀ 15.27

[**a**] (**284v7**) (sthānam etad bhikṣavo vidyate yad anyatīrthikaparivrājakā evaṃ vadeyuḥ |[644] kiṃ bhavan)t(aḥ ś)r(amaṇena)[645] gautamena <vyākṛtam iti |>[646] śāśvato l(o)k(a)ḥ[647] <|> idam eva satyaṃ moham anyad iti <|> aśāśvataḥ <|> śāśvataś cāśāśvataś ca <|> (**284v8**) (nai)va śāśvato nāśāśv(ataś) c(a) | ant(a)v(ān; ananta)ḥ[648] <|> ant(a)v(āṃś) c(ānan)t(avāṃś) c(a | nai)vānt(avān nā)nantavān* <|> sa jīvas tac charīram; anyo jīvo 'nyac charīraṃ; bhavati tathāgataḥ paraṃ maraṇā<n>; n(a) bha(v)ati t(a)thāgataḥ paraṃ maraṇā(**285r1**)(d; bhavati ca na bhavati ca | naiva bhavati na na bhavati paraṃ maraṇād; idam eva)[649] satyaṃ moham anyad iti <|>

[**b**] pṛṣṭair neti[650] syur vacanīyāḥ[651] <|>

644. Cf. 283r1–2, 283r7, 283v8, 284v1, 285r1, 285r3, 285r5, 285r7, 285r8–v1, 285v7, and BLSF III.1 Or.15009/565 (= DĀ(U.H.) Hs. 130): v7 /// + ..*ḥ evaṃ vadeyuḥ vyākṛtaṃ śrama* .. + + ///.

645. Cf. 285r3–4 and DN III 135.24–25: *kin nu kho āvuso hoti Tathāgato param maraṇā.*

646. Cf. 285r4, BLSF III.1 Or.15009/565 (= DĀ(U.H.) Hs. 130): v7 /// + ..*ḥ evaṃ vadeyuḥ vyākṛtaṃ śrama* .. + + ///, and DN III 136.27–28: *kiṃ pan' āvuso samaṇena Gotamena vyākatan ti?*. The reading suggested by Or.15009/565 v7 would place *vyākṛtaṃ* before *śramaṇena gautamena*, however, I place it after, as this corresponds to the readings both here in the *Prāsādika-sūtra* as preserved in the Virginia Collection (best preserved in 285r5) and in the DN.

647. Cf. DĀ 36.49 (*Pṛṣṭhapāla-sūtra*), DĀ 36.56 (*Pṛṣṭhapāla-sūtra*), Abhidh-k-bh(P) 294.1–3.

648. Cf. Abhidh-k-bh(P) 294: *antavān anantaḥ.*

649. Cf. DĀ 36.49 (*Pṛṣṭhapāla-sūtra*) and DĀ 36.56 (Melzer 2010, 280). Abhidh-k-bh(P) 294.1–3, DhskD 12r10–12v2, and Pras 446.9–14.

650. Ms. reads *naiti.*

651. Ms. reads *vasanīyāḥ*. Cf. 283r8, 284r1, 284v2, and 285v1.

DĀ 15.27

[a] [Buddha:] "(It is possible, monks, that wanderers who are adherents of another faith might speak in this way:) 'Sirs, [has it been explained] by the ascetic Gautama: "The world is eternal. Just this is true; anything else is false." "[The world] is not eternal." "[The world] is eternal and not eternal." "[The world] is neither eternal nor not eternal." "[The world] is finite." "[The world] is infinite." "[The world] is both finite and infinite." "[The world] is neither finite nor infinite." "Life is the body." "Life is different from the body." "A tathāgatha does not exist after death." "(He does exist [after death]." "He does and does not." "He neither does nor does not exist after death. Just this) is true; anything else is false."'

[**b**] "They are to be addressed: 'No,' by those questioned."

~15.27~

DĀ(U.H.) Hs. 130 (=BLSF III.1 Or.15009/565) (*Prāsādika-sūtra*)

R

7[652] /// + .. ḥ evaṃ vadeyuḥ vyākṛtaṃ śrama + + ///

DN III 135.23–136.16 (DN 29.30)[653]

30. ṭhānaṃ kho pan' etaṃ cunda vijjati yaṃ aññatitthiyā paribbājakā evaṃ vadeyyuṃ—kin nu kho āvuso hoti tathāgato param maraṇā? idam eva saccaṃ, mogham aññan ti? evaṃ-vādino cunda añña-titthiyā paribbājakā evam assu vacanīyā—avyākataṃ kho āvuso bhagavatā: hoti tathāgato param maraṇā, idam eva saccaṃ, mogham aññan ti. ṭhānaṃ kho pan' etaṃ cunda vijjati, yaṃ añña-titthiyā paribbājakā evaṃ vadeyyuṃ—kiṃ pan' āvuso na hoti tathāgato param maraṇā? idam eva saccaṃ, mogham aññan ti? evaṃ-vādino cunda añña-titthiyā paribbājakā evam assu vacanīyā—etam pi kho āvuso bhagavatā avyākataṃ: na hoti tathāgato param maraṇā, idam eva saccaṃ, mogham aññan ti. ṭhānaṃ kho pan' etaṃ cunda vijjati, yaṃ añña-titthiyā paribbājakā evaṃ vadeyyuṃ—kin nu kho āvuso hoti ca na hoti ca tathāgato param maraṇā ... pe ... n' eva hoti na na hoti tathāgato param maraṇā, idam eva saccaṃ, mogham aññan ti? evaṃ-vādino cunda añña-titthiyā paribbājakā evam assu vacanīyā—etam pi kho āvuso bhaga-

652. DĀ 15.27.

653. This section of the DN does not parallel closely with the DĀ.

vatā avyākataṃ: n' eva hoti na na hoti tathāgato param maraṇā, idam eva saccaṃ, mogham aññan ti.

T I 1 75c12–28

[a] 或有外道梵志作如是說。世間常存唯此爲實。餘者虛妄。或復說言。此世無常唯此爲實。餘者虛妄。或復有言。世間有常無常唯此爲實。餘者虛妄。或復有言。此世間非有常非無常唯此爲實餘者虛妄。或復有言。此世間有邊唯此爲實。餘者爲虛妄。或復有言。世間無邊唯此爲實。餘者虛妄。或復有言。世間有邊無邊唯此爲實。餘者虛妄。或復有言。世間非有邊非無邊唯此爲實。餘者虛妄。或復有言。是命是身此實餘虛。或復有言。非命非身此實餘虛。或復有言。命異身異此實餘虛。或復有言。非異命非異身此實餘虛。或復有言。如來終此實餘虛。或復有言。如來不終此實餘虛。或復有言。如來終不終此實餘虛。或復有言。如來非終非不終。此實餘虛。諸有此見。名本生本見。

T I 1 75c28–76a1

[b] 今爲汝記。謂此世常存。乃至如來非終非不終。唯此爲實餘者虛妄。是爲本見本生。爲汝記之。

DĀ 36.49 (*Pṛṣṭhapāla-sūtra*) (Melzer 2010, 276):

36.49 na khalu {m}upādhyāya tasya bhavato gautamasyaiva bhāṣitasyā(**419r3**)rtham ājānīmo yad uta śāśvato loka idam eva satyaṃ moham anyad iti; a<śāśvato loka |> śāśvataś cāśāśvataś ca <|> naiva śāśvato nāśāśvata ◦ {an}antavān antaḥ; anantavān antaḥ; {an}antavā {gā}(**419r4**)ś (c)<ā>(nantav)āṃś cā <|> naivāntavā<n> nānantavān <|> sa jīvas tac charīraṃ <| anyo jīvo 'nyac charīraṃ |> bhavati tathāgata paraṃ maraṇā<ṃ> <|> na bhavati <|> bhavati ca na bhavati <ca |> naiva bhavati na na bhavati tathāgataḥ paraṃ maraṇād i(**419r5**)dam e(va sat)y(a) mo(ha)m anyad iti <|>

DĀ 36.56 (*Pṛṣṭhapāla-sūtra*) (Melzer 2010, 280):

36.56 (**419v4**) so ham acirap<r>akrānte bhavati gautame{na} svakai<ḥ> s{v}abrahmacāribhir vākpratodakai<ḥ> saṃcanmarīkṛto <|> na khalūpādhyāyaivaṃ tasya bhavato gautamasya bhāṣita-syārtham <ā>jānīmo yad uta śāśva(**419v5**)to lokaḥ; idam <e>va satyaṃ moham anyad iti; aśāśvataḥ; yāvad bhavati tathāgataḥ paraṃ maraṇād idam eva satyaṃ moham anyad iti;

Abhidh-k-bh(P) 294.1–3:

tadyathā śāśvato loko 'śāśvataḥ | śāśvataś cāśāśvataś ca | naiva śāśvato nāśāśvataḥ | antavān anantaḥ | antavāṃś cānantaś ca | naivāntāvān nānantavān | bhavati tathāgataḥ paraṃ maraṇān, na bhavati tathāgataḥ paraṃ maraṇāt yāvad anyo jīvo 'nyac charīram ity ayaṃ bhikṣavaḥ sthāpanīyaḥ praśna iti |

DhskD 12r10–12v2
aśāśvato (12v1) lokaḥ (|) śāśvataś caśāśvataś ca (|) naiva śāśvato nāśāśvataḥ (|) antavān lokaḥ (|) anantavān lokaḥ (|) antavāṃś cānantavāṃś ca (|) naivāntavān anantavāṃś ca (|) sa jīvas tac charīraṃ (|) anyo jīvo 'nyac charīraṃ bhavati (|) tathāgataḥ paraṃ maraṇān na bhavati (|) tathāgataḥ (12v2) paraṃ maraṇād bhavati ca na bhavati ca (|) naiva bhavati na na bhavati paraṃ maraṇād (|)

Pras 446.9–14:
iha caturdaśāvyākṛtavastūni bhagavatā nirdiṣṭāni | tad yathā | śāśvato lokaḥ aśāśvato lokaḥ śāśvataś caśāśvataś ca lokaḥ naiva śāśvato nāśāśvataś ca loka iti catuṣṭayaṃ | antavān lokaḥ anantavān lokaḥ | antavāṃś cānantavāṃś ca lokaḥ naivāntavān nānantavāṃś ca loka iti dvitīyam | bhavati tathāgataḥ paraṃ maraṇān na bhavati tathāgataḥ paraṃ maraṇād bhavati ca na bhavati ca tathāgataḥ paraṃ maraṇān naiva bhavati na na bhavati ca tathāgataḥ paraṃ maraṇād iti tṛtīyam | sa jīvas taccharīram anyo jīvo 'nyac charīram iti || tāny etāni caturdaśa vastūny avyākṛtatvād avyākṛtavastūnīty ucyante ||

SĀ(H) I Bl. 159V2–162V1 5 (*Anāthapiṇḍada*)
5. (athānyataro 'nyatīrtikaparivrājako 'nātha)piṇḍadaṃ gṛhapatim idam a(vocat. mama dṛṣṭiḥ śāsvato loka idaṃ satyaṃ moham anyat. apara evam āha mama dṛṣṭir aśāśvato loka idaṃ satyaṃ mohaṃ a)nyat* apara evam āha śāśvataś (cāśāśva)ta(ś ca loka. apara evam āha naiva śāśvato nāśāśvataś ca lokaḥ. antavān lokaḥ. anantavān. antavāṃś cā)nantavāṃś ca. naivāntavāṃ nānantavāṃ. yo jī(vas tac charīram. anyo jīvo 'nyac charīram. bhavati tathāgataḥ paraṃ maraṇāt. na bhavati. bhavati ca na bhavati ca. a)para evam āha mama dṛṣṭir naiva bhavati (naiva na bhavati tathāgataḥ paraṃ maraṇāt. idaṃ satyaṃ moham anyat.)

▪ ▪ ▪ ▪ ▪

DĀ 15.28

[a] sthānam etad bhikṣavo vidyate y(ad anyatīrthikapa)ri(v)rā(j)a(kā evaṃ vadeyuḥ |)[654] **(285r2)** (kasmād bhavantaḥ śramaṇena gautamena ime dharmā ekāṃśenāvyākṛtā iti |)[655]

654. Cf. 283r1–2, 283r7, 283v8, 284v1, 285r3, 285r5, 285r7, 285r8–v1, and 285v7

655. Cf. 285r3, 285r5, 285r6, DĀ 36.62 (*Pṛṣṭhapāla-sūtra*), and DN III 136.18–19: *kasmā pan'*

[b] (pṛṣṭair evaṃ)[656] syur vacanīyāḥ <|>[657] ete {r}hi[658] bhavanto dharmā nārthopasaṃhitā na dharmopasaṃhitā na brahmacaryop(a)s(aṃ)hi(tā nābhijñāyai na saṃbodhaye na nirvāṇāya) **(285r3)** s(aṃvarttanta iti | tasmād ime dharmā bhagavatā ekāṃśenāvy)ākṛtā[659] iti <|>

DĀ 15.28

[a] [Buddha:] "It is possible, monks, that wanderers who are adherents of another faith (might speak in this way: 'Why, sirs, have these doctrines not been definitively explained by the ascetic Gautama?')

[b] "They are to be addressed (thus by those questioned): 'Because, sirs, these doctrines are not associated with the goal [of salvation], not associated with [the Buddha's] doctrine, not associated with the holy life; they (do not) lead to (supernormal knowledge, to perfect awakening, to nirvāṇa. Therefore, these doctrines) are not definitively explained (by the Blessed One).'"

~15.28~

DN III 136.16–25 (DN 29.31)

[a] 31. ṭhānaṃ kho pan' etaṃ cunda vijjati yaṃ añña-titthiyā paribbājakā evaṃ vadeyyuṃ — kasmā pan' etaṃ āvuso samaṇena gotamena avyākatan ti?

[b] evaṃ-vādino cunda añña-titthiyā paribbājakā evam assu vacanīyā — na h' etaṃ āvuso attha-saṃhitaṃ na dhamma-saṃhitaṃ na ādibrahmacariyakaṃ na nibbidāya na virāgāya na nirodhāya na upasamāya na abhiññāya na sambodhāya na nibbānāya saṃvattati. tasmā taṃ bhagavatā avyākatan ti.

T I 1.17 —

~15.28b~

DĀ 36.62 (*Pṛṣṭhapāla-sūtra*) (Melzer 2010, 282)

---

etaṃ āvuso samaṇena gotamena avyākatan ti.

656. Cf. 283r8, 284r1, 284v2, 285r1, and 285v1. See note 572 above.

657. Cf. 283r8, 284r1, 284v2, 285r1, and 285v1.

658. Cf. DĀ 36.62 and 36.64 (*Pṛṣṭhapāla-sūtra*): *ete hi.*

659. Cf. 285r2, 285r5, 285r6, and DĀ 36.62 (*Pṛṣṭhapāla-sūtra*).

36.62 kasmāt te mayā pṛṣṭhapāla naikāṃśikam ekāṃśenaikāntīkṛtvā lokasya bhavati sthiti prajñaptā; ete hi pṛṣṭhapāla dharmā n<ā>rthopasaṃhitā ° na dharmopasaṃ(**420r4**)(hitā na) brahmacaryo-pasaṃhitā {nā}nābhijñāyai <na> saṃbodhaye na nirvāṇāya saṃvarttaṃte <|> tasmā<t> te mayā pṛṣṭhapāla naikāṃśikam ekāṃśenaikāntīkṛtvā lokasya bhavati sthiti prajñaptā <|>

▪ ▪ ▪ ▪ ▪

DĀ 15.29

[**a**] sthānam etad bhikṣavo vidyate yad anyatīrthikaparivrājakā evaṃ vadeyu(ḥ[660] | kiṃ bhavantaḥ śramaṇena gautamena) (**285r4**) (vyākṛtam iti |)[661]

[**b**] (pṛṣtair evaṃ syur vacanīyāḥ |[662] yad utedaṃ duḥkham ār)y(asatyam i)ti[663] bhavaṃto vyākṛtam itīdaṃ duḥkhasamuda{yo}yam[664] idaṃ duḥkha-

660. Cf. 283r1–2, 283r7, 283v8, 284v1, 285r1, 285r5, 285r7, 285r8–v1, and 285v7.

661. Cf. 284v7.

662. Cf. 283r8, 284r1, 284v2, 285r1, and 285v1.

663. Cf: DĀ 36.63 (*Pṛṣṭhapāla-sūtra*): *yad utedaṃ duḥkham āryasatyam* and DĀ 20.178: *so 'ham idaṃ (338v1) duḥkham āryasatyam iti.*

664. There is no consensus among texts on the usage of pronouns before, or even the case of, the *āryasatya*s as presented in this type of list. One variously finds the *āryasatya*s in this list presented as either nominative or accusative. This is complicated here as we are able to read two pronouns, *ayam* and *idam* before *duḥkhanirodham* and the case of *duḥkhasamudaya* in the ms. would be read as nominative if no emendations were made. I have emended to: *duḥkhasamuda{yo}yam idaṃ* reading the whole list in the accusative, but it would have been just as possible to emend the readings to favor both *ayam* and a nominative presentation: *duḥkhasamudayo 'ya{m ida}ṃ duḥkhanirodha{m}*, etc. The fact that *duḥkhanirodham* is accusative however, would make this a slightly problematic reading. On the other hand, the word *duḥkhanirodhaḥ* is masculine so it would be preferable to read *ayam* over *idam*. Indeed, *ayam* is attested in the majority of similar passages in several other texts: DN III 136.31.EFGH 26.72 and 73, CPS E.23–24 (= Abhidh-k-vy II 645.20–26), SBV I 118.34, SBV II 250.26 (and others that are less similar). These texts also state all four of the *āryasatya*s that mark the theme of this section in the nominative. Unfortunately, even the closest DĀ parallels (besides the Pali, which one notes is listed above as reading *ayam*), are not consistent with DĀ 20.178 (*Kāyabhāvanā-sūtra*) favoring *idam* and the accusative: *i(daṃ duḥ)kh(a)s(amuda)yam idaṃ duḥkhanirodham idaṃ duḥkhanirodhagāminī{ṃ} pratipad ārya(s)atyam iti*, DĀ 36.63 (*Pṛṣṭhapāla-sūtra*), also favoring both *idam* and the accusative reading: *idaṃ duḥkhasamudayam*, and DĀ 25.48 (*Tridaṇḍi-sūtra*) favoring *ayam* and the nominative (at least as edited by Choi): *a)(366v7)yaṃ (d)u(ḥ)khasa(m)udayo{m i} 'yaṃ duḥkhanirodha{m i}<ḥ i>yaṃ duḥkhanirodhagāminī{ṃ} pratipad āryasatyam iti*. The reading in DĀ 25.48 (*Tridaṇḍi-sūtra*) demonstrates inconsistencies similar to those we find here

nirodham[665] iy(a)ṃ (d)u(ḥ)kha(n)i(ro)dh(a)gāminī prati(pad āryasatyam iti |) (**285r5**) (yathābhūtaṃ prajānātīti |)[666]

DĀ 15.29

[**a**] [Buddha:] "It is possible, monks, that wanderers who are adherents of another faith might speak in this way: ('What, sirs, has been explained by the ascetic Gautama?')

[**b**] "(They are to be addressed thus by those questioned): 'Sirs, it is explained that he accurately knows: this is the noble truth of suffering, this is [the noble truth of] the arising of suffering, this is [the noble truth of] the elimination of suffering, this is the noble truth of the practice leading to the end of suffering.'"

~15.29~

DN III 136.26–33 (DN 29.32)

[a] 32. ṭhānaṃ kho pan' etaṃ cunda vijjati yaṃ añña-titthiyā paribbājakā evaṃ vadeyyuṃ—kiṃ pan' āvuso samaṇena gotamena vyākatan ti?

---

in the *Prāsādika-sūtra* suggesting some equivocation as to how this list was transmitted. While I suspect a reading of *ayam* and nominative case is preferable, I break from Choi and follow the readings of Melzer and Zhen.

However, the four *āryasatyas* are only quite rarely found in the accusative, and I have only been able to find two other instances besides Melzer's and Zhen's editions, NidSa 23.13: *yataś cāryaśrāvako duḥkhaṃ yathā(bhū)taṃ prajānāti | duḥkhasamudayaṃ duḥkhanirodhaṃ duḥkha(niro)dhagāmi(nīṃ pra)tipadaṃ yathābhūtaṃ prajānāti* | and Mvu III 257: *duḥkhaṃ duḥkhasamudayaṃ duḥkhanirodhaṃ mārgaṃ* || bolstering my belief that the passage should be read with the phrases in question in the nominative case. In an article devoted to these grammatical issues surrounding the four *āryasatyas*, Norman notes: "The general tendency of the manuscripts, however, to read *–samudayaṃ* and *–nirodhaṃ* indicates that this is what the Pali tradition felt was correct, and consequently refrained from 'correcting.'" (Norman 1991, 211 (= Norman 1982)). Norman concludes by suggesting that the correct pronoun usage is *idam, ayam, ayam,* and *ayam* Norman 1992, 213, 219, and 222 (= Norman 1982). However, it should be remembered that the "correct" usage is not always attested in practice as we see here. A case in point is that *iyam* occurs extremely regularly with *duḥkkanirodhagāminim* in Sanskrit texts as, indeed, it does here.

665. Note the *jihvāmūlīya*.

666. Cf. DĀ 25.48 (*Tridaṇḍi-sūtra*): *duẖkhanirodhagāminī{ṃ} pratipad āryasatyam iti yathābhūtaṃ prajānāti* and DĀ 20.178 (*Kāyabhāvanā-sūtra*): *duḥkhanirodhagāminī{ṃ} pratipad ārya(s)atyam iti yathābhūtaṃ prajānāmi* as well as DĀ 36.63 (*Pṛṣṭhapāla-sūtra*), NidSa 23.13.a, EFGH 26.72 and 26.73, CPS E. 23–24 (= Abhidh-k-vy II 645.20–26), SBV I 118.32–119.4, and SBV II 250.23–31.

[b] evaṃ-vādino cunda añña-titthiyā paribbājakā evam assu vacanīyā—idaṃ dukkhan ti kho āvuso bhagavatā vyākataṃ, ayaṃ dukkha-samudayo ti kho āvuso bhagavatā vyākataṃ, ayaṃ dukkha-nirodha ti kho āvuso bhagavatā vyākataṃ, ayaṃ dukkha-nirodhogāminī paṭipadā ti kho āvuso bhagavatā vyākatan ti.

T I 1.17 —

~15.29b~

DĀ 20.178 (*Kāyabhāvanā-sūtra*) (Liu Zhen 2008, 132):
so 'ham idaṃ (338v1) duḥkham āryasatyam iti yathābhū(ta̤)ṃ (pra)jā(nāmi) <|> i(daṃ duḥ)kh(a)s(amuda)yam idaṃ duḥkhanirodham idaṃ duḥkhanirodhagāminī{ṃ} pratipad ārya(s)atyam iti yathābhūtaṃ prajānāmi <|>

MN I 249.6 (MN 36 *Mahāsaccaka-sutta*)
So: idaṃ dukkhan - ti yathābhūtaṃ abbhaññāsiṃ, ayaṃ dukkhasamudayo ti yathābhūtaṃ abbhaññāsiṃ, ayaṃ dukkhanirodho ti yathābhūtaṃ abbhaññāsiṃ, ayaṃ dukkhanirodhagāminī paṭipadā ti yathābhūtaṃ abbhaññāsiṃ; ime āsavā ti yathābhūtaṃ abbhāññāsiṃ [*sic*], ayaṃ āsavasamudayo ti yathābhūtaṃ abbhaññāsiṃ, ayaṃ āsavanirodho ti yathābhūtaṃ abbhaññāsiṃ, ayaṃ āsavanirodhagāminī paṭipad ti yathābhūtaṃ abbhaññāsiṃ.

DĀ 36.63 (*Pṛṣṭhapāla-sūtra*) (Melzer 2010, 282):
36.63 kiṃ ca (**420r5**) t(e) mayā pṛṣṭhapālaikā śikam ekāṃśenaikāntīkṛtvā lokasya bhavati sthiti prajñaptā <|> yad utedaṃ duḥkham āryasatyam idaṃ duḥkhasamudayam idaṃ duḥkhanirodham idaṃ duḥkhanirodha(**420r6**)gāminīpratipad āryasatyam <|> idaṃ te mayā pṛṣṭhapālaikāṃ śikam ekāṃśenānekāntīkṛtvā lokasya bhavati sthiti prajñaptā <|>

NidSa 23.13.a
yataś cāryaśrāvako duḥkhaṃ yathā(bhū)taṃ prajānāti | duḥkhasamudayaṃ duḥkhanirodhaṃ duḥkha(niro)dhagāmi(nīṃ pra)tipadaṃ yathābhūtaṃ prajānāti |

EFGH 26.72–73:
26.72 anāryā parṣat katamā | (yeyaṃ parṣad idaṃ duḥkham āryasatyam iti yathābhū)(H6R2)taṃ na prajānāty, ayaṃ duḥkha-samudayo, 'yaṃ duḥkha-

nirodha, iyaṃ duḥkha-nirodha-gāminī pratipad ārya-satyam iti yathābhūtaṃ na prajānāti | i(yam ucyate anāryā parṣat |

26.73 āryā parṣat kata)(H6R3)mā | yeyaṃ parṣad idaṃ duḥkham āryasatyam iti yathābhūtaṃ prajānāty, ayaṃ duḥkha-samudayo 'yaṃ duḥkha-nirodha iyaṃ duḥkha-nirodha-gāminī pra(tipad āryasatyam iti yathābhūtaṃ prajānāti | i)(H6R4)yam ucyate āryā parṣad |

CPS E. 23–24 (= Abhidh-k-vy II 645.20–26):
23 (sa rātryāḥ paścime yāme āsravakṣayajñānasākṣīkriyāya abhijñāyāṃ cittam abhinirnāmayati |) 24 (idaṃ duḥkham āryasatyam iti yathābhūtaṃ prajānāti | ayaṃ duḥkhasamudayaḥ | ayaṃ duḥkhanirodhaḥ | iyaṃ duḥkhanirodhagāminī pratipad āryasatyam iti yathābhūtaṃ prajānāti | tasyaivaṃ jānata evaṃ paśyataḥ kāmāsravāc cittaṃ vimucyate | bhavāsravād avidyāsravāc cittaṃ vimucyate | vimuktasya vimukto 'smīti jñānadarśanaṃ bhavati | kṣīṇā me jātir uṣitaṃ brahmacaryaṃ kṛtaṃ karaṇīyaṃ nāparam asmād bhavaṃ prajānāmīti |)

DĀ 27.102 (*Lohitya-sūtra I*) (Choi 2016)
sa evaṃ samā(h)i(te) citte pariśuddhe paryavadāte anaṃgaṇe vigatopakleśe ṛjubhūte karmaṇye sthite āni<ṃ>jyaprāpte āsravakṣayajñānasākṣātkṛyā{ṃ}yāṃ vidyāyāṃ cittam abhinirṇamayati <|> sa i(**382r1**)daṃ duḥkham āryasatyam i(ti) yathābhūtaṃ prajānāti <|> idaṃ duḥkhasamudaya<ṃ> yāvan nāparam asmā<d bhavaṃ> prajānāmī̱>ti |>

DĀ 25.48 (*Tridaṇḍi-sūtra*) (Choi 2016)
sa evaṃ samāhite citte pariśuddhe paryavad(āte anaṃga)(**366v6**)ṇe vigatopakleśe ṛjubhūte karmaṇye sthite āniṃjyaprāpte āsravakṣayajñānasākṣātkriyāyāṃ vidyāyāṃ cittam abhinirṇamayati <|> sa idaṃ duḫkham āryasatyam iti yathābhūtaṃ (p)r(ajāti ⁝ a)(**366v7**)yaṃ (d)u(ḥ)khasa(m)udayo{m i} 'yaṃ duḫkhanirodha{m i}<ḥ i>yaṃ duḫkhanirodhagāminī{ṃ} pratipad āryasatyam iti yathābhūtaṃ prajānāti <|> tasyaivaṃ jānata evaṃ pasyataḥ kāmāsravāc cittaṃ vimucyate <|> bhavāsravād a(v)i(dyāsravā)(**366v8**)c cittaṃ vimucyate <|> vimuktasya vimuktam eva jñānadarśanaṃ bhavati <|> kṣīṇā me jātir uṣitaṃ brahmacaryaṃ kṛtaṃ karaṇīyaṃ nāparam asmād bhavaṃ prajānāmīti ⁝

SBVG 386v2 (from DĀ 27.102 in Choi 2016) (Cf. SBV I 118.32–119.4)
sa idaṃ duḥkham āryasatym iti yathābhūtam prajānāti ⁝ ayaṃ duḥkhasamudayo

'yaṃ[667] duḥkhanirodha iyaṃ duḥkhanirodhagāminī pratipad āryasatyam iti[668] yathābhūta<ṃ> prajānāti <|> tasyaivaṃ jānata evaṃ (**386v3**) paśyataḥ kāmāsravāc cittaṃ vimucyate <|> bhavāsravād avidyāsravā{d aviyāsravā}c cittaṃ vimucyate <|> vimuktasya vimuktam eva jñānadarśanaṃ bhavati <|> kṣīṇā me jātir uṣitaṃ brahmacaryaṃ kṛtaṃ karanīyaṃ nāparam asmād bhavaṃ prajānāmīti ⁞

SBVG 515r2–4 (from DĀ 27.102 in Choi 2016, 310) (Cf. SBV II 250.23–31)

85. sa evaṃ samāhite citte pariśuddhe paryavadāte anaṃgaṇe vigatopakleśe ṛjubhūte karmaṇye sthite āniṃjyaprāpte āsravakṣayajñāna(**515r3**)sākṣātkriyāyām vidyāyāṃ[669] cittam abhinirṇamayati <|> sa idaṃ duḥkham āryasatyam iti yathābhūtaṃ prajānāti ⁞ ayaṃ duḥkhasamudayo 'yaṃ duḥkhanirodhaḥ iyam duḥkhanirodhagāminī pratipad āryasatyam iti yathābhūtaṃ prajānāti <|> tasyaivaṃ jānata evaṃ paśyata<ḥ> kāmā(**515r4**)sravāc cittaṃ[670] vimucyate <|> bhavāsravād avidyāsravāc cittaṃ[671] vimucyate <|> vimuktasya vimuktam eva jñānadarśanaṃ bhavati <|> kṣīṇā me jātiḥ uṣitaṃ brahmacaryaṃ kṛtaṃ karaṇīyaṃ nāparam asmād bhavaṃ prajānāmīti <|>

▪ ▪ ▪ ▪ ▪

DĀ 15.30

[**a**] (sthānam etad bhikṣavo vidyate yad anyatīrthika)parivrājakā[672] evaṃ vadeyuḥ <|> kasmād bhavantaḥ śramaṇena gautamena ime dharmā ekāṃ(śe)na[673] vyākṛtā iti <|>

[**b**] pṛṣṭair evaṃ[674] sy(u)r vacan(ī)yāḥ <|> (**285r6**) (ete hi bhavanto dharmā arthopasaṃhitā dharmopasaṃhi)tāḥ brahmacaryopasaṃhitāḥ abhijñāyai saṃbodhaye nirvāṇāya saṃvarttanta iti <|> tasmād ime dharmā bhagavatā ekāṃ(śena vyākṛtā iti |)[675]

667. Ms. reads *duḥkhamudaya ayaṃ.*

668. Ms. reads *ity ayathābhūta.*

669. Ms. reads *divyāyāṃ.*

670. Ms. reads *kāmāśravāś cittaṃ.*

671. Ms. reads *avidyāsravāṃś cittaṃ.*

672. Cf. 283r1–2, 283r7, 283v8, 284v1, 285r1, 285r3, 285r7, 285r8–v1, and 285v7.

673. Cf. 285r2, 285r3, 285r6, and DĀ 36.64: *ekāṃśena.*

674. See note 572 above.

675. Cf. Cf. 285r2, 285r3, 285r5, and DĀ 36.64 (*Pṛṣṭhapāla-sūtra*): *ete hi pṛṣṭhapāla dharmā <a>rthopasaṃhitā <dharmopasaṃhitā> brahmacaryopasamhitā abhijñāyai sa bodhaye*

DĀ 15.30

[**a**] [Buddha:]: "(It is possible, monks, that) wanderers who are adherents of another faith might speak in this way: 'Why, sirs, have these doctrines been definitively explained by the ascetic Gautama?'

[**b**] "They are to be addressed thus by those questioned: '(Because, sirs, these doctrines are associated with the goal) [of salvation], associated with [the Buddha's] doctrine, associated with the holy life; they lead to supernormal knowledge, to perfect awakening, to nirvāṇa. Therefore, these doctrines are definitively (explained) by the Blessed One.'"

~15.30~

DN III 137.1–8 (DN 29.33)

[a] 33. ṭhānaṃ kho pan' etaṃ cunda vijjati yaṃ añña-titthiyā paribbājakā evaṃ vadeyyuṃ—kasmā pan' etaṃ āvuso samaṇena gotamena vyākatan ti?

[b] evaṃ-vādino cunda añña-titthiyā paribbājakā evam assu vacanīyā—etaṃ hi āvuso attha-saṃhitaṃ, etaṃ dhamma-saṃhitaṃ, etaṃ ādi-brahmacariyakaṃ, ekanta-nibbidāya virāgāya nirodhāya upasamāya abhiññāya sambodhāya nibbānāya saṃvattati. tasmā taṃ bhagavatā vyākatan ti.

T I 1.17 —

~15.30b~

DĀ 36.64 (Pṛṣṭhapāla-sūtra) (Melzer 2010, 282):

36.64 kasmāt te mayā pṛṣṭhapālaikā śikam ekāṃśena nekāntī(**420r7**)(kṛtvā l)o(kas)y(a) bhavati sthitiḥ prajñaptā; ete hi pṛṣṭhapāla dharmā <a>rthopasaṃhitā <dharmopasaṃhitā> brahmacaryopasamhitā abhijñāyai sa bodhaye nirvāṇāya saṃvartta<ṃ>te <|> tasmāt te mayā pṛṣṭhapāla ekāṃśikam ekāṃśenānekāntī(**420r8**)kṛtvā lo(kasya) bhavati sthitiḥ prajñaptā <|>

▪ ▪ ▪ ▪ ▪

nirvāṇāya saṃvartta<ṃ>te <|> tasmāt te mayā pṛṣṭhapāla ekāṃśikam ekāṃśenānekāntī(420r8)*kṛtvā lo(kasya) bhavati sthitiḥ prajñaptā.*

DĀ 15.31

[a] **(285r7)** (sthānam etad bhikṣavo vidyate yad anyatīrthikaparivrājakā eva)ṃ v(a)deyur;[676] asthiradharmāṇaḥ śramaṇāḥ śākyaputrīyāḥ na sthiradharmāṇas; tathā hy eṣām ekaṃ vyākṛtam ekaṃ na[677] vyāk(ṛ)t(am) i(ti)[678] <|>

[b] (pṛṣṭair evaṃ[679] syur vacanī)**(285r8)**(yā |)[680] + ti <|> santy asmākaṃ dharmāḥ sthirāḥ śāntāḥ praṇītāḥ asaṃhāryā asaṃkṣobhyāḥ s(arvabālapṛthagja)naiḥ[681] <|>

DĀ 15.31

[a] [Buddha:] "(It is possible, monks, that wanderers who are adherents of another faith) might speak in this way: 'The ascetics who follow the Śākya are those whose doctrines are uncertain, not those whose doctrines are certain. Accordingly, for them one is explained [and] one is not explained.'

[b] "(They are to be addressed thus by those questioned): [...] 'Our doctrines are certain, calm, superb, immovable, and unperturbed by all foolish, common folk.'"

~15.31~
DN III 132.33–133.10 (DN 29.26)
[a] 26. ṭhānaṃ kho pan' etaṃ cunda vijjati yaṃ aññatitthiyā paribbājakā evaṃ vadeyyuṃ — aṭṭhita-dhammā samaṇā sākya-puttiyā viharantīti.

[b] evaṃ-vādino cunda añña-titthiyā paribbājakā evam assu vacanīyā — atthi kho āvuso tena bhagavatā jānatā passatā arahatā sammāsambuddhena sāvakānaṃ dhammā desitā paññattā yāva-jīvaṃ anatikkamanīyā.

676. Cf. 283r1–2, 283r7, 283v8, 284v1, 285r1, 285r3, 285r5, 285r7, 285r8–v1 and 285v7.

677. Ms. reads *ekan nā*. However, it is quite possible that the *-ā-* in *na* is actually short as the quality of the ms. is very poor here. Cf. 286r1.

678. Cf. 286r1, which reads *vyākṛta{ḥ}m ekaṃ na vyākṛtam iti*.

679. See note 572 above.

680. Cf. 283r8, 284r1, 284v2, 285r5, and 285v1. While I am quite confident that this phrase belongs here, with the gap in the ms. as large as it is, it is possible (although less likely) that this phrase may occur further down in the gap, perhaps leaving the previous section with an extra sentence at its end.

681. Cf. 285v1 and 285v7.

seyyathā pi āvuso inda-khīlo vā ayo-khīlo vā gambhīra-nemo sunikhāto acalo asampavedhī, evam eva kho āvuso tena bhagavatā jānatā passatā arahatā sammā-sambuddhena sāvakānaṃ dhammā desitā paññattā yāva-jīvaṃ anatikkamanīyā.

T I 1.17 —

▪ ▪ ▪ ▪ ▪

DĀ 15.32

[**a**] (sthāna)m e(tad bhikṣavo vidyate yad anya)(**285v1**)tīrthika(parivrāja)kā ev(aṃ) v(a)d(e)yuḥ <|>[682] katame te bhavatāṃ dharm(āḥ sth)i(rā)<ḥ> śāntāḥ praṇītā asaṃhāryāḥ asaṃk(ṣ)obhyāḥ sarvabālapṛthagjanair iti <|>[683]

[**b**] pṛṣṭair evaṃ[684] syur vacanīyā; yo 'sau bhavanto bhikṣ(u)(**285v2**) r bh(avat)i śaikṣo 'saṃprāptamānaso 'nuttaraṃ yogakṣemaṃ nirvāṇam abhiprārthayamāna(rūp)o (b)ahulaṃ viharati <|>[685] tasya saptānāṃ bodhipakṣyāṇāṃ dharmāṇām āsev(anānvayāt*[686] bhavanānva-yat)*

682. Cf. 283r1–2, 283r7, 283v8, 284v1, 285r1, 285r3, 285r5, 285r7, and 285v7.

683. Cf. 285r8 and 285v7.

684. See note 572 above.

685. Cf. SBV II 145.

686. Ms. reads *dharmāṇā hasev*. It is unfortunate that the ms. is damaged here but despite this, the best way to make sense of what we read here is to assume a mistake. From the context it is clear that *dharma* should be in genitive plural but the final *m* (or *ṃ*) is missing. I believe the most likely scenario is that the scribe wrote *ha* where he meant to write *mā* for *dharmāṇām āsevanānvayat*. *Āsevaṇanvayat* fits quite well with the following words *bhāvanānvayat* and *bahulīkārānvayāt* (see the following note for discussion on this reconstruction) with the three often appearing together: cf. in *Prāsādika-sūtra* at 283r5: *nāsevitavyo na bhāvayitavyo na bahulīkarttavyo*, 283r6: *āsevi{yi}tavyo bhāvayitavya bahulīkartta(v)y(o)*, 283r8: *nāsevitavyo na bhāvayitavyo na bahulīkarttavyo*, 283v7: *nāsevitavyo na bhāvayitavyo na bahulīkarttavyo*, 284r1: *ā(sev)it(avyo) <bhāvayitavyo> bahulīkartta(vy)o*, and 284v1: *ā(sevi)t(a)vyo bh(ā)<va>yi(tavyo bahul)ī(kartavyo)* and Śrāv-bh II 48: -II-3-a-(1)-iv: *yad asya yogina āsevanānvayād bhāvanānvayād bahulīkārānvayāc chamathavipaśyanāyā yah pratibimbālambano manaskāraḥ sa paripūryate* |, Śrāv-bh II 54: -II-3-a-(2)-2-ii-(d): *pragrahanimittam upekṣānimittam āsevanānvayād bhāvanānvayād bahulīkārānvayāt sarvadauṣṭhulyānāṃ pratipraśrabdher āśrayapariśuddhim anuprāpnoti sparśayati sākṣātkaroti* |, Śrāv-bh II 90: -II-3-b-(5)-ii-(a)-(5): *tasya ca prayogasyāsevanānvayād bhāvanānvayād bahulīkārānvayāt kāyaprasrabdhir utpadyate, cittaprasrabdhiś ca* |, Śrāv-bh II 100: -II-3-b-(5)-ii-(f): *api tu khalu tasyāsevanānvayād bhāvanānvayād bahulīkārānvayāt* |, Śrāv-bh II 104: -II-3-b-(5)-ii-(f): *yadā ca tac cittam āsevanānvayād bhāvanānvayād bahulīkārānvayān nivaraṇasamu-dācārād dūrīkṛtaṃ bhavati nivaraṇebhyo viśodhitam* |, (bahu)(285v3)(līkārā)nvayāt[687] samyaṅmanasikārānvayāt kāmā{ṃpra}sravā<c>[688] cittaṃ <vi>mucyate <|> bhavāsravād avidyāsravā<c>[689] cittaṃ vimucyate <|> vimuktasya vimukt(o 'smīti jñānadarśanaṃ bhavati | kṣīṇā me) (285v4) (jāti)r[690] uṣitaṃ brahmacaryaṃ kṛtaṃ karaṇīyaṃ nāparam asmād bhavaṃ prajānāmīti <|>

DĀ 15.32

[a] [Buddha:] "It is possible, (monks, that) wanderers who are adherents of another faith might speak in this way: 'What are these doctrines of yours,

---

Śrāv-bh II 106: -II-3-b-(5)-ii-(f): *yenāsyāsevanānvayād bhāvanānvayād bahulīkārānvayād avaśiṣṭebhyo bhāvanāprahātavyebhyaḥ kleśebhyaś cittaṃ vimucyate* |, Śrāv-bh II 206: -II-12-b-(2)-i-(c): *teṣām eva ca kuśalānāṃ dharmāṇāṃ pratilabdhānāṃ saṃmukhībhūtānām āsevanānvayāt parinispattiṃ niṣṭhāgamanam adhikṛtyāha bhāvanāparipūraya iti* |, and Śrāv-bh II 226: -II-12-b-(4)-iii: *sa eṣām indriyāṇām eteṣāṃ ca balānām āsevanānvayād bhāvanānvayād bahulīkārānvayān nirvedhabhāgīyāni kuśalamūlāny utpādayati mṛdumadhyādhimātrāṇi* |. Cf. also the following, which also contain these three words but in different formations: Saṅg IV.33 (four times): *asti samādhibhāvanā āsevitā bhāvitā bahulīkṛtā*, Saṅg VI.16 (=Daśo VI.7(1–5)a) *cetaḥsamādir āsevito bhāvito bahulīkṛto*, MPS 15.10 (twice); 15.13 (twice); 18.4; and 18.5: *catvāra ṛddhipādā āsevitā bhāvitā bahulīkṛtā*, DhskD 26r10: *sa tam utpannaṃ mārgam āsevayati bhāvayati bahulīkurute tasya imaṃ mārgam* |, DhskD 26v1: *āsevayato bhāvayato bahulīkurvataḥ tac cittam āsthihati saṃsthihati upasthihati ekotībhavati samāvarte* |, SHT (IV) 162 b R7: *///(u)[pa]sthānāny (āse)[v]itāni bh(āvitāni ba)hulīkṛtāni*, SHT (I) 620 R2: *///bhāvayata maitrāyām āsevitā///*, SHT (IV) 162 c5 A1: *///(bo)dhyaṅgāny āsevitā(n)[i]///*, SHT (V) 1325 B1: *///[sa]mādir āsevito bhāvito bahu[lī](kṛto)///*, and SHT (VI) 1515: *///(āsevit)ā bhāvitā bahulī(k)ṛ///*.

687. Cf. SĀ(VP) 10v3, 10v7, and 10v10: *saptānāṃ bodhipakṣyāṇān [sic] dharmāṇāṃ bhāvanānvayāt*, this phrase is used earliar in the *Prāsādika-sūtra* at 283r5: *nāsevitavyo na bhāvayitavyo na bahulīkarttavyo*, 283r6: *āsevi{yi}tavyo bhāvayitavya bahulīkartta(v)y(o)*, 283r8: *nāsevitavyo na bhāvayitavyo na bahulīkarttavyo*, 283v7: *nāsevitavyo na bhāvayitavyo na bahulīkarttavyo*, 284r1: *ā(sev)it(avyo)<bhāvayitavyo>bahulīkartta(vy)o*, and 284v1: *ā(sevi)t(a)vyo bh(ā)<va>yi(tavyo bahul)ī(kartavyo)* as well as these phrases in the *Prasādanīya-sūtra* 292r5: *bhāvanānvayād bahulīkārānvayāt samyaṅmanasikārānvayāt*, 296r5: *bhāvanānvayā<d> bahulīkārānvayā<t> samyaṅma(nas)i(kā)r(ā)nvayā<t>*, 296v1: *bhāvanānvayā<d> bahulīkārānvayā<t> (sa)m(ya)ṅmanasikārānvayā<t>*, and 296v5: *bhāvanānvayā<d> bahulīkarānvayā<t> samyaṅmanasikārānvay(āt)*. In addition to their frequent use in this sūtra strongly favoring my reconstruction, I feel all the more confident in reconstructing *bhāvanānvayat* and *bahulīkārānvayāt* here, as they often appear before *samyaṅmanasikārānvayāt* as seen above in the quotations from the *Prasādanīya-sūtra*.

688. Ms. reads *prasravacittaṃ*.

689. Ms. reads *avidyāsravacittaṃ*.

690. Cf. CPS E. 23–24 (= Abhidh-k-vy II 645.20–26), SBV II 145, SBV II 250, SĀ(VP) 10v3, 10v7, and 10v10, and DĀ 20.179 (*Kāyabhāvanā-sūtra*).

sirs, that are certain, calm, superb, immovable, and unperturbed by all foolish, common folk?'

[b] "They are to be addressed thus by those questioned: 'Sirs, he who is a monk, a student, one who has not mentally reached his goal, often dwells striving greatly for unsurpassed peace from bondage, nirvāṇa. His mind, due to concern with the following: (concern with cultivating), concern with intensely practicing, and concern with properly mentally attending to the seven factors related to awakening, is liberated from the [negative] influence of sensual pleasure. [His] mind is liberated from the [negative] influence of existence, from the [negative] influence of ignorance. For one who is liberated (there is the knowledge and discernment: "I am) free. (My) births (are exhausted), I have lived the holy life, I have done what is to be done, and therefore I know there is not another existence [for me].'"

DĀ 15.32

[c][691] yo 'sau bhavanto bhikṣur bhavaty arẖaṃ[692] (kṣ)ī(ṇāsravaḥ kṛtakṛtyaḥ kṛtakaraṇī)(**285v5**)y(o 'pa)hṛt(a)bhāro[693] 'nuprāptasvakārtha<ḥ> parikṣīṇabhavasaṃyojanaḥ samyagājñāsuvimuktacittaḥ <|> abhavyaḥ tasmiṃ samaye paṃcasthānāny a(dh)y(ācar)<i>tu(ṃ);[694] k(atamāni

691. The passage bears a strong similarity to the passages found in DĀ 15.24d and DĀ 15.25d.

692. Ms. reads *arthaṃ*, which makes little sense here. A scribal error of *rtha* for *rha* is especially obvious when one notes the various formations of *arhat* are used in this phrase in several texts. Cf. Avś(V) 237: *bhikṣur arhan kṣīṇāśravaḥ*, CPS 27a.1 (= SBV I 231): *cārhadbhiḥ kṣīṇāsravaiḥ*, CPS 27b.2 (= SBV I 232–233): *cārhadbhiḥ kṣīṇāsravaiḥ*, CPS 27c.1 (= SBV I 233–234): *cārhadbhiḥ kṣīṇāsravaiḥ*, Saṅg V.16: *abhavyo 'rhad bhikṣuḥ kṣīnāsravaḥ*, and DĀ 24 (the currently unedited *Mahāsamāja-sūtra*) 354r6: *arhadbhiẖ [kṣ]īṇā[s]ravai[ḥ].*

693. Cf. Avś(V) 237: *kṣīṇāśravaḥ kṛtakṛtyaḥ kṛtakaraṇīyo 'pahṛtabhāro*, which is the only other instance of this common phrase I have been able to find in nominative singular (all others are in instrumental plural). Also note these instances in DĀ 24 (the currently unedited *Mahāsamāja-sūtra* 354r5–6: *...arhadbhiḥ kṣīṇāsravaiḥ kṛtakṛtyaiẖ kṛtakaraṇīyair apahṛ = = ta* (354r6) *bhārair anuprāptasvakārthaiḥ parikṣīṇabhavasaṃyoja○naiḥ [s]. [ṃ]* .. + + .. *[s]uvimuktavicittais*, and 354r8: *...arhadbhiẖ [kṣ]īṇā[s]ravai[ḥ] ..tak[ṛ]* .. .. .. + *[ka]ra[ṇī]y[ai]r apahṛtabhārair anuprāptasvakārthaiḥ parikṣīṇabhavasamyojanais samyagājñā suvimukta[c]i[ttai]* .. (see also MSjSū(Re-ed) 1.2). Similar phrases occur verbatim to one another, all instrumental plural, in CPS and SBV (CPS 27a.1 = SBV I 231, CPS 27b.2 = SBV I 232–233, and CPS 27c.1 = SBV I 233–34), in addition to SHT (I) 496 R4: *(a)[va]h[ṛ]dabhārer anuprāptasvakārthaiḥ*, and still other, similar phrases occurring in numerous texts.

694. Cf. SHT (V) 1123 Ac: */// (a)bhav[y]aḥ sa tasmiṃ samaye [pa]ṃ[ca] sthānāny adhyā-*

paṃca)[695] <|> abh(av)yo 'rhadbhikṣuḥ (285v6) kṣīṇāsravaḥ [1] saṃciṃtya prāṇinaṃ jīvitād vyaparopayituṃ [2] <adattaṃ steyasaṃkhyātam ādātum* |>[696] [3] abrahmacaryaṃ maithunaṃ dharmaṃ pratisevituṃ [4] saṃprajānaṃ mṛṣāvācaṃ bhāṣituṃ [5] sannidhikāra-paribhogena[697] vā kāmān paribhoktum iti <|> ime te ('smākaṃ) bhava(nt)o (285v7) dharmā<ḥ> sthirāś śāntāḥ praṇītā asaṃhāryā asaṃkṣobhyās (sa)rv(a)bālapṛthagjanaiḥ[698] <|>

DĀ 15.32

[c][699] [Buddha:] "'Sirs, he who is a monk, an arhat, one whose [negative] influences have been exhausted, (one who has done his duty), one who has done what is to be done, one who has laid aside his burden, one who has reached his own aim, one for whom the fetter of existence has been exhausted, one whose mind has been completely liberated by proper, highest knowledge is at that time unable to transgress upon five occasions. What (are these five)? A monk who is an arhat, one whose [negative] influences have been exhausted, is unable to [1] intentionally deprive a living creature of life, [2] <to take what is not given so as to be considered theft>, [3] to indulge in sexual intercourse [and] impure conduct, [4] to deliberately tell lies, [5] or to enjoy sensual pleasure via the enjoyment of storing provisions.

(caritum) (or °*cartum?*), DN III 133.14: *abhabbo so nava ṭhānāni ajjhācarituṃ* and MN I 523: *abhabbo so pañca ṭhānāni ajjhācarituṃ*.

695. Although not attested in a parallel, this usage of asking what numbered subjects are, immediately after they are first stated, is quite common in the *Prasādanīya-sūtra*. Cf. DĀ 16.4 (292v1): *katamāni dvādaśa*, DĀ 16.5 (292v4): *katamāḥ sapta*, DĀ 16.9 (293v8): *katamāni catvāri*, DĀ 16.15 (297v5): *katamā catasraḥ*, and DĀ 16.18 (298v6): *katameṣāṃ caturṇāṃ*.

696. While the text states that there are five impossible states, it only lists four, and it appears that the scribe omitted one of the members of the list. Cf. Saṅg V.16: *abhavyo 'dattaṃ steyasaṃkhyātam ādātum*, which fortunately attests to what must be the missing item in this fivefold list. This is also clear from the Pali, DN III 133.15–16: *abhabbo khīṇāsavo bhikkhu adinnaṃ theyyasaṃkhātaṃ ādātuṃ*, DN III 235.4–11 (*Saṅgīti-sutta*): *abhabbo khīṇāsavo bhikkhu adinnaṃ theyya-saṃkhātaṃādātuṃ*, and MN I 523 (*Sandaka-sutta*): *abhabbo khīṇā-savo bhikkhu adinnaṃ theyyasaṅkhātaṃ ādātuṃ*. Cf. also 283v4: *saṃcintya prāṇinaṃ jīvitād vyaparopyādattam ādāya* and 284r5: *saṃciṃtya prāṇi(na)ṃ jīvitād vyaparopyādattam ādāya*.

697. Ms. reads *sannidhīkāraparibhogena*. S.v. *saṃnidhi-kāra-paribhoga* in SWTF.

698. Cf. 285r8 and 285v1.

699. This passage shares a strong similarity with the content of DĀ 15.24d and DĀ 15.25d.

These, sirs, are (our) doctrines that are certain, calm, superb, immovable, and unperturbed by all foolish, common folk.'"

~15.32~

DN III 133.10–27 (DN 29.26)[700]

[c] yo so āvuso bhikkhu arahaṃ khīṇāsavo vusitavā kata-karaṇīyo ohita-bhāro anuppattasadattho parikkhīṇa-bhava-saṃyojano sammad-aññā vimutto, abhabbo so nava ṭhānāni ajjhācarituṃ. abhabbo āvuso khīṇāsavo bhikkhu sañcicca pāṇaṃ jīvitā voropetuṃ. abhabbo khīṇāsavo bhikkhu adinnaṃ theyyasaṃkhātaṃ ādātuṃ. abhabbo khīṇāsavo bhikkhu methunaṃ dhammaṃ paṭisevituṃ. abhabbo khīṇāsavo bhikkhu sampajāna-musā bhāsituṃ. abhabbo khīṇāsavo bhikkhu sannidhi-kārakaṃ kāme paribhuñjituṃ, seyyathā pi pubbe agāriya-bhūto. abhabbo khīṇāsavo bhikkhu chandāgatiṃ gantuṃ. abhabbo khīṇāsavo bhikkhu dosāgatiṃ gantuṃ. abhabbo khīṇāsavo bhikkhu mohāgatiṃ gantuṃ. abhabbo khīṇāsavo bhikkhu bhayāgatiṃ gantuṃ. yo so āvuso bhikkhu arahaṃ khīṇāsavo vusitavā katakaraṇīyo ohita-bhāro anuppatta-sadattho parikkhīṇa-bhavasaṃyojano sammad-aññā vimutto, abhabbo so imāni nava ṭhānāni ajjhācaritun ti.

T I 1.17 —

~15.32c~

SHT (V) 1123 M 644 (Sūtra-Fragment *mit einer Erörterung der „fünf unmöglichen Zustände"*)[701]

A

a /// [yā]van=n=āpa[ram=a)sm(ā)d=bhava(ṃ) pra[jān](ī)maḥ [y]. [s. [ā) + ///

b /// [sa]myagājñāya suvimuktacittaḥ pratiṣevete [s). + ///

c ///+ + bhav[y]aḥ sa tasmiṃ samaye [pa]ṃ[ca] sthānāny=adhyā .. ///

d /// (mai)[th]unaṃ dharma pratiṣevituṃ saṃprajāna mṛṣāvā[d]. ///

e /// + + [k](a)r[m]ā[n]i [pa]ṃ[ca sthā) + + + + .. + + + + + ///

~15.32b~

SBVG 515r3–4 (Cf. SBV II 250.23–31)

700. The DN only parallels DĀ 15.32c; 15.32a&b are not found in the *Sampasādanīya-sutta*.

701. Although this may be from the *Prāsādika-sūtra*, since the same passage occurs in several sūtras, I cannot confirm the source.

tasyaivaṃ jānata evaṃ paśyata<ḥ> kāmā(515r4)sravāc cittaṃ[702] vimucyate <|> bhavāsravād avidyāsravāc cittaṃ[703] vimucyate <|> vimuktasya vimuktam eva jñānadarśanaṃ bhavati <|> kṣīṇā me jātiḥ uṣitaṃ brahmacaryaṃ kṛtaṃ karaṇīyaṃ nāparam asmād bhavaṃ prajānāmīti <|>

SĀ(VP) 10v1–5 (pp. 576–577) (Cf. 10v6–10 for the same prhase)
śrāvastyāṃ nidā[naṃ tatra bhagavān bhikṣūn āmaṃtra]yati sma • rūpam bhikṣa[va] (2) anityaṃ yad anityaṃ tad duḥkhaṃ yad duḥkhaṃ tad anātmā yad anātmā tan naitan mama [naiṣo ham asmi naiṣa me] ātmety evam etad yathābhūtaṃ samyakprajñayā draṣṭavyaṃ • vedanā saṃjñā saṃskārā vijñānam anityaṃ yad anityaṃ tad duḥkham ya(3)d duḥkhaṃ tad anātmā yad anātmā tan naitan mama naiṣo ham asmi na me ātmety e[vam etad ya]thābhūtaṃ samyakprajñayā draṣṭavyaṃ evaṃ jānato bhikṣava evaṃ paśyataḥ śrutavata āryaśrāvakasya *saptānāṃ bodhipakṣyāṇān [sic] dha(4)rmāṇāṃ bhāvanānvayāt kāmāsravāc cittaṃ vimucyate vimuktasya vimukto smīti [jñānaṃ bha]vati • kṣīṇā me jātir uṣitaṃ brahmacaryaṃ kṛtaṃ karaṇīyaṃ nāparaṃ asmād bhavaṃ prajānāmi* • yāvad bhikṣavo bhavāgraṃ yāvat satvā (5) vasa [*sic*] ete grā ete śreṣṭhāḥ ete pravarāḥ ete praṇītāḥ yad utārhaṃta [idam a]vocat ◎

CPS E. 24 (= Abhidh-k-vy II 645.20–26):
24 (idaṃ duḥkham āryasatyam iti yathābhūtaṃ prajānāti | ayaṃ duḥkhasamudayaḥ | ayaṃ duḥkhanirodhaḥ | iyaṃ duḥkhanirodhagāminī pratipad āryasatyam iti yathābhūtaṃ prajānāti | *tasyaivaṃ jānata evaṃ paśyataḥ kāmāsravāc cittaṃ vimucyate* | *bhavāsravād avidyāsravāc cittaṃ vimucyate* | *vimuktasya vimukto 'smīti jñānadarśanaṃ bhavati* | *kṣīṇā me jātir uṣitaṃ brahmacaryaṃ kṛtaṃ karaṇīyaṃ nāparam asmād bhavaṃ prajānāmīti* |)

DĀ 20.179 (*Kāyabhāvanā-sūtra*) (Liu Zhen 2008, 132):
tasya mamaivaṃ jānata evaṃ paśyataḥ kā(338v2)māsravāc cittaṃ vimucyate bhavāsravād avidyāsravāc cittaṃ vimucyate <|> vimuktasya vimuktam eva jñānadarśanaṃ bhavati <|> kṣīṇā me jātir uṣitaṃ brahmacaryaṃ <kṛtaṃ karaṇīyaṃ> nāparam asmād bhavaṃ prajānāmi | iti <|>

702. Ms. reads *kāmāśravāś cittaṃ.*

703. Ms. reads *avidyāsravāṃś cittaṃ.*

MN I 23 (MN 4 *Bhayabherava-sutta*)
tassa me evaṃ jānato evaṃ passato kāmāsavā pi cittaṃ vimuccittha. bhavāsavā pi cittaṃ vimuccittha. avijjāsavā pi cittaṃ vimuccittha, vimuttasmiṃ vimuttam—iti ñāṇaṃ ahosi; khīṇā jāti, vusitaṃ brahmacariyaṃ, kataṃ karaṇīyaṃ nāparaṃ itthattāyāti abbhaññāsiṃ.

MN I 249.14 (MN 36 *Mahāsaccaka-sutta*)
tassa me evaṃ jānato evaṃ passato kāmāsavā pi cittaṃ vimuccittha, bhavāsavā pi cittaṃ vimuccittha, avijjāsavā pi cittaṃ vimuccittha, vimuttasmiṃ vimuttam—iti ñāṇaṃ ahosi; khīṇā jāti, vusitaṃ brahmacariyaṃ, kataṃ karaṇīyaṃ nāparaṃ itthattāyāti abbhaññāsiṃ.

MN III 36 (MN 112 *Chabbisodhana-sutta*)
tassa me evaṃ jānato evaṃ passato kāmāsavā pi cittaṃ vimuccittha, bhavāsavā pi cittaṃ vimuccittha, avijjāsavā pi cittaṃ vimuccittha, vimuttasmiṃ vimuttam iti ñāṇaṃ ahosi: khīṇā jāti, vusitaṃ brahmacariyaṃ, kataṃ karaṇīyaṃ, nāparaṃ itthattāyāti abbhaññāsiṃ.

AN IV 179 (AN *Mahāvagga* XI.15–XII.1)
tassa me evaṃ jānato evaṃ passato kāmāsavā pi cittaṃ vimuccittha, bhavāsavā pi cittaṃ vimuccittha, avijjāsavā pi cittaṃ vimuccittha, vimuttasmiṃ vimuttam iti ñāṇaṃ ahosi. khīṇā jāti, vusitaṃ brahmacariyaṃ, kataṃ karaṇīyaṃ, nāparaṃ itthattāyā ti abbhaññāsiṃ.

Vin III 5 (Suttavibhaṅga, Pārājika 1)
tassa me evaṃ jānato evaṃ passato kāmāsavāpi cittaṃ vimuccittha, bhavāsavāpi cittaṃ vimuccittha, diṭṭhāsavāpi cittaṃ vimuccittha, avijjāsavāpi cittaṃ vimuccittha, vimuttasmiṃ vimuttam iti ñāṇaṃ ahosi, khīṇā jāti, vusitaṃ brahmacariyaṃ, kataṃ karaṇīyaṃ, nāparaṃ itthattāyā 'ti abbhaññāsiṃ.

~15.32c~
DĀ 24 (*Mahāsamāja-sūtra*) 354r5–6 (see also MSjSū(Re-ed) 1.2)
...arhadbhiḥ kṣīṇāsravaiḥ kṛtakṛtyaiḥ kṛtakaraṇīyair apahṛ = = ta (354r6) bhārair anuprāptasvakārthaiḥ parikṣīṇabhavasaṃyoja○naiḥ [s]. [ṃ] .. + + .. [s]uvimuktavicittais, and (354r8) ...arhadbhiḥ [kṣ]īṇā[s]ravai[ḥ] ..tak[ṛ] .. .. .. + [ka]ra[ṇī]y[ai]r apahṛtabhārair anuprāptasvakārthaiḥ parikṣīṇabhavasamyojanais samyagājñā suvimukta[c]i[ttai] ..

Avś(V) 237
kaṃ punas tvam ānanda sthavirakaṃ bhikṣuṃ saṃjānīyāḥ? sthavirako bhadanta bhikṣur arhan kṣīṇāśravaḥ kṛtakṛtyaḥ kṛtakaraṇīyo ’pahṛtabhāro ’nuprāptasvakārthaḥ parikṣīṇabhavasaṃyojanaḥ samyagājñāsuvimuktacittaḥ | tāny api bhikṣuśatāni sarvāṇy arhanti kṣīṇāsravāṇi kṛtakṛtyāni kṛtakaraṇīyāny apahṛtabhārāṇy anuprāptasvakārthaḥ parikṣīṇabhavasaṃyojanaḥ samyagājñāsuvimuktacittāni ||

CPS 27a.1 = SBV I 231
(atha bhagavān gayāyāṃ gayāśīrṣe caitya eva viharati sārdhaṃ bhikṣusahasreṇa sarvaiḥ purāṇajaṭilaiḥ sarvaiś cārhadbhiḥ kṣīṇāsravaiḥ kṛtakṛtyaiḥ kṛtakaraṇīyair avahṛtabhārair anuprāptasvakārthaiḥ parikṣīṇabhavasaṃyojanaiḥ samyagājñayā suvimuktacittaiḥ |)

CPS 27b.2 = SBV I 232–233
(sa keśaśmaśrūṇy avatārya kāṣāyāṇi vastrāṇy ācchādya samyag eva śraddhayāgārād anagārikāṃ pravrajitaḥ | so ’nuttarāṃ samyaksaṃbodhim abhisaṃbuddho gayāyāṃ) (122.5) viharati gayāśīrṣe caitye (sārdhaṃ bhikṣusahasreṇa sarvaiḥ purāṇajaṭilaiḥ sarvaiś cārhadbhiḥ (SBV I 233) kṣīṇāsravaiḥ kṛtakṛtyaiḥ kṛtakaraṇīyair avahṛtabhārair anuprāptasvakārthaiḥ pa)(122.6)rikṣīṇabh(avasaṃyojanaiḥ samyagājñayā suvimuktacittaiḥ |)

CPS 27c.1 = SBV I 233–234
(atha bhagavān mahatā bhikṣusaṃghena sārdhaṃ bhikṣusahasreṇa sarvaiḥ (SBV I 234) purāṇajaṭilaiḥ sarvaiś cārhadbhiḥ kṣīṇāsravaiḥ kṛtakṛtyaiḥ kṛtakaraṇīyair avahṛtabhārair anuprāptasvakārthaiḥ parikṣīṇabhavasaṃyojanaiḥ samya)(21.3)gājñayā suvimuktacittair (māgadheṣu janapadeṣu caryāṃ caran) ye(na yaṣṭivanaṃ supratiṣṭhito māgadhakānāṃ caityas tena caryāṃ prakrāntaḥ |)

Saṅg V.16
(pañcābhavyasthānāni | abhavyo ’rhad bhikṣuḥ kṣīnāsravaḥ saṃcintya prāṇinaṃ jīvitād vyaparopitum | abhavyo ’dattaṃ steyasaṃkhyātam ādātum | abhavyo maithunaṃ dharmaṃ pratisevitum | abhavyaḥ saṃprajānan mṛṣā vaditum |) .. ..

DN III 235.4–11 (*Saṅgīti-sutta*, DN 33.2 I (x))
(x) pañca abhabba-ṭṭhānāni. abhabbo āvuso khīṇāsavo bhikkhu sañcicca pāṇaṃ jīvitā voropetuṃ. abhabbo khīṇāsavo bhikkhu adinnaṃ theyya-

saṃkhātaṃādātuṃ. abhabbo khīṇāsavo bhikkhu methunaṃ dhammaṃ paṭisevituṃ. abhabbo khīṇāsavo bhikkhu sampajāna-musā bhāsituṃ. abhabbo khīṇāsavo bhikkhu sannidhi-kārakaṃ kāme paribhuñjituṃ, seyyathā pi pubbe agāriya-bhūto.

Śrāv-bh(Sh) 509–510[704]
[4] ..... parinirvṛt(o) bhavati | yathā na saṃsṛto/(tau) nānyatra yad duḥkhaṃ tan niruddhaṃ tavyupaśāntaṃ tac chītībhūtaṃ bhava iṃ [sic] gataṃ | śāntaṃ śāntam idaṃ padaṃ | yad uta sarvopadhipratiniḥsarvasaṃjñākṣayo virāgo nirodho nirvāṇaṃ tasyemāni liṃgān yevaṃ bhāgīyāni veditavyāni | [510] pañcasthānāny u .... bhikṣuḥ kṣīṇāsravaḥ prati | vi vine | kta [sic] manyamasaṃ tathā [5] prāpayituṃ mandadātram abrahmacaryaṃ maithunaṃ dharmaṃ pratiṣevituṃ | saṃprajānā(no) mṛṣāpa [sic] bhāṣitum abhavyaḥ mandavikāreṇa kāmān paribhoktuṃ | tathā bhavyaḥ svayaṃ kṛtaṃ sukhaṃ duḥkhaṃ pratyetuṃ | pūrvavad yāvat svayaṃkāyakāro (')hetusamutpannam ugraduḥkhaṃ praṇītam amavyāya kṛtastubhiḥ-(tiḥ) | satrāsaṃ māṃsaṃ bhakṣya(vya) ....

Śrāv-bh II 232–234: -II-12-b-(6)-i
yo 'py āryakāntāni śīlāny ucyante | kena kāraṇena | dīrghakālaṃ hy etad āryāṇāṃ satāṃ samyaggatānām iṣṭaṃ kāntaṃ priyaṃ mana-āpaṃ "kaccid ahaṃ tad vāgduścaritasya kāyaduścaritasya mithyājīvasyākaraṇaṃ saṃvaraṃ pratilabheyam" | yad asya dīrgharātram iṣṭaṃ kāntaṃ priyaṃ mana-āpaṃ tad anena tasmin samaye pratilabdhaṃ bhavati | tasmād āryakāntam ity ucyate | tathā hi sa labdheṣv āryakānteṣu śīleṣu, na saṃprajāno mṛṣāṃ vācaṃ bhāṣate, na saṃcintya prāṇinaṃ jīvitād vyaparopayati, nādattam ādatte, (Śrāv-bh II 234) na kāmeṣu mithyā carati, na cādharmeṇa cīvarādīni paryeṣate | iti tāny āryakāntāni śīlāny adhipatiṃ kṛtvā mārgabhāvanākāle yā vāk pravartate yac ca kāyakarma yaś cājīvaḥ, te 'pi samyagvākkarmāntājīvā ity ucyante |

MN I 523 (MN 76 *Sandaka-sutta* 3.6)
yo so sandaka bhikkhu arahaṃ khīṇāsavo vusitavā katakaraṇīyo ohitabhāro anuppattasadattho parikkhīṇabhavasaṃyojano samma-d-aññā vimutto, abhabbo so pañca ṭhānāni ajjhācarituṃ: abhabbo khīṇāsavo bhikkhu sañcicca pāṇaṃ jīvitā voropetuṃ, abhabbo khīṇā-savo bhikkhu adinnaṃ theyyasaṅkhātaṃ ādātuṃ, abhabbo khīṇāsavo bhikkhu methunaṃ dhammaṃ patisevituṃ, abhabbo khīṇāsavo bhikkhu sampajānamusā bhāsituṃ, abhabbo khīṇāsavo bhikkhu

704. See note 619.

sannidhikārakaṃ kāme paribhuñjituṃ seyyathā pi pubbe agāriyabhūto. yo so sandaka bhikkhu arahaṃ khīṇāsavo vusitavā katakaraṇīyo ohitabhāro anuppattasadattho parikkhīṇabhavasaṃyojano samma-d-aññā-vimutto, abhabbo so imāni pañca ṭhānāni ajjhācaritun-ti.

▪ ▪ ▪ ▪ ▪

DĀ 15.33

sthānam etad bhikṣavo vidyate yad anyatīrthikaparivrājakā evaṃ vadeyus; tiryag bhavantaḥ śramaṇasya gautamasya .. + + + + (**286r1**) tā (jñā) nada(rśa)naṃ[705] pravarttate <|> anāgatena tathā{gatā}[706] hy anenaikaṃ vyākṛta{ḥ}m ekaṃ na vyākṛtam iti <|> tad idaṃ[707] bhikṣavo anyatīrthikaparivrājakā anyathābhāgīyena jñānena anyabhāgīyajñā(na)ṃ[708] .. .i .ā nayi(**286r2**)tavyaṃ manya<n>te[709] <|> tat teṣāṃ asadṛśaṃ |

705. Cf. DN III 134.2–3: *atītaṃ kho addhānaṃ ārabbha samaṇo Gotamo atīrakaṃ ñāṇadassanaṃ paññāpeti.* I have not been able to reconstruct the gap here but it should convey some information about the past as in the DN. It is unclear why this sentence begins with *tiryak* when we would expect *ātītam* from the Pali and, indeed, the content of the *Prāsādika-sūtra* as we see in the next passage below. Perhaps *tiryak* here has to do with *atīrakam* (boundless, limitless, literally "not shored") in the Pali and became *tiryak* due to some Middle-Indic influence. In any case, this has made it difficult to reconstruct this sentence with confidence. Note this passage from MPS 42.6: *sadhu sādhv ānanda prasādena tvam* (227 *Ba*) *evaṃ vadasi* | *ta(thāgatasya tv an)*(223.3)*uttare jñānadarśanaṃ pravartate.* This is not a parallel, but *anuttare jñānadarśanaṃ pravartate*, "he sets forth unsurpassed knowledge and insight," demonstrates a similar usage we see in the Pali: *atīrakaṃ ñāṇadassanaṃ paññāpeti*, "he imparts boundless knowledge and insight," and it seems likely that we can expect a similar phrase here, even if we are unable to make a complete reconstruction.

706. Cf. 285r7: *tathā hy eṣām ekaṃ vyākṛtam ekaṃ na vyāk(r)t(am).* I find it likely that where the scribe had meant to write *tathā* he had inadvertently continued the word to the very familiar *tathāgata*, lengthening the final *a* as he would be used to before writing *hi*, which often comes after *tathā*.

707. It is possible that *tad idam* here refers to a question that has been lost but is still visible in the *Pāsādika-sutta*: DN III 134.5–6 *tayidaṃ kiṃ su tayidaṃ kathaṃ sū ti?* and occurs directly before the corresponding Pali phrase to what we see in the *Prāsādika-sūtra*.

708. Ms. reads *arya*°.

709. Ms. reads *manyeta*. CF. DN III 134.8: *maññanti*.

DĀ 15.33

[Buddha:] "It is possible, (monks, that) wanderers who are adherents of another faith might speak in this way: 'Conversely, sirs, the knowledge and insight of the ascetic Gautama endures [...].[710] Accordingly, by the future one is explained [and] one is not explained.' This here, monks, [is when] adherents of another faith think that knowledge belonging elsewhere is to be [...] by knowledge belonging yet somewhere else. This is different from those."

~15.33~

DN III 134.1–13 (DN 29.27)

27. ṭhānaṃ kho pan' etaṃ cunda vijjati yaṃ aññatitthiyā paribbājakā evaṃ vadeyyuṃ—atītaṃ kho addhānaṃ ārabbha samaṇo gotamo atīrakaṃ ñāṇa-dassanaṃ paññāpeti, no ca kho anāgataṃ addhānaṃ ārabbha atīrakaṃ ñāṇa-dassanaṃ paññāpeti; tayidaṃ kiṃ su tayidaṃ kathaṃ sūti? ten' eva añña-titthiyā paribbājakā añña-vihitakena ñāṇa-dassanena añña-vihitakaṃ ñāṇadassanaṃ paññāpetabbaṃ maññanti, yatheriva bālā avyattā. atītaṃ kho cunda addhānaṃ ārabbha tathāgatassa satānusāri-viññāṇaṃ hoti. so yāvatakaṃ ākaṅkhati tāvatakaṃ anussarati. anāgatañ ca kho addhānaṃ ārabbha tathāgatassa bodhijaṃ ñāṇaṃ uppajjati—ayam antimā jāti, n' atthi dāni punabbhavo ti.

T I 1 75b25–28

或有外道梵志作是說言。沙門瞿曇。盡知過去世事。不知未來事。彼比丘。彼異學梵志智異智觀亦異所言虛妄。

▪ ▪ ▪ ▪ ▪

DĀ 15.34

[**a**] atītaṃ cāpi bhikṣavo bhavati tac ca bhavaty abhūtam atatvam anarthopasaṃhitaṃ sarvathā tat tathāgato na vyākaroti • atītaṃ cāpi bhikṣavo bha(vati tac ca) bha(**286r3**)(vati) bhūtaṃ ta(tva)m ‹an›arthopasaṃhitaṃ[711] tad api tathāgato na vyākaroti | atītaṃ cāpi bhikṣavo bhavati tac ca

710. The content of this gap may be similar in theme to the content of the DN. Cf. LDB 435–36: "As regards past times, Gotama displays boundless knowledge and insight, but not about the future."

711. Cf. DN III 134.15–16: *atītaṃ ce pe cunda hoti bhūtaṃ tacchaṃ anattha-saṃhitaṃ, tam pi Tathāgato na vyākaroti*. This reading makes more sense in context as well.

bhavati bhūtaṃ tatvam arthopasaṃhi(ta)ṃ (ta)tr(a)[712] kālajñas ta(**286r4**)-thāgatas tasya[713] vyākaraṇāya smṛtaḥ saṃprajānaṃ;

[**b**] anā(ga)taṃ[714]

[**c**] pratyutpannaṃ cāpi bhikṣavo bhavati tac ca bhavaty abhūtam atatvam anarthopasaṃhitaṃ (sarvath)ā (tat tathāga)to na vyā(**286r5**)k(a)roti <|> pratyutpannaṃ cāpi bhikṣavo bhavati tac ca bhava(t)i (bhūtā)ṃ (tatvam anar)thopasaṃhitaṃ tad api tathāgato na vyākaroti <|> pratyu(t-pannaṃ cāp)i bhikṣa(vo bhavati tac ca bhavati bhūtaṃ)[715] (**286r6**) tatvam arthopasaṃhitaṃ tatr(a)[716] kālajñas tathāgatas[717] {tathāga}tasya[718] vyākaraṇā<ya>[719] smṛtaḥ (saṃprajā)n(a)(ṃ);[720]

712. Cf. 286r6 and DN III 134. 17–19: *atītaṃ ce pi cunda hoti bhūtaṃ taccham atthasaṃhitam, tatra kālaññū hoti tathāgato tassa pañhassa veyyākaraṇāya*. For similar passages that show *tatra* (or *atra*) before *kālajñaḥ* but are not direct parallels to the *Prāsādika-sūtra* cf. 286r3, Avś(V) 40: *tathāgatā evātra kālajñāḥ* |, Avś(V) 42 (= 148): *vayam atra kālajñā bhaviṣyāma iti* |, Div(V) 467.5: *tatra kālajñā bhaviṣyāmaḥ* |, and Śay-v 49 (= 53): *tatra kālajñā buddhā bhagavantaḥ arthopasaṃhitāyāṃ pṛcchāyām*.

713. DN III 134.19 reads: *tassa pañhassa* (that question), which is likely what the *tasya* here refers to.

714. This section is the middle part of a triad and its content has been abbreviated where only the first word and topic of this passage appears, *anāgatam*. If the content were resupplied it would read: *<cāpi bhikṣavo bhavati tac ca bhavaty abhūtam atatvam anarthopasaṃhitaṃ sarvathā tat tathāgato na vyākaroti | anāgataṃ cāpi bhikṣavo bhavati tac ca bhavati bhūtāṃ tatvam anārthopasaṃhitaṃ tad api tathāgato na vyākaroti | anāgataṃ cāpi bhikṣavo bhavati tac ca bhavati bhūtaṃ tatvam arthopasaṃhitaṃ tatra kālajñas tathāgatas tasya vyākaraṇāya smṛtaḥ saṃprajānaṃ;>*

Cf. 286r4–6 and DN III 134.19–25: *anāgataṃ ce pi cunda hoti abhūtaṃ atacchaṃ anattha-saṃhitaṃ, na taṃ tathāgato vyākaroti. anāgataṃ ce pi cunda hoti bhūtaṃ tacchaṃ anattha-saṃhitaṃ, tam pi tathāgato na vyāka-roti. anāgataṃ ce pi cunda hoti bhūtaṃ tacchaṃ atthasaṃhitaṃ tatra kālaññū hoti tathāgato tassa pañhassa veyyākaraṇāya saṃkhittaṃ.*

715. Cf. 286r2–4.

716. Cf. 286r6, Avś(V) 40: *tathāgatā evātra kālajñāḥ* |, Avś(V) 42 (= 148): *vayam atra kālajñā bhaviṣyāma iti* |, Div(V) 467.5: *tatra kālajñā bhaviṣyāmaḥ* |, and Śay-v 49 (= 53): *tatra kālajñā buddhā bhagavantaḥ arthopasaṃhitāyāṃ pṛcchāyām.*

717. Ms. reads *tathāgatos*.

718. This appears to be caused by a dittographic error.

719. Ms. reads *vyākaraṇa*. Cf. 286r4 and DN III 134.19 and 134.24–25: *tathāgato tassa pañhassa veyyākaraṇāya.*

720. Cf. 286r4.

[d] atīte bhikṣavas tathāgatasya smṛtyanusārijñānaṃ yena tathāgat. .. .. dh(a)ṃ .. .. + + + + + + + + ... **(286r7)** .. + + + + ...ṃ .. (| ayam a)ntimā jātir[721] <|> iyaṃ me bhave(t paśc)i(mā ja)tir[722] iti

DĀ 15.34

[a] [Buddha:] "If, monks, there is the past and it is unreal, false, and not associated with the goal, this the Tathāgata does not explain at all. If, monks, there is the past (and it) is real, true, and [yet] not associated with the goal [of salvation], this also the Tathāgata does not explain. If, monks, there is the past and it is real, true, and associated with the goal, in that case the Tathāgata is one who knows the proper time to explain it, mindful and deliberate.

[b] "[The same can be said for] the future.[723]

[c] "If, monks, there is the present and it is unreal, false, and not associated with the goal, (this) the Tathāgata does not explain at all. If, monks, there is the present and it is real, (true), and [yet] not associated with the goal, this also the Tathāgata does not explain. If, monks, (there is) the present (and it is real), true, and associated with the goal [of salvation], in that case the Tathāgata is one who knows the proper time to explain it, mindful and deliberate.

[d] "Regarding the past, monks, the knowledge acting in conformity with the mindfulness of the Tathāgata, by which the Tathāgata [...] '(This) is the final birth. This should be my last birth.'"

~15.34~

DN III 134.14–135.6 (DN 29.28)

721. Cf. DN III 134.13: *ayam antimā jāti.*

722. Cf. MAV 5d.2: *iyaṃ me bhave(t paśc)imā jāti.*

723. This is the middle section in a triad and the content has been abbreviated. If the content were resupplied it would be read like this: <If, monks, there is> the future <and it is unreal, false, and not associated with the goal, this the Tathāgata does not explain at all. If, monks, there is the future and it is real, true, and [yet] not associated with the goal, this also the Tathāgata does not explain. If, monks, there is the future and it is real, true, and associated with the goal [of salvation], in that case the Tathāgata is one who knows the proper time to explain it, mindful and deliberate.>

[a] 28. atītañ ce pi cunda hoti abhūtaṃ atacchaṃ anatthasaṃhitaṃ, na taṃ tathāgato vyākaroti. atītaṃ ce pi cunda hoti bhūtaṃ tacchaṃ anattha-saṃhitaṃ, tam pi tathāgato na vyākaroti. atītaṃ ce pi cunda hoti bhūtaṃ tacchaṃ attha-saṃhitaṃ, tatra kālaññū hoti tathāgato tassa pañhassa veyyākaraṇāya.

[b] anāgataṃ ce pi cunda hoti abhūtaṃ atacchaṃ anattha-saṃhitaṃ, na taṃ tathāgato vyākaroti. anāgataṃ ce pi cunda hoti bhūtaṃ tacchaṃ anattha-saṃhitaṃ, tam pi tathāgato na vyākaroti. anāgataṃ ce pi cunda hoti bhūtaṃ tacchaṃ atthasaṃhitaṃ tatra kālaññū hoti tathāgato tassa pañhassa veyyākaraṇāya saṃkhittaṃ.

[c] paccuppannaṃ ce pi cunda hoti abhūtaṃ atacchaṃ anattha-saṃhitaṃ, na taṃ tathāgato vyākaroti. paccuppannaṃ ce pi cunda hoti bhūtaṃ tacchaṃ anattha-saṃhitaṃ, tam pi tathāgato na vyākaroti. paccuppannaṃ ce pi cunda hoti bhūtaṃ tacchaṃ atthasaṃhitaṃ, tatra kālaññū hoti tathāgato tassa pañhassa veyyākaraṇāya.

[d] iti kho cunda atītānāgata-paccuppannesu dhammesu tathāgato kāla-vādī bhūta-vādī attha-vādī dhamma-vādī vinaya-vādī. tasmā tathāgato ti vuccati.

T I 1 75b28–75c07

[a–c] 如來於彼過去事。若在目前無不知見。於未來世生於道智。過去世事虛妄不實不足喜樂。無所利益。佛則不記。或過去事有實無可喜樂。無所利益佛亦不記。若過去事有實可樂。而無利益佛亦不記。若過去事有實可樂有所利益。如來盡知然後記之。未來現在亦復如是。如來於過去未來現在。應時語實語義語利語法語律語無有虛也。

▪ ▪ ▪ ▪ ▪

DĀ 15.35

yat t(ad) bh(ik)ṣ(ava)s sarvaśaḥ sarvatra bhāyai[724] samyak tat[725] sarvaṃ tathāgatena jñātaṃ dṛṣṭaṃ viditaṃ vijñāt(aṃ sam)y(ag evābh)i(saṃ-

724. *Bhā* is very damaged in the ms. and could possibly also be a *tā*. I have ultimately gone with *bhāyai*, which makes little sense, as the damaged akṣara looks slightly more like a *bhā* than a *tā* and while *bhāyai* makes little sense, *tāyai* makes no sense.

725. Ms. reads *tvaṃ*.

b)uddh(am |)[726] + + + + + (**286v1**) ..ṃ + + + (yasyā)ṃ (ca rātr)au[727] (bodhisattvo 'nuttaraṃ samyaksa)ṃ(bodh)i(m abh)i(sa)ṃ(b)uddho; ya(s)y(ā)ṃ (ca rā)trau tathāgato nirupadhiśeṣe nirvāṇadhātau parini(r)vā(s)y(a)ty;[728] atrāntare .y. .. .. + ... + + + + + + + + + (**286v2**) .. + .. + ...v. .. .. .(av)ip(a)rīt(a)m avipary(a)s(ta)ṃ;[729] (tasmāt) ta(thā)gata[730] ity ucyate ||

DĀ 15.35

[Buddha:] "Monks, whatever perfection shines[731] wholly [and] entirely, that is all known, perceived, learned, understood, and completely, fully, perfectly realized by the Tathāgata.[732] [...] between the night when the Bodhisattva fully [and] perfectly realized unsurpassed, complete, perfect awakening and the night when the Tathāgata will achieve parinirvāṇa in the sphere of nirvāṇa free from any remainder of the substratum of existence, [...][733] not wrong, not contrary. (Therefore), he is called Tathāgata."

726. Cf. a very similar phase in the *Prasādanīya-sūtraī*, DĀ 16.18 (298v4): *sa(rv)aṃ bha(ga) vatā jñānaṃ dṛṣṭaṃ viditaṃ vijñātaṃ samyag evābhisaṃbuddhaṃ* as well as DbSū(4) 6.2, (= 6.1, 6.3, 6.4, 6.5, 6.6, 6.7, 6.8, 6.9, and 6.10): *jñātaṃ dṛṣṭaṃ viditaṃ vijñātaṃ samyag evābhisaṃbuddhaṃ*. Unfortunately these similar phrases do not occur within any larger parallels to the text here.

727. Ms. reads + *.iṃ*.

728. Cf. MPS 25.58: *(yasyāṃ rātrau bodhisat)(59.3)vo 'nuttarāṃ samyaksaṃbodhim a(168.1) bhisaṃbuddho yasyāṃ ca rātrau tathāgato 'nupadhiśeṣe nirvāṇ(adhātau parinirvāsyate |)*.

729. Cf. Śrāv-bh II 118: -II-3-d-(2)-ii: *bhūtaṃ caitat tathā avitathā aviparītam aviparyastaṃ duḥkhaṃ duḥkhārthena, yāvan mārgo mārgārthena tasmāt satyam ity ucyate* | and Śikṣ 142.1–2: *iti hi bhikṣavo jāṅgulyāṃ vidyāyāṃ udāhṛtāyāṃ sarvabhūtasamāgate sarvaṃ tathâvitathānanyathābhūtaṃ satyam aviparītam aviparyastaṃ* |. The portion of the ms. I have been unable to reconstruct here is likely similar in theme (if not exact content) to the corresponding section in *Pāsādika-sutta*, DN III 135.13–15: *yaṃ etasmiṃ antare bhāsati lapati niddisati, sabbaṃ taṃ tath' eva hoti no aññathā* (LDB 436: "...whatever he proclaims, says, or explains is so and not otherwise.").

730. Cf. DN III 135.6, 11, 15–16, and 20–21, which all read: *tasmā tathāgato ti vuccati.*

731. See note 724 above. Obviously, this translation of "shines" is unsure.

732. Note the extremely similar phrase in the *Prasādanīya-sūtra*, DĀ 16.18: "(Sir, whatever) is to be known, to be perceived, to be obtained, and to be realized (by a faithful son of a good family), that is all known, perceived, learned, understood, and completely, fully, perfectly realized by the Blessed One."

733. The portion of the ms. I have been unable to reconstruct here is likely similar in theme (if not exact content) to the corresponding section in *Pāsādika-sutta*, DN III 135.13–15: *yaṃ*

~15.35~

DN III 135.7–22 (DN 29.29)

29. yaṃ kho cunda sadevakassa lokassa samārakassa sabrahmakassa sassamaṇa-brāhmaṇiyā pajāya sadevamanussāya diṭṭhaṃ sutaṃ mutaṃ viññātaṃ pattaṃ pariyesitaṃ anuvicaritaṃ manasā, sabbaṃ tathāgatena abhisambuddhaṃ. tasmā tathāgato ti vuccati. yañ ca cunda rattiṃ tathāgato anuttaraṃ sammā-sambodhiṃ abhisambujjhati, yañ ca rattim anupādisesāya nibbānadhātuyā parinibbāyati, yaṃ etasmiṃ antare bhāsati lapati niddisati, sabbaṃ taṃ tath' eva hoti no aññathā. tasmā tathāgato ti vuccati. yathā-vādī cunda tathāgato tathākārī, yathā-kārī tathā-vādī. iti yathā-vādī tathā-kārī, yathā-kārī tathā-vādī, tasmā tathāgato ti vuccati. sadevake loke samārake sabrahmake sassamaṇa-brāhmaṇiyā pajāya sadevamanussāya tathāgato abhibhū anabhibhūto aññadatthu-daso vasavattī. tasmā tathāgato ti vuccati.

T I 1 75c07–12

佛於初夜成最正覺及末後夜。於其中間有所言說盡皆如實。故名如來。復次如來所說如事。事如所說。故名如來。以何等義名等正覺。佛所知見所滅所覺。佛盡覺知。故名等正覺。

MPS 28.57–58

57 (katamau dvau |)

58 (yasyāṃ rātrau bodhisat)(59.3)vo 'nuttarāṃ samyaksaṃbodhim a(168.1) bhisaṃbuddho yasyāṃ ca rātrau tathāgato 'nupadhiśeṣe nirvāṇ(adhātau parinirvāsyate |).

DN II 134.5–7 (DN 16.4.37) (*Mahāparinibbāna-sutta*)

Katamesu dvisu? yañ ca ānanda rattiṃ tathāgato anuttaraṃ sammāsambodhiṃ abhisambujjhati, yañ ca rattiṃ anupādisesāya nibbānadhātuyā parinibbāyati.

YL 164 R4

(niru)padhiśe(ṣe) ni(r)v(ā)ṇa(dhātau pari)nirvāṇaṃ (bhaviṣyati).

DbSū(4) 6.2 (cf. DbSū(4) 6.1 & 6.3–10, which are very similar)

---

etasmiṃ antare bhāsati lapati niddisati, sabbaṃ taṃ tath' eva hoti no aññathā (LDB 436: "... whatever he proclaims, says, or explains is so and not otherwise.").

6.2 taṃ c(ai)naṃ tathāgataṃ karmasv(a)kajñānabale praśnaṃ pṛccheyu(ḥ ya)thā ta(t tathā)g(a)tena karmasvakajñānabalaṃ *jñātaṃ dṛṣṭaṃ viditaṃ vijñātaṃ samyag evābhisaṃbuddhaṃ* tathā t(a)t tathā(gataḥ praśnaṃ pṛṣṭo vy)ākuryāt*

▪ ▪ ▪ ▪ ▪

DĀ 15.36

siṃha (i)ti bhikṣavo v(a)d(a)nto .ā .. + + + ... + + + + + + (**286v3**) .. + + + + + + + + + + + + + + + id(aṃ) tatra tathāg(a)t(as)ya (samyaksiṃhan)ādaṃ[734] nāditasya[735] <|> tadyathā utpalāni vā padmāni vā kumudāni (vā) puṇḍarīk(āni vā udake jātāny u)(**286v4**)(dake vṛddhāny udakād abhyudgatāni tiṣ)ṭh(a)nty (a)nupaliptāny uda(k)e(na | evam eva) tathāgato loke jāto loke (vṛ)ddho lokād abhyud(ga)ta(s) tiṣṭhaty anupalipto loke(na |)[736] + + + + + + + + + (**286v5**) + + + + + + + + + + + + + ... te anupalipto .. ..

734. Ms. reads .. .. *.āda*. Cf. DĀ 16 (*Prasādanīya-sūtra*) 290v7: *samyaksiṃhanādo nāditaḥ* and NidSa 24.26: *samyaksiṃhanādo nāditaḥ*.

735. Ms. reads *naditasya*. See previous note.

736. While the first half of this passage with the various lotuses is rather common, I have only been able to find the complete metaphor comparing the flowers to a tathāgata in Pali sources. Among these the best parallels are SN III 140 (*Khanda-saṃyutta*): *seyyathāpi bhikkhave uppalam vā padumaṃ vā puṇḍarīkaṃ vā udake jātam udake saṃvaddhaṃ udakā accuggamma ṭhāti anupalittam udakena* || || *evam eva kho bhikkhave tathāgato loke saṃvaddho lokam abhibhuyya viharati anupalitto lokenāti* || || and AN II 38.30–39.3: *seyyathāpi brāhmaṇa uppalaṃ vā padumaṃ vā puṇḍarīkaṃ vā udake jātaṃ udake saṃvaḍḍhaṃ udakaṃ accuggamma ṭhāti anupalittaṃ udakena, evam eva kho brāhmaṇa loke jāto loke saṃvaḍḍho lokaṃ abhibhuyya viharāmi anupalitto lokena*. Note how these two parallels distuinguish between *accuggamma* (rise up) for the flowers and *abhibhuyya* (overcome from *abhi√bhū*) for the tathāgata, while in the *Prāsādika-sūtra* we see *abhyudgata*, which corresponds to *accuggama*, used for both flowers and tathāgata. The meanings of *accuggama* and *abhibhuyya* are quite similar and it is possible that in the *Prāsādika-sūtra* the distinction was not made. It is also possible that the usage in the *Prāsādika-sūtra* is that of a pun. Indeed, *abhyudgam* can refer to either the sun rising or a water-plant growing above the surface of the water, s.v. *abhigacchati* in BHSD and *abhigam* and *atyudgata* in SWTF.

Less exact Pali parallels may be found in AN V 152.12–16: *seyyathā pi bāhuna uppalaṃ vā padumaṃ vā puṇḍarīkaṃ vā udake jātaṃ udake saṃvaḍḍhaṃ udakā accuggamma tiṭṭhati anupalittaṃ udakena, evam eva kho bāhuna imehi dasahi dhammehi tathāgato nissaṭo visaṃyutto vippamutto vimariyādikatena cetasā viharatī ti* and DN II 38.25–39.5 (*Mahāpadāna-sutta*) (nearly = to SN I 138 (*Brahma-saṃyutta*)): *appekaccāni uppalāni vā padumāni vā puṇḍarīkāni vā udake jātāni udake saṃvaḍḍhāni udakā accuggamma ṭhanti anupalittāni udakena, — evam eva kho bhikkhave vipassī bhagavā arahaṃ sammāsambuddho buddha-cakkhunā lokaṃ volokento addasa satte appa-rajakkhe mahā-rajakkhe tikkhindriye*

DĀ 15.36

[Buddha:] "Monks saying, 'Lion' [...] this, in that case, for that Tathāgata who roars a (complete lion's) roar [...]. For example, blue lotuses,[737] or red lotuses, (or) night lotuses, (or) white lotuses (born in the water [and] grown in the water, stand risen from the water), unsullied by water. (In this very way), the Tathāgata, born in the world [and] grown in the world, stands risen from the world, unsullied by the world. [...] unsullied [...]."

~15.36~

DN —

T I 1.17 —

DĀ 27.73 (*Lohitya-sūtra I*) (Choi 2016)

(**378v4**) tadyathā utpalāni vā padmāni vā kumudāni vā puṇḍarīkāni vā udake jātāny udake vṛddhāny udake nimagnakośāni tiṣṭhanti <|> teṣāṃ yāvac ca mūlaṃ yāvac ca prāptām atrāntarān[738] nāsti (**378v5**) kiṃcid asphuṭaṃ bhavati {d}aspharaṇīyaṃ yad uta śītalena vāriṇā · evam eva sa imam eva kāyaṃ niṣprītikena sukhenābhiṣyandayati pa<ri>ṣyandayati pariprīṇāti parispharati <|> (**378v6**) nāsty asya kiṃcit sarvartaḥ kāyād asphuṭaṃ bhavati · {d}aspharaṇīyaṃ yad uta niṣprītikena su(kh)ena <|>

---

mudindriye svākāre dvākāre suviññāpaye duviññāpaye appekacce paraloka-vajja-bhaya-dassāvino viharante.

As mentioned above, the first half of this phrase is found in several Sanskrit texts, most notably in DĀ 27.72 (*Lohitya-sūtra* I): *tadyathā utpalāni vā padmāni vā kumudāni vā puṇḍarīkāni vā udake jātāny udake vṛddhāny udake nimagnakośāni tiṣṭhanti*. Cf. also Arthav 25.11–26.3 *tadyathāpi nāma bhikṣavaḥ utpalāni vā padmāni vā kumudāni vā puṇḍarīkāni vā udake jātāni, udake vṛddhāni* and very similar readings in Arthav(V) 320.9–14) and SBV II 244. A less similar parallel is found in KP 38 (nearly = to KP(VD) 38): *tadyathāpi nāma kāśyapa padmam udake jātam udakena na lipyate | evam eva kāśyapa bodhisattvo loke jāto lokadharme na lipyate* |.

737. *Utpalāni* above. An *utpala* is not the same plant as the lotus (lotuses are in the Nelumbonaceae family, of which there are but two extant members), but rather is a waterlily. However, it is also specifically defined as the "blue lotus" (*nymphaea caerulea*, also known as the Egyptian lotus) in both MW and PTSD. S.v. *utpala* in MW and *uppala* in PTSD. I use "blue lotus" in the translation above to keep with the theme of variously colored types of lotuses expressed in the sentence, but it is also possible that *utpala* here simply refers to water lilies generally.

738. Cf. SWTF, s.v. *agrāntara* and *atrāntara*.

SN III 140 (SN 22.94.26–27) (*Khanda-saṃyutta*) (= AN II 38–39 and AN V 152.12–16)
26 Seyyathāpi bhikkhave uppalam vā padumaṃ vā puṇḍarīkaṃ vā udake jātam udake saṃvaddhaṃ udakā accuggamma ṭhāti anupalittam udakena || ||

27 Evam eva kho bhikkhave Tathāgato loke saṃvaddho lokam abhibhuyya viharati anupalitto lokenāti || ||

AN II 38.30–39.3 (*Cakka-vagga*)
3. yesaṃ kho ahaṃ brāhmaṇa āsavānaṃ appahīnattā devo bhaveyyaṃ te me āsavā pahīnā ucchinnamūlā tālāvatthukatā anabhāvakatā āyatiṃ anuppādadhammā, yesaṃ kho ahaṃ brāhmaṇa āsavānaṃ appahīnattā gandhabbo bhaveyyaṃ yakkho bhaveyyaṃ manusso bhaveyyaṃ te me āsavā pahīnā ... anuppādadhammā. *seyyathāpi brāhmaṇa uppalaṃ vā padumaṃ vā puṇḍarīkaṃ vā udake jātaṃ udake saṃvaḍḍhaṃ udakaṃ accuggamma ṭhāti anupalittaṃ udakena, evam eva kho brāhmaṇa loke jāto loke saṃvaḍḍho lokaṃ abhibhuyya viharāmi anupalitto lokena.* buddho ti maṃ brāhmaṇa dhārehīti.

AN V 152.12–16 (*Thera-vagga*)
4. seyyathā pi bāhuna uppalaṃ vā padumaṃ vā puṇḍarīkaṃ vā udake jātaṃ udake saṃvaḍḍhaṃ udakā accuggamma tiṭṭhati anupalittaṃ udakena, evam eva kho bāhuna imehi dasahi dhammehi tathāgato nissaṭo visaṃyutto vippamutto vimariyādikatena cetasā viharatī ti.

DN II 38.25–39.5 (DN 14.3.6) (*Mahāpadāna-sutta*) (nearly = SN I 138)
seyyatha pi nāma uppaliniyaṃ vā paduminiyaṃ vā puṇḍarīkiniyaṃ vā appekaccāni uppalāni vā padumāni vā puṇḍarīkāni vā udake jātāni udake saṃvaḍḍhāni udakānuggatāni anto-nimugga-posīni, appekaccāni uppalāni vā padumāni vā puṇḍarīkāni vā udake jātāni udake saṃvaḍḍhāni samodakaṃ ṭhitāni, *appekaccāni uppalāni vā padumāni vā puṇḍarīkāni vā udake jātāni udake saṃvaḍḍhāni udakā accuggamma ṭhanti anupalittāni udakena,—evam eva* kho bhikkhave vipassī bhagavā arahaṃ sammāsambuddho buddha-cakkhunā lokaṃ volokento addasa satte appa-rajakkhe mahā-rajakkhe tikkhindriye mudindriye svākāre dvākāre suviññāpaye duviññāpaye appekacce paraloka-vajja-bhaya-dassāvino viharante.

SN I 138 (SN 6.1.1.12) (*Brahma-saṃyutta*) (= DN II 38.25–39.5)
12. seyyathāpi nāma uppaliniyaṃ vā paduminiyaṃ vā puṇḍarīkiniyaṃ vā appekaccāni uppalāni vā padumāni vā puṇḍarīkāni vā udake jatāni udake saṃvaddhāni

udakānuggatāni anto-nimuggaposīni || appekaccāni uppalāni vā padumāni vā puṇḍarikāni vā udake jātāni udake saṃvaddhāni samodakam ṭhitāni || *appekaccāni uppalāni vā padumāni vā puṇḍarīkāni vā udake jātāni udake saṃvaddhāni udakā accuggamma tiṭṭhanti anupalittāni udakena* || *evam eva* bhagavā buddhacakkhunā lokaṃ volokento addasa satte apparajakkhe mahārajakkhe tikkhindriye mudindriye svākāre dvākāre suviññāpaye duviññāpaye appekacce paralokavajjabhayadassāvino viharante || ||

Arthav 25.11–26.3

tadyathāpi nāma bhikṣavaḥ utpalāni vā padmāni vā kumudāni vā puṇḍarīkāni vā udake jātāni, udake vṛddhāni, udake magnāni, sarvāṇi tāni śītalena vāriṇā 'bhiṣyanditāni pariṣyanditāni paripūritāti [sic] pariprīṇitāni parisphuritāni; evam eva bhikṣavo bhikṣur araṇyagato vā vṛkṣamūlagato vā śūnyāgāragato vā imam eva kāyam adhyātmaṃ vivekajena samādhijena prītisukhenābhiṣyandati [sic] paripūrayati pariprīṇayati parisphurayati | tasya nāsti sarvataḥ kāyād asphuṭaṃ bhavaty asphuraṇīyaṃ [sic] yad uta adhyātmaṃ vivekajena prītisukhena |

Arthav(V) 320.9–14

tadyathāpi nāma bhikṣavaḥ utpalāni vā padmāni vā kumudāni vā puṇḍarīkāni vā udake jātāni udake magnāni, sarvāṇi tāni śītalena vāriṇābhiṣyanditāni pariṣyanditāni paripūritāni pariprīṇitāni parisphuritāni | evam eva bhikṣur araṇyagato vā vṛkṣamūlagato vā śūnyāgāragato vā imam eva kāyam adhyātmaṃ pratyātmaṃ vivekajena prītisukhenābhiṣyandayati pariṣyandayati paripūrayati parisphurayati pariprīṇayati, tasya nāsti sarvataḥ kāyam asphuṭaṃ bhavaty aspharaṇīyaṃ yad uta adhyātmakaṃ vivekajena prītisukhena |

SBV II 244 (T402b) (* * * = lacuna)

74. *tadyathā utpalāni vā padmāni vā kumudāni vā puṇḍarīkāni vā ‹udake jātāni udake vṛddhāni* * * * tiṣṭhanti; teṣām agrato mūlataś * * * na kiṃcid asphuṭaṃ bhavaty aspharaṇīyaṃ yad uta śīta›lena vāriṇā; evam eva imam eva kāyaṃ niṣprītikena sukhenābhiṣyandayati ‹pariṣyandayati› pariprīṇāti ‹parispharati; nāsya kiṃcit sarvataḥ kāyād asphuṭaṃ bhavaty aspharaṇīyaṃ yad uta niṣprītikena sukhena.›

KP 38

38 *tadyathāpi nāma kāśyapa padmam udake jātam udakena na lipyate* |
evam eva kāśyapa bodhisattvo loke jāto lokadharme na lipyate | tatredamucyate 10 ||
padmaṃ yathā kokanadaṃ jaleruhaṃ jalena no lipyati kardamena vā |
loke smi jāto tathā bodhisattvo na lokadharmehi kadāci lipyate ||

KP(VD) 38 (fol. 24r (KP-SI P/2))
38 *tadyathāpi nāma kāśyapa padmam udake jātam udakena na lipyate* | *evam eva kāśyapa bodhisatvo*

3 *loke jāto lokadharme(hi) na lipyate* | tatredam ucyate 10 || padmaṃ yathā kokanadaṃ jaleruhaṃ jalena no lipyati

4 kardamena vā | lokesmi jāto tathā bodhisatvo na lokadharmehi kadāci lipyate ||

The Beginning, the End, and the Fivefold Fallacy of Nirvāṅa in the Present Existence (DĀ 15.37–41)

DĀ 15.37[739]
(yāni tān)i[740] bhikṣavaḥ pūrvāntasaha(gatāni d)ṛṣṭigatāni vyākṛtāni mayā yathā tā(n)i (v)yāk(ar)tta(v)y(ān)i <|> (yath)ā[741] tāni **(286v6)** (na vyākarttavyāni kim ahaṃ tāni tathā)[742] vyākariṣye <|> yāni tāny aparāntasahagatāni dṛṣṭigatāni vyākṛtāni tāni mayā (yathā t)ā(n)i (vyākartta)v(y)āni <|> yathā tāni na vyāk(a)rttavyāni[743] kim ahaṃ **(286v7)** (tāni tathā vyākariṣye |)[744]

DĀ 15.37
[Buddha:] "Monks, whatever views associated with the beginning [there are], they have been explained by me as they are to be explained. Shall I (thus) explain (them) as they (are not to be explained)? Whatever views associated with the end [there are], they have been explained by me as they are to be explained. (Shall) I (thus explain them) as they are not to be explained?"

~15.37~
DN III 137.9–14 (DN 29.34)
34. ye pi te cunda pubbanta-sahagatā diṭṭhi-nissayā, te pi vo mayā vyākatā yathā te vyākattabbā, yathā ca kho te na vyākattabbā, kiṃ no ahaṃ tathā vyākarissāmi? ye pi te cunda aparanta-sahagatā diṭṭhi-nissayā, te pi vo mayā

739. This section serves to introduce the coming sections: DĀ 15.38 and 15.40 dealing with the beginning of existence in the past (*pūrvāntaḥ*) and DĀ 15.39 and 15.41 dealing with the end (*aparāntaḥ*) of existence in the future.

740. Cf. 287r4.

741. Cf. 286v6, 286v7, and 288r2–3.

742. Cf. This line, 286v7, and 288r3.

743. Cf. 286v5.

744. Cf. 286v6 and 288r3.

vyākatā yathā te vyākattabbā, yathā ca kho te na vyākattabbā, kiṃ vo ahaṃ te tathā vyākarissāmi?

T I 1.17 —

SHT (IV) 412 Fragment 60, A1 (Unidentified fragment)[745]

A
1 ///.ā pūrvān=na saga[tā]ni ///

B
6 /// yam=atr=ottare prajā[n](ā)ti ///

DĀ(U.H.) Hs. 127 R5 and 7 (*Pañcatraya-sūtra*)
5 /// + [ni] pratini[ḥ]sṛjya aparān[t]asahagatāni ///
7 ///t.++[ṣṭi]ga[tā]ni pratiniḥsṛjya dṛ[ṣṭe] dhar[m]e///

DĀ(U.H.) Hs. 128 V3 (*Pañcatraya-sūtra*)
V
3 (aparāntasagatā)ni [dṛ]ṣṭigatān[y]///

■ ■ ■ ■ ■

DĀ 15.38[746]
[a] (kata)māni[747] tāni bhikṣavaḥ pūrvāntasahagatāni dṛṣṭigatāni yāni mayā vyākṛtāni y(athā tān)i (v)y(ākart)ta(v)yā(n)i <|> (yathā tān)i na vyāka(rttavyā)ni[748] **(287r1)** + + + + + + .y. .i[749] k(im aha)ṃ[750] tāni tathā vyākariṣye <|>

745. It is unlikely that this is from the *Prāsādika-sūtra* as the wording on the other side of the folio does not appear in what would be the corresponding section of the *Prāsādika-sūtra*.

746. DĀ 15.38 corresponds to DĀ 15.40.

747. Cf. 287r5.

748. Cf. 286v5

749. These unreconstructed akṣaras are not easily explainable. Based on parallel readings in 286v5–6, 286v6–7, 287r4–5, and 288r3 we can expect *yathā tāni na vyākarttavyāni kim ahaṃ tāni tathā vyākariṣye* with some certainty, which plainly leaves no room for the akṣaras between the two parts of the sentence that we see here. It is possible that here the scribe made a dittographical error and wrote superflously what he had already written in the previous folio. A likely reconstruction under such a hypothesis would be something like: *tāni na vyākarttavyāni*, which ends 286v7, with the understanding that it was accidentally repeated at the beginning of 287r1. The opposite seems to have happened in the following section, DĀ 15.39a) where the scribe seems to have committed a haplography, see note 768 below.

750. Cf. 286v6 and 288r3.

[b][751] santi bhikṣava eke śramaṇabrāhmanāḥ pūrvāntakalpakā evaṃdṛṣṭaya evaṃvādinaḥ <|>

[1] śāśvataḥ ātmā lokaś ca <|> aśāśvataḥ <|> śāśva(**287r2**)(taś cāśāśvataś ca | n)aiv(a) śāś(v)a(t)o[752] nāśāśvataḥ ātmā lokaś ca <|>

[2] śāśvataḥ ātmā duẖkhaṃ[753] ca <| a>śāśvataḥ[754] <|> śāśvataś cāśāśvataś ca <|> naiva śāśvato nāśāśvataḥ ātmā duẖkhaṃ[755] ca <|>

[3] svayaṃkṛta ātmā loka(**287r3**)(ś ca | parakṛtaḥ | svayaṃkṛtaś ca parakṛtaś)[756] cāsvayaṃkārāparakārahetusamutpannaḥ[757] ātmā lokaś ca <|>

[4] svayaṃkṛta ātmā duẖkhaṃ[758]ca <|> parakṛtaḥ <|> svayaṃkṛtaś ca parakṛtaś cāsvayaṃkā(**287r4**)(rāparakārahetusamutpanna)ḥ[759] ātmā duẖkhaṃ[760] ca <|>

751. DĀ 15.38b corresponds to 15.40b.

752. Cf. 284v7–8 and 288r7.

753. Note *jihvāmūlīya*.

754. Cf. 287r1 and 288r7.

755. Note *jihvāmūlīya*.

756. Cf. this line and 288r8.

757. Interestingly, the DN reads *asayaṃ-kāro aparaṃ-kāro adhicca-samuppanno* (DN III 138.1) (LDB 437: "They are neither self-created nor created by another but have arisen by chance"), where *adhiccasamuppanna* (*adhṛtyasamutpannaḥ*, Skt.) has the exact opposite meaning as *hetusamutpannaḥ*. NidSa always (NidSa 6.7, 6.9, 6.10, 6.11, 20.9d, 20.10, 22.6b, and 22.7) reads *asvayaṃkāraparakārahetusamutpannaṃ*, which could be understood either as it is taken in the *Prāsādika-sūtra*, "arisen from a cause that is neither self-made nor made by another," where the *a* negates both *svayaṃkāra* and *parakāra*, or as "arisen by a cause and not by their own work but the work of another," where *parakāra* is not negated. It is not entirely clear which of the three readings is preferred, but I suspect that *asvayaṃkāraparakāra* in the NidSa should be understood as *asvayaṃkāra-aparakāra*, as we see in the *Prāsādika-sūtra*. Sv. *a-svayaṃkāra-parakāra-hetu-samutpannaḥ* and *a-svayaṃkāra-aparakāra-hetu-samutpannaḥ* in SWTF.

758. Note *jihvāmūlīya*.

759. Cf. 287r3.

760. Note *jihvāmūlīya*.

[**c**] imāni tāni (bh)ikṣavaḥ pūrvāntasahagatāni dṛṣṭigatāni yāni mayā vyākṛtāni yathā tāni <vyā>karttavyāni[761] <|> yathā tā(**287r5**)(ni na vyākarttavyāni kim ahaṃ tāni tathā vyāka)riṣye[762] <|>

DĀ 15.38

[**a**] [Buddha:] "Monks, what are these views associated with the beginning that have been explained by me as they are to be explained? Shall I thus explain them [...] as they are not to be explained?

[**b**][763] "Monks, there are some ascetics and brahmins who speculate about the beginning, who hold such views, who profess so:

[1] The self and the world [are] eternal. [They are] not eternal. [They are both] eternal and not eternal. The self and the world [are] neither eternal nor not eternal.

[2] The self and suffering [are] eternal. [They are] not eternal. [They are both] eternal and not eternal. The self and suffering [are] neither eternal nor not eternal.

[3] The self and the world [are] self-made. [They are] (made by another). [They are both] (self-made and made by another). The self and the world arise due to a cause that is neither by their own work nor the work of another.

[4] The self and suffering [are] self-made. [They are] made by another. [They are both] self-made and made by another. The self and suffering arise from a cause that is neither by their own work nor the work of another.

[**c**] "Monks, these are those views associated with the beginning that have been explained by me as they are to be explained. (Shall I thus) explain (them) as they (are not to be explained)?"

~15.38~

DN III 137.15–17 (DN 29.34)

761. Cf. 286v5, 286v6, 286v7, and 288r3.

762. Cf. 286v5, 286v6, 286v7, and 288r3.

763. DĀ 15.38b corresponds to 15.40b.

[a] katame te cunda pubbanta-sahagatā diṭṭhi-nissayā ye vo mayā vyākatā yathā te vyākattabbā yathā ca te na vyākattabbā?

DN III 137.17–138.11 (DN 29.34)
[b] santi cunda eke samaṇa-brāhmaṇā evaṃ-vādino evaṃ-diṭṭhino—sassato attā ca loko ca, idam eva saccaṃ mogham aññan ti. santi pana cunda eke samaṇa-brāhmaṇā evaṃ-vādino evaṃ-diṭṭhino—
asassato attā ca loko ca ... pe ...
sassato ca asassato ca attā ca loko ca ... pe ...
n' eva sassato nāsassato attā ca loko ca ... pe ...
sayaṃ-kato attā ca loko ca ... pe ... paraṃ-kato attā ca loko ca ... pe ...
sayaṃ-kato ca paraṃ-kato ca attā ca loko ca ... pe ...
asayaṃ-kāro aparaṃ-kāro adhicca-samuppanno attā ca loko ca. idam eva saccaṃ, mogham aññan ti.
sassataṃ sukha-dukkhaṃ:
asassataṃ sukha-dukkhaṃ:
sassatañ ca asassatañ ca sukha-dukkhaṃ:
n' eva sassataṃ nāsassataṃ sukha-dukkhaṃ:
sayaṃ-kataṃ sukha-dukkhaṃ:
paraṃ-kataṃ sukha-dukkhaṃ:
sayaṃ-katañ ca paraṃ-katañ ca sukha-dukkhaṃ.
asayaṃ-kāraṃ aparaṃ-kāraṃ adhicca-samuppannaṃ sukha-dukkhaṃ. idam eva saccaṃ, mogham aññan ti.

DN III 139.17–20 (DN 29.36)
[c] ime kho te cunda pubbantasahagatā diṭṭhi-nissayā, ye vo mayā vyākatā yathā te vyākattabbā, yathā ca te na vyākattabbā, kiṃ vo ahaṃ te tattha vyākarissāmi?

T I 1 76a20–23 (= DĀ 15.38b3–4)
[b3&b4] 或有沙門婆羅門作是說。此世間自造。復有沙門婆羅門言。此世間他造。或復有言。自造他造。或復有言。非自造非他造。忽然而有。

~15.38b~[764]
NidSa 6.7, (Cf. very similar passages: NidSa 6.9, 6.10, 6.11, 20.9d, 20.10, 22.6b, and 22.7)

764. This parallel for DĀ 15.38b is the same as that for DĀ 15.40b.

6.7 (kin nv āyuṣmān mahāko)ṣṭhila svayaṃkṛtaṃ jarāmaraṇam | aho svit parakṛtam | aho svit svayaṃkṛtañ ca parakṛ(tañ ca | aho svid asvayaṃkāraparakārahetusamutpannaṃ jarāmaraṇam | na hy evāyuṣmañ) chāriputra svayaṃkṛtaṃ ja(r)ā(ma)raṇam | na parakṛtaṃ | na svayaṃkṛtañ ca parakṛtañ ca | nāpy asvayaṃkārapa(rakārahetusamutpannaṃ jarāmaraṇam | api tu jātipratyayaṃ jarāmaraṇam |)

DĀ 15.39[765]

[a] katamāni tāni bhikṣavo 'parāntasahagatāni[766] dṛṣṭigatāni yāni mayā vyākṛtā(n)i (yathā tāni vyākarta)(**287r6**)vyā(n)i (| yathā tāni na vyākartavyāni)[767] <kim ahaṃ tāni tathā vyākariṣye |>[768]

[b] (santi bhikṣava eke śra)m(a)ṇ(ab)rāhmaṇā{ḥ}[769] aparāntakalpakā evaṃdṛṣṭaya evaṃvādino;

[b1] [1] rūpī ātmā bhavaty; ataḥ paraṃ saṃ(jñī | [2] arūpī | [3] rūpī cārūpī) (**287r7**) (ca | [4] n)ai(va rūpī nār)ūp(ī) ātm(ā) bh(avat)y; (ataḥ paraṃ saṃjñī |)[770]

765. DĀ 15.39 corresponds to DĀ 15.41 in content with DĀ 15.39b&c especially corresponding to 15.41b&c

766. Ms. reads *pūrvāntasahagatāni*, clearly an error.

767. Cf. 287r4–5.

768. This phrase is necessary to complete the sense of the statement and is attested in the previous two sections (DĀ 15.37, 15.38a, and 15.38c). It is most likely that the scribe committed a haplography and omitted a section of the repetitive "*yathā tāni vyākartavyāni | yathā tāni na vyākartavyāni*" formula, which explains the necessity to add in the following *kim ahaṃ*... This seems to be the opposite of what happened previously in DĀ 15.38a above where the scribe likely made a dittography, see note 749 above.

769. Cf. 287r1, 287v4, 287v8, DĀ 47 (the currently unedited *Brahmajāla-sūtra*) 452v7: *santi bhikṣavaḥ eke śramaṇabrāhmāṇā evaṃ dṛṣṭaya evaṃvādino*, and DN III 139.24–25: *santi cunda eke samaṇa-brāhmaṇā evaṃ-vādino evaṃ-diṭṭhino — arūpī attā hoti*...

770. Cf. 288v7.

[5] (a)nt(a)v(ā)n[771] ātmā bhavaty; ataḥ paraṃ saṃjñī <|> [6] anantaḥ <|> [7] a{na}ntavāṃś cānantavāṃś ca <|> [8] naivā{na}ntavān nānantavān[772] ātmā[773] bhavaty; ataḥ (paraṃ saṃjñī |)[774]

[9] (e)(**287v1**)katvasaṃjñī <|> [10] nānātvasaṃjñī <|> [11] parīttasaṃj(ī | [12] apramāṇasaṃjñī |

[13] e)k(ā)ntasukhī[775] <|> [14] ekāntaduḫkhī[776] <|> [15] sukhaduḫkhī[777] <|> [16] aduḫkhāsukhī[778] ātmā bhavaty; ataḥ paraṃ saṃjñī <|>

[b2] [1] rūpī ātmā bhavaty; ataḥ paraṃ <naiva>[779] saṃj(ñ)ī <|> [2] (arūpī | [3] rūpī cārūpī ca | naiva) (**287v2**) [4] rūp(ī nā)rū(pī) ā(tmā bhavaty; ataḥ paraṃ naiva[780] saṃjñī |)[781]

[5] (antavān ātmā bhavat)y; (a)taḥ[782] paraṃ naiva saṃjñī <|> [6] ananta{ta}ḥ <|> [7] a{na}ntavāṃś cānantavāṃś ca <|> [8] naivā{na}ntavān nānantavāṃn ātmā bhavaty; (ataḥ paraṃ naiva saṃjñī |)[783]

771. Cf. 288v7.

772. Ms. reads *naivāntavāṃś cānantavān*. Cf. 288v8.

773. Ms. reads *ānya*. Cf. 288v8.

774. Cf. 288v8.

775. Cf. 288v8 and DĀ 17 (the currently unedited *Pañcatraya-sūtra*) 299v8–300r1: *arūpiṇam ekatvasaṃjñinaṃ* (300r1) *nānāt[v]asaṃjñinaṃ parīttasaṃjñinam apramāṇasaṃjñinam* and 300r3: *arūpiṇam ekatvasaṃjñinaṃ <nānātvasaṃjinaṃ> parīttasaṃjñi(n)am.*

776. Note *jihvāmūlīya*.

777. Note *jihvāmūlīya*.

778. Note *jihvāmūlīya*.

779. Cf. DN I 32.10 (*Brahmajāla-sutta*): *rūpī attā hoti arogo param maraṇā asaññī ti naṃ paññāpenti.*

780. Cf. DN I 32.13–15 (*Brahmajāla-sutta*): *n' ev' antavā nānantavā attā hoti arogo param maraṇā asaññī ti naṃ paññāpenti.*

781. Cf. 289r1.

782. Cf. 289r1.

783. Cf. 289r2.

[b3] [1] (rūpī ātmā bhavaty; a)(**287v3**)t(aḥ paraṃ n)ai(va)s(a)ṃ-(jñ)ī(nāsaṃjñī | [2] arūpī | [3] rūpī cārūpī ca | [4] naiva) rū(p)ī[784] nārūpī ātmā bhavaty; ataḥ paraṃ naiva-saṃjñīnāsaṃjñī <|>

[5] antavān ātmā bhavaty; a(taḥ paraṃ naivasaṃjñīnāsaṃjñī <|> [6] anantaḥ | [7] anta)(**287v4**)(vaṃś cānantavaṃś ca <|> [8] naivāntavān nānantavan ātmā bha)vaty;[785] ataḥ paraṃ naivasaṃjñīnāsaṃjñī <|>

DĀ 15.39a–b

[a] [Buddha:] "Monks, what are these views associated with the end that have been explained by me (as they are to be explained)? <Shall I thus explain them> (as they are not to be explained)?

[b] "(Monks, there are some) ascetics and brahmins who speculate about the end, who hold such views, who profess so:

[b1] [According to the view of the *Saṃjñīvāda*:] [1] The self is corporeal. Beyond this life it is aware. [2] It is (incorporeal. [3] It is [both] corporeal and incorporeal.) [4] The self is neither (corporeal) nor incorporeal. (Beyond this life it is aware.)

[5] The self is finite. Beyond this life it is aware. [6] It is infinite. [7] It is [both] finite and infinite. [8] The self is neither finite nor infinite. Beyond this life it is (aware).

[9] It is possessed of a uniform awareness. [10] It is possessed of a diverse awareness. [11] It is possessed of a limited awareness. [12] (It is possessed of an unlimited awareness.)

[13] It is possessed of absolute happiness. [14] It is possessed of absolute suffering. [15] It is possessed of [both] happiness and suffering. [16] The self is possessed of neither suffering nor happiness. Beyond this life it is aware.

784. Cf. 289r2.

785. Cf.289r3–4 and DĀ 47 (the currently unedited *Brahmajāla-sūtra*) 452v2–3: *ataḥ paraṃ naivasaṃjñ[ī]-nāsaṃ(jñ)ī <|> (anantavān | antavāṃś cānantavā)ṃ[ś ca] naivāntavā*(**452v3**)*n nānantavān ātmā bhavaty.*

[**b2**] [According to the view of the *Asaṃjñīvāda*:] [1] The self is corporeal. Beyond this life it is <not at all> aware. [2] (It is incorporeal. [3] It is [both] corporeal and incorporeal. [4] The self is) neither corporeal nor incorporeal. (Beyond this life it is not at all aware.)

[5] (The self) is (finite). Beyond this life it is not at all aware. [6] It is infinite. [7] It is [both] finite and infinite. [8] The self is neither finite nor infinite. (Beyond this life it is not at all aware.)

[**b3**] [According to the view of the *Naivasaṃjñīnāsaṃjñīvāda*:] [1] (The self is corporeal). Beyond this life it is neither aware nor unaware. [2] It is (incorporeal. [3] It is [both] corporeal and incorporeal.) [4] The self is (neither) corporeal nor incorporeal. Beyond this life it is neither aware nor unaware.

[5] The self is finite. Beyond this life it is (neither aware nor unaware. [6] It is infinite. [7] It is [both] finite and infinite. [8] The self) is neither finite nor infinite. Beyond this life it is neither aware nor unaware.

DĀ 15.39c–e

[c] santi bhikṣava eke śramaṇabrāhmaṇā{ḥ} aparāntakalpakā evaṃ(d)ṛṣṭ(aya evaṃvādinaḥ |)[786]

[1] (**287v5**) (yataś cāyam ātmā rūpī | audārikaś cāturma)hābhūtiko[787] jīvati tiṣṭhati dhṛyate yāpayati <|> tāvat sarogaḥ sagaṇḍaḥ saśalyaḥ sajvaraḥ saparidāho; yataś[788] cāyam ātmo[789] 'cchidya(**287v6**)(te[790] | vinaśyati | na bhavati paraṃ mara)ṇād[791] <|> etāvad ayam ātmā samyaksusamucchinno bhavati <|>

786. Cf. 287r1, 287r6, 287v8, and DĀ 47 (the currently unedited *Brahmajāla-sūtra*) 452v7: *santi bhikṣavaḥ eke śramaṇabrāhmāṇā evaṃ dṛṣṭaya evaṃvādino.*

787. Cf. 287v8, 289r4, and DĀ 47 (the currently unedited *Brahmajāla-sūtra*) 452v7–8: *santi bhikṣavaḥ eke śramaṇabrāhmāṇā evaṃ dṛṣṭaya evaṃvādino yayāṃ ā[tmā rūpī] audārika[ś cāt]urm[a]hā*(452v8)*bhūtikaḥ.*

788. Ms. reads *yata[c].*

789. Ms. reads *ātmā.*

790. Cf. 287v8 and 289r7.

791. Cf. 289r5 and Abhidh-k-vy 457.15–17 *yataś cāyam ātmā ucchidyate vinaśyati na bhavati. iyatā 'yam ātmā samyak samucchinno bhavatīti.*

[2] divyaẖ[792] kāmāvacaro divyo rūpāvacaraḥ arūpi ākāśānaṃtyāyatanopago 'rū(287v7)(pī vijñānānantyāyatanopago)[793] 'rūpī ākiṃcanyāyatanopago 'rūpī naivasaṃjñānāsaṃjñāyatanopago jīvati tiṣṭhati dhṛyate yāpayati <|> tāvat sarogaḥ sagaṇḍas saśalyas sajvaraḥ sapa(287v8)(ridāho; yataś cāyam) [794] ātmā ucchidyate <|> {na} vinaśyati <|> na bhavati paraṃ maranād <|> etāvad ayam ātmā samyak<su>samucchinno[795] bhavati <|>

[d][796] saṃti bhikṣava eke śramaṇabrāhmanā evaṃdṛṣṭaya evaṃvādino;

[1] yataś cāyam ātmā paṃcabhiḥ kāmaguṇaiḥ (288r1) samarpitaḥ samanvaṃgībhūtaḥ krīḍati ramate paricārayati <|> etāvad ayam ātmā <parama>dṛṣṭadharmanirvāṇaprāpto[797] bhavati <|>

[2] yataś cātmā vivikta<ṃ> kāmai<ḥ> pūrvavat* yāvac (c)aturthaṃ[798] dhyānam upasaṃpa(288r2){saṃpa}dya[799] viharati <|> etāvad ayam ātmā paramadṛṣṭadharmanirvāṇaprāpto bhavati <|>

[e] imāni tāvad bhikṣavo 'parāntasahagatāni dṛṣṭigatāni yāni mayā vyākṛtāni yathā tā(288r3)ni vyākarttavyāni <|> yathā tāni na vyākarttavyāni kim ahaṃ tāni tathā vyākariṣye <|>

DĀ 15.39c–e

[c] [Buddha:] "Monks, there are some ascetics and brahmins who speculate about the end, who hold such views, who profess so:

792. Note *jihvāmūlīya*.

793. Cf. 289r6.

794. Cf. 287v5, 289r7, and Abhidh-k-vy 457.15–17: *tāvat sarogaḥ sagandhaḥ saśalyaḥ sajvaraḥ saparidāhakaḥ. yataś cāyam ātmā ucchidyate vinaśyati na bhavati.*

795. Cf. 287v6, 289r8, and DĀ 47 (the currently unedited *Brahmajāla-sūtra*), 452v8: *yataś cāyam ātmā samyak susamucchinno bhavati.*

796. Compare with DĀ 15.24b and DĀ 15.25b regarding *kāmaguṇa*.

797. Cf. 288r2 and 289v8.

798. Cf. 284r4, 284r6, *Prasādanīya-sūtra* 298v6: *viviktaṃ kāmair yāvac caturthaṃ upasaṃ(padya v)i(harat)i*, DĀ 47 (the currently unedited *Brahmajāla-sūtra*) 453r3–4: *etāvad ayam ātmā viviktaṃ kamair yā(453r4)vac caturthaṃ dhyānam (u)pasa<ṃ>padya viharati*, and MPS 34.97 (= 34.94, 34.95, and 34.96): *viviktaṃ kāmaiḥ pūrvavad.*

799. The second *saṃpa* is the result of dittography.

[According the the view of *Ucchedavāda*:] [1] (Insofar as[800] this self is corporeal, coarse), consisting of the four great elements, lives, remains, is maintained, and is sustained to that end, [it is] diseased, afflicted with ulcers, tormented,[801] fevered, and anguished. Insofar as this self is eradicated, (perishes, and ceases to exist after death) to that end, this self is completely and entirely destroyed.

[2] [And so on, up to:] The divine inhabitants of the sphere of desire, the divine inhabitants of the sphere of materiality, the incorporeal gods in the stage of the infinity of space, the incorporeal gods in the stage of the infinity of consciousness, the incorporeal gods in the stage of nothingness, the incorporeal gods in the stage of neither awareness nor unawareness live, remain, are maintained, and are sustained; therefore they are diseased, afflicted with ulcers, tormented, fevered, and anguished. (Insofar as this) self is eradicated, perishes, and ceases to exist after death, to that end, this self is completely and entirely destroyed.

[d] [Buddha:] "Monks, there are some ascetics and brahmins who hold such views, who profess so:

[According to the view of the *Dṛṣṭadharmanirvāṇavāda*:] [1] Insofar as this self is affected by [and] provided with the five sensual pleasures, plays, enjoys itself, and amuses itself, to that end, this self is one that attains ‹ultimate› nirvāṇa in this present state of existence.

[2] Insofar as this self dwells free from passion, having reached up to the fourth dhyāna as before with the previous [three dhyānas], to that end, this self is one that attains ultimate nirvāṇa in this present state of existence.

[e] "Therefore, monks, are those views associated with the end that have been explained by me as they are to be explained. Shall I thus explain them as they are not to be explained?

800. "Insofar as ... to that end ..." = *yataḥ* ... *tāvat* ... above and below in the following sections. Sv. *yato* –3 in PTSD: "*yato* ... *ettāvatā* because ... therefore," which is how the sense is taken in the parallel sections from the *Brahmajāla-sutta*.

801. *Saśalya* would literally translate to "pierced by an arrow" but *saśalyaḥ* carries the additional, figurative meaning of anything tormenting or causing pain. S.v. *śalya* in SWTF and MW and *saśalya* in MW. See note 566 above for a similar usage.

~15.39~

DN III 139.21–140.5 (DN 29.37)

[a] 37. katame ca te cunda aparanta-sahagatā diṭṭhinissayā ye vo mayā vyākatā yathā te vyākattabbā yathā ca te na vyākattabbā?

[b] santi cunda eke samaṇa-brāhmaṇā evaṃ-vādino evaṃdiṭṭhino—rūpī attā hoti arogo param maraṇā, idam eva saccaṃ, mogham aññan ti.

santi pana cunda eke samaṇa-brāhmaṇā evaṃ-vādino evaṃ-diṭṭhino—arūpī attā hoti. ...

rūpī ca arūpī ca attā hoti. ...

n' eva rūpī nārūpī attā hoti. ...

saññī attā hoti. ...

asaññī attā hoti. ...

n' eva saññī nāsaññī attā hoti. ...

attā ucchijjati vinassati, na hoti param maraṇā, idam eva saccaṃ, mogham aññan ti.

DN III 140.34–141.2 (DN 29.39)

[e] ime kho cunda aparanta-sahagatā diṭṭhi-nissayā ye vo mayā vyākatā, yathā te vyākattabbā; yathā ca te na vyākattabbā, kiṃ vo ahaṃ te tathā vyākarissāmi?

T I 1 76a1–12

[b] 所謂未見未生者我亦記之。何者＊未見＊未生。我所記者。色是我。從想有終。此實餘虛。無色是我。從想有終。亦有色亦無色是我。從想有終。非有色非無色是我。從想有終。我有邊。我無邊。我有邊無邊。我非有邊非無邊。從想有終。我有樂。從想有終。我無樂。從想有終。我有苦樂。從想有終。我無苦樂。從想有終。一想是我。從想有終。種種想是我。從想有終。少想是我。從想有終。無量想是我。從想有終。此實餘虛。是爲邪見本見本生。我之所記。

~15.39b~[802]

DĀ 47 (the currently unedited *Brahmajāla-sūtra*) 452r8–252v4

santi bhikṣava eke śramaṇā brāhmaṇā aparāntakalpakāḥ saṃjñivādinaḥ saṃjñī ātmā bhavaty; ataḥ param ity eke bhivadanto bhivadanti <|> yad uta ṣoḍhaśasu vastuṣu te vā punar bhavantaḥ śrama(**452v1**)(ṇabrāhma)ṇā[ḫ] ki(mā)ga(m)y(a kiṃ

802. All of the parallels below for DĀ 15.39b are the same as those for DĀ 15.41b.

niśṛtya kiṃ) prati[ṣ]ṭhāya aparāntaka[lp]ak(ā)[ḥ] n(ai)v[a]saṃjñināsaṃjñivādino naivasaṃjñīnāsaṃjñī bhavaty; ataḥ param ity eke bhivadanto bhivadanti yad utā[ṣṭā](daśasu vastuṣu te vā punar bhavantaḥ) [ś]ram[a]ṇā (**452v2**) (brāh)maṇā evaṃdṛṣṭaya [e]v[a](ṃ)v(ā)[d]i(no; rūp)ī ātmā bhavaty;
ataḥ pa[r]aṃ naivasaṃjñ<ī>nāsaṃjñī <|> arūpī <|> rūpī cārūpī ca <|> naiva rūpī nārūpī ātmā bhavaty;
ataḥ paraṃ naivasaṃjñ[ī]nāsaṃ(jñ)ī <|> (anantavān | antavāṃś cānantavā)ṃ[ś ca] naivāntavā(**452v3**)n nānantavān ātmā bhavaty;
ataḥ paraṃ naivasaṃjñīnāsaṃjñī <|>
idam [a]ṣṭamaṃ vastu yadāgamya yanniśṛtya yatpratiṣṭhāya aparāntakalpakā naivasaṃjñināsaṃjñivādino naiva(saṃjñināsaṃjñi ātmā bhavaty ata)ḥ param ity [e](**452v4**)ke bhivadanto bhivadanti <|>

DĀ 17 (the currently unedited *Pañcatraya-sūtra*) 299v8–300r1:
arūpiṇam ekatvasaṃjñinaṃ (**300r1**) nānāt[v]asaṃjñinaṃ parīttasaṃjñinam apramāṇasaṃjñinam ato vā punar upāti vartamānā vijñānānaṃtyāyatanam ity eke 'bhivadaṃto 'bhivadanti <|>

DĀ 17 (the currently unedited *Pañcatraya-sūtra*) 300r3:
arūpiṇam ekatvasaṃjñinaṃ <nānātvasaṃjinaṃ> parīttasaṃjñi(n)am apramāṇasaṃjñinam ato vā punar upāti vartamānā vijñānānaṃtyāy(ata)n(a)m ity eke 'bhivadaṃto 'bhivadanti •

FrgmDĀ c R4–5 (*Brahmajāla-sūtra*)
R4 /// + + + + + ○ ātmā .. ///

R5 /// + + + .. [te ā]tmā ataḥ param ity e[k]. ///

~15.39b1~[803]
DN I 30.24–31.15 (*Brahmajāla-sutta*, DN 1.2.37–38)
37. santi, bhikkhave, eke samaṇa-brāhmaṇā aparantakappikā aparantānudiṭṭhino, aparantaṃ ārabbha anekavihitāni adhivutti-padāni abhivadanti catu-cattārīsāya vatthūhi. te ca bhonto samaṇa-brāhmaṇā kim āgamma kim ārabbha aparantakappikā aparantānudiṭṭhino aparantaṃ ārabbha aneka-vihitāni adhivutti-padāni abhivadanti catu-cattārīsāya vatthūhi?

803. The parallels listed here for DĀ 15.39b1 are the same as those for DĀ 15.41b1.

38. santi, bhikkhave, eke samaṇa-brāhmaṇā uddhamāghatanikā saññi-vādā, uddham āghatanā saññiṃ attānaṃ paññāpenti soḷasahi vatthūhi. te ca bhonto samaṇabrāhmaṇā kim āgamma kim ārabbha uddham-āghatanikā saññi-vādā uddham āghatanā saññiṃ attānaṃ paññāpenti soḷasahi vatthūhi?
rūpi attā hoti arogo param maraṇā saññī ti naṃ paññāpenti. arūpī attā hoti arogo param maraṇā saññī ti naṃ paññāpenti. rūpī ca arūpī ca ... pe ... n' eva rūpī nārūpī ... antavā attā hoti ... anantavā ... antavā ca anantavā ca ... n' ev' antavā nānantavā ... ekatta-saññī attā hoti ... nānattasaññī ... parittā-saññī ... appamāṇā-saññī ... ekanta-sukhī attā hoti ... ekanta-dukkhī ... sukha-dukkhī ... adukkham-asukhī attā hoti arogo param maraṇā saññī ti naṃ paññāpenti.

Brmj(W) §161[804]
dge sloṅ dag dge sbyoṅ daṅ bram ze k'a cig di latr lta žiṅ di skad du smra ba dag yod, de p'an c'ad bdag gzugs daṅ ldan pai du śes can daṅ, de p'an c'ad bdag gzugs daṅ ldan pa ma yin pa daṅ, gzugs daṅ ldan pa yaṅ ma yin la, gzugs daṅ mi ldan pa yaṅ yin pa daṅ, gzugs daṅ ldan pa yaṅ ma yin la, gzugs daṅ mi ldan pa yaṅ ma yin pai du śes can daṅ, de p'an c'ad bdag mt'a daṅ ldan pai du śes can mt'a daṅ mi ldan pa daṅ, de p'an c'ad bdag mt'a daṅ ldan pa yaṅ yin la, mt'a daṅ mi ldan pa yaṅ yin pa daṅ, mt'a daṅ ldan pa yaṅ ma yin la, mt'a daṅ mi ldan pa yaṅ ma yin pai du śes can daṅ, de p'an c'ad bdag gcig pai du śes can daṅ, t'a dad pai du śes can daṅ, c'uṅ ṅui du śes can daṅ, ts'ad med pai du śes can daṅ gcig tu bde ba can daṅ, gcig tu sdug bsṅal ba can daṅ, bde ba daṅ sdug bsṅal ba can daṅ, bde ba daṅ, sdug bsṅal ba can ma yin pai du śes can.

~15.39b2~[805]

DN I 32.4–15 (*Brahmajāla-sutta*, DN 1.3.1–2)
3.1. santi, bhikkhave eke samaṇa-brāhmaṇā uddhamāghatanikā asaññi-vādā, uddham āghatanā asaññiṃ attānaṃ paññāpenti aṭṭhahi vatthūhi. te ca bhonto samaṇa-brāhmaṇā kim āgamma kim ārabbha uddhamāghatanikā asaññi-vādā uddham āghatanā asaññiṃ attānaṃ paññāpenti aṭṭhahi vatthūhi?

3.2 rūpī attā hoti arogo param maraṇā asaññī ti naṃ paññāpenti. arūpī ... pe ... rūpī ca arūpī ca ... n' eva rūpī nārūpī ... antavā ca ... anantavā ... antavā ca anantavā ca ... n' ev' antavā nānantavā attā hoti arogo param maraṇā asaññī ti naṃ paññāpenti.

804. For German translation see Brmj(W)tr §161. (See also Weller 1933, 393).
805. The parallels to DĀ 15.39b2 are the same as those for DĀ 15.41b2.

Brmj(W) §171[806]
dge sloṅ dag dge sbyoṅ daṅ bram ze k'a cig di ltar lta žin di skad du smra ba dag yod de, de p'an c'ad bdag ni .... gzugs can yin ži du śes can yaṅ yin pa daṅ, de p'an c'ad ... dbag ni gzugs can ma yin pa daṅ, gzugs can yin la, gzugs can ma yin pa yaṅ pa daṅ, gzugs can ma yin la, gzugs can ma yin pa yaṅ ma yin žiṅ du śes can yaṅ ma yin pa daṅ, de p'an c'ad bdag ni mt'a daṅ ldan žiṅ du śes can yin pa daṅ, de p'an c'ad bdag ni mt'a daṅ mi ldan pa daṅ, mt'a daṅ ldan pa aṅ yin la mt'a daṅ mi ldan pa a yin pa daṅ, mt'a daṅ ldan pa yaṅ ma yin la mt'a daṅ mi ldan pa aṅ ma yin žin du śes can yaṅ yin pa ...

~15.39b3~[807]

DN I 33.3–15 (*Brahmajāla-sutta*, DN 1.3.5–6)
5. santi, bhikkhave, eke samaṇa-brāhmaṇā uddham-āgha tanikā n' eva-saññi-nāsaññi-vādā, uddham āghatanā n' eva saññiṃ nāsaññiṃ attānaṃ paññāpenti aṭṭhahi vatthūhi. te ca bhonto samaṇa-brāhmaṇā kim āgamma kim ārabbha uddham-āghatanikā n' eva-saññi-nāsaññi-vādā uddham āghatanā n' eva saññiṃ nāsaññiṃ attānaṃ paññāpenti aṭṭhahi vatthūhi?

6. rūpī attā hoti arogo param maraṇā n' eva saññī nāsaññī ti naṃ paññāpenti. arūpī ... rūpī ca arūpī ca ... n' eva rūpī nārūpī ... antavā ... anantavā ... antavā ca anantavā ca ... n' ev' antavā nānantavā attā hoti arogo param maraṇā n' eva saññī nāsaññī ti naṃ paññāpenti.

Brmj(W) §178[808]
dge sloṅ dag dge sbyoṅ daṅ, bram ze k'a cig di ltar lta žiṅ di skad du smra ba dag de p'an c'ad bdag ni gzugs can yin iṅ du śes can yaṅ ma yin la du śes can ma yin pa yaṅ ma yin pa daṅ, de p'an c'ad bdag ni gzugs can ma yin pa daṅ, gzugs can yaṅ ma yin la gzugś can ma yin pa yaṅ ma yin pa daṅ, gzugs can yaṅ ma yin pa la gzugs can ma yin pa yaṅ ma yin žiṅ, du śes can yaṅ ma yin la, ... du śes can ... ma yin pa yaṅ ma yin pa daṅ, de p'an c'ad bdag ni mt'a daṅ ldan pa yin žiṅ du śes can yaṅ ma yin la, du śes can ma yin pa yaṅ ma yin pa daṅ, de p'an c'ad .... bdag ni mt'a daṅ mi ldan pa daṅ, mt'a daṅ ldan pa yaṅ yin la, mt'a daṅ mi ldan pa yaṅ .... yin pa daṅ mt'a daṅ ldan pa

806. For German translation see Brmj(W)tr §171. See also Weller 1933, 394.
807. The parallels to DĀ 15.39b3 are the same as those for DĀ 15.41b3.
808. For German translation see Brmj(W)tr §178. See also Weller 1933, 395.

yaṅ ma yin la mt'a daṅ mi ldan pa yaṅ ma yin žiṅ du śes can yaṅ ma yin la, du śes can ma yin pa yaṅ ma yin pa.

~15.39c~[809]

Yogācārabhūmi YBhū(Bh)150.19–151.3 (*Yogācārabhūmi* possibly quoting the *Prāsādika-sūtra*)[810]

501S [ucchedavādaḥ:]

ucchedavādaḥ katamaḥ | yathāpīhaikatyaḥ śramaṇo vā brāhmaṇo vaivaṃdṛṣṭir bhavaty evaṃ vādī yāvad ātmā rūpy audārikaś cāturmahābhūtikas tiṣṭhati dhriyate yāpayati

tāvat sarogaḥ sagaṇḍaḥ saśalyaḥ sajvaraḥ saparitāpaḥ | yataś cātmo 'cchidyate vinaśyati na bhavati paraṃ maraṇād iyat ātmā samucchinno bhavati || evaṃ divyaḥ kāmāvacaro divyo rūpāvacaro 'rūpyākāśānantyāyatanaopago yāvan naivasaṃjñānāsaṃjñāyatanopagaḥ | yathāsūtram eva vistaraḥ | tad yathā saptocchedavādinaḥ ||

DN I 34.1–36.3 (*Brahmajāla-sutta*, DN 1.3.9–17)

9. santi, bhikkhave, eke samaṇa-brāhmaṇā uccheda-vādā, sattassa ucchedaṃ vināsaṃ vibhavaṃ paññāpenti sattahi vatthūhi. te ca bhonto samaṇa-brāhmaṇā kim āgamma kim ārabbha uccheda-vādā sattassa ucchedaṃ vināsaṃ vibhavaṃ paññāpenti sattahi vatthūhi?

10. idha, bhikkhave, ekacco samaṇo vā brāhmaṇo vā evaṃ-vādī hoti evaṃ-diṭṭhī: yato kho bho ayaṃ attā rūpī cātum-mahā-bhūtiko mātā-pettika-sambhavo, kāyassa bhedā ucchijjati vinassati, na hoti param maraṇā, ettāvatā kho bho ayaṃ attā sammā samucchinno hotīti. itth' eke sato sattassa ucchedaṃ vināsaṃ vibhavaṃ paññāpenti.

11. taṃ añño evam āha: atthi kho bho eso attā yaṃ tvaṃ vadesi. n' eso n' atthīti vadāmi. no ca kho bho ayaṃ attā ettāvatā sammā samucchinno hoti. atthi kho bho añño attā dibbo rūpī kāmāvacaro kabaliṅkārāhāra-bhakkho. taṃ tvaṃ na jānāsi na passasi. taṃ ahaṃ jānāmi passāmi. so kho bho attā yato kāyassa bhedā ucchijjati vinassati na hoti param maraṇā, ettāvatā kho bho ayaṃ attā sammā samucchinno hotīti. itth' eke sato sattassa ucchedaṃ vināsaṃ vibhavaṃ paññāpenti.

809. The parallels to DĀ 15.39c are the same as those for DĀ 15.41c.

810. Although it is equally possible that it is quoting the *Brahmajāla-sūtra*.

12. taṃ añño evam āha: atthi kho bho eso attā yaṃ tvaṃ vadesi. n' eso n' atthīti vadāmi. no ca kho bho ayaṃ attā ettāvatā sammā samucchinno hoti. atthi kho bho añño attā dibbo rūpī manomayo sabbaṅga-paccaṅgī ahīnindriyo. taṃ tvaṃ na jānāsi na passasi. taṃ ahaṃ jānāmi passāmi. so kho bho attā yato kāyassa bhedā ucchijjati vinassati na hoti param maraṇā, ettāvatā kho bho ayam attā sammā samucchinno hotīti. itth' eke sato sattassa ucchedaṃ vināsaṃ vibhavaṃ paññāpenti.

13. taṃ añño evam āha: atthi kho bho eso attā yaṃ tvaṃ vadesi. n' eso n' atthīti vadāmi. na ca kho bho ayaṃ attā ettāvatā sammā samucchinno hoti. atthi kho bho añño attā sabbaso rūpa-saññānaṃ samatikkamā paṭighasaññānaṃ attha-gamā nānatta-saññānaṃ amanasi-kārā ananto ākāso ti ākāsānañcāyatanūpago. taṃ tvaṃ na jānāsi na passasi. taṃ ahaṃ jānāmi passāmi. so kho bho attā yato kāyassa bhedā ucchijjati vinassati na hoti param maraṇā, ettāvatā kho bho ayaṃ attā sammā samucchinno hotīti. itth' eke sato sattassa ucchedaṃ vināsaṃ vibhavaṃ paññāpenti.

14. taṃ añño evam āha: atthi kho bho eso attā yaṃ tvaṃ vadesi. n' eso n' atthīti vadāmi. no ca kho bho ayaṃ attā ettāvatā sammā samucchinno hoti. atthi kho bho añño attā sabbaso ākāsānañcāyatanaṃ samatikkamma anantaṃ viññāṇan ti viññānāṇañcāyatanūpago. taṃ tvaṃ na jānāsi na passasi. taṃ ahaṃ jānāmi passāmi.

so kho bho attā yato kāyassa bhedā ucchijjati vinassati na hoti param maraṇā, ettāvatā kho bho ayaṃ attā sammā samucchinno hotīti. itth' eke sato sattassa ucchedaṃ vināsaṃ vibhavaṃ paññāpenti.

15. taṃ añño evam āha: atthi kho bho eso attā yaṃ tvaṃ vadesi. n' eso n' atthīti vadāmi. no ca kho bho ayaṃ attā ettāvatā sammā samucchinno hoti. atthi kho bho añño attā sabbaso viññāṇañcāyatanaṃ samatikkamma n' atthi kiñcīti ākiñcaññāyatanūpago. taṃ tvaṃ na jānāsi na passasi. taṃ ahaṃ jānāmi passāmi. so kho bho attā yato kāyassa bhedā ucchijjati vinassati na hoti param maraṇā, ettāvatā kho bho ayaṃ attā sammā samucchinno hotīti. itth' eke sato sattassa ucchedaṃ vināsaṃ vibhavaṃ paññāpenti.

16. taṃ añño evam āha: "atthi kho bho eso attā yaṃ tvaṃ vadesi. n' eso n' atthīti vadāmi. no ca kho bho ayaṃ attā ettāvatā sammā samucchinno hoti. atthi kho bho añño attā sabbaso ākiñcaññāyatanaṃ samatikkamma santaṃ etaṃ paṇītam etan ti n'eva-saññā-nāsaññāyatanūpago. taṃ tvaṃ na jānāsi na passasi. taṃ ahaṃ jānāmi passāmi. so kho bho attā yato kāyassa bhedā ucchijjati vinassati na hoti param

maraṇā, ettāvatā kho bho ayaṃ attā sammā samucchinno hotīti. itth' eke sato sattassa ucchedaṃ vināsaṃ vibhavaṃ paññāpenti.

17. ime kho te, bhikkhave, samaṇa-brāhmaṇā ucchedavādā sato sattassa ucchedaṃ vināsaṃ vibhavaṃ paññāpenti sattahi vatthūhi. ye hi keci, bhikkhave, samaṇā vā brāhmaṇā vā uccheda-vādā sato sattassa ucchedaṃ vināsaṃ vibhavaṃ paññāpenti, sabbe te imeh' eva sattahi vatthūhi etesaṃ vā aññatarena, n' atthi ito bahiddhā.

DĀ 47 (the currently unedited *Brahmajāla-sūtra*), 452v7–9
santi bhikṣavaḥ eke śramaṇabrāhmāṇā evaṃdṛṣṭaya evaṃvādino yayāṃ ā[tmā rūpī] audārika[ś cāt]urm[a]hā(**452v8**)bhūtikaḥ jīv[at]i (t)i(ṣṭhati dhriya)te yāpaya[t]i <|> tāvat sarogaḥ sagaṇḍaḥ saśalyaḥ sajvaraḥ saparidāhaḥ <|> yataś cāyam ātmā samyak susamucchinno bhavati <|> divyaḫ[811] kāmāvacaro divyo rūpāvacara ārūpi ākā(**452v9**)śāna(ṃtyāyatanopag). + .. + + + naivasaṃjñānāsaṃjñāyatanopagaḥ jīvati tiṣṭhati |

Vibh 383.25–31 (numeration added for reader's convenience)
tattha katamā sata diṭṭhiyo?
idh' ekacco samaṇo vā brāhmaṇo vā evaṃvādī hoti evaṃdiṭṭhī: yato kho bho [1] ayaṃ attā rūpī [2] cātummahābhūtiko [3] mātāpettikasambhavo [4] kāyassa bhedā ucchijjati [5] vinassati [6] na hoti param maraṇā, [7] ettāvatā kho bho ayaṃ attā sammā samucchinno hotīti, itth' eke sato sattassa ucchedaṃ vināsaṃ vibhavaṃ paññāpenti.

Abhidh-k-vy 457.14–17 (Ital. = root text)
yathoktaṃ sūtre. yāvad ayam ātmā jīvati tiṣṭhati dhriyate yāpayati. tāvat sarogaḥ sagaṇḍaḥ saśalyaḥ sajvaraḥ saparidāhakaḥ. yataś cāyam ātmā ucchidyate vinaśyati na bhavati. iyatā 'yam ātmā samyak samucchinno bhavatīti.

DĀ 44 (the currently unedited *Rājan-sūtra*), 437v4–9
ihaiva jīvo *jīvati (437v5) (sa pretyocchidyate vi)naśyati na bhavati para<ṃ> mā<ra>ṇād; cā◯turmahābhūtikaṃ puruṣasya samucchrayam** <|> sa yasmiṃ samaye kālaṃ karoti tasya pṛthivī upaiti āpo vāyus tejaskāyo vāyuṃ v(ayu)(**437v6**)-(kāyaḥ ākaśa)m (i)ndriyāṇy anuparivarttate | āsandīpaṃ◯camāḥ puruṣāḥ puruṣasmṛtam ādāya smaśānam anupravrajaty[812] ādahanāt paraṃ na prajñāyate

811. Note *jihvāmūlīya.*
812. Ms. reads *anupravrajety.*

bhasmībhavaty āhutayaḥ kapotava(rṇā)(**437v7**)(ny asthīny ava)tiṣṭhanti iti <|> tṛptoprajñātaṃ dānaṃ paṇḍitopajñātaḥ pratigrahaḥ tatra ye[813] 'sthitivādinaḥ sarve te riktaṃ[814] tucchaṃ mṛṣā vilapanti iti <|> bālaś ca paṇḍitaḥ{ś} cobhāv api[815] pretyocchidyete vi(naś)y(ato na bhavataḥ) (**437v8**) para<ṃ> mā<ra>ṇād iti <|>

DĀ 36.36–38 (*Pṛṣṭhalapāla-sūtra*) (Melzer 2010, 273)
36.36 rūpiṇam ahaṃ bho gautama puruṣasyaudārikaṃ cāturmahābhūtikam ātmānaṃ prajñāpayaṃ prajñāpay(ā)mi <|>

36.37 (418v2) rūpī cet pṛṣṭhapāla puruṣasyaudārika<ś> *cāturmahābhūtika ātmā syāt tiṣ(ṭh)ed* asy(a) sa<ṃjñā> ātmā samyak tathaiva · anyā cāsya saṃjñā utpadyeta ⁝ anyā nirudhyeta <|>

36.38 rūpiṇam ahaṃ bho{ḥ} gautama manomayaṃ pu(418v3)ruṣ<asy>ā(t)mānaṃ prajñāpayan {na} prajñāpayāmi <|>

FrgmDĀ c V4–R3 (reconstruction)
V4 /// (caturmahā)bhūtik(a) + .. .i .. + ///
V5 /// (vi)naśyati na bhavati paraṃp(arayā) ///
R1 ///(arūpākāśānantyāyatanopa)gāḥ arūpavijñānānaṃtyā(yatanopagāḥ) ///
R2 /// (.. tit ā .... ◯ ro[g]. + + ///
R3 /// (āt)m(ā) samyaksu(vyucchinnaḥ) ///

SBVG A504b6–9 (Cf. SBV II 221)
ihaiva jīvo *jīvati; sa pretyocchidyate; vinaśyati; na bhavati paraṃ mara*(**A504b7**)*ṇāt*; cāturmahābhautikaḥ* puruṣasya samucchrayaḥ; yasmin samaye kālaṃ ◯ karoti tasya pṛthivyāṃ[816] pṛthivīkāya upaiti; apsu apkāyaḥ; tejasi tejaḥkāyaḥ; vāyau vāyukāyaḥ; ākāśe indriyāṇy anuparivartante; āsandīpañcamāḥ[817] puruṣāḥ[818] {pu(**A504b8**)ruṣaṃ} puruṣam ādāya śmaśānam anu-vrajanty ādahanāt paraṃ <na> prajñāyate; bhasmībhavanty āhutayaḥ; kapotavarṇāny asthīny avatiṣṭhante iti; dṛptopajñātaṃ dānaṃ; paṇḍitopajñātaḥ pratigrahaḥ; tatra ye 'stivādinaḥ sarve

813. Ms. reads *ya*.

814. Ms. reads *raktaṃ*.

815. Ms. reads *avi*.

816. Ms. reads *pṛthivī*.

817. Ms. reads *āsandīpañcamāt**.

818. Ms. reads *puruṣāt*.

te riktaṃ tucchaṃ mṛṣā pralapanti iti; bālaś ca paṇḍi(A504b9)taś cobhāv apy etau pretyocchidyete vinaśyato[819] na bhavataḥ paraṃ maraṇāt.

Pravr-v I 9v2–7

9v2 /// kimanuśaṃsaṃ brahmacaryam iti | sa evam āha | | aham asmi māṇavakā evaṃdṛṣṭir evaṃvādī nāsti dattaṃ nāsti

9v3 /// upapāduko na santi loke 'rhantaḥ samyaggatāḥ samyakpratipannāḥ ye imaṃ ca lokaṃ paraṃ ca lokaṃ

9v4 /// jīvo *jīvati sa pretyocchidyate vinaśyati na bhavati paraṃ maraṇād atha cāturmahābhautikaḥ*

9v5 /// indriyāṇy anuparivartante | āsandīpañcamāḥ puruṣāḥ puruṣaṃ mṛtam ādāya śmaśānam anuvrajanty ādahanāt

9v6 /// 'stivādinaḥ sarve te riktaṃ tucchaṃ mṛṣā vipralapante iti bālaś ca paṇḍitaś cobhāv api pretyocchidyete

9v7 /// varjanīyaḥ paṇḍitair mārgas sapratibhayo yatheti viditvā gāthāṃ bhāṣete | |

~15.39d~[820]

DN I 36.17–38.11 (*Brahmajāla-sutta*, DN 1.3.19–25)

19. santi, bhikkhave, eke samaṇa-brāhmaṇā diṭṭhadhamma-nibbāna-vādā, sato sattassa parama-diṭṭhadhamma-nibbānaṃ paññāpenti pañcahi vatthūhi. te ca bhonto samaṇa-brāhmaṇā kim āgamma kim ārabbha diṭṭha-dhamma-nibbāna-vādā sato sattassa diṭṭha-dhammanibbānaṃ paññāpenti pañcahi vatthūhi?

20. idha, bhikkhave, ekacco samaṇo va brāhmaṇo vā evaṃ-vādī hoti evaṃ-diṭṭhī: yato kho bho ayaṃ attā pañcahi kāma-guṇehi samappito samaṅgi-bhūto paricāreti, ettāvatā kho bho ayaṃ attā parama-diṭṭha-dhamma-nibbānaṃ patto hotīti. itth' eke sato sattassa parama-diṭṭhadhamma-nibbānaṃ paññāpenti.

21. taṃ añño evam āha: atthi kho bho eso attā yaṃ tvaṃ vadesi. n' eso n' atthīti vadāmi. no ca kho bho ayaṃ attā ettāvatā parama-diṭṭha-dhamma-nibbānappatto

819. Ms reads *vidaśyeto*.

820. The parallels for DĀ 15.39d are the same as those for DĀ 15.41d.

hoti. taṃ kissa hetu? kāmā hi bho aniccā dukkhā vipariṇāma-dhammā, tesaṃ vipariṇām-aññathā-bhāvā uppajjanti soka-parideva-dukkha-domanass-upāyāsā. yato kho bho ayaṃ attā vivicc' eva kāmehi vivicca akusaladhammehi savitakkaṃ savicāraṃ vivekajaṃ pīti-sukhaṃ paṭhamajjhānaṃ upasampajja viharati, ettāvatā kho bho ayaṃ attā parama-diṭṭha-dhamma-nibbānaṃ patto hotīti. itth' eke sato sattassa parama-diṭṭha-dhamma-nibbānaṃ paññāpenti.

22. taṃ añño evam āha: "atthi kho bho eso attā yaṃ tvaṃ vadesi. n' eso n' atthīti vadāmi. no ca kho bho ayaṃ attā ettāvatā parama-diṭṭha-dhamma-nibbānappatto hoti. taṃ kissa hetu? yad eva tattha vitakkitaṃ vicāritaṃ etena etaṃ oḷārikaṃ akkhāyati. yato kho bho ayaṃ attā vitakka-vicārānaṃ vūpasamā ajjhattaṃ sampasādanaṃ cetaso ekodi-bhāvaṃ avitakkaṃ avicāraṃ samādhijaṃ pīti-sukhaṃ dutiyajjhānaṃ upasampajja viharati, ettāvatā kho bho ayaṃ attā parama-diṭṭha-dhamma-nibbānaṃ patto hotīti. itth' eke sato sattassa parama-diṭṭhadhamma-nibbānaṃ paññāpenti.

23. taṃ añño evam āha: "atthi kho bho eso attā yaṃ tvaṃ vadesi. n' eso n' atthīti vadāmi. no ca kho bho ayaṃ attā ettāvatā parama-diṭṭha-dhamma-nibbānappatto hoti. tam kissa hetu? yad eva tattha pīti-gataṃ cetaso ubbillāvitattaṃ etena etaṃ oḷārikaṃ akkhāyati. yato kho bho ayaṃ attā pītiyā ca virāgā upekhako ca viharati sato ca sampajāno sukhañ ca kāyena paṭisaṃvedeti yan taṃ ariyā ācikkhanti upekhako satimā sukha-vihārī ti tatiyajjhānaṃ upasampajja viharati, ettāvatā kho bho ayaṃ attā parama-diṭṭha-dhamma-nibbānaṃ patto hotīti. itth' eke sato sattassa parama-diṭṭha-dhamma-nibbānaṃ paññāpenti.

24. taṃ añño evam āha: atthi kho bho eso attā yaṃ tvaṃ vadesi. n' eso n' atthīti vadāmi. no ca kho bho ayaṃ attā ettāvatā parama-diṭṭha-dhamma-nibbānappatto hoti. taṃ kissa hetu? yad eva tattha sukham iti cetaso ābhogo etena etaṃ oḷārikaṃ akkhāyati. yato kho bho ayaṃ attā sukhassa ca pahānā dukkhassa ca pahānā pubb' eva somanassa-domanassānaṃ atthagamā adukkhaṃ asukhaṃ upekhā-sati-pārisuddhiṃ catutthajjhānaṃ upasampajja viharati, ettāvatā kho bho ayaṃ attā paramadiṭṭha-dhamma-nibbānaṃ patto hotīti. itth' eke sato sattassa parama-diṭṭha-dhamma-nibbānaṃ paññāpenti.

25. ime kho te, bhikkhave, samaṇa-brāhmaṇā diṭṭhadhamma-nibbāna-vādā sato sattassa parama-diṭṭhadhamma-nibbānaṃ paññāpenti pañcahi vatthūhi. ye hi keci, bhikkhave, samaṇā vā brāhmaṇā vā diṭṭha-dhammanibbāna-vādā sato sattassa

parama-diṭṭha-dhamma-nibbānaṃ paññāpenti, sabbe te imeh' eva pañcahi vatthūhi etesaṃ vā aññatarena, n' atthi ito bahiddhā.

DĀ 47 (the currently unedited *Brahmajāla-sūtra*) 453r3–4
santi bhikṣava[ḥ] eke śramaṇābrāhmaṇā evaṃdṛṣṭaya evaṃvādino yataś cāyaṃ ātmā paṃcabhiḥ kāmagunaiḥ samarpitaḥ samanvaṃgībhūtaḥ krī◊ḍati ramate parivārayati <|> etāvad ayam ātmā viviktaṃ kamair yā(453r4)vac caturthaṃ dhyānam (u)pasa<ṃ>padya viharati etāvad ayam ātmā ◯ (paramad)ṛṣṭadharmanirvāṇaprāpto bhavati <|>

DĀ 27.66 (*Lohitya-sūtra I*) (Choi 2016)
evam eva imāni paṃc(a nivaraṇāni yathā) (377v2)riṇaṃ yathā rogaṃ yathā dāsyaṃ yathā bandha<na>ṃ yathā bhayam evam ātmanaḥ prahīṇāni samanupaśyati <|> sa paṃca nivara(ṇā)ni prahāya cetasa upakleśakarāṇi prajñādaurbalyakarāṇi vighāta(pa)kṣyā(377v3)ṇy anirvāṇasaṃvarttanīyāni *(v)iviktaṃ kāmair viviktaṃ pāpakair akuśalair dharmais savitarkaṃ savicāraṃ vivekajaṃ prītisukhaṃ prathama<ṃ> dhyānam upasaṃpadya viharati* <|> sa imam eva kā(377v4)yaṃ vivekajena prītisukhenābhiṣyandayati pariṣyandayati paripriṇayati parispharati <|> (n)āsty asya kiṃcit sarvataḥ kāyād asphuṭam bhavati spharaṇīyaṃ yad uta vivekajena prī(377v5)tisukhena |

DĀ 31 (the currently unedited *Maṇḍiśa-sūtra I*), 390v5
sa viviktaṃ kāmair yāva prathamaṃ dhyānam upasaṃpadya viharati <|>

DĀ 36.23 (*Pṛṣṭhalapāla-sūtra*) (Melzer 2010, 267)
viviktaṃ kāmair yāv(417v1)t prathamaṃ dhyānam upasaṃpadya viharati <|> tasya yā pūrvaṃ kā(ma)sukha{ṃ} saṃjñā sā niruddhā bhavati • vivekaja{ṃ} prītisukha{ṃ}saṃ<jñī> pṛṣṭhapāla{s} tasmiṃ samaye āryaśrāvako viharati tasyāṃ ca śikṣāyāṃ śikṣita iti <|>

DĀ 36.43 (*Pṛṣṭhalapāla-sūtra*) (Melzer 2010, 274)
iha pṛṣṭhapālaiko viviktaṃ kāmair yāvat prathamaṃ dhyāna(418v6)m upasaṃpadya viharati <|> idam atraike saṃjñānām agryaṃ prajñāpayantaḥ prajñāpayanti <|>

MPS 34.92–97
34.92 n(a) m(a)ma pratirūpaṃ syād yad ahaṃ dhārme prāsāde *pañca(kāmaguṇair*

sama)rpitaḥ samanvaṅgībhūtaḥ krīḍeyaṃ rameyaṃ paricārayeyaṃ || yannv ah(aṃ) dhārme prāsāda ekena puruṣeṇopasthāyakena rājarṣir brahmacary(aṃ careyam ||)

34.93 (atha rā)jā mahāsudarśana ekena puruṣenopasthāyakena dhārme prāsāde rājarṣir brahmacaryam acārṣīt ||

34.94 atha rājā mahāsudarśano dhārme prāsāde (p)r(aviśya s)auv(ar)ṇ(aṃ) kūṭ(ā)-gāra(m a)dhiruhya rājate paryaṅke niṣadya *viviktaṃ kāmaiḥ pūrvavad yāvat prathamaṃ dhyānam upasaṃpadya vyahā(rṣīt ||)*

34.95 sauvarṇāt kūṭāgā(rā)n niṣkramya rājataṃ (kūṭāgā)ram adhiru(hya) s(au)varṇe paryaṅke niṣadya *viviktaṃ kāmai(ḥ) pūr(va)vad yāvat pr(atha)maṃ dhyānam upasaṃpadya vyahārṣīt* ||

34.96 rājatāt kū(ṭāgārān ni)ṣk(ra)mya vaiḍ(ūryamayaṃ kūṭāgāram adhiruhya sphaṭikama)ye paryaṅke niṣadya *viviktaṃ kāmaiḥ p(ū)rvavad y(ā)vat pratha-(ma)ṃ dhyānam upasaṃpad(ya vya)hārṣīt* ||

34.97 vaiḍūryamay(ā)t (kū)ṭā(gārān niṣkramya sphaṭikamayaṃ kūṭāgāram adhiruhya vaiḍūryamaye paryaṅke niṣadya *viviktaṃ kāmaiḥ pūrvavad yāvat prathamaṃ dhyānam upasaṃpadya vyahārṣīt* ||)

DĀ(U.H.) Hs. 93 (*Mahāparinirvāṇa-sūtra*) (= MPS 34.90–101)
V
t ///++++++++..+++///
u /// + + + jayitvā pratyekapratyek. ///
v /// .[y]. [d]. ha. dharme p[r]āsāde [pa]ṃcabhiḥ [k]. ///
w /// [s]. de ekena pu[r]u[ṣ]. [ṇopa]sthāya ///
x /// rm. prāsāde rājarṣibrahmacaryam a ///
y /// + viviktaṃ kāmaiḥ pūrvavad yāva + ///
z ///+....[ṣ].[dy].[v]i.i[k].ṃ++++///
R
1 ///.[ph]...k.m.[y].[p]..[y].+++///
2 /// .[y]a sphaṭikamayaṃ kūṭāgāra .. + ///
3 /// [d]ya vyāhārṣī[t*] || atha catura[ś]. ///
4 ///lu devī jānī[y]ā[ś].iradṛṣṭo[s].///
5 /// + ..ḥ āgamay. [t]. .. [vad a]haṃ + ///
6 ///++..lu senā[pa]te jānī[y].///
7 ///++++++..++++///

DĀ(U.H.) Hs. 13 R3 (*Brahmajāla-sūtra* or *Pañcatraya-sūtra*)
3 /// + + . [o] + .. n ad.e d.āś. ṣir bhavant[i] tasmād avirodha iti 9 || yada brahmajāle aparāntakalpikā dṛṣ(ṭa)dharma ///

DhskD 4r5–6
api (DhskD 4r6) tv avidyāyāṃ satyām avidyāsaṃcetanāhetor viviktaṃ kāmair yāvat prathamaṃ dhyānam upasaṃpadya viharati |

Abhidh-sam-bh 146
iha bhikṣavo bhikṣuś cittasyotpādakuśalo bhavati iha bhikṣur viviktaṃ kāmair yāvac caturthadhyānam upasaṃpadya viharati |

MSuAv 14
atha rājā mahāsudarśana(ḥ) su(varṇamayaṃ) (GBM 1559.5) (kūṭāgāraṃ prav)iśya rupyamaye paryaṃke paryaṃke(na) niṣadya viviktaṃ kāmair viviktaṃ pāpakair akuśalair dharmaiḥ savitarkaṃ savicāraṃ vivekajaṃ (GBM 1559.6) (prītisukhaṃ prathamaṃ dhyāna)m upasaṃpadya viharati. rupyamayā paryaṃkād avatīrya suvarṇamayāt kūṭāgārān niṣkramya rupyamayaṃ kūṭāgāraṃ praviśya suvarṇamaye (GBM 1559.7) (paryaṃke paryaṃkena niṣadya) *viviktaṃ kāmair yāvat prathamaṃ dhyānam upasaṃpadya viharati.* suvarṇamayāt paryaṃkād avatīrya rupyamayāt kūṭāgārān niṣkramya vaiḍū(ryamayaṃ) (GBM 1559.8) (kūṭāgāraṃ pravi)śya sphaṭikamaye paryaṃke paryaṃkena niṣadya viviktaṃ kāmair yāvat prathamaṃ dhyānam upasaṃpadya viharati. sphaṭikamayāt paryaṃkā(d avatīrya) (GBM 1560.1) (vaiḍūryamayāt kū)ṭāgāran niṣkramya sphaṭikamayaṃ kūṭāgāraṃ praviśya vaiḍūryamaye paryaṃke paryaṃkena niṣadya *viviktaṃ kamair yāvat prathamaṃ dhyānam upasaṃ(padya)* (GBM 1560.2) *(viharati.)*

▪ ▪ ▪ ▪ ▪

DĀ 15.40[821]

[a] tatra bhikṣavo <ye>[822] te śramaṇabrāhmaṇāḥ pūrvāntakalpakā evaṃdṛṣṭaya evamvādi(**288r4**)no; śāśvata ātmā lokaś cety abhivadanto 'bhivadanti <|> tān aham upasaṃkra(m)ā(m)y;[823] upasaṃkramyaivaṃ

821. DĀ 15.40 corresponds to DĀ 15.38.

822. Cf. 288v3.

823. Cf. 288v1, 288v4, DĀ 36.66 (*Pṛṣṭhalapāla-sūtra*) (Melzer 2010, 270): *ātān a̱ham upasaṃkramāmi*, and NidSA 22.21: *tān aham upasaṃkramāmi.*

vadāmi <|> satyaṃ kila bhavanta[824] evaṃdṛṣṭaya evaṃvādinaḥ <|> śāśvataḥ ātmā loka(**288r5**)ś ceti <|> te mayā[825] pṛṣṭā om i(ti pratijānante | tān a)ham[826] evaṃ vadā(m)i <|> (ast)y[827] (e)tad bhavantaḥ evaṃ ucyate <|> yat punar atra bhavantaḥ sthāmaśaḥ[828] parāmṛśyābhinivişyānuvyav(a)h(a)ranti[829] <|> i(**288r6**)(dam e)va[830] satyaṃ moham anyad iti <|> idam atrāhaṃ nānujānāmi <|> tat kasya het(oḥ |)[831] a(n)y(athā)saṃjñino[832] hi bhavanta ihaike śramaṇabrāh(ma)ṇā<ḥ[833] |>

[**b**] (tatra bh)i(kṣavo ye te śramaṇabrāhma)(**288r7**)ṇā{ḥ} <evaṃdṛṣṭaya evaṃvādinaḥ |>[834]

[1] <śāśvataḥ ātmā lokaś ca |> aśāśvataḥ <|> (ś)ā(ś)v(ata)ś cāśāśvataś ca <|> naiva (śāśvat)o nāśā(śvata)ḥ āt(m)ā[835] lokaś ca <|>

[2] śāśvataḥ (ā)t(m)ā duḥkhaṃ ca <| a>śāśvataś;[836] śāśvataś cāśāśvataś ca <|> nai(va śāś)v(ato nāśāśvataḥ ātmā duḥkhaṃ ca |)[837]

824. Ms reads bhavanti. Cf. 288v1, 288v4, DĀ 36.66 (*Pṛṣṭhalapāla-sūtra*): *satyaṃ kila bhavanta evaṃdṛṣṭaya*, and NidSA 22.21: *satyaṃ kila bhavantaḥ svayaṃkṛtaṃ*.

825. Ms. reads *mama*. Cf. 288v2, 288v5, and NidSa 22.21: *may(ā)*.

826. Cf. 288v2 288v5, and NidSa 22.21: *te may(ā pṛṣṭā evam iti prati)jānanti | tān a(ham e)vaṃ vadāmi*.

827. Cf. 288v2: *apy* (emended to *asty*), 288v5: *asty*, and NidSa 22.21: *asty etad bhadanta evam ucyate*.

828. MW reads sthānaśaḥ. Cf. 288v2, 288v5, NidSa 22.21: *yat punar a(t)r(a bha)vantaḥ sthāmaśaḥ*.

829. Cf. 288v2, 288v5–6 and NidSa 22.21: *sthāmaśaḥ parāmṛśyābhiniviśyānuvyavaharanti*.

830. Cf. 288v2, 288v6 and NidSa 22.21: *idam eva satyaṃ moham anyat*.

831. *Hetor* is attested in direct parallels of this passage in both 288v3 and 288v6, which applied both *sandhi* between *hetoḥ* and *anyathāsaṃjñinaḥ*. However, in this instance it appears *sandhi* was not applied, which is appropriate as a *tat kasta hetoḥ* is a complete interrogative statement.

832. Cf. 288v3 and 288v6.

833. Cf. 288v3 and 288v6.

834. Cf. 288v3–4 amd 288v6–7.

835. Cf. 287r1–2.

836. Cf. 287r1 and 288r7.

837. Cf. 287r2.

[3](**288r8**) <svayaṃkṛta ātmā> lokaś ca <|> parakṛtaḥ <|> svayaṃkṛtaś ca par(akṛ)t(aś) cāsvayaṃkārāpar(a)kārāh(e)tus(a)mutpannaḥ[838] ātmā lokaś ca <|>

[4]svayaṃkṛta ātmā duḥkhaṃ ca <|> parakṛtaḥ <|> svayaṃkṛtaś ca pa(rak)ṛ(taś cāsvayaṃkārāparakāra)(**288v1**)hetusamutpannāḥ[839] ātmā duẖkhaṃ[840] ca <|>

[c] tān[841] aham (u)pasaṃkra<mā>my; upa<saṃ>kramyaivaṃ[842] vadāmi <|> satyaṃ kila bhavanta evaṃdṛṣṭaya evaṃvādinaḥ <|> asvayaṃkārāparakārāhetusamut(pannāḥ ātmā duḥkhaṃ ceti | te ma)(**288v2**)yā[843] pṛṣṭā om iti pra<ti>jānante[844] <|> tān aham evaṃ vadāmy; asty[845] etad bhavanta{ḥ} evam ucyate <|> yat punar atra bhavantaḥ sthāmaśaḥ parāmṛśyābhiniviśyānuvyavaharan(t)i[846] <|> i(dam eva satyaṃ moham anyad iti | i)(**288v3**)da(m)[847] atrāhaṃ nānujānāmi <|> tat kasya hetor; anyathāsaṃjñino hi bhavanta ihaike{na}[848] śra(m)aṇabrāhmaṇā<ḥ[849] |>

838. Cf. 287r3.

839. Cf. 2873–4.

840. Note *jihvāmūlīya*.

841. The phrase *tatra bhikṣavo ye te śramaṇabrāhmaṇāḥ pūrvāntakalpakā evaṃdṛṣṭaya evamvādino; śāśvata ātmā lokaś cety abhivadanto 'bhivadanti* is attested in sections that parallel this one, cf. especially 288r3–4 but also 288v3–4, which contains the phrase with a different quotation: *ataḥ para<ṃ> saṃj(ñ)īti*, but it is not included here. Its absence does not negatively affect the meaning as the phrase reoccurs often to introduce the various *dṛṣṭis* discussed and can be assumed to be implied from its previous use above.

842. Cf. 288r4, 288v4, DĀ 36.66 (*Pṛṣṭhalapāla-sūtra*): *tān aham upasaṃkramāmi upasaṃkramyaivaṃ*, and NidSa 22.21: *tān aham upasaṃkramāmi | upasaṃkram(y)aivaṃ.*

843. Cf. 288r4–5 and 288v4–5 (for *ceti te mayā*), 288r8 and 288v1 (for *samutpannāḥ ātmā duḥkhaṃ ca*), and NidSa 22.21 *te may(ā pṛṣṭā).*

844. Cf. 288r5, 288v5, and NidSa 22.21: *te may(ā pṛṣṭā evam iti prati)jānanti | tān a(ham e)vaṃ vadāmi.*

845. Ms reads *apy*. Cf. 288r5, 288v5 and NidSa 22.21: *asty etad bhadanta evam ucyate.*

846. Cf. 288r5 and NidSa 22.21: *parāmṛśyābhiniviśyānuvyavaharanti.*

847. Cf. 284v7, 285r1, 285v6, and NidSa 22.21: *idam eva satyaṃ moham anyat | idam atrā(haṃ nānujānā)mi.*

848. Cf. 288r6 and 288v6.

849. Cf. 288r6 and 288v6.

DĀ 15.40

[a] [Buddha:] "In that case, monks, these ascetics and brahmins <are the ones who> speculate about the beginning, who hold such views, who profess so. They make assertions, [such as] asserting 'The self and the world are eternal.' I approach them, [and] having approached them I say: 'Sirs, is it really true that you hold such views, profess so: "The self and the world are eternal"?' Questioned by me (they affirm), 'Yes.' I speak (to them) in this way: 'Sirs, it is said this is so. Further, sirs, whatever in this respect you all[850] steadfastly, persistently, insistently, assert [as]: "Just this is true; anything else is false," that I do not allow in this matter. Why is this? Because, sirs, in this case some ascetics and brahmins are of different opinions.'

[b] "(In that case), monks, (these) ascetics and brahmins (are the ones who) <hold such views, who profess so>:

[1] '<The self and the world are [are] eternal.> [They are] not eternal. [They are both] eternal and not eternal. The self and the world [are] neither eternal nor not eternal.

[2] The self and suffering [are] eternal. [They are] not eternal. [They are both] eternal and not eternal. (The self and suffering) [are] neither eternal (nor not eternal).

[3] <The self> and the world [are] <self-made>. [They are] made by another. [They are both] self-made and made by another. The self and the world arise due to a cause that is neither by their own work nor the work of another.

[4] The self and suffering [are] self-made. [They are] made by another. [They are both] self-made (and) made by another. The self and suffering arise from a cause that is (neither by their own work nor the work of another).'

[c] "I approach them, [and] having approached them I say: 'Sirs, is it really true that you hold such views, profess so: ("The self and suffering) arise

850. Here and in proceeding sections, this entire phrase is in the third person plural but translated as second person plural as would be intended in the hypothetical conversation being described.

from a cause that is neither by their own work nor the work of another"?' Questioned by me they affirm, 'Yes.' I speak to them in this way: 'Sirs, it is said this is so. Further, sirs, whatever, in this respect you all steadfastly, persistently, insistently, assert [as]: "(Just) this (is true; anything else is false)," that I do not allow in this matter. Why is this? Because, sirs, in this case some ascetics and brahmins are of different opinions.'

~15.40~

DN III 138.12–21 (DN 29.35)

[a] 35. tatra cunda ye te samaṇa-brāhmaṇā evaṃ-vādino evaṃ-diṭṭhino—sassato attā ca loko ca, idam eva saccaṃ, mogham aññan ti, tyāhaṃ upasaṃkamitvā evaṃ vadāmi—atthi nu kho idaṃ, āvuso, vuccati sassato attā ca loko cāti? yañ ca kho te evam āhaṃsu—idam eva saccaṃ, mogham aññan ti, taṃ tesaṃ nānujānāmi. taṃ kissa hetu? aññathā-saññino pi h' ettha cunda sant' eke sattā. imāya pi kho ahaṃ cunda paññattiyā n' eva attano samasamaṃ samanupassāmi kuto bhiyyo, atha kho aham eva tattha bhiyyo yadidaṃ adhippaññatti.

DN III 138.22–139.17 (DN 29.36)

[b] 36. tatra cunda ye te samaṇa-brāhmaṇā evaṃ-vādino evaṃ-diṭṭhino:
asassato attā ca loko ca:
sassato ca asassato ca attā ca loko ca:
n' eva sassato nāsassato attā ca loko ca:
sayaṃ-kato attā ca loko ca:
paraṃ-kato attā ca loko ca:
sayaṃ-kato ca paraṃ-kato ca attā ca loko ca:
asayaṃ-kāro ca aparaṃ-kāro ca adhicca-samuppanno attā ca loko ca:
sassataṃ sukha-dukkhaṃ:
asassataṃ sukha-dukkhaṃ:
sassatañ ca asassatañ ca sukha-dukkhaṃ:
n' eva sassataṃ nāsassataṃ sukha-dukkhaṃ:
sayaṃ-kataṃ sukha-dukkhaṃ:
paraṃ-kataṃ sukha-dukkhaṃ:
sayaṃ-katañ ca paraṃ-katañ ca sukha-dukkhaṃ:
asayaṃ-kāraṃ aparaṃ-kāraṃ adhicca-samuppannaṃ sukha-dukkhaṃ.
idam eva saccaṃ, mogham aññan ti:

[c] tyāhaṃ upasaṃkamitvā evaṃ vadāmi—atthi kho idaṃ, āvuso, vuccati 'asayaṃ-kāraṃ aparaṃ-kāraṃ adhiccasamuppannaṃ sukha-dukkhan ti? yañ ca kho te evam āhaṃsu,—idam eva saccaṃ, mogham aññan ti, taṃ tesaṃ nānujānāmi. taṃ kissa hetu? aññathā-saññino pi h' ettha cunda sant' eke sattā. imāya pi kho ahaṃ cunda paññattiyā n' eva attano sama-samaṃ samanupassāmi kuto bhiyyo, atha kho aham eva tattha bhiyyo yadidaṃ adhippaññatti.

T I 1 76a12–20
[a] 或有沙門婆羅門。有如是論有如是見。此世常存此實餘虛。乃至無量想是我。此實餘虛。彼沙門婆羅門。復作如是説如是見此實餘者虛妄。當報彼言。汝實作此論。云何此世常存此實餘虛耶。如此語者佛所不許。所以者何。此諸見中各有結使。我以理推。諸沙門婆羅門中。無與我等者。況欲出過。此諸邪見但有言耳。不中共論。乃至無量想是我。亦復如是。

~15.40a–c~[851]
Caṅgī(U.H.) 12–13
iha bharadvāja ekatyena dṛ(ṣṭa)ṃ bhoti <|> so evaṃ me dṛṣṭam tti vācāṃ bhāṣati <|> na ca puna sthāmaśaḥ praḷaṃśaḥ pragṛhya abhiniviśya abhivyavaharati | (**5r1** idam eva satyaṃ mogham anya tti | i)ha bharadvāja ekatyena śrutaṃ (bho)ti | so evaṃ me śrutaṃ ti vācāṃ bhāṣati <|> na ca pun(a) s(a)ḥ sth(ā)m(a)ś(a)ḥ praḷa(ṃ)-śaḥ || pe || yāva idam eva satyaṃ mogham aṃnyad iti || p(e) || (**5r2** iha bharadvāja ekyatena hmutaṃ bho)t(i) <|> so evaṃ me hmutam iti vācāṃ (bhāṣati | na ca puna sthāmaśaḥ <praḷaṃśaḥ> pragṛhya abhinivśya{ḥ} abhivyavaharati idam eva satyaṃ mogham anya tti || pe || iha bharadvāja eka(**5r3**tyena vijñātaṃ bhoti | so e)v(aṃ) me vijñātam iti vācāṃ bhāṣati <|> na ca puna sthāmaśaḥ pra(ḷa)ṃśaḥ pragṛhya abhiniviśya abhivyavaharati idam eva satyaṃ mogham aṃnyat idi <|>

DN II 282.25–31 (DN 21.2.5) *Sakkapañha-sutta*
anekadhātu nānādhātu kho devānam inda loko. tasmiṃ anekadhātu-nānādhātu-smiṃ loke yaṃ yad eva sattā dhātuṃ abhinivisanti taṃ tad eva thāmasā parāmassa abhinivissa voharanti: idam eva saccaṃ mogham aññan ti. tasmā na sabbe samaṇa-brāhmaṇā ekanta-vādā ekanta-sīlā ekanta-chandā ekanta-ajjhosānā ti.

851. The parallels for DĀ 15.40a&c are the same as those for DĀ 15.41a&e.

ŚprSū 89
khalu tasmāt satvā yam eva dhātuṃ saṃjānaṃti tam e(va dhātuṃ) sthāmaśaḥ parāmṛśyābhini-viśyānuvyavaharanti | idam eva satyaṃ moham anyat |

SBV II 90.11–13
tad eva vastu sthāmaśaḥ parāmṛsya abhinivisyānuvyavaharati <|> idam eva satyaṃ moham anyad iti <|>

NidSa 22.21–22.23
22.21 ta(t)r(a ye kecic chramaṇa)br(ā)hmaṇāḥ svayaṃkṛtaṃ sukhaduḥkhaṃ prajñapayanti tān aham upasaṃkramāmi | upasaṃkram(y)aivaṃ vadāmi | satyaṃ kila bhavantaḥ svayaṃkṛtaṃ sukhaduḥkhaṃ (p)rajñapayanti | te may(ā pṛṣṭā evam iti prati)jānanti | tān a(ham e)vaṃ vadāmi | asty etad bhadanta evam ucyate | yat punar a(t)r(a bha)vantaḥ sthāmaśaḥ parāmṛśyābhiniviśyānuvyavaharanti | idam eva satyaṃ moham anyat | idam atrā(haṃ nānujānā)mi |

22.22 tat kasmād dhetoḥ | anyathāsa(m)utpannaṃ mayā bhavantaḥ sukhaduḥkhaṃ prajñaptam | te mama pṛccha(n)t(i) | kathaṃ samutpannaṃ bhagavatā gautamena sukhaduḥkham prajñaptam | tān aham e(vaṃ va)dāmi | (pratītyasamu)tpannaṃ mayā sukhaduḥaṃ prajñaptam |

22.23 evaṃ parakṛtaṃ svayaṃkṛtañ ca parakṛtañ ca asvayaṃkārapa(rak)ārahetusamutpannaṃ sukhadukhaṃ prajñapayanti tān aham upasaṃkramāmi pūrvavad yāvat |

~15.40b~[852]

▪ ▪ ▪ ▪ ▪

DĀ 15.41a[853]

[a] tatra bhikṣavo ye te śramaṇ(abrāhmaṇāparāntakalpakā evaṃdṛṣṭaya) (288v4)evaṃ(v)ādino;[854] rūpī ātmā bhavaty; ataḥ para<ṃ> saṃj(ñ)īti <|>

852. The parallels to DĀ 15.40b are the same to that of DĀ 15.38b and may be found there. See note 764 above.

853. DĀ 15.41 corresponds to DĀ 15.39 in content with DĀ 15.41b&c especially corresponding to 15.39b&c

854. Cf. 287r7 (DĀ 15.39b), which is a member of the parallel section to this one that is being responded to. Cf. especially 288r4: *tatra bhikṣavo te śramaṇabrāhmaṇāḥ pūrvāntakalpakā evaṃdṛṣṭaya evamvādi*(288r4)*no* (DĀ 15.40a) which parallels this section in its

tān aham upasaṃkramāmy (u)pasaṃkramy(ai)vaṃ[855] vadāmi <|> satyaṃ kila bhavanta{ḥ} evaṃdṛṣṭayo eva(ṃ)vādin(aḥ | rūpī ātmā bhavaty; a)taḥ (**288v5**) paraṃ saṃjñīti <| te> mayā pṛṣṭā om iti pratijāna<n>te[856] <|> tān aham eva(ṃ) vadā(m)y; asty etad bhavanta evam ucyate <|> ya(t) punar atra bhavanta<ḥ> sthāmaśaḥ parāmṛ(ś)y(ā)bh(in)i(v)i(ś)y(ā)nu(v)y(ava)-ha(**288v6**)ranti[857] <|> idam eva satya<ṃ> moham anyad iti idam atrāhaṃ nānujānāmi <|> tat kasya hetor; anyathāsaṃjñino hi bhavanta ihaike śramaṇabrāhmaṇāḥ <|>

DĀ 15.41a

[Buddha:] "In that case, monks, these ascetics (and brahmins) are the ones who (hold such views), [...] who profess so: 'The self is corporeal. Beyond this life it is aware.' I approach them [and] having approached them I say: 'Sirs, is it really true that you hold such views, profess so: ("The self is corporeal.) Beyond this life it is aware"?' Questioned by me <they> affirm, 'Yes.' I speak to them in this way: 'Sirs, it is said this is so. Further, sirs, whatever, in this respect you all steadfastly, persistently, insistently, assert [as]: "Just this is true; anything else is false," that I do not allow in this matter. Why is this? Because, sirs, in this case some ascetics and brahmins are of different opinions.'

DĀ 15.41b

[b] tatra bhikṣa(vo) ye (**288v7**) te śramaṇabrāhmaṇā evaṃdṛṣṭaya evaṃvādino;

[b1][1][858] [2] arūpī <|> [3] rūpī cārūpī ca <|> [4] naiva rūpī nārūpī ā(t)mā bhavaty; ataḥ paraṃ saṃjñī <|>

---

scope as a response to a previous statement although the phrase in 288r4 refers to *pūrvāntakalpakā* as opposed to *aparāntakalpakā*. The phrase *tatra bhikṣavo ye te śramaṇabrāhmaṇāḥ evaṃdṛṣṭaya evavādinaḥ* is attested multiple times in the portions of the ms. (note for example: 288r6–7 and 288v6–7).

855. Cf. 288r4, 288v1, DĀ 36.66 (*Pṛṣṭhalapāla-sūtra*): *tān aham upasaṃkramāmi upasaṃkramyaivaṃ*, and NidSa 22.21: *tān aham upasaṃkramāmi | upasaṃkram(y)aivaṃ*.

856. Cf. 288r5, 288v2, and NidSa 22.21: *te may(ā pṛṣṭā evam iti prati)jānanti*.

857. Cf. 288r5, 288v2, and NidSa 22.21: *yat punar a(t)r(a bha)vantaḥ sthāmaśaḥ parāmṛśyābhiniviśyānuvyava-haranti*.

858. *Rūpī ātmā bhavaty; ataḥ paraṃ saṃjñī* would be expected here as is seen in the previous instance of this list, cf. 287r6, and is contextually required. However, this sentence

[5] antavān ātmā bhavaty; ataḥ paraṃ saṃjñī <|> [6] anantaḥ <|> [7] a{na}ntavāṃ(**288v8**)ś cānantavāṃś ca <|> [8] naivā{na}ntavāṃ nānantavā<n ātmā>[859] bhavaty; ataḥ para<ṃ> saṃjñī <|>

[9] ekatvasaṃjñī <|> [10] nānātvasaṃjñī <|> [11] parīttasaṃjñī <|> [12] apramaṇasaṃjñī <|>

[13] ekāntasukhī <|> [14] ekāntaduḫkhī[860] <|> [15] sukhaduḫkhī[861] <|> [16] aduḫkhāsu-khī[862] ātmā bhava(**289r1**)(t)y; (ataḫ paraṃ sa)ṃ(jñ)ī[863] <|>

[b2] [1] (rūp)ī (ātmā bhavaty; a)taḥ[864] paraṃ <naiva>[865] saṃjñī <|> [2] arūpī <|> [3] rūpi cārūpī ca <|> [4] naiva rūpī nārūpī ātmā bhavaty; ataḥ paraṃ <naiva>[866] saṃjñī <|>

[5] antavān ātmā bhavaty; ataḥ paraṃ naiva saṃjñī <|> [6] anantaḥ <|> [7] a{na}ntavāṃś cāna(**289r2**)(ntavāṃś ca | [8] naivān)t(avān[867] nā)nantavān[868] ātmā bhavaty; ataḥ paraṃ naiva saṃjñī <|>

---

is expressed in the preceding paragraph, which serves as an introduction to the list, cf. 288v4–5.

859. Cf. 287r7.

860. Note *jihvāmūlīya.*

861. Note *jihvāmūlīya.*

862. Note *jihvāmūlīya.*

863. Cf. 287v1.

864. Cf. 287v1.

865. Cf. DN I 32.10 (*Brahmajāla-sutta*): *rūpī attā hoti arogo param maraṇā asaññī ti naṃ paññāpenti.*

866. Cf. DN I 32.13–15 (*Brahmajāla-sutta*): *n' ev' antavā nānantavā attā hoti arogo param maraṇā asaññī ti naṃ paññāpenti.*

867. This reconstruction leaves a one-akṣara deficit to the line due to the fact that *naivāntavān* is always incorrectly written as *naivānantavān* in this ms. If this section of the ms. were not damaged, it would surely read *naivānantavān*, which I would have then emended to *naivā{na}ntavān.*

868. Cf. 287v2.

[b3] [1] rūpī ātmā bhavaty; a(taḥ) paraṃ naivasaṃjñīnāsaṃjñī <|> [2] arūpī <|> [3] rūpī cārūpī ca <|> [4] naiva rūpī nārūpī <ātmā> bhavaty; ataḥ paraṃ nai(**289r3**)(vasaṃjñī)nāsaṃjñī[869] <|>

[5] {an}antavān ātmā bhavaty; ataḥ paraṃ naivasaṃjñīnāsaṃjñ(ī | {antav)ān[870] ātmā bhavaty; ataḥ paraṃ naivasaṃjñīnāsaṃjñī <|>}[871] [6] anantaḥ <|> [7] {an}antavāṃś cānantavaṃ(ś ca | [8] naiv)ā(**289r4**)(ntavān nānantavān ātmā bhavaty; ataḥ paraṃ) naivasaṃj(ñ)ī(nāsa)ṃ(jñ)ī[872] <|>

DĀ 15.41b

[b] [Buddha:] "In that case, monks, these ascetics and brahmins are the ones who hold such views, who profess so:

[b1] [According to the view of the *Saṃjñīvāda*:] [1] [The self is corporeal. Beyond this life it is aware.][873] [2] It is incorporeal. [3] It is [both] corporeal and incorporeal. [4] The self is neither corporeal nor incorporeal. Beyond this life it is aware.

[5] The self is finite. Beyond this life it is aware. [6] It is infinite. [7] It is [both] finite and infinite. [8] <The self> is neither finite nor infinite. Beyond this life it is aware.

[9] It is possessed of a uniform awareness. [10] It is possessed of a diverse awareness. [11] It is possessed of a limited awareness. [12] It is possessed of an unlimited awareness.

869. Cf. 287v3.

870. Cf. 287v3.

871. In addition to the difference of the first words (*anantavān* and *antavān*), this passage is exactly the same as the one preceding it and is contextually incorrect. It is, perhaps, an example of the scribe inadvertently repeating what he had written.

872. Cf. 287v3–4 and DĀ 47 (the currently unedited *Brahmajāla-sūtra*) 452v2–3: *ataḥ paraṃ naiva-saṃjñ[ī]nāsaṃ(jñ)ī* <|> *(anantavān | antavāṃś cānantavā)ṃ[ś ca] naivāntavā*(**452v3**)*n nānantavān ātmā bhavaty* <|> *ataḥ paraṃ naivasaṃjñīnāsaṃjñī.*

873. This sentence, *rūpī ātmā bhavaty; ataḥ paraṃ saṃjñī*, which begins this list as is seen in the first iteration of the list above, cf. 287r6, is contextually required. However, this sentence is expressed in the preceding paragraph, which serves the function of an introduction to the list, cf. 288v4–5.

[13] It is possessed of absolute happiness. [14] It is possessed of absolute suffering. [15] It is possessed of [both] happiness and suffering. [16] The self is possessed of neither suffering nor happiness. (Beyond this life) it is aware.

[b2] [According to the view of the *Asaṃjñīvāda*:] [1] The (self is) corporeal. Beyond this life it is <not at all> aware. [2] It is incorporeal. [3] It is [both] corporeal and incorporeal. [4] The self is neither corporeal nor incorporeal. Beyond this life it is <not at all> aware.

[5] The self is finite. Beyond this life it is not at all aware. [6] It is infinite. [7] It is [both] finite and infinite. [8] The self is neither finite nor infinite. Beyond this life the self is not at all aware.

[b3] [According to the view of the *Naivasaṃjñīnāsaṃjñīvāda*:] [1] The self is corporeal. Beyond this life it is neither aware nor unaware. [2] It is incorporeal. [3] It is [both] corporeal and incorporeal. [4] <The self> is neither corporeal nor incorporeal. Beyond this life it is neither aware nor unaware.

[5] The self is finite. Beyond this life it is neither aware nor unaware. [6] It is infinite. [7] It is [both] finite and infinite. [8] (The self is neither finite nor infinite. Beyond this life) it is neither aware nor unaware."

DĀ 15.41c–d

[c][874] [1] (yata)ś (c)āyam ātmā rūpī <|> audārikaś cāturmahābhūtiko jī(va)ti ti(ṣṭhati dhriyate yāpayati | tāva)**(289r5)**t sar(o)gaḥ sagaṇḍaḥ s(aśal)y(aḥ saj)v(araḥ sapar)i(dā)h(o); y(a)t(a)ś c(ā)y(a)m ā(t)m(ā

874. The section, DĀ 15.39c, which parallels this section, begins with the phrase: *santi bhikṣava eke śramaṇabrāhmaṇāḥ aparāntakalpakā evaṃ(d)ṛṣṭ(aya evaṃvādinaḥ |)* (287v5), a phrase found at the beginning of many of the surrounding sections in this part of the text (although *tatra bhikṣavo ye te* would be a preferable beginning if the phrase were employed here). It is possible that the scribe neglected to include it here simply because he forgot. However, as it is not certain that this phrase belongs here, nor is it absolutely necessary as such a phrase would be implied throughout this part of the text) I have not added it to the reconstruction above.

ucchidya)te[875] <|> vinaśyati na bhavati {•}[876] paraṃ maraṇād <|> etāvad a(yam ātmā samyaksusamucchinno bha)(**289r6**)v(a)ti[877] <|>

[2] divyaḥ kāmāvacaro divyo rūpāvacaraḥ arūpī ā{tmā}kāśānaṃ(t)yā(ya)-tanopagaḥ arūpī vijñānānaṃtyāyata{na}nop(a)g(o 'rūpī ākiṃcanyāyatano)-(**289r7**)p(ago)[878] 'rūpī naivasamjñānāsaṃjñāyatanopag(o) jīvati tiṣṭhati dhriyate yāpayati <|> tāvat sarogaḥ sagaṇḍaḥ saśalyaḥ sajvaraḥ saparidāho; yataś cā<yam ā>tmā u(cchidyate | vinaśyati | na bhava)(**289r8**)ti[879] paraṃ maraṇād <|> etāvad ayam ātmā (sam)y(ak)susamucchinno[880] bhavati <|>

[d][881] santi bhikṣava eke[882] śramaṇābrāh(m)aṇā evaṃdṛṣṭaya evaṃvādi-(no |)

875. Cf. 287v7 and 289r7, which both refrain from *sandhi* while 287v5 reads *ātmo̱ 'cchidyate.*

876. Cf. DĀ 44 (the currently unedited *Rājan-sūtra*): 437v7–8: *na bhavataḥ*) (**437v8**) *para<ṃ> mā<ra>ṇād iti*, DN II 34.9 (*Brahmajāla-sutta*) and Vibh 383.31: *na hoti param maranā*, SBV II 221 (A50b6–7): *na bhavati paraṃ mara*(**A504b7**)*ṇāt**.

877. Cf. 287v5–6, DĀ 47 (the currently unedited *Brahmajāla-sūtra*), 452v7–8: *yayāṃ ā[tmā rūpī] audārika[ś cāt]urm[a]hā*(**452v8**)*bhūtikaḥ jīv[at]i (t)i(ṣṭhati dhriya)te yāpaya[t]i <|> tāvat sarogaḥ sagaṇḍaḥ saśalyaḥ sajvaraḥ saparidāhaḥ yataś cāyam ātmā samyak susamucchinno bhavati*, and Abhidh-k-vy 457.17: *yāvad ayam ātmā jīvati tiṣṭhati dhriyate yāpayati. tāvat sarogaḥ sagaṇḍaḥ saśalyaḥ sajvaraḥ saparidāhakaḥ. yataś cāyam ātmā ucchidyate vinaśyati na bhavati. iyatā 'yam ātmā samyak samucchinno bhavatīti.*

878. Cf. 287v6–7.

879. Cf. 289r4 and Abhidh-k-vy 457.16–17: *yataś cāyam ātmā ucchidyate vinaśyati na bhavati.*

880. Cf. 287v8 and DĀ 47 (the currently unedited *Brahmajāla-sūtra*), 452v8: *yataś cāyam ātmā samyaksusamu-cchinno bhavati.*

881. Compare with DĀ 15.24b and DĀ 15.25b regarding *kāmaguṇa.*

882. It would be preferable if *tatra bhikṣavo ye te* were here instead of *santi bhikṣava eke*, as *santi bhikṣava eke* is used in the corresponding sections above (in this case DĀ 15.39e) while *tatra bhikṣavo ye te* is used for these type of sections, which serve as rebuttals. The meaning is not grossly different between the two wordings but there does appear to be a sense of introduction and conclusion to a thought at play, a "here/there" type of construction. It is possible that *tatra bhikṣavo ye te* is used here to introduce this particular section (DĀ 15.41d), and that the largely unreconstructed section, DĀ 15.42, that follows is a response. It is also possible that there was simply a textual corruption and the intended reading of *tatra bhikṣavo ye te* improperly transmitted as *santi bhikṣava eke.*

[1] (ya)tāś cāyam ātmā paṃca(bhiḥ kāmaguṇaiḥ samarpitaḥ sa)(**289v1**)-(manvaṃgībhūtaḥ krīḍati ramate paricārayati | etāvad ayam ātmā paramadṛṣṭadharmanirvāṇaprāpto bhavati |)[883]

[2] (yataś cātmā viviktaṃ kāmaiḥ pūrvavat* yāvac caturthaṃ dhyānam upasaṃpadya viharati | etā)(**289v2**)(vad ayam ātmā paramadṛṣṭadharmanirvāṇaprāpto bhavati |)[884]

DĀ 15.41c–d

[c] [According to the view of the *Ucchedavāda*:] [1] "Insofar as this self is corporeal, coarse, consists of the four great elements, lives, remains, (is maintained, and is sustained), to that end, [it is] diseased, afflicted with ulcers, tormented,[885] fevered, and anguished. Insofar as this self is eradicated, perishes, and ceases to exist after death, to that end, this (self) is (completely and entirely destroyed).

[2] [And so on, up to:] The divine inhabitants of the sphere of desire, the divine inhabitants of the sphere of materiality, the incorporeal gods in the stage of the infinity of space, the incorporeal gods in the stage of the infinity of consciousness, the (incorporeal) gods in the stage of nothingness, and the incorporeal gods in the stage of neither awareness nor unawareness live, remain, are maintained, and are sustained; therefore they are diseased, afflicted with ulcers, tormented, fevered, and anguished. Insofar as this self is eradicated, (perishes, and ceases) to exist after death, to that end, this self is completely and entirely destroyed.

[d] [Buddha:] "Monks, there are some ascetics and brahmins who hold such views, who profess so:

[According to the view of the *Dṛṣṭadharmanirvāṇavāda*:] [1] Insofar as this self (is affected by [and] provided with) the five (sensual pleasures, plays, enjoys itself, and amuses itself, to that end, this self is one that attains ultimate nirvāṇa in this present state of existence.)

883. Cf. 287v8–288r2.

884. Cf. 287v8–288r2.

885. See note 801 above.

[2] (Insofar as this self dwells free from passion, having reached up to the fourth dhyāna as before with the previous [three dhyānas], to that end, this self is one that attains ultimate nirvāṇa in this present state of existence.)"

DĀ 15.41e

[e] (tān aham upasaṃkramāmy; upasaṃkramyaivaṃ vadāmi | satyaṃ kila bhavanta evaṃdṛṣṭaya evaṃvādinaḥ |) + + + + + + + + + + + (**289v3**) + + + + + + + + + + + + + + + + ... + + + + + + + + + + ... (te mayā pṛṣṭā om iti pratijānante | tān aham evaṃ vadāmy asty; etad bhavanta evam ucyate | yat punar atra) (**289v4**) (bhavantaḥ sthāmaśaḥ parāmṛśyābhiniviśyānuvyāvaharanti | idam e)v(a) s(atyaṃ moham anyad iti | idam atrāhaṃ nānujānāmi | tat kasya hetor; anyathāsaṃjñino hi) (**289v5**) (bhavanta ihai)k(e) śram(a)ṇabra(hma)ṇ(āḥ |)[886]

DĀ 15.41e

[e] [Buddha:] "I approach them, [and] having approached them I say: 'Sirs, is it really true that you hold such views, profess so:' [...] (Questioned by me they affirm, 'Yes.' I speak to them in this way: 'Sirs, it is said this is so. Further, sirs, whatever, in this respect you all steadfastly, persistently, insistently, assert [as]:) "Just (this is) true, (anything else is false," that I do not allow in this matter. Why is this? Because, sirs, in this case) some ascetics and brahmins (are of different opinions).'"

~15.41~

DN III 140.6–16 (DN 29.38)

[a] 38. tatra cunda ye te samaṇa-brāhmaṇā evaṃ-vādino evaṃ-diṭṭhino—rūpī attā hoti arogo param maraṇā, idam eva saccaṃ, mogham aññan ti, tyāhaṃ upasaṃkamitvā evaṃ vadāmi—atthi kho idaṃ, āvuso, vuccati 'rūpī attā hoti arogo param maraṇā ti? yañ ca kho te evam āhaṃsu idam

886. Cf. 288v3–6 in (DĀ 15.41a) as well as 288r3–6 (DĀ 15.40a) and 288v1–3 (DĀ 15.40c), which are similarly constructed. While I believe that it is most appropriate to follow DĀ 15.40c in the reconstruction of the beginning of this paragraph, it is not entirely clear whether it should begin with *tān aham upasaṃkramāmy*... as in 288v1 (DĀ 15.40c), or with *tatra bhikṣavo ye te*... as with 288r3 and 288v3 (DĀ 15.40a and DĀ 15.41a). Thus a reconstruction beginning with *tatra bhikṣavo ye te*... is also a possibility. Additionally, it is impossible to say exactly what the quotation of the improper *dṛṣṭi* to be refuted here would be, although it surely must be something stated in the directly preceding sections (DĀ 15.41b, 15.41c, or 15.41d). Considering the rather long lacuna remaining, it is quite possible that some or perhaps all of the *dṛṣṭi*s in DĀ 15.41b, 15.41c, or 15.41d are mentioned.

eva saccaṃ, mogham aññan ti, taṃ tesaṃ nānujānāmi. taṃ kissa hetu? aññathā-saññino pi h' ettha cunda sant' eke sattā. imāya pi kho ahaṃ cunda paññattiyā n' eva attano sama-samaṃ samanupassāmi kuto bhiyyo, atha kho cunda aham eva tattha bhiyyo yadidaṃ adhippaññatti.

[b] DN III 140.17–34 (DN 29.39)
39. tatra cunda ye te samaṇa-brāhmaṇā evaṃ-vādino evaṃ-diṭṭhino—
arūpī attā hoti ... pe ...
rūpī ca arūpī ca attā hoti. ...
n' eva rūpī nārūpī attā hoti. ...
saññī attā hoti. ...
asaññī attā hoti. ...
n' eva saññī nāsaññī attā hoti. ...
attā ucchijjati vinassati, na hoti param maraṇā, idam eva saccaṃ, mogham aññan ti:

tyāhaṃ upasaṃkamitvā evaṃ vadāmi—atthi kho idaṃ, āvuso, vuccati attā ucchijjati vinassati, na hoti param maraṇā ti? yañ ca kho te cunda evam āhaṃsu—idam eva saccaṃ, mogham aññan ti, taṃ tesaṃ nānujānāmi. taṃ kissa hetu? aññathā saññino pi h' ettha cunda sant' eke sattā. imāya pi kho ahaṃ cunda paññattiyā n' eva attano sama-samaṃ samanupassāmi kuto bhiyyo, atha kho aham eva tattha bhiyyo yadidaṃ adhippaññatti.

T I 1.17 —

~15.41a&e~[887]

~15.41b~[888]

~15.41b1~[889]

887. The parallels for DĀ 15.41e are the same as those for DĀ 15.40a&c and may be found there. See note 851 above.

888. All of the parallels below for DĀ 15.41b are the same as those found under DĀ 15.39b and may be found there. See note 802 above.

889. The parallels listed here for DĀ 15.41b1 are the same as those found under DĀ 15.39b1 and may be found there. See note 803 above.

~15.41b2~[890]

~15.41b3~[891]

~15.41c~[892]

~15.41d~[893]

890. The parallels to DĀ 15.41b2 are the same as those to DĀ 15.39b2 and may be found there. See note 805 above.

891. The parallels to DĀ 15.41b3 are the same as those to DĀ 15.39b3 and may be found there. See note 807 above.

892. The parallels to DĀ 15.41c are the same as those found under DĀ 15.39c and may be found there. See note 809 above.

893. The parallels for DĀ 15.41d are the same as those of DĀ 15.39d and may be found there. See note 820 above.

Final Refutation and Concluding Frame (DĀ 15.42)

DĀ 15.42

tatra bhi(kṣavo ye) te ś(ra)m(a)ṇa(brā)h(ma)ṇ(ā evaṃdṛṣṭaya evaṃvādin).[894] + **(289v6)** .. .. + + .. + + + + .i + + + + + + + + + + + + ... + + + + + + + (etāvad ayam ātmā paramadṛṣṭadharmanir)vāṇ(a)prāpto bhav(a)ti[895] • tad (a)**(289v7)**(p)i[896] .. .. .. s. .. + .i + (śaśvata ātmā l)okaś c(e)ti[897] <|> t(a)d[898] a**(289v8)**pi sp. .. + + ..ṃ .. .. + ... + .. + (etāvad aya)m ātmā paramadṛṣṭadharmanirvā**(290r1)**(ṇa)prāpto[899] bhavati <|> tad (a)pi [900] rm. s. .r. .y. + ...dṛṣṭigatānā**(290r2)**m anutpādā(ś ca)tvāri s(mṛtyupasthānāni)[901] +

894. Cf. 288r6–7 and 288v6–7.

895. Cf. 288r1, 288r2, and 289v8.

896. Cf. 289v7–8 and 290r1.

897. Cf. 288r4 and 288r4–5.

898. Cf. 289v6–7 and 290r1.

899. Cf. 288r2.

900. Cf.289v6–7 and 289v7–8.

901. Here we expect something similar to the *Pāsādika-sutta* in the DN with *pūrvānta-sahagatānaṃ* or *aparāntasahagatānaṃ* before *dṛṣṭigatānām* or possibly *pūrvāntāparāntasahagatānaṃ* in compound. Cf. DN III 141.3–6 and 141.10–14: *imesañ ca cunda pubbanta-sahagatānaṃ diṭṭhi-nissayānaṃ imesañ ca aparanta-sahagatānaṃ diṭṭhi-nissayānaṃ pahānāya samatikkamāya evaṃ mayā cattāro satipaṭṭhānā desitā paññattā*. Cf also DĀ(U.H.) Hs. 131 Vt: *(°an)up(a)śy(a)n(ā)smṛtyupasth(ānaṃ)* and SHT (IV) 32 Fragm. 66 Bl. 183 V1 .. .. smṛtyupasthānaṃ vedanā + + + ttadharmeśu dharmānupa +, which are very similar but not exact parallels.

+ + + + (me)dh(a)sy(a)[902] śākyasyāmra(**290r3**)(vaṇ).[903] +

DĀ 15.42

[Buddha:] "In that case, monks, these (are those) ascetics and brahmins (who hold such views, who profess so): [...] (to that end, this self) is one that attains supreme nirvāṇa in this present state of existence. This also [...] 'The self and the world are eternal.' This also [...] (therefore), this self is one that attains supreme nirvāṇa in this present state of existence. This also [...] these four establishments of mindfulness, [which are for] the non-production of these views[904] [...]" [...] the mango forest of the Śākyan Medha [...]."

~15.42~

SHT (IV) 32 Fragm. 66 Bl. 183 (*Prāsādika-sūtra*)

V

1[905] .. .. smṛtyupasthānaṃ vedanā + + + ttadharmeśu dharmānupa +

2 medhyasya śākyasy=āmravane .. + + + rmeṣu prāsādaṃ pra[ve] +

3 adhivacanaṃ ||[906] antarod(d)ā ○ nam* durākhyātaś=ca svākhyāt(o) na [v]. + + ⏑ – ⏑ – | – – – – ⏑ – – – | – – – –

902. Cf. 274v5 and 275r5.

903. Ms. reads *śākyasyāśra*. Cf. 274v5 and especially 275r5. Cf. also SHT (IV) 32 Fragm. 66 Bl. 183 V2: *medhyasya śākyasy=āmravane*. See note 277 above.

904. The views in question are almost certainly *pūrvāntasahagata* and *aparāntasahagata* (those associated with the beginning and those associated with the end) as discussed in the previous sections. Cf. DN III 141.3–6 and 141.10–14: *imesañ ca cunda pubbanta-sahagatānaṃ diṭṭhi-nissayānaṃ imesañ ca aparanta-sahagatānaṃ diṭṭhi-nissayānaṃ pahānāya samatikkamāya evaṃ mayā cattāro satipaṭṭhānā desitā paññattā*. LDB 438: "And, Cunda, for the destruction of all such views about the beginning and the end, for transcending them, I have taught and laid down the four foundations of mindfulness."

905. DĀ 15.42.

906. DĀ 15.43 starts here.

4 ś=ca cīvaram* sukhallik(āḥ) ○ saptaphalā vyākṛtāvyākṛtena ca – – – – ˘ – – – | – – – – ˘ –

5 cikā || uddānam* apanna + + + ntha[k]o bhārgavaś=[śa]l[y]o bhaya-bhai(rava) + + + + + + + + + + + + + + + + +

6 prasādanīyena paścimaḥ || ○ ||

DN III 141.3–14 (DN 29.41)

40. imesañ ca cunda pubbanta-sahagatānaṃ diṭṭhinissayānaṃ imesañ ca aparanta-sahagatānaṃ diṭṭhi-nissayānaṃ pahānāya samatikkamāya evaṃ mayā cattāro satipaṭṭhānā desitā paññattā. katame cattāro? idha cunda bhikkhu kāye kāyānupassī viharati ātāpī sampajāno satimā, vineyya loke abhijjhā-domanassaṃ, vedanāsu ... citte ... dhammesu dhammānupassī viharati ātāpī sampajāno satimā, vineyya loke abhijjhā-domanassaṃ. imesañ ca cunda pubbanta-sahagatānaṃ diṭṭhi-nissayānaṃ imesañ ca aparanta-sahagatānaṃ diṭṭhi-nissayānaṃ pahānāya samatikkamāya evam mayā ime cattāro satipaṭṭhānā desitā paññattā ti.

DN 141.15–25 (DN 29.40)

41. tena kho pana samayena āyasmā upavāno bhagavato piṭṭhito ṭhito hoti bhagavantaṃ vījayamāno. atha kho āyasmā upavāno bhagavantaṃ etad avoca: acchariyaṃ bhante, abbhutaṃ bhante, pāsādiko vatāyaṃ bhante dhamma-pariyāyo, atipāsādiko vatāyaṃ bhante dhamma-pariyāyo. ko nāmo ayaṃ bhante dhamma-pariyāyo ti?
tasmāt iha tvaṃ upavāna imaṃ dhamma-pariyāyaṃ pāsādiko ti eva naṃ dhārehīti.idam avoca bhagavā. attamano āyasmā upavāno bhagavato bhāsitaṃ abhinandīti.

T I 1 76b5–22

佛告諸比丘。若欲滅此諸邪惡見者。於四念處當修三行。云何比丘滅此諸惡。於四念處當修三行。比丘謂內身身觀。精勤不懈憶念不忘。除世貪憂。外身身觀。精勤不懈憶念不忘。除世貪憂。內外身身觀憶念不忘。除世貪憂。受意法觀亦復如是。是爲滅衆惡法。於四念處。三種修行。有八解脱。云何爲八。色觀色初解脱。內有色想外觀色二解脱。淨解脱三解脱。度色想滅有對想住空處四解脱。捨空處住識處五解脱。捨識處住不用處六解脱。捨不用處住有想無想處七解脱。滅盡定八解脱。爾時阿難在世尊後執扇扇佛。即偏露右肩右膝著地。叉手白佛言。甚奇世尊。此法清淨微妙第一當云何名。云何奉持。佛告阿難。此經名爲清淨。汝當清淨持之。爾時阿難聞佛所說。歡喜奉行。

⁝ Summary Verse (DĀ 15.43)

DĀ 15.43

(|| antaroddānam* ||[907]
durākh)yāt(a)ś[908] ca svākhyāto n(a)vaś śāstā **(290r4)** tathāgat(a)ḥ[909]
u(dra)ko[910] ye te dharmā[911] nā(nādṛṣṭiś[912] ca cīvaram)[913]
(su)khālaya(saptaphalā[914] v)y(ākṛtāvyākṛtena[915] ca)[916]
+ + + +[917] .. (p)ū(r)v(ā)ntāparāntena[918] paṃcakāḥ (||) ||[919]

907. Cf. 299v1 in *Prasādanīya-sūtra*: || *anta(ro)ddānam** || and SHT (IV) 32 Fragm. 66 Bl. 183 V3: || *antarod(d)ā ◯ nam**.

908. Cf. 276r8, 276v2, 276v4, 276v7, 276v8, 277r2, and 277r5.

909. Cf. SHT (IV) 32 Fragm. 66 Bl. 183 V3: *durākhyātaś=ca svākhyāt(o) na [v].* + + ⏑ – ⏑ – |.

910. Cf. 281r2 and 281r3.

911. Note that this half-*pāda* only contains seven syllables. Compare with DĀ(U.H.) Hs. 131 Vv: */// ◯ ko [ya] ime dharma* where *ya ime* is used instead of *ye te* with better metrical results.

912. Cf. 281v5, 282r2, 282r5, and 282v1.

913. Cf. 282v4 for *cīvaram*. For the *pāda* cf. DĀ(U.H.) Hs. 131 Vv: */// ◯ ko [ya] ime dharmā nānādṛṣṭi ///* and SHT (IV) 32 Fragm. 66 Bl. 183 V3–4: – – – – ⏑ – – – | – – – – *(4) ś=ca cīvaram**.

914. Cf. 283r4, 283r5, 283r6, 283r8, 283v7, 284r1, 284r7, 284v1, and 284v6 for *sukālaya* and for *saptaphala*.

915. Cf. 285r3, 285r4, 285r5, 285r6, and 285r7.

916. Cf. SHT (IV) 32 Fragm. 66 Bl. 183 V4: *sukhallik(āḥ) ◯ saptaphalā vyākṛtāvyākṛtena ca* – – – – ⏑ – – – |.

917. The distance between the extant akṣaras on this line, especially when compared with 289r4, which this folio sits atop, suggests that as many as five akṣaras remain unaccounted for. However, it is very likely that the akṣaras here were justified in such a way that they had a larger than usual amount of space between them so that the final line of the summary verse could extend to the end of the line in the folio.

918. Cf. 286v5, 286v7, 287r1, 287r4, and 288r3,

919. A loose *anuṣṭubh* metre.

DĀ 15.43

Summary Verse:

[DĀ 15.4–5:] Ill-Proclaimed [Dharma and Vinaya] (*durākhyātaḥ*)
[DĀ 15.6–7:] Well-Proclaimed [Dharma and Vinaya] (*svākhyātaḥ*)
[DĀ 15.8–15:] A Tathāgata Who Is a New Teacher (*navaś śāstā tathāgataḥ*)
[DĀ 15.16:] Udraka [Rāmaputra] (*udrakaḥ*)
[DĀ 15.17:] Those Doctrines That [are Conducive to Dwelling Happily] (*ye te dharma*)
[DĀ 15.18–21:] [Monks of] Various Views (*nānādṛṣṭiḥ*)
[DĀ 15.22:] Robes [and that which is Allowed by the Buddha] (*cīvaram*)
[DĀ 15.23–25:] Devotion to Pleasure (*sukhālayaḥ*)
[DĀ 15.26:] Seven Fruits (*saptaphalāḥ*)
[DĀ 15.27–36:] That Which Is and Is Not Explained [by the Ascetic Gautama] (*vyākṛtāvyākṛtena*)
[...][920]
[DĀ 15.37, 15.38, 15.40, and 15.42:] The Beginning (*pūrvāntaḥ*)
[DĀ 15.37, 15.39, 15.41 and 15.42:] The End (*aparāntaḥ*)
[DĀ 15.39.d and 15.41.d:][921] The Fivefold [Fallacy of Nirvāṇa in the Present Existence] (*paṃcakāḥ*)

~15.43~

DN —

T I 1.17 —

920. As we cannot be sure of even the number of aksaras missing, it is difficult to say what would have been written within this gap. Every section of the sūtra seems to fall under at least one of the key words given in the summary verse, which makes hazarding a guess a very unappealing prospect. It is possible that there is no missing keyword and that what is missing is a filler word or phrase used for the sake of metre. If I were to hazard a guess on a missing keyword, if indeed there is one, I would suspect that there may be a lost keyword from one of the sections of the text that have suffered heavy damage themselves, such as DĀ 15.35 or 15.36, two consecutive sections that are both damaged and do not fall neatly under any of the extant keywords.

921. Also note DĀ 15.24b 15.25b, which discuss the same five sensual pleasures referred to here.

SHT (IV) 32 Fragm. 66 Bl. 183 (*Prāsādika-sūtra*)[922]
V
1[923] .. .. smṛtyupasthānaṃ vedanā + + + ttadharmeśu dharmānupa +
2 medhyasya śākyasy=āmravane .. + + + rmeṣu prāsādaṃ pra[ve] +
3 adhivacanaṃ ||[924] antarod(d)ā ◯ nam* durākhyātaś=ca svākhyāt(o) na [v]. + + ⏑ – ⏑ – | – – – – – ⏑ – – – | – – – –
4 ś=ca cīvaram* sukhallik(āḥ) ◯ saptaphalā vyākṛtāvyākṛtena ca – – – – ⏑ – – – | – – – – ⏑ –
5 cikā || uddānam* apanna + + + ntha[k]o bhārgavaś=[śa]l[y]o bhayabhai(rava) + + + + + + + + + + + + + + + + +
6 prasādanīyena paścimaḥ || ◎ ||

DĀ(U.H.) Hs. 131 (= BLSF III.1 Or.15009/406) (*Prāsādika-sūtra*) (Hoernle without number (photo 173)) (Vv–w parallel the *antaroddāna*)[925]
V
t /// + .[up]. [śy]. [n]. [s]mṛ[tyupasth]. .. .. [t]. ///
u /// [t]. sya dharmapary[ā]yasya pras[ā]da .. ///
v /// ◯ ko [ya] ime dharmā nānādṛṣṭi ///
w /// ◯ parāṃta paṃcikā || uddānam* || ///
x /// ◯ yabhairava śrāvastyāṃ vai[śa]lyāṃ ro ///
y /// .. [na ca] paścimaḥ || prasādan[ī] .. ///
z /// +.. .. [m]e [t]. .. [bh]. .. ..ṃ .[i] + + ///

922. The parallel to DĀ 15.43 spans lines 1–6. The remainder of this fragment corresponds to the summary verse for the *Prasādanīya-sūtra* at DĀ 16.20. See also note 1371.

923. DĀ 15.42

924. DĀ 15.43 starts here.

925. The parallel to DĀ 15.43 in this fragment spans lines t–w. The remainder of the fragment corresponds to DĀ 16.20. See also note 1373.

The *Prasādanīya-sūtra*

Introductory Frame: Śāriputra's Lion's Roar (DĀ 16.1)

DĀ 16.1.1

(290r5) bh(a)g(a)vāṃ (nālandāyaṃ v)ih(a)ra(t)i pāvā(r)i(kāmbavane | āyuṣmāṃ śāri)putraḥ[926] .. + + + + + + + + + + + + + + + + + + + ..ṃ + + + + + + + + + + + (290r6) + (evaṃ sati[927] prasanno 'ha)ṃ (bha)da(nta bhagavato yan nābhūn na bhavi)(290r7)(ṣ)y(ati nāpy etarhi vidyate yad anyaḥ śramaṇo vā brāhmaṇo vā bhagavato 'ntikād bhūyo 'bhijñataraḥ syād yad uta saṃbodhaya iti |)[928]

DĀ 16.1.2

[a] (udārā khalu te iyaṃ śāriputra ārṣabhī vāg bhāṣitā ekāṃśa) (290r8) (udgṛhītaḥ parṣadi samyaksiṃhanādo nāditaḥ[929] | evaṃ sati prasanno 'haṃ bhadanta bhagavato yan nābhūn na bhaviṣyati nāpy etarhi vidyate yad anyaḥ śramaṇo vā brāhmaṇo vā bhagavato 'ntikā)(290v1)d[930] bhūyo 'bhijñatara<ḥ> syād yad uta saṃbodhaya[931] iti <|> kiṃ punas te śāriputra

926. Cf. DN III 99.2–7: *ekaṃ samayaṃ bhagavā nāḷandāyaṃ viharati pāvārikambavani. atha kho āyasmā sāriputto yena bhagavā ten' upasaṃkami, upasaṃkamitvā bhagavantaṃ abhivādetvā eka-m-antaṃ nisīdī. eka-m-antaṃ nisinno kho āyasmā sāriputto bhagavantaṃ etad avoca.* While I have not been able to reconstruct this section in its entirety, the DĀ is very likely quite similar to the Pali of the DN.

927. *Evaṃ sati* here might seem unlikely, but it is attested later in the sūtra where the Buddha quotes Śāriputra's statement in full. Cf. DĀ 16.1.5, 290v7–8.

928. Cf. 290v7–8 and DN III 99.8–11 99.13–16, and 100.19–22.

929. Cf. NidSa 24.26: *(āyu)ṣmatā bhadanta śāriputre(ṇ)a udārārṣabhī vā(g bhāṣi)taikāṃśa u(dgṛhītaḥ pari)ṣadi samyaksiṃhanādo nāditaḥ.*

930. Cf. 290v6–8 and DN III 99.8–16: *uḷārā kho te ayaṃ sāriputta āsabhī vācā bhāsitā, ekaṃso gahito, sīha-nādo nadito: evaṃ pasanno ahaṃ bhante bhagavati, na cāhu na ca bhavissati na c' etarahi vijjati añño samaṇo vā brāhmaṇo vā bhagavatā bhiyyo 'bhiññataro yadidaṃ sambodhiyan ti* and DN III 100.19–22.

931. Ms. reads *saṃbodhāya*. Cf. 290v8, 291r5, 291r8, 291v4, and 291v5.

ye abhūvaṃ atīte 'dhvani tathāgatārhantaḥ samyaksaṃbuddhās te tvayā buddhā bhagavantaś cetasā s(phar)i(tvā viditā evaṃśīlā bata) (**290v2**) te bu(ddh)ā̱[932] bhagavanto 'bhūvaṃn ity apy evaṃdharmāṇa{ḥ} evaṃprajñā (eva)mabhijñā[933] evaṃvimuktaya{ḥ} evaṃbahulavihāriṇo bata te buddhā bhagavanta̱[934] {n}ity api <|>

[**b**] no bhada(nta |)[935]

DĀ 16.1.3

[**a**] (kiṃ punas te śāriputra ye bhaviṣya)(**290v3**)<nty anāgate 'dhvani>[936] tathāgato̱ ̱'rhantaḥ[937] samyaksaṃbuddhās te tvayā buddhā bhagavantaś cetasā spharitvā viditā evaṃśīlā bata te buddhā bhagavaṃto bhaviṣyaṃty anāgate ('dh)v(anīty apy) + + +[938] (evaṃdharmā)(**290v4**)ṇaḥ[939] evaṃprajñā evamabhijñā evaṃvimukta̱ya[940] evaṃbahulavihāriṇo bata te buddhā bhagavaṃto bhaviṣyaṃty anāgate 'dhvanīti <|>

[**b**] no bhadanta <|>

932. Ms. reads *buddho*. Cf. 290v3 and 290v5.

933. Cf. 290v4 and 290v5.

934. Ms. reads *bhagavanto*.

935. Cf. 290v4 and 290v6.

936. Cf. 290v1 and DN III 100.4–5: *kim pana sāriputta ye te bhavissanti anāgatam addhānaṃ arahanto sammāsambuddhā*. This reconstruction is longer than the gap in the ms. but it is impossible to determine what is missing.

937. Ms. reads *tathāgatārhantaḥ* here, which would not be appropriate, as the following *samyaksaṃbuddhās* would then also need to be included in the compound. Be that as it may, this odd compound does occur in other sūtra and *vinaya* texts. See, for example, Śikṣ 169.16–170.1: *sarvalokadhātuṣu tathāgatārhantaḥ samyaksaṃbuddhās*. However, these occurences are rare and in older editions. This suggests that such compounds are the result of scribes not taking care of the proper usage of the terms *tathāgataḥ*, *arhantaḥ*, and *samyaksaṃbuddhaḥ* and editors from years past not having encountered this phrase often enough to confidently edit the erroneous compound.

938. I suspect that there were filler marks here in the ms. or some textual corruption that caused these seemingly extraneous akṣaras.

939. Cf. 290v2 and 290v5.

940. Ms. reads *evaṃvimuktiṃya*.

DĀ 16.1.4

[**a**] ahaṃ tā(vat te śāriputra etarhi ta)(**290v5**)thāgato[941] 'rhan samyaksaṃbuddhaḥ evaṃ cetasā spharitvā viditaḥ evaṃśīlo batāyaṃ buddho bhagavānn ity api evaṃdharmā evaṃprajña evamabhijña e(vaṃvim)ukti (evaṃbahulavihārī)[942] (**290v6**) batāyaṃ buddho bhagavāṃ ity api <|>

[**b**] no bhadanta <|>

DĀ 16.1.5

[**a**] na te śāriputrātītānāgatapratyutpannānāṃ {ma} samyaksaṃbuddhānāṃ cetaḥparyāyo viditaḥ <|> atha kin nu te {sa}tvayā[943] iyam ev(aṃ)rū(**290v7**)pā udārā ārṣabhī vāg bhāṣitā ekāṃśa udgṛhītaḥ parṣadi samyaksiṃhanādo nāditaḥ[944] <|> evaṃ sati prasanno 'haṃ bhadanta bhagavato yan nābhūn na bhaviṣyati nāpy etarhi vidyate yad anyaḥ (**290v8**) śramaṇo vā brāhmaṇo vā bhagavato 'ntikād bhūyo 'bhijñatara<ḥ> syād yad uta saṃbodhaya iti <|>

[**b**] na me bhadantātītānāgatapratyutpannānāṃ tathāgatānām a(r)hatā(ṃ samyaksaṃbuddhānāṃ cetaḥ)paryāyo[945] (**291r1**) vidito 'pi dharmaparyāyo me vidita<ḥ |> iha mama bhagavāṃ dharmaṃ deśayaty uttarād uttarataraṃ praṇītāt praṇītataraṃ; hīnapraṇītakṛṣṇaśuklasapratibhāgapratī(t)y(asa)mutpannān[946] dharmān vistareṇa saṃpra(**291r2**)kāśayati <|> yathā yathā me bhagavāṃ dharmaṃ deśayaty uttarād uttarataraṃ <praṇītāt>[947] praṇītataraṃ; hīnapraṇītakṛṣṇaśuklasapratibhāgapratītyasamutpannāṃ dharmāṃ vistareṇa saṃprakāśayati <|> tathā ta(**291r3**)thā{n} ekāṃ dharmān abhijñayā parijānā(my; ek)āṃ[948] dharmān abhijñayā pratijahāmi <|> ekāṃ dharmān abhijñayā sākṣāt karomy; ekāṃ dharmān abhijñayā bhāvayāmi <|> dharmeṣu ca niṣṭhāṃ gacchāmi <|> (**291r4**) śāstari ca prasādaṃ

941. Cf. DN III 100.11: *kim pana sāriputta ahaṃ te etarahi.*

942. Cf. 290v2 and 290v4.

943. Ms. reads *satvāya.*

944. Ms. reads *naditaḥ.*

945. Cf. 290v6.

946. Cf. 291r2. Ms. reads *hīnapraṇītakṛṣṇaśukle.*

947. Cf. 291r1.

948. Cf. later in this line.

pravedaye{t}; samyaksa(ṃb)uddh(o)[949] b(a)t(a)[950] bhagavāṃn ity api jāne <|>[951]

DĀ 16.1.1

The Blessed One dwelled (in Nālandā) at the mango grove of Pāvārika. (The Venerable) Śāriputra [...] [Śāriputra:] "(This being so), sir, I (have serene confidence in the Blessed One that it has not been), will not be, (nor is it now possible that another ascetic or brahmin could be more knowledgeable than the Blessed One in regard to perfect awakening.)"

DĀ 16.1.2

[a] [Buddha:] "(Lofty indeed, Śāriputra, is this bull's speech of yours in the assembly, unequivocally roaring a complete lion's roar, [saying:] 'This being so, sir, I have serene confidence in the Blessed One that it has not been, will not be, nor is it now possible that another ascetic or brahmin) could be more knowledgeable than (the Blessed One) in regard to perfect awakening.' What about, Śāriputra, those tathāgatas, arhats, these complete, perfect buddhas of the past? Have you grasped firmly with your mind (what they know), [in order to say:] 'Certainly these buddhas, these blessed ones (were of such conduct), these buddhas, these blessed ones were of such dharma, such insight, such supernormal knowledge, such a liberation, and such a way of life'?"

[b] [Śāriputra:] "No, Sir."

DĀ 16.1.3

[a] [Buddha:]"(What about, Śāriputra,) those tathāgatas, arhats, those complete, perfect buddhas (who will be) <in the future>? Have you grasped firmly with your mind what they know, [in order to say:] 'Certainly these

949. Cf. 290v8.

950. Cf. 290v2, 290v3, 290v4, 290v5 292v3, and 299r5.

951. These phrases, the thesis of the sūtra, end the introductory frame here in DĀ 16.1.5b (291r3–4): *dharmeṣu ca niṣṭhāṃ gacchāmi* <|> (291r4) *śāstari ca prasādaṃ pravedayet; samyaksa(ṃb)uddh(o) b(a)t(a) bhagavāṃn ity api jāne*, and are echoed in the conclusion of the frame narrative in DĀ 16.19a (299r4–5): *dharmeṣu ca niṣṭhāṃ gacchiṣyanti* <|> *śāstari ca pra(s)ādaṃ pra(v)edayiṣyaṃte* <|> (299r5) *samyaksaṃbuddho bata bhagavān ity api jñāsyanti* and DĀ 16.19b (299r7): *dharmeṣu ca niṣṭhāṃ gami(ṣ)ya(nt)i (| śāstari ca prasādaṃ prave)dayiṣyante* <|> *samyaksaṃbuddho bha(gavān ity api jñāsyanti).*

buddhas, these blessed ones will be of such conduct in the future; these buddhas, these blessed ones will be of [...] such dharma, such insight, such supernormal knowledge, such a liberation, and such a way of life in the future'?"

[**b**] [Śāriputra:] "No, Sir."

DĀ 16.1.4

[**a**] [Buddha:] "At least (then, Śāriputra), I am a tathāgata, an arhat, a complete, perfect buddha. Have you grasped firmly with your mind what I know [in order to say:] 'Certainly this buddha, this blessed one is of such conduct; this buddha, this blessed one is of such dharma, such insight, such supernormal knowledge, such a liberation, and (such a way of life)'?"

[**b**] [Śāriputra:] "No, Sir."

DĀ 16.1.5

[**a**] [Buddha:] "Śāriputra, you do not know the way of thought of those complete, perfect buddhas of the past, future, and present. Rather, how is it that you say this lofty bull's speech of yours in the assembly in this way, unequivocally roaring a complete lion's roar, [saying:] 'This being so, sir, I have serene confidence in the Blessed One that there has not been, there will not be, nor can there be another ascetic or brahmin more knowledgeable than the Blessed One in regard to perfect awakening.'?"

[**b**] [Śāriputra:] "No, sir, I do not know the way of thought of those tathāgatas, arhats, (those complete, perfect buddhas) of the past, future, and present. However, I do know the dharma discourses. In this case the Blessed One teaches me dharma more superior than superior, more superb than superb. He extensively illuminates these dharmas that are dependently originated together with their counterparts that are good and bad, superb and inferior. In whatever way the Blessed One teaches me dharma more superior than superior, more superb <than superb>, he extensively illuminates these dharmas that are dependently originated together with their counterparts that are good and bad, superb and inferior.[952] In that way I

952. S.v. *kṛṣṇaśukla-sapratibhāga-pratītyasamutpanna* in SWTF.

comprehend some dharmas with supernormal knowledge.[953] I abandon some dharmas with supernormal knowledge. I directly experience some dharmas with supernormal knowledge. I cultivate some dharmas with supernormal knowledge. I become perfect regarding dharma. I proclaim serene faith in the Teacher. I know: 'The Blessed One is certainly a complete, perfect buddha.'"

~16.1.1 ~

T I 18 255a15–23

如是我聞。一時佛在阿拏迦城菴羅園中。與大衆俱。爾時尊者舍利弗。食時著衣持鉢。入阿拏迦城。於其城中。次第乞已。復還本處。收衣洗足。敷座而食。 飯食訖已。往詣佛所。頭面禮足。於一面立。合掌向佛。而作是言。世尊。我今 於佛深起信心。何以故。謂佛神通最勝無比。所有過現未來沙門婆羅門等。尚無有能知佛神通。況復過者。豈能證於無上菩提

~16.1.2a, 16.1.3a, 16.1.4a~

T I 18 255a24–b6

佛言。善哉善哉。舍利弗。汝能善說。甚深廣義。汝當受持於大衆中作師子吼。廣爲宣說。舍利弗復白佛言。世尊。我今於佛所起信心。乃爲過去未來現在 無有能者。亦無沙門婆羅門等。知於佛通過於佛者。豈能證於無上菩提。佛告 舍利弗。於意云何。所有三世諸佛如來應供正等正覺。具清淨戒智慧解脱神通妙 行。我以通力皆悉了知。彼諸如來應供正等正覺亦復如是。知我所有具清淨戒智 慧解脱神通妙行。舍利弗。汝勿謂今釋迦牟尼佛獨具此通。

~16.1.2b, 16.1.3b, 16.1.4b~

T I 18 255b6–12

舍利弗言。不也世尊。我不作是言。唯佛具此神通。我知三世如來應供正等正覺。清淨戒法智慧解脱神通妙行皆悉同等。佛言。舍利弗。如是如是。所有

953. While the ms. clearly uses the term *abhijñā* here, it is possible that it is not meant to refer to supernormal knowledge but rather to something more akin to intuition, or simply to the general sort of knowledge that comes from logically thinking things through (s.v. *abhijānāti* in BHSD). This understanding may be bolstered by the refrain used at the end of nearly every section of DĀ 16: *tad bhagavān aśeṣam abhijānāti | tat te 'śeṣam abhijānata uttare 'bhijñeyaṃ nāsti yasyābhijñānād anyaḥ śramaṇo vā brahmaṇo vā bhagavato 'ntikād bhūyo 'bhijñataraḥ syād yad uta saṃbodhaya iti.* Nonetheless, it is unclear whether Śāriputra understands the above by recalling his own experience or by means of his supernormal knowledge.

三 世諸佛如來正等正覺。皆悉具此神通等法。汝但爲彼衆生。宣布如是甚深之法。 一心受持。於大衆中。作師子吼。而爲廣說。

~16.1.5~

T I 18 255b12–17

舍利弗白佛言。世尊。我佛宣説廣大甚深最勝妙法。乃至善不善業。及諸緣生法。我皆如實一一了知。了一法已復修一法。修一法已復滅一法。滅一法已復 證一法。是故我今於佛起信。是眞正等正覺

~16.1.1 ~

DN III 99.2–11 (DN 28.1)

ekaṃ samayaṃ bhagavā nāḷandāyaṃ viharati pāvārikambavani. atha kho āyasmā sāriputto yena bhagavā ten' upasaṃkami, upasaṃkamitvā bhagavantaṃ abhivādetvā eka-m-antaṃ nisīdī. eka-m-antaṃ nisinno kho āyasmā sāriputto bhagavantaṃ etad avoca. evaṃ pasanno ahaṃ bhante bhagavati na cāhu na ca bhavissati na c' etarahi vijjati añño samaṇo vā brāhmaṇo vā bhagavatā bhiyyo 'bhiññataro yadidaṃ sambodhiyan ti.

~16.1.2~

DN III 99.12–100.3 (DN 28.1)

[a] uḷārā kho te ayaṃ sāriputta āsabhī vācā bhāsitā, ekaṃso gahito, sīhanādo nadito: evaṃ pasanno ahaṃ bhante bhagavati na cāhu na ca bhavissati na c' etarahi vijjati añño samaṇo vā brāhmaṇo vā bhagavatā bhiyyo 'bhiññataro yadidaṃ sambodhiyan ti. kiṃ nu sāriputta ye te ahesuṃ atītam addhānaṃ arahanto sammā-sambuddhā, sabbe te bhagavanto cetasā ceto paricca viditā—evaṃ-sīlā te bhagavanto ahesuṃ iti pi, evaṃ-dhammā te bhagavanto ahesuṃ iti pi, evaṃ-paññā te bhagavanto ahesuṃ iti pi, evaṃ-vihārī te bhagavanto ahesuṃ it ipi, evaṃ-vimuttā te bhagavanto ahesuṃ iti pī ti?

[b] no h' etaṃ bhante.

~16.1.3~

DN III 100.4–10 (DN 28.1)

[a] kiṃ pana sāriputta ye te bhavissanti anāgatam addhānaṃ arahanto sammā-sambuddhā, sabbe te bhagavanto cetasā ceto paricca viditā,—evaṃ-sīlā te bhagavanto bhavissanti iti pi, evaṃ-dhammā ... evaṃ-paññā ... evaṃ-vihārī ... evaṃ-vimuttā te bhagavanto bhavissanti it ipī ti?

[b] no h' etaṃ bhante.

~16.1.4~

DN III 100.11–15 (DN 28.1)

[a] kiṃ pana sāriputta ahaṃ te etarahi arahaṃ sammā-sambuddho cetasā ceto paricca vidito—evaṃ-sīlo bhagavā iti pi, evaṃ dhammo ... evaṃ-pañño ... evaṃ-vihārī ... evaṃ-vimutto bhagavā iti pī ti?

[b] no h' etaṃ bhante.

~16.1.5~

DN III 100.16–22 (DN 28.1)

[a] ettha carahi te sāriputta atītānāgata-paccuppannesu arahantesu sammā-sambuddhesu ceto-pariya-ñāṇaṃ n' atthi. atha kiñ carahi te ayaṃ sāriputta uḷārā āsabhī vācā bhāsitā, ekaṃso gahito, sīha-nādo nadito—evaṃ pasanno ahaṃ bhante bhagavati na cāhu na ca bhavissati na c' etarahi vijjati aññe samaṇo vā brāhmaṇo vā bhagavatā bhiyyo 'bhiññataro yadidaṃ sambodhi-yan ti?

DN III 100.23–102.9 (DN 28.2)

[b] na kho me bhante atītānāgata-paccuppannesu arahantesu sammā-sambuddhesu ceto-pariya-ñāṇaṃ atthi. api ca me bhante dhammanvayo vidito. seyyathā pi bhante rañño paccantimaṃ nagaraṃ daḷhuddāpaṃ daḷhapākāra-toraṇaṃ eka-dvāraṃ, tatr' assa dovāriko paṇḍito viyatto medhāvī aññātānaṃ nivāretā, ñātānaṃ pavesetā. so tassa nagarassa samantā anupariyāya pathaṃ anukkamante na passeyya pākāra-sandhiṃ vā pākāra-vivaraṃ vā antamaso bilāla-nissakkana-mattam pi. tassa evam assa,—ye kho keci oḷārikā pāṇā imaṃ nagaraṃ pavisanti vā nikkhamanti vā, sabbe te iminā va dvārena pavisanti vā nikkhamanti vā ti. evam eva kho me bhante dhammanvayo vidito. ye te ahesuṃ atītam addhānaṃ arahanto sammā-sambuddhā, sabbe te bhagavanto pañca nīvaraṇe pahāya, cetaso upakkilese paññāya dubbalī-karaṇe, catusu satipaṭṭhānesu supatiṭṭhita-cittā, satta bojjhaṅge yathā-bhūtaṃ bhāvetvā anuttaraṃ sammāsambodhiṃ abhisambujjhiṃsu. ye pi te bhante bhavissanti anāgatam addhānaṃ arahanto sammā-sambuddhā, sabbe te bhagavanto pañca nīvaraṇe pahāya, cetaso upakkilese paññāya dubbalī-karaṇe, catusu satipaṭṭhānesu supatiṭṭhita-cittā, satta bojjhaṅge yathā-bhūtaṃ bhāvetvā, anuttaraṃ sammā-sambodhiṃ abhisambujjhissanti. bhagavā pi bhante etarahi ara-

haṃ sammā-sambuddho pañca nīvaraṇe pahāya, cetaso upakkilese paññāya dubbalīkāraṇe, catusu satipaṭṭhānesu supatiṭṭhita-citto, satta bojjhaṅge yathā-bhūtaṃ bhāvetvā, anuttaraṃ sammāsambodhiṃ abhisambuddho. idhāhaṃ bhante yena bhagavā ten' upasaṃkamiṃ dhamma-savanāya. tassa me bhante bhagavā dhammaṃ desesi uttaruttariṃ paṇīta-paṇītaṃ kaṇha-sukka-sappaṭibhāgaṃ. yathā yathā me bhante bhagavā dhammaṃ desesi uttaruttariṃ paṇīta-paṇītaṃ kaṇha-sukka-sappaṭibhāgaṃ, tathā tathā 'haṃ tasmiṃ dhamme abhiññā idh' ekaccaṃ dhammaṃ dhammesu niṭṭham agamaṃ, satthari pasīdiṃ,—sammāsambuddho bhagavā, svākkhāto bhagavatā dhammo, supaṭipanno saṃgho ti.

~16.1.1~

T I 1 76b24–76c3

如是我聞。一時佛在那難陀城波波利菴婆林。與大比丘衆千二百五十人俱。時長老舍利弗於閑靜處默自念言。我心決定知過去未來現在沙門婆羅門智慧神足功德力。無有與如來無所著等正覺等者。時舍利弗從靜室起往至世尊所。頭面禮足在一面坐。白佛言。向於靜室默自思念。過去未來現在沙門婆羅門智慧神足功德道力。無有與如來無所著等正覺等者。

~16.1.2~

T I 1 76c3–8

[a] 佛告舍利弗。善哉善哉。汝能於佛前說如是語。一向受持正師子吼。餘沙門婆羅門無及汝者。云何舍利弗。汝能知過去諸佛心中所念。彼佛有如是戒如是法如是智慧如是解脫如是解脫堂不。

T I 1 76c8

[b] 對曰不知。

~16.1.3~

T I 1 76c8–10

[a]云何舍利弗。汝能知當來諸佛心中所念。有如是戒如是法如是智慧如是解脫如是解脫堂不。

T I 1 76c10

[b] 答曰不知。

~16.1.4~

T I 1 76c11–13

[a] 云何舍利弗。如我今如來至眞等正覺心中所念。如是戒如是法如是智如是解脱如是解脱堂。汝能知不。

T I 1 76c13
[b] 答曰不知。

~16.1.5~
T I 1 76c13–19
[a] 又告舍利弗。過去未來現在如來至眞等正覺心中所念。汝不能知。何故決定作是念。因何事生是念。一向堅持而師子吼。餘沙門婆羅門。若聞汝言我決定知過去未來現在沙門婆羅門智慧神足功德道力無有與如來無所著等正覺等者。當不信汝言。

T I 1 76c19–26
[b] 舍利弗白佛言。我於過去未來現在諸佛心中所念。我不能知。佛總相法我則能知。如來爲我説法轉高轉妙。説黒白法縁無縁法照無照法。如來所説轉高轉妙。我聞法已

~16.1~
Abhidh-k-ṭ Derge Ju 3a4–4a6 (Derge no. 4094); Peking Tu 3b4–4b7 (Peking no. P5595) (quoting the *Prasādanīya-sūtra*)[954]

~16.1.1~
Derge Ju 3a4–7 (cf. Peking Tu 3b4–7)
'di ltar de dag la sangs rgyas kyi chos dang zhes bya ba la | bcom ldan 'das na len dra'i a mra'i tshal na bzhugs te | de nas tshe dang ldan pa shā ri'i bu nang du yang dag 'jog las langs te | bcom ldan 'das ga la ba der nye bar song ste | nye bar 'ongs nas bcom ldan 'das kyi zhabs la spyi bos phyag byas nas phyogs gcig tu 'dug go || phyogs gcig tu 'dug nas tshe dang ldan pa shā ri'i bus bcom ldan 'das la 'di skad ces gsol to || btsun pa bcom ldan 'das la bdag mngon par rab tu dang ste | dge sbyong ngam | bram ze gzhan gang zhig bcom ldan 'das las mngon par shes pa khyad par du 'phags pa gang yang ma byung | 'byung bar mi 'gyur | da ltar yang med de | 'di lta ste | mngon par rdzogs par byang chub pa zhes bya'o ||

954. The Tibetan Abhidh-k-ṭ parallels in DĀ16.1 and DĀ 16.2 below follows the reading found in the Derge read against the Peking. Citations to the Peking are given for the reader's convenience but variant readings found within the Peking are generally not noted.

~16.1.2~

Derge Ju 3a7–3b3 (cf. Peking Tu 3b7–4a3)
[a] bcom ldan 'das kyis bka' stsal pa | shā ri'i bu btsun pa bcom ldan 'das la bdag 'di ltar mngon par rab tu dang ste | dge sbyong ngam bram ze gzhan gang zhig bcom ldan 'das las mngon par shes pa khyad par du 'phags pa gang yang ma byung | 'byung bar mi 'gyur | da ltar yang med de | 'di lta ste | mngon par rdzogs par byang chub pa'o zhes rgya che ba dang | drang srong gi ngag gi brjod pa mtha' gcig tu nges par 'dzin pa | 'khor gyi nang du seng ge'i sgra sgrogs pa legs so legs so || shā ri'i bu ci gang byung bar gyur pa 'das pa'i dus kyi de bzhin gshegs pa dgra bcom pa yang dag par rdzogs pa'i sangs rgyas de dag sangs rgyas bcom ldan 'das 'di lta bu'i tshul khrims dang ldan | sangs rgyas bcom ldan 'das kyi chos 'di lta bu byung | 'di lta bu'i shes rab dang | 'di lta bu'i mngon par shes pa dang | 'di lta bu'i rnam par grol ba dang | 'di lta bu'i mang du gnas pa dang ldan pa'i sangs rgyas bcom ldan 'das byung ngo zhes khyod kyis sems kyis dmigs shing rig gam |

Derge Ju 3b3 (cf. Peking Tu 4a3)
[b] btsun pa ma lags so ||

~16.1.3~

Derge Ju 3b4–5 (cf. Peking Tu 4a3–5)
[a] gang ma 'ongs pa'i dus na 'byung bar 'gyur ba'i de bzhin gshegs pa dgra bcom pa yang dag par rdzogs pa'i sangs rgyas de dag sangs rgyas bcom ldan 'das 'di lta bu'i tshul khrims dang ldan pa | 'di lta bu'i chos | 'di lta bu'i shes rab | 'di lta bu'i mngon par shes pa | 'di lta bu'i rnam par grol ba | 'di lta bu'i mang du gnas pa dang ldan pa sangs rgyas bcom ldan 'das rnams 'byung bar 'gyur ro zhes rig gam |

Derge Ju 3b5 (cf. Peking Tu 4a5)
[b] btsun pa ma lags so ||

~16.1.4~

Derge Ju 3b5–6 (cf. Peking Tu 4a5–7)
[a] da ltar byung ba'i de bzhin gshegs pa dgra bcom pa yang dag par rdzogs pa'i sangs rgyas nga 'di lta bu'i tshul khrims dang ldan pa | 'di lta bu'i shes rab | 'di lta bu'i mngon par shes pa | 'di lta bu'i rnam par grol ba | 'di lta bu'i mang du gnas pa dang ldan zhes bya bar yang rig gam |

Derge Ju3b6 (cf. Peking Tu4a7)
[b] btsun pa ma lags so ||

~16.1.5~
Derge Ju 3b6–4a2 (cf. Peking Tu 4a7–4b1)
[a] shā ri'i bu khyod kyis 'das pa dang ma 'ongs pa dang da ltar byung ba'i de bzhin gshegs pa dgra bcom pa yang dag par rdzogs pa'i sangs rgyas rnams kyi sems kyi rnam grangs mi shes na bsam pa cis | ji ste btsun pa bcom ldan 'das la bdag mngon par rab tu dang ste | dge sbyong ngam bram ze gzhan gang zhig bcom ldan 'das las mngon par shes pa khyad par du 'phags pa gang yang ma byung 'byung bar mi 'gyur ba da ltar med de | 'di lta ste | rdzogs par byang chub pa zhes bya'o zhes ngag gis brjed pa drang srong gi ngag gis brjod pa rgya che ba mtha' gcig tu nges par 'dzin pa 'khor gyi nang du seng ge'i sgra sgrogs |

Derge Ju 4a2–6 (cf. Peking Tu 4b2–7)
[b] btsun pa bdag gis 'das pa dang ma 'ongs pa dang da ltar byung ba'i de bzhin gshegs pa dgra bcom pa de dag gi thugs kyi rnam grangs ma 'tshal mod kyi | 'on kyang chos kyi rnam grangs 'tshal te | 'dir bcom ldan 'das kyis bdag la chos bstan pa gang bla na med pa | gong na med pa | gya nom pa | ches gya nom pa | dman pa dang khyad par du 'phags pa dkar po dang nag po mi 'dra ba'i rten cing 'brel par 'byung ba gsal bar mdzad de | ji lta ji ltar bcom ldan 'das kyis bdag la chos bstan pa bla na med pa | gong na med pa | gya nom pa | ches gya nom pa | dman pa dang khyad par du 'phags pa'i chos dkar po dang nag po mi 'dra ba'i rten cing 'brel par 'byung ba rgyas par gsal bar mdzad pa de lta de ltar bdag la chos gcig mngon par yongs su shes pa dang | chos gcig spangs pa mngon par shes pa dang | chos gcig mngon sum du bya ba mngon par shes pa dang | chos gcig bsgom pa mngon par shes pa dang | chos rnams la rtogs pa nye bar 'gro ba dang | ston pa la rab tu dang bar gyur cing yang dag par rdzogs pa'i sangs rgyas bcom ldan 'das la rtag tu ngo mtshar bar yang shes so ||

Mahāparinibbāna-sutta[955]
~16.1.1~
DN II 81.28–82.6 (*Mahāparinibbāna-sutta*, DN 16.15–16)
15. atha kho bhagavā ambalaṭṭhikāyaṃ yathābhirantaṃ viharitvā āyasmantaṃ

955. See also *Nālanda-sutta*, SN 47.12, SN V 159.1–161.17 for a similar parallel.

ānandaṃ āmantesi: āyām ānanda yena nāḷandā ten' upasaṃkamissāmāti. evaṃ bhante ti kho āyasmā ānando bhagavato paccassosi. atha kho bhagavā mahatā bhikkhu-saṃghena saddhiṃ yena nāḷandā tad avasari. tatra sudaṃ bhagavā nāḷandāyaṃ viharati pāvārikambavane.

16. atha kho āyasmā sāriputto yena bhagavā ten' upasaṃkami, upasaṃkamitvā bhagavantaṃ abhivādetvā ekamantaṃ nisīdi. ekamantaṃ nisinno kho āyasmā sāriputto bhagavantaṃ etad avoca: evaṃ-pasanno ahaṃ bhante bhagavati na cāhu na ca bhavissati na c' etarahi vijjati añño samaṇo vā brāhmaṇo vā bhagavatā bhiyyo 'bhiññataro yadidaṃ sambodhiyan' ti.

~16.1.2~

DN II 82.7–17 (*Mahāparinibbāna-sutta*, DN 16.16)

[a] uḷārā kho te ayaṃ sāriputta āsabhī vācā bhāsitā, ekaṃso gahito sīha-nādo nadito: evaṃ-pasanno ahaṃ bhante bhagavati na cāhu na ca bhavissati na c' etarahi vijjati añño samaṇo vā brāhmaṇo vā bhagavatā bhiyyo 'bhiññataro yadidaṃ sambodhiyan ti. kin nu sāriputta ye te ahesuṃ atītam addhānaṃ arahanto sammāsambuddhā, sabbe te bhagavanto cetasā ceto paricca viditā evaṃ-sīlā te bhagavanto ahesuṃ iti pi, evaṃdhammā evaṃ-paññā evaṃ-vihārī evaṃ-vimuttā te bhagavanto ahesuṃ iti pīti?

[b] no h' etaṃ bhante.

~16.1.3~

DN II 82.25–29 (*Mahāparinibbāna-sutta*, DN 16.16)

[a] kiṃ pana sāriputta ahaṃ te etarahi arahaṃ sammāsambuddho cetasā ceto paricca vidito evaṃ-sīlo bhagavā iti pi, evaṃ-dhammo evaṃ-pañño evaṃ-vihārī evaṃvimutto bhagavā iti pīti?

[b] no h' etaṃ bhante.

~16.1.4~

DN II 82.25–29 (*Mahāparinibbāna-sutta*, DN 16.16)

[a] kiṃ pana sāriputta ahaṃ te etarahi arahaṃ sammāsambuddho cetasā ceto paricca vidito evaṃ-sīlo bhagavā iti pi, evaṃ-dhammo evaṃ-pañño evaṃ-vihārī evaṃvimutto bhagavā iti pīti?

[b] no h' etaṃ bhante.

~16.1.5~

DN II 82.30–83.5 (*Mahāparinibbāna-sutta*, DN 16.16)

[a] etth' eva hi te sāriputta atītānāgata-paccuppannesu arahantesu sammā-sambuddhesu ceto-pariya-ñāṇaṃ n' atthi. atha kiñ carahi te ayaṃ sāriputta uḷārā āsabhī vācā bhāsitā ekaṃso gahito sīha-nādo nadito, evaṃ-pasanno ahaṃ bhante bhagavati na cāhu na ca bhavissati na c' etarahi vijjati añño samaṇo vā brāhmaṇo vā bhagavatā bhiyyo 'bhiññataro yadidaṃ sambodhiyan ti?

DN II 83.6-8 (*Mahāparinibbāna-sutta*, DN 16.17)

[b] 17. na kho me bhante atītānāgata-paccuppannesu arahantesu sammā-sambuddhesu ceto-pariya-ñāṇaṃ atthi.

Nà luó jiāntuó (那羅犍陀)[956]

~16.1.1~

T II 130c7–11

如是我聞。一時佛住那羅揵陀賣衣者菴羅園。爾時。舍利弗詣世尊所。稽首禮足退坐一面。白佛言。世尊。我深信世尊。過去當來今現在諸沙門婆羅門所有智慧。無有與世尊菩提等者。況復過上。

~16.1.2~

T II 130c11–16

[a]佛告舍利弗。善哉善哉。舍利弗。善哉所說。第一之說。能於衆中作師子吼。自言深信世尊。言過去當來今現在沙門婆羅門所有智慧。無有與佛菩提等者。況復過上。佛問舍利弗。汝能審知過去三藐三佛陀所有增上戒。舍利弗白佛言。不知。世尊復問舍利弗。知如是法如是慧如是明如是解脫如是住不。

T II 130c18–19

[b] 舍利弗白佛言。不知。

~16.1.3~

T II 130c19–21

[a] 佛告舍利弗。汝復知未來三藐三佛陀所有增上戒。如是法如 是慧如是明如是解脫如是住不。

T II 130c21–22

[b] 舍利弗白佛言。不知。

956. *Zá āhán jīng* (雜阿含經) (Chinese SĀ) 498, T II 130c7–131a24 (T 99.498).

~16.1.4~

T II 130c22–24

[a] 佛告舍利弗。汝復能知今現在佛所有增上戒。如是法如是慧如是明如是解脱如是住不。

T II 130c21–22

[b] 舍利弗白佛言。不知世尊。

~16.1.5~

T II 130c25–29

[a]知世尊佛告舍利弗。汝若不知過去未來今現在諸佛世尊心中所有諸法。云何如是讚歎。於大衆中作師子吼。説言。我深信世尊。過去當來諸沙門婆羅門所有智慧。無有與世尊菩提等者。況復過上。

T II 130c29–131a07

[b]舍者弗白佛言。世尊。我不能知過去當來今現在諸佛世尊心之分齊。然我能知諸佛世尊法之分齊。我聞世尊説法。轉轉深。轉轉勝。轉轉上。轉轉妙。我聞世尊説法知一法即斷一法。知一法。即證一法。知一法即修習一法。究竟於法。於大師所。得淨信。心得淨。世尊。是等正覺世尊。

Perfect Awakening (DĀ 16.2)

DĀ 16.2.1

[**a**] sace<t> tvā śāriputra kaścid upasaṃkramyaivaṃ pṛcched abhūvan[957] bho śāriputrātīte 'dhvany e<ke>[958] śramaṇabrāhmaṇā (**291r5**) ye śramaṇasya gautamasyāntikād bhūyo 'bhijñatarā[959] yad uta saṃbodhaya iti <|> evaṃ (p)ṛṣṭas tvaṃ śāriputra kiṃ v<y>ākuryāḥ[960] <|>

[**b**] sacen mā bhadanta kaścid upasa(ṃkramyaivaṃ pṛcchet ta)syāhaṃ (p)ṛṣṭo[961] (**291r6**) neti[962] vyākuryāṃ;

DĀ 16.2.2

[**a**] sace<t> tvā śāriputra kaścid upasaṃkramyaivaṃ pṛcched bhavi(ṣ)y(an)-ti (n)u bhoḥ śāriputrānāgate[963] 'dhvany eke śramaṇa(br)āh(ma)ṇ(ā) ye (śrama)ṇ(asya) gautama(s)y(ān)ti(kād bhū)yo[964] (**291r7**) 'bhijñatarā yad uta saṃbodhaya[965] iti | evaṃ pṛṣṭas tvaṃ śāri(pu)tra[966] kiṃ vyākuryāḥ <|>

957. Ms. reads *abhūvad.*

958. Ms. reads *dhvanya.* Cf. 291r6.

959. Ms. reads *bhijñatara.*

960. Cf. 291r5, 291r7, 291v1, 291v2, 291v4, 291v6, and 291v7.

961. Cf. 291r7, 291v1, 291v4, and 291v6.

962. This negative answer by Śāriputra (seen throughout this section) was immortalized by Mātṛceta in his *Varṇārhavarṇastotra* where he praises Śāriputra (see VAV(UH) 1.16 and 1.17). This may also be a reference to the *neti neti* (not this, not that) found in Upaniṣad literature, suggesting the possibility of a transmission of this work within communities familiar with the Indian philosophical milieu of the era. Further such evidence is seen in DĀ 15.16 where the Buddha discusses his time studying with his old teacher, Udraka Rāmaputra.

963. Ms. reads *śāriputr{{ā}} rājate.*

964. Cf. 290v8, 291r5, 291r8, 291v4, and 291v5 as well as DN III 113.29: *kim pan' āvuso sāriputya bhavissanti anāgatam addhānam aññe samaṇā vā brāhmaṇā vā bhagavatā bhiyyo 'bhiññatarā sambodhiyan ti.*

965. Ms. reads *saṃbodhāya.*

966. Cf. 291r6, 291r8, 291v2, 291v4, 291v6, and 291v7.

[**b**] sacen mā bhadanta kaścid[967] upasaṃkramyaivaṃ pṛcche<t> tasyāhaṃ pṛṣṭo neti (v)y(āk)u(ryāṃ)[968] <|>

DĀ 16.2.3

[**a**] (sacet tvā śariputra kaścid upasaṃkra)(**291r8**)myaivaṃ[969] pṛcche{t*}d[970] asti nu bhoḥ śāriputra kaścid[971] etarhi pratyutpanne śramaṇo <vā> brāhmaṇo vā yaḥ śramaṇasya gautamasyāntikād bhūyo 'bhijñataro yad uta saṃbodha(ya iti | evaṃ pṛṣṭas tvaṃ śāri)(**291v1**)putra[972] kiṃ vyākuryā<ḥ |>

[**b**] sacen mā bhadanta kaścid[973] upasaṃkramyaivaṃ pṛcche<t> tasyāhaṃ pṛṣṭo neti vyākuryāṃ;

DĀ 16.2.4

[**a**] sace<t> tvā śāriputra kaścid[974] upasaṃkramyaivaṃ pṛcched abhūva(ṃ) bho (śāriputrātīte 'dhvany eke śra)(**291v2**)maṇabrāhmaṇā[975] ye samasamā[976] śramaṇena gautamena yad (u)ta[977] saṃbodhaya[978] iti <|> evaṃ pṛṣṭas tvaṃ śāriputra {vaṃ} kiṃ vyāku(r)y(āḥ)[979] <|>

967. Ms. reads *ka[c]cid.*

968. Cf. 291v1, 291v4, and 291v6.

969. Cf. 291r5, 291r6, 291v1, 291v3, 291v5, and 291v7.

970. Ms. reads *pṛcchat*d.*

971. Ms. reads *kaccid.*

972. Cf. 291r5, 291r7, 291v2, 291v4, 291v6, and 291v7.

973. Ms. reads *kaccid.*

974. Ms. reads *kaccid.*

975. Cf. 291r4.

976. Ms. reads *mama saha.* Cf. 291v5; DN III 114.7, 10, and 13; as well as Abhidh-k-bh(P) 184.23–24: *asti kaścid etarhi śramaṇo vā brāhmaṇo vā samasamaḥ śramaṇena gautamena yadutābhisaṃbodhāya.*

977. Cf. 291r5, 291r7, 291r8, and 291v4.

978. Ms. reads *saṃbodhāya.* Cf. 290v8, 291r5, 291r8, 291v4, and 291v5.

979. Cf. 291r5, 291r7, 291v1, 291v4, 291v6, and 291v7.

[**b**] s(a)c(e)n mā[980] bhadanta ka(śc)id[981] (upasaṃkramyaivaṃ pṛcchet tasyāhaṃ pṛṣṭa)[982] (**291v3**) om iti vyākuryāṃ;

DĀ 16.2.5

[**a**] sace<t> tvā śāriputra kaścid upasaṃkramyaivaṃ pṛcched bhavi(ṣ)ya<n>ti[983] nu bhoḥ śāriputra anāgate 'dhvany eke śram(aṇabrāhmaṇā ye samasamā) śr(amaṇena gau)(**291v4**)t(a)m(e)na[984] yad uta saṃbodhaya iti <|> evaṃ pṛṣṭas tvaṃ śāriputra kiṃ vyākuryāḥ <|>

[**b**] sacen mā bhadanta kaścid upasaṃkramyaivaṃ pṛcchet tasyāhaṃ pṛṣṭa om iti vyākuryā(ṃ)[985] <|>

DĀ 16.2.6

[**a**] (sacet tvā śāriputra)[986] kaści(**291v5**)d upasaṃkramyaivaṃ pṛcched asti nu bhoḥ śāriputra kaścid etarhi pratyutpanne 'dhvani śramaṇo vā brāhmaṇo vā yas samasamaḥ śramaṇena gau(tamena yad uta)[987] saṃbodhaya i(**291v6**)ti <|> evaṃ pṛṣṭas tvaṃ śāriputra kiṃ vyākuryā<ḥ |>

[**b**] sacen mā bhadanta kaścid upasaṃkramyaivaṃ pṛcchet tasyāhaṃ pṛṣṭo neti vyākuryāṃ;

980. Ms. reads *s. c. tv[ā]* where the scribe apparently repeated the beginning of the previous section: *sace<t> tvā śāriputra*, but the mistake was partially corrected, as Śāriputra's name is erroneously written and then deleted twice in this section. Cf. 291r5, 291r7, 291v1, 291v4, 291v6, and 291v7.

981. Cf. 291r5, 291r7, 291v1, 291v4, 291v6, and 291v8.

982. Cf. 291v4.

983. Cf. 291r6 and DN III 114.8.

984. Cf. 291v2 and Abhidh-k-bh(P) 184.25–185.1: *sa cen* [sic] *māṃ bhadanta kaścid upasaṃkramyāivaṃ pṛcchet tasyāhaṃ pṛṣṭa evaṃ vyākuryāṃ, nāsti kaścid etarhi śramaṇo vā brāhmaṇo vā samasamo bhagavatā yad utābhisaṃbodhāya.*

985. Cf. 291r6, 291v1, 291v3, and 291v6.

986. Cf. 291r4, 291r6, 291v1, 291v3, and 291v6.

987. Cf. 291r5, 291r7, 291r8, 291v2, and 291v4 as well as Abhidh-k-bh(P) 184.25–185.1: *sa cen [sic] māṃ bhadanta kaścid upasaṃkramyāivaṃ pṛcchet tasyāhaṃ pṛṣṭa evaṃ vyākuryāṃ, nāsti kaścid etarhi śramaṇo vā brāhmaṇo vā samasamo bhagavatā yad utābhisaṃbodhāya.*

DĀ 16.2.7

[a] sace<t> tvāṃ[988] śāriputra kaś(c)id upasaṃkramy(ai)vaṃ[989] pṛcchet ka(**291v7**)smā<t> tvaṃ bhoḥ śāriputrātītānāgatapratyutpannāṃ śramaṇa{brāhmaṇā}brāhmaṇān[990] ekān abhyanumoda(se)[991] ekāṃ nābhya(n)umoda<se>[992] iti <|> evaṃ pṛṣṭas tvaṃ śāriputra kiṃ vyāku(ry)āḥ[993] <|>

[**b**] sacen mā bhada(**291v8**)nta kaścid upasaṃkramyaivaṃ pṛcchet tasyāhaṃ pṛṣṭa evaṃ vyākuryā<m>[994] abhūvan[995] bhadantātīte[996] 'dhvany eke śramaṇabrāhmaṇāḥ y(e)[997] samasamā[998] bhagavatā yad uta saṃbodhaya <i>ti[999] <|> bhaviṣya<n>ty anā(ga)te[1000] 'dhvany eke śra(**292r1**)maṇabrāhmaṇā ye samasamā[1001] bhagavatā saṃbodhaya iti • saṃmukhaṃ me bha-danta bhagavato 'ntikāc chrutaṃ saṃmukham udgṛhītaṃ asthānam anava(k)āśo yad apūrvācaramau dvau tathāgatāv arha(**292r2**)ntau samyaksaṃbuddhau loka utpadyate <| n>edaṃ[1002] sthānaṃ vidyate • sthānam etad vidyate yad eka<ḥ |> etad ānuttaryaṃ bhadanta bhagavato[1003] yad uta saṃbodhaye <|> tad bhagavān aśeṣam abhijānāti <|> tat te 'śeṣam a(**292r3**)(bhi)jā(na)ta{ḥ} uttare[1004] 'bhijñeyaṃ nāsti yasyābhijñānād

988. Ms. reads *sace tvaṃ*. Note how all other instances in these passages read *sace tvā* (emended to *sacet tvā* in reconstruction).

989. Cf. 291r5, 291r6, 291r7, 291v1, 291v3, 291v4, 291v5, 291v6, 291v7, and 291v8.

990. Dittography.

991. Ms. reads *anyanumoda*.

992. Ms. reads *nānya .umoda*.

993. Cf. 291r5, 291r7, 291v1, 291v2, 291v4, and 291v6.

994. Cf. 291r6, 291v1, 291v3, and 291v6.

995. Ms. reads *abhū[t]ad*.

996. Ms. reads *bhadantotīte*.

997. Cf. 291v2.

998. Ms. reads *mama sa[m]ā*.

999. Ms. reads *saṃbodhāyeti*.

1000. Cf. DN III 114.21–22: *bhavissanti anāgataṃ*.

1001. Ms. reads *mama samā*. Cf. 291v5 and DN III 114.21–23: *bhavissanti anāgataṃ addhānaṃ arahanto sammā-sambuddhā mayā samasamā sambodhiyan ti*.

1002. Ms. reads *evaṃ*. Cf. DN III 114.27: *n' etaṃ ṭhanaṃ vijjatī ti*.

1003. Ms. reads *bhagavataḥ*.

1004. Ms. reads *[utt]aro*.

anyaḥ śramaṇo{na} vā brāhmaṇo{na}[1005] vā bhagavato 'ntikād bhūyo 'bhijñatara<ḥ> syād yad uta saṃbodhaye <|>

DĀ 16.2.1

[**a**] [Buddha:] "Śāriputra, if someone having approached you were to question you in this way, 'Hey, Śāriputra, were there in former times any ascetics or brahmins more knowledgeable than the ascetic Gautama in regard to perfect awakening?' Questioned thus, Śāriputra, how would you respond?"

[**b**] [Śāriputra:] "Sir, if someone having approached me (were to question) me in this way, questioned, I would respond to him, 'No.'"

DĀ 16.2.2

[**a**] [Buddha:] "Śāriputra, if someone having approached you were to question you in this way, 'Hey, Śāriputra, now then, will there be in the future any ascetics or brahmins more knowledgeable than the ascetic Gautama in regard to perfect awakening?' Questioned thus, Śāriputra, how would you respond?"

[**b**] [Śāriputra:] "Sir, if someone having approached me were to question me in this way, questioned, I would respond to him, 'No.'"

DĀ 16.2.3

[**a**] [Buddha:] "(Śāriputra, if someone) having approached you were to question you in this way, 'Hey, Śāriputra, then is there now in the present an ascetic or brahmin more knowledgeable than the ascetic Gautama in regard to perfect awakening?' (Questioned thus), Śāriputra, how would you respond?"

[**b**] [Śāriputra:] "Sir, if someone having approached me were to question me in this way, questioned, I would respond to him, 'No.'"

1005. Ms reads *śramaṇena vā brāhmaṇena*. This formula: *etad ānuttaryaṃ bhadanta ... syād yad uta saṃbodhaye* (with the appropriate topic for each respective section), ends sections DĀ 16.2–16.17. Cf. 292r2–3, 292r6–8, 292v2–3, 292v5–7, 292v8–293r1, 293v3–4, 293v6–7, 294r4–6, 295r3–4, 295r7–v1, 296r2–3, 296v8–297r2, 297v3–4, 297v8–298r2, 298r7–8, and 298v2–3.

DĀ 16.2.4

[**a**] [Buddha:] "Śāriputra, if someone having approached you were to question you in this way, 'Hey, (Śāriputra, were there in former times any) ascetics or brahmins who were equal to the ascetic Gautama in regard to perfect awakening?' Questioned thus, Śāriputra, how would you respond?"

[**b**] [Śāriputra] "Sir, if someone (having approached me were to question me in this way, questioned, I) would respond to him, 'Yes.'"

DĀ 16.2.5

[Buddha:] "Śāriputra, if someone having approached you were to question you in this way, 'Hey, Śāriputra, now then, will there be in the future any ascetics or brahmins (who are equal) to the ascetic Gautama in regard to perfect awakening?' Questioned thus, Śāriputra, how would you respond?"

[**b**] [Śāriputra] "Sir, if someone having approached me were to question me in this way, questioned, I would respond to him, 'Yes.'"

DĀ 16.2.6

[**a**] [Buddha:] "(Śāriputra, if) someone having approached (you) were to question you in this way, 'Hey, Śāriputra, then is there now in the present an ascetic or brahmin equal to the ascetic Gautama in regard to perfect awakening?' Questioned thus, Śāriputra, how would you respond?"

[**b**] [Śāriputra:] "Sir, if someone having approached me were to question me in this way, questioned, I would respond to him, 'No.'"

DĀ 16.2.7

[**a**] [Buddha:] "Śāriputra, if someone having approached you were to question you in this way, 'Hey, Śāriputra, why do you approve of some past, future, and present ascetics and brahmins and disapprove of others?' Questioned thus, Śāriputra, how would you respond?"

[**b**] [Śāriputra:] "Sir, if someone having approached me were to question me in this way, questioned, I would respond to him in this way: 'There were, sir, in former times ascetics and brahmins equal to the Blessed One in regard to perfect awakening. There will be in the future ascetics and brahmins equal to the Blessed One in regard to perfect awakening. In his presence, sir, I

have heard from the Blessed One and taken from him that it is impossible for two tathāgatas, arhats, two complete, perfect buddhas to arise simultaneously in the world.[1006] This possibility cannot exist. It is [only] possible that there is one. Sir, this is the supremacy of the Blessed One regarding perfect awakening. The Blessed One knows this in its entirety. For you, knowing this in its entirety, there is nothing further to be known from the knowledge of which another ascetic or brahmin could be more knowledgeable than the Blessed One in regard to perfect awakening.'"

~16.2~

BLSF III.1 Or.15007/548 (*Prasādanīya-sūtra*)

recto

a[1007] [t]v(aṃ) [ś](ā)[r](i)pu(t)[r]. + ///
b[1008] cched bhavi[ś](ya)ṃ + ///
c vyāku[ry](ā)[ḥ] + + ///
d[1009] kaśc[i]d etarhi [pr]. ///
e[1010] pṣṛṭas [sic][1011] tvaṃ śāri[pu] ///
f[1012] saṃkra[m](y)[ai](va)[ṃ] + ///
g[1013] (k)iṃ [v](yā) + + + + ///

verso

a[1014] [nāg]. + + + + ///
b[1015] kaścid u .. + + ///
c[1016] ṇo vā brāhma .. ///
d[1017] danta kaścid u .. ///
e[1018] gata[prat]. + + ///
f[1019] pasaṃ[k]r. + + + ///
g(v)i[ṣ](ya)ṃ[ty] (a)[nā] + + ///

1006. This statement is the *locus classicus* of the normative understanding of the impossibility of more than one buddha existing in a *lokadhātu* simultaneously at any given time.

1007. DĀ 16.2.1a.

1008. DĀ 16.2.2a.

1009. DĀ 16.2.3a.

1010. DĀ 16.2.7a.

1011. The ms., which is available online, reads *pṛṣṭas* as one would expect.

1012. DĀ 16.2.3b.

1013. DĀ 16.2.4a.

1014. DĀ 16.2.5a.

1015. DĀ 16.2.5b.

1016. DĀ 16.2.6a.

1017. DĀ 16.2.6b.

1018. DĀ 16.2.7a.

1019. DĀ 16.2.7b.

BLSF III.1 Or.15007/235 (*Prasādanīya-sūtra*)

recto	*verso*
a /// .. [ṣ]. .. + + + ///	a /// + + .. [m]. + + + ///
b[1020] /// .. kaścid et(ar)[h](i) ///	
c[1021] /// + kramyaivaṃ pṛ .[e] ///	
d /// dasi • eka[ty]. + ///	
e[1022] /// .. samasa[mā] + ///	
f /// + .ā ..ṃ + + + ///	

~16.2.1~

T I 18 255b18–20

[a] 佛告舍利弗。汝今往問餘人。過去世中。可有沙門婆羅門而能了知眞實通力等過佛者。乃至成佛菩提。汝當往問彼作何答

T I 18 255c01

[b] 爾時舍利弗白佛言。世尊。是義不然。[1023]

~16.2.5~[1024]

T I 18 255b21–23[1025]

[a] 復次舍利弗。汝復往彼問於餘人。未來世中可有沙門婆羅門與佛等者。乃至成佛菩提。汝當往問。彼作何答

~16.2.6~

T I 18 255b24–26

[a]復次舍利弗。汝可往彼復問於餘人。現在世中可有沙門婆羅門與佛等者。乃至成佛菩提

1020. DĀ 16.2.6a.

1021. DĀ 16.2.6b.

1022. DĀ 16.2.7b.

1023. This answer only comes after all the questions equivalent to DĀ 16.2.1a, 5a, 6a, and 7a. Note that this negative does not not apply to 5a.

1024. DĀ 16.2.2–16.2.4 are not present.

1025. Only DĀ 16.2.5a is present here. The positive answer in DĀ 16.2.5b is missing.

~16.2.7~

T I 18 255b27–29

[a]復次舍利弗。又復往彼問於餘人。所有過去未來現在世中。沙門婆羅門等歸依何人。汝當往問。彼作何答

T I 18 255c1–6

[b]我從佛聞。記念受持。無有二佛並出於世。唯佛世尊是眞正等正覺。是正遍知者。具足最上神通之力。世尊。我不見有沙門婆羅門而能知此通力。況復過於佛者。乃至成佛菩提

~16.2.1~

DN III 113.25–114.4 (DN 28.20)[1026]

sace maṃ bhante evaṃ puccheyya—kin nu kho āvuso sāriputta, ahesuṃ atītam addhānaṃ aññe samaṇā vā brāhmaṇā vā bhagavatā bhiyyo 'bhiññatarā sambodhiyan ti? evaṃ puṭṭho ahaṃ bhante no ti vadeyyaṃ.

~16.2.2~

DN III 113.28–114.1 (DN 28.20)

[a] kim pan' āvuso sāriputta bhavissanti anāgatam addhānaṃ aññe samaṇā vā brāhmaṇā vā bhagavatā bhiyyo 'bhiññatarā sambodhiyan ti?

[b]evaṃ puṭṭho ahaṃ bhante no ti vadeyyaṃ.

~16.2.3~

DN III 114.1–4 (DN 28.20)

[a] kim pan' āvuso sāriputta, atth' etarahi añño samaṇo vā brāhmaṇo vā bhagavatā bhiyyo 'bhiññataro sambodhiyan ti?

[b]evaṃ puṭṭho ahaṃ bhante no ti vadeyyaṃ.

1026. There are numeration discrepancies between the PTS numbering for the edition of the *Sampasādanīya-sutta* and the translations by Rhys Davids & Rhys Davids and Walshe. In both translations this section is numbered 28.19. However, the number in the 2006 printing of the PTS edition is 28.20. The problem seems to be with infelicities appearing in the various printings of the PTS edition. For example, in the 1992 printing there is no section 19 at all. I follow the numbering used by the most recent printing (2016) of the PTS edition. These discrepancies should be noted by those who wish to examine the translations from Pali.

~16.2.4~
DN III 114.4–8 (DN 28.20)
[a] sace pana maṃ bhante evaṃ puccheyya—kin nu kho āvuso sāriputta ahesuṃ atītam addhānaṃ añ̃ñe samaṇā vā brāhmaṇā vā bhagavatā samasamā sambodhiyan ti?

[b] evaṃ puṭṭho ahaṃ bhante evan ti vadeyyaṃ.

~16.2.5~
DN III 114.8–11 (DN 28.20)
[a] kim pan' āvuso sāriputta, bhavissanti anāgatam addhānaṃ añ̃ñe samaṇā vā brāhmaṇa vā bhagavatā samasamā sambodhiyan ti?

[b] evaṃ puṭṭho ahaṃ bhante evan ti vadeyyaṃ.

~16.2.6~
DN III 114.11–14 (DN 28.20)
[a] pan' āvuso sāriputta atth' etarahi añ̃ño samaṇo vā brāhmaṇo bhagavatā samasamo sambodhiyan ti?

[b] evaṃ puṭṭho ahaṃ bhante no ti vadeyyaṃ.

~16.2.7~
DN III 114.14–115.9 (DN 28.20)
[a] sace pana maṃ bhante evaṃ puccheyya—kasmā pan' āyasmā sāriputto ekaccaṃ abbhanujānāti ekaccaṃ nābbhanujānātīti?

[b] evaṃ puṭṭho ahaṃ bhante evaṃ vyākareyyaṃ—sammukhā me taṃ āvuso bhagavato sutaṃ, sammukhā paṭiggahītaṃ: ahesuṃ atītam addhānaṃ arahanto sammā-sambuddhā mayā samasamā sambodhiyan ti. sammukhā me taṃ āvuso bhagavato sutaṃ, sammukhā paṭiggahītaṃ: bhavissanti anāgataṃ addhānaṃ arahanto sammā-sambuddhā mayā samasamā sambodhiyan ti. sammukhā me taṃ āvuso bhagavato sutaṃ, sammukhā paṭiggahītaṃ: aṭṭhānam etaṃ anavakāso yaṃ ekissā loka-dhātuyā dve arahanto sammā-sambuddhā apubbaṃ acarimaṃ uppajjeyyuṃ. n' etaṃ ṭhānaṃ vijjatī ti. kaccāhaṃ bhante evaṃ puṭṭho evaṃ vyākaramāno vuttavādī c' eva bhagavato homi, na ca bhagavantaṃ abhūtena abbhācikkhāmi, dhammassa cānudhammaṃ vyākaromi, na ca koci sahadhammiko vādānuvādo gārayhaṃ ṭhānaṃ āgacchatī ti.

taggha tvaṃ sāriputta evaṃ puṭṭho evaṃ vyākaramāno vutta-vādī c' eva mama hosi, na ca maṃ abhūtena abbhācikkhasi, dhammassa cānudhammaṃ vyākarosi, na ca koci sahadhammiko vādānuvādo gārayhaṃ ṭhānaṃ āgacchatī ti.

~16.2.4–6~[1027]

T I 1 78c19–28

佛告舍利弗。若有外道異學來問汝言。過去沙門婆羅門。與沙門瞿曇等不。汝當云何答。彼復問言。未來沙門婆羅門。與沙門瞿曇等不。汝當云何答彼復問言。現在沙門婆羅門。與沙門瞿曇等不。汝當云何答。時舍利弗白佛言。設有是問過去沙門婆羅門與佛等不。當答言有。設問未來沙門婆羅門瞿曇等不。當答言有。設問現在沙門婆羅門與佛等不。當答言無。

~16.2.7~

T I 1 78c28–29

[a]佛告舍利弗。彼外道梵志或復問言。汝何故或言有或言無。汝當云何答。

T I 1 78c29–79a8

[b]舍利弗言。我當報彼。過去三耶三佛與如來等。未來三耶三佛與如來等。我躬從佛聞。欲使現在有三耶三佛與如來等者。無有是處。欲使現在有三耶三佛與如來等者。無有是處。

世尊。我如所聞依法順法作如是答。將無答耶。佛言如是答依法順法不違也。所以然者。過去三耶三佛與我等。未來三耶三佛與我等。欲使現在有二佛出世。無有是處。

Cf. T I 1 76c26–28

世尊智慧無餘。神通無餘。諸世間所有沙門婆羅門。無有能與如來等者。況欲出其上。

~16.2.7~

Abhidh-k-bh(P) 184.16–185.2 (quoting the *Prasādanīya-sūtra*)[1028]

na ca dvau saha buddhavat |

1027. There are no parallels for DĀ 16.2.1–4 here.

1028. This is without doubt a quotation from the *Prasādanīya-sūtra*, and yet, in his *Upāyikā* to the *Abhidh-k-bh*, Śamathadeva (possibly erroneously) states a different name for the sūtra being quoted when discussing the context of the quotation. Abhidh-k-ṭ Ju188b3–4; Tu215b2: *khams mang po ba'i mdo las ji skad bshad pa lta bu ste | gang snga phyi med par de bzhin gshegs pa dgra bcom pa yang dag par*. Later he states that this is the seventh sūtra of the *Dīrghāgama*: Abhidh-k-ṭ Ju188b5; Tu215b4. It is unclear why Śamathadeva makes

[b] sūtra uktam asthānam anavakāśo yad apūrvācaramau dvau tathāgatāv arhantau samyaksaṃbuddhau loka utpadyeyātāṃ nedaṃ sthānaṃ vidyate, sthānam etad vidyate yadaikas [sic] tathāgataḥ | yathā tathāgata evaṃ cakravartināv iti | idam atra saṃpradhāryam | kim atra trisāhasramahāsāhasro lokadhātur loka iṣṭa utāho sarvalokadhātava iti | nānyatra buddhā utpadyante ity eke | kiṃ kāraṇam | mā bhūt bhagavataḥ śaktivyāghātaḥ iti | eka eva hi bhagavān sarvatra śaktaḥ | yatra buddha eko na śaktaḥ syād vineyān vinetuṃ tatrānyo 'pi na śakta iti |

[a] uktaṃ ca sūtre sa cet [sic] tvāṃ śāriputra kaścid upasaṃkramyaivaṃ pṛcchet, asti kaścid etarhi śramaṇo vā brāhmaṇo vā samasamaḥ śramaṇena gautamena yad utābhisaṃbodhāya | evaṃ ca pṛṣṭaḥ kiṃ vyākuryāḥ |

[b] sa cen [sic] māṃ bhadanta kaścid upasaṃkramyaivaṃ pṛcchet tasyāhaṃ pṛṣṭa evaṃ vyākuryāṃ, nāsti kaścid etarhi śramaṇo vā brāhmaṇo vā samasamo [185] bhagavatā yad utābhisaṃbodhāya | tat kasya hetoḥ | saṃmukhaṃ me bhagavato 'ntkāc chrutaṃ saṃmukham udgṛhītaṃ asthānam anavakāśo yad apūrvācaramau tathāgatau loka utpadyeyātāṃ nedaṃ sthānaṃ vidyata iti |

~16.2~

Abhidh-k-ṭ Derge Ju4a6–5a5 (Derge no. 4094); Peking Tu4b7–5b8 (Peking no. P5595) (quoting the *Prasādanīya-sūtra*)[1029]

~16.2.1~

Derge Ju4a6–7 (cf. Peking Tu4b7–8)

[a] shā ri'i bu khyod kyi drung du kha cig nye bar 'ongs te 'di lta bu'i dri ba 'byung ste | 'das pa'i dus na dge sbyong ngam bram ze dge sbyong gau ta ma las khyad par du 'phags pa byung ngam | 'di lta ste | rdzogs par byung chub pa la'o zhes khyod la 'di ltar 'dri ba de la ji ltar lan gdab par bya |

---

attribution with a seemingly incorrect name for the sūtra and its place within the *Dīrghāgama*. This may be due to some problem that arose when the *Upāyikā* was translated from Sanskrit to Tibetan. It may also be that Śamathadeva made use of a different transmission of the *Dīrghāgama* than the one that produced this *Dīrghāgama* manuscript. Or, even if he made use of the same transmission, he may have used an earlier classification of the sūtra order within the *Dīrghāgama* that later changed. See also DiSimone 2018, 143, and DĀ(U.H.), 242 for further discussion.

1029. See note 954 above.

Derge Ju4a7(cf. Peking Tu4b8–5a1)
[b] btsun pa bdag gi drung du kha cig nye bar 'ongs te de ltar 'dri ba de la bdag gis med do zhes lan gdab par bya'o ||

~16.2.2~
Derge Ju4a7–4b1(cf. Peking Tu5a1–2)
[a] shā ri'i bu khyod kyi drung du kha cig nye bar 'ongs te 'di skad du 'dri ste | ma 'ongs pa'i dus na gzhan dge sbyong ngam bram ze dge sbyong gau ta ma[1030] las ches khyad par du 'phags pa 'byung bar 'gyur ram | 'di lta ste | rdzogs par byang chub pa la'o zhes 'di skad du 'dri na | shā ri'i bu ji ltar lan 'debs |

Derge Ju4b1–2 (cf. Peking Tu5a2)
[b] btsun pa bdag gi drung du kha cig nye bar 'ongs te 'di ltar 'dri na 'dri ba de la med do zhes lan gdab par bgyi'o ||

~16.2.3~
Derge Ju4b2–3 (cf. Peking Tu5a3–4)
[a] shā ri'i bu khyod kyi drung du kha cig nye bar 'ongs te 'di skad du 'dri ste | shā ri'i bu da ltar byung ba'i dus na dge sbyong ngam bram ze gzhan kha cig dge sbyong gau ta ma las khyad par du 'phags pa yod dam | 'di lta ste | mngon par rdzogs par byang chub pa la'o zer na de ltar 'dri ba de la shā ri'i bu ji ltar lan 'debs |

Derge Ju4b3 (cf. Peking Tu5a4)
[b] btsun pa bdag gi drung du kha cig nye bar 'ongs te 'di ltar 'dri na 'dri ba de la med do[1031] zhes lan gdab par bgyi'o ||

~16.2.4~
Derge Ju4b3–4 (cf. Peking Tu5a4–6)
[a] shā ri'i bu khyod kyi drung du kha cig nye bar 'ongs nas 'di ltar 'dri ste | shā ri'i bu 'das pa'i dus na gzhan dge sbyong ngam bram ze dge sbyong gau ta ma dang 'di lta ste | mngon par byang chub pa la mnyam zhing mnyam pa yod dam zhes 'di ltar 'dri na | shā ri'i bu ji ltar lan gdab |

1030. Emended from Peking. Derge: *ga ta ma.*

1031. Emended from Peking. Derge: *med da.*

Derge Ju4b4 (cf. Peking Tu5a6)
[b] btsun pa kha cig bdag gi drung du nye bar 'ongs te 'dri na 'dri ba de la yod do zhes lan gdab par bgyi'o ||

~16.2.5~
Derge Ju4b4–5 (cf. Peking Tu5a6–7)
[a] shā ri'i bu khyod kyi drung du kha cig nye bar 'ongs te 'di ltar 'dri ste | shā ri'i bu ma 'ongs pa'i dus na gzhan dge sbyong ngam bram ze dge sbyong gau ta ma 'di lta ste | mngon par byang chub pa la mnyam zhing mnyam pa 'byung bar 'gyur ram zhes 'di ltar 'dri ba de la shā ri'i bu ji ltar lan gdab |

Derge Ju4b6 (cf. Peking Tu5a8)
[b] btsun pa bdag gi drung du kha cig nye bar 'ongs te 'di ltar 'dri na 'dri ba de la bdag gis yod do zhes lan gdab par bgyi'o ||

~16.2.6~
Derge Ju4b6–7 (cf. Peking Tu5a8–5b1)
[a] shā ri'i bu khyod kyi drung du kha cig nye bar 'ongs te 'di ltar 'dri ste | shā ri'i bu da ltar byung ba'i dus na dge sbyong ngam bram ze dge sbyong gau ta ma dang mngon par byang chub pa la mnyam zhing mnyam pa yod dam zhes 'di ltar 'dri na shā ri'i bu ji ltar lan gdab par bya |

Derge Ju4b7 (cf. Peking Tu5b1–2)
[b] btsun pa bdag gi drung du kha cig nye bar 'ongs te 'di ltar 'dri na 'dri ba de la bdag gis med do zhes lan gdab par bgyi'o ||

~16.2.7~
Derge Ju4b7–5a1 (cf. Peking Tu5b2–3)
[a] shā ri'i bu khyod kyi drung du kha cig || nye bar 'ongs shing 'di skad du 'dri ste shā ri'i bu 'das pa dang ma 'ongs pa dang da ltar byung ba'i dge sbyong dang bram ze kha cig rjes su yi rang la kha cig rjes su yi rang ba ma yin pa ci'i phyir zhes 'di ltar 'dri na | shā ri'i bu ji skad du lan gdab par bya |

Derge Ju5a1–5 (cf. Peking Tu5b3–8)
[b] btsun pa kha cig bdag gi drung du nye bar 'ongs te 'di ltar 'dri na 'dri ba de la bdag gis 'di ltar lan gdab par bya ste | 'das pa'i dus na dge sbyong ngam bram ze bcom ldan 'das dang mngon par byang chub pa la mnyam zhing mnyam par byung bar gyur to || ma 'ongs pa'i dus na gzhan dge sbyong dang

bram ze bcom ldan 'das dang mngon par byang chub pa la mnyam zhing mnyam par 'byung bar 'gyur ro || gnas ma yin zhing go skabs med de | de gang snga phyi med par de bzhin gshegs pa dgra bcom pa yang dag par rdzogs pa'i sangs rgyas gnyis 'jig rten du 'byung ba ni gnas ma yin zhing go skabs med la | gang gcig 'byung ba ni go skabs yod do zhes bcom ldan 'das las bdag gis mngon sum du thos shing mngon sum du 'byung ngo || btsun pa bcom ldan 'das bla na med pa 'di lta ste mngon par byang chub pa'o || de bcom ldan 'das kyis ma lus pa mngon par shes shing ma lus pa mngon par rab tu mkhyen nas | dge sbyong ngam bram ze bcom ldan 'das las 'di lta ste | mngon par byang chub pa zhes bya ba mngon par shes pa khyad par du 'phags pa dus phyis mngon par shes par bya ba mngon par shes pa gzhan med do ||

Classification of Wholesome Factors (DĀ 16.3)

DĀ 16.3

aparam api me[1032] bhadanta bha(**292r4**)gavata[1033] ānuttaryaṃ yadā me bhagavāṃ dharmaṃ deśayati yad uta[1034] kuśaladharmaprajñaptiṣu[1035] <|> iha bhadantaika<ḥ> śramaṇo vā brāhmaṇo vāraṇyagato vā (vṛkṣamūlagato v)ā śūnyāgāra(**292r5**)gato vā ātaptānvayāt prah(ā)ṇ(ā)nvayāt* bhāvanānvayād[1036] bahulīkārānvayāt[1037] samyaṅmanasikārānvayāt[1038] tadrūpaṃ śānta<ṃ> cetaḥsamādhi<ṃ>[1039] spṛśati yathā (samāhite cit)te[1040] anekavi(**292r6**)dhān pāpakā<n> akuśalā<n> dharmān abhinivarjya anekavidhān kuśalān dharmān samādāya varttate sākṣādbhavyatāyāṃ na ca pari(ta)syati <|> e(tad ānuttaryaṃ bhadanta bhagavato yad u)(**292r7**)ta kuśaladharmaprajñaptiṣu <|> tad bhagavān aśeṣam a(bh)i(jānāt)i <|> tat te 'śeṣam abhi<jā>nata[1041] uttare 'bhijñeyaṃ nāsti yasyābhijñā<nād a>nyaḥ śramaṇo

1032. Ms. reads *ye*.

1033. Ms. reads *bhagav[a]t[o]*.

1034. This formula: *aparam api me bhadanta ... deśayati yad uta* (and the topic of the respective section), begins sections DĀ 16.3–16.17. Cf. 292r3–4, 292r8, 292v3–4, 292v7, 293r1–2, 293v4–5, 293v7–8, 294r6, 295r4–5, 295v1, 296r3–4, 297r2, 297v4–5, 298r2, and 298v1.

1035. Ms. reads *kuśaladharmaprajñaptiṣṭhā*.

1036. Ms. reads *bhavanatvayād*.

1037. Ms. reads *bahulīkarātvayāt*.

1038. Ms. reads *samyaṅmanasikāratvayāt*.

1039. Ms. reads *[sa]māvi*.

1040. This phrase, *ekaḥ śramaṇo vā brāhmaṇo vā araṇyagato vā vṛkṣamūlagato vā śunyāgāragato vā ātaptānvayāt prahāṇānvayād bhāvanānvayād bahulīkarānvayāt samyaṅmanasikārānvayāt tadrūpaṃ śāntaṃ cetaḥsamādhiṃ spṛśati yathā samāhite citte*, occurs four times throughout the *Prasādanīya-sūtra* in 16.3, 16.13a, 16.13b, and 16.13c. Cf. 292r4–5, 296r4–5, 296r8–v1, and 296v4–5.

1041. Ms. reads *abhinati*.

vā brahma(ṇo vā bhagavato 'ntikād bhūyo 'bhijñataraḥ syā)**(292r8)**d[1042]
yad uta saṃbodha̱ya[1043] iti <|>

DĀ 16.3

[Śāriputra:] "'For me, sir, there is another way in which the Blessed One is supreme when he teaches me dharma, and that is regarding the classification of wholesome factors. In this case, sir, an ascetic or brahmin, or one who has gone to the wilderness, (or one who has gone to the foot of a tree), or one who has gone to a solitary place, due to concern with ardor, concern with effort, concern with cultivation, concern with intense practice, and concern with proper mental attention, he experiences such a kind of calm concentration of mind that when his mind (is settled), having cast away numerous evil, unwholesome factors and having taken up numerous wholesome factors, he abides in direct cultivation and will not be disturbed. (Sir), this (is the way in which the Blessed One is supreme), and that is regarding the classification of wholesome factors. The Blessed One knows this in its entirety. For you, knowing this in its entirety, there is nothing further to be known from the knowledge of which another ascetic or brahmin could (be more knowledgeable than the Blessed One) in regard to perfect awakening.'"

~16.3~

BLSF III.1 Or.15007/235 (*Prāsādanīya-sūtra*)
verso
b[1044] /// .. dā me bhag(a) + ///
c /// .. d bhāvanānva[y]. ///
d /// .. nekavidhāṃ ku .. ///
e /// .. aśeṣa[m] (a)[bh]i + ///

T I 18 255c7–15

爾時舍利弗復白佛言。我見世尊有種種最勝之法。最勝法者。謂佛世尊當說法時。所得善利。佛悉能知。若有沙門婆羅門等。住於山野樹下塚間。及在空舍。入三摩地。斷諸煩惱。修習圓滿。增益善法。正心記念。又彼沙門婆羅門等。斷諸惡法。而修善法。乃至證得果位。如是等法。佛悉能知。是即名爲佛最勝法。無有沙門婆羅門知此通力過於佛者。乃至成佛菩提

DN III 102 (DN 28.3)

1042. On the formula: *etad anuttaryaṃ bhadanta ...: syād yad uta saṃbodhaye*, see note 1005 above.

1043. Ms. reads *saṃbodhaya*.

1044. DĀ 16.3.

3. aparam pana bhante etad ānuttariyaṃ yathā bhagavā dhammaṃ deseti kusalesu dhammesu. tatr' ime kusalā dhammā seyyathidaṃ cattāro satipaṭṭhānā, cattāro sammappadhānā, cattāro iddhipādā, pañc' indriyāni, pañca balāni, satta bojjhaṅgā, ariyo aṭṭhaṅgiko maggo. idha bhante bhikkhu āsavānaṃ khayā anāsavaṃ cetovimuttiṃ paññāvimuttiṃ diṭṭhe va dhamme sayaṃ abhiññā sacchikatvā upasampajja viharati. etad ānuttariyaṃ bhante kusalesu dhammesu. taṃ bhagavā asesam abhijānāti, taṃ bhagavato asesam abhijānato uttari abhiññeyyaṃ n' atthi, yad abhijānaṃ añño samaṇo vā brāhmaṇo vā bhagavatā bhiyyo 'bhiññataro assa, yadidaṃ kusalesu dhammesu.

T I 1 76c28–77a03
世尊說法復有上者。謂制法。制法者。謂四念處四正勤四神足四禪五根五力七覺意八賢聖道。是爲無上制。智慧無餘。神通無餘。諸世間所有沙門婆羅門。皆無有與如來等者。況欲出其上者。

Abhidh-k-vy V.8, 448.3–10 (quoting the *Brahmajāla-sūtra*)
brahmajāla-sūtre vītarāgāṇāṃ kāmadhātv-ālaṃ banānāṃ dṛṣṭīnāṃ samudācāra uktaḥ. pūrva-janma-darśanānisāreṇa ya evam utpanna-dṛṣṭikāḥ. te pūrvāṃtakalpakāḥ. śāśvatavādino bahavas tatroktāḥ. teṣām udāharaṇam ekaṃ darśayiṣyāmaḥ. ihaikatyaḥ śramaṇo vā brāhmaṇo vā 'raṇyagato vā vṛkṣa-mūla-gato vā śūny-'āgāragato vā ataptānvayāt. prahāṇānvayāt. bhāvanā'nvayāt bahulī-kārānvayāt samyaṅmanasikārānvayāt. tad-rūpaṃ śāṃtaṃ cetaḥ-samādhiṃ spṛśati. yathā samāhite citte viṃśatiṃ saṃvarta-vivarta-kalpān samanusmarati. tasyaivaṃ bhavati.

Abhidh-k-vy 449.8–10
sa vṛddher anvayād indriyāṇāṃ paripākāt keśaśmaśrūṇy avatārya kāṣāyāṇi vastrāṇy ācchādya samyag eva śradhhayā agārād anagārikāṃ pravrajyāṃ pravrajati. so 'raṇyagato vā vṛkṣamūlagato vā vistareṇa yāvat tadrūpaṃ śāṃtaṃ cetaḥsamādhiṃ spṛśati. yathā samāhite citte pūrvakam ātmabhāvaṃ samanusmarati. tasyaivaṃ bhavati.

Classification of the Sense Spheres (DĀ 16.4)

DĀ 16.4

aparam api me[1045] bhadanta bhagavata ānuttaryaṃ yadā[1046] me bhagavāṃ dharmaṃ deśayati yad utāyatanaprajñaptiṣu[1047] <|> ye kecid bhadanta śra(maṇā vā brāhmaṇā vā dvādaśāyatanā)(**292v1**)ni[1048] prajñāpayantaḥ prajñāpayanti sarve te dvādaśāyatanāni • katamāni dvādaśa <|> [1] cakṣurāyatanaṃ [2] rūpāyatanaṃ [3] śrotrāyatanaṃ[1049] [4] śabdāyatanaṃ [5] ghrāṇāyatanaṃ [6] ga(ndhāyatanaṃ [7] jihvāyatanaṃ [8] rasāyatanaṃ [9] kāyāyata)(**292v2**)naṃ[1050] [10] spraṣṭavyāyatanaṃ [11] mana-āyatanaṃ [12] dharmāyatanaṃ; etad ānuttaryaṃ bhadanta bhagavato yad utāyatanaprajñaptiṣu <|> tad bhagavāṃn aśeṣam abhijānāti[1051] <|> tat t(e) 'ś(e)ṣam (abhijānata uttare 'bhijñeyaṃ nāsti) (**292v3**) ya(s)yābhijñānād anyaḥ śramaṇo vā brāhmaṇo vā bhagavato 'ntikād bhūyo 'bhijñataraḥ[1052] syād <ya>d uta[1053] saṃbodhaye[1054] •

1045. Ms. reads *ye*.

1046. Ms. reads *yadi*.

1047. On the formula: *aparam api me bhadanta ... deśayati yad uta*, see note 1034 above.

1048. Cf. 292v4: *ye kecid bhadanta śramaṇā vā brāhmaṇā vā sapta{ḥ} pudgalaḥ <prajñāpayantaḥ> prajñāpayanti sarve te saptapudgalāḥ*, which shows the formula for numerical lists within the *Prasādanīya-sūtra*. In this formula, numbers are redundantly duplicated. It is not the most eloquent Sanskrit, but it seems to be intentional.

1049. Ms. reads *vrotrāyatanaṃ*.

1050. Cf. DĀ 15.25b (*Prāsādika-sūtra*), 284r1–2: *[1] cakṣurvijñē*(284r2)*yāni (rūpāṇī)-ṣṭāni kāntāni priyāṇi manāpāni kāmopasaṃhitāni r(a)ṃjanīyāni [2] śrotavijñeyāṃ śabdhāṃ [3] ghrāṇavijñeyā{ṃ} gandhā{ṃ} [4] jihvāvijñeyā{n} rasāḥ [5] kāyavijñ(e)yāni spraṣṭavyānīṣṭāni*. DN III 102.24–28: *cha-y-imāni, bhante, ajjhattika-bāhirāni āyatanāni. cakkhuñ c' eva rūpā ca, sotañ c' eva saddā ca, ghānañ c' eva gandhā ca, jivhā c' eva rasā ca, kāyo c' eva phoṭṭhabbā ca, mano c' eva dhammā ca.*

1051. Ms. reads *abhijānati*.

1052. Ms. reads *bhijñataraṃ*.

1053. Ms. reads *syād bata saṃbodhaye*.

1054. On the formula: *etad ānuttaryaṃ bhadanta ... syād yad uta saṃbodhaye*, see note 1005 above.

DĀ 16.4

[Śāriputra:] "'For me, sir, there is another way in which the Blessed One is supreme when he teaches me dharma, and that is regarding the classification of the sense spheres. Sir, there are some ascetics (or brahmins) who, expounding twelve sense spheres, all expound twelve sense spheres. What are the twelve sense spheres? They are [in their respective pairs]: [1] visual perception and [2] object of sight, [3] auditory perception and [4] sound, [5] olfaction and [6] odor, [7] (gustation and [8] flavor), [9] tactile perception and [10] tangible object, [11] mind and [12] mental object. Sir, this is the way in which the Blessed One is supreme, and that is regarding the classification of the sense spheres. The Blessed One knows this in its entirety. For you, (knowing) this in its entirety, (there is nothing further to be known) from the knowledge of which another ascetic or brahmin could be more knowledgeable than the Blessed One in regard to perfect awakening.'"

~16.4~

BLSF III.1 Or.15007/235 (*Prāsādanīya-sūtra*)

verso

f[1055] ///+ [g]a[vat]. + + + ///

T I 18 255c16–22

復次我佛世尊具最勝法。謂佛世尊善能分別十二處法。及能爲他廣大宣說。無有沙門婆羅門能了知此十二處法。及能分別十二處者。所謂眼處色處。耳處聲處。鼻處香處。舌處味處。身處觸處。意處法處。如是等法。唯佛世尊。悉能了知。是即名爲佛最勝法。無有沙門婆羅門等過於佛者。乃至成佛菩提

DN III 102.23–103.2

4. aparaṃ pana bhante etad ānuttariyaṃ yathā bhagavā dhammaṃ deseti āyatanapaṇṇattīsu. cha-y-imāni bhante ajjhattika-bāhirāni āyatanāni. cakkhuñ c' eva rūpā ca, sotañ c' eva saddā ca, ghānañ c' eva gandhā ca, jivhā c' eva rasā ca, kāyo c' eva phoṭṭhabbā ca, mano c' eva dhammā ca. etad ānuttariyaṃ bhante āyatanapaṇṇattīsu. taṃ bhagavā asesam abhijānāti, taṃ bhagavato asesam abhijānato uttari abhiññeyyaṃ n' atthi, yad abhijānaṃ añño samaṇo vā brāhmaṇo vā bhagavatā bhiyyo 'bhiññataro assa yadidaṃ āyatanapaṇṇattīsu.

T I 1 77a5–11

世尊說法又有上者。謂制諸入。諸入者。謂眼色耳聲鼻香舌味身觸意法。如過去如來至眞等正覺亦制此入。所謂眼色乃至意法。正使未來如來至眞等正覺亦制此入。所謂眼色乃至意法。今我如來至眞等正覺亦制此入。所謂眼色乃至意法。此法無上無能過者。智慧無餘。神通無餘。諸世間沙門婆羅門。無能與如來等者。況欲出其上。

Classification of Individuals (DĀ 16.5)

DĀ 16.5

aparam api me[1056] bhadanta (bhagava)ta ā(nuttaryaṃ yadā me bhagavāṃ dharmaṃ deśaya)(**292v4**)ti y(a)d[1057] uta pudgalaprajñaptiṣu <|> ye kecid bhadanta śramaṇā vā brāhmaṇā vā sapta{ḥ}[1058] pudgalaḥ <prajñāpayantaḥ>[1059] prajñāpayanti sarve te saptapudgalāḥ <| katamāḥ sapta |>[1060] [1] śraddhānusāriṇ(aṃ) [2] dharmā(nus)āriṇaṃ [3] śra(ddhāv)i(mu)kt(aṃ)[1061] [4] dṛ(**292v5**)ṣṭiprāptaṃ [5] kāyasākṣiṇaṃ [6] prajñāvimuktam [7] ubhayatobhāgavimukta<ṃ |> etad ānuttaryaṃ {bha}bhadanta[1062] bhagavato yad uta pudgala{ḥ}prajñaptiṣu <|> tad bhagavān aśe(ṣam abhijānāti | ta)t te aśeṣa(**292v6**)m abhijānata uttare 'bhijñeyaṃ nāsti yasyābhijñānād anyaḥ {paiśunyam arthamatīṃ dharatīn niruktivatīṃ kālenātiprakīrṇāsāvadānāṃ sopadeś(āṃ dharm)y(āṃ ar)th(opa)sa<ṃ>hitāṃ[1063] vācaṃ (**292v7**) (bhāṣa)t(e)[1064] tad} <śramaṇo vā brāhmaṇo vā bhagavato 'ntikād bhūyo 'bhijñataraḥ syād yad uta saṃbodhaye |>[1065]

1056. Ms. reads *te*.

1057. On the formula: *aparam api me bhadanta ... deśayati yad uta*, see note 1034 above.

1058. Ms. reads *sataḥ*.

1059. Cf. 292v1 and 293v5.

1060. Cf. 295v5–6.

1061. Cf. Saṅg 7.2: *yaduta sapta pudgalāḥ | śraddh(ānusārī dharmānusārī śraddhādhimukto dṛṣṭiprāptaḥ kāyasākṣī prajñā)(86.4)(vi)mu(k)ta u(bhayat)obhāgavimuktaḥ*, DN III 105.28–29: *satt' ime, bhante, puggalā. ubhato-bhāga-vimutto paññā-vimutto kaya-sakkhi diṭṭhi-ppatto saddhā-vimutto dhammānusārī saddhānusārī*, and DN III.253.27–254.2 (*Saṅgīti-sutta*): *satta puggalā dakkhiṇeyyā. ubhato bhāga-vimotto, pañña-vimotto, kaya-sakkhī, diṭṭhi-ppatto, saddhā-vimotto, dhammānusāri, saddhānusārī.*

1062. Dittography.

1063. Cf. 292v8.

1064. Cf. 292v8.

1065. The text is corrupted here and it appears that at some point a scribe must have gotten confused or lost his place and inadvertently transposed a line from the next section (cf. 292v7–8) into the this section while omitting the ending and beginning of this and the next

DĀ 16.5

[Śāriputra:] "'For me, sir, there is another way in which the Blessed One is supreme (when he) teaches (me) dharma, and that is regarding the classification of individuals. Sir, there are some ascetics or brahmins who, <expounding> seven [classifications of] individuals, all expound seven [classifications of] individuals. <What are the seven?> They are: [1] he who acts in accordance with faith, [2] he who acts in accordance with dharma, [3] he who is liberated by faith, [4] he who has gained the [proper] view, [5] he who has directly experienced reality, [6] he who is liberated through insight, and [7] he who is liberated both ways. Sir, this is the way in which the Blessed One is supreme, and that is regarding the classification of individuals. The Blessed One (knows) this in its entirety. For you, knowing this in its entirety, there is nothing further to be known from the knowledge of which <another ascetic or brahmin could be more knowledgeable than the Blessed One in regard to perfect awakening>.'"

~16.5~

T I 18 255c23–29

復次我佛世尊有最勝法。謂佛世尊善能了知補特伽羅法理。及爲他說。無有沙門婆
羅門等知如是法。及爲他説補特伽羅法者。而身七種。所謂隨信行。隨法行。信解。見至。身證。慧解脱。俱解脱。如是七種補特伽羅最上之法。唯佛世尊悉能了知。是即名爲佛最勝法

DN III 105.25–30 (DN 28.8)

8. aparaṃ pana bhante etad ānuttariyaṃ yathā bhagavā dhammaṃ deseti puggala-paṇṇattīsu. satt' ime bhante puggalā. ubhato-bhāga-vimutto paññā-vimutto kaya-sakkhi diṭṭhi-ppatto saddhā-vimutto dhammānusārī saddhānusārī. etad ānuttariyaṃ bhante puggala-paṇṇattīsu.

T I 1.18 —

Saṅg VII.2

(84.4) yaduta sapta pudgalāḥ | śraddh(ānusārī dharmānusārī śraddhādhimukto dṛṣṭiprāptaḥ kāyasākṣī prajñā)(86.4)(vi)mu(k)ta u(bhayat)obhāgavimuktaḥ |

---

section. On the formula: *etad ānuttaryaṃ bhadanta ... syād yad uta saṃbodhaye*, see note 1005 above.

DN III 253.26–254.2 (DN 33, *Saṅgīti-sutta*)
satta puggalā dakkhiṇeyyā. ubhato bhāga-vimotto, pañña-vimotto, kaya-sakkhī, diṭṭhi-ppatto, saddhā-vimotto, dhammānusāri, saddhānusārī.

Conduct in Speech (DĀ 16.6)

DĀ 16.6

<aparam api me bhadanta bhagavata>[1066] ānuttaryaṃ yadā me[1067] bhagavāṃ dharmaṃ deśayati yad uta bhāṣyasamudācāratāyāṃ; na bhagavāṃn saṃprajānan[1068] mṛṣāvācaṃ bhāṣate <|> na saṃrambhahetoḥ paiśunyam arthamatīṃ dharmamatīṃn niruktivatīṃ kāle(**292v8**)nātiprakīrṇāsāvadhānāṃ[1069] sopadeśāṃ dharmyāṃ arthopasaṃhitāṃ vācaṃ bhāṣate <| e>tad ānuttaryaṃ bhadanta bhagavato[1070] yad <uta> bhāṣyasamudācāratāyāṃ; tad bhagavān aśeṣam abhijānāti <|> tat te aśeṣa(**293r1**)m abhijānata uttare 'bhijñeyaṃ nāsti yasyābhijñ(ānā)<d a>nyaḥ śramaṇo vā <brāhmaṇo vā>[1071] bhagavato 'ntikād bhūyo 'bhijñatara<ḥ> syād yad uta saṃbodhaye <|>

DĀ 16.6

[Śāriputra:] "'<For me, sir, there is another way in which the Blessed One> is supreme when he teaches me dharma, and that is regarding conduct in speech. The Blessed One does not deliberately tell lies. Nor does he speak on account of vehemence or slanderously [but rather,] he speaks purposefully, with his mind focused on dharma, explanatorily, at the proper time; not overly careless and confused [but rather,] prescriptively, virtuously, and associated with the goal [of salvation]. Sir, this is the way in which

1066. As noted at the end of 16.5, at some point in the copying tradition for this text a scribe appears to have gotten confused or lost his place and inadvertently transposed a line from the next section (cf. 292v7–8) into this section while omitting the beginning and ending of this and the previous section.

1067. Ms. reads *bhadanta*. On the formula: *aparam api me bhadanta ... deśayati yad uta*, see note 1034 above.

1068. Ms. reads *saṃprajānaṃ*.

1069. Ms. reads *kalenātiprakīrṇā{{ṃ}}sāvadānāṃ*.

1070. Ms. reads *bhagavatā*.

1071. On the formula: *etad ānuttaryaṃ bhadanta ... syād yad uta saṃbodhaye*, see note 1005 above.

the Blessed One is supreme, and that is regarding conduct in speech. The Blessed One knows this in its entirety. For you, knowing this in its entirety, there is nothing further to be known from the knowledge of which another ascetic or ‹brahmin› could be more knowledgeable than the Blessed One in regard to perfect awakening.'"

~16.6~

BLSF II.1 Or.15009/59 (*Prasādanīya-sūtra*)[1072]

recto

1[1073] ///+ + + + ... bhagavān dha+///

2 /// + + + .. rmavatīṃ niruktava + ///

3 /// + + gavato [ya] .. [va]bhāṣya + ///

T I 18 256a1–6

復次我佛世尊有最勝法。謂佛世尊出眞實語無有虛妄。亦無綺語而不兩舌。所出言辭是眞大利。是最勝法。有因有緣。能於大衆中。出微妙音說甚深義。如是最上眞實之法。唯佛世尊悉能了知。是即名爲佛最勝法

DN III 106.20–25 (DN 28.11)

11. aparaṃ pana bhante etad ānuttariyaṃ, yathā bhagavā dhammaṃ deseti bhassa-samācāre. idha bhante ekacco na c' eva musāvādupasaṃhitaṃ vācaṃ bhāsati, na ca vebhūtiyaṃ na ca pesuṇiyaṃ na ca sārambhajaṃ jayāpekkho, mantā mantā vācaṃ bhāsati nidhānavatiṃ kālena. etad ānuttariyaṃ bhante bhassa-samācāre.

T I 1 77b05–11

如來說法復有上者。謂言清淨。言清淨者。世尊於諸沙門婆羅門。不說無益虛妄之言。言不求勝。亦不朋黨。所言柔和。不失時節。言不虛發。是爲言清淨。此法無上。智慧無餘。神通無餘。諸世間沙門婆羅門。無有與如來等者。況欲出其上。

1072. Referred to as *Prāsādika-sūtra* in BLSF II.1.

1073. DĀ 16.6.

Attainments of Discernment (DĀ 16.7)

DĀ 16.7a

[a] aparam api me bhadanta bhagavat(a)[1074] ānuttaryaṃ yadā me bhagavāṃ dharmaṃ de(**293r2**)śayati yad uta darśanasamāpattiṣu <|> paṃcem(ā)ni[1075] bhadanta samāpattayaḥ <|> iha bhadanta <e>ke śramaṇā vā brāhmaṇā vā imam eva<ṃrūpaṃ>[1076] kāyam ūrdhvaṃ[1077] pādatalād adhaḥ keśamastakā(t)[1078] <tva>kparyantaṃ yathāsthitaṃ yathā(**293r3**)(praṇihi)t(aṃ) pūrṇa(ṃ)[1079] nānāprakārasyāśucinaḥ pratyavekṣa<n>te[1080] <|> saṃty asmiṃ kāye keśā romāṇi nakhā dantā rajomalaṃ[1081] tvaṅ* māṃsam asthi snāyu śirā[1082] vṛkkā hṛdayaṃ plīhā klomaka[1083] āntrāṇy a(**293r4**)ntr(a)guṇ(ā)[1084] āmāśayaḥ pakvāśayaḥ audaryakaṃ ya{t}kṛt[1085] pu<rī>ṣam[1086] aśrūṇi śvedaḥ kheṭaḥ śiṃghaṇako vasā lasīkā majjā medaḥ pittaṃ śleṣmā pūyaṃ śoṇitaṃ m(as)t(aka)ṃ[1087] mastakaluṃgaṃ (**293r5**)

1074. On the formula: *aparam api me bhadanta ... deśayati yad uta*, see note 1034 above.

1075. Cf. DN III 104.16, *catasso imā, bhante, dassanasamāpattiyo*, which states four instead of five.

1076. Cf. 293r5 and 293r7.

1077. Ms. reads *kaya pūrvaṃ*.

1078. Ms. reads *keśamastak*.

1079. Ms. reads *pūrva*.

1080. Cf: Poṣ §5.2 (p. 260): *eta yūyaṃ bhikṣava imam eva kāyam ūrdhvaṃ pādatalād adhaḥ keśamastakāt tvakparyantaṃ yathāsthitaṃ yathāpraṇihitaṃ pūrṇaṃ nānāprakārasyāśuceḥ pratyavekṣadhvaṃ*.

1081. Bendall takes this as two distinct units (cf. Śikṣ, 209) but it also appears as a *dvandva* compound. S.v. *rajojala* and *rajomala* in SWTF and BHSD.

1082. Ms. reads *śira*.

1083. Ms. reads *klomaśa*.

1084. Cf. Poṣ §5.2 (p. 260): *āntrāṇy antraguṇāny* and DN III 104.27: *anta-guṇaṃ*.

1085. Cf. Śikṣ 209.9, Poṣ §5.2 (p. 260): *yakṛt* and DN III 104.26 and Khp 2.6: *yakana*.

1086. Ms. reads *[pū]○ṣam*. Cf. Śikṣ 209.9 and Poṣ §5.2 (p. 260): *purīṣam*, as well as DN III 104.27 and Khp 2.7: *karīṣa*.

1087. Cf. Śikṣ 209.10 and Poṣ §5.2 (p. 260): *mastakam*.

prasrāva iti <|>[1088] yasyaiva<ṃ>[1089] syād iyaṃ pra(thama)ṃ (dar)ś(ana)-samāpatti<ḥ[1090] |>

DĀ 16.7a

[a] [Śāriputra:] "'For me, sir, there is another way in which the Blessed One is supreme when he teaches me dharma, and that is regarding the attainments of discernment. Sir, there are five attainments. In this case, sir, some ascetics or brahmins consider the body <composed> in this way upward from the soles of the feet and downward from the hair of the head, encased in skin, in whatever state or disposition, filled with many kinds of impurities: "In this body there is: hair, body hair, nails, teeth, dirt and filth, skin, flesh, bones, sinews, nerves, kidneys, heart, spleen, lungs, entrails, mesentery, stomach cavity and duodenum,[1091] intestines,[1092] liver, excrement, tears, sweat, phlegm, mucus, fat, lymph, marrow, synovial fluid,[1093] bile, rheum, pus, blood, the head, the brain, and urine." This should be the first attainment of discernment for whomever [considers] in this way.'"

DĀ 16.7b–d

[**b**]punar aparaṃ bhadanta ihaika<ḥ> śramaṇo vā brāhmaṇo vā imam evaṃrūpaṃ kāyaṃ yāvad[1094] pra(srāvaḥ | adh)i(v)i(dhy)ā(dh)i(vidh)ya (**293r6**) (tvaṅmā)ṃsa(śo)ṇitam[1095] asthipuruṣakaṃ pratyavekṣate <|> vijñānasrota iti <|> yasyaivaṃ syād iyaṃ dvitīyaṃ darśanasamāpatti<ḥ> •

1088. This list of the 37 impurities of the body is common throughout Buddhist literature. Parallel examples of this list are noted in ~**16.7a**~ below.

1089. Cf. 293r6, 293r7, and 293v1.

1090. Cf. 293r6 and 293r8, which read *dvitīyaṃ darśanasamāpatti* and *tṛtīyaṃ darśanasamāpattiḥ*.

1091. *Āmāśayaḥ* and *pakvāśaḥ*. Bendall and Rouse translate these as "upper and lower stomach," cf. Bendall and Rouse 1922, 202.

1092. *Audaryakam*. Edgerton notes: Bendall assumes bladder, but states that "Tib. gives *leṅ ga* = Skt. *liṅga*; perhaps error for *loṅ ga* = Intestines, entrails, guts" (s.v. *audaryaka* in BHSD).

1093. For marrow (*majjā*), synovial fluid (*medaḥ*), Bendall and Rouse translate *majjā* as lard and *medaḥ* as marrow. However, both terms seem to mean marrow or something similar with only shades of difference. *Medaḥ* seems closer to what I translate as synovial fluid and perhaps the two terms were mixed in Bendall and Rouse's translation. Sv. *medhaḥ* in MW: "the juice of meat, broth" etc., but also "marrow".

1094. Ms. reads *yāvat*.

1095. Cf. 293r7 and 293r8.

[c] punar aparaṃ bh(a)d(a)n(ta) i(h)ai(ka)ḥ (śramaṇo vā brāhmaṇo vā)[1096] ima(**293r7**)m evaṃ<rūpaṃ>[1097] kāyaṃ yāvad[1098] prasrāvaḥ <|> adhividhyādhividhya tvaṃmā<ṃ>saśoṇit(a)m asthi{ṣu}puruṣakaṃ pratyavekṣate <|> vijñānasrotaḥ pratyavekṣate • iha loke pratiṣṭhi(taṃ paraloke pratiṣṭhitaṃ ceti | yasyaivaṃ syā)(**293r8**)(d)[1099] iyaṃ tṛtīyaṃ darśanasamāpattiḥ <|>

[d] punar aparaṃ bhadanta ihaika<ḥ> śramaṇo vā brāhmaṇo vā <imam evaṃrūpaṃ kāyaṃ> yāvad <prasrāvaḥ[1100] |> adhividhyādhividhya[1101] tvaṅ{*}māṃsaśoṇitam asthipuruṣakaṃ pratyave(kṣate | vijñānasrotaḥ pratyavekṣate |)[1102] (**293v1**) i(ha) loke pratiṣṭhitam iti <|> yasyaivaṃ syād iyaṃ caturthī darśanasamāpatti<ḥ |>

DĀ 16.7b-d

[**b**] [Śāriputra:]"'Moreover, sir, in this case an ascetic or brahmin [considers] the body composed in this way up to "urine". Moving on, he considers the skeleton [covered by] blood, flesh, and skin: "This is the stream of consciousness." This should be the second attainment of discernment for whomever [considers] in this way.

[**c**] "'Moreover, sir, in this case an ascetic or brahmin [considers] the body <composed> in this way up to "urine". Moving on, he considers the skeleton [covered by] blood, flesh, and skin: "This is the stream of consciousness," he considers, "established here in this world (and established in the world beyond)." This should be the third attainment of discernment (for whomever [considers] in this way).

[**d**] "'Moreover, sir, in this case an ascetic or brahmin [considers] <the body composed in this way> up to <"urine">. Moving on, he considers the skeleton [covered by] blood, flesh, and skin: "(This is the stream of

1096. Cf. 293r5, 293r8, and 293v1.

1097. Cf. 293r5.

1098. Ms. reads *yāvat*.

1099. Cf. 293r5, 293r6, and 293v2.

1100. Cf. 293r5 and 297r7.

1101. Ms. reads *adhividhyādhividhyā*.

1102. Cf. 293r7 and 293v1–2.

consciousness," he considers), "established here in this world." This should be the fourth attainment of discernment for whomever [considers] in this way.'"

DĀ 16.7e–f

[e] punar aparaṃ bhadanta ihaikaḥ śramaṇo vā brāhmaṇo vā imam eva<ṃrūpaṃ> kāyaṃ yāvad <prasrāvaḥ[1103] |> adhividhya<adhividhya>[1104] tvaṅ{*}m(ā)ṃ(saśoṇitam asthipuruṣa)(**293v2**)kaṃ[1105] pratyavekṣate <|> vijñānasrotaḥ pratyavekṣate <|> iha lok(e a)pratiṣṭhitam[1106] paraloke apratiṣṭhitam {apratiṣṭhite}[1107] vā <|> punaḥ kvacit pariśuddhaṃ paryavadātam iti <|> ya(syaivaṃ syād iyaṃ pañcamā darśanasamā)(**293v3**)pattiḥ[1108] <|>

[f] bhagavāṃ bhadanta divyena cakṣuṣā yāvad <sugatau svargaloke> d(e)veṣūpapa(dyata)[1109] iti <|> etad ānuttaryaṃ bhadanta bhagavato yad uta darśanasamāpatti(ṣu | tad bhagavān aśeṣam abhijānāti | tat te aśeṣam a)(**293v4**)bhijānata uttare 'bhijñeyaṃ nā(st)i (yasy)ābhijñānād anyaḥ śramaṇo vā brāhmaṇo vā bhagavato 'ntikād bhūyo 'bhijñatara<ḥ> syād yad uta (saṃbodhaye |)[1110]

1103. Cf. 293r5 and 293r7.

1104. Cf. 293r7 and 293r8, both read *adhividhyādhividhya*.

1105. Cf. 293r7 and 8.

1106. Ms. reads .. *[pr]atiṣṭhite*.

1107. Dittography.

1108. Cf. 293r5, 293r6, 293r7–8, and 293v1.

1109. Cf. 16.13c (296v8) where this phrase: *bhagavāṃ bhadanta divyena cakṣuṣā yāvat sugatau svargaloke deveṣūpapadyata iti*, also occurs. This is an abbreviation of a description of the *divyacakṣus* varyingly found in both Pali and Sanskrit literature. See the *Sampasādanīya-sutta*: DN III 111.15–112.5 (DN 28.17) and *Samaññaphala-sutta*: DN I 82.22–83.3. These are quoted in §6.2 of the introduction above. See also similar usages in the *Udumbārikāsīhanāda-sutta*: DN III 52 (DN 25.19), *Mahāparinibbāna-sutta*: DN II 86 (DN 16.1.24) and its Sanskrit parallel MPS 4.17, and Śikṣ 158.16–159.6 among numerous other instances. As noted in §6.2 of the introduction, it is odd that the vision of the birth and death granted by the *divyacakṣus* appears in both the Pali and Dharmaguptaka Chinese translations as an independent section.

1110. On the formula: *etad ānuttaryaṃ bhadanta ... syād yad uta saṃbodhaye*, see note 1005 above.

DĀ 16.7e-f

[e] [Śāriputra:] "'Moreover, sir, in this case an ascetic or brahmin [considers] this body <composed> in this way up to <"urine">. Moving on, he considers the skeleton [covered by] blood, flesh, and skin: "This is the stream of consciousness," he considers, "not established here in this world or in the world beyond. Further, somewhere it is perfectly pure and completely cleansed. (This should be the fifth attainment of discernment) for whomever [considers] (in this way).

[f] "'Sir, with his divine eye the Blessed One [sees] all the way to birth <in a good condition, a celestial world> of the gods. Sir, this is the way in which the Blessed One is supreme, and that is regarding the attainments of discernment. (The Blessed One knows this in its entirety. For you), knowing (this in its entirety), there is nothing further to be known from the knowledge of which another ascetic or brahmin could be more knowledgeable than the Blessed One in regard to (perfect awakening).'"

~16.7~

BLSF II.1 Or.15009/59 (*Prasādanīya-sūtra*)[1111]

recto

4[1112] /// + + yati da(r)[ś]. [n]. [s]. .. [pa]tti[ṣu] ///

5 /// + .. thāsthitaṃ yathāpraṇ[i] + ///

6 ///.. sam a .i .[ā] + + rāvṛk.+ + ///

verso

1 /// phenaḥ [ś]. .. + + .. sā l. + + ///

2[1113] /// + [d]ar[ś]a[na]sam[ā] pattiḥ punar. + ///

3 /// .. tam asthipuruṣaṃ pratyave[kṣ]. ///

4[1114] /// + .ikṣur imam eva kāyaṃ [y]. ///

5[1115] /// + + + [n]asamāpattiḥ puna + ///

6 /// + + + + .ai[v]aṃ syād iyaṃ ///

1111. Referred to as *Prāsādika-sūtra* in BLSF II.1.

1112. DĀ 16.7a.

1113. DĀ 16.7b.

1114. DĀ 16.7c.

1115. DĀ 16.7d.

T I 18 256a7–11
[a]復次我佛世尊有最勝法。謂佛世尊以三摩鉢底。觀有漏身不淨可惡。所謂身分上下。髮毛爪齒。皮肉筋骨。如是等種種不淨之物。充滿其身。佛悉能知。是不究竟。是可厭離。此名第一三摩鉢底

T I 18 256a12–14
[b]復次世尊。若有沙門婆羅門等。於身上下所有皮肉骨髓諸臭穢等有漏不淨。能以智慧如實觀者。是爲第二三摩鉢底

T I 18 256a15–17
[c]復次世尊。若有沙門。以智慧觀有漏身。盡此一世而不究竟。若能如是觀者。是爲第三三摩鉢底

T I 18 256a18–20
[d]復次世尊。若有沙門。能以智慧觀有漏身。今世不究竟。乃至後世亦不究竟。若能如是觀者。是爲第四三摩鉢底

T I 18 256a21–24
[e]復次世尊。若有沙門。能以智慧。如前觀察有漏之身。今世後世。皆不究竟。乃至後後世亦不究竟。不淨可惡。若能如是觀者。是爲第五三摩鉢底

T I 18 256a25–28
[f]復次世尊。如是有漏不淨。不究竟法。唯佛世尊。以清淨天眼過於肉眼。悉見衆生生滅好醜善趣惡趣。乃至生於天界。皆如實知。是即名爲佛最勝法

DN III 104.15–104.28 (DN 28.7)
[a] 7. aparaṃ pana bhante etad ānuttariyaṃ, yathā bhagavā dhammaṃ deseti dassana-samāpattīsu. catasso imā bhante dassana-samāpattiyo. idha bhante ekacco samaṇo vā brāhmaṇo vā ātappam anvāya padhānam anvāya anuyogam anvāya appamād amanvāya sammāmanasikāram anvāya tathā-rūpaṃ ceto-samādhiṃ phusati, yathā samāhite citte imam eva kāyaṃ uddhaṃ pāda-talā adho kesa-matthakā taca-pariyantaṃ pūraṃ nānappakārassa asucino paccavekkhati:—atthi imasmiṃ kāye kesā lomā nakhā dantā taco maṃsaṃ nahāru aṭṭhi aṭṭhi-miñjā vakkaṃ hadayaṃ yakanaṃ kilomakaṃ pihakaṃ papphāsaṃ antaṃ anta-guṇaṃ udariyaṃ karīsaṃ pittaṃ semhaṃ pubbo lohitaṃ sedo medo assu vasā kheḷo siṅghānikā lasikā muttan ti. ayaṃ paṭhamā dassana-samāpatti.

DN III 104.28–105.13 (DN 28.7)
[b] puna ca paraṃ bhante idh' ekacco samaṇo vā brāhmaṇo vā ātappam anvāya anuyogam anvāya appamādam anvāya sammā-manasikāra anvāya tathā-rūpaṃ ceto-samādhiṃ phusati, yathā samāhite citte imam eva kāyaṃ uddhaṃ pāda-talā adho kesa-matthakā taca-pariyantaṃ pūraṃ nānappakārassa asucino paccavekkhati: atthi imasmiṃ kāye kesā lomā nakhā dantā taco maṃsaṃ nahārū aṭṭhī aṭṭhī-miñjā vakkaṃ hadayaṃ yakanaṃ kilokaṃ pihakaṃ papphāsaṃ antaṃ antaguṇaṃ udariyaṃ karīsaṃ pittaṃ semhaṃ pubbo lohita sedo medu assu vasa kheḷo siṅhānikā lasikā muttaṃ. atikkamma ca purisassa chavi-maṃsa-lohitaṃ aṭṭhiṃ paccavekkhati. ayaṃ dutiyā dassana-samāpatti.

DN III 105.13–18 (DN 28.7)
[c] puna ca paraṃ bhante idh' ekacco samaṇo vā brāhmaṇo vā ātappam anvāya anuyogam anvāya appamādam anvāya sammā-manasikāra anvāya tathā-rūpaṃ ceto-samādhiṃ phusati, yathā samāhite citte imam eva kāyaṃ uddhaṃ pāda-talā adho kesa-matthakā taca-pariyantaṃ pūraṃ nānappakārassa asucino paccavekkhati: atthi imasmiṃ kāye kesā lomā nakhā dantā taco maṃsaṃ nahārū aṭṭhī aṭṭhī-miñjā vakkaṃ hadayaṃ yakanaṃ kilokaṃ pihakaṃ papphāsaṃ antaṃ antaguṇaṃ udariyaṃ karīsaṃ pittaṃ semhaṃ pubbo lohita sedo medu assu vasa kheḷo siṅhānikā lasikā muttaṃ. atikkamma ca purisassa chavi-maṃsa-lohitaṃ aṭṭhiṃ paccavekkhati. purisassa ca viññāṇa-sotaṃ pajānāti, ubhayato labbocchinnaṃ idha-loke patiṭṭhitañ-ca para-loke patiṭṭhitañ ca. ayaṃ tatiyā dassana-samāpatti.

DN III 105.18–24 (DN 28.7)
[d–f] puna ca paraṃ bhante ... pe ... atikkamma ca purisassa chavi-maṃsa-lohitaṃ aṭṭhiṃ paccavekkhati, purisassa ca viññāṇa-sotaṃ pajānāti ubhayato abbocchinnaṃ idha-loke appatiṭṭhitañ-ca para-loke appatiṭṭhitañ-ca. ayaṃ catutthā dassana-samāpatti. etad ānuttariyaṃ bhante dassana-samāpattīsu.

T I 1 77b11–16
[a] 如來説法復有上者。謂見定。彼見定者。謂有沙門婆羅門。種種方便入定意三昧。隨三昧心。觀頭至足觀足至頭皮膚内外。但有不淨髮毛爪甲。肝肺腸胃脾腎五臟。汗肪髓腦屎尿涕淚臭。不淨無一可貪。是初見定。

T I 1 77b16–18
[b] 諸沙門婆羅門。種種方便入定意三昧。隨三昧心除去皮肉外諸不淨。唯觀白骨及與牙齒。是爲二見定。

T I 1 77b18–22
[c] 諸沙門婆羅門。種種方便入定意三昧。隨三昧心除去皮肉外諸不淨及白骨。唯觀心識在何處住。爲在今世。爲在後世。今世不斷後世不斷。今世不解脱後世不解脱。是爲三見定。

T I 1 77b22–26
[d] 諸沙門婆羅門。種種方便入定意三昧。隨三昧心除去皮肉外諸不淨。及除白骨。復重觀識。識在後世不在今世。今世斷後世不斷。今世解脱後世不解脱。是爲四見定。

T I 1 77b26–77c01
[e] 諸有沙門婆羅門種種方便入定意三昧。隨三昧心除去皮肉外諸不淨。及除白骨。復重觀識。不在今世不在後世。二俱斷二俱解脱。是爲五見定。

T I 1 77c01–03
[f] 此法無上。智慧無餘。神通無餘。諸世間沙門婆羅門。無與如來等者。況欲出其上。

~16.7a~[1116]

DN II 293.10–18 (*Mahāsatipaṭṭhāna-sutta*, DN 22)

5. puna ca paraṃ bhikkhave bhikkhu imam eva kāyaṃ uddhaṃ pādatalā adho kesamatthakā taca-pariyantaṃ pūraṃ nānappakārassa asucino paccavekkhati: atthi imasmiṃ kāye kesā lomā nakhā dantā taco maṃsaṃ nahārū aṭṭhī aṭṭhi-miñjā vakkaṃ hadayaṃ yakanaṃ kilomakaṃ pihakaṃ papphāsaṃ antaṃ anta-guṇaṃ udariyaṃ karīsaṃ pittaṃ semhaṃ pubbo lohitaṃ sedo medo assu vasā kheḷo siṅghāṇikā lasikā muttan ti.

Khp 2.4–9 (*Khuddakapāṭha* III, *Dvattiṃsākāraṃ*)

Atthi imasmiṃ kāye kesā lomā nakhā dantā taco, maṃsaṃ nahārū aṭṭhi aṭṭhimiñjā vakkaṃ, hadayaṃ yakanaṃ kilomakaṃ pihakaṃ papphāsaṃ, antaṃ antaguṇaṃ

1116. The following passages do not parallel the topic of DĀ 16.7 but rather attest to the list of the thirty-seven impurities of the body. See note 1088 above.

udariyaṃ karīsaṃ, pittaṃ semhaṃ pubbo lohitaṃ sedo medo assu vasā khelo siṅghāṇikā lasikā muttaṃ, matthake matthaluṅgam.

Śikṣ 209.7–11 (quoting *Ratnamegha-sūtra*)
yad uta santy asmin kāye keśā romāṇi nakhā dantā rajo malaṃ tvak māṃsāsthi snāyuḥ śirā vṛkkā hṛdayaṃ plīhakaḥ klomakaḥ | antrāṇy antraguṇāmāśayaḥ pakvāśayaḥ | audaryakaṃ yakṛt purīṣam aśru svedaḥ kheṭaḥ siṅghāṇakaṃ vasā lasikā majjā medaḥ pittaṃ śleśmā pūyaṃ śoṇitaṃ mastakaṃ mastakaluṅgaṃ prasrāvaḥ |

Arthav(V) 316
iha khalu bhikṣavo bhikṣuḥ striyaṃ dṛṣṭvā utpanne rāge bāhyātmikayoḥ śarīrayoraśubhākāreṇa yathābhūtadarśī bhavati - santyasmin kāye keśā romāṇi nakhā dantā rajomalatvaṅmāṃsam, asthisnāyusirā vṛkkā hṛdayam(ā) maka āmāśayaḥ pakkāśayaḥ antrāṇi antraguṇā odarīyakaṃ yakṛt parīṣamaśru svedaḥ khelakaḥ siṃghāṇako vasā lasīkā majjā medaḥ pittaṃ śleṣmā pūyaṃ śoṇitaṃ mastakaluṅgamuccāraprasravaiḥ pūrṇaṃ nānāprakārakamaśuciriti | iyamucyate bhikṣavaḥ samyaksmṛtiḥ ||

Arthav(V) 318
iha bhikṣavo bhikṣu rimam eva kāyamūrdhvaṃ pādatalādadhaḥ keśamastakādiparyantaṃ yathāsthitaṃ tathāpraṇihitaṃ pūrṇaṃ nānāprakārasyāśucer yathābhūtaṃ samyak prajñayā pratyavekṣate – yad uta ayaṃ kāyaḥ anupūrveṇa samudāgato 'pūrvavināśī paramāṇusaṃcayaḥ suṣira unnāmonnāmanānmānavavraṇasumukharomakūpasrāvī valmīkavadāśīviṣanivāsaḥ |

Arthav(V) 320
evameva bhikṣavo bhikṣur imam eva kāyaṃ yathāsthitaṃ yathāpraṇihitaṃ yāvat pratyavekṣate | iyaṃ samādhibhāvanā āsevitā bahulīkṛtā kāmarāgaprahāṇāya saṃvartate |

Śrāv-bh II 58–60: -II-3-b-(1)-i-(a)
tatrādhyātmam upādāya | tadyathā keśā, romāṇi, nakhā, dantā, rajaḥ, [60] malaṃ, tvak, māṃsaṃ, asthi, snāyu, sirā, vṛkkā, hṛdayaṃ, plīhakaṃ, klomam, antrāṇi, antraguṇaḥ, āmāśayaṃ, pakvāśayaṃ, yakṛt, purīṣam, aśru, svedaḥ, kheṭaḥ, śiṅghāṇakaṃ, vasā, lasīkā, majjā, medaḥ, pittaṃ, śleṣmā, pūyaḥ, śoṇitam, mastakaṃ, mastakaluṅgaṃ, prasrāvaḥ ||

Śrāv-bh II 172: -II-12-a-(2)
tatrordhvamadhaḥsaṃjñī imam eva kāyaṃ yathāsthitaṃ yathāpraṇihitam ūrdhvaṃ pādatalād adhaḥ keśamastakāt pūrṇaṃ nānāvidhasyāśuceḥ pratyavekṣate | santy asmin kāye keśā romāṇīti pūrvavat | tatra paścātpuraḥsaṃjñī | yathāpi tad ekatyena pratyavekṣaṇānimittam eva sādhu ca suṣṭhu ca sūdgṛhītaṃ bhavati sumanasīkṛtam sujuṣṭaṃ supratividdham | tadyathā sthito niṣaṇṇaṃ pratyavekṣate, niṣaṇṇo vā nipannam, purato vā gacchantaṃ pṛṣṭhato gacchan pratyavekṣate | sā khalv eṣā traiyadhvikānāṃ saṃskārāṇāṃ pratītyasamutpannānāṃ vipaśyanākārā pratyavekṣā paridīpitā |

Śrav-bh(Sh) 286
paścātpura imam eva kāyaṃ yathāsthitaṃ yathāpraṇihitaṃ ūrdhvaṃ pādatalādadhaḥ keśamastakāt pūrṇaṃ nānāvidhasyāśuceḥ pratyavekṣate | santy asmin kāye keśā romāṇīti pūrvavat | tatra paścāt punaḥ | saṃjñī tathā tadekatyena pratyavekṣaṇānimittameva |

Poṣ §5.2 (p. 260)
bhagavān āha | niṣadyā ucyate yogaḥ | eta yūyaṃ bhikṣava imam eva kāyam ūrdhvaṃ pādatalād adhaḥ keśamastakāt tvakparyantaṃ yathāsthitaṃ yathāpraṇihitaṃ pūrṇaṃ nānāprakārasyāśuceḥ pratyavekṣadhvaṃ | santy asmin kāye keśā romāṇi nakhā dantā rajo malaṃ tvaṅ māṃsam asthi snāyu sirā vṛkkā hṛdayaṃ plīhā klomaka āntrāṇy antraguṇāny āmāśayaḥ pakvāśaya audaryakaṃ yakṛt purīṣam aśru svedaḥ kheṭaś śiṃghāṇako vasā lasīkā majjā medaḥ pittaṃ śleṣmā pūyaḥ śoṇitaṃ mastakaṃ (54r (= GBM 6.1058)) mastakaluṅgaṃ mūtraṃ ca iti |

Practices (DĀ 16.8)

DĀ 16.8

(aparam api me bhadanta bhagava)ta{ḥ}[1117] ā(**293v5**)nuttaryaṃ ya̱<dā>[1118] me bhagavāṃ dharmaṃ deśayati yad uta pratipatsu <|> ye kecic chramaṇā vā brāhmaṇā vā sap̱ta{ḥ}[1119] pratipadaḥ prajñāpayan(t)aḥ prajñāpa(yant)i (sarve) t(e sap)t(a) b(o)dhyaṃgāni • k(a)(**293v6**)(tama)ni[1120] sapta <|> smṛtisaṃbo(dh)yaṃga<ṃ> dharma<pra>vicayavīryaprītipraś̱rabdhisamādhyupekṣāsaṃbodhyaṃgam[1121] <|> etad ānuttaryaṃ bhadanta bhagavato yad uta pratipatsu <|> tad bhagavān aśeṣam abhi(**293v7**)(jānāti | tat) t(e)[1122] aśeṣam abhijānata uttare 'bhijñeyaṃ nāsti yasyābhijñānād anyaḥ śramaṇo vā brāhmaṇo vā bhagavato 'ntikād bhūyo 'bhijñatara<ḥ> syād yad uta saṃbodhaye <|>

DĀ 16.8

[Śāriputra:] "'(For me, sir, there is another way) in which the Blessed One is supreme when he teaches me dharma, and that is regarding practices. Sir, there are some ascetics or brahmins who, expounding seven practices, (all) expound the seven limbs of awakening. What are these seven? They are: [1] the limb of awakening [consisting of] mindfulness, [2] the limbs of awakening [consisting of] discriminating comprehension of dharma, [3] vigor, [4] joy, [5] serenity, [6] meditative concentration, and [7] equanimity. Sir,

1117. On the formula: *aparam api me bhadanta ... deśayati yad uta*, see note 1034 above.

1118. Ms. reads *yā*.

1119. Ms. reads *sataḥ*. The *Sampasādanīya-sutta* refers to four and not seven, c.f. DN III 106.6–21, and uses this sevenfold description (*saptabodhyaṅga*) in the section on *padhāna*, c.f. DN III 105.31–106.5.

1120. Cf. 292v1 and 292v4 as well PvSP 208: *yad uta saptabodhyaṅgāni katamāni sapta smṛtisaṃbodhyaṅgaṃ*.

1121. Cf. Śrāv-bh II 176: II-12-b: *smṛtisaṃbodhyaṅgasya dharmapravicayavīryaprītipraśrabdhisamādhyupekṣāsaṃbodhyaṅgasya ca*.

1122. On the formula: *etad ānuttaryaṃ bhadanta ... syād yad uta saṃbodhaye*, see note 1005 above.

this is the way in which the Blessed One is supreme, and that is regarding practices. The Blessed One knows this in its entirety. For you, knowing this in its entirety, there is nothing further to be known from the knowledge of which another ascetic or brahmin could be more knowledgeable than the Blessed One in regard to perfect awakening.'"

~16.8~

T I 18 256a29–b5
復次我佛世尊有最上勝法。謂世尊説法時。若有沙門婆羅門歸向聽受。求寂靜者。彼皆依止七覺分。七覺分者。謂擇法覺分。精進覺分。喜覺分。輕安覺分。捨覺分。念覺分。定覺分。如是七法。唯佛世尊悉能了知。是即名爲佛最勝法[1123]

DN III 106.6–19 (DN 28.10) (content actually parallels DN III 105.31–106.5)
10. aparaṃ pana bhante etad-ānuttariyaṃ yathā bhagavā dhammaṃ deseti paṭipadāsu. catasso imā bhante paṭipadā, dukkhā paṭipadā dandhābhiññā, dukkhā paṭipadā khippābhiññā, sukhā paṭipadā dandhābhiññā, sukhā paṭipadā khippābhiññā. tatra bhante yāyaṃ paṭipadā dukkhā dandhābhiññā, ayaṃ bhante paṭipadā ubhayen' eva hīnā akkhāyati dukkhattā ca dandhattā ca. tatra bhante yāyaṃ paṭipadā dukkhā khippābhiññā, ayaṃ bhante paṭipadā dukkhattā hīnā akkhāyati. tatra bhante yāyaṃ paṭipadā sukhā dandhābhiññā, ayaṃ bhante paṭipadā dandhattā hīnā akkhāyati. tatra bhante yāyaṃ paṭipadā sukhā khippābhiññā, ayaṃ bhante paṭipadā ubhayen' eva paṇītā akkhāyati sukhattā ca khippattā ca. etad ānuttariyaṃ bhante paṭipadāsu.

DN III 105.31–106.5 (DN 28.9)
9. aparaṃ pana bhante etad ānuttariyaṃ, yathā bhagavā dhammaṃ deseti padhānesu. satt' ime bhante bojjhaṅgā, sati-sambojjhaṅgo, dhamma-vicaya-sambojjhaṅgo, vīriya-sambojjhaṅgo, pīti-sambojjhaṅgo, passaddhi-sambojjhaṅgo, samādhi-sambojjhaṅgo, upekkhā-sambojjhaṅgo. etad ānuttariyaṃ bhante padhānesu.

1123. Note that the order of the seven limbs is slightly different here: [2] 擇法, [3] 精進, [4] 喜, [5] 輕安, [7] 捨, [1] 念, [6] 定.

T I 1 77a17–23

如來說法復有上者。所謂道也。所謂道者。諸沙門婆羅門以種種方便入定慧意三昧。隨三昧心修念覺意。依欲依離依滅盡依出要法精進喜猗定捨覺意。依欲依離依滅盡依出要。此法最上。智慧無餘。神通無餘。諸世間沙門婆羅門。無能與如來等者。況欲出其上。

⁝ Efforts (DĀ 16.9)

DĀ 16.9

aparam api <me> bhadanta bha(**293v8**)gavata ānuttaryaṃ yadā me bhagavāṃ dharmaṃ deśa(ya)ti[1124] yad uta prahā̱ṇe̱<ṣu[1125] |> catvārīmāni bhadanta prahāṇāni <|> katamāni catvāri <|> [1] asṯi{ṃ}[1126] prahāṇaṃ duẖkhaṃ[1127] ḏẖandhābhijñam;[1128] [2] asti prahāṇaṃ duẖkhaṃ[1129] kṣiprābhijña(**294r1**)(m; [3] asti prahā)ṇaṃ[1130] sukhaṃ dhaṃdhābhijñam; [4] asti prahāṇaṃ sukhaṃ kṣiprābhijña<ṃ> na bahujanyaṃ pṛthu̱bhūtaṃ[1131] na yāvad {eva} devamanuṣyebhyaḥ samyak(suprakāśitaṃ)[1132] <|> tatra bhadanta ya(d) i(da)ṃ (pra)hāṇaṃ[1133] duẖkhaṃ dhandhābhijñaṃ (**294r2**) (dhandhatvāt[1134] tadduḥkha)tvād[1135] dhīnam ākhyātaṃ; tatra yad idaṃ prahāṇaṃ duẖkhaṃ kṣiprābhijñaṃ tadduḥkhatvād dhīnam ākhyātaṃ; tatra yad idaṃ prahāṇaṃ ḏukẖa<ṃ>[1136] dhandhābhijñaṃ dhandhatvā̱<d>[1137] dhī(nam ākhy)ātaṃ;[1138] tatra yad idaṃ prahā(**294r3**)(ṇaṃ su)kh(aṃ)[1139] kṣ(i)prābhijñaṃ na bahujanyaṃ pṛthubhūtaṃ na

1124. On the formula: *aparam api me bhadanta ... deśayati yad uta*, see note 1034 above.

1125. Ms. reads *prahaṇā.*

1126. Ms. reads *asmiṃ.*

1127. Note *jihvāmūlīya.*

1128. Ms. reads *vandhābhijñam.*

1129. Note *jihvāmulīya.*

1130. Cf. later in line.

1131. Ms. reads *pṛthībhūtaṃ.*

1132. Cf. 278v8, 279r4, 279r7, 279v4, and 294r3.

1133. Cf. 294r2.

1134. Cf. DN III 106.12: *dandhattā*

1135. Cf. *tadduḥkhatvād* in this line.

1136. Ms. reads *duẖkha.*

1137. Ms. reads dhandhatva.

1138. Cf. 294r2 and 292r4.

1139. Cf. 292r1.

yāvad devamanuṣyebhyaḥ samyaksuprakāśitaṃ tad abahujanyatvād apṛthubhūtvā<d> na yāva<d> devamanuṣye(bhya)ḥ samyak(su)prakāśita(**294r4**)tvād dhīnam ākhyātaṃ; bhagavato bhadanta prahāṇaṃ sukhaṃ kṣiprābhijñaṃ bahujanyaṃ pṛthubhūtaṃ yāva<d> devamanuṣyebhyaḥ samyaksuprakā(ś)ita(m) <|> e(tad ānuttaryaṃ bhadanta bhagavato yad uta) (**294r5**) prahāṇeṣ<u[1140] |> tad bhagavān{n} aśeṣam[1141] (abh)i(jānāti) <|> tat te aśeṣam abhijānata uttare 'bhi(j)ñ(e)yaṃ nāsti yasyābhijñānād anyaḥ śra(maṇo vā brāhmaṇo vā bhagavato 'ntikād bhūyo 'bhi)(**294r6**)-jñatara<ḥ>[1142] syād yad uta saṃbodhaye <|>

DĀ 16.9

[Śāriputra:] "'For me, sir, there is another way in which the Blessed One is supreme when he teaches me dharma, and that is regarding efforts. Sir, there are four efforts. What are these four? [1] There is painful effort and slow understanding. [2] There is painful effort and quick understanding. [3] There is pleasurable effort and slow understanding. [4] There is pleasurable effort and quick understanding, which does not pertain to many people and is not widespread, and consequently it is not well (and properly explained) to gods and men. In that case, sir, this painful effort and slow understanding is said to be inferior due to the painfulness (and slowness) of it. In that case, this painful effort and quick understanding is said to be inferior due to the painfulness of it. In that case, this pleasurable effort and slow understanding is said to be inferior due to slowness. In that case, this pleasurable effort and quick understanding, which does not pertain to many people and is not widespread, and consequently it is not well and properly explained to gods and men, is said to be inferior due to the fact that it is does not pertain to many people and is not widespread, as well as to the fact that it is not well and properly explained to gods and men. The effort of the Blessed One, sir, is pleasurable and the understanding is quick, which pertains to many people and is widespread, and consequently it is well and properly explained to gods and men. Sir, this is the way in which the Blessed One is supreme, and that is regarding efforts. The Blessed One knows this in its entirety. For you, knowing this in its entirety, there is nothing further

1140. Ms. reads *prahāṇāt*.

1141. Ms. reads *aśeṣaḥ*.

1142. On the formula: *etad ānuttaryaṃ bhadanta ... syād yad uta saṃbodhaye*, see note 1005 above.

to be known from the knowledge of which another ascetic (or brahmin) could (be more) knowledgeable (than the Blessed One) in regard to perfect awakening.'"

~16.9~

T I 18 256b6–10

復次我佛世尊有最勝法。謂善分別四正勤法。四正勤者。謂已作惡令斷。未作惡令止。已作善令增長。未作善令發生。如是等法。於天上人間。廣大宣說。而作利益。是即名爲佛最勝法[1143]

DN III 105.31–106.5 (DN 28.9) (content actually parallels DN III 106.6–19)

9. aparaṃ pana bhante etad ānuttariyaṃ, yathā bhagavā dhammaṃ deseti padhānesu. satt' ime bhante bojjhaṅgā, sati-sambojjhaṅgo, dhamma-vicaya-sambojjhaṅgo, vīriya-sambojjhaṅgo, pīti-sambojjhaṅgo, passaddhi-sambojjhaṅgo, samādhi-sambojjhaṅgo, upekkhā-sambojjhaṅgo. etad ānuttariyaṃ bhante padhānesu.

DN III 106.6–19 (DN 28.10)

10. aparaṃ pana bhante etad ānuttariyaṃ yathā bhagavā dhammaṃ deseti paṭipadāsu. catasso imā bhante paṭipadā, dukkhā paṭipadā dandhābhiññā, dukkhā paṭipadā khippābhiññā, sukhā paṭipadā dandhābhiññā, sukhā paṭipadā khippābhiññā. tatra bhante yāyaṃ paṭipadā dukkhā dandhābhiññā, ayaṃ bhante paṭipadā ubhayen' eva hīnā akkhāyati dukkhattā ca dandhattā ca. tatra bhante yāyaṃ paṭipadā dukkhā khippābhiññā, ayaṃ bhante paṭipadā dukkhattā hīnā akkhāyati. tatra bhante yāyaṃ paṭipadā sukhā dandhābhiññā, ayaṃ bhante paṭipadā dandhattā hīnā akkhāyati. tatra bhante yāyaṃ paṭipadā sukhā khippābhiññā, ayaṃ bhante paṭipadā ubhayen' eva paṇītā akkhāyati sukhattā ca khippattā ca. etad ānuttariyaṃ bhante paṭipadāsu.

T I 1 77a23–77b5

1143. While the theme of four correct efforts is present here, the fourfold list itself is slightly different: [1] effort of cutting off bad conduct that has already happened, [2] effort of preventing bad conduct yet to happen, [3] effort of nourishing good conduct that has already happened, and [4] effort of create good conduct yet to happen.

如來說法復有上者。所謂爲滅。滅者謂苦滅遲得。二俱卑陋。苦滅速得。唯苦卑陋。樂滅遲得。唯遲卑陋。樂滅速得。然不廣普。以不廣普故名卑陋。如今如來樂滅速得。而復廣普。乃至天人見神變化。舍利弗白佛言。世尊。所說微妙第一。下至女人亦能受持。盡有漏成無漏。心解脫慧解脫。於現法中自身作證。生死已盡梵行已立。所作已辦不受後有。是爲如來說無上滅。此法無上。智慧無餘。神通無餘。諸世間沙門婆羅門。無能與如來等者。況欲出其上。

Abhidh-k-bh(P) 382
mārga eva punaḥ pratipad ity ukto nirvāṇapratipādanāt | catasraḥ pratipadaḥ | asti pratipad duḥkhā dhandhābhijñā | asti duḥkhā kṣiprābhijñā | evaṃ sukhāpi dvidhā | tatra dhyāneṣu mārgaḥ pratipat sukhā caturdhyāneṣu mārgaḥ sukhā pratipad aṅgaparigrahaśamathavipaśyanāsamatābhyām ayatnavāhitvāt | duḥkhānyabhūmiṣu | anyāsv anāgamyadhyānāntarārūpyabhūmiṣu mārgo duḥkhā pratipad aṅgāparigrahāc chamathavipaśyanānyūnatvāc ca yatnavāhitvāt | śamathanyūne hy anāgamyadhyānāntare vipaśyanānyūnā ārūpyā iti | sā punar dvividhāpi pratipat, dhandhābhijñā mṛdumateḥ kṣiprābhijñetarasya tu || || mṛdvindriyasya sukhā duḥkhā vā pratipad dhandhābhijñā, tīkṣṇendriyasya kṣiprābhijñā | dhandhābhijñāsyāṃ pratipadi, seyaṃ dhandhābhijñā | evaṃ kṣiprābhijñā | dhandhasya vā pudgalasyeyam iti dhandhābhijñā |

Śrāv-bh II 34–35: -II-2-a-(5)
kathaṃ pratipatprabhedena pudgalavyavasthānaṃ bhavati | eṣāṃ yathoddiṣṭānāṃ yathāparikīrtitānāṃ pudgalānāṃ catasṛbhiḥ pratipadbhir niryāṇaṃ bhavati | katamābhiś catasṛbhiḥ | asti pratipad duḥkhā dhandhābhijñā| asti pratipad duḥkhā kṣiprābhijñā | asti pratipat sukhā dhandhābhijñā | asti pratipat sukhā kṣiprābhijñā | tatra mṛdvindriyasya pudgalasya mauladhyānālābhino yā pratipad iyam ucyate duḥkhā dhandhābhijñā | tatra tīkṣṇendriyasya pudgalasya mauladhyānālābhino yā pratipad iyam ucyate duḥkhā kṣiprābhijñā | tatra mṛdvindriyasya pudgalasya mauladhyānalābhino yā pratipad iyam ucyate sukhā dhandhābhijñā | tatra tīkṣṇendriyasya pudgalasya mauladhyānalābhino yā pratipad iyam ucyate sukhā kṣiprābhijñā | evaṃ pratipatprabhedena pudgalavyavasthānaṃ veditavyam |

Abhidh-sam 71
catasraḥ pratipadaḥ katamāḥ | duḥkhā pratipad dhandhābhijñā duḥkhā pratipat kṣiprābhijñā sukhā pratipad dhandhābhijñā sukhā pratipat kṣiprābhijñā ||

Artha(V) 317
(11) tatra katamāścatasraḥ pratisaṃvidaḥ? asti duḥkhā pratipad dhandhābhijñā |

asti duḥkhā pratipat kṣiprābhijñā | asti sukhā pratipad dhandhābhijñā | asti sukhā pratipat kṣiprābhijñā | tatra katamā sā duḥkhā pratipad dhandhābhijñā |

Abhidh-d 355
punarmārgo bhagavatā mokṣapurapratipādanāt pratipacchabdenoktaḥ catasraḥ pratipadaḥ | asti pratipat sukhā dhandhābhijñā | asti sukhā kṣiprābhijñā | asti duḥkhā dhandhābhijñā | asti duḥkhā kṣiprābhijñā |

⁝ Knowledge of the Range of Supernormal Power (DĀ 16.10)

DĀ 16.10a–b

[a] aparam api <me> bhadanta bhagavata ānuttaryaṃ yadā me bhagavāṃ dharmaṃ deśayati yad uta (ṛddh)i(viṣayajñe[1144] | iha bhadantaikaḥ śramaṇo vā brāhma)(**294r7**)ṇo[1145] vā anekavidham ṛddhiviṣayaṃ pratyanubhavaty <|> ek(o) bhūtvā bahudhā bhavati yāvad[1146] imau vā punaḥ sūryacandramasāv evaṃmahardhikāv eva(ṃ)m(a)h(ān)u(bhāvau pāṇinā āmārṣṭi parimārṣṭi |)[1147] (**294r8**) asty eṣā bhadanta ṛddhir[1148] ahaṃ nāstīti vadāmi • sā caiṣā hīnā grāmyā prākṛtā pārthagjanikā nālamāryānalamāryasaṃkhyātā[1149] nābhijñāyai na saṃb(odhaye na nirvāṇāya saṃvartate |)[1150]

[b] [1] (**294v1**) bhagavān bhadanta ye loke priyarūpaṃ sātarūpam ākāṃkṣaṃs tatra tathāgataḥ pratikūla{ṃ}saṃjñī viharati <| prati>kūlasaṃjñī tatra tathāgato viharati[1151] smṛtas saṃprajānaṃ(n |) i(yaṃ bhadanta

1144. Cf. 295r3.

1145. Cf. 295r3 and 295r5.

1146. This passage is abbreviated. A complete parallel passage can be found in DĀ27.85 (*Lohitya-sūtra I*) (Choi 2016): *tadyathā eko bhūtvā bahudhā bhavati <|> bahudhā bhūtvā eko bhavaty; āvirbhāva<ṃ> tirobhāva<ṃ> jñānadarśanena pratyanubha(**380r2**)vati <|> tiraḫkuḍyaṃ tiraśśailaṃ tiraḫprākāram asajjamānaḫ kāyena gacchati tadyathā ākāśe <|> pṛthivyā<ṃ> unmajjananimajjanaṃ karoti tadya<thā> udake <| udake> abhindas{s}roto{ś ā}gacchati <tadyathā> pṛthivyā<m; ā>kāśe paryaṃkena krāmati tadya(**380r3**)thā pakṣī śakunaka<ḥ |> imau vā punas sūryācandramasāv evaṃmahardhikāv evaṃmahānubhāvau pāṇinā āmārṣṭi parimārṣṭi.*

1147. Cf. DĀ 27.85 (*Lohitya-sūtra II*): *imau vā punas sūryācandramasāv evaṃmahardhikāv evaṃmahānubhāvau pāṇinā āmārṣṭi parimārṣṭi.*

1148. Ms reads *ṛddhin.*

1149. Ms reads *nālāmāryānālamārya°.*

1150. Cf. DĀ 15.30.1 (*Prāsādika-sūtra*) 285r6: *abhijñāyai saṃbodhaye nirvāṇāya saṃvarttanta iti.*

1151. Ms. reads *viharataḥ.*

bhagavata ṛddhir i)(**294v2**)ty[1152] ucyate <|> [2] bhagavān bhadanta ye loke apriyarūpam asāta{ta}rūpam ākāṃkṣa<ṃ>s tatra tathāgato 'pratikūlasaṃjñī viharaty; apratikūlasaṃjñī tatra t(a)thāg(at)o (viharati smṛtaḥ saṃprajānann | i)(**294v3**)yaṃ [1153] bhadanta bhagavata riddhir[1154] ity ucyate <|> [3] bhagavān bhadanta ye {l}loke priyarūpaṃ cāpy apṛyarūpaṃ[1155] ca sātarūpaṃ cāsātarūpaṃ (cākāṃkṣaṃ)[1156] + + + + + + + + + + + + + + +[1157] (**294v4**) smṛtaḥ saṃprajānan <|> iyaṃ bhadanta (bhagavata)[1158] ṛddhir ity ucyate <|>

DĀ 16.10a–b

[a] [Śāriputra:] "'For me, sir, there is another way in which the Blessed One is supreme when he teaches me dharma, and that is regarding the knowledge of the range of supernormal power. (In this case, sir, some ascetic) or brahmin realizes the various ranges of supernormal power. Being one, he becomes many until[1159] he reaches and (grasps and seizes) the sun and moon by hand, those objects of great might and supernormal power. Sir, there is the seeking of supernormal power, [and to that] I say, "This is forbidden." Seeking this is inferior, vulgar, simple, characteristic of common folk, not worthy of a noble one, not accounted as worthy of a noble one;

1152. Ms. reads *m ucyate.* Cf. 294v1, 2, 3, 4, 5, 6, 7, 8, 295r1, and 2.

1153. Cf 294v1.

1154. Note the use of *ri* for *ṛ*.

1155. Note the nonstandard usage of *ṛ* for *ri*.

1156. Cf. 294v1 and 294v2.

1157. Cf. While I have some idea of what might have been written in this gap, there does not seem to be enough space to fit a reconstruction based on the *Sampasādanīya-sutta*. Cf. DN III 113.6–10 *sace ākaṃkhati — paṭikūlañ ca appaṭikūlañ ca tad ubhayaṃ abhinivajjetvā upekhako vihareyyaṃ sato sampajāno ti, upekhako tattha viharati sato sampajāno. ayaṃ bhante iddhi anāsavā anupadhikā ariyā ti vuccati.*

1158. Cf. 294v3.

1159. This passage is abbreviated in the *Prasādanīa-sūtra* but a complete parallel is found in DĀ 27.85 (*Lohitya-sūtra II*) (Choi 2016): "For example, being one, he becomes many. Having become multiple, he becomes one. He enjoys appearing and disappearing with knowledge and insight. He goes without hesitation through a wall, through a mountain, through a rampart as if it were through an open space. He emerges up and dives down to the earth as if it were in water. He goes on the water without breaking the (surface of) water as if it were on the earth. He goes across in the sky with his legs crossed like a winged bird. Or also he touches and grasps with his hand the sun and the moon of such great supernatural power and of such great might."

(it does not lead) to supernormal knowledge, to perfect awakening, (to nirvāṇa).

[**b**] [1] "'As the Blessed One wishes, sir, the Tathāgata dwells in a world of pleasant appearance, of a pleasing appearance feeling disgust. The Tathāgata dwells there feeling disgust mindful and deliberate. This, (sir), is called (a supernormal power of the Blessed One). [2] As the Blessed One wishes, sir, the Tathāgata dwells in a world of an unpleasant appearance, of an unpleasing appearance not feeling disgust. The Tathāgata (dwells) there not feeling disgust (mindful and deliberate). This is called a supernormal power of the Blessed One. [3] (As) the Blessed One (wishes), sir, [...] in a world of a pleasant appearance and an unpleasant appearance, of a pleasing appearance and an unpleasing appearance [...] mindful and deliberate. This is called a supernormal power of the Blessed One.'"[1160]

DĀ 16.10c

[**c**] [1] bhagavāṃ bhadanta rūpī rūpāṇi paśyatīyaṃ bhadanta bhagavata ṛddhi(r) i(ty ucyate |)[1161] [2] (bhagavāṃ bhadantādhyātmam arūpa)-(**294v5**)saṃjñī[1162] bahirdhārūpāṇi paśyatīyaṃ (bhadanta)[1163] bhagavata ṛddhir ity ucyate <|> [3] bhagavān bhadanta śubhaṃ vimokṣaṃ kāyena sākṣātkṛtv(opasaṃpadya viharatīyam bhadanta bhagava)(**294v6**)(ta ṛ)ddhir[1164] it(y u)cyate[1165] <|> [4] bhagavān bhadanta sarva(ś)o rūpa-saṃjñānāṃ samatikramāt pratighasaṃjñānām asta<ṃ>gamā<n> nānātvasaṃjñānām amanasikārād <an>antam[1166] ākāśam ity

1160. DĀ 16.10b is rather strange. It is unclear what it is describing. Note that T I 18 does not seem to include a parallel for DĀ 16.10b2.

1161. Cf. 294v2, 292v3, 292v4, 292v5, 292v6, 292v7, 292v8, and 295r1.

1162. Cf. PvSP(K) VI–VIII 57: *adhyātmam arūpasaṃjñāṃ bahirddhārūpāṇi paśyaty ayaṃ dvitīyo vimokṣaḥ* and Śrāv-bh II 36–38: -II-2-a-(8): *adhyātmam arūpasaṃjñī bahirdhā rūpāṇi paśyati.*

1163. Cf. 294v3 and 294v4.

1164. Cf. 295r2, PvSP(K) VI–VIII 57: *śubhaṃ vimokṣaṃ kāyena sākṣātkṛtvopasaṃpadya viharaty ayaṃ tṛtīyo vimokṣaḥ,* and Śrāv-bh II 36–38: -II-2-a-(8): *śubhaṃ vimokṣaṃ (kāyena sākṣātkṛtvopasaṃpadya viharati.*

1165. Cf. 294v2, 292v3, 292v4, 292v5, 292v6, 292v7, 292v8, and 295r1.

1166. Ms. reads *atram.*

ā(kāśā)(**294v7**)(nantyāyatanam upa)saṃpadya[1167] viharatīyaṃ bhadanta bhagavataḥ ṛddhir ity ucyate <|> [5] bhagavān bhadanta sarvaśa ākāśānaṃtyāyatanaṃ samatikramyānantaṃ vijñānam iti vijñānānantyāyata(**294v8**)(nam upasaṃpad)y(a vi)h(a)r(a)ti[1168] <|> iyaṃ bhadanta bhagavata ṛddhir ity ucyate <|> [6] bhagavān bhadanta sarvaśo vijñānānantyāyatanaṃ samatikramya (nās)ti (k)iṃcid[1169] ity ākiṃcanyāyatanam upasaṃpa(d)ya[1170] viharati <|> iyaṃ bhadanta (**295r1**) bhagavata ṛddhir ity ucyate <|> [7] bhagavān bhadanta sarvaśa ākiṃcanyāyatanaṃ samatikramya naivasaṃjñānāsaṃjñāyatanam upasaṃpadya viharatīyaṃ bhadanta bhagavata riddhir ity ucyate <|> [8] bhagavān bhadanta (**295r2**) (sarvaśo)[1171] naivasaṃjñānāsaṃjñāyatanaṃ samatikramya saṃjñāveditanirodhaṃ kāyena sākṣātkṛtvopasaṃpadya viharati <|> iyaṃ bhadanta bhagavata ri<ddhir i>ty[1172] ucyate <|> etad ānuttaryaṃ[1173] bhadanta bhagavato (**295r3**) yad uta ṛddhiviṣayajñe <|> etad[1174] bhagavān aś{r}eṣam[1175] abhijānāti <|> tat te aśeṣam abhijānata uttare 'bhijñeyaṃ nāsti yasyābhijñānād anyaḥ śramaṇo vā brāhmaṇo vā bhagava(**295r4**)to 'ntikād bhūyo 'bhijñataraḥ[1176] syād yad uta saṃbodhaye <|>

DĀ 16.10c

[c] [Śāriputra:] [1] "'Sir, the Blessed One, corporeal, sees matter. This, sir, (is called) the supernormal power of the Blessed One. [2] (Sir, the Blessed

1167. Cf. PvSP(K) VI–VIII 57: *sa sarvaśo rūpasaṃjñānāṃ samatikramāt pratighasaṃjñānām astaṅgamāṃ nānātvasaṃjñānām amanasikārād anantam ākāśam ity ākāśānantyāyatanam upasaṃpadya viharati* and Śrāv-bh II 36–38: -II-2-a-(8): *śubhaṃ vimokṣaṃ (kāyena sākṣātkṛtvopasaṃpadya viharati.*

1168. Cf. 294v7, 294v8, and 295r1. Note also that the final and initial vowels of *viharati* and *iyam* are not coalesced by *sandhi* as is usual in this section of the text.

1169. Cf. PvSP(K) VI–VIII 57: *vijñānānantyāyatanasamatikramān nāsti kiṃ canety ākiñcanyāyatanam upasaṃpadya viharati.*

1170. Cf. 294v7 and 295r1.

1171. Cf. 294v6, 294v67, and 294v8.

1172. Cf. 294v3, 294v4, 294v5, 294v6, 294v8, and 295r1.

1173. Ms. reads *etād vāvuttaryaṃ.*

1174. Ms. reads *ṛddhiviṣayajñān etad.*

1175. Ms. reads *aśroṣam.* On the formula: *etad ānuttaryaṃ bhadanta ... syād yad uta saṃbodhaye,* see note 1005 above.

1176. Ms. reads *abhijñatarata.*

One), not aware of matter (in himself), sees matter outwardly. This, (sir), is called the supernormal power of the Blessed One. [3] Sir, the Blessed One (dwells having attained) and directly experienced pure liberation. This, sir, is called the supernormal power of the Blessed One. [4] Sir, through complete transcendence from the awareness of matter, cessation of the awareness of sensory reaction, and inattention to awareness of variety, the Blessed One dwells having attained the stage of the infinity of space, [thinking:] "space is infinite." This, sir, is called the supernormal power of the Blessed One. [5] Sir, completely transcending the stage of the infinity of space, the Blessed One dwells having attained the stage of the infinity of consciousness, [thinking:] "Consciousness is infinite." This, sir, is called the supernormal power of the Blessed One. [6] Sir, completely transcending the stage of the infinity of consciousness, the Blessed One dwells having attained the stage of nothingness, [thinking:] "There is not anything." This, sir, is called the supernormal power of the Blessed One. [7] Sir, completely transcending the stage of nothingness, the Blessed One dwells having attained the stage of neither awareness nor unawareness. This, sir, is called the supernormal power of the Blessed One. [8] Sir, (completely) transcending the stage of neither awareness nor unawareness, the Blessed One dwells having attained and having directly experienced the elimination of awareness and sensation. This, sir, is called the supernormal power of the Blessed One. Sir, this is the way in which the Blessed One is supreme, and that is regarding the knowledge of the range of supernormal power. The Blessed One knows this in its entirety. For you, knowing this in its entirety, there is nothing further to be known from the knowledge of which another ascetic or brahmin could be more knowledgeable than the Blessed One in regard to perfect awakening.'"

~16.10~

T I 18256b11–20

[a] 復次我佛世尊有最勝法。謂佛世尊能以正智現大神通。其神通者。謂從一現多。攝多爲一。或現空無所有。或現城隍山石隨身而去。或現從地以手捫摸虛空乃至梵界。或現履水如地。或現空中跏趺而坐。或現行相。譬如日月行於虛空。如是神通。若有沙門婆羅門等。見此通力。生不信者。我說彼等皆是愚迷凡夫。彼非聖者。彼不具通。不求正覺。亦不樂求寂靜涅槃。而此通力。是即名爲佛最勝法

T I 18 256b21–26
[b] 復次世尊。世間所欲。喜色善色等。有所求者。如來爲彼衆生。隨根而行。是即名爲如來神通復次世尊。世間所有喜不喜色。善不善色。彼二倶離捨而不住。善知宿命。是即名爲如來神通

T I 18 256b27–c13
[c] [1] 復次世尊。色中見色是即名爲如來神通 [2] 復次世尊。內無色想見諸外色。是即名爲如來神通 [3] 復次世尊。身善解脱證得行住。是即名爲如來神通 [4] 復次世尊。空無邊處決定證得。是即名爲如來神通 [5] 復次世尊。識無邊處決定證得。是即名爲如來神通 [6] 復次世尊。無所有處決定證得。是即名爲如來神通 [7] 復次世尊。非想非非想處決定證得。是即名爲如來神通 [8] 復次世尊。了知受想受想滅已。是即名爲如來神通。如是等最勝神通境界。唯佛世尊悉能了知。是即名爲佛神通力

DN III 112.6–113.15 (DN 28.18)
[a] 18. aparaṃ pana bhante etad ānuttariyaṃ yathā bhagavā dhammaṃ deseti iddhi-vidhāsu. dve 'mā bhante iddhiyo. atthi bhante iddhi yā sāsavā sa-upadhikā no ariyā ti vuccati. atthi bhante iddhi yā anāsavā anupadhikā ariyā ti vuccati. katamā ca bhante iddhi yā sāsavā sa-upadhikā no ariyā ti vuccati? idha bhante ekacco samaṇo vā brāhmaṇo vā ātappam anvāya padhānam anvāya anuyogam anvāya appamādam anvāyasammā-manasikāram anvāya tathā-rūpaṃ ceto-samādhiṃ phusati yathā-samāhite citte aneka-vihitaṃ iddhi-vidhaṃ paccanubhoti. eko pi hutvā bahudhā hoti, bahudhā pi hutvā eko hoti, āvibhāvaṃ tiro-bhāvaṃ tiro-kuḍḍaṃ tiro-pākāraṃ tiro-pabbataṃ asajjamāno gacchati seyyathā pi ākāse, pathaviyā pi ummujja-nimujjaṃ karoti seyyathā pi udake, udake pi abhijjamāno gacchati seyyathāpi pathaviyaṃ, ākāse pi pallaṅkena kamati seyyathā pi pakkhī-sakuṇo, ime pi candima-sūriye evaṃ-mahiddhike evaṃ-mahānubhāve pāṇinā parimasati parimajjati, yāva brahma-lokā pi kāyena vasaṃ vatteti. ayaṃ bhante iddhi yā sāsavā sa-upadhikā no ariyā ti vuccati.

[b] katamā ca bhante iddhi yā anāsavā anupadhika ariyā ti vuccati? idha bhante bhikkhu sace ākaṃkhati—paṭikūle appaṭikūla-saññī vihareyyan ti, appaṭikūla-saññī tattha viharati. sace ākaṃkhati—appaṭikūle paṭikūla-saññī vihareyyan ti, paṭikūla-saññī tattha viharati. sace ākaṃkhati—paṭikūle ca appaṭikūle ca appaṭikūla-saññī vihareyyan ti, appaṭikūla-saññī tattha viharati. sace ākaṃkhati—paṭikūle ca appaṭikūle ca paṭikūla-saññī vihareyyan ti, paṭikūla-saññī tattha viharati. sace ākaṃkhati—paṭikūlañ

ca appaṭikūlañ ca tad ubhayaṃ abhinivajjetvā upekhako vihareyyaṃ sato sampajāno ti, upekhako tattha viharati sato sampajāno. ayaṃ bhante iddhi anāsavā anupadhikā ariyā ti vuccati.
[c] etad ānuttariyaṃ bhante iddhi-vidhāsu. taṃ bhagavā asesam abhijānāti. taṃ bhagavato asesam abhijānato uttarim abhiññeyyaṃ n' atthi, yad abhijānaṃ añño samaṇo vā brāhmaṇo vā bhagavatā bhiyyo 'bhiññataro assa yadidaṃ iddhi-vidhāsu.

T I 1 78b26
如來說法復有上者。謂神足證。神足證者。

~16.10a~
DĀ27.85 (*Lohitya-sūtra I*) (Choi 2016)
sa evaṃ samāhite citte pariśuddhe paryavadāte anaṃgane vigatopakleśe ṛjubhūte karmaṇye sthite āni<ṃ>jyāprāpte ṛddhiviṣaya(380r1)jñānasākṣātkṛyāyām abhijñāyāṃ cittam abhinirṇamayati <|> so 'nekavidham ṛddhiviṣayaṃ pratyanubhavati <|> tadyathā eko bhūtvā bahudhā bhavati <|> bahudhā bhūtvā eko bhavaty; āvirbhāva<ṃ> tirobhāva<ṃ> jñānadarśanena pratyanubha(380r2)vati <|> tirahkuḍyaṃ tiraśśailaṃ tiraḥprākāram asajjamānah kāyena gacchati tadyathā ākāśe <|> pṛthivyā<ṃ> unmajjananimajjanaṃ karoti tadya<thā> udake <| udake> abhindas{s}roto{ś ā}gacchati <tadyathā> pṛthivyā<m; ā>kāśe paryaṃkena krāmati tadya(380r3)thā pakṣī śakunaka<ḥ |> imau vā punas sūryācandramasāv evaṃmahardhikāv evaṃmahānubhāvau pāṇinā āmārṣṭi parimārṣṭi <|> yāvad brahmalokaṃ

SBVG 514r9–514v3 (=SBV II 249.3–17) (from DĀ27.85 (*Lohitya-sūtra I*) (Choi 2016))
sa evaṃ samāhite citte (514r10) pariśuddhe paryavadāte anaṃgaṇe vigatopakleśe rijubhūte karmaṇye sthite āniṃjyaprāpte pūrvanivāsā<nu>smṛtijñānasākṣātkriyāyā<ṃ vidyāyāṃ> cittam abhi- nirṇamayati <|> so 'nekavidhaṃ pūrvanivāsaṃ samanusmarati <|> tadyathā ekām api jātiṃ dve tisraś catasraḥ paṃca ṣaṭsaptāṣṭau nava daśa{d} viṃśa(514v1)taṃ tṛṃśataṃ catvāriṃśatam paṃcāśataṃ jātiśataṃ jātisahasraṃ jātiśatasahasram anekāny api jātiśatāni anekāny api jātisahasrāṇy anekāny api jātiśatasahasrāṇi saṃvarttakalpam api vivarttakalpam api saṃvarttavivarttakalpam api anekān api saṃ(514v2)vartta<kalpā>n anekān api vivarttakalpān anekān api saṃvarttavivarttakalpāṃ samanusmarati | amī nāma te bhavantaḥ satvā{ḥ} yatrāham āsam evaṃnāmā evaṃjātya evaṃgotra evamāhāra evaṃsukhaduḥkhapratisaṃvedī evaṃdīrghāyur evamcirasthitika{ḥ} evamāyuṣparyantaḥ <|> so 'haṃ (514v3) tasmāt sthānāc cyuto 'mutropapannaḥ tasmād api

cyuto 'mutropapannaḥ tasmād api cyuta ihopapanna iti | sākāraṃ soddeśam anekavidhaṃ pūrvenivāsam anusmarati <|>

~16.10c~

DN II 111.35–112.20 (*Mahāparinibbāna-sutta*, DN 16)
aṭṭha kho ime ānanda vimokkhā. katame aṭṭha? rūpī rūpāni passati, ayaṃ paṭhamo vimokkho. ajjhattaṃ arūpasaññī bahiddhā rūpāni passati, ayaṃ dutiyo vimokkho. subhan t'eva adhimutto hoti, ayaṃ tatiyo vimokkho. sabbaso rūpasaññānaṃ samatikkamā paṭighasaññānaṃ atthagamā, nānattasaññānaṃ amanasikārā ananto ākāso ti ākāsānañcāyatanaṃ upasampajja viharati, ayaṃ catuttho vimokkho. sabbaso ākāsānañcāyatanaṃ samatikkamma anantaṃ viññāṇan ti viññāṇañcāyatanaṃ upasampajja viharati, ayaṃ pañcamo vimokkho. sabbaso viññāṇañcāyatanaṃ samatikkamma natthi kiñcī ti ākiñcaññāyatanaṃ upasampajja viharati, ayaṃ chaṭṭho vimokkho. sabbaso ākiñcaññāyatanaṃ samatikkamma nevasaññānāsaññāyatanaṃ upasampajja viharati. ayaṃ sattamo vimokkho. sabbaso nevasaññānāsaññāyatanaṃ samatikkamma saññāvedayitanirodhaṃ upasampajja viharati, ayaṃ aṭṭhamo vimokkho. ime kho, ānanda, aṭṭha vimokkhā.

DN II 70.28–71.17 (*Mahānidāna-sutta*, DN 15)
aṭṭha kho ime ānanda vimokkhā. katame aṭṭha? rūpī rūpāni passati ayaṃ paṭhamo vimokkho. ajjhattaṃ arūpasaññī bahiddhā rūpāni passati, ayaṃ dutiyo vimokkho. subhan t' eva adhimutto hoti, ayaṃ tatiyo vimokkho. sabbaso rūpasaññānaṃ samatikkamā paṭighasaññānaṃ atthagamā nānattasaññānaṃ amanasikārā ananto ākāso ti ākāsānañcāyatanaṃ upasampajja viharati, ayaṃ catuttho vimokkho. sabbaso ākāsānañcāyatanaṃ samatikkamma anantaṃ viññāṇan ti viññāṇañcāyatanaṃ upasampajja viharati, ayaṃ pañcamo vimokkho. sabbaso viññāṇañcāyatanaṃ samatikkamma natthi kiñcī ti ākiñcaññāyatanaṃ upasampajja viharati, ayaṃ chaṭṭho vimokkho. sabbaso ākiñcaññāyatanaṃ samatikkamma nevasaññānāsaññāyatanaṃ upasampajja viharati, ayaṃ sattamo vimokkho. sabbaso nevasaññānāsaññāyatanaṃ samatikkamma saññāvedayitanirodhaṃ upasampajja viharati, ayaṃ aṭṭhamo vimokkho. ime kho, ānanda, aṭṭha vimokkhā.

PvSP(K) I.2 25–26
aṣṭau vimokṣāḥ katame aṣṭau? rūpī rūpāṇi paśyati, ayaṃ prathamo vimokṣaḥ, adhyātmam arūpasaṃjñī bahirdhā rūpāṇi paśyati, ayaṃ dvitīyo vimokṣaḥ, śubhatāyām adhimukto bhavati, ayaṃ tṛtīyo vimokṣaḥ, sarvaśo rūpasaṃjñānāṃ samatikramāt, pratighasaṃjñānām astaṅgamāt, nānātvasaṃjñānām amanasikārād

anantam ākāśam ity ākāśānantyāyatanam upasaṃpadya viharati, ayaṃ caturtho vimokṣaḥ, sarvaśa ākāśānantyāyatanasamatikramād anantaṃ vijñānam iti vijñānānantyāyatanam upasaṃpadya viharati, ayaṃ pañcamo vimokṣaḥ, sarvaśo vijñānānantyāyatanasamatikramāt, nāsti kiñcid ity ākiñcanyāyatanam upasaṃpadya viharati, ayaṃ ṣaṣṭho vimokṣaḥ, sarvaśa ākiñcanyāyatanasamatikramāt, naiva saṃjñānāsaṃjñāyatanam upasaṃpadya viharati, ayaṃ saptamo vimokṣaḥ, sarvaśo naivasaṃjñānāsaṃjñāyatanasamatikramāt saṃjñāvedayitanirodham upasaṃpadya viharati, ayam aṣṭam vimokṣaḥ, ima aṣṭau vimokṣāḥ.

PvSP(K) VI–VIII 57–58
katame ca subhūte aṣṭau vimokṣā? rūpī rūpāṇi paśyaty ayaṃ prathamo vimokṣaḥ. adhyātmam arūpasaṃjñāṃ bahirddhārūpāṇi paśyaty ayaṃ dvitīyo vimokṣaḥ. śubhaṃ vimokṣaṃ kāyena sākṣātkṛtvopasaṃpadya viharaty ayaṃ tṛtīyo vimokṣaḥ. sa sarvaśo rūpasaṃjñānāṃ samatikramāt pratighasaṃjñānām astaṅgamāṃ nānātvasaṃjñānām amanasikārād anantam ākāśam ity ākāśānantyāyatanam upasaṃpadya viharati. ākāśānantyāyatanasamatikramād anantaṃ vijñānam iti vijñānānantyāyatanam upasaṃpadya viharati. vijñānānantyāyatanasamatikramān nāsti kiṃ canety ākiñcanyāyatanam upasaṃpadya viharati. ākiñcanyāyatanasamatikramān naivasaṃjñānāsaṃjñāyatanasamāpattim upasaṃpadya viharati, naivasaṃjñānāsaṃjñāyatanasamāpattisamatikramāt saṃjñāvedayitanirodham [58] upasaṃpadya viharati, ime ucyante aṣṭau vimokṣāḥ.

AdSP(C) I 107–8
tatra samādhiṣu sthitvā aṣṭau vimokṣān anulomapratilomaṃ samāpadyate ca vyutthiṣṭhate ca. katamān aṣṭau? iha subhūte bodhisattvo mahāsattvo rūpī rūpāṇi paśyaty, ayaṃ prathamo vimokṣaḥ. adhyātmarūpasaṃjñī bahirddhārūpāṇi paśyaty, ayaṃ [108] dvitīyo vimokṣaḥ. śubhaṃ cādhimukto bhavaty, ayaṃ tritīyo vimokṣaḥ. sa sarvaśo rūpasaṃjñānāṃ samatikramāt pratighasaṃjñānām asta(ṃ)gamān nānātvasaṃjñānām amanasikārād anantam ākāśam ity ākāśānāntyāyatanam upasaṃpadya viharaty, ayaṃ caturtho vimokṣaḥ. sa sarvaśa ākāśānāntyāyatana samatikramād anantaṃ vijñānam iti vijñānanantyāyatanam upasaṃpadya viharaty, ayaṃ paṃcamo vimokṣaḥ. sa sarvaśo vijñānānantyāyatanasamatikramān nāsti kiṃcid ity ākiṃcanyāyatanam upasaṃpadya viharaty, ayaṃ ṣaṣṭho vimokṣaḥ. sa sarvaśa ākiṃcanyāyatanasamatikramān naiva-saṃjñānāsaṃjñāyatanam upasaṃpadya viharaty, ayaṃ saptamo vimokṣaḥ. sa sarvaśo naivasaṃjñānāsaṃjñāyatanasamatikramāt saṃjñāvedayitanirodham [f. 243a] upasaṃpadya viharaty, ayam aṣṭamo vimokṣaḥ.

Śrāv-bh II 36–38: -II-2-a-(8)

tatra katham samāpattiprabhedena pudgalavyavasthānaṃ bhavati | tadyathā kāyasākṣy aṣṭau vimokṣān kāyena sākṣātkṛtvopasaṃpadya viharati | na ca sarveṇa sarvam āsravakṣayam anuprāpto bhavati | rūpī rūpāṇi paśyati | adhyātmam arūpasaṃjñī bahirdhā rūpāṇi paśyati | śubhaṃ vimokṣaṃ (kāyena sākṣātkṛtvopasaṃpadya viharati | akāśānantyāyatanam, vijñānānantyāyatanam, ākiñcanyāyatanam, naivasaṃjñānāsaṃjñāyatanam,) saṃjñāvedayitanirodham anulomapratilomaṃ samāpadyate ca, vyuttiṣṭhate ca | evaṃ samāpattiprabhedena pudgalavyavasthānaṃ bhavati |

Knowledge of the Recollection of Former States of Existence (DĀ 16.11)

DĀ 16.11

aparam api bhadanta bhagavata ānuttaryaṃ yadā me bhagavāṃ dharmaṃ de(śayat)i (yad uta[1177] pūrvan)i(vāsānusmṛ)ti(**295r5**)jñāne[1178] <|> iha bhadantaika<ḥ> śramaṇo vā brāhmaṇo vā anekavidhaṃ pūrvanivāsaṃ samanusmarati <|> tadyathā ekām api jāti<ṃ dve ti>sraḥ[1179] catasraḥ yāvad[1180] ihotpanna .. .. .i khalv ahaṃ bhada(**295r6**)nta varṣā ugrakoṭīgaṇanasaṃkhyāmātrakena satvānām āyuṣparyantaṃ vadāmi <|> bhagavāṃ bhadanta yatra tatra uṣitapū(rv)o (bhavati yad)i (vā rū)piṣ(u ya)di vā arūpiṣ(u ya)di[1181] (**295r7**) vā saṃjñiṣu yadi vā asaṃjñiṣu yadi vā naivasaṃjñānāsaṃjñiṣu tatra tatra bhagavāṃ {nā}sākāraṃ{s}[1182] soddeśam[1183] anekavidhaṃ pūrvanivāsaṃ samanu(smarati[1184] | etad ānuttaryaṃ bhadanta

1177. On the formula: *aparam api me bhadanta ... deśayati yad uta,* see note 1034 above.

1178. Cf. 295r8.

1179. Cf. DN III 110.29: *ekam pi jātiṃ dve pi jātiyo tisso pi catasso pi.*

1180. This passage is abbreviated but a complete parallel is found in DĀ 27.85 (*Tridaṇḍi-sūtra*) (Choi 2016): *tadyathā ekām api jāti<ṃ> dve tisraś catasraḥ paṃca ṣaṭ saptāṣṭau nava daśa viṃśa tṛṃśa catvāriṃśat pa(ñcāśat jāti)*(**366r6**)*śataṃ jātisahasraṃ anekāny api jātiśatāny anekāny api jātisahasrāṇi anekāny api jātiśatasahasrāṇi saṃvarttakalpavivarttakalpam api saṃvarttavivarttakalpa(m anekān a)*(**366r7**)*pi saṃvarttakalpān anekān api vivarttakalpān anekān api saṃvarttavivarttakalpān samanusmara{ṃ}ty; amī nāma te bhavantaḥ satvā yatrāham āsam evaṃnāmā evaṃjātir evaṃgotra evamāhāra (eva)ṃ(sukhaduḥkha)*(**366r8**)*pratisaṃvedī evaṃdīrghāyur e(vaṃ)cirasthitika eva{ṃvaya}māyuṣparyanta<ḥ |> so 'haṃ tasmāc cyuto 'mutropapanna<ḥ> tasmād api cyuto 'mutropapannaḥ tasmād api cyuta ihopa(panna iti).*

1181. Cf. DN III 111.10–11: *abhinivuttha-pubbaṃ* (cf. note 6 for °*pubbo* variant) *hoti yadi vā rūpīsu yadi vā arūpīsu yadi vā saññīsu yadi vā asaññīsu yadi vā n'-eva-saññī-nāsaññīsu.*

1182. Ms. reads *nātmākāraṃs.*

1183. Ms. reads *sadaśam.* Cf. DN III 111.7–8: *iti sākāraṃ sa-uddesaṃ aneka-vihitaṃ pubbenivāsaṃ anussarati.*

1184. Cf. 295r5.

bhagavato ya)(**295r8**)d uta pūrvanivāsānusmṛtijñāne{na}[1185] <|> tad bhagavān aśeṣam abhijānāti <|> tat te aśeṣam abhijānata{ḥ} uttare abhijñeyaṃ nāsti yasyābhijñānād anyaḥ (ś)r(amaṇo vā brāhmaṇo vā bhagava)(**295v1**)-to[1186] 'ntikād bhūyo 'bhijñatara<ḥ> syād yad uta saṃbodhaye <|>

DĀ 16.11

[Śāriputra:] "'For me, sir, there is another way in which the Blessed One is supreme when he teaches me dharma, and that is (regarding) the knowledge of the recollection of (former) states of existence. In this case, sir, some ascetic or brahmin remembers his various former states of existence. For example, one birth, two, three, four, up to[1187] arising here. Certainly, sir, I say the lifespan of beings is merely calculated to the extreme limit [...] years. Sir, wherever the Blessed One previously stayed, whether in the sphere of materiality or in the sphere of immateriality, whether in the stage of awareness, or the stage of unawareness, or the stage of neither awareness nor unawareness,[1188] the Blessed One remembers those various former states of existence with their characteristic features and their details. Sir, this is the way in which the Blessed One is supreme, and that is regarding the knowledge of the recollection of former states of existence. The Blessed One knows this in its entirety. For you, knowing this in its entirety, there is nothing further to be known from the knowledge of which another ascetic or brahmin could be more knowledgeable than the Blessed One in regard to perfect awakening.'"

1185. Cf. 295r5, DN III 110.25 and DN III 111.14.

1186. On the formula: *etad ānuttaryaṃ bhadanta ... syād yad uta saṃbodhaye*, see note 1005 above.

1187. This passage is abbreviated, but a complete parallel is found in DĀ 27.85 (*Tridaṇḍisūtra*) (Choi 2016) (quotation slightly edited): "For example, [he] recollects also one birth, two, three, four, five, six, seven, eight, nine, ten, twenty, thirty, forty, fifty, a hundred births, a thousand births, also many hundreds of births, also many thousands of births, also many hundreds and thousands of births, also periods of destruction of the world, also periods of evolution of the world, also periods of destruction and evolution of the world. 'When those people were being called by those names, I had such a name, such a birth, such a family, such food, such an experience of happiness and misery, such a long life, such a length of existence, and such an end of life. From there I died and was reborn in the other life, from there again I died and was reborn in another life, and from there again, I died and was reborn in this life.'"

1188. These terms are also discussed in DĀ 15.41c2 above.

~16.11~

T I 18 256c14–21

復次我佛世尊有最勝法。謂沙門婆羅門等。所有過去一生多生所作因緣果報思念等事。乃至壽量。我於俱胝歲數而不能知。唯佛世尊。知彼沙門婆羅門於過去時中處處所止。或色界中。或無色界中。或有想處。或無想處。或非有想非無想處。彼種種所作因緣果報等事。悉能了知。是即名爲佛最勝法

DN 110.24–111.14 (DN 28.16)

16. aparaṃ pana bhante etad ānuttariyaṃ, yathā bhagavā dhammaṃ deseti pubbe-nivāsānussati-ñāṇe. idha bhante ekacco samaṇo vā brāhmaṇo vā ātappam anvāya ... pe ... tathā-rūpaṃ ceto-samādhiṃ phusati, yathā samāhite citte aneka-vihitaṃ pubbe-nivāsaṃ anussarati—seyyathidaṃ, ekam pi jātiṃ dve pi jātiyo tisso pi jātiyo catasso pi jātiyo pañca pi jātiyo dasa pi jātiyo vīsatim pi jātiyo tiṃsam pi jātiyo cattārīsam pi jātiyo paññāsam pi jātiyo jāti-satam pi jāti-sahassam pi jāti-sata-sahassam pi aneke pi saṃvaṭṭa-kappe aneke pi vivaṭṭa-kappe aneke pi saṃvaṭṭa-vivaṭṭa-kappe, amutrāsiṃ evaṃ-nāmo evaṃ-gotto evaṃ-vaṇṇo evam-āhāro evaṃ-sukha-dukkha-paṭisaṃvedī evam-āyu-pariyanto. so tato cuto amutra udapādiṃ. tatrāpāsiṃ evaṃ-nāmo evaṃ-gotto evaṃ-vaṇṇo evam-āhāro evaṃ-sukha-dukkha-paṭisaṃvedī evam-āyu-pariyanto. so tato cuto idhūpapanno ti—ti sākāraṃ sa-uddesaṃ aneka-vihitaṃ pubbe-nivāsaṃ anussarati. santi bhante devā yesaṃ na sakkā gaṇanāya vā saṅkhāto vā āyum saṅkhātuṃ, api ca yasmiṃ yasmiṃ atta-bhāve abhinivuṭṭha-pubbam hoti yadi vā rūpīsu yadi vā arūpīsu yadi vā saññīsu yadi vā asaññīsu yadi vā n'-eva-saññī-nāsaññīsu, iti sākāraṃ sa-uddesaṃ pubbe-nivāsaṃ anussarati. etad ānuttariyaṃ bhante pubbe-nivāsānussati-ñāṇe.

T I 1 78b6–16

如來説法復有上者。謂自識宿命智證。諸沙門婆羅門種種方便入定意三昧。隨三昧心自憶往昔無數世事。一生二生乃至百千生成劫敗劫。如是無數我於某處生。名字如是種姓如是。壽命如是。飲食如是。苦樂如是。從此生彼從彼生此。若干種相。自憶宿命無數劫事。晝夜常念本所經歷。此是色此是無色。此是想此是無想。此是非無想盡憶盡知。此法無上。

DĀ 27.85 (*Tridaṇḍi-sūtra*) (Choi 2016)

sa evaṃ samāhite citte pariśuddhe paryavadāte anaṃgaṇe vigatopakleśe ‹ṛjubhūte› karmaṇye sthite āniṃjyaprāpte pūrvanivāsānusmṛtijñānasākṣā(tk)ri(yāyāṃ vi)(**366r5**)(d)y(āyā)ṃ (c)i(tta)m abhinirṇamayati ‹|› so 'nekavidhaṃ pūrvanivāsaṃ samanusmrati <|> tadyathā ekām api jāti<ṃ> dve tisraś catasraḥ paṃca ṣaṭ saptāṣṭau nava daśa viṃśa tṛṃśa catvāriṃśat pa(ñcāśat jāti)(366r6)-śataṃ jātisahasraṃ anekāny api jātiśatāny anekāny api jātisahasrāṇi anekāny api jātiśatasahasrāṇi saṃvarttakalpavivarttakalpam api saṃvarttavivarttakalpa(m anekān a)(366r7)pi saṃvarttakalpān anekān api vivarttakalpān anekān api saṃvarttavivarttakalpān samanusmara{ṃ}ty; amī nāma te bhavantaḥ satvā yatrāham āsam evaṃnāmā evaṃjātir evaṃgotra evamāhāra (eva)ṃ(sukhaduḥkha)(366r8) pratisaṃvedī evaṃdīrghāyur e(vaṃ)cirasthitika eva{ṃvaya}māyuṣparyanta<ḥ |> so 'haṃ tasmāc cyuto 'mutropapanna<ḥ> tasmād api cyuto 'mutropapannaḥ tasmād api cyuta ihopa(panna iti | sākāraṃ soddeśam aneka)(366v1)vidha<ṃ> pūrvanivāsaṃ samanusmarati |

SBVG 514r9–514v3 (in DĀ 27.97, Choi 2016) (= SBV II 249.3–17)
sa evaṃ samāhite citte (514r10) pariśuddhe paryavadāte anaṃgaṇe vigatopakleśe rijubhūte karmaṇye sthite āniṃjyaprāpte pūrvanivāsā<nu>smṛtijñānasākṣātkriyāyā<ṃ vidyāyāṃ> cittam abhinirṇamayati <|> so 'nekavidhaṃ pūrvanivāsaṃ samanusmarati <|> tadyathā ekām api jātiṃ dve tisraś catasraḥ paṃca ṣaṭsaptāṣṭau nava daśa{d} viṃśa(514v1)taṃ tṛṃśataṃ catvāriṃśatam paṃcāśataṃ jātiśataṃ jātisahasraṃ jātiśatasahasram anekāny api jātiśatāni anekāny api jātisahasrāṇy anekāny api jātiśatasahasrāṇi saṃvarttakalpam api vivarttakalpam api saṃvarttavivarttakalpam api anekān api saṃ(514v2)vartta<kalpā>n anekān api vivarttakalpān anekān api saṃvarttavivarttakalpāṃ samanusmarati | amī nāma te bhavantaḥ satvā{ḥ} yatrāham āsam evaṃnāmā evaṃjātya evaṃgotra evamāhāra evaṃsukhaduḥkhapratisaṃvedī evaṃdīrghāyur evamcirasthitika{ḥ} evamāyuṣparyantaḥ <|> so 'haṃ (514v3) tasmāt sthānāc cyuto 'mutropapannaḥ tasmād api cyuto 'mutropapannaḥ tasmād api cyuta ihopapanna iti | sākāraṃ soddeśam anekavidhaṃ pūrvenivāsam anusmarati <|>

PvSP(K) I 99 (= PvSP 86.1–87.2)
pūrvanivāsānusmṛtijñānena sa ekām api jātim anusmarati, dve tisro yāvaj jātiśatasahasrāṇy apy anusmarati, sa ekam api cittam anusmarati yāvac cittaśatam api, ekam api divasaṃ divasaśatam api, ekam api māsaṃ māsaśatam api, ekam api varṣaṃ varṣaśatam api, ekam api kalpaṃ kalpaśatam api, anekāni api kalpaśatāny anekāny api kalpasahasrāṇy anekāny api kalpaśatasahasrāṇy anekāny api kalpakoṭiniyutaśatasahasrāṇi anusmarati yāvat pūrvāntakoṭīm apy anusmarati, amutrāham āsam evaṃnāmā evaṃgotra evaṃjātir evamāhāra evaṃcirasthitikaḥ, evamāyuṣparyantaḥ, sa tataś cyuto 'mutropapannaḥ, tataś cyuta ihāsmy upapanna iti, sa evaṃ sākāraṃ sādṛśaṃ sanirdeśam anekavidhaṃ pūrvanivāsam

anusmarati, tena ca pūrvanivāsānusmṛtyabhijñānena na manyate, tathā hi tajjñānam ajñānam acintyatām upādāya, so 'haṃ prajānāmīti na manyate, sa tad eva jñānaṃ nopalabhate svabhāvaśūnyatām upādāya svabhāvaviviktatām upādāya svabhāvānupalabdhitām upādāya, na sa pūrvanivāsānusmṛticetanām apy utpādayati, na pūrvanivāsānusmṛtyabhinirhāracetanāṃ vā anyatra sarvākārajñatāmanasikārāt. evaṃ hi śāriputra bodhisattvo mahāsattvaḥ prajñāpāramitāyāṃ caran pūrvanivāsānusmṛtisākṣātkriyājñānam abhinirharati.

Daśa-bh 35.
so 'nekavidhaṃ pūrvanivāsam anusmarati | ekām api jātim anusmarati | dve tisraś catasraḥ pañca daśa viṃśati triṃśataṃ catvāriṃśataṃ pañcaśataṃ jātiśatam anusmarati | anekāny api jātiśatāni | anekāny api jātiśatasahasrāṇi | saṃsaṃvartakalpam api vivartakalpam apy anekān api saṃvartavivartakalpān apu anusmarati | kalpaśatam api kalpasahasram api kalpaśatasahasram api kalpakoṭīm api kalpakoṭiśatam api kalpakoṭīsahasram api kalpakoṭīśatasahasram api yāvad anekāny api kalpakoṭīniyutaśatasahasrāṇy anusmarati | amutrāham āsam evaṃnāmā | evaṃgotra evaṃjātir evamāhāra evamāyuḥpramāṇa evaṃcirasthitika evaṃsukhapratisaṃvedi | so 'haṃ tataś cyuto 'tropapannaḥ | tataś cyuta ihopapannaḥ | iti sākāraṃ soddeśaṃ sanimittam anekavidhaṃ pūrvanivāsam anusmarati |

Abhidh-k-vy 646
punar apram āyuṣmantas tathāgato 'nekavidhaṃ pūrvanivāsam anusmarati. tadyathaikām api jātiṃ dve tisraś catasraḥ paṃca ṣaṭ saptāṣṭau nava daśa viṃśatiṃ yāvad anekān api saṃvartavivartakalpān anusmarati. amī nāma te bhavantaḥ sattvāḥ. yatrāham āsa evaṃnāma evaṃjātya evaṃgotra evamāhāra evaṃsukhaduḥkhapratisaṃvedī evam dīrgh'āyur evaṃcirasthitikaḥ evamāyuṣparyantaḥ so 'haṃ tasmāt sthānāc cyuto 'mutropapannaḥ tasmād api cyuta ihopapanāḥ. iti s'ākāraṃ sa-nidānaṃ soddeśam anekavidhaṃ pūrvanivāsam anusmarati. yad āyuṣmantas tathāgataḥ pūrvavat. idam aṣṭamaṃ tathāgatabalaṃ. yena baleneti pūrvavat.

DN I 13.11–14.1 (*Brahmajāla-sutta* DN 1.31)
31. idha bhikkhave ekacco samaṇo vā brāhmaṇo vā ātappam anvāya padhānam anvāya anuyogam anvāya appamādam anvāya sammāmanasikāram anvāya tathārūpaṃ cetosamādhiṃ phusati yathā samāhite citte anekavihitaṃ pubbe nivāsaṃ anussarati—seyyathīdaṃ: ekam pi jātiṃ dve pi jātiyo tisso pi jātiyo catasso pi jātiyo pañca pi jātiyo dasa pi jātiyo vīsatim pi jātiyo tiṃsam pi jātiyo cattārīsam pi jātiyo paññāsam pi jātiyo jātisatam pi jātisahassam pi jātisatasahassam pi anekāni

pi jātisatāni anekāni pi jātisahassāni anekāni pi jātisatasahassāni. amutrāsiṃ evannāmo evaṃgotto evaṃvaṇṇo evamāhāro evaṃsukhadukkhapaṭisaṃvedi evamāyupariyanto. so tato cuto amutra upapādiṃ. tatrāpāsiṃ evannāmo evaṃgotto evaṃvaṇṇo evamāhāro evaṃsukhadukkhapaṭisaṃvedī evamāyupariyanto. so tato cuto idhūpapanno ti iti sākāraṃ sa-uddesaṃ anekavihitaṃ pubbenivāsaṃ anussarati.

⁝ Method of Reading Minds (DĀ 16.12)

DĀ 16.12

[a] aparam api me bhadanta bhagavata ānuttaryaṃ yadā me bhagavāṃ dharmaṃ deśayati yad uta ā(deśanāvidhau[1189] | iha bhadantaikaḥ śrāmaṇo vā brāhmaṇo)[1190] **(295v2)** vā nimittena vā parikathayā vā ādiśaty; evaṃ <te> ma(na i)tthaṃ[1191] te mana anyathā te mana<ḥ[1192] |> cira{ṃ}kṛtaṃ cirabhāṣitam apy ādiśati <|> rahaẖkṛtaṃ[1193] (rahobhāṣitam apy ādiśati dūre 'py ādiśaty; antike 'py ādiśati atītam anā)**(295v3)**gataṃ[1194] pratyutpannam apy ādiśati • atī<tānā>gatapratyutpannam apy ādiśati[1195] <|> cittam apy ādiśati <|> cetasām[1196] api dharmān nādiśa(t)i <|> y(ac) c(a) t(athā ādiśati tat sarvaṃ tat tathaiva bhavati nānyathā |)[1197]

[b] (pu)**(295v4)**nar aparam ihaiko na haiva nimittena vā parikathayā vā ādiśati <|> api tu de(vā)nāṃ vā (ma)nuṣyāṇāṃ vā śābdaṃ śrutvā ā(d)i(śati | evaṃ) te (mana itthaṃ te mano 'nyathā te mano; yāva)**(295v5)**d ādiśa{n}ti[1198] sarvaṃ tat tathaiva bhavati nānyathā <|>

1189. Cf. 296r2 along with DN III 103.21 and DN III 104.14: *ādesana-vidhāsu.*

1190. Cf. 296r4, 296r8, 296v4 as well as 293r5, 293r8, 293v1.

1191. Cf. 295v5.

1192. Ms. reads *manu.*

1193. Note *jhivāmūlīya.*

1194. Cf. 295v7.

1195. It is possible that the repetition of phrases concerning the past, future, and present here is the result of a dittographical error by the scribe, but this line in this section of the manuscript where the first instance is reconstructed is too damaged to allow one to draw any firm conclusions.

1196. Ms. reads *caitasām.* Cf. 295v8.

1197. Cf. 295v8.

1198. Cf. 295v2 and 295v6–8, cf. also DĀ 29 (*Kaivarti-sūtra*) S14 for an example of the use of *yāvat* demonstrating a gloss in content: *evaṃ te mana itthaṃ yāvat sarvaṃ tat tathaiva bhavati nānyathā.*

[c] punar aparam ihaiko na haiva nimittena vā pa{.. ..}rikathayā[1199] vā ādiśati (| na haiva) dev(ānāṃ vā manuṣyāṇaṃ)[1200] vā śabdaṃ (**295v6**) śrutvā ādiśati <|> api tu parasatvānāṃ parapudgalānāṃ vitarkitaṃ <vicāri-taṃ>[1201] manasā mānasaṃ jñātvā ādiśati <|> evaṃ t(e mana) itthaṃ te manānyathā te <ma>naḥ[1202] <|> cirakṛtaṃ cira(**295v7**)bhāṣitam apy ādiśati <|> rahaẖkṛtaṃ[1203] rahobhāṣitam apy ādiśati <|> dūre 'py ādiśaty; antike 'py ādiśati <|> atītam apy ādiśaty <|> anāgatam apy ādiśati <|> pūrvavac cittam apy ādi(**295v8**)śati <|> cetasām api dharmān nādiśati <|> yac ca tathā ādiśati tat sarvaṃ tat tathaiva bhavati nānyathā <|>

[d] bhagavān bhadanta paraṃ paśyaty avitarkam avicāraṃ samādhiṃ samāpannaṃ dṛṣṭvā ca punas te evaṃ bhavati <|> (**296r1**) .. .. + + (na) vitarkayati na vicārayati <|> yathā praṇihitāś cāsya manaḥsaṃskārāḥ pravarttante <|> idānīm ayam āyuṣmāṃ tasmāt s(amā)dher[1204] vyutthāya imāṃś cemāṃś ca vitarkān vitarkayi(**296r2**)(ṣ)y(atī)ti <|> (sa tasmāt) [1205] samādher vyutthāya tāṃs tāṃ vita(r)kān vitarkayati <|> etad ānuttaryaṃ bhadanta (bhagava)to <yad uta> ādeś(anāvi)dhau[1206] <|> tad bhagavā(n aśe)ṣ(a)m (abhijā)nāti <|> t(at te) a(śe)ṣam abhijānata uttare 'bhi(**296r3**)-jñeyaṃ nāsti yasyābhijñānād anyaḥ śramaṇo vā brāhmaṇo vā bhagav(ato 'ntikād bhūyo 'bhijña)tara<ḥ> (s)y(ād)[1207] yad uta saṃbodhaye <|>

1199. *Parikathayā* is the correct reading here, and the two damaged akṣaras between the *pa* and *arikathayā* do not serve a purpose. Perhaps there were filler marks that have been destroyed, or perhaps this folio was written over twice in an attempt to correct mistakes.

1200. Cf. 296v4.

1201. Cf. 296r1, BLSF II.1 Or.15009/137r6 (= DĀ(U.H.) 137): */// + rapudgalānāṃ vā vitarkitaṃ vicaritaṃ manasā manoj[ñ]ā ///* and DĀ 29 (*Kaivarti-sūtra*) S13: *api tu parasatvānāṃ parapudgalānāṃ vitarkitaṃ vicāritaṃ vā mana<sā> mānasaṃ jñātvā ādiśaty* and DN III 104.1: *api ca kho vitakkayato vicārayato.*

1202. Cf. DĀ 29 (*Kaivarti-sūtra*) S15: *evaṃ te mana itthaṃ te yāvat sarvaṃ tat tathaiva bhavati nānyathā.*

1203. Ms. reads *rahatkṛtaṃ*. Note that this has been emended to *rahaẖkṛtaṃ* (i.e., *jihvāmūlīya*) as in 295v2 above, which may be difficult to discern due to the underline used to denote an emendment to the reading.

1204. Cf. 296r2.

1205. Cf. BLSF II.1 Or.15009/137v2. (= DĀ(U.H.) 137): *[s]a tasmāt samādher vyutthāya.*

1206. Cf. 295v1 along with DN III 103.21 and DN III 104.14: *ādesana-vidāsu.*

1207. On the formula: *etad ānuttaryaṃ bhadanta ... syād yad uta saṃbodhaye*, see note 1005 above.

DĀ 16.12

[a] [Śāriputra:] "'For me, sir, there is another way in which the Blessed One is supreme when he teaches me dharma, and that is regarding the method of reading minds. (In this case, sir, an ascetic) or (brahmin) tells by signs or verbal cues. [Saying]: "Your mind is thus, your mind is this way, your mind is another way." He also tells (what was done long ago and what was said long ago). He also tells what was done secretly (and what was said secretly. He also tells what is remote, he also tells what is near, he also tells the past), future, and present. He also tells the past, future, and present.[1208] He also tells thoughts. However, he does not tell the factors of minds. That which he tells this way, it is all just like this and not otherwise.

[b] "'Moreover, in this case [another] one absolutely does not tell by signs or verbal cues. Rather, he tells by hearing the speech of gods or men. [Saying]: "Your (mind is thus, your mind is this way, your mind is another way)," up to: all that he tells is just like this and not otherwise.

[c] "'Moreover, in this case [yet another] one absolutely does not tell by signs or verbal cues. He (absolutely does not) tell by hearing the speech of gods or (men). Rather, he tells by mentally knowing the reflections, deliberations, and intellect of other beings and other men. [Saying]: "Your (mind) is thus, your mind is this way, your mind is another way." He also tells what was done long ago and what was said long ago. He also tells what was done secretly and what was said secretly. He also tells what is remote. He also tells what is near. He also tells the past. He also tells the future. He also tells previous thoughts. However, he does not read the factors of minds. That which he tells this way, it is all just like this and not otherwise.

[d] "'Sir, the Blessed One sees another, [a monk], and having seen [him] engaged in meditative concentration without reflection and without deliberation, again, he thinks thus: "[...] does not reflect nor does he deliberate. According to how his mental functions become fixed, having now emerged from that meditative concentration, this venerable one will reflect on these and those reflections." [Then] having emerged from that meditative concentration, [the venerable one] reflects on these and those reflections. Sir, this is the way in which the Blessed One is supreme, and that is regarding

1208. See note 1195 above.

the method of reading minds. The Blessed One knows this in its entirety. For (you), knowing this in its entirety, there is nothing further to be known from the knowledge of which another ascetic or brahmin could be (more) knowledgeable (than) the Blessed One in regard to perfect awakening.'"

~16.12b–d~

BLSF II.1 Or.15009/137 (= DĀ(U.H.) 136) (*Prasādanīya-sūtra*)

recto

1 /// .. .. [v]. [t]. [m]. [nā] i.[th]. [t]. [m]. .. + ... + + ... + + ///
2 /// [n]āgata pratyutpannam apy ādiśati dūre h[y] ādiśati [antik]e + ///
3 /// ◯ diśati tat t. «thai»va bhavati nānyathā [•[1209] puna]r aparam i + ///
4 /// ◯ manuṣyāṇāṃ vā śaṣṭaṃ śrutvā ādiśati + .. n. mana + ///
5 /// ◯ na haiva nimittena vā parikathayā vā ādiśati .. ///
6 /// + rapudgalānāṃ vā vitarkitaṃ vicaritaṃ manasā manoj[ñ]ā ///
7 /// + .. bhad. nta .. + + + .. + .[i] + r.. + .ā + ..ṃ + [m]ādhiṃ .. ///

verso

1 ///.. ra y. t. .. + + + + + + + + + + + + ... + ///
2[1210] /// .. ti • [s]a tasmāt samādher vyutthāya tāṃs tāṃ vitarkāṃ vit. ///
3 /// ◯ śeṣam abhijānāti pūrvavad yāva [s]aṃbodhāya • a ///

~16.12~

T I 18 256c22–28

[a] 復次我佛世尊有最勝法。謂世尊説法時。皆如實説。或有沙門婆羅門等。以愚癡故。生彼此意。起疑惑心。謂佛説法。皆以事相言説。所説之法。三世同説。若近若遠。及心意法。亦如是説。彼所説法。皆不如實。作是疑者。佛悉能知。是則名爲佛最勝法

T I 18 256c29–257a3

[b] 復次我佛世尊説法時。若有沙門婆羅門自不生疑。後聞人言。佛所説法皆不如實。聞是言已。便復起疑。亦謂世尊以事相言説。起是謗者。佛亦能知。是即名爲佛最勝法。

T I 18 257a4–9

[c] 復次我佛世尊説法時。若沙門婆羅門等。本不生疑。不謂世尊事相言説。後聞人言。隨彼生疑。而復告語他人。令他亦生疑惑。由疑惑故。生彼此意。

1209. DĀ 16.12c begins here.

1210. DĀ 16.12d.

作如是言。此事如前。皆非眞實。此是衆生種種異心。佛於如是。皆悉了知。是即名爲佛最勝法

T I 18 257a10–14

[d] 復次我佛世尊。見有沙門在三摩地無疑無説。佛悉能知彼之行願。又復或見沙門從定而出。佛亦能知。彼所有事及有疑惑故彼出定。如是疑惑佛皆決了。是即名爲佛最勝法

DN III 103.20–104.14 (DN 28.6)

[a] 6. aparaṃ pana bhante etad ānuttariyaṃ, yathā bhagavā dhammaṃ deseti ādesana-vidhāsu. catasso imā bhante ādesana-vidhā. idha bhante ekacco nimittena ādisati—evam pi te mano, ittham pi te mano, iti pi te cittan ti. so bahuṃ ce pi ādisati—tath' eva taṃ hoti, no aññathā, ayaṃ paṭhamā ādesan-avidhā.

[b] puna ca paraṃ bhante idh' ekacco na h' eva kho nimittena ādisati, api ca kho manussānaṃ vā amanussānaṃ vā devatānaṃ vā saddaṃ sutvā ādisati—evam pi te mano, ittham pi te mano, iti pi te cittan ti. so bahuñ ce pi ādisati—tath' eva taṃ hoti no aññathā, ayaṃ dutiyā ādesana-vidhā.

[c] puna ca paraṃ bhante idh' ekacco na h' eva kho nimittena ādisati, na pi manussānaṃ vā amanussānaṃ vā devatānaṃ vā saddaṃ sutvā ādisati, [104] api ca kho vitakkayato vicārayato vitakka-vipphāra-saddaṃ sutvā ādisati—evam pi te mano, ittham pi te mano, iti pi te cittan ti. so bahuñ ce pi ādisati—tath' eva taṃ hoti no aññathā, ayaṃ tatiyā ādesana-vidhā.

[d] puna ca paraṃ bhante idh' ekacco na h' eva kho nimittena ādisati, na pi manussānaṃ vā amanussānaṃ vā devatānaṃ vā saddaṃ sutvā ādisati, na pi vitakkayato vicārayato vitakka-vipphāra-saddaṃ sutvā ādisati, api ca kho avitakkaṃ avicāraṃ samādhiṃ samāpannassa cetasā ceto paricca pajānāti—yathā imassa bhoto mano-saṃkhārā paṇihitā, tathā imassa cittassa anantarā amuṃ nāma vitakkaṃ vitakkessatī ti. so bahuñ ce pi ādisati—tath' eva taṃ hoti no aññathā, ayaṃ catutthā ādesana-vidhā. etad ānuttariyaṃ bhante ādesana-vidhāsu.

T I 1 77c25–28

[a] 如來説法復有上者。謂觀察。觀察者。謂有沙門婆羅門以想觀察。他心爾趣此心爾趣。彼心作是想時。或虚或實。是爲一觀察。

T I 1 77c28–78a01
[b] 諸沙門婆羅門不以想觀察。或聞諸天及非人語。而語彼言。汝心如是。汝心如是。此亦或實或虛。是二觀察。

T I 1 78a01–05
[c] 或有沙門婆羅門。不以想觀察。亦不聞諸天及非人語。自觀己身又聽他言。語彼人言。汝心如是汝心如是。此亦有實有虛。是爲三觀察。

T I 1 78a05–11
[d] 或有沙門婆羅門不以想觀察。亦不聞諸天及非人語。又不自觀觀他。除覺觀已得定意三昧。觀察他心而語彼言。汝心如是汝心如是。如是觀察則爲眞實。是爲四觀察。此法無上。智慧無餘。神通無餘。諸世間沙門婆羅門。無有與如來等者。況欲出其上。

~16.12a~

DĀ 29 (*Kaivarti-sūtra*) S12 (Zhou 2008, 7)
S12 na haiva nimittena vā parikathayā vā ādiśaty api <tu> devā<nāṃ> manusyāṇāṃ [sic] vā śabdaṃ śrutvā ādiśati evaṃ te <ma>na yāvat sarva<ṃ> tat tathaiva bhavati nānyathā

AN I 170–71 (*Saṇgārava-sutta*, AN III. 60. 6)
katamañ ca brāhmaṇa ādesanāpāṭihāriyaṃ? idha brāhmaṇa ekacco nimittena ādisati, evam pi te mano ittham pi te mano iti pi te cittan ti. so bahuñ ce pi ādisati, tath'; eva taṃ hoti no aññathā.

~16.12b~

DĀ 29 (*Kaivarti-sūtra*) S13 (Zhou 2008, 7)
S13 na haiva nimittena vā parikathayā vā ādiśati napi devānāṃ vā manuṣyāṇāṃ vā śabda<ṃ> śrutvā ādiśati api tu parasatvānāṃ parapudgalānāṃ vitarkitaṃ vicāritaṃ vā mana<sā> mānasaṃ jñātvā ādiśaty evaṃ mana yāvat sarvaṃ <tat> tathaiva bhavati nānyathā

AN I 171 (*Saṇgārava-sutta*, AN III. 60. 6)
idha pana brāhmaṇa ekacco na h'; eva kho nimittena ādisati, api ca kho manussānaṃ vā amanussānaṃ vā devatānaṃ vā saddaṃ sutvā ādisati, evam pi te mano ittham pi te mano iti pi te cittan ti. so bahuñ ce pi ādisati tath'; eva taṃ hoti no aññathā.

~16.12c~

DĀ 29 (*Kaivarti-sūtra*) S14 (Zhou 2008, 7–8)

S14 śramaṇaṃ vā brāhmaṇaṃ vā nimittena vā parikathayā vā ādiśantaṃ yāvat sarvaṃ tat tathaiva bhavati nānyathā ca dṛṣṭ<v>ā ca punar anya<ta>masyāśrāddhasya gṛhapater vā gṛhapatiputrasya vā ārocayed yat khalu bhoḥ puruṣa jānīthā ihāham adrākṣam anyatamaṃ śramaṇaṃ vā brāhmaṇaṃ vā nimittena vā parikathayā vā ādiśantam evaṃ te mana itthaṃ te mana yāvat sarvaṃ tat tathaiva bhavati nānyathā

AN 171 (*Saṅgārava-sutta*, AN III. 60. 6)

idha pana brāhmaṇa ekacco na h'; eva kho nimittena ādisati na pi manussānaṃ vā amanussānaṃ vā devatānaṃ vā saddaṃ sutvā ādisati, api ca kho vitakkayato vicārayato vitakkavipphārasaddaṃ sutvā ādisati, evam pi kho te mano ittham pi te mano iti pi te cittan ti. so bahuñ ce pi ādisati tath'; eva taṃ hoti no aññathā.

~16.12d~

DĀ 29 (*Kaivarti-sūtra*) S15 (Zhou 2008, 8)

S15 sa evaṃ vaded atra nu bhoḥ puruṣa kim āścaryaṃ yatredānī<ṃ> tvam adrākṣīr anyatama<ṃ> vā śramaṇaṃ vā bra<hma>ṇaṃ vā nimittena <vā> parikathaya vā ādiśantam evaṃ te mana itthaṃ te yāvat sarvaṃ tat tathaiva bhavati nānyathā tat kasya hetor asti khalu bhoḥ puruṣa īkṣaṇikā nāma vidyā yām ihaika udgṛhya par<ya>vāpya nimittena vā parikathayā vā ādiśati yāva tat sarvaṃ tat tathaiva nānyathā

AN 171 (*Saṅgārava-sutta*, AN III. 60. 6)

idha pana brāhmaṇa ekacco na h'; eva kho nimittena ādisati na pi manussānaṃ vā amanussānaṃ vā devatānaṃ vā saddaṃ sutvā ādisati na pi vitakkayato na pi vicārayato na vitakkavipphārasaddaṃ sutvā ādisat, api ca kho avitakkaṃ avicāraṃ samādhiṃ samāpannassa citasā ceto paricca pajānāti, yathā imassa bhoto manosaṅkhāre paṇihitā imassa cittassa anantarā amun nāma vitakkaṃ vitakkissatī ti. so bahuñ ce pi ādisati tath'; eva taṃ hoti no aññathā. idaṃ vuccati brāhmaṇa ādesanāpāṭihāriyaṃ.

Theories of Eternalism (DĀ 16.13)

DĀ 16.13a

[a] a(param a)pi (me bha)d(a)nt(a bha)g(avata ā)nu(tta)ryaṃ yadā <me>[1211] bhaga(**296r4**)vāṃ dharmaṃ deśayati yad uta śāśvata(vād)itāyāṃ[1212] <|> iha bhadantai(kaḥ śramaṇo vā brahma)ṇ(o vā ara)ṇyagato vā vṛkṣamūla(gato) v(ā śūnyāgāragato vā ātaptānvayāt prahā)ṇā(**296r5**)nvayā<d> bhāvanānvayā<d> bahulīkārānvayā<t> samyaṅma(nas)i(kā)r(ā)nvayā<t> t(a)drū(paṃ śāntaṃ cetaḥ)samādhiṃ spṛśati yathā sam(āhite citte[1213] viṃśataṃ[1214] saṃvarttavivarttakalpān samanusma)(**296r6**)rati[1215] <|> tasyaivaṃ bhavati <|> etāvad ayaṃ loka<ḥ> saṃvṛ(taś) c(a) vivṛtaś[1216] ca yāvad eva mayānvayam <abhijñāy>ābhisaṃbuddha[1217] <|> itaḥ pū(rvam aha)ṃ (jāna etāvad ayaṃ lokaḥ saṃvṛttaś ca vivṛttaś ca |)[1218] (**296r7**) itaḥ paścād ahaṃ ca jāna etāvad[1219] ayaṃ lok(aḥ sa)ṃ(va)rttayiṣyate ca vivar(tay)i(ṣ)yate[1220] (c)eti[1221] <|> sa na haiva lokasya paryantadarśī bh(avati | api

1211. On the formula: *aparam api me bhadanta ... deśayati yad uta*, see note 1034 above.

1212. Cf. 296r8 and 297r1.

1213. See note 1040 above.

1214. Cf. DN III 109.20–21: *vīsam pi saṃvaṭṭa-vivaṭṭāni.* Note how the number doubles in the two succeeding sections of 16.13 so in 16.13.2 (296v1–2): *catvāriṃśatam*) and 16.13.3 (296v6): *aśītim.*

1215. Cf. 296v1–2 and 296v5–6.

1216. Cf. 296v3 and 296v7 but note that 296v7 reads *saṃvṛttaś ca vivṛttaś ca.*

1217. Ms. reads *abhisaṃbaddha*. Cf. 296v6.

1218. Cf. 296v3 and 296v7 and BLSF II.1 Or.15009/137v6 (= DĀ(U.H.) 137): */// [n]āmi etāval lokaḥ saṃvṛtta[ś ca] vi[v]ṛttaś ca ita .. .. + ///.*

1219. Note the *sandhi* usage here that is not employed elsewhere in this section (apart from where I have reconstructed it) with all other instances reading *jāne etāvad* (see 296v3 and 296v7).

1220. Cf. 296v2, 296v3, and 296v7. Note that the other instances read *saṃvartiṣyate* and *vivartiṣyate.*

1221. Cf. 296v3 and 296v7.

tu pūrvānte jñānadarśanaṃ pravarttate |)[1222] (**296r8**) aparānte (ajñāna)m iti <|> yasyaivaṃ[1223] syād iyaṃ prathamā śāśvatavādit(ā)[1224] <|>

DĀ 16.13a

[a] [Śāriputra:] "'For me, sir, there is another way in which the Blessed One is supreme when he teaches me dharma, and that is regarding the theories of eternalism. In this case, sir, (an ascetic or) brahmin, or one who has gone to the wilderness, or one who has gone to the foot of a tree, or (one who has gone to a solitary place, due to concern with ardor), concern with effort, concern with cultivation, concern with intense practice, and concern with proper mental attention, he experiences a kind of (calm), concentration of mind such that when (his mind) is settled, he remembers (the dissolution and evolution of twenty world cycles). It occurs to him: "Insofar as this world is dissolved and evolved, this succession is completely understood by me through <supernormal knowledge>. To that end, (I know) that previously (this world dissolved and evolved). To that end, I know that hereafter, this world will dissolve and evolve." He is absolutely not one who knows the end of the world. (Rather, knowledge and discernment emerge) in regard to the beginning. In regard to the end he is ignorant. For one to whom this would occur, this is the first theory of eternalism.'"

DĀ 16.13b

[**b**] (p)unar aparaṃ bhadanta ihaikaḥ śramaṇo vā b(r)āhmaṇo vā a(raṇyagato vā vṛkṣamūlagato vā śūnyāgāra)(**296v1**)gato[1225] vā āta(p)t(ān)v(ayā)<t> prahāṇānvayā<d> bhāvanānvayā<d> bahulīkārānvayā<t> (sa)m(ya)ṅmanasikārānvayā<t>[1226] tadrūpaṃ śāntaṃ cetaḥsamādhi(c)e(taḥ)-

1222. Cf. 296v3–4 and 296v7–8.

1223. Ms. reads *pasyaivaṃ*.

1224. Cf. 296v4 and 296v8.

1225. Note that imprints from the *a* and *y* from *araṇyagato* can be made out on 295v1 above the unrelated fragment reading *samādhiṃ spṛśati*.

1226. Ms. reads *samyaṅmanasikāratayā*.

samādhi}ṃ[1227] spṛśati (yathā samāhite citte[1228] ca)(**296v2**)tvāriṃśataṃ[1229] saṃvarttavivarttakalpān samanusmarati <|> (ta)syaivaṃ bhavati <|> etāvad (ayaṃ) lokaḥ saṃvarttiṣyate ca vivarttiṣyate ca yāvad ev(a ma)yānvayam a(bh)i(jñayābhisaṃbuddha; itaḥ paścā)(**296v3**)d[1230] ahaṃ jāne etāvad {v}ayaṃ lokaḥ saṃvarttiṣyate ca viva(rtt)i(ṣya)te[1231] ceti <|> itaḥ pūrvam ahaṃ jāne etāvad ayaṃ lokaḥ saṃvṛtaś ca vi(v)ṛ(taś) c(e)t(i |) s(a) n(a haiva lokas)y(a par)y(an)t(adar)ś(ī) bh(avati |)[1232] (**296v4**) api tv aparānte jñānadarśanaṃ pravarttate (pūrvā)nte[1233] ajñā(nam iti |)[1234] yasyaivaṃ sy(ād) i(yaṃ dv)i(t)ī(yā[1235] śā)śvatavāditā{ṃ}[1236] <|>

DĀ 16.13b

[b] [Śāriputra:] "'Moreover, sir, in this case an ascetic or brahmin, or one who has gone to the wilderness, (or one who has gone to the foot of a tree), or one who has gone to a solitary place, due to concern with ardor, concern with effort, concern with cultivation, concern with intense practice, and concern with proper mental attention, he experiences a kind of calm, concentration of mind (such that when his mind is settled), he remembers the dissolution and evolution of forty world cycles. It occurs to him: "Insofar as (this) world will dissolve and evolve, this succession is completely understood by me through supernormal knowledge. (Hence), I know that hereafter this world will dissolve and evolve. Hence, I know that previously this world dissolved and evolved." He is (absolutely) not one who knows the end of the world. Rather, knowledge and discernment emerge in regard

1227. It appears that at some point in the course of copying the text, a scribe introduced a textual corruption where *cetaḥsamādhi* was written twice. Whether this duplication was introduced by scribe C or he just diligently copied the mistake is impossible to say.

1228. See note 1040 above.

1229. Cf. 292r5, 296r5, and 296v5.

1230. Cf. 296r6 and 296v6.

1231. Cf. 296r7, 296v2, and 296v7.

1232. Cf. 296r7 and 296v7.

1233. Cf. 296v7–8 and s.v. *pūrvanta* in BHSD and SWTF.

1234. Cf. 296r8 and 296v8. Note however, the reconstruction of *ajñānam* is not attested to textually but fits contextually.

1235. Cf. 296r8: *yasyaivaṃ syād iyaṃ prathamā śāśvatavādit(ā)* and 296v8: *yasyaivaṃ syād iyaṃ tṛtīyā śāśvatavāditā.*

1236. Ms. reads *śvatavādināṃ*

to the end. In regard to the beginning he is ignorant. For he who would be thus, this is the second theory of eternalism.'"

DĀ 16.13c

[c] punar aparaṃ bhadanta ihaikaḥ śr(amaṇo) vā brāhmaṇ(o) vā a(raṇyagato) (**296v5**) vā vṛkṣamūlagato vā śunyāgāragato vā ātaptānvayāt prahāṇānvayād bhāvanānvayā<d> bahu(l)īkārānvayā<t> samyaṅmanasikārānvay(āt ta)drū(paṃ śānta)ṃ (cetaḥsamādhiṃ sp)ṛ(śati ya)th(ā)[1237] (**296v6**) samāhite citte aśītiṃ saṃvartta<vivartta>kalpān samanusmarati <|> tasyai-vaṃ bhavati <|> etāvad ayaṃ loka<ḥ> (saṃ)varttate ca vivarttate ca yāvad eva mayā(n)v(a)y(am a)bhijñayābhisaṃbuddha;[1238] ita<ḥ> pūrva(**296v7**)(m aha)ṃ (jā)ne[1239] etāvad ayaṃ lokaḥ saṃvṛttaś ca vivṛttaś ca <|> itaḥ paścād apy ahaṃ jāne etāvad ayaṃ lokaḥ saṃvartti(ṣ)yate ca[1240] vivarttiṣyate c(e)ti[1241] <|> s(a na) haiva lokasya paryantadarśī bhavati <|> api tu pū(**296v8**)(rvāntāpa)rānte[1242] ('s)y(a)[1243] jñāna(darśa)naṃ[1244] pravarttata iti <|> yasyaivaṃ syād iyaṃ tṛtīyā[1245] śāśvatavāditā <|> bhagavāṃ bhadanta divyena cakṣuṣā yāvat sugatau svargaloke deveṣūpapadyata iti[1246] <|> etad ānuttaryaṃ bhada(**297r1**)nta bhagavato yad uta śāśvatavāditāyāṃ; tad bhagavān aśeṣam abhijānāti <|> tat te aśeṣam abhijānata uttare 'bhijñeyaṃ nāsti yasyābhijñānād anyaḥ śramaṇo vā brāhmaṇo vā bhagavato (**297r2**) 'ntikād bhūyo 'bhijñatara<ḥ> syād yad uta saṃbodhaye <|>

DĀ 16.13c

[c] [Śāriputra:] "'Moreover, sir, in this case an ascetic or brahmin, or one who has gone to the wilderness, or one who has gone to the foot of a tree,

1237. See note 1040 above.

1238. Cf. 296r5–6 and 296v2.

1239. Cf. 296v3.

1240. Ms. reads *na*.

1241. Cf. 296r7 and 296v3.

1242. Cf. 296r8 and s.v. *pūrvantāparānte* in SWTF.

1243. This reconstruction is not attested textually and should be considered an educated guess based upon what would be possible in the limited space here in the ms.

1244. Cf. 296v4.

1245. Ms. reads *tṛtayā*.

1246. Note this phrase: *bhagavāṃ bhadanta divyena cakṣuṣā yāvat sugatau svargaloke deveṣūpapadyata iti*, also occurs in 16.7.6 (293v3). See note 1109 above.

or one who has gone to a solitary place, due to concern with ardor, concern with effort, concern with cultivation, concern with intense practice, and concern with the proper mental attention, he experiences a kind of calm, (concentration of mind) such that when his mind is settled, he remembers the dissolution and evolution of eighty world cycles. It occurs to him: "Insofar as this world dissolves and evolves, this succession is completely understood by me through supernormal knowledge. Hence, I know that previously this world dissolved and evolved. Hence, I know that hereafter this world will dissolve and evolve." He is absolutely (not) one who knows the end of the world. Rather, knowledge and discernment emerge for him in regard to the beginning and the end. For he who would be thus, this is the third theory of eternalism. Sir, with his divine eye the Blessed One [sees all possible births] up to birth in a good condition, a celestial world of the gods. Sir, this is the way in which the Blessed One is supreme, and that is regarding the theories of eternalism. The Blessed One knows this in its entirety. For you, knowing this in its entirety, there is nothing further to be known from the knowledge of which another ascetic or brahmin could be more knowledgeable than the Blessed One in regard to perfect awakening.'"

~16.13a~

BLSF II.1 Or.15009/137 (= DĀ(U.H.) 136) (*Prasādanīya-sūtra*)

verso

3 /// ○ śeṣam abhijānāti pūrvavad yāva [s]aṃbodhāya •[1247] a ///

4 /// ○ śvatavidhāne iha bhadanta [ś]rama .o [vā] b[r]āhma + ///

5 /// ○ nusmarati tasyaivaṃ bhavati etāval l[o]kaḥ saṃ .[ṛ]+ ///

6 /// [n]āmi etāval lokaḥ saṃvṛtta[ś ca] vi[v]ṛttaś ca ita .. .. + ///

7 ///......rśī bhavati • [a]pi tu. .r[v]ā .e .. .. [p]a[t]e + ///

~16.13b–c~

BLSF III.1 Or.15009/408 (= DĀ(U.H.) Hs. 137); (*Prasādanīya-sūtra*)

recto

a /// + .. + + + + + + + ... + + ///

b /// .y. [t]e ca [y]āvad e[v]a mayā svayam abhijñāyā[bh]i ///

c[1248] /// .. taḥ pūrvaṃ na jānāmi • etāval lokaḥ saṃvṛ ///

d /// + + ..ṃ p[r]a[ty]e .. pūrvānt[e] ajñānam iti yasyaivaṃ ///

1247. DĀ 16.13a begins here.

1248. DĀ 16.13b

e /// + [a]raṇ[ya]gato vā pūrvavad [y]āvad yathā samā[h]i[t]e ///
f /// + [va]r[t]a te .. [y]āvad eva mayā svayam abhij[ñ]āyā ///
g[1249] /// + mi • (et)āva[l] (l)[o]k[a]ḥ ..ṃvar[tiṣ]ḍ. + + .. .i + + ///
verso
a /// + + + + + + +.. .. + .. + .[ū/ṛ] + + + + + ///
b /// + n a[p]i pūrvavad y[ā]vad [d]eveṣūpa[pad]yate • et. ///
c /// + rvavad yāvat saṃbodhāya •[1250] apara[m] api [m]e bhadaṃ ///

~16.13~

T I 18 257a15–21
[a] 復次我佛世尊有最勝法。謂佛世尊善能了知諸不究竟法。若有沙門婆羅門。在於山中。住等引心。以自通力。知二十增減劫事。彼作是念。我於過去世中。所有增減劫事。我悉能知。世尊彼沙門婆羅門。而於未來及今現在增減等事。而不能知。唯佛世尊具知三世增減等事。是名了知第一不究竟法

T I 18 257a22–27
[b] 復次世尊。若有沙門婆羅門等。止於深山。住等引心。以自通力。知四十增減劫事。彼作是念。未來世中。所有增減。我已悉知。世尊彼沙門婆羅門。而不知彼過去現在增減劫事。唯佛世尊。具知三世。是名了知第二不究竟法

T I 18 257a28–b6
[c] 復次世尊。若有沙門婆羅門等。在於深山。住等引心。以自通力。知八十增減劫事。彼作是念。所有過去未來增減等事。我悉能知。世尊彼沙門婆羅門。唯今現世所有邊際。而不能知。唯佛世尊一一了知三世邊際。是即名爲了知第三不究竟法。如是世尊以清淨天眼過於肉眼。悉見衆生生滅之法。乃至生於天界。是即名爲佛最勝法

DN III 108.20–109.11 (DN 28.15)
[a] 15. aparaṃ pana bhante etad ānuttariyaṃ, yathā bhagavā dhammaṃ deseti sassata-vādesu. tayo 'me bhante sassata-vādā. idha bhante ekacco samaṇo vā brāhmaṇo vā ātappam anvāya padhānam anvāya anuyogam anvāya appamādam anvāya sammā-manasikāram anvāya tathā-rūpaṃ ceto-samādhiṃ phusati, yathā samāhite citte aneka-vihitaṃ pubbe-nivāsaṃ anussarati—seyyathidaṃ, ekam pi jātiṃ dve pi jātiyo tisso pi jātiyo catasso pi jātiyo pañca pi jātiyo dasa pi jātiyo vīsam pi jātiyo tiṃsam pi jātiyo cat-

1249. DĀ 16.13c
1250. DĀ 16.14a begins here.

tālīsam pi jātiyo paññāsam pi jātiyo jāti-satam pi jāti-sahassam pi jāti-sata-sahassam pi anekāni pi jāti-satāni anekāni pi jāti-sahassāni anekāni pi jāt-isata-sahassāni. amutrāsiṃ evaṃ-nāmo evaṃ-gotto evaṃ-vaṇṇo evam-āhāro evaṃ-sukha-dukkha-paṭisaṃvedī evam-āyu-pariyanto. so tato cuto amutra udapādiṃ. tatrāpāsiṃ evaṃ-nāmo evaṃ-gotto evaṃ-vaṇṇo evam-āhāro evaṃ-sukha-dukkha-paṭisaṃvedī evam-āyu-pariyanto. so tato cuto idhūpapanno ti—iti sākāraṃ sa-uddesaṃ aneka-vihitaṃ pubbe-nivāsaṃ anussarati. so evam āha: atītaṃ p' ahaṃ addhānaṃ jānāmi, saṃvaṭṭi vā loko vivaṭṭi vā ti,—anāgataṃ p' ahaṃ addhānaṃ jānāmi, saṃvaṭṭissati vā loko vivaṭṭissati vā ti. sassato attā ca loko ca vañjho kūṭaṭṭho esika-ṭṭhāyi-ṭṭhito, te ca sattā sandhāvanti saṃsaranti cavanti upapajjanti, atthi tv eva sassati-saman ti. ayaṃ paṭhamo sassata-vādo.

DN III 109.11–110.4 (DN 28.15)
[b]puna ca paraṃ bhante idh' ekacco samaṇo vā brāhmaṇo vā ātappam anvāya padhānam anvāya anuyogam anvāya appamādam anvāya sammā-manasikāram anvāya tathā-rūpaṃ ceto-samādhiṃ phusati, yathā samāhite citte aneka-vihitaṃ pubbe-nivāsaṃ anussarati—seyyathidaṃ ekam pi saṃvaṭṭa-vivaṭṭaṃ dve pi saṃvaṭṭa-vivaṭṭāni tīṇi pi saṃvaṭṭa-vivaṭṭāni cattāri pi saṃvaṭṭa-vivaṭṭāni pañca pi saṃvaṭṭa-vivaṭṭāni dasa pi saṃvaṭṭa-vivaṭṭāni amutrāsiṃ evaṃ-nāmo evaṃ-gotto evaṃ-vaṇṇo evam-āhāro evaṃ-sukha-dukkha-paṭisaṃvedī evam-āyu-pariyanto. so tato cuto amutra upapādiṃ. tatrāpāsiṃ evaṃ-nāmo evaṃ-gotto evaṃ-vaṇṇo evam-āhāro evaṃ-sukha-dukkha-paṭisaṃvedī evam-āyu-pariyanto. so tato cuto idhū-papanno ti—iti sākāraṃ sa-uddesaṃ aneka-vihitaṃ pubbe-nivāsaṃ anussarati. so evam āha: atītaṃ kho aham addhānaṃ jānāmi saṃvaṭṭi pi loko vivaṭṭi pi loko, anāgataṃ ca kho ahaṃ addhānaṃ [110] jānāmi saṃvaṭṭissati vā loko vivaṭṭissati vā ti. sassato attā ca loko ca vañjho kūṭaṭṭho esikaṭṭhāyiṭṭhito, te ca sattā sandhāvanti saṃsaranti cavanti upapajjanti, atthi tv eva sassati-saman ti. ayaṃ dutiyo sassata-vādo.

DN III 110.4–23 (DN 28.15)
[c] puna ca paraṃ bhante idh' ekacco samaṇo vā brāhmaṇo vā ātappam anvāya ... pe ... tathā-rūpaṃ ceto samādhiṃ phusati yathā samāhite citte aneka-vihitaṃ pubbe-nivāsaṃ anussarati—seyyathidaṃ dasa pi saṃvaṭṭa-vivaṭṭāni vīsam pi saṃvaṭṭa-vivaṭṭāni tiṃsam pi saṃvaṭṭa-vivaṭṭāni cattārīsam pi saṃvaṭṭa-vivaṭṭāni. amutrāsiṃ evaṃ-nāmo evaṃ-gotto evaṃ-vaṇṇo evam-āhāro evaṃ-sukha-dukkha-paṭisaṃvedī evam-āyu-pariyanto.

so tato cuto amutra udapādiṃ. tatrāpāsiṃ evaṃ-nāmo evaṃ-gotto evaṃ-vaṇṇo evam-āhāro evaṃ-sukha-dukkha-paṭisaṃvedī evam-āyu-pariyanto. so tato cuto idhūpapanno ti—iti sākāraṃ sa-uddesaṃ aneka-vihitaṃ pubbe-nivāsaṃ anussarati. so evam āha: atītaṃ p' ahaṃ addhānaṃ jānāmi saṃvaṭṭi pi loko vivaṭṭi pi loko, anāgataṃ p' ahaṃ addhānaṃ jānāmi saṃvaṭṭissati pi loko vivaṭṭissatipi loko ti. sassato attā ca loko ca vañjho kūṭaṭṭho esikaṭṭhāyiṭṭhito, te ca sattā sandhāvanti saṃsaranti cavanti upapajjanti, atthi tv eva sassati-saman ti. ayaṃ tatiyo sassatavādo. etad ānuttariyaṃ bhante sassata-vādesu. etad ānuttariyaṃ bhante sassata-vādesu.

~13a&c~

T I 1 77c10–17

[a] 諸沙門婆羅門。種種方便入定意三昧。隨三昧心憶識四十成劫敗劫。彼作是言。此世間常此爲眞實。餘者虛妄。所以者何。以我憶識故知成劫敗劫。我復能過是知過去成劫敗劫。我不知未來劫之成敗。此說知始不說知終。此人朝暮以無智說言。世間常存唯此眞實。餘者虛妄。此是二常法。

T I 1 77c17–25

[c] 諸沙門婆羅門。種種方便入定意三昧。隨三昧心憶識八十成劫敗劫。彼言此世間常。餘者虛妄。所以者何。以我憶識故知有成劫敗劫。復過是知過去成劫敗劫。未來劫之成敗我亦悉知。此人朝暮以無智說言。世間常存唯此爲實。餘者虛妄。是爲三常存法。此法無上。智慧無餘。神通無餘。諸世間沙門婆羅門。無有能與如來等者。況欲出其上。

Cf. T I 1 77c03–10

如來說法復有上者。謂說常法。常如來說法復有上者。謂說常法。常隨三昧心憶識世間二十成劫敗劫。彼作是言。世間常存此爲眞實。餘者虛妄。所以者何。由我憶識故知有此成劫敗劫。其餘過去我所不知。未來成敗我亦不知。此人朝暮以無智說言。世間常存唯此爲實。餘者爲虛。是爲初常法。

~16.13.a–c~

Abhidh-k-vy V.8, 448.3–10 (quoting the *Brahmajāla-sūtra*)

brahmajāla-sūtre vītarāgāṇāṃ kāmadhātv-ālaṃ banānāṃ dṛṣṭīnāṃ samudācāra uktaḥ. pūrva-janma-darśanānisāreṇa ya evam utpanna-dṛṣṭikāḥ. te *pūrvāṃtakalpakāḥ. śāśvatavādino bahavas tatroktāḥ*. teṣām udāharaṇam ekaṃ darśayiṣyāmaḥ. ihaikatyaḥ śramaṇo vā brāhmaṇo vā 'raṇyagato vā vṛkṣa-mūla-gato vā śūny-'āgāra-gato vā ataptānvayāt. prahāṇānvayāt. bhāvanā'nvayāt bahulī-kārānvayāt samyaṅmanasikārānvayāt. tad-rūpaṃ śāṃtaṃ cetaḥ-samādhiṃ spṛśati. yathā samāhite citte viṃśatiṃ saṃvarta-vivarta-kalpān samanusmarati. tasyaivaṃ bhavati.

Abhidh-k-vy 449.8–10
sa vṛddher anvayād indriyāṇāṃ paripākāt keśaśmaśrūṇy avatārya kāṣāyāṇi vastrāṇy ācchādya samyag eva śradhhayā agārād anagārikāṃ pravrajyāṃ pravrajati. so 'raṇyagato vā vṛkṣamūlagato vā vistareṇa yāvat tadrūpaṃ śāṃtaṃ cetaḥsamādhiṃ spṛśati. yathā samāhite citte pūrvakam ātmabhāvaṃ samanusmarati. tasyaivaṃ bhavati.

~16.13b–c~

DN I 13.11–14.1 (*Brahmajāla-sutta* DN I.31)
31. idha bhikkhave ekacco samaṇo vā brāhmaṇo vā ātappam anvāya padhānam anvāya anuyogam anvāya appamādam anvāya sammāmanasikāram anvāya tathārūpaṃ cetosamādhiṃ phusati yathā samāhite citte anekavihitaṃ pubbe nivāsaṃ anussarati —seyyathīdaṃ: ekam pi jātiṃ dve pi jātiyo tisso pi jātiyo catasso pi jātiyo pañca pi jātiyo dasa pi jātiyo vīsatim pi jātiyo tiṃsam pi jātiyo cattārīsam pi jātiyo paññāsam pi jātiyo jātisatam pi jātisahassam pi jātisatasahassam pi anekāni pi jātisatāni anekāni pi jātisahassāni anekāni pi jātisatasahassāni. amutrāsiṃ evannāmo evaṃgotto evaṃvaṇṇo evamāhāro evaṃsukhadukkhapaṭisaṃvedi evamāyupariyanto. so tato cuto amutra upapādiṃ. tatrāpāsiṃ evannāmo evaṃgotto evaṃvaṇṇo evamāhāro evaṃsukhadukkhapaṭisaṃvedī evamāyupariyanto. so tato cuto idhūpapanno ti iti sākāraṃ sa-uddesaṃ anekavihitaṃ pubbenivāsaṃ anussarati.

Method of Instruction (DĀ 16.14)

DĀ 16.14[1251]

[**a**] aparam api me bhadanta bhagavata ānuttaryaṃ[1252] yadā me bhagavāṃ dharmaṃ deśayati yad uta anuśāsanavidhau <|> jānāti bhagavāṃn aya<ṃ> pudgalaḥ kālya(**297r3**)m avoditaḥ[1253] sāyaṃ viśeṣāya paraiṣyati <|> sāyaṃ vā avoditaḫ[1254] kālyaṃ viśeṣāya paraiṣyatīti[1255] <|> sa evaṃ yathānuśiṣṭa<ḥ>[1256] samyak pratipadyamāno nacirād eva trayāṇāṃ saṃyo(**297r4**)janānāṃ prahāṇāt srota-āpanno bhavaty; avinipātadharmā niyataṃ saṃbodhiparāyaṇaḥ saptakṛtvobhava{ti}paramāḥ[1257] saptakṛtvo devāṃś (ca m)anuṣyāṃś[1258] ca saṃdhāvy(a) saṃsṛty(a) d(uḥ)(**297r5**)khasyāntaṃ[1259] kariṣyatīti • ity api bhagavāṃ jānāti <|>

[**b**] jānāti bhagavāṃn ayaṃ[1260] pudgalaḥ kālyam avoditaḥ sāyaṃ viśeṣāya paraiṣyati <|> sā(ya)ṃ (vā av)o(d)i(ta)ḥ (kālyaṃ viśeṣāya pa)(**297r6**)raiṣyatīti <|> sa evaṃ yathānuśiṣṭaḥ samyak prati<padya>mā(n)o[1261] nacirād eva trayāṇāṃ saṃyojanānāṃ prahāṇād rāgadveṣamohā(nā)ṃ (ca

1251. DĀ 16.14a–d echos DĀ 16.16a–d with very similar content running in the opposite order. Thus 14a relates to 16d, 14b relates to 16c, 14c relates to 16b, and 14d relates to 16a.

1252. Ms. reads *anuttaryaṃ*.

1253. Ms. reads *aveditaḥ*.

1254. Note *jihvāmūlīya*.

1255. Ms. reads *pareṣyatīti*.

1256. Cf. 297r6, 297r7, and 297v2.

1257. Ms. reads *satvakṛtvobhavatiparamaḥ*. Cf. 297r6–7: *(saptakṛ)tvobhavaparama<ḥ>* and s.v. *saptakṛd* in BHSD: "*saptakṛd*-(or, in Divy, MSV, °*kṛtvo*-)-*bhavaparama*" and *saptakṛtvaparama* in SWTF.

1258. Cf. 298r7.

1259. Read saṃdhāvya saṃsṛtya duḥ. Cf. 298r7.

1260. Ms. reads āyaṃ.

1261. Cf. 297r3.

ta)n(u)t(vāt sakṛdāgāmī bhaviṣyati | sakṛd imaṃ)[1262] (297r7) lokam āgatya duḥkhasyāntaṃ kariṣyatīti <|> ity api bhagavāṃ jānāti <|>

[c] <jānāti>[1263] bhagavān ayaṃ pudgalaḥ kālyam avoditaḥ[1264] sāyaṃ viśeṣāya paraiṣyati <|> s(āyaṃ vā avoditaḥ kālyaṃ viśeṣāya parai)(297r8)-ṣyatīti <|> sa {v}evaṃ yathānuśi(ṣṭa)ḥ[1265] samyak pratipadyamāno nacirād eva paṃcānām avarabhāgīyānāṃ saṃyojanānāṃ prahāṇād upapāduko bhaviṣyati <|> ta(t)r(a sa parinirvāyī anāgāmī)[1266] (297v1) anāvṛttika-dharmā punar imaṃ loka<m iti |> ity api bhagavāṃ jānāti <|>

[d] <jānāti>[1267] bhagavān ayaṃ pudgalaḥ kālyam avoditaḥ sāyaṃ viśeṣāya paraiṣyati (| sāyaṃ vā avoditaḥ kālyaṃ viśeṣāya paraiṣya)(297v2)tīti[1268] <|> sa evaṃ yathānuśiṣṭaḥ samyak pratipadyamāno nacirād evāsravāṇāṃ <kṣayād anāsravāṃ>[1269] cetovimuktiṃ prajñāvimuktiṃ dṛṣṭa eva dharme svayam abhijñayā (sākṣātkṛtvopasaṃpadya pravedayiṣya)(297v3)te • kṣīṇā me jātir uṣitaṃ brahmacaryaṃ kṛtaṃ karaṇīyaṃ n(ā)param[1270] asmād bhavaṃ prajān{ī}āmīti[1271] <|> ity api bhagavāṃ jānāti <|> etad ā(n)u(ttaryaṃ bhadanta bhagavato yad uta anuśāsanavidhau[1272] | ta)(297v4)d bhagavān aśeṣam abhijānāti <| tat te aśeṣam abhijānata> uttare[1273] 'bhijñeyaṃ nāsti

1262. Cf. 298r5.

1263. Cf. 297r5, which ends 16.14a and begins 16.14b where we see *jānāti* twice as is necessary: *ity api bhagavāṃ jānāti <|> jānāti bhagavāṃn ayaṃ.*

1264. Ms. reads aviditaḥ.

1265. Cf. 297r3, 297r6, and 297v2.

1266. Cf. 298r4.

1267. Cf. 297r5, which ends 16.14a and begins 16.14b where we see *jānāti* twice as is necessary: *ity api bhagavāṃ jānāti <|> jānāti bhagavāṃn ayaṃ.*

1268. Cf. 297r3.

1269. Cf. DbSū(3) 15.10a: *kṣayād anāsravāṃ c(e)t(o)vimuktiṃ*, DbSū(4) 5.10a: *kṣayād anā(s)r(a)vāṃ ceto(vimuktiṃ)*, Abhidh-k-vy 642.21: *kṣayād anāsravāṃ cetovimuktiṃ*, Note DĀ 37.76 (*Pṛṣṭapāla-sūtra*) reads: *kṣayād anāsravāṃś ce*(421r8)*(tovimu)kti(ṃ).*

1270. Cf. 298r2–298r3.

1271. The scribe mistakenly wrote the diacritics for both *ī* and *ā* on to the base *na* akṣara of *prajānāmi.*

1272. Cf. 297r2.

1273. Ms. reads *uttara.*

ya(s)yābhijñā<nā>d anyaḥ śramaṇo vā brāhmaṇo vā bhagavato 'ntikād bhūyo 'bhijñatara<ḥ> (s)yā(d) yad ut(a) s(aṃ)bodh(a)y(e |)[1274]

DĀ 16.14

[a] [Śāriputra:] "'For me, sir, there is another way in which the Blessed One is supreme when he teaches me dharma, and that is regarding the method of instruction. The Blessed One knows: "This man was taught in the morning and in the evening he will attain distinction. Or, he was taught in the evening and in the morning he will attain distinction. Thus, practicing properly just as he was taught, due to his abandonment of the three fetters, he soon becomes a stream-enterer. No longer liable to fall, certainly destined for perfect awakening, having run through no more than seven further existences and having transmigrated seven times as gods and men, he will make an end to suffering." This indeed the Blessed One knows.

[b] "'The Blessed One knows: "This man was taught in the morning and in the evening he will attain distinction. (Or,) he was taught in the evening and (in the morning) he will attain (distinction). Thus, practicing properly just as he was taught, soon, due to his abandonment of the three fetters (and) diminishment of lust, hatred, and delusion, (he will become a once-returner). Coming to (this) world (once) [more], he will make an end to suffering." This indeed the Blessed One knows.

[c] "'The Blessed One <knows>: "This man was taught in the morning and in the evening he will he will attain distinction. (Or, he was taught) in the evening (and in the morning) he will attain (distinction). Thus, practicing properly just as he was taught, soon, due to his abandonment of the five lower fetters, he will be spontaneously arisen. In that case (he is one who attains parinirvāṇa, a nonreturner), no longer liable to return again to this world." This indeed the Blessed One knows.

[d] "'The Blessed One <knows>: "This man was taught in the morning and in the evening he will attain distinction. (Or, he was taught in the evening and in the morning) he will attain (distinction). Thus, practicing properly just as he was taught, soon, <due to his exhaustion> of [negative]

1274. On the formula: *etad ānuttaryaṃ bhadanta ... syād yad uta saṃbodhaye*, see note 1005 above.

influences, (having attained and having directly experienced) freedom from [negative] influence, liberation of the mind, and liberation through insight in this very existence through his own supernormal knowledge, he will proclaim: 'My births are exhausted, I have lived the holy life, I have done what is to be done, therefore I know there is not another existence [for me].'" This indeed the Blessed One knows. (Sir), this (is the way in which the Blessed One is) supreme, (and that is regarding the method of instruction). The Blessed One knows this in its entirety. <For you, knowing this in its entirety>, there is nothing further to be known from the knowledge of which another ascetic or brahmin could be more knowledgeable than the Blessed One in regard to perfect awakening.'"

~16.14a~

BLSF III.1 Or.15009/408 (= DĀ(U.H.) Hs. 137); (*Prasādanīya-sūtra*)
verso
c /// + rvavad yāvat saṃbodhāya •[1275] apara[m] api [m]e bhadaṃ ///
d /// + .. gavān ayaṃ pudgalaḥ sāyam a[va]vaditaḥ ///
e /// .. thānuśiṣṭaḥ samyak pratipadyamāno nacira ///
f /// [y]. taṃ saṃ[b]odhiparāyaṇaḥ saptakṛtvaḥ parama ///
g /// + + .. + .. + + ..ṃ [p](u)d[g](a)laḥ sāya[m]. .. .. .i ///

~16.14~

T I 18 257b7–11
[a] 復次我佛世尊有最勝法。謂佛世尊以調伏法。了知諸補特伽羅心所樂法。從應爲説是補特伽羅。既了知已。如理修行。斷三煩惱。不久證於須陀洹果。逆生死流。七往天上。七來人間。盡苦邊際。如是世尊皆悉了知。

T I 18 257b11–14
[b] 又復世尊。知彼補特伽羅意樂之法。如理修行。斷三煩惱。及斷貪瞋癡。不久證於斯陀含果。一來人間。盡苦邊際。如是世尊悉皆了知。

T I 18 257b14–17
[c] 又復世尊。善知補特伽羅意樂之法。如理修行。斷五煩惱及隨煩惱。不久證於阿那含果。如是世尊悉皆了知。

1275. DĀ 16.14a begins here.

T I 18 257b17–21

[d] 又復世尊。善知補特伽羅。如理修行。非久漏盡。證解脱法。我生已盡梵行已立。所作已辦。不受後有。如是等法。世尊一一皆悉了知。是即名爲佛最勝法

DN III 107.7–27 (DN 28.13)

[a] 13. aparaṃ pana bhante etad ānuttariyaṃ, yathā bhagavā dhammaṃ deseti anusāsana-vidhāsu. catasso imā bhante anusāsana-vidhā. jānāti bhante bhagavā para-puggalaṃ paccattaṃ yoniso-manasikārā—ayaṃ puggalo yathānusiṭṭhaṃ tathā paṭipajjamāno, tiṇṇaṃ saṃyojanānaṃ parikkhayā sotāpanno bhavissati avinipātadhammo niyato sambodhi-parāyaṇo ti.

[b] jānāti bhante bhagavā para-puggalaṃ paccattaṃ yoniso-manasikārā—ayaṃ puggalo yathānusiṭṭhaṃ tathā paṭipajjamāno tiṇṇaṃ saṃyojanānaṃ parikkhayā raga-dosa-mohānaṃ tanuttā sakad-āgāmī bhavissati, sakid eva imaṃ lokaṃ ‹āgantvā dukkhassantaṃ karissatī ti›.

[c] ‹jānāti bhante› bhagavā para-puggalaṃ paccattaṃ yoniso-manasikārā—ayaṃ puggalo yathānusiṭṭhaṃ tathā paṭipajjamāno pañcannaṃ orambhāgiyānaṃ saṃyojanānaṃ parikkhayā opapātiko bhavissati, tattha parinibbāyī anāvattidhammo tasmā lokā ti.

[d] jānāti bhante bhagavā para-puggalaṃ paccattaṃ yoniso-manasikārā—ayaṃ puggalo yathānusiṭṭhaṃ tathā paṭipajjamāno āsavānaṃ khayā anāsavaṃ ceto-vimuttiṃ paññā-vimuttiṃ diṭṭhe va dhamme sayaṃ abhiññā sacchikatvā upasampajja viharissatī ti. etad ānuttariyaṃ bhante anusāsana-vidhāsu.

T I 1 78a19–21

[a]或時有人不違教誡。三結盡。得須陀洹。極七往返必成道果。不墮惡趣。是爲四教誡。

T I 1 78a16–18

[b] 或時有人不違教誡。三結盡。薄淫怒癡。得斯陀含還至此世而取滅度。是爲三教誡。

T I 1 78a15–16
[c] 或時有人不違教誡。盡五下結。於彼滅度。不還此世。是爲二教＊誡。或時有人不違教誡。三結盡。薄淫怒癡。得斯陀含還至此世而取滅度。是爲三教誡。

T I 1 78a11–15
[d] 如來說法復有上者。所謂教誡。教誡者。或時有人不違教誡。盡有漏成無漏。心解脫。智慧解脫。於現法中自身作證。生死已盡梵行已立。所作已辦不復受有。是爲初教誡。

T I 1 78a21–23
[d] 此法無上。智慧無餘。神通無餘。諸世間沙門婆羅門無有與如來等者。況欲出其上。

~16.14a~[1276]
MPS 9.16
9.16 sātirekāṇy asyāṃ nādikāyāṃ pañcopāsakaśatāny abhyatītān(i) kālagatāni yāni (trayāṇāṃ saṃyojanānāṃ prahāṇāc chrotaāpannā avinipā)tadharmāṇo niyataṃ saṃbodhiparāyaṇāḥ saptakṛtvaḥparamāḥ sap(takṛtvo de)vāṃś ca manuṣyāṃ(ś ca saṃdhāvya saṃsṛtya duḥkhasyāntaṃ kariṣyanti ||)

DN II 93.7–10 (*Mahāparinibbāna-sutta*, DN 16.2.7)
Sātirekāni Ānanda pañcasatāni Nādike upāsakā kālakatā tiṇṇaṃ saṃyojanānaṃ parikkhayā sotāpannā avinipātā-dhammā niyatā sambodhiparāyanā.

Śrāv-bh II 12: (II)-A-II-1-a-(17)
saptakṛdbhavaparamaḥ pudgalaḥ katamaḥ | yo 'yaṃ pudgalas trayāṇāṃ saṃyojanānāṃ prahāṇāt satkāyadṛṣṭeḥ śīlavrataparāmarśasya vicikitsāyāḥ srota-āpanno bhavati | avinipātadharmā niyataḥ saṃbodhiparāyaṇaḥ saptakṛdbhavaparamaḥ saptakṛtvo devāṃś ca manuṣyāṃś ca saṃdhāvya saṃsṛtya duḥkhasyāntaṃ karoti, ayam ucyate saptakṛdbhavaparamaḥ pudgalaḥ |

Abhidh-k-vy, 492.12–14
sa eṣāṃ trayāṇāṃ saṃyojanānāṃ prahāṇāt srota-āpanno bhavaty avinipātadharmā saṃbodhiparāyaṇaḥ saptakṛdbhavaparamaḥ saptakṛtvo devāṃś ca manuṣyāṃś ca saṃsṛtya saṃdhāvya duḥkhasyāṃtaṃ kariṣyatīti.

1276. = ~16.16d~ below.

Abhidh-k-vy, 554
srota-āpanno bhavann avinipātakadharmā niyataṃ saṃbodhi-parāyaṇaḥ saptakṛtvaḥ-paramaḥ saptakṛtvo devāṃś ca manuṣyāṃś ca saṃdhāvya saṃsṛtya duḥkhasyāṃtaṃ karotīti.

~16.14b~[1277]
MPS 9.15
9.15 sāti(rekāṇi bhikṣavo nādikāyāṃ tryupāsa)kaśatāni abhyatītāni kālagatāni yāni trayāṇāṃ saṃyojanānāṃ prahāṇād rāgadveṣamohānāṃ ca tanutvā(t kālaṃ kṛtvā sakṛdāgāminaḥ sakṛd imaṃ lokam āgamya duḥkhasyāntaṃ ka)riṣyanti ||

DN II 93.4–7 (*Mahāparinibbāna-sutta*, DN 16.2.7)
sādhikā navuti ānanda nādike upāsakā kālakatā tiṇṇaṃ saṃyojanānaṃ parikkhayā rāga-dosa-mohānaṃ tanuttā sakadāgāmino sakid eva imaṃ lokaṃ āgantvā dukkhass' antaṃ karissanti.

~16.14c~[1278]
MPS 9.12–9.14
9.12 karkaṭaka up(āsakaḥ pañcānām avarabhāgīyā)nāṃ saṃ(yojanānāṃ prahāṇād aupapādukās tatra parinirvāyy anāgāmy anāvṛttidharmā pu)nar imaṃ lokaṃ |

9.13 nikaṭaḥ kaḍaṅgaraḥ pūrvavad yāvad yaśottara upāsakaḥ pañ(cānām avarabhāgīyānāṃ pūrvavad) yāvat punar imaṃ lo(kam |)

9.14 (santi bhikṣavo nādikā)(187.4)yām ardhatṛtīyāny upāsakaśatāni kālagatāni yāni pañcānām a(varabhāgīyānāṃ saṃyojanān)āṃ prahāṇād aupapādukās tatra parinirvāyiṇo (187.5) 'nāgāmino 'nāvṛttidharmāṇaḥ punar imaṃ lokam |

DN II 92.22–93.4 (*Mahāparinibbāna-sutta*, DN 16.2.7)
kakudho ānanda upāsako pañcannaṃ orambhāgiyānaṃ saṃyojanānaṃ parikkhayā opapātiko tattha-parinibbāyī anāvatti-dhammo tasmā lokā. kāliṅgo ānanda upāsako ... pe ... nikaṭo ānanda upāsako ... kaṭissabho ānanda upāsako ... tuṭṭho ānanda upāsako ... santuṭṭho ānanda upāsako ... bhaddo ānanda upāsako ... subhaddo ānanda upāsako pañcannaṃ orambhāgiyānaṃ saṃyojanānaṃ parikkhayā opapātiko tattha-parinibbāyī anāvatti-dhammo tasmā lokā. paro-paññāsa ānanda nādike

1277. = ~16.16c~ below.
1278. = ~16.16b~ below.

upāsakā kālakatā pañcannaṃ orambhāgiyānaṃ saṃyojanānaṃ parikkhayā opapātikā tattha-parinibbāyino anāvatti-dhammā tasmā lokā.

~16.14d~[1279]

DĀ 36.76 (*Pṛṣṭapāla-sūtra*) (Melzer 2010, 273)

.. .. (ahaṃ pṛṣṭha)pāla evaṃ vadāmi · etu bhikṣur mama śrāvakaḥ aśaṭho amāyāvī ṛjuṛjukajātīyaḥ; aham enam evaṃ vadāmy aham anuśāsmy aham asmai dharmaṃ deśayāmi; sa (421r7) (bhikṣuḥ sāya)m avoditaḥ kālyaṃ vi(ś)e(ṣ)ā(ya) pa(r)ai(ṣyat)i (kā)l<y>am avoditaḥ sāyaṃ viśeṣāya paraiṣyati <|> sa evaṃ yathānuśiṣṭaḥ samyak pratipadymānaḥ nacirād evāsravāṇāṃ kṣayād anāsravāṃś ce(421r8)(tovimu) kti(ṃ) prajñāvimuktiṃ dṛṣṭ(a eva dharme svayam abhijñay)ā sākṣātkṛtvopasaṃpadya pravedayiṣyate • kṣīṇā me jātir uṣ(i)taṃ brahmacaryaṃ kṛtaṃ karaṇīyaṃ nāparam asmād bhavaṃ prajānāmīti |

DbSū(3) 15.10a

(punar aparaṃ tathāgata)ḥ āsravāṇāṃ kṣayād anāsravāṃ c(e)t(o)vimuktiṃ prajñāvimuktiṃ dṛṣṭa eva dharme svaya(m abhijñāya sākṣīkṛtvopasaṃpadya praveda)yati kṣīṇā me jātir uṣitaṃ brahmacaryaṃ kṛtaṃ karaṇīyaṃ nāparam asmād bh(a)va(ṃ) pr(ajānāmi |)

DbSū(4) 5.10a

punar aparaṃ tathāgataḥ āsravāṇāṃ kṣayād anā(s)r(a)vāṃ ceto(vimuktiṃ pra)j(ñ)ā(v)im(u)ktiṃ dṛṣṭa eva dharme s(va)yam abhijñāya sākṣīkṛtvopasaṃpadya pravedayati k(ṣ)īṇā (me jātir) u(ṣitaṃ) brahmacarya(ṃ) kṛta(ṃ) kara(ṇī)yaṃ nāparam asmād bhavaṃ (p)r(a)jānāmi |

Abhidh-k-vy 642.21

punar aparam āyuṣmantas tathāgataḥ āsravāṇāṃ kṣayād anāsravāṃ cetovimuktiṃ prajñāvimuktiṃ dṛṣṭa eva dharme svayam abhijñāya sākṣātkṛtvopasaṃpadya prativedayate kṣīṇā me jātir uṣitaṃ brahmacaryaṃ kṛtaṃ karaṇīyaṃ nāparam asmād bhavaṃ prajānāmīti.

SBV II 143

anena tvaṃ śroṇa vihāreṇa viharan nacirād eva āsravāṇāṃ kṣayād anāsravāṃ cetovimuktiṃ prajñāvimuktiṃ dṛṣṭa eva dharme svayam abhijñayā sākṣātkṛtvā, upas-

1279. = ~16.16a~ below.

aṃpadya pravedayase kṣīṇā me jātiḥ; uṣitaṃ brahmacaryaṃ; kṛtaṃ karaṇīyaṃ; nāparam asmād bhavaṃ prajānāmi iti.

PvSP(K) I-2 84 (=PvSP 210.19–21)
sa āsravāṇāṃ kṣayād anāsravāṃ cetovimuktiṃ prajñāvimuktiṃ dṛṣṭa eva dharme svayam abhijñāya sākṣātkṛtvā upasaṃpadya viharati, kṣīṇā me jātir uṣitaṃ brahmacaryaṃ kṛtaṃ karaṇīyaṃ nāparamithyātvam iti yathābhūtaṃ prajānāti.

Descent into the Womb (DĀ 16.15)

DĀ 16.15

[1280]a(param api)[1281] (**297v5**) me bhadanta bhagavata ānuttaryaṃ[1282] yadā me bhagavāṃ dharmaṃ deśayati yad uta <gar>bhāvakrāntiṣu[1283] <|> catasraḥ imā garbhāvakrāntayaḫ[1284] <|> katamā catasraḥ <|> [1] asti garbho 'sa(ṃ)prajāna(ṃ)[1285] (**297v6**) mātuḥ kukṣim avakrāmaty a{yaṃ}-saṃprajānaṃs tiṣṭhaty asaṃprajāna<ṃ>[1286] niṣkrāmati <|> [2] asti garbhas saṃprajānan mātuḥ kukṣim avakrāmati <a>saṃprajānaṃ<s> tiṣṭhati {saṃprajānaṃ niṣkrāmati}[1287] (**297v7**) asaṃprajānaṃ niṣkrāmati | [3] asti ga(r)bhaḥ saṃprajānan mātuḥ kukṣim avakrāmati saṃprajānaṃs tiṣṭhaty asaṃprajānaṃ niṣkrāmati | [4] asti garbhaḥ saṃpra(jā)nan[1288] mātuḥ kukṣim avakrāmati saṃprajā(**297v8**)na(ṃ)<s>[1289] tiṣṭhati saṃprajānaṃ niṣkrāmati <|> bodhisatvo bhagavāṃ saṃprajānaṃ mātuḥ kukṣim avakrāntaḥ saṃprajānaṃ sthitaḥ saṃprajānan niṣkrāntaḥ <|> etad <ān>uttaryaṃ bhadanta bhagavato yad(u)ta garbhā(**298r1**)(va)krāntiṣu[1290] <|> tad bhagavān aśeṣam abhijānāti <|> tat te aśeṣam abhijānata{ḥ} uttare 'bhijñeyaṃ nāsti <yasyā>bhijñānād anyaḥ śramaṇo vā brāhmaṇo vā bhagavato 'ntikād bhūyo 'bhijñatara<ḥ> syād ya(d)uta[1291] saṃbo(**298r2**)dhaye <|>

1280. Cf. DN III 103.10: *asampajāno mātu kucchismiṃ ṭhāti.*

1281. On the formula: *aparam api me bhadanta ... deśayati yad uta,* see note 1034 above.

1282. Ms. reads *anuttaryaṃ.*

1283. Ms. reads *bhavākrāntiṣu.* Cf. 298r1–2: *garbhāvakrāntiṣu* and DN III 103.6: *gabbhāvakkantīsu.*

1284. Note *jihvāmūlīya.*

1285. Cf. 297v6, 297v7, and 297v8.

1286. Cf 297v7 and 297v8.

1287. Dittography.

1288. Cf. earlier in this line and surrounding lines.

1289. Cf. 297v6.

1290. Cf. 297v5 and DN III 103.19: *gabbhāvakkantīsu.*

1291. On the formula: *etad ānuttaryaṃ bhadanta ... syād yad uta saṃbodhaye,* see note 1005 above.

DĀ 16.15

[Śāriputra:] "'For me, sir, there is another way in which the Blessed One is supreme when he teaches me dharma, and that is regarding descent into the womb. There are four descents into the womb. What are these four? [1] There is the womb where one enters a mother's belly unknowingly, stays there unknowingly, and leaves unknowingly. [2] There is the womb where one enters a mother's belly knowingly, stays there unknowingly, and leaves unknowingly. [3] There is the womb where one enters a mother's belly knowingly, stays there knowingly, and leaves unknowingly. [4] There is the womb where one enters a mother's belly knowingly, stays there knowingly, and leaves knowingly. The Bodhisattva, the Blessed One, entered in his mother's belly knowingly, he stayed there knowingly, and he left knowingly. Sir, this is the way in which the Blessed One is supreme, and that is regarding descent into the womb. The Blessed One knows this in its entirety. For you, knowing this in its entirety, there is nothing further to be known from the knowledge ‹of which› another ascetic or brahmin could be more knowledgeable than the Blessed One in regard to perfect awakening.'"

~16.15~

T I 18 257b22–27

復次我佛世尊有最勝法。謂佛世尊善能了知四種胎藏。一者不知入胎。亦復不知住出。二者有知入胎。不知住出。三者有知入住。不知出胎。四者有入住出皆悉了知。如是四種。知有差別。唯佛世尊。一一了知。是即名爲佛最勝法

DN III 103.3–19 (DN 28.5)

5. aparaṃ pana bhante etad ānuttariyaṃ, yathā bhagavā dhammaṃ deseti gabbhāvakkantīsu. catasso imā bhante gabbhāvakkantiyo. idha bhante ekacco asampajāno c' eva mātu kucchiṃ okkamati, asampajāno mātu kucchismiṃ ṭhāti, asampajāno mātu kucchismā nikkhamati. ayaṃ paṭhamā gabbhāvakkanti. puna ca paraṃ bhante idh' ekacco sampajāno pi kho mātu kucchiṃ okkamati, asampajāno mātu kucchismiṃ ṭhāti, asampajāno mātu kucchismā nikkhamati. ayaṃ dutiyā gabbhāvakkanti. puna ca paraṃ bhante idh' ekacco sampajāno mātu kucchiṃ okkamati, sampajāno mātu kucchismiṃ ṭhāti, asampajāno mātu kucchismā nikkhamati. ayaṃ tatiyā gabbhāvakkanti. puna ca paraṃ bhante idh' ekacco sampajāno c' eva mātu kucchiṃ okkamati, sampajāno mātu kucchismiṃ ṭhāti, sampajāno mātu kucchismā nikkhamati. ayaṃ catutthā gabbhāvakkanti. etad ānuttariyaṃ bhante gabbhāvakkantīsu.

T I 1 77a11–17

世尊說法又有上者。謂識入胎。入胎者。一謂亂入胎亂住亂出。二者不亂入亂住亂出。三者不亂入不亂住而亂出。四者不亂入不亂住不亂出。彼不亂入不亂住不亂出者。入胎之上。此法無上。智慧無餘。神通無餘。諸世間沙門婆羅門。無能與如來等者。況欲出其上。

Knowledge of the Liberation of Other People (DĀ 16.16)

DĀ 16.16[1292]

[**a**] (a)param[1293] api me bhadanta bhagavata ānuttaryaṃ yadā me bhagavāṃ dharmaṃ deśayati yad uta <parapudgalavimuktijñāne | jānāti bhagavān ayaṃ>[1294] pudgalaḥ āsravāṇāṃ kṣayād anāsravā<ṃ>[1295] cetovimuktiṃ prajñāvimuktiṃ dṛṣṭa eva dharme svayam abhijñayā (**298r3**) s(āk)ṣ(ā)tkṛtvo(pasa)ṃpadya[1296] pravedayiṣyate <|> kṣīṇā me jātir uṣitaṃ brahmacaryaṃ kṛtaṃ karaṇīyaṃ nāparam asmād bhavaṃ prajānāmīti <|> ity api bhagavāṃ jānāti <|>

[**b**] <jānāti>[1297] bhagavān ayaṃ pudgalaḥ (**298r4**) paṃ(cān)ām av(a)r(a)bh(ā)gīyā(n)āṃ saṃyojan(ā)nāṃ (p)rahāṇād[1298] upapāduko bhaviṣyati <|> tatra sa parinirvāyī anāgāmī anāvṛttikadharmā punar imaṃ lokam <iti |>[1299] ity api bha<ga>vāṃ jānāti <|>

1292. See note 1251 above.

1293. On the formula: *aparam api me bhadanta … deśayati yad uta*, see note 1034 above.

1294. The topic and beginning of the first sentence of the body of this section have been omitted by the scribe due to an act of haplography. The beginning of the first sentence may be safely reconstructed due to the regularity of 16.16, as well as 16.14, whose content is very similar. The topic, *pudgalavimuktijñāne* has been reconstructed from the Pali of DN III 108.2 and DN III 108.16: *para-puggala-vimutti-ñāṇe*.

1295. Cf. DbSū(3) 15.10a: *kṣayād anāsravāṃ c(e)t(o)vimuktiṃ*, DbSū(4) 5.10a: *kṣayād anā(s)r(a)vāṃ ceto(vimuktiṃ)*, Abhidh-k-vy 642.21: *kṣayād anāsravāṃ cetovimuktiṃ*, Note DĀ 37.76 (*Pṛṣṭapāla-sūtra*) reads: *kṣayād anāsravāṃś ce*(421r8)*(tovimu)kti(ṃ)*.

1296. Cf. 295r2 and 297v2.

1297. Cf. 297r5, which ends 16.14a and begins 16.14b where we see *jānāti* twice as is necessary: *ity api bhagavāṃ jānāti* <|> *jānāti bhagavāṃn ayaṃ*.

1298. Cf. 297r8.

1299. Haplography.

[c] **(298r5)** <jānāti>[1300] bhagavān a̱yaṃ[1301] pudgalaḥ trayāṇāṃ saṃyojanānāṃ pra(hāṇ)ād rāgadveṣamohānāṃ ca tanutvāt sakṛdāgāmī bhaviṣyati <|> sakṛd imaṃ lo(kam) āgatya duḫkhasyāntaṃ[1302] (kar)iṣ(y)atīti[1303] <|> **(298r6)** ity api bhagavāṃ jānāti <|>

[d] <jānāti>[1304] bhagavān ayaṃ pudgalaḥ (tra)yāṇāṃ (saṃyo)janānāṃ[1305] prahāṇāt srota-āpanno bhaviṣyati <| a>vi(n)i(pātadharmā niyataṃ saṃbodhiparāyaṇaḥ saptakṛ)**(298r7)**tvobhavaparama<ḥ>[1306] saptakṛtvo devāṃś ca manuṣyāṃś ca saṃdhāvya saṃsṛtya duḥkhasyāntaṃ kariṣyatīti <|> ity api bhagavāṃ jānīte <|> etad ānuttaryaṃ bha(danta bhagavato yad uta parapudgalavimuktijñāne[1307] | tad bha)**(298r8)**gavā(n aś)e(ṣa)m abhijānāti <|> tat te aśeṣam abhijānata uttare 'bhijñeya̱<ṃ>[1308] nāsti y(as)yābhijñānād anyaḥ śramaṇo vā brāhmaṇo vā bhagava(to 'nt)i(kād bh)ū(yo 'bhi)jñ(ataraḥ syād yad uta saṃbodhaye |)[1309]

DĀ 16.16

[a] [Śāriputra:] "'For me, sir, there is another way in which the Blessed One is supreme when he teaches me dharma, and that is regarding <the knowledge of the liberation of other people. The Blessed One knows: "This> person, due to his exhaustion of [negative] influences, having attained and having directly experienced freedom from [negative] influence, liberation of the mind, and liberation through insight in this very existence, through his own supernormal knowledge will proclaim: "My births are exhausted, I

1300. See note 1297 above.

1301. Ms. reads *āyaṃ*.

1302. Note *jihvāmūlīya*.

1303. Cf. 297r6–7.

1304. See note 1297 above.

1305. Cf. 297r6, 298r5, and 298r6.

1306. Cf. 297r3–4.

1307. As noted above, the topic of this section has been lost and has been reconstructed based on the Pali found in DN III 108.2 and DN III 108.16: *para-puggala-vimutti-ñāṇe*.

1308. Ms. reads *bhijñeye*.

1309. On the formula: *etad ānuttaryaṃ bhadanta ... syād yad uta saṃbodhaye*, see note 1005 above.

have lived the holy life, I have done what is to be done, therefore I know there is not another existence [for me]." This indeed the Blessed One knows.

[b] "'The Blessed One <knows>: "This person, due to his abandonment of the five lower fetters, will be spontaneously arisen. In that case he is one who attains parinirvāṇa, a nonreturner, no longer liable to return again to this world." This indeed the Blessed One knows.

[c] "'The Blessed One <knows>: "This person, due to his abandonment of the three fetters and diminishment of lust, hatred, and delusion, he will become a once-returner. Coming to this world once [more], he will make an end to suffering." This indeed the Blessed One knows.

[d] "'The Blessed One <knows>: "This man, due to his abandonment of the three fetters, will become a stream-enterer. No longer liable to fall, <certainly destined for perfect awakening>, having run through no more than seven further existences and having transmigrated seven times as gods and men, he will make an end to suffering." This indeed the Blessed One knows. Sir, this (is the way in which the Blessed One) is supreme, (and that is regarding the knowledge of the liberation of other people). The Blessed One knows (this) in its entirety. For you, knowing this in its entirety, there is nothing further to be known from the knowledge of which another ascetic or brahmin (could be) more knowledgeable than the Blessed One (in regard to perfect awakening).'"

~16.16~

T I 18 257b28–c1

復次我佛世尊有最勝法。謂佛世尊。善能了知諸補特伽羅。隨所斷障而證聖果。如是等法。佛悉了知。是即名爲佛最勝法

DN III 108.1–19 (DN 28.14)

[d] 14. aparaṃ pana bhante etad ānuttariyaṃ yathā bhagavā dhammaṃ deseti para-puggala-vimutti-ñāṇe. jānāti bhante bhagavā para-puggalaṃ paccattaṃ yoniso-manasikārā—ayaṃ puggalo tiṇṇaṃ saṃyojanānaṃ parikkhayā sotāpanno bhavissati avinipāta-dhammo niyato sambodhi-parāyaṇo ti.

[c] jānāti bhante bhagavā para-puggalaṃ paccattaṃ yoniso-manasikārā,— ayaṃ puggalo tiṇṇaṃ saṃyojanānaṃ parikkhayā raga-dosa-mohānaṃ tanuttā sakadāgāmī <bhavissati>[1310] sakid eva imaṃ lokaṃ āgantvā dukkhass' antaṃ karissatī ti.

[b] jānāti bhante bhagavā paraṃ puggalaṃ paccattaṃ yoniso-manasikārā,—ayaṃ puggalo pañcannaṃ orambhāgiyānaṃ saṃyojanānaṃ parikkhayā opapātiko <bhavissati>[1311] tattha parinibbāyī anāvatti-dhammo tasmā lokā ti.

[a] jānāti bhante bhagavā paraṃ puggalaṃ paccattaṃ yoniso-manasikārā, — ayaṃ puggalo āsavānaṃ khayā anāsavaṃ ceto-vimuttiṃ paññā-vimuttiṃ diṭṭhe va dhamme sayaṃ abhiññā sacchikatvā upasampajja viharissatī ti. etad ānuttariyaṃ bhante paraṃ puggalaṃ vimutti-ñāṇe.

T I 1 78b1–6
如來説法復有上者。謂解脱智。謂解脱智者。世尊。由他因縁内自思惟言。此人是須陀洹。此是斯陀含。此是阿那含。此是阿羅漢。此法無上。智慧無餘。神通無餘。諸世間沙門婆羅門無有與如來等者。況欲出其上。

~16.16a~[1312]

~16.16b~[1313]

~16.16c~[1314]

~16.16d~[1315]

1310. Cf. DN III 107.17.

1311. Cf. DN III 107.21.

1312. The corresponding parallel passages may be found in ~16.14d~ above.

1313. The corresponding parallel passages may be found in ~16.14c~ above.

1314. The corresponding parallel passages may be found in ~16.14b~ above.

1315. The corresponding parallel passages may be found in ~16.14a~ above.

Knowledge of the Purity of Moral Conduct of Men (DĀ 16.17)

DĀ 16.17

(**298v1**)apara(m ap)i m(e) bhadanta bhagavata ānuttaryaṃ yadā me bhagavāṃ dharmaṃ deśayati y(adu)ta[1316] p(u)ruṣaśīlaviśuddhijñāne[1317] <|> śrāddha<ḥ> syāt satyaś ca aśuddh. + + .i + .i .. + + + + + + + + + (**298v2**) ko na ca kāmeṣu evam[1318] āpadyeta na ca satveṣu mithyā pratipadyeta smṛtaś cāna + ...[1319] (| etad ānuttaryaṃ bhada)nta bhagavato yad uta puruṣa(ś)ī(laviśuddhijñāne[1320] | tad bhagavān aśeṣam abhijānāti | ta)(**298v3**)t te aśeṣam abhijānata uttare 'bhijñeyaṃ nāsti yasyābhijñ(ā)nād any(aḥ) śramaṇ(o) vā brāhmaṇo vā bhagavato 'ntikād bhūyo 'bhijñ(a)t(ara syād yad uta saṃbodhaye |)[1321]

DĀ 16.17

[Śāriputra:] "'For me, sir, there is another way in which the Blessed One is supreme when he teaches me dharma, and that is regarding the knowledge of the purity of moral conduct of men. One should be faithful, truthful, and [...] and one should not engage in passion in this way, nor should one practice falsely among beings [...][1322] and mindful. Sir, (this is the way

1316. On the formula: *aparam api me bhadanta ... deśayati yad uta*, see note 1034 above.

1317. Cf. 298v2.

1318. Ms. reads *avam*.

1319. I have been unable to reconstruct these pages in the ms. The corresponding passage in the *Sampasādanīya-sutta*, DN III 106.27–107.5: *idha bhante ekacco sacco c'assa saddho ca, na ca kuhako, na ca lapako, na ca nemittiko, na ca nippesiko, na ca lābhena lābhaṃ nijigiṃsitā, indriyesu gutta-dvāro, bhojane mattaññū, sama-kārī, jāgariyānuyogam anuyutto, atandito, āraddha-vīriyo, ñāyī, satimā, kalyāṇa-paṭibhāno, gatimā, dhitimā, mutimā, na ca kāmesu giddho, sato ca nipako ca*, is similar in scope but does not appear to parallel the *Prsādanīya-sūtra* closely enough to give a firm basis for a reconstruction.

1320. Cf. 298v1.

1321. On the formula: *etad ānuttaryaṃ bhadanta ... syād yad uta saṃbodhaye*, see note 1005 above.

1322. The Pali of the *Saṃpasādanīya-sutta* while thematically similar does not match the

in which) the Blessed One (is supreme), and that is regarding the knowledge of the purity of moral conduct of men. (The Blessed One knows this in its entirety.) For you, knowing this in its entirety, there is nothing further to be known from the knowledge of which another ascetic or brahmin (could be) more knowledgeable than the Blessed One (in regard to perfect awakening).'"

~16.17~

T I 18 257c2–7
復次我佛世尊有最勝法。謂佛世尊。了知有人已具信根。戒行清淨。智慧具足。眞實無妄。無我無懈。無諸幻惑。亦無散亂。亦不貪欲。不以邪道引示衆生。常行正念。如是等法。唯佛世尊。悉能了知。是即名爲佛最勝法

DN III 106.26–107.6 (DN 28.12)
12. aparaṃ pana bhante etad ānuttariyaṃ, yathā bhagavā dhammaṃ deseti purisa-sīla-samācāre. idha bhante ekacco sacco c' assa saddho ca, na ca kuhako, na ca lapako, na ca nemittiko, na ca nippesiko, na ca lābhena lābhaṃ nijigiṃsitā, indriyesu gutta-dvāro, bhojane mattaññū, sama-kārī, jāgariyānuyogam anuyutto, atandito, āraddha-vīriyo, ñāyī, satimā, kalyāṇa-paṭibhāno, gatimā, dhitimā, mutimā, na ca kāmesu giddho, sato ca nipako ca. etad ānuttariyaṃ bhante purisa-sīla-samācāre.

T I 1 78a23–78b01
如來說法復有上者。爲他說法使戒清淨。戒清淨者。有諸沙門婆羅門所語至誠無有兩舌。常自敬肅捐除睡眠。不懷邪諂口不妄言。不爲世人記於吉凶。不自稱說從他所得。以示於人更求他利。坐禪修智辯才無礙。專念不亂。精勤不怠。此法無上。智慧無餘。神通無餘。諸世間沙門婆羅門。無有與如來等者。況欲出其上。

Prasādanīya-sūtra closely enough to enable a reconstruction. Cf. DN III 106.27–107.5: *idha bhante ekacco sacco c' assa saddho ca, na ca kuhako, na ca lapako, na ca nemittiko, na ca nippesiko, na ca lābhena lābhaṃ nijigiṃsitā, indriyesu gutta-dvāro, bhojane mattaññū, sama-kārī, jāgariyānuyogam anuyutto, atandito, āraddha-vīriyo, ñāyī, satimā, kalyāṇa-paṭibhāno, gatimā, dhitimā, mutimā, na ca kāmesu giddho, sato ca nipako ca* and its translation, LBD 430: "One should be truthful and faithful, not using deception, patter, hinting or belittling, not always on the make for further gains, but with sense-doors guarded, abstemious, a peace-maker, given to watchfulness, active, strenuous in effort, a meditator, mindful, of fitting conversation, steady-going, resolute and sensible, not hankering after sense-pleasures but mindful and prudent."

Higher Mental States (DĀ 16.18)

DĀ 16.18

(yat tad bhadanta śrāddhena)[1323] **(298v4)** kulaputreṇa jñātavyaṃ draṣṭavyaṃ prāptavyaṃ boddhavyaṃ tat sa(rv)aṃ bha(ga)vatā[1324] jñātaṃ[1325] dṛṣṭaṃ viditaṃ vijñātaṃ samyag evābhisaṃbuddhaṃ;[1326] na bhagavān kām(as)ukh(ālayānu)yoge[1327] hīne (grāmye prākṛ)**(298v5)**-{kṛ}te[1328] pārth(a)gjanike[1329] garbham[1330] āpanno nātmaklamathānuyoge duḥkhe 'nārye anarthopasaṃhite[1331] <|> caturṇāṃ ca bhagavān ādhicaitasikānāṃ dṛṣṭ(adha)rma(s)u(kha)vihārāṇāṃ[1332] ni(k)ā(mal)ā**(298v6)**-bhy[1333] <a>kṛcchralābhī[1334] <|> katameṣāṃ caturṇāṃ; bhagavāṃ bhadanta viviktaṃ kāmair yāvac caturthaṃ dhyānam upasaṃ(padya v)i(harat)i <|> .. .. (na) bhagavāṃ kāmasukhālayānuyoge hīne grāmye prākṛ**(298v7)**te

1323. Cf. DN III 113.16: *yan taṃ bhante saddhena*. S.v. *srāddha* in SWTF: *vertrauensvoll, gläubig* and in BHSD: = Pali *saddha*, believing, having true faith.

1324. Ms. reads *bha(ga)vato*. Cf. *Prāsādika-sūtra* (286r7): *sarvaṃ tathāgatena jñātaṃ dṛṣṭaṃ viditaṃ vijñāt(aṃ sam)y(ag evābh)i(saṃb)uddh(am |)*.

1325. Ms. reads *jñānaṃ*.

1326. Ms. reads *evābhisaṃbuddhe*. Cf. very similar phrases that occur in the *Prāsādika-sūtra*, DĀ 15.35 (286r7): *sarvaṃ tathāgatena jñātaṃ dṛṣṭaṃ viditaṃ vijñāt(aṃ sam)y(ag evābh)i(saṃb)uddh(am |)* and DbSū(4) 6.2, (= 6.1, 6.3, 6.4, 6.5 6.6, 6.7, 6.8, 6.9 and 6.10: *jñātaṃ dṛṣṭaṃ viditaṃ vijñātaṃ samyag evābhisaṃbuddhaṃ*.

1327. Ms. reads *kāmasukhālayānuyoga*.

1328. Cf. 298v6. The reconstruction assumes a dittographical error.

1329. Cf. *Prāsādika-sūtra*, DĀ 15.23.2 (283r4): *sukhālayānuyogo hī(no grāmya)ḥ (p)r(ā)kṛtaḥ pārthagjaniko*.

1330. Ms. reads *garba*. Cf. 298v7.

1331. Ms. reads *anarśopasaṃhite*. Cf. 298v7.

1332. Ms. reads *dṛṣṭadharmasukhavihāriṇāṃ*.

1333. Ms. reads °*bhī*.

1334. Cf. 298v7 and SHT (V) 1118 V5 (*Nagaropamā-sūtra*): /// *[k]ānāṃ dṛṣṭadharmasukhavihārāṇāṃ nikāmalābhī [bhavaty]=akṛcchra[l](ā)*.

pār(tha)gjanike garbham āpanno nātmaklamathānuyoge duḫkhe[1335] anārye anarthopasaṃhite <|> eṣāṃ ca bhagavā<ṃ> caturṇām ā(dhicaitasikānāṃ d)ṛṣṭadharmasukhavihārāṇāṃ[1336] nikāmalābhy akṛcchralābhī <|>

DĀ 16.18

[Śāriputra:] "'(Sir, whatever) is to be known, to be perceived, to be obtained, and to be realized (by a faithful son of a good family), that is all known, perceived, learned, understood, and completely, fully, perfectly realized by the Blessed One.[1337] The Blessed One has not acquired the womb in devotion to worldly enjoyment, which is inferior, (vulgar), simple, and characteristic of common folk, nor in devotion to self-mortification, which is painful, ignoble, and not associated with the goal [of salvation]. The Blessed One is one who easily and effortlessly obtains that happy dwelling in the present state of existence of the higher mental states of the four [dhyānas]. What are the four? Sir, the Blessed One dwells having reached the fourth dhyāna, which is free from passion. [...] the Blessed One has (not) acquired the womb in devotion to worldly enjoyment, which is inferior, vulgar, simple, and characteristic of common folk, nor in devotion to self-mortification, which is painful, ignoble, and not associated with the goal [of salvation]. The Blessed One is one who easily and effortlessly obtains that happy dwelling in the present state of existence of the higher mental states of these four [dhyānas].'"

~16.18~

SHT (V) 1118 V5 (*Nagaropamā-sūtra*):

5 /// [k]ānāṃ dṛṣṭadharmasukhavihārāṇāṃ nikāmalābhī [bhavaty]= akṛcchra[l](ā)

T I 18 257c08–14

爾時舍利弗復白佛言。世尊。世間所有愚癡凡夫。貪諸欲樂。勞苦己身。求無義利。諸佛如來。於此不然。唯樂利他。非求自樂。善了心法。見法寂靜。住

1335. Note *jihvāmūlīya*.

1336. Cf. 298v5.

1337. Note the extremely similar phrase above in the *Prāsādika-sūtra* at DĀ 15.35: "Monks, whatever perfection shines wholly [and] entirely, that is all known, perceived, learned, understood, and completely, fully, perfectly realized by the Tathāgata."

安樂句。無欲無苦。得四禪定。是故世尊。若有上根善男子等。當如是見。當如是聞。當如是覺。當如是知。是即名爲眞上根者

DN III 113.16–24 (DN 28.20)
20. yan taṃ bhante saddhena kula-puttena pattabbaṃ āraddha-viriyena thāmavatā purisa-thāmena purisa-viriyena purisa-parakkamena purisa-dhorayhena, anuppattaṃ tam bhagavatā. na ca bhante bhagavā kāmesu kāmasukhallikānuyoga-yutto hīnaṃ gammaṃ pothujjanikaṃ anariyaṃ anattha-saṃhitaṃ, na ca atta-kilamathānuyogam anuyutto dukkhaṃ anariyaṃ anattha-saṃhitaṃ, catunnaṃ bhagavā jhānānaṃ abhicetasikānaṃ diṭṭha-dhammasukha-vihārānaṃ nikāma-lābhī akiccha-lābhī akasira-lābhī.

T I 1 78c12–19
猶如世尊精進勇猛有大智慧。有知有覺得第一覺。故名等覺。世尊。今亦不樂於欲。不樂卑賤凡夫所習。亦不勞勤受諸苦惱。世尊。若欲除弊惡法。有覺有觀。離生喜樂遊於初禪。如是便能除弊惡法。有覺有觀。離生喜樂遊於初禪。二禪三禪四禪亦復如是。精進勇猛有大智慧。有知有覺得第一覺。故名等覺。

Concluding Frame: Serene Faith in the Teacher (DĀ 16.19)

DĀ 16.19

[a] tena kha(**298v8**)(lu sama)y(e)nāyuṣmān[1338] nāgasapālo bhagavataḥ pṛ(ṣṭha)ta<ḥ>[1339] sthito 'bhūd vyajanaṃ gṛhītvā bhagavantaṃ vījayamānaḥ <|> athāyu(ṣ)m(ān nā)g(asa)pālo[1340] bhagavantam idam avocat* <|> ime bhadanta anyatīrthika(**299r1**)parivrājakā eṣām aṃgānām[1341] anyatamānyata(m). saṃ .. m ātmanaḥ saṃmukhībhūtaṃ paśyeyur apīdānī<ṃ> mahatī cailap(a)tākā (u)cchrayitvā[1342] sarvāṃ nālandāṃ anvāhiṇḍata<ṃ>ty[1343] ā .. .. n ity a(p)i vaya(**299r2**)(m evaṃ)mahardhikā evaṃmahānubhāvā iti <|> atha ca punar bha<ga>vāṃ <evaṃ>mahardhika[1344] eva<ṃ>mahānubhāvo necchati pare .. m a .. + + + + ..[1345] .y(a)tra bhagavāṃn alpecchaḥ sādhu bhadanta āyuṣmataḥ śāripu(**299r3**)tra(s)yāyaṃ[1346] dharmaparyāyo 'bhīkṣṇaṃ bhāṣituṃ pratibhāyad bhikṣubhyo bhikṣuṇībhya{ḥ} upāsakebhya{ḥ} upāsik(ābhyaḥ)[1347] + +[1348]

1338. Cf. *Prāsādika-sūtra*, DĀ 15.1.1(276v5): *tena khalu samaye(na).*

1339. S.v. *pṛṣṭhatas* entry 2 in SWTF: *bhagavataḥ pṛṣṭhataḥ sthito.*

1340. Cf. earlier in line.

1341. Ms. reads *aṃganām.*

1342. Cf. DN III 115.16: *paṭākaṃ parihareyyum.*

1343. Ms. reads *anvāhiṇḍitaty.*

1344. Cf. earlier in this line and DN III 115.12–13: *yatra hi nāma tathāgato evaṃ mahiddiko evaṃ mahānubhāvo.*

1345. The ms. is very damaged here and I have not been able to make a dependable reconstruction. The *Sampasādanīya-sutta* is similar but not close enough to use for a reconstruction, DN III 115. 13–14: *atha ca pana na attānaṃ pātukarissati.*

1346. Ms. reads *ahaṃ.*

1347. Cf. 299r6. It is very likely that the reading should be *upāsikābhyo*, as can be seen in 299r6. However, the lacuna both here and in 299r6 below make a certain reconstruction impossible.

1348. Despite the two occurrances of this phrase (299r3 and 299r6) and a similar phrase

(nānā)tīrthikaśramaṇabrāhmaṇacarakaparivrājakebhyas; ta(**299r4**)tra yeṣāṃ bhaviṣyati bhagavato 'ntike kāṃkṣā vā vimatir vā <|> te kāṃkṣā prahāsyanti <|> dṛṣṭim ṛjvīkariṣyanti <|> dharmeṣu ca niṣṭhāṃ gacchiṣyanti[1349] <|> śāstari ca pra(s)ādaṃ pra(v)edayiṣyaṃte <|> (**299r5**) samyaksaṃbuddho bata bhagavān ity api jñāsyanti <|>[1350]

[**b**] tatra bhagavān āyuṣmantaṃ śāriputram āmantrayate <|> tasmāt tarhi śāriputrāyaṃ dharmaparyā(yo 'bh)īk(ṣṇaṃ) bhāṣituṃ pratibhātu bhik(ṣu)(**299r6**)bhyo[1351] bhikṣuṇībhyaḥ upāsakebhya upāsikābhyo .. ..[1352] nānātīrthikaśramaṇabrāhmaṇac(a)rakaparivrājakebhyas <|> tatra ye(ṣā)ṃ (bhav)i(ṣyat)i (bhagavato 'ntike kāṃkṣā vā vimati)(**299r7**)r[1353] vā <|> te kāṃkṣā prahāsyanti <|> dṛṣṭim ṛjvīkariṣyanti <|> dharmeṣu ca niṣṭhāṃ gami(ṣ)ya(nt)i (| śāstari ca prasādaṃ prave)dayiṣyante <|> samyaksaṃbuddho bha(gavān ity api jñāsyanti |[1354] bhagavata 'dhivāsayati[1355] śāri)(**299r8**)-putras tūṣṇīṃ(bh)āvena <|> asmiṃ khalu dharmaparyāye bhāṣyamāṇe mahājana(k)āyasya bhagav(a)to 'ntike cittam abhiprasannaṃ; tasmād asya dharmaparyāyasya prasāda[1356] .. .. + + + + + + + + +

DĀ 16.19

in NidSa 5.38 (= NagSū I.38): *bhikṣūṇīnām upāsakānām upāsikānāṃ nānātīrthyaśramaṇa(brāhma)ṇacarakaparivrājakānām ārocayāmi* |, I have not been able to reconstruct these two akṣaras. Notice that these two akṣaras do not occur in the phrase as it appears in NidSa.

1349. Note the peculiar conjugation of √*gam* here.

1350. These phrases, the thesis of the sūtra, end the introductory frame in DĀ 16.1.5b (291r3–4): *dharmeṣu ca niṣṭhāṃ gacchāmi* <|> (**291r4**) *śāstari ca prasādaṃ pravedayet; samyaksa(ṃb)uddh(o) b(a)t(a) bhagavāṃn ity api jāne*, and are echoed here in the concluding frame narrative in DĀ 16.19a (299r4–5): *dharmeṣu ca niṣṭhāṃ gacchiṣyanti* <|> *śāstari ca pra(s)ādaṃ pra(v)edayiṣyaṃte* <|> (**299r5**) *samyaksaṃbuddho bata bhagavān ity api jñāsyanti* and DĀ 16.19b (299r7): *dharmeṣu ca niṣṭhāṃ gami(ṣ)ya(nt)i (| śāstari ca prasādaṃ prave)dayiṣyante* <|> *samyaksaṃbuddho bha(gavān ity api jñāsyanti).*

1351. Cf. 299r3.

1352. See note 1348 above, which outlines the same issue at 299r3.

1353. Cf. 299r3–4.

1354. See note 1350 above.

1355. S.v. *adhivāsayati* in BHSD: "or the sentence may begin *adhivāsayati*, then subject nom., then gen. of person, then *tūṣṇībhāvena*." Note that the word order in this reconstruction is different from what Edgerton suggests.

1356. Ms. reads *prasada*.

[**a**] At that time, the venerable Nāgasapāla was standing behind the Blessed One, having taken up a fan, and fanning the Blessed One. The venerable Nāgasapāla then said this to the Blessed One: "Sir, if these wanderers who are adherents of another faith were to see one or another of these qualities [...] present in themselves, immediately raising a great cloth banner, they would roam about the whole of Nālandā [...] [saying]: 'We are of such great supernormal power, we are they whose power is so great." Moreover, the Blessed One who is of such great supernormal power and whose power is so great does not wish [...] in which case the Blessed One, one who has few wishes [...].[1357] How wonderful, sir, this doctrinal discourse of venerable Śāriputra should constantly appear clearly in mind to tell to monks, nuns, laymen, laywomen, [...] and various ascetics, brahmins, and itinerant wanderers who are adherents of another faith. In that case, those who will have doubt or confusion in the presence of the Blessed One, they will abandon that doubt. They will correct their view. They will become perfect regarding dharma. They will proclaim serene faith in the Teacher. They will know: 'The Blessed One is certainly a complete, perfect buddha.'"

[**b**] Then, the Blessed One addressed the venerable Śāriputra: "Therefore, in that case, Śāriputra, make this doctrinal discourse constantly appear clearly in mind to tell to monks, nuns, laymen, laywomen, [...] and various ascetics, brahmins, and itinerant wanderers who are adherents of another faith. In that case, those who will have (doubt) or (confusion with regard to the Blessed One), they will abandon that doubt. They will correct their view. They will become perfect regarding dharma. They will proclaim (serene faith in the Teacher. They will know): 'The Blessed One is certainly a complete perfect buddha.'" Śāriputra silently (consented to the Blessed One). While this doctrinal discourse was being spoken, the minds of a large crowd became serenely confident in the Blessed One. Therefore, the faith of this doctrinal discourse [...].

~16.19~

T I 18 257c15–20

1357. For the two gaps in the this sentence we can expect something similar to what is found in the *Sampasādanīya-sutta*, LDB 425: "It is wonderful, Lord, it is marvellous how content the Blessed Lord is, how satisfied and restrained, when being endowed with such power and influence he does not make a display of himself!"

[a] 爾時會中。有一尊者。名曰龍護。手執寶拂。侍立佛側。時尊者龍護白佛言。世尊。我見諸邪外道尼乾子等。於佛世尊。先不起信。唯於邪道。競說勝能。是故我今建立表刹宣示於世。咸使聞知佛勝功德。於佛世尊。是大丈夫。最尊最上。無有等者

T I 18 257c21–258a5

[b] 爾時世尊告尊者龍護言。汝莫作是說。莫宣示他人佛勝功德。我今不欲如是稱揚。於是尊者龍護讃世尊言。善哉善哉。是眞正等正覺爾時佛告尊者舍利弗。汝當善以如是正法。廣爲苾芻苾芻尼。優婆塞優婆夷。及諸沙門婆羅門。流布宣說。乃至諸魔外道尼乾子等。所有邪見不信佛者。聞此正法。令起深信。歸向於佛。而生正見。了知正法。又復告言。汝舍利弗。應當如是流布宣說 爾時世尊謂尊者舍利弗。言已。默然而住。於是尊者舍利弗。承佛威力。說是法已。禮佛而退。時諸會衆。得聞正法。歡喜作禮。信受奉行

DN III 115.10–29 (DN 28.21)

[a] 21. evaṃ vutte, āyasmā udāyī bhagavantaṃ etad avoca: acchariyaṃ bhante abbhutaṃ bhante tathāgatassa appicchatā santuṭṭhitā sallekhatā, yatra hi nāma tathāgato evaṃ mahiddhiko evaṃ mahānubhāvo, atha ca pana na attānaṃ pātukarissati. ekamekañ ce pi ito bhante dhammaṃ aññatitthiyā paribbājakā attani samanupasseyyuṃ, te tāvataken' eva paṭākaṃ parihareyyuṃ. acchariyaṃ bhante abbhutaṃ bhante tathāgatassa appicchatā santuṭṭhitā sallekhatā. yatra hi nāma tathāgato evaṃ mahiddhiko evaṃ mahānubhāvo, atha ca pana na attānaṃ pātukarissatī ti.
passa kho tvaṃ, udāyi: tathāgatassa appicchatā santuṭṭhitā sallekhatā, yatra hi nāma tathāgato evaṃ mahiddhiko evaṃ mahānubhāvo, atha ca pana na attānaṃ pātukarissatī ti. ekamekañ ce pi ito, udāyi, dhammaṃ aññatitthiyā paribbājakā attani samanupasseyyuṃ, te tāvataken' eva paṭākaṃ parihareyyuṃ. passa kho tvaṃ, udāyi: tathāgatassa appicchatā santuṭṭhitā sallekhatā, yatra hi nāma tathāgato evaṃ mahiddhiko evaṃ mahānubhāvo, atha ca pana na attānaṃ pātukarissatī ti.

T I 1 79a8–23

爾時尊者欝陀夷。在世尊後執扇扇佛。佛告之曰。欝陀夷。汝當觀世尊少欲知足。今我有大神力有大威德。而少欲知足不樂在欲。欝陀夷。若餘沙門婆羅門。於此法中能勤苦得一法者。彼便當豎幡告四遠言。如來今者少欲知足。今觀如來少欲知足。如來有大神力有大威德。不用在欲。爾時尊者欝陀夷。正衣服偏露右肩右膝著地。叉手白佛言。甚奇世尊。少有少欲知足如世尊者。世尊。有大神力有大威德。不用在欲。若復有餘沙門婆羅門。於此法中能勤苦得

一法者。便能豎幡告四遠言。世尊。今者少欲知足。舍利弗。當爲諸比丘比丘尼優婆塞優婆夷數説此法。彼若於佛法僧於道有疑者。聞説此法無復疑網。

~16.19b~

DN III 116.1–10 (DN 28.22)

22. atha kho bhagavā āyasmantaṃ sāriputtaṃ āmantesi: tasmā-t-iha tvaṃ, sāriputta, imaṃ dhamma-pariyāyaṃ abhikkhaṇaṃ bhāseyyāsi bhikkhūnaṃ bhikkhunīnaṃ upāsakānaṃ upāsikānaṃ. yesampi hi, sāriputta, moghapurisānaṃ bhavissati tathāgate kaṅkhā vā vimati vā, tesam pi imaṃ dhamma-pariyāyaṃ sutvā yā tathāgate kaṅkhā vā vimati vā, sā pahīyissatī ti. iti h' idaṃ āyasmā sāriputto bhagavato sammukhā sampasādaṃ pavedesi. tasmā imassa veyyākaraṇassa sampasādanīyan t' eva adhivacanan ti.

T I 1 79a23–29

爾時世尊告舍利弗。汝當爲諸比丘比丘尼優婆塞優婆夷數説此法。所以者何。彼於佛法僧於道有疑者。聞汝所説當得開解。對曰。唯然世尊。時舍利弗即便數數爲諸比丘比丘尼優婆塞優婆夷説法。以自清淨故。故名清淨經。爾時舍利弗聞佛所説。歡喜奉行。

~16.19a–b~

NidSa 5.38 (= NagSū I.38)

so 'ham imān dharmān svayam abhijñ(āya sākṣīkṛtvā) bhikṣūṇām ārocayāmi | bhikṣūṇīnām upāsakānām upāsikānāṃ nānātīrthyaśramaṇa(brāhma)ṇacarakaparivrājakānām ārocayāmi |

Summary Verses (DĀ 16.20)

DĀ 16.20a
(||) (**299v1**) anta(ro)ddānam* ||
saṃbodhikuśalāyatanaṃ pudgalā bhāṣyadarśanam*
pratiprahāṇam[1358] ṛddhiś ca nivāsādeśanena ca •
śāśvatam cānuśāstiś ca ga(rbhā)vakrānti[1359] pudgalā[1360]
(puruṣaśīlaviśuddhim[1361] ādhicai)(**299v2**)tasikena[1362] ca • || ||[1363]

DĀ 16.20a
Summary Verse:
[DĀ 16.1–2:] Perfect Awakening (*saṃbodhiḥ*)
[DĀ 16.3:] [The Classification of] Wholesome Factors (*kuśalaḥ*)
[DĀ 16.4:] [The Classification of] the Sense Spheres (*āyatanam*)
[DĀ 16.5:] [The Classification of] Individuals (*pudgalāḥ*)
[DĀ 16.6:] [Conduct in] Speech (*bhāṣyaḥ)*
[DĀ 16.7:] [Attainments of] Discernment (*darśanam*)
[DĀ 16.8:] Practices (*prati(pad)*)
[DĀ 16.9:] Efforts (*prahāṇam*)
[DĀ 16.10:] [Knowledge of the Range of] Supernormal Power (*ṛddhiḥ*)
[DĀ 16.11:] [Knowledge of the Recollection of Former] States of Existence (*nivāsaḥ*)
[DĀ 16.12:] [The Method of] Reading Minds (*adeśanena*)
[DĀ 16.13:] [Theories of] Eternalism (*śāśvatam*)
[DĀ 16.14:] [The Method of] Instruction (*anuśāsitḥ*)

1358. This appears to be an abbreviated reference to *pratipad* (cf. DĀ 16.8) and *prahāṇa* (cf. DĀ 16.9) in order to fit the meter and to the detriment of the intended meaning.

1359. Cf. 16.15 (297v4–298r2).

1360. Cf. 16.16 (298r2–298r8).

1361. Cf. 16.17 (298v1–298v3).

1362. Cf. 16.18 (298v3–298v7).

1363. *Anuṣṭubh* metre.

[DĀ 16.15:] Descent Into the Womb (*garbhāvakrāntiḥ*)
[DĀ 16.16:] [Knowledge of the Liberation of Other] People (*pudgalāḥ*)
[DĀ 16.17:] [Knowledge of] (the Purity of Moral Conduct of Men) (*puruṣaśīlaviśuddhim*)
[DĀ 16.18:] Higher Mental States (*ādhicaitasikena*)

~16.20a~
T I 18 —

DN —

T I 1.18 —

DĀ 16.20b[1364]
apannakaḥ sarveko{ṃ}[1365] bhargavaḥ śalyāva-
bhayabhairavo romaharṣaṇo jinadabhaś ca
(g)ovindaḥ[1366] prāsādikaḥ prasādanīye d. + +
+ + + + + + + + + + + + + + +[1367]
(kā)(**299v3**)maṭhikaḥ kayabhāvanā bodhaḥ saṃkara<ka>ś[1368] caiva
ā(ṭāṇā)ṭamahāsamājena bhavati paścimaṃ || ||[1369]

DĀ 16.20b
[The *Yuga-nipāta* is]:
The *Apannaka-sūtra* [folios unidentified]
The *Sarveka-sūtra* [folios unidentified]
The *Bhārgava-sūtra* [folios unidentified]
The *Śalya-sūtra* [folios unidentified]
The *Bhayabhairava-sūtra* [folios unidentified]
The *Romaharṣaṇa-sūtra* [folios unidentified]

1364. This section is made up almost entirely of the sūtra titles from the *Yuga-nipāta*.

1365. Read *sarveko*.

1366. Read *govinda*.

1367. This gap should surely be filled with the *Pañcatraya-sūtra* and the *Māyājāla-sūtra*, the only texts missing from the *Yuga-nipāta*.

1368. The text is titled *Saṃkaraka-sūtra* but does not include the additional akṣara in the metrical syllabic count.

1369. *Anuṣṭubh* metre.

The *Jinayabha-sūtra* [folios unidentified]
The *Govinda-sūtra* [266–274v5]
The *Prāsādika-sūtra* [274v5–290r4]
The *Prasādanīya-sūtra* [290r5–299v3] [...]
(The *Pañcatraya-sūtra* [299v3–306r5]
The *Māyājāla-sūtra* [306r5–317v5])[1370]
The *Kāmaṭhika-sūtra* [317v5–329r4]
The *Kāyabhāvanā-sūtra* [329r4–340r2]
The *Bodha-sūtra* [340r2–344v4]
as well as the *Saṃkaraka-sūtra* [344v4–348r8]
The *Āṭāṇāṭa-sūtra* [348r1–354r4]
and the *Mahāsamāja-sūtra* [354r5–360v1] is at the end.

~16.20b~
SHT (IV) 32 Fragm. 66 Bl. 183 (*Prāsādika-sūtra*)[1371]
V
1[1372] .. .. smṛtyupasthānaṃ vedanā + + + ttadharmeśu dharmānupa +
2 medhyasya śākyasy=āmravane .. + + + rmeṣu prāsādaṃ pra[ve] +
3 adhivacanaṃ ||[1373] antarod(d)ā ◯ nam* durākhyātaś=ca svākhyāt(o) na [v]. + + ᵕ – ᵕ – | – – – – ᵕ – – – | – – – –
4 ś=ca cīvaram* sukhallik(āḥ) ◯ saptaphalā vyākṛtāvyākṛtena ca – – – – ᵕ – – – | – – – – ᵕ –
5 cikā || uddānam* apanna + + + ntha[k]o bhārgavaś=[śa]l[y]o bhay-abhai(rava) + + + + + + + + + + + + + + + + + +
6 prasādanīyena paścimaḥ || ◎ ||

DĀ(U.H.) Hs. 131 (= BLSF III.1 Or.15009/406) (*Prāsādika-sūtra*) (Vv–w parallel the *antaroddāna*)[1374]

1370. See note 1367 above.

1371. The parallel for DĀ 16.20 begins on line 6 of the below SHT fragment. This SHT fragment and the following Hoernle fragment contain parallel witnesses to the summary verses for both the end of DĀ 15 and DĀ 16. See also note 922 above and 1374 below.

1372. DĀ 15.42

1373. DĀ 15.43 starts here.

1374. Parallel to DĀ 16.20 begins from line w. The previous lines correspond to the summary verse at the end of the *Prāsādika-sūtra* at DĀ 15.43. See also note 925 above.

V

t /// + .[up]. [śy]. [n]. [s]mṛ[tyupasth]. .. .. [t]. ///
u /// [t]. sya dharmapary[ā]yasya pras[ā]da .. ///
v /// ○ ko [ya] ime dharmā nānādṛṣṭi ///
w /// ○ parāṃta paṃcikā || uddānam* || ///
x /// ○ yabhairava śrāvastyāṃ vai[śa]lyāṃ ro ///
y /// .. [na ca] paścimaḥ || prasādan[ī] .. ///
z /// +.. .. [m]e [t]. .. [bh]. .. ..ṃ .[i] + + ///

T I 18 —

DN —

T I 1.18 —

Bibliography

Allon, Mark, Richard Salomon, Geraldine Jacobson, and Ugo Zoppi. 2006. "Radiocarbon Dating of Kharoṣṭhī Fragments from the Schøyen and Senior Manuscript Collections." In *Buddhist Manuscripts*, vol. 3, edited by Jens Braarvig, 279–91. Manuscripts in the Schøyen Collection. Oslo: Hermes Publishing.

Anālayo, Bhikkhu. 2020a. "'Mūlasarvāstivādin and Sarvāstivādin': Oral Transmission Lineages of *Āgama* Texts" In *Research on the Saṃyukta-āgama*, edited by Bhikkhunī Dhammadinnā, 387–426. Dharma Drum Institute of Liberal Arts Research Series 8. Taipei: Dharma Drum Corporation.

———. 2020b. "*Āgama* and *aṅga* in the Early Buddhist Oral Tradition." *Singaporean Journal of Buddhist Studies* 3: 9–37.

Anālayo, Bhikkhu, and Stefania Travagnin. 2020. "Assessing the Field of *Āgama* Studies in Twentieth-century China: With a Focus on Master Yinshun's 印順 Three-*aṅga* Theory." In *Research on the Saṃyukta-āgama*, edited by Dhammadinnā, 933–1007. Dharma Drum Institute of Liberal Arts Research Series 8. Taipei: Dharma Drum Corporation.

Barua, A. 1949. *The Peṭakopadesa*. London: The Pali Text Society.

Bechert, Heinz. 1980. *Die Sprache der ältesten buddhistischen Überlieferung*. Göttingen: Vandenhoeck & Ruprecht.

———. 1990. *Abkürzungsverzeichnis zur buddhistischen Literatur in Indien und Südostasien*. Sanskrit-Wörterbuch der buddhistischen Texte aus den Turfan-Funden, Beiheft 3. Göttingen: Vandenhoeck & Ruprecht.

Bechert, Heinz, and Petra Kieffer-Pülz. 1989. *Ernst Waldschmidt: Ausgewählte kleine Schriften*. Stuttgart: Franz Steiner.

Bendall, Cecil. 1897–1902. *Çikshāsamuccaya: A Compendium of Buddhistic Teaching, Compiled by Çāntideva Chiefly from Earlier Mahāyāna-Sūtras*. Bibliotheca Buddhica 1. St. Petersburg: Imperial Academy of Sciences. (Repr. Osnabrück: Biblio Verlag, 1970.)

Bendall, Cecil, and W. H. D. Rouse, trans. 1971 (1922). *Śikshā-samuccaya: A Compendium of Buddhist Doctrine*. Delhi: Motilal Banarsidass.

Bhattacarya, Vidushekhara, ed. 1957. *The Yogācārabhūmi of Ācārya Asaṅga: The Sanskrit Text Compared with the Tibetan Version, Part 1*. Calcutta: University of Calcutta.

Braarvig, Jens, ed. 2002. *Buddhist Manuscripts*, vol. 2. Manuscripts in the Schøyen Collection 3. Oslo: Hermes Publ.

Brough, John. 1962. *The Gāndhārī Dharmapada*. London: Oxford University Press.

Burnouf, Eugène, Katia Buffetrille, and Donald S. Lopez. 2010. *Introduction to the History of Indian Buddhism*. Chicago: University of Chicago Press.

Choi, Jin kyoung. 2016. *Three Sūtras from the Gilgit Dīrghāgama Manuscript*. PhD dissertation, Ludwig-Maximilians-Universität, Munich.

Choong, Mun-keat. 2020. "Ācāriya Buddhaghosa and Master Yinshun 印順 on the Three-*aṅga* Structure of Early Buddhist Texts." In *Research on the Saṃyukta-āgama*, edited by Dhammadinnā, 883–931. Dharma Drum Institute of Liberal Arts Research Series 8. Taipei: Dharma Drum Corporation.

Chung, Jin-il. 2009. "Ein Drittes und ein Viertes Daśabala-Sūtra." *Sanko Bunka Kenkyūjo Nenpo* 40: 1–32 [17–29].

Clarke, Shayne, ed. 2014. *Vinaya Texts*. Gilgit Manuscripts in the National Archives of India, Facsimile Edition, vol. 1. Tokyo and New Delhi: The International Research Institute for Advanced Buddhology, Soka University, and The National Archives, India.

Conze, Edward. 1962/74. *The Gilgit Manuscript of the Aṣṭādaśasāhasrikā-prajñāpāramitā: Chapters 55 to 70 and Chapters 70 to 82*. Rome: Istituto Italiano per il Medio ed Estremo Oriente.

Dietz, Siglinde. 1984. *Fragmente des Dharmaskandha: Ein Abhidharma-Text in Sanskrit aus Gilgit*. Abhandlungen der Akademie der Wissenschaften in Göttingen, Philologisch-Historische Klasse, 142. Göttingen: Vandenhoeck & Ruprecht.

DiSimone, Charles. 2018. "An Unidentified *Āgama* Quotation and the Beginning of the *Prasādanīya-Sūtra*." In *Reading Slowly: A Festschrift for Jens E. Braarvig*, edited by Lutz Edzard, Jens W. Borgland, and Ute Hüsken, 137–57. Wiesbaden: Harrassowitz Verlag.

———. 2019. "Scribal Technique and Birch Bark Folio Repair Utilized in the Production of the Mūlasarvāstivāda *Dīrghāgama* Manuscript by a Scriptorium in Gilgit Around the 8th Century CE." Critical review for *Buddhist Studies* 25: 9–45.

Drewes, David. 2015. "Oral Texts in Indian Mahāyāna." *Indo-Iranian Journal* 58: 117–41.

Dutt, Nalinaksha. 1934. *The Pañcaviṁśatisāhasrikā Prajñāpāramitā*. London: Luzac & Co.

Edgerton, Franklin, 1972 (1953). *Buddhist Hybrid Sanskrit Grammar and Dictionary*. Delhi: Motilal Banarsidass.

Enomoto, Fumio, Jens-Uwe Hartmann, Hisashi Matsumura, eds. 1989. *Sanskrittexte aus dem buddhistischen Kanon: Neuentdeckungen und Neueditionen, Erste Folge*. SWTF Beiheft 2. Göttingen: Vandenhoeck & Ruprecht.

Feer, L. 1884–98. *Saṃyutta-nikāya of the Sutta-Piṭaka*. London: The Pali Text Society.

Gnoli, Raniero, ed. (with the assistance of T. Venkatacharya). 1977–78. *The Gilgit Manuscript of the Saṅghabhedavastu: Being the 17th and Last Section of the Vinaya of the Mūlasarvāstivādin*. Rome: Istituto Italiano per il Medio ed Estremo Oriente.

Gnoli, Raniero. 1978. *The Gilgit Manuscript of the Śayanāsanavastu and the Adhikaraṇavastu, Being the 15th and 16th Sections of the Vinaya of the Mūlasarvāstivādin*. Serie Orientale Roma 50. Rome: Istituto Italiano per il Medio ed Estremo Oriente.

Harrison, Paul, and Jens-Uwe Hartmann, eds. 2014. *From Birch Bark to Digital Data: Recent Advances in Buddhist Manuscript Research: Papers Presented at the Conference, Indic Buddhist Manuscripts: The State of the Field, Stanford, June 15–19, 2009*. Vienna: Verlag der Österreichischen Akademie der Wissenschaften.

Hartmann, Jens-Uwe. 1987. *Das Varṇārhavarṇastotra des Matṛceṭa*. Göttingen: Vandenhoeck & Ruprecht.

———. 1989. "Fragmente aus dem Dīrghāgama der Sarvāstivādins." In *Sanskrittexte aus dem buddhistischen Kanon: Neuentdeckungen und Neueditionen, Erste Folge*, edited by Fumio Enomoto, Jens-Uwe Hartmann, and Hisashi Matsumura, 37–67. Göttingen: Vandenhoeck & Ruprecht.

———. 1992. *Untersuchungen zum Dīrghāgama der Sarvāstivādins*. Habilitation thesis, Georg-August-Universität, Göttingen.

———. 2002: "More Fragments of the Caṅgīsūtra." In *Buddhist Manuscripts*, vol. 2. *Manuscripts in the Schøyen Collection 3*, edited by Jens Braarvig, 1–16. Oslo: Hermes Publications.

———. 2014. "The *Dīrgha-āgama* of the (Mūla-)Sarvāstivādins: What Was the Purpose of This Collection?" In *Research on the Dīrgha-āgama*, edited by Dhammadinnā, 135–66. Taipei: Dharma Drum Corporation.

———. Forthcoming. Edition of the *Pravāraṇā-sūtra* (currently untitled).

Hartmann, Jens-Uwe, and Klaus Wille. 2014. "The Manuscript of the *Dīrghāgama* and the Private Collection in Virginia." In *From Birch Bark to Digital Data: Recent Advances in Buddhist Manuscript Research: Papers Presented at the Conference, Indic Buddhist Manuscripts: The State of the Field, Stanford, June 15–19, 2009*, edited by Paul Harrison and Jens-Uwe Hartmann, 137–56. Vienna: Verlag der Österreichischen Akademie der Wissenschaften.

Hikata, Ryusho. 1983. *Suvikrāntavikrāmi-Paripṛcchā Prajñāpāramitā-Sūtra*. Kyoto: Rinsen.

von Hinüber, Oskar. 1994. "Die neun Aṅgas: Ein früher Versuch zur Einteilung buddhistischer Texte." *Wiener Zeitschrift für die Kunde Südasiens* 37: 121–35.

———. 2014. "The Gilgit Manuscripts: An Ancient Buddhist Library in Modern Research." In *From Birch Bark to Digital Data: Recent Advances in Buddhist Manuscript Research: Papers Presented at the Conference, Indic Buddhist Manuscripts: The State of the Field, Stanford, June 15–19, 2009*, edited by Paul Harrison and Jens-Uwe Hartmann, 79–135. Vienna: Verlag der Österreichischen Akademie der Wissenschaften

Hirakawa, Akira. 1963. "The Rise of Mahāyāna Buddhism and Its Relationship to the Worship of Stupas." *The Memoirs of the Research Department of the Toyo Bunko* 22: 57–106.

Hirakawa, Akira, and Paul Groner. 1990. *A History of Indian Buddhism from Śākyamuni to Early Mahāyāna*. Honolulu: University of Hawaii Press.

Hoernle, A. F. R. 1897. "Three Further Collections of Ancient Manuscripts from Central Asia." *Journal of the Asiatic Society (of Bengal)* 66.1: 242–43.

Hosoda, N. 1989. "Sanskrit Fragments from the Parivrājakasaṃyukta of the Saṃyuktāgama (I)." In *Indian Philosophy and Buddhism, Essays in Honour of Professor Kotatsu Fujita*, 185–206. Kyoto: Heirakuji shoten.

Hu-von Hinüber, Haiyan. 1994. *Das Poṣadhavastu: Vorschriften für die buddhistische Beichtfeier im Vinaya der Mūlasarvāstivādins*. Reinbek: Verlag für Orientalistische Fachpublikationen.

Ishihama Yumiko and Fukuda Yoichi. 1989. *A New Critical Edition of the Mahāvyutpatti / Shintei hon'yaku myōgi taishū* 新訂翻譯名義大集; *Sanskrit-Tibetan-Mongol Dictionary of Buddhist Terminology*. Studia tibetica 16. Tokyo: Toyo Bunko.

Jaini, Padmanabh S. 1959. *Abhidharmadīpa with Vibhāshāprabhāvṛitti*. Patna: Kashi Prasad Jayaswal Research Institute.

de Jong, Jan Willem. 1976a. "Book Review: Śrāvakabhūmi of Ācārya Asaṅga [= Tibetan Sanskrit Works Series 14] by Karunesha Shukla." *Indo-Iranian Journal* 18.3/4: 307–10.

———. 1976b. "Book Review: The Sūtra on the Foundation of the Buddhist Order (Catuṣpariṣatsūtra) [= Religious Texts Translation Series Nisaba, vol. 1] by Ria Kloppenborg." *Indo-Iranian Journal* 18.3/4: 324–27 (= de Jong 1979, 280–81).

———. 1979. *Buddhist Studies.* Edited by Gregory Schopen. Berkeley: Asian Humanities Press.

Karashima, Seishi (辛嶋 静志). 2015. "Who Composed the Mahāyāna Scriptures? The Mahāsāṃghikas and Vaitulya Scriptures." ARIRIAB 18 (創価大学国際仏教学高等研究所年報 / 創価大学-国際仏教学高等研究所 [編 18]): 113–62.

Karashima, Seishi (辛嶋 静志), and Klaus Wille, eds. 2006. *The British Library Sanskrit Fragments: Buddhist Manuscripts From Central Asia (I)*. Tokyo: International Research Institute for Advanced Buddhology, Soka University.

———. 2009. *The British Library Sanskrit Fragments: Buddhist Manuscripts From Central Asia (II)*. Tokyo: International Research Institute for Advanced Buddhology, Soka University.

———. 2015. *The British Library Sanskrit Fragments: Buddhist Manuscripts From Central Asia (III)*. Tokyo: International Research Institute for Advanced Buddhology, Soka University.

Karashima, Seishi (辛嶋 静志), Youngjin Lee, Jundo Nagashima, Fumio Shoji, Kenta Suzuki, Ye Shaoyong, and Stefano Zacchetti, eds. 2016. *Mahāyāna Texts: Prajñāpāramitā Texts (1)*. Gilgit Manuscripts in the National Archives of India, Facsimile Edition, vol. 2.1. Tokyo and New Delhi: The International Research Institute for Advanced Buddhology, Soka University, and The National Archives, India.

Kimura, Takayasu. 1986–2009. *Pañcaviṃśatisāhasrikā Prajñāpāramitā*. Tokyo: Sankibō Busshorin.

Kudo, Noriyuki, ed. 2017. *Avadānas and Miscellaneous Texts*. Gilgit Manuscripts in the National Archives of India, Facsimile Edition, vol. 3. Tokyo and New Delhi: The International Research Institute for Advanced Buddhology, Soka University, and The National Archives, India.

Kudo, Noriyuki, Takanori Fukita, and Hironori Tanaka, eds. 2018. *Gilgit Manuscripts in the National Archives of India, vol. 2.3: Samādhirājasūtra*. Tokyo and New Delhi: The International Research Institute for Advanced Buddhology, Soka University, and The National Archives, India.

Lal, Banarsi. 1994 (1974). *Āryamañjuśrīnāmasaṃgīti with Amṛtakaṇikā-Ṭippaṇī by Bhikṣu Raviśrījñāna and Amṛtakaṇikodyata-Nibandha of Vibhūticandra*. Varanasi: Central Institute of Higher Tibetan Studies.

Lamotte, Étienne. 1980. *Le Traité de la Grande Vertu de Sagesse de Nāgārjuna (Mahāprajñāpāramitāśāstra): Tome V: Chapitres XLIX–LII, et Chapitres XX (2ème série)*. Louvain: Institut Orientaliste.

———. 1988a. *History of Indian Buddhism: From the Origins to the Saka Era*. Louvain-la-Neuve: Université Catholique de Louvain, Institut Orientaliste.

———. 1988b. "Assessment of Textual Interpretation in Buddhism." In *Buddhist Hermeneutics*, edited by Donald S. Lopez, 11–28. Honolulu: University of Hawaii Press.

La Vallée Poussin, Louis de. 1903–13. *Mūlamadhyamakakārikās (Mādhyamikasūtras) de Nāgārjuna avec la Prasannapadā commentaire de Candrakīrti*. Bibliotheca Buddhica 4. St. Petersburg: Imperial Academy of Sciences.

———. 1911. "Documents Sanskrits de la seconde collection M. A. Stein." *Journal of the Royal Asiatic Society of Great Britain and Ireland* (July): 773–77.

———. 1913. "Documents Sanskrits de la seconde collection M.A. Stein: Fragments du Samyuktagama." *Journal of the Royal Asiatic Society of Great Britain and Ireland* (July): 569–80.

Li, Channa. 2019. "Śāriputra." In *Brill's Encyclopedia of Buddhism, Volume Two: Lives*, edited by Jonathan A. Silk, Richard Bowring, Vincent Eltschinger, and Michael Radich, 209–19. Leiden: Brill.

Manné, Joy. 1990. "Categories of Sutta in the Pāli Nikāyas and Their Implications for Our Appreciation of the Buddhist Teaching and Literature." *Journal of the Pali Text Society* 15: 29–87.

Matsuda, Kazunobu. 1986. *Newly Identified Sanskrit Fragments of the Dharmaskandha in the Gilgit Manuscripts (1), Sanskrit Fragments Transliterated.* Kyoto: Bun'eido.

Matsumura, H. 1988. *The Mahāsudarśanāvadāna and the Mahāsudarśanasūtra.* Bibliotheca Indo-Buddhica 47. Delhi: Sri Satguru Publications.

Melzer, Gudrun. 2010. *Ein Abschnitt aus dem Dīrghāgama.* PhD dissertation, Ludwig-Maximilians-Universtität, Munich.

———. 2014. "A Palaeographic Study of a Buddhist Manuscript from the Gilgit Region." In *Manuscript Cultures: Mapping the Field*, edited by Jörg B. Quenzer, Dmitry Bondarev, and Jan-Ulrich Sobisch 227–72. Berlin: de Gruyter.

Mette, Adelheid, Noriyuki Kudo, Ruriko Sakuma, Chanwit Tudkeao, and Jiro Hirabayashi, eds. 2017. *Further Mahāyānasūtras.* Gilgit Manuscripts in the National Archives of India, Facsimile Edition, vol. 2.4. Tokyo and New Delhi: The International Research Institute for Advanced Buddhology, Soka University, and The National Archives, India.

Mittal, Kusum, Dieter Schlingloff, and Valentina Stache-Rosen. 1957/62. *Dogmatische Begriffsreihen im älteren Buddhismus.* STT 4, 4a. Berlin: Akademie-Verlag.

Monier-Williams, Monier, Ernst Leumann, and Carl Cappeller. 1899. *A Sanskrit-English Dictionary Etymologically and Philologically Arranged with Special Reference to Cognate Indo-European Languages.* Oxford: The Clarendon Press.

Morris, Richard, and E. Hardy. 1885–1900. *The Aṅguttara-Nikāya.* London: The Pali Text Society.

Nattier, Jan. 2004. "The Twelve Divisions of Scriptures (十二部經) in the Earliest Chinese Buddhist Translations." ARIRIAB 7 (創価大学国際仏教学高等研究所年報 / 創価大学-国際仏教学高等研究所 [編 7]): 167–96.

Norman, K. R. 1982. "The Four Noble Truths: A Problem of Pāli Syntax" In *Indological and Buddhist Studies: Volume in Honour of Professor J.W. de Jong on his Sixtieth Birthday*, edited by L. A. Hercus, 377–91. Canberra: [Australian National University], Faculty of Asian Studies. (= Norman 1991, 210–23).

———. 1991. *Collected Papers, Vol. 2.* Oxford: The Pali Text Society.

Oldenberg, Hermann. 1993 (1881). *The Vinaya Piṭakam, Vol. 3: The Suttavibhaṅga, First Part (Pārājika, Saṃghādisesa, Aniyata, Nissaggiya).* London: The Pali Text Society.

Potter, Karl H. 1996. *Encyclopedia of Indian Philosophies, Vol. 7*. Delhi: Motilal Banarsidass.

Pradhan, Prahlad. 1950. *Abhidharmasamuccaya: Critically Edited and Studied*. Santiniketan: Visva-Bharati.

———. 1975. *Abhidharmakośabhāṣyam of Vasubandhu*, rev. 2nd ed. Patna: K. P. Jayaswal Research Institute.

Rahder, Johannes. 1926. *Daśabhūmikasūtra*. Leuven: J.-B. Istas.

Ramers, Peter. 1996. *Die "Drei Kapitel über die Sittlichkeit" im Śrāmaṇyaphala-Sūtra die Fassungen des Dīghanikāya und Saṃghabhedavastu, verglichen mit dem Tibetischen und Mongolischen; Einführung, Text, Übersetzung, Kommentar*. PhD dissertation, Bonn.

Rhys Davids, C. A. F. 1904. *The Vibhaṅga, Being the Second Book of the Abhidhamma Piṭaka*. London: The Pali Text Society.

Rhys Davids, T. W., and J. Estlin Carpenter. 2006 (1890–1911). *The Dīgha Nikāya*. Lancaster: The Pali Text Society.

Rhys Davids, T. W., and C. A. F. Rhys Davids. 1965 (1921). *Dialogues of the Buddha Part 3: Translated from the Pali of the Dīgha Nikāya*. London: The Pali Text Society.

Rhys Davids, T. W., and William Stede. 1921–25. *The Pali Text Society's Pali-English Dictionary*. London: The Pali Text Society.

Sakaki, Ryōzaburō (榊 亮三郎). 1916. *Mahāvyutpatti / Bon-zō-kan-wa shiyaku taikō, Hon'yaku myōgi taishū* (梵藏漢和四譯對校飜譯名義大集). Kyoto: Shingonshū Kyōto Daigaku (眞言宗京都大學).

Salguero, C. Pierce. 2014. *Translating Buddhist Medicine in Medieval China*. Philadelphia: University of Pensylvania Press.

Samtani, N. H. 1971. *The Arthaviniścaya-sūtra and Its Commentary (Nibandhana)*. Patna: Jayaswal Research Institute.

Schlingloff, Dieter. 1964. *Ein buddhistisches Yogalehrbuch*. STT 7. Berlin: Akademie-Verlag.

Schmidt, Richard, and Otto Boehtlingk. 1924. *Nachträge zum Sanskrit-Wörterbuch in kürzerer Fassung von Otto Böhtlingk. Bearb. von Richard Schmidt*. Hannover: Lafaire.

Senart, Émile. 1882–97 (3 volumes). *Le Mahāvastu*. Paris: Imprimerie Nationale.

Shukla, Karunesh. 1973/1991. *Śrāvakabhūmi of Ācārya Asaṅga*, vols. 1–2. Tibetan Sanskrit Works Series 14 and 28. Patna: Jayaswal Research Institute.

Skilling, Peter. 2002. "Review of C. Chojnacki et al. (ed.), *Vividharatnakaraṇḍakakathā, Festgabe für Adelheid Mette*." *Indo-Iranian Journal* 45: 373–77.

———. 2013. "Vaidalya, Mahāyāna, and Bodhisatva in India: An Essay toward Historical Understanding." In *The Bodhisattva Ideal: Essays on the Emergence of Mahāyāna*, edited by Bhikkhu Nyanatusita, 69–119. Kandy, Sri Lanka: Buddhist Publication Society.

Smith, Helmer. 1978 (1915). *The Kuddhaka-Pāṭha Together with Its Commentary Paramatthajotikā I*. London: The Pali Text Society.

Śrāvakabhūmi Study Group (The Institute for Comprehensive Studies of Buddhism, Taisho University)/大正大学綜合佛教研究所声聞地研究会, trans. and ed. 1998. *Śrāvakabhūmi, The First Chapter, Revised Sanskrit Text and Japanese Translation*/瑜伽論声聞地. 第一瑜伽処: サンスクリット語 テキスト と 和訳. Tokyo: Sankibo Press.

Śrāvakabhūmi Study Group (The Institute for Comprehensive Studies of Buddhism, Taisho University)/大正大学綜合佛教研究所声聞地研究会, trans. and ed. 2007. *Śrāvakabhūmi, The Second Chapter with Asamāhitā bhūmiḥ, Śrutamayī bhūmiḥ, Cintāmayī bhūmiḥ, Revised Sanskrit Text and Japanese Translation*/瑜伽論声聞地. 第二瑜伽処. 付, 非三摩呬多地. 聞所成地. 思所成地 : サンスクリット語 テキスト と 和訳. Tokyo: Sankibo Press.

Stache-Rosen, Valentina (after preliminary work by Kusum Mittal). 1968. *Dogmatische Begriffsreihen im älteren Buddhismus I und II: Das Saṅgītisūtra und sein Kommentar Saṅgītiparyāya*. STT 9. Berlin: Akademie-Verlag.

von Staël-Holstein, Alexander. 1926. *The Kāçyapaparivarta. A Mahāyānasūtra of the Ratnakūṭa Class* (大寶積經迦葉品梵藏漢六種合刋). Shanghai: Commercial Press (商務印書館).

Suzuki, D. T., ed. 1955–61. *The Tibetan Tripiṭaka, Peking Edition*. (168 vols.) Tōkyō and Kyōto: Tibetan Tripitaka Research Institute.

Takakusu, J., and K. Watanabe, eds. 1924ff. *Taishō Shinshū Daizōkyō* or *Taishō Issaikyō*, 100 vols. Tōkyō: Taishō Issai-kyō Kankō Kwai Taishō.

Tatia, N., ed. 1976. *Abhidharmasamuccayabhāṣyam*. Patna: Jayaswal Research Institute.

Trenckner, V., and R. Chalmers. 1993 (1888–99). *The Majjhima-Nikāya*. Oxford: The Pali Text Society.

Trenckner, V., Dines Andersen, Helmer Smith, Hans Hendriksen, Ludwig Alsdorf, Kenneth Roy Norman, and Oskar von Hinüber. 1924–2011ff. *A Critical Pali Dictionary*. Copenhagen: The Royal Danish Academy of Sciences and Letters.

Tripāṭhī, Chandrabhāl. 1962. *Fünfundzwanzig Sūtras des Nidānasaṃyukta*. STT 8. Berlin: Akademie-Verlag.

———. 1995. *Ekottarāgama-Fragmente der Gilgit-Handschrift*. Studien zur Indologie und Iranistik, Monographie 2. Reinbek: I. Wezler Verlag für Orientalistische Fachpublikationen.

Vaidya, P. L., ed. 1958a. *Avadānaśataka*. Buddhist Sanskrit Texts 19. Darbhanga: Mithila Institute.

———. 1958b. *Lalitavistara*. Buddhist Sanskrit Texts 24. Darbhanga: Mithila Institute.

———. 1959. *Divyāvadāna*. Buddhist Sanskrit Texts 20. Darbhanga: Mithila Institute.

———. 1961. *Mahāyāna-Sūtra-Saṁgraha*. Buddhist Sanskrit Texts 17. Darbhanga: Mithila Institute.

Vira, Raghu, and Lokesh Chandra. 1959–74. *Gilgit Buddhist Manuscripts, A Facsimile Edition*. New Delhi: International Academy of Indian Culture.

Vogel, C., and K. Wille. 1984. *Some Hitherto Unidentified Fragments of the Pravrajyāvastu Portion of the Vinayavastu Manuscript Found Near Gilgit*. Nachrichten der Akademie der Wissenschaften in Göttingen, Philologisch-Historische Klasse. Göttingen: Vandenhoeck & Ruprecht.

Vorobyova-Desyatovskaya, M.I., S. Karashima, and N. Kudo. 2002. *The Kāśyapaparivarta, Romanized Text and Facsimiles*. Bibliotheca Philologica et Philosophica Buddhica 5. Tokyo: International Research Institute for Advanced Buddhology.

Waldschmidt, Ernst. 1932. *Bruchstücke buddhistischer Sutras aus dem zentralasiatischen Sanskritkanon I*. Leipzig: Deutsche Morgenländische Gesellschaft.

———. 1952–62. *Das Catuṣpariṣatsūtra, Eine kanonische Lehrschrift über die Begründung der buddhistischen Gemeinde, Teil 1–3*. Berlin: Akademie-Verlag.

———. 1953/56. *Das Mahāvadānasūtra, Ein kanonischer Text über die sieben letzten Buddhas, Sanskrit verglichen mit dem Pāli, Nebst einer Analyse der in der chinesischen Übersetzung überlieferten Parallelversionen, Auf Grund von Turfan-Handschriften hrsg, Teil 1–2*. Berlin: Akademie-Verlag.

———. 1955. "Die Einleitung des Saṅgīti-sūtra." *Zeitschrift der Deutschen Morgenländischen Gesellschaft* 105: 298–318.

———. 1980. "Central Asian Sūtra Fragments and Their Relation to the Chinese Āgamas." In *Die Sprache der ältesten buddhistischen Überlieferung*, edited by Heinz Bechert, 136–74. Göttingen: Vandenhoeck & Ruprecht. (Reprinted in Bechert and Kieffer-Pülz 1989, 370–408.)

———. 1986 (1950–51). *Das Mahāparinirvāṇasūtra, Text in Sanskrit und Tibetisch, verglichen mit dem Pāli; nebst einer Übersetzung der chinesischen Entsprechung im Vinaya der Mūlasarvāstivādins, Teil 1–3*. Kyoto: Rinsen Book Co. (Orig. ed. Berlin: Akademie-Verlag.)

Waldschmidt, Ernst, W. Clawiter, L. Holzmann, L. Sander, H. Bechert, K. Wille, W. Voigt, D. George, and H. Feistel. 1965, 1968, 1971, 1980, 1985, 1989, 1995, 2000, 2004, 2008, and 2012. *Sanskrithandschriften aus den Turfan-Funden*, 11 vols. Verzeichnis der orientalischen Handschriften in Deutschland. Wiesbaden/Stuttgart: Franz Steiner.

Waldschmidt, Ernst, Heinz Bechert, Georg von Simson, Michael Schmidt, and Jens-Uwe Hartmann, eds. 1973ff. *Sanskrit-Wörterbuch der buddhistischen Texte aus den Turfan-Funden*, volumes 1–4. Göttingen: Vandenhoeck & Ruprecht.

Walshe, Maurice, trans. 1995 (1987). *The Long Discourses of the Buddha: A Translation of the Dīgha Nikāya*. Boston: Wisdom Publications.

Weller, Friedrich. 1933. "Über das Brahmajālasūtra, I Teil: Der tibetische Text." *Asia Major* 9: 195–332 and 381–440.

———. 1934. *Brahmajālasūtra: Tibetischer und Mongolischer Text*. Leipzig: O. Harrassowitz.

———. 1935–36. "Das tibetische Brahmajālasūtra." Zeitschrift für Indologie und Iranistik 10: 1–61.

Wogihara, Unrai. 1989 (1932–36). *Sphuṭārthā Abhidharmakoçavyākhyā: The Works of Yaśomitra*. (repr.) Tokyo: Sankibo.

Wynne, Alexander. 2007. *The Origin of Buddhist Meditation*. London: Routledge.

Zhen, Liu. 2008. *Versenkung und Askese: Eine neue Sanskrit-Quelle zur Buddha-Legende*. PhD dissertation: Ludwig-Maximilians-Universität, München.

Zhou, Chunyang. 2008. *Das Kaivartisūtra der neuentdeckten Dīrghāgama-Handschrift: Ein Edition und Rekonstruktion des Textes*. MA thesis, Georg-August-Universität, Göttingen.

Index

About the Author

Charles DiSimone is an associate professor of Buddhist studies at Ghent University and is principal investigator of the European Research Council starting grant project "Corpora in Greater Gandhāra: Tracing the Development of Buddhist Textuality and Gilgit/Bamiyan Manuscript Networks in the First Millennium of the Common Era." Since graduating from the doctoral program in Buddhist studies at Ludwig Maximilians University (LMU) in Munich, he has held posts at the Buddhist Digital Resource Center, Mahidol University, LMU, and Ghent.

⁝ What to Read Next from Wisdom Publications

The Long Discourses of the Buddha
A Translation of the Dīgha Nikāya
Maurice Walshe

"An amazing work that speaks to us across 2,500 years."
—*Mountain Record*

Questioning the Buddha
A Selection of Twenty-Five Sutras
Peter Skilling

"In this volume, prose and verse join beautifully to celebrate the Dharma. The selections show how rich, how diverse, and how wonderful the Kangyur is—and how little we know about it."
—from the foreword by Dzongsar Jamyang Khyentse

The Buddhist Literature of Ancient Gandhāra
An Introduction with Selected Translations
Richard Salomon

"There is no doubt that this work will serve as a terrific guidebook especially for those who are interested in Buddhist philology. Therefore, it would not be surprising to find this book added to the curricula of many Buddhist studies programs as well as in the bookshelves of Buddhist scholars around the world."
—*International Journal of Buddhist Thought & Culture*

About Wisdom Publications

Wisdom Publications is the leading publisher of classic and contemporary Buddhist books and practical works on mindfulness. To learn more about us or to explore our other books, please visit our website at wisdomexperience.org or contact us at the address below.

Wisdom Publications
132 Perry Street
New York, NY 10014 USA

We are a 501(c)(3) organization, and donations in support of our mission are tax deductible.

Wisdom Publications is affiliated with the Foundation for the Preservation of the Mahayana Tradition (FPMT).